Gubernatorial Elections
1787-1997

Gubernatorial Elections
1787-1997

Congressional Quarterly Inc.
Washington, D.C.

Printed and bound in the United States of America

The paper used in this publication meets the minimum requirements of the American National
Standard for Information Science—Permanence of Paper for Printed Library Materials, ANSI
Z39.48-1984.

Cover illustration credits (clockwise from top right): Congressional Quarterly; Congressional
Quarterly; Smithsonian Institution; Library of Congress; R. Michael Jenkins

Library of Congress Cataloging-in-Publication Data

Gubernatorial elections, 1787-1997
    p.   cm.
  Includes bibliographical references (p.   ) and indexes.
  ISBN 1-56802-396-0 (alk. paper)
    1. Governors—United States—Election—History.   2. Elections—
United States—States—History.   I. Congressional Quarterly, Inc.
JK2447.G76   1998
324.973—dc21   97-50560

Contents

Preface vii

Gubernatorial Elections 1
 Length of Governor Terms (box) 2
 Limitations on Governor Terms (box) 3
 Party Lineup of Governors (box) 4

The Historical Significance of Southern Primaries 5
 Preference and Runoff Primaries (table) 7

Governors of the States, 1787-1998 9

General Election Returns, 1787-1997 37

Primary Election Returns, 1919-1997 93

Political Party Abbreviations 155

Bibliography 157

General Election Candidates Index 159

Primary Candidates Index 175

Preface

The governors of the 50 states historically have been the most restricted of the government officials elected in the United States' system of government. From the very beginning of the Republic, some states placed term limits on their governors. By the end of 1997—when term limits were still being discussed for members of Congress—37 states limited the number of consecutive terms their governors could serve. As for the length of a single term, there was almost complete uniformity across the nation. Forty-eight states set gubernatorial terms at four years—only New Hampshire and Vermont had two-year terms for their governors.

At the start of 1998, the Republicans maintained a big majority among governors in the nation: there were 32 Republicans to 17 Democrats, with one independent in Maine. The Democrats had held the majority of governorships for most of the last half of the 20th century, including a long period from 1971 to 1994. The Republican tide that swept the GOP into control of the U.S. Congress in 1995 also turned over the majority status in the state executive mansions to the GOP for the first time in 24 years.

In the 1996 and 1997 gubernatorial elections, the American populace seemed satisfied with the new status quo. In 1996, 11 states held gubernatorial contests. All seven incumbent governors seeking reelection—four Democrats and three Republicans—won easily. Two states, Indiana and Washington, replaced retiring Democrats with Democrats. The only state to choose a Democrat to succeed a Republican was the traditionally Republican state of New Hampshire, while the only state to go the opposite way was the equally Democratic West Virginia. In 1997, there were two gubernatorial elections: New Jersey reelected its Republican governor to a second term, and Virginia, the only state with a one-term limit, replaced its GOP governor with another Republican.

Gubernatorial Elections 1787-1997 is a unique collection of popular vote returns and election data on the contests for the chief executive post in state government. General election results are provided for every gubernatorial race decided by popular vote (including runoff and special elections) back to the state's admission to the union. Election returns prior to 1974 were obtained primarily from the Inter-University Consortium for Political and Social Research (ICPSR) at the University of Michigan. Congressional Quarterly and its *America Votes* series have added to the ICPSR data, supplying the election returns for congressional races from 1974 to 1997.

The introduction examines the historical changes that have occurred in the process of choosing U.S. governors. Only five of the original thirteen states selected their governors through popular ballots. The state legislatures in the other eight states decided who became governors. Popular election was not used in every state until after the Civil War. The introduction also looks at the changing lengths of gubernatorial terms, majority vote requirements and the establishment of term limits. A separate discussion examines the historical significance of Southern primaries. Because of the overwhelming dominance of the Democratic Party in the South during the first half of the 20th century, the party's primaries there until the 1960s usually determined the winner of the governor's race.

Next is a listing of all governors from 1787 to 1998. This list gives the length of the terms and the political affiliations of all governors in U.S. history. Notes identify special elections and partial-term appointments. The date when each state ratified the Constitution or was admitted into the Union is also noted.

Following this gubernatorial listing are the general election and primary vote results. General election returns are provided for all gubernatorial races from 1787 to 1997, including special elections. Primary vote returns (and runoff elections) are given for most states back to 1956; results for Southern primaries are provided back to 1919. All election results contain the total vote count for each candidate along with political party affiliation and the percentage of the vote received. For both general election and primary returns, all candidates receiving at least 5 percent of the total vote are included.

The book concludes with a listing of political party abbreviations; a bibliography, which provides the starting point for further reading about gubernatorial elections; and two indexes — gubernatorial candidates for general election and gubernatorial candidates for primary election.

Gubernatorial Elections

Governors were not popular during the period of the American Revolution. To the revolutionists, the British-appointed governors were symbols of the mother country's control and tyranny.

Before the Revolutionary War, colonial assemblies were able to assert their control over appropriations and thus became the champions of colonial rights against the governors. Thus, when forming their own state constitutions, the newly freed Americans tended to look with suspicion on the office of governor and gave most of the power to the legislative bodies.

For these reasons, early American governors found themselves hemmed in by restrictions. Among such restrictions were both the length of the term of office and the method of election.

To this day, the 50 state governors are among the most restricted of the officials elected under the United States' system of government. Presidents have been limited to two terms since 1951 by constitutional amendment but states only recently have begun trying to limit the length of service of their members of Congress. (The Supreme Court struck down congressional term limits as unconstitutional in 1995.) By contrast, more than half the states limit their governors to two consecutive terms or less. Almost all, however, had abandoned the original one- or two-year terms in favor of four-year terms that required fewer elections and permitted more stability in the nation's statehouses.

Length of Terms

As of 1789 all four New England states—Connecticut, Massachusetts, New Hampshire and Rhode Island (Vermont was admitted in 1791 and Maine in 1820)—held gubernatorial elections every year. Some of the Middle Atlantic states favored somewhat longer terms; New York and Pennsylvania had three-year terms for their governors, although New Jersey instituted a one-year term. The Border and Southern states had a mix: Maryland and North Carolina governors served a one-year term, South Carolina had a two-year term, and Delaware, Virginia and Georgia had three-year terms. No state had a four-year term.

Over the years states have changed the length of gubernatorial terms. With some occasional back and forth movement, the general trend has been toward longer terms. New York, for example, has changed the term of office of its governor four times. Beginning in 1777 with a three-year term, the state switched to a two-year term in 1820, back to a three-

year term in 1876, back to a two-year term in 1894, and to a four-year term beginning in 1938.

Maryland provides another example of a state that has changed its gubernatorial term several times. Beginning with one year in 1776, the state extended the term to three years in 1838, then to four years in 1851. Regular gubernatorial elections were held every second odd year from then through 1923, when the state had one three-year term so that future elections would be held in even-numbered years, beginning in 1926. Thus, the state held gubernatorial elections in 1919, 1923 and 1926 and then every four years after that.

The trend toward longer gubernatorial terms shows up clearly in a comparison of the length of terms in 1900 and 1996. Of the 45 states in the Union in 1900, 22, almost half, had two-year terms. One (New Jersey) had a three-year term, while Rhode Island and Massachusetts were the only states left with one-year terms. The remaining 20 states had four-year gubernatorial terms. *(Length of terms, box, p. 2)*

By the beginning of 1998, 43 of those same states had four-year terms, and the five states admitted to the Union after 1900—Oklahoma (1907), Arizona and New Mexico (1912), Alaska and Hawaii (1959)—also had four-year gubernatorial terms. This left only two states with two-year terms: New Hampshire and Vermont.

Arkansas, one of the last holdouts, voted in 1984 to switch to a four-year term, effective in 1986. Rhode Island voters in 1992 approved a constitutional change to a four-term beginning in 1995.

Sources

The Book of the States, 1996-1997, vol. 31. Lexington, Ky.: Council of State Governments, 1996.

Lipson, Leslie, *The American Governor from Figurehead to Leader*. 1939. Reprint. Westport, Conn.: Greenwood Press, 1969.

Offices of secretaries of state of Connecticut, Georgia, Hawaii, Maine, Massachusetts, New Hampshire, Rhode Island, Vermont, Washington and West Virginia.

Length of Governor Terms

State	1900	1996	Year of Change to Longer Term
Alabama	2	4	1902
Alaska [1]	—	4	—
Arizona [1]	—	4	1970
Arkansas	2	4	1986
California	4	4	—
Colorado	2	4	1958
Connecticut	2	4	1950
Delaware	4	4	—
Florida	4	4	—
Georgia	2	4	1942
Hawaii [1]	—	4	—
Idaho	2	4	1946
Illinois	4	4	—
Indiana	4	4	—
Iowa	2	4	1974
Kansas	2	4	1974
Kentucky	4	4	—
Louisiana	4	4	—
Maine	2	4	1958
Maryland	4	4	—
Massachusetts [2]	1	4	1920, 1966
Michigan	2	4	1966
Minnesota	2	4	1962
Mississippi	4	4	—
Missouri	4	4	—
Montana	4	4	—
Nebraska	2	4	1966
Nevada	4	4	—
New Hampshire	2	2	—
New Jersey	3	4	1949
New Mexico [1]	—	4	1970
New York	2	4	1938
North Carolina	4	4	—
North Dakota	2	4	1964
Ohio	2	4	1958
Oklahoma [1]	—	4	—
Oregon	4	4	—
Pennsylvania	4	4	—
Rhode Island [3]	1	4	1912, 1994
South Carolina	2	4	1926
South Dakota	2	4	1974
Tennessee	2	4	1954
Texas	2	4	1974
Utah	4	4	—
Vermont	2	2	—
Virginia	4	4	—
Washington	4	4	—
West Virginia	4	4	—
Wisconsin	2	4	1970
Wyoming	4	4	—

1. *Oklahoma was admitted to the Union in 1907, Arizona and New Mexico in 1912, and Alaska and Hawaii in 1959. Oklahoma, Alaska and Hawaii have always had four-year gubernatorial terms; Arizona began with a two-year term and switched to four years in 1970. New Mexico (1912) began with a four-year term, changed to two years in 1916, and back to four years in 1970.*

2. *Massachusetts switched from a one- to a two-year term in 1920 and to a four-year term in 1966.*

3. *Rhode Island switched from a one- to a two-year term in 1912 and to a four-year term in 1994.*

Source: *Book of the States, 1996-1997,* vol. 31. Lexington, Ky.: Council of State Governments, 1996; *Congressional Quarterly Weekly Report.*

Trend to Isolation

Along with the change to longer terms for governors came another trend—away from holding gubernatorial elections in presidential election years. Except for North Dakota, every state in the 20th century that switched to four-year gubernatorial terms scheduled its elections in non-presidential years. Moreover, Florida, which held its quadrennial gubernatorial elections in presidential years, changed to non-presidential years in 1966. To make the switch, the state shortened to two years the term of the governor elected in 1964, then resumed the four-year term in 1966. Thus, Florida held gubernatorial elections in 1960, 1964, 1966, 1970 and 1974.

Illinois made a similar switch in 1976-78, leaving nine states—Delaware, Indiana, Missouri, Montana, North Carolina, North Dakota, Utah, Washington and West Virginia—holding quadrennial gubernatorial elections at the same time as the presidential election. New Hampshire and Vermont still had two-year terms, so every other gubernatorial election in these two states occurred in a presidential year.

Arkansas and Rhode Island, the two most recent converts to four-year terms, chose to select their governors in non-presidential election years, beginning in 1986 for Arkansas and 1994 for Rhode Island.

Methods of Election

Yet another way in which Americans of the early federal period restricted their governors was by the method of election. In 1789, only in New York and the four New England states did the people directly choose their governors by popular vote. In the remaining eight states, governors were chosen by the state legislatures, thus enhancing the power of the legislatures in their dealing with the governors. But several factors—including the democratic trend to elect public officials directly, the increasing trust in the office of governor and the need for a stronger and more independent chief executive—led to the gradual introduction of popular votes in all the states.

By the 1860s the remaining eight original states all had switched to popular ballots. Pennsylvania was first, in 1790, and was followed by Delaware in 1792, Georgia in 1824, North Carolina in 1835, Maryland in 1838, New Jersey in 1844, Virginia in 1851 and South Carolina in 1865, after the Civil War.

All the states admitted to the Union after the original 13, with one exception, made provision from the very beginning for popular election of their governors. The exception was Louisiana, which from its admission in 1812 until a change in the state constitution in 1845 had a unique system of gubernatorial elections. The people participated by voting in a first-step popular election. In a second step, the legislature was to select the governor from the two candidates receiving the highest popular vote.

Because of the domination of the Democratic Party in the South for many years after the Civil War, the Democratic primary was more important than the general election in the selection of governors and other officials in some Southern states. Victory in the party's primary often was tantamount to election, with the winner unopposed or facing token Republican opposition in the November election. *(The Historical Significance of Southern Primaries, p. 5)*

Although the so-called Solid South has become more of a two-party region in recent decades, the South continues to produce some anomalies in the election of governors. Louisiana, for example, holds an open primary for governor late in every fourth odd-numbered year. Candidates from all parties run on the same ballot. Any candidate who receives a majority is elected. If no candidate receives 50 percent, a runoff is held between the two top finishers.

Number of Terms

Another limitation placed on governors is a restriction on the number of terms they are allowed to serve. In the early years at least three states had such limitations: governors of Maryland were eligible to serve three consecutive one-year terms and then were required to retire for at least one year; Pennsylvania allowed its governors three consecutive three-year terms and then forced retirement for at least one term; and in New Jersey, according to the constitution of 1844, a governor could serve only one three-year term before retiring for at least one term.

In 1996, 37 states had a limitation on the number of consecutive terms their governors could serve. Out of these 37, only Virginia limited its governor to one term, and only Utah had a three-term limit. 35 states allowed their governors to seek re-election once but required that they step down after two terms for an interim of at least one term. Five states—Arkansas, Delaware, Mississippi, Missouri and Ohio—imposed an absolute two-term limit. That is, a governor could serve only two terms, however spaced, in his lifetime. The remaining 13 states imposed no limits on the number of consecutive terms a governor could serve. *(Table on right.)*

Majority Vote Requirement

One peculiarity of gubernatorial voting that has almost disappeared from the American political scene is the requirement that the winning gubernatorial candidate receive a majority of the popular vote. Otherwise, the choice devolves upon the state legislature or upon a runoff between the two highest candidates.

All six New England states had such a provision in their state constitutions at one time. New Hampshire, Vermont, Massachusetts and Connecticut had the provision when they entered the Union between 1788 and 1791. Rhode Island required a majority election but did not adopt a provision for legislative election until 1842; Maine adopted a majority provision when it split off from Massachusetts to form a separate state in 1820. Elsewhere, Georgia put the majority provision in its constitution when it switched from legislative to popular election of governors in 1825; Mississippi put it in its 1890 constitution; and Arizona adopted a runoff in 1990.

The purpose of the majority provision appears to have been to safeguard against a candidate's winning with a small fraction of the popular vote in a multiple field. In most of New England, the provision was part of the early state constitutions, formed largely in the 1780s, before the development of the two-party system.

The prospect of multiple-candidate fields diminished with the coming of the two-party system. Nevertheless, each of these states had occasion to use the provision at least once. Sometimes, in an extremely close election, minor party candidates received enough of a vote to keep the winner from getting a majority of the total vote. And at other times strong third-party movements or disintegration of the old party structure resulted in the election's being thrown into the state legislature.

Five of the nine states that originally had a majority requirement have repeated it. Georgia maintains it but instead of legislative election, now provides for a runoff

Limitations on Governor Terms

In most states with limits of one or two consecutive terms, governors may serve again after a one-term hiatus. Thus in a state with a two-term limitation, the governor must retire after two consecutive terms. After a one-term interim, he or she may serve again.

State	Maximum Number of Consecutive Terms (as of 1996)
Alabama	2
Alaska	2
Arizona	2
Arkansas [1]	2
California	2
Colorado	2
Connecticut	No limit
Delaware [1]	2
Florida	2
Georgia	2
Hawaii	2
Idaho	No limit
Illinois	No limit
Indiana [2]	2
Iowa	No limit
Kansas	2
Kentucky	2
Louisiana	2
Maine	2
Maryland	2
Massachusetts	2
Michigan	2
Minnesota	No limit
Mississippi [1]	2
Missouri [1]	2
Montana [3]	2
Nebraska	2
Nevada	2
New Hampshire	No limit
New Jersey	2
New Mexico	2
New York	No limit
North Carolina	2
North Dakota	No limit
Ohio [1]	2
Oklahoma	2
Oregon [2]	2
Pennsylvania	2
Rhode Island	2
South Carolina	2
South Dakota	2
Tennessee	2
Texas	No limit
Utah	3
Vermont	No limit
Virginia	1
Washington [4]	No limit
West Virginia	2
Wisconsin	No limit
Wyoming [3]	No limit

1. Arkansas, Delaware, Mississippi, Missouri and Ohio have absolute two-term limits. That is, no person may serve more than two gubernatorial terms in his or her lifetime.

2. Indiana and Oregon prohibit a person from serving more than eight years in any 12-year period.

3. Montana and Wyoming prohibit a person from serving more than eight years in any 16-year period.

4. Washington prohibits a person from serving more than eight years in any 14-year period.

Source: *Book of the States, 1996-1997*, vol. 31. Lexington, Ky.: Council of State Governments, 1996.

Party Lineup of Governors

The figures below show the number of governor-ships held by the two parties after each election since 1950.

Year	Democrat	Republican	Independent
1950	23	25	0
1952	18	30	0
1954	27	21	0
1956	29	19	0
1958	35	14	0
1960	34	16	0
1962	34	16	0
1964	33	17	0
1966	25	25	0
1968	19	31	0
1970	29	21	0
1972	31	19	0
1974	36	13	1
1976	37	12	1
1978	32	18	0
1980	26	24	0
1982	34	16	0
1984	34	16	0
1986	26	24	0
1988	28	22	0
1990	27	21	2
1992	30	18	2
1994	19	30	1
1996	18	31	1

Source: *Book of the States, 1996-1997*, vol. 31. Lexington, Ky.: Council of State Governments, 1996; *Congressional Quarterly Weekly Report.*

between the top two contenders three weeks after the general election. Mississippi's majority vote provision has never been used because the Democratic Party nominee always had received a majority (until 1991, when the Republican winner secured a majority).

Following are the states that had the majority vote provision for governor (except Mississippi), the years in which the choice devolved on the legislature because of it, and the year, if any, in which the requirement was repealed or changed:

Arizona. Arizona adopted and used a runoff provision in 1990 following impeachment of a governor elected with less than a majority.

Connecticut. No gubernatorial candidate received a majority of the popular vote, thus throwing the election into the legislature, in the following years subsequent to 1824: 1833, 1834, 1842, 1844, 1846, 1849, 1850, 1851, 1854, 1855, 1856, 1878, 1884, 1886, 1888 and 1890. Following the election of 1890, the legislature was unable to choose a new governor, so the outgoing governor, Morgan G. Bulkeley, R, continued to serve through the entire new term (1891-93). The provision was repealed in 1901. The years prior to 1824 in which the provision was used, if any, were unavailable from the Connecticut secretary of state's office.

Georgia. Although the majority vote requirement was initiated in 1825, when Georgia first elected its governor by popular vote, it was not used until the 20th century. In 1966, with an emerging Republican Party, a controversial Democratic nominee and an independent Democrat all affecting the gubernatorial race, no candidate received a majority. The legislature chose Democrat Lester Maddox. It was the controversy surrounding this experience that led to the change from legislative choice to a runoff between the top two contenders. Earlier, in 1946, the Georgia legislature also attempted to choose the governor, under unusual circumstances not covered by the majority vote requirement. The governor-elect, Eugene Talmadge, D, died before taking office. When it met, the legislature chose Talmadge's son, Herman E. Talmadge, as the new governor. Herman Talmadge was eligible for consideration on the basis that he received enough write-in votes in the general election to make him the second-place candidate. But the state Supreme Court voided the legislature's choice and declared that the lieutenant governor-elect, Melvin E. Thompson, D, should be governor. The runoff provision was first used in the 1992 election for U.S. senator.

Maine. Maine entered statehood in 1820 with a majority vote provision for governor but repealed it in 1880. During this 60-year span, the legislature was called on to choose the governor nine times, in 1840, 1846, 1848, 1852, 1853, 1854, 1855, 1878 and 1879.

Massachusetts. Like the other New England states, Massachusetts originally had a requirement for majority voting in gubernatorial elections. However, after the legislature was forced to choose the governor for six straight elections from 1848 to 1853, Massachusetts repealed the provision in 1855. The years in which it was used were 1785, 1833, 1842, 1843, 1845, 1848, 1849, 1850, 1851, 1852 and 1853.

New Hampshire. New Hampshire's mandated majority vote for governor was in force from 1784 through 1912, when it was repealed. The outcome of the following gubernatorial elections was determined by the legislature: 1785, 1787, 1789, 1790, 1812, 1824, 1846, 1851, 1856, 1863, 1871, 1874, 1875, 1886, 1888, 1890, 1906 and 1912.

Rhode Island. Under the constitution of 1842, Rhode Island required a majority to win the gubernatorial election. Under this mandate, the legislature chose the governor in the years 1846, 1875, 1876, 1880, 1889, 1890 and 1891. Because of a disagreement between the two houses of the state legislature, the ballots for governor were not counted in 1893, and Gov. D. Russell Brown, R, continued in office for another term of one year. The provision for majority voting then was repealed.

Before 1842 there was also a requirement for a popular majority, but the legislature was not allowed to choose a new governor if no candidate achieved a majority. Three times—in 1806, 1832 and 1839—there was no majority in a gubernatorial election, with a different outcome each time. In 1806 the lieutenant governor-elect served as acting governor for the term. In 1832 the legislature mandated a new election, but still no majority choice was reached; three more elections were held, all without a majority being achieved, so the same state officers were continued until the next regular election. And in 1839, when neither the gubernatorial nor lieutenant governor's race yielded a winner by majority, the senior state senator acted as governor for the term.

Vermont. Vermont's provision for majority gubernatorial election resulted in the legislature's picking the governor 20 times: 1789, 1797, 1813, 1814, 1830, 1831, 1832, 1834, 1841, 1843, 1845, 1846, 1847, 1848, 1849, 1852, 1853, 1902, 1912 and 1986. On another occasion, 1835, the legislature failed to choose a new governor because of a deadlock and the lieutenant governor-elect served as governor for the term. The Vermont provision remains in force.

The Historical Significance of Southern Primaries

Because of the overwhelming dominance of the Democratic Party in the South during the first half of the 20th century, the party's primaries became, in effect, the region's significant elections. The 11 states that constitute the South—all members of the Civil War Confederacy—are Alabama, Arkansas, Florida, Georgia, Louisiana, Mississippi, North Carolina, South Carolina, Tennessee, Texas and Virginia.

In his classic study *Southern Politics in State and Nation*, V. O. Key Jr. concluded, "In fact, the Democratic primary is no nominating method at all. The primary is the election. . . ." That was in 1949, shortly before Republicans began seriously challenging Democrats for hegemony in the region.

But Key's observation holds true for the 20th century up through the time of his study and for much of the period since, depending on the particular state and election involved. Of the 114 gubernatorial elections held in the 11 former Confederate states in the period 1919-1948, the Democratic nominee won 113 times. The exception was Tennessee's election of a Republican governor in the Harding presidential landslide of 1920.

The Southern shift to the Republican Party began on the presidential level in 1964, when Barry Goldwater's criticisms of civil rights laws found a wide audience. In 1972 Republican presidential nominee Richard Nixon carried all 11 states of the Old South with at least 65 percent of the vote. In 1984 and 1988 Ronald Reagan and George Bush did almost as well, carrying every Southern state with at least 58 percent (Reagan) or 54 percent (Bush) of the vote. Although the Democrats regained the White House in 1992 and 1996, the party's all-Southern ticket of Bill Clinton of Arkansas and Al Gore of Tennessee carried only four Southern states in both elections. In 1992 Clinton and Gore won Arkansas, Georgia, Louisiana and Tennessee. In 1996 the ticket lost Georgia but picked up Florida—the first time the state had gone Democratic since 1976.

From the 1960s to the 1990s, the Republican Party picked up governorships slowly. The first GOP gubernatorial victories in the South coming in Arkansas and Florida in 1966. Thereafter, Republicans won their first governorships in Virginia (1969), Tennessee (1970), North Carolina (1972), South Carolina (1974), Texas (1978), Louisiana (1979), Alabama (1986) and Mississippi (1991). Since Reconstruction in the 1870s, Georgia has been the only Southern state not to have elected a Republican governor.

By the start of 1998, the GOP outnumbered the Democrats eight to three in Southern governorships. On the federal level, the Republican Party, which took over majority status in the South after the 1994 midterm elections, had increased its advantage to 15 to 7 in Senate seats and 77 to 54 in U.S. House seats in the 11 Southern states. The only area where the Democratic Party held onto its traditional Southern dominance was at the state legislative level. In 1998 the Democratic Party maintained a commanding advantage in both houses of the state government in six Southern states. The Democrats split control of the legislature with the GOP in another four Southern states. Florida was the only Southern state to have its two state legislative bodies controlled by the Republican Party.

Runoff Primaries

The South along with the rest of the nation instituted the use of primaries during the first two decades of the 20th century. By 1920 all 11 Southern states were choosing their Democratic gubernatorial nominees through the primary process.

But because the primaries were, for all practical purposes, the deciding election, many legislators began to doubt the effectiveness of a system that frequently allowed a candidate in a multi-candidate race to win a plurality of the popular vote—and thus the Democratic nomination that ensured election—even though he received only a small percentage of the total primary vote.

So, most Southern states adopted the runoff primary—a second election following the first primary, usually by two to four weeks—that matched only the top two contenders from the first primary. The runoff system was adopted in Alabama in 1931, Arkansas in 1939, Florida in 1929, Georgia in 1917 (with the county unit system, *see p. 7*), Louisiana in

Sources

Heard, Alexander, and Donald S. Strong. *Southern Primaries and Elections, 1920-1949.* 1950. Reprint. Salem, N.H.: Ayers, 1970.

Key, V. O. Jr. *Southern Politics in State and Nation.* New York: Alfred A. Knopf, 1949.

Secretaries of state and state handbooks of the 11 Southern states.

1922, Mississippi in 1902, North Carolina in 1915, South Carolina in 1915 and Texas in 1918. (Arkansas had adopted the runoff in 1933, abandoned it in 1935, then reinstituted it in 1939.) Virginia adopted the runoff in 1969 but repealed it in 1971.

After 1969 Tennessee remained the only Southern state to nominate by plurality. In that state's 1974 gubernatorial race, Ray Blanton won the Democratic nomination with only 22.7 percent of the vote in a field of 12 candidates. Blanton went on to win the governorship in November.

Runoffs are not always obligatory. In most states, if the second-place finisher in the primary does not want a runoff, the first-place candidate is then the winner without a runoff. In the North Carolina Democratic gubernatorial primary of 1968, for example, front-runner Robert W. Scott narrowly missed winning a majority of the vote in the first primary, winding up with 48.1 percent. However, the second-place candidate, J. Melville Broughton Jr., who received 33.4 percent, declined a runoff. None was held and Scott automatically became the Democratic nominee.

Jackson's Anti-runoff Campaign

Jesse L. Jackson, contender for the 1984 Democratic presidential nomination, mounted an attack against the runoff feature in the spring of that year. Jackson hoped to persuade the 10 other Southern states to join Tennessee in avoiding the runoff.

Jackson argued that runoffs injured black candidates' chances of victory because in the second election whites, who comprised the majority of registered voters, usually voted on the basis of race.

Jackson carried his plea to the Democratic National Convention, which defeated his move to abolish runoffs, by a vote of 2,500.8 to 1,253.2. Supporters argued that runoffs prevented the election of fringe candidates when more qualified candidates split the vote in hotly contested primaries. In addition, conservative Southerners opposed having a national convention decide the election procedures required in their states.

Preferential Primaries

Three Southern states—Alabama, Florida and Louisiana—tried to avoid the effort and expense of runoff elections by experimenting with a preferential system of primary voting. All three later switched to the runoff system—Alabama after the election of 1930, Florida after the election of 1928 and Louisiana (whose system was similar to Alabama's) after the election of 1920. Louisiana modified its system yet again in 1975, this time to a two-step process: an initial non-partisan primary followed by a general election runoff between the two top finishers.

Under the preferential system a voter, instead of simply marking an X opposite one candidate's name, writes the digits 1 *or* 2, beside the names of two candidates. This indicates the "preference" order the voter gives each of the candidates, the number one indicating his first choice, the number two his second choice. To determine the winner, without a runoff, second-choice votes are added to the first-choice votes and the candidate with the highest combined total wins.

Alabama. Under the Alabama system, each voter expressed a first and second choice. If no candidate received a majority of the first choices, all but the two leaders were eliminated. All second choices expressed for the two leaders

were then added to their first-choice totals, the candidate with the highest combined total winning.

In the Democratic gubernatorial primary in 1926, the candidates were Bibb Graves and three persons whose first names are not available: McDowell, Carmichael and Patterson. Graves, with 61,493 first-choice votes, led the field but received only 27.6 percent of the total. McDowell ran second with 59,699 first-choice votes, or 26.8 percent; Carmichael had 54,072 first-choice votes, or 24.3 percent, and Patterson was last with 47,411 first-choice votes, or 21.3 percent. Thus, in many Southern states a runoff would have been necessary. But instead of a runoff all second-choice votes cast for the two leaders—Graves and McDowell—were added to their first-choice ballots. A total of 21,978 second-choice votes were cast for Graves by voters whose first choice had gone to one of the other three candidates. Added to his first-choice vote of 61,493, this gave Graves a grand total of 83,471 votes. McDowell received 7,943 second-choice votes—to raise his grand total to 67,642 votes, but not enough to surpass Graves' total, who was declared the winner.

Florida. The Florida system of preference voting differed somewhat from the Alabama system. In Florida, as in Alabama, each voter expressed a first and second choice. Also as in Alabama, if no candidate received a majority of first choices, all candidates but the two highest first-choice candidates were eliminated. To determine the winner, the second choices expressed for the two highest *on the ballots of eliminated candidates only* were added to the first-choice totals. (In Alabama, the second choices for the two leaders expressed on ballots for *all* candidates, including the two leaders, were added to the first-choice totals.)

For example, in the Florida Democratic gubernatorial election of 1924 there were five candidates. John W. Martin received 55,715 first-choice votes, to lead the field. His closest rival, Sidney J. Catts, received 43,230 votes. But a third major contender, Frank E. Jennings, received 37,962 first-choice votes, depriving either Martin or Catts of a majority. In addition, two other candidates also received first-choice votes—Worth W. Trammell with 8,381 and Charles H. Spencer with 1,408. The percentages stood Martin 38.0, Catts 29.5, Jennings 25.9, Trammell 5.7 and Spencer 0.9 percent.

To determine the winner, the second-choice votes cast for Martin (17,339) and Catts (6,067) by voters who had cast first-choice votes for Jennings, Trammell and Spencer were added to Martin's and Catts' first-choice totals. The result was Martin 73,054 and Catts 49,297, a clear win for Martin.

The preference system, however, did not prove useful. Apparently it was too confusing for voters, most of whom did not bother to cast second-choice votes. In the Alabama election discussed above, for example, there were 130,814 first-choice votes, but only 34,768 second-choice votes.

Louisiana. Not satisfied with either the partisan runoff or the preferential primary, Louisiana adopted a law in 1975 that allowed its voters to participate in an initial open primary followed by a runoff general election between the two top finishers. In the primary, all candidates of all parties were to be on the ballot, but party designations were optional and at the individual candidate's discretion. A candidate receiving more than 50 percent of the primary vote would be unopposed in the general election. If no candidate received more than 50 percent of the vote, the two candidates receiving the greatest number of votes—regardless of party—would oppose each other in the runoff general election.

Thus, in 1975, when the governor was chosen under this

new system, six candidates, all Democrats, entered the initial open primary held on Nov. 1. There were no Republican, independent or minor party candidates. Gov. Edwin W. Edwards, D, received 62.4 percent of the vote, and only his name appeared on the Dec. 13 general election ballot. (Louisiana by 1978 dispensed with the runoff general election if the primary winner received more than 50 percent of the vote.) If Edwards had placed first with less than 50 percent of the vote, the runoff general election would have been between him and the second-place finisher, even though the other candidate was also a Democrat. In 1978 the law went into effect for House and Senate races.

Georgia: County Unit System

Another variant of the primary system was Georgia's county unit system. Each county in the state was apportioned a certain number of unit votes. The candidate who received the largest number of popular votes in the county was awarded all the county's unit votes, even if he won only a plurality and not a majority. A candidate had to have a majority of the state's county unit votes to win the primary; otherwise a runoff became necessary. The runoff also was held on the basis of the county unit system.

For example, as of 1946, there were 410 county unit votes. The eight most populous counties had six unit votes each, the next 30 most populous counties had four each, and the remaining 121 counties had two each. The system was weighted toward rural and sparsely populated areas, because every county, no matter how small, had at least two unit votes.

The Georgia county unit system sometimes produced winners who received less than a majority of popular votes. Political scientist Key found that in two of 16 gubernatorial races between 1915 and 1948 the winner of a majority of county units received less than a majority of the popular votes. In a third case, that of 1946, the winner of the county unit vote, Eugene Talmadge, actually received fewer popular votes than his chief opponent, James V. Carmichael. The popular vote stood: Carmichael, 313,389 (45.3 percent); Talmadge, 297,245 (43.0 percent); E. D. Rivers, 69,489 (10.0 percent); and Hoke O'Kelly, 11,758 (1.7 percent). But the county unit totals were: Talmadge, 244 (59.5 percent); Carmichael, 144 (35.1 percent); Rivers, 22 (5.4 percent); and O'Kelly, 0 (0.0 percent).

Talmadge's victory was attributable to the rural orientation of the county unit system. His popularity in farm areas gave him an almost clean sweep of the small counties, allowing him to amass more county unit votes than Carmichael, whose strength was centered in the underrepresented urban areas. However, Talmadge died shortly after the November election, precipitating a crisis in Georgia's gubernatorial succession.

The county unit system fell before the Supreme Court's "one-person, one-vote" doctrine. In the 1963 case, *Gray v. Sanders*, the court declared the Georgia county unit system unconstitutional because of the disparity in representation between the urban and rural areas.

White Primaries

Closely connected with the history of Southern Democratic primaries is the issue of race. In many Southern states, blacks were long barred from participation in the Democratic primary, either on a statewide basis or in various counties. To exclude blacks from the primaries, the

---

Preference and Runoff Primaries

State	Preferential Primary	Runoff Primary Adopted
Alabama	Until 1931	1931
Arkansas	—	1939[1]
Florida	Until 1929	1929
Georgia	—	1917[2]
Louisiana[3]	Until 1922	1922
Mississippi	—	1902
North Carolina	—	1915
South Carolina	—	1915
Tennessee[4]	—	—
Texas	—	1918
Virginia[5]	—	—

1. Arkansas adopted the runoff in 1933, abandoned it in 1935 and reinstituted it in 1939.
2. Runoff held under county unit system; see text opposite.
3. Louisiana used the runoff "for a time prior to 1916," according to political scientist V. O. Key Jr.; in 1975 Louisiana adopted an initial non-partisan primary followed by a general election runoff.
4. Tennessee has never used the preferential or runoff primary. Candidates are nominated by winning a plurality; see text, p. 6.
5. Virginia adopted the runoff primary in 1969 and repealed it in 1971.

Sources: Heard, Alexander, and Donald S. Strong. *Southern Primaries and Elections.* 1950. Reprint. Salem, N.H.: Ayers, 1970. Key, V. O. Jr. *Southern Politics in State and Nation.* New York: Alfred A. Knopf, 1949. Virginia secretary of state.

Democratic Party was designated as a private association or club. The practice was defended as constitutional because the 15th Amendment, ratified in 1870, prohibited only *states*, not private associations, from denying the right to vote to persons on account of race or color. However, in 1944 the Supreme Court, in the case of *Smith v. Allwright*, declared the white primary unconstitutional, holding that it was an integral part of the election machinery for choosing state and federal officials.

Poll Tax. Another device used in limiting both black and white voters was the poll tax, which required the payment of a fee before voting. The amount of the poll tax ranged from one to two dollars, but in Alabama, Mississippi, Virginia and Georgia before 1945 the tax was cumulative. Thus, a new voter in Georgia could face up to $47 in fees. Various regulations as to the time and manner of payment of the tax also substantially reduced the number of voters. In Mississippi, for example, a person wanting to vote in the Democratic primary (usually held in August) had to pay his poll tax on or before the first day of the two preceding Februarys— long before most voters had even begun to think about the election.

The poll tax was barred in federal elections by ratification of the 24th Amendment in January 1964. The amendment simply stated that the "right of citizens of the United States to vote in any primary or other election . . . shall not be denied or abridged by the United States or any other State by reason of failure to pay any poll tax or other tax."

Literacy Tests. The literacy test was another method used to limit the Southern franchise to whites. Voters were required to read and/or write correctly—usually a section of the state or federal Constitution. Sometimes, voters who could not pass the test could have the materials read to them, to see if they could "understand" or "interpret" it correctly.

This provision allowed local voting officials, inevitably whites, to judge whether voters passed the tests; it usually resulted in whites passing and blacks failing.

However, in his study of Southern politics, Key concluded that informal pressures—including economic reprisals and other sanctions—were more important in limiting the black franchise than were the official suffrage limitations.

By the 1970s most formal bars to voting in the South, and many informal ones, had been lifted, either by constitutional amendment, federal laws, state action or protest movements.

Governors of the States, 1787-1998

Sources: Governors of the States, 1787-1998

This section *(pp. 11-35)* contains a listing of state governors from 1787 to January 1998. For those governors who, as of their state's ratification of the Constitution, began their service prior to 1787, the date upon which they began their gubernatorial term is listed. Arranged alphabetically by state, the lists provide the name, political affiliation and dates of service of each state's governors in chronological order.

The following sources were used for the names, party affiliations and dates of service for governors.

● *Governors of the States 1900-1974.* Lexington, Ky.: Council of State Governments, 1974. Compiled by Samuel R. Solomon.

● *The Book of Governors.* Los Angeles: Washington Typographers, 1935. Compiled by William W. Hunt.

● Kallenbach, Joseph E., and Jessamine S. Kallenbach. *American State Governors, 1776-1976.* 3 vols. Dobbs Ferry, N.Y.: Oceana Publishing, 1977.

● *Congressional Quarterly Weekly Report.*

● State manuals published by the state governments.

● State governors' offices and Internet sites.

● Gubernatorial election returns provided by the Inter-University Consortium for Political and Social Research (ICPSR), appearing on pages 39 to 88.

● *The Encyclopedia Americana.* 30 vols. Danbury, Conn.: Grolier Education, 1982.

Names, Party Affiliation and Dates of Service

For the 20th century, *The Governors of the States 1900-1974* was the primary source for the names of governors and dates of service. The party designations appearing in the ICPSR election returns were used to assign party affiliation. Where the ICPSR returns indicated two or more party designations, only the major party is listed. *(For a list of political party abbreviations used in this section, see p. 36.)*

For the 18th and 19th centuries, state manuals and Hunt's *The Book of Governors* were used for names and dates of service. Hunt provides the names of state governors and dates of service—in some cases complete dates (month, day and year), in other cases only month and year and in still other cases only the dates of gubernatorial elections. Congressional Quarterly has used the most precise dates available from Hunt and state manuals.

Because political parties did not exist formally in the early years of the Republic, classification of governors by party during this period can be difficult or misleading. In cases where party affiliation was not appropriate or could not be determined, no party designation appears. After 1824, the starting date for the ICPSR gubernatorial election returns, the ICPSR data were used where they provided information on party affiliation. State manuals and *The Encyclopedia Americana,* which gives governors' party affiliation for some states, were also consulted.

Footnotes

Footnotes, based on information from the above sources, have been used to indicate the following circumstances:

● Deaths, resignations or removals from office and succession of lieutenant governors or other officials to governorships.

● Circumstances surrounding disputed elections.

For details on the 20th-century trend toward longer gubernatorial terms and limitations on the number of consecutive terms, as well as unusual gubernatorial election procedures in some states, see "Introduction," pages 1 to 4.

Governors of the States, 1787-1998

ALABAMA

(Became a state Dec. 14, 1819)

Governors	Dates of Service	
William W. Bibb (D-R)	Nov. 9, 1819	July 15, 1820
Thomas Bibb (D-R)	July 15, 1820	Nov. 9, 1821
Israel Pickens (D-R)	Nov. 9, 1821	Nov. 25, 1825
John Murphy (JAC D)	Nov. 25, 1825	Nov. 25, 1829
Gabriel Moore (JAC D)	Nov. 25, 1829	March 3, 1831
Samuel B. Moore (D)	March 3, 1832	Nov. 26, 1831
John Gayle (D)	Nov. 26, 1831	Nov. 21, 1835
Clement C. Clay (D)	Nov. 21, 1835	July 17, 1837
Hugh McVay (D)	July 17, 1837	Nov. 21, 1837
Arthur P. Bagby (D)	Nov. 21, 1837	Nov. 22, 1841
Benjamin Fitzpatrick (D)	Nov. 22, 1841	Dec. 10, 1845
Joshua L. Martin (I)	Dec. 10, 1845	Dec. 16, 1847
Reuben Chapman (D)	Dec. 16, 1847	Dec. 17, 1849
Henry W. Collier (D)	Dec. 17, 1849	Dec. 20, 1853
John A. Winston (D)	Dec. 20, 1853	Dec. 1, 1857
Andrew B. Moore (D)	Dec. 1, 1857	Dec. 2, 1861
John Gill Shorter (D)	Dec. 2, 1861	Dec. 1, 1863
Thomas H. Watts (W)	Dec. 1, 1863	May 1865
Lewis E. Parsons[1]	June 21, 1865	Dec. 20, 1865
Robert M. Patton (W)	Dec. 20, 1865	July 14, 1868
William Hugh Smith (R)	July 14, 1868	Nov. 26, 1870
Robert B. Lindsay (D)	Nov. 26, 1870	Nov. 17, 1872
David P. Lewis (R)	Nov. 17, 1872	Nov. 24, 1874
George S. Houston (D)	Nov. 24, 1874	Nov. 28, 1878
Rufus W. Cobb (D)	Nov. 28, 1878	Dec. 1, 1882
Edward A. O'Neal (D)	Dec. 1, 1882	Dec. 1, 1886
Thomas Seay (D)	Dec. 1, 1886	Dec. 1, 1890
Thomas G. Jones (D)	Dec. 1, 1890	Dec. 1, 1894
William C. Oates (D)	Dec. 1, 1894	Dec. 1, 1896
Joseph F. Johnston (D)	Dec. 1, 1896	Dec. 1, 1900
William D. Jelks (D)[2]	Dec. 1, 1900	Dec. 26, 1900
William J. Samford (D)[3]	Dec. 26, 1900	June 11, 1901
William D. Jelks (D)[4]	June 11, 1901	April 25, 1904
Russell M. Cunningham (D)[5]	April 25, 1904	March 5, 1905
William D. Jelks (D)	March 5, 1905	Jan. 14, 1907
Braxton B. Comer (D)	Jan. 14, 1907	Jan. 17, 1911
Emmet O'Neal (D)	Jan. 17, 1911	Jan. 18, 1915
Charles Henderson (D)	Jan. 18, 1915	Jan. 20, 1919
Thomas E. Kilby (D)	Jan. 20, 1919	Jan. 15, 1923
William W. Brandon (D)	Jan. 15, 1923	Jan. 17, 1927
Bibb Graves (D)	Jan. 17, 1927	Jan. 19, 1931
Benjamin M. Miller (D)	Jan. 19, 1931	Jan. 14, 1935
Bibb Graves (D)	Jan. 14, 1935	Jan. 17, 1939
Frank M. Dixon (D)	Jan. 17, 1939	Jan. 19, 1943
Chauncey M. Sparks (D)	Jan. 19, 1943	Jan. 20, 1947
James E. Folsom (D)	Jan. 20, 1947	Jan. 15, 1951
Gordon Persons (D)	Jan. 15, 1951	Jan. 17, 1955
James E. Folsom (D)	Jan. 17, 1955	Jan. 19, 1959
John M. Patterson (D)	Jan. 19, 1959	Jan. 14, 1963
George C. Wallace (D)	Jan. 14, 1963	Jan. 16, 1967
Lurleen B. Wallace (D)[6]	Jan. 16, 1967	May 7, 1968
Albert P. Brewer (D)[7]	May 7, 1968	Jan. 18, 1971
George C. Wallace (D)	Jan. 18, 1971	Jan. 15, 1979
Forrest "Fob" James Jr. (D)	Jan. 15, 1979	Jan. 17, 1983
George C. Wallace (D)	Jan. 17, 1983	Jan. 19, 1987
Guy Hunt (R)[8]	Jan. 19, 1987	April 22, 1993
James E. Folsom Jr. (D)[9]	April 22, 1993	Jan. 16, 1995
Forrest "Fob" James Jr. (R)[10]	Jan. 16, 1995	

Alabama
1. Provisional governor, appointed by president.
2. Jelks, as president of the state Senate, took office as acting governor due to the illness of governor-elect Samford.
3. Died June 11, 1901.
4. As president of the state Senate, Jelks became governor on Samford's death. Subsequently re-elected in 1902.
5. As lieutenant governor, he became acting governor due to the illness of Jelks.
6. Died May 7, 1968.
7. As lieutenant governor, he succeeded to office.
8. Removed from office upon conviction of misusing campaign funds.
9. As lieutenant governor, he succeeded to office.
10. Switched to Republican Party in 1994.

ALASKA

(Became a state Jan. 3, 1959)

Governors	Dates of Service	
William A. Egan (D)	Jan. 3, 1959	Dec. 5, 1966
Walter J. Hickel (R)[1]	Dec. 5, 1966	Jan. 29, 1969
Keith H. Miller (R)[2]	Jan. 29, 1969	Dec. 5, 1970
William A. Egan (D)	Dec. 5, 1970	Dec. 2, 1974
Jay S. Hammond (R)	Dec. 2, 1974	Dec. 6, 1982
Bill Sheffield (D)	Dec. 6, 1982	Dec. 1, 1986
Steve C. Cowper (D)	Dec. 1, 1986	Dec. 3, 1990
Walter J. Hickel (ALI)	Dec. 3, 1990	Dec. 5, 1994
Tony Knowles (D)	Dec. 5, 1994	

Alaska
1. Resigned Jan. 29, 1969.
2. As secretary of state, he succeeded to office.

ARIZONA

(Became a state Feb. 14, 1912)

Governors	Dates of Service	
George W. P. Hunt (D)	Feb. 14, 1912	Jan. 1, 1917
Thomas E. Campbell (R)[1]	Jan. 1, 1917	Dec. 25, 1917
George W. P. Hunt (D)[2]	Dec. 25, 1917	Jan. 6, 1919
Thomas E. Campbell (R)	Jan. 6, 1919	Jan. 1, 1923
George W. P. Hunt (D)	Jan. 1, 1923	Jan. 7, 1929
John C. Phillips (R)	Jan. 7, 1929	Jan. 5, 1931
George W. P. Hunt (D)	Jan. 5, 1931	Jan. 2, 1933
Benjamin B. Moeur (D)	Jan. 2, 1933	Jan. 4, 1937
Rawghile C. Stanford (D)	Jan. 4, 1937	Jan. 2, 1939
Robert T. Jones (D)	Jan. 2, 1939	Jan. 6, 1941
Sidney P. Osborn (D)[3]	Jan. 6, 1941	May 25, 1948
Dan E. Garvey (D)[4]	May 25, 1948	Jan. 1, 1951
J. Howard Pyle (R)	Jan. 1, 1951	Jan. 3, 1955
Ernest W. McFarland (D)	Jan. 3, 1955	Jan. 5, 1959
Paul J. Fannin (R)	Jan. 5, 1959	Jan. 4, 1965
Sam Goddard (D)	Jan. 4, 1965	Jan. 2, 1967
Jack Williams (R)	Jan. 2, 1967	Jan. 6, 1975
Raul Castro (D)[5]	Jan. 6, 1975	Oct. 20, 1977

Wesley Bolin (D)[6]	Oct. 20, 1977	March 4, 1978
Bruce Babbitt (D)[7]	March 4, 1978	Jan. 5, 1987
Evan Mecham (R)[8]	Jan. 5, 1987	April 4, 1988
Rose Mofford (D)[9]	April 5, 1988	March 6, 1991
Fife Symington (R)[10]	March 6, 1991	Sept. 5, 1997
Jane Hull (R)[11]	Sept. 5, 1997	

Arizona

1. Campbell was initially declared the winner, but the election was contested. After an extended recount, Hunt was declared the winner by 43 votes.
2. Hunt served out the remainder of the term following his successful challenge to Campbell's election.
3. Died May 25, 1948.
4. As secretary of state, he succeeded to office. Subsequently elected.
5. Resigned Oct. 20, 1977, to become ambassador to Argentina.
6. As secretary of state, he succeeded to office. Died March 4, 1978.
7. As attorney general, he succeeded to office. Subsequently elected.
8. Impeached; removed from office April 4, 1988.
9. As secretary of state, she succeeded to office.
10. Resigned Sept. 5, 1997.
11. As secretary of state, she succeeded to office.

ARKANSAS

(Became a state June 15, 1836)

Governors	Dates of Service	
James S. Conway (D)	Sept. 13, 1836	Nov. 4, 1840
Archibald Yell (D)[1]	Nov. 4, 1840	April 29, 1844
Samuel Adams (D)[2]	April 24, 1844	Nov. 5, 1844
Thomas S. Drew (D)[3]	Nov. 5, 1844	Jan. 10, 1849
Richard C. Byrd (D)[4]	Jan. 11, 1849	April 19, 1849
John S. Roane (D)	April 19, 1849	Nov. 15, 1852
Elias N. Conway (D)	Nov. 15, 1852	Nov. 16, 1860
Henry M. Rector (ID)	Nov. 16, 1860	Nov. 4, 1862
Thomas Fletcher[5]	Nov. 4, 1862	Nov. 15, 1862
Harris Flannigan (D)	Nov. 15, 1862	April 18, 1864
Isaac Murphy (UN)	April 18, 1864	July 2, 1868
Powell Clayton (R)[6]	July 2, 1868	March 17, 1871
Ozra A. Hadley (R)[7]	March 17, 1871	Jan. 6, 1873
Elisha Baxter (R)	Jan. 6, 1873	Nov. 12, 1874
A. H. Garland (D)	Nov. 12, 1874	Jan. 11, 1877
William R. Miller (D)	Jan. 11, 1877	Jan. 13, 1881
Thomas J. Churchill (D)	Jan. 13, 1881	Jan. 13, 1883
James H. Berry (D)	Jan. 13, 1883	Jan. 17, 1885
Simon P. Hughes (D)	Jan. 17, 1885	Jan. 17, 1889
James P. Eagle (D)	Jan. 17, 1889	Jan. 10, 1893
William M. Fishback (D)	Jan. 10, 1893	Jan. 18, 1895
James P. Clarke (D)	Jan. 18, 1895	Jan. 12, 1897
Daniel Webster Jones (D)	Jan. 12, 1897	Jan. 8, 1901
Jeff Davis (D)	Jan. 8, 1901	Jan. 8, 1907
John S. Little (D)[8]	Jan. 8, 1907	Feb. 11, 1907
John I. Moore (D)[9]	Feb. 11, 1907	May 11, 1907
Xenophon O. Pindall (D)[10]	May 14, 1907	Jan. 11, 1909
George W. Donaghey (D)	Jan. 11, 1909	Jan. 15, 1913
Joseph T. Robinson (D)[11]	Jan. 15, 1913	March 10, 1913
William K. Oldham (D)[12]	March 10, 1913	March 13, 1913
Junius M. Futrell (D)[13]	March 13, 1913	July 23, 1913
George W. Hays (D)	July 23, 1913	Jan. 9, 1917
Charles H. Brough (D)	Jan. 9, 1917	Jan. 11, 1921
Thomas C. McRae (D)	Jan. 11, 1921	Jan. 13, 1925
Thomas J. Terrall (D)	Jan. 13, 1925	Jan. 11, 1927
John E. Martineau (D)[14]	Jan. 11, 1927	March 4, 1928
Harvey Parnell (D)[15]	March 4, 1928	Jan. 10, 1933
Junius M. Futrell (D)	Jan. 10, 1933	Jan. 12, 1937
Carl E. Bailey (D)	Jan. 12, 1937	Jan. 14, 1941
Homer M. Adkins (D)	Jan. 14, 1941	Jan. 9, 1945
Benjamin T. Laney (D)	Jan. 9, 1945	Jan. 11, 1949
Sidney S. McMath (D)	Jan. 11, 1949	Jan. 13, 1953
Frances A. Cherry (D)	Jan. 13, 1953	Jan. 11, 1955
Orval E. Faubus (D)	Jan. 11, 1955	Jan. 10, 1967

Winthrop Rockefeller (R)	Jan. 10, 1967	Jan. 12, 1971
Dale Bumpers (D)[16]	Jan. 12, 1971	Jan. 3, 1975
Bob Riley (D)[17]	Jan. 3, 1975	Jan. 14, 1975
David Pryor (D)[18]	Jan. 14, 1975	Jan. 3, 1979
Joe Purcell (D)[19]	Jan. 3, 1979	Jan. 9, 1979
Bill Clinton (D)	Jan. 9, 1979	Jan. 19, 1981
Frank D. White (R)	Jan. 19, 1981	Jan. 11, 1983
Bill Clinton (D)[20]	Jan. 11, 1983	Dec. 12, 1992
Jim Guy Tucker (D)[21]	Dec. 12, 1992	July 15, 1996
Mike Huckabee (R)[22]	July 15, 1996	

Arkansas

1. Resigned April 29, 1844.
2. As president of the state Senate, he succeeded to office.
3. Resigned Jan. 10, 1849.
4. As president of the state Senate, he succeeded to office.
5. Acting governor.
6. Resigned March 17, 1871.
7. Succeeded to office.
8. Resigned Feb. 11, 1907.
9. Acting governor.
10. Elected president of the state Senate, he then succeeded to office as governor.
11. Resigned March 10, 1913.
12. As president of the state Senate, he succeeded to office.
13. As president of the state Senate, he succeeded to office.
14. Resigned March 4, 1928.
15. As lieutenant governor, he succeeded to office. Subsequently elected.
16. Resigned Jan. 3, 1975.
17. As lieutenant governor, he succeeded to office.
18. Resigned Jan. 3, 1979.
19. As lieutenant governor, he succeeded to office.
20. Resigned Dec. 12, 1992, having been elected president of the United States.
21. As lieutenant governor, he succeeded to office. Resigned July 15, 1996.
22. As lieutenant governor, he succeeded to office.

CALIFORNIA

(Became a state Sept. 9, 1850)

Governors	Dates of Service	
Peter H. Burnett (ID)[1]	Dec. 20, 1849	Jan. 9, 1851
John McDougal (ID)[2]	Jan. 9, 1851	Jan. 8, 1852
John Bigler (D)	Jan. 8, 1852	Jan. 9, 1856
J. Neely Johnson (AM)	Jan. 9, 1856	Jan. 8, 1858
John B. Weller (D)	Jan. 8, 1858	Jan. 9, 1860
Milton S. Latham (D)[3]	Jan. 9, 1860	Jan. 14, 1860
John G. Downey (D)[4]	Jan. 14, 1860	Jan. 10, 1862
Leland Stanford (R)	Jan. 10, 1862	Dec. 10, 1863
Frederick F. Low (UN R)	Dec. 10, 1863	Dec. 5, 1867
Henry H. Haight (D)	Dec. 5, 1867	Dec. 8, 1871
Newton Booth (R)[5]	Dec. 8, 1871	Feb. 27, 1875
Romualdo Pacheco (R)[6]	Feb. 27, 1875	Dec. 9, 1875
William Irwin (D)	Dec. 9, 1875	Jan. 8, 1880
George C. Perkins (R)	Jan. 8, 1880	Jan. 10, 1883
George Stoneman (D)	Jan. 10, 1883	Jan. 8, 1887
Washington Bartlett (D)[7]	Jan. 8, 1887	Sept. 13, 1887
Robert W. Waterman (R)[8]	Sept. 13, 1887	Jan. 8, 1891
Henry H. Markham (R)	Jan. 8, 1891	Jan. 11, 1895
James H. Budd (D)	Jan. 11, 1895	Jan. 3, 1899
Henry T. Gage (R & UL)	Jan. 3, 1899	Jan. 6, 1903
George C. Pardee (R)	Jan. 6, 1903	Jan. 8, 1907
James N. Gillett (R)	Jan. 8, 1907	Jan. 3, 1911
Hiram W. Johnson (R, PROG)[9]	Jan. 3, 1911	March 15, 1917
William D. Stephens (RP & PROG)[10]	March 15, 1917	Jan. 9, 1923
Friend William Richardson (R)	Jan. 9, 1923	Jan. 4, 1927
Clement C. Young (R)	Jan. 4, 1927	Jan. 6, 1931
James Rolph Jr. (R)[11]	Jan. 6, 1931	June 2, 1934
Frank F. Merriam (R)[12]	June 2, 1934	Jan. 2, 1939
Culbert L. Olson (D)	Jan. 2, 1939	Jan. 4, 1943

Earl Warren (R)[13]	Jan. 4, 1943	Oct. 5, 1953
Goodwin J. Knight (R)[14]	Oct. 5, 1953	Jan. 5, 1959
Edmund G. Brown (D)	Jan. 5, 1959	Jan. 2, 1967
Ronald Reagan (R)	Jan. 1, 1967	Jan. 6, 1975
Edmund G. Brown Jr. (D)	Jan. 6, 1975	Jan. 3, 1983
George Deukmejian (R)	Jan. 3, 1983	Jan. 7, 1991
Pete Wilson (R)	Jan. 7, 1991	

California

1. Resigned Jan. 9, 1851.
2. As lieutenant governor, he succeeded to office.
3. Resigned Jan. 14, 1860.
4. As lieutenant governor, he succeeded to office.
5. Resigned Feb. 27, 1875.
6. As lieutenant governor, he succeeded to office.
7. Died Sept. 13, 1887.
8. As lieutenant governor, he succeeded to office.
9. Elected as Republican in 1910. Elected as Progressive in 1914. Resigned March 15, 1917.
10. As lieutenant governor, he succeeded to office. Subsequently elected.
11. Died June 2, 1934.
12. As lieutenant governor, he succeeded to office. Subsequently elected.
13. Resigned Oct. 5, 1953.
14. As lieutenant governor, he succeeded to office. Subsequently elected.

COLORADO

(Became a state Aug. 1, 1876)

Governors	**Dates of Service**	
John L. Routt (R)	Nov. 3, 1876	Jan. 14, 1879
Frederick W. Pitkin (R)	Jan. 14, 1879	Jan. 9, 1883
James B. Grant (D)	Jan. 9, 1883	Jan. 13, 1885
Benjamin H. Eaton (R)	Jan. 13, 1885	Jan. 11, 1887
Alva Adams (D)	Jan. 11, 1887	Jan. 10, 1889
Job A. Cooper (R)	Jan. 10, 1889	Jan. 13, 1891
John L. Routt (R)	Jan. 13, 1891	Jan. 10, 1893
Davis H. Waite (POP & SL D)	Jan. 10, 1893	Jan. 8, 1895
Albert W. McIntire (R)	Jan. 8, 1895	Jan. 12, 1897
Alva Adams (D)	Jan. 12, 1897	Jan. 10, 1899
Charles S. Thomas (FUS)	Jan. 10, 1899	Jan. 8, 1901
James B. Orman (FUS)	Jan. 8, 1901	Jan. 13, 1903
James H. Peabody (R)	Jan. 13, 1903	Jan. 10, 1905
Alva Adams (D)[1]	Jan. 10, 1905	March 16, 1905
James H. Peabody (R)	March 16, 1905	March 17, 1905
Jesse F. McDonald (R)[2]	March 17, 1905	Jan. 8, 1907
Henry A. Buchtel (R)	Jan. 8, 1907	Jan. 12, 1909
John F. Shafroth (D)	Jan. 12, 1909	Jan. 14, 1913
Elias M. Ammons (D)	Jan. 14, 1913	Jan. 12, 1915
George A. Carlson (R)	Jan. 12, 1915	Jan. 9, 1917
Julius C. Gunter (D)	Jan. 9, 1917	Jan. 14, 1919
Oliver H. Shoup (R)	Jan. 14, 1919	Jan. 9, 1923
William E. Sweet (D)	Jan. 9, 1923	Jan. 13, 1925
Clarence J. Morley (R)	Jan. 13, 1925	Jan. 11, 1927
William H. Adams (D)	Jan. 11, 1927	Jan. 10, 1933
Edwin C. Johnson (D)[3]	Jan. 10, 1933	Jan. 3, 1937
Ray H. Talbot (D)[4]	Jan. 3, 1937	Jan. 12, 1937
Teller Ammons (D)	Jan. 12, 1937	Jan. 10, 1939
Ralph L. Carr (R)	Jan. 10, 1939	Jan. 12, 1943
John C. Vivian (R)	Jan. 12, 1943	Jan. 14, 1947
William L. Knous (D)[5]	Jan. 14, 1947	April 15, 1950
Walter W. Johnson (D)[6]	April 15, 1950	Jan. 9, 1951
Dan Thornton (R)	Jan. 9, 1951	Jan. 11, 1955
Edwin C. Johnson (D)	Jan. 11, 1955	Jan. 8, 1957
Stephen L. R. McNichols (D)	Jan. 8, 1957	Jan. 8, 1963
John A. Love (R)[7]	Jan. 8, 1963	July 16, 1973
John D. Vanderhoof (R)[8]	July 16, 1973	Jan. 14, 1975
Richard D. Lamm (D)	Jan. 14, 1975	Jan. 13, 1987
Roy Romer (D)	Jan. 13, 1987	

Colorado

1. The 1904 election between Alva Adams (D) and James H. Peabody (R) caused a dispute surrounding charges of fraud which had to be settled by the Legislature. Both contenders were asked to withdraw. Adams served as governor for 66 days and Peabody for one day.
2. As lieutenant governor, he succeeded to office.
3. Resigned Jan. 3, 1937.
4. As lieutenant governor, he succeeded to office.
5. Resigned April 15, 1950.
6. As lieutenant governor, he succeeded to office.
7. Resigned July 16, 1973.
8. As lieutenant governor, he succeeded to office.

CONNECTICUT

(Ratified the Constitution Jan. 9, 1788)

Governors	**Dates of Service**	
Samuel Huntington[1]	May 11, 1786	Jan. 5, 1796
Oliver Wolcott (FED)[2]	Jan. 5, 1796	Dec. 1, 1797
Jonathan Trumbull (FED)[3]	Dec. 1, 1797	Aug. 7, 1809
John Treadwell (FED)	Aug. 7, 1809	May 9, 1811
Roger Griswold (FED)[4]	May 9, 1811	Oct. 25, 1812
John Cotton Smith (FED)	Oct. 25, 1812	May 8, 1817
Oliver Wolcott Jr. (D-R)	May 8, 1817	May 2, 1827
Gideon Tomlinson (D-R, NR)[5]	May 2, 1827	March 1831
John S. Peters (NR)	March 1831	May 4, 1833
Henry W. Edwards (D)	May 4, 1833	May 7, 1834
Samuel A. Foote (NR)	May 7, 1834	May 6, 1835
Henry W. Edwards (D)	May 6, 1835	May 2, 1838
William W. Ellsworth (W)	May 2, 1838	May 4, 1842
Chauncey F. Cleveland (D)	May 4, 1842	May 1844
Roger S. Baldwin (W)	May 1844	May 6, 1846
Isaac Toucey (D)	May 6, 1846	May 5, 1847
Clark Bissell (W)	May 5, 1847	May 2, 1849
Joseph Trumbull (W)	May 2, 1849	May 4, 1850
Thomas H. Seymour (D)[6]	May 4, 1850	Oct. 13, 1853
Charles H. Pond (D)[7]	Oct. 13, 1853	May 1854
Henry Dutton (W)	May 3, 1854	May 1855
William T. Minor (AM)	May 3, 1855	May 6, 1857
Alexander H. Holley (R)	May 6, 1857	May 5, 1858
William A. Buckingham (R)	May 5, 1858	May 2, 1866
Joseph R. Hawley (R)	May 2, 1866	May 1, 1867
James E. English (D)	May 1, 1867	May 5, 1869
Marshall Jewell (R)	May 5, 1869	May 4, 1870
James E. English (D)	May 4, 1870	May 1871
Marshall Jewell (R)	May 16, 1871	May 7, 1873
Charles R. Ingersoll (D)	May 7, 1873	Jan. 3, 1877
Richard D. Hubbard (D)	Jan. 3, 1877	Jan. 9, 1879
Charles B. Andrews (R)	Jan. 9, 1879	Jan. 5, 1881
Hobart B. Bigelow (R)	Jan. 5, 1881	Jan. 3, 1883
Thomas M. Waller (D)	Jan. 3, 1883	Jan. 8, 1885
Henry B. Harrison (R)	Jan. 8, 1885	Jan. 7, 1887
Phineas C. Lounsbury (R)	Jan. 7, 1887	Jan. 10, 1889
Morgan G. Bulkeley (R)[8]	Jan. 10, 1889	Jan. 4, 1893
Luzon B. Morris (D)	Jan. 4, 1893	Jan. 9, 1895
O. Vincent Coffin (R)	Jan. 9, 1895	Jan. 6, 1897
Lorrin A. Cooke (R)	Jan. 6, 1897	Jan. 4, 1899
George E. Lounsbury (R)	Jan. 4, 1899	Jan. 9, 1901
George P. McLean (R)	Jan. 9, 1901	Jan. 7, 1903
Abiram Chamberlain (R)	Jan. 7, 1903	Jan. 4, 1905
Henry Roberts (R)	Jan. 4, 1905	Jan. 9, 1907
Rollin S. Woodruff (R)	Jan. 9, 1907	Jan. 6, 1909
George L. Lilley (R)[9]	Jan. 6, 1909	April 21, 1909
Frank B. Weeks (R)[10]	April 21, 1909	Jan. 4, 1911
Simeon E. Baldwin (D)	Jan. 4, 1911	Jan. 6, 1915
Marcus H. Holcomb (R)	Jan. 6, 1915	Jan. 5, 1921
Everett J. Lake (R)	Jan. 5, 1921	Jan. 3, 1923
Charles A. Templeton (R)	Jan. 3, 1923	Jan. 7, 1925
Hiram Bingham (R)[11]	Jan. 7, 1925	Jan. 8, 1925
John H. Trumbull (R)[12]	Jan. 8, 1925	Jan. 7, 1931
Wilbur L. Cross (D)	Jan. 7, 1931	Jan. 4, 1939
Raymond E. Baldwin (R)	Jan. 4, 1939	Jan. 8, 1941
Robert A. Hurley (D)	Jan. 8, 1941	Jan. 6, 1943

Raymond E. Baldwin (R)[13]	Jan. 6, 1943	Dec. 27, 1946
Wilbert Snow (D)[14]	Dec. 27, 1946	Jan. 8, 1947
James L. McConaughy (R)[15]	Jan. 8, 1947	March 7, 1948
James C. Shannon (R)[16]	March 7, 1948	Jan. 5, 1949
Chester Bowles (D)	Jan. 5, 1949	Jan. 3, 1951
John D. Lodge (R)	Jan. 3, 1951	Jan. 5, 1955
Abraham Ribicoff (D)[17]	Jan. 5, 1955	Jan. 21, 1961
John Dempsey (D)[18]	Jan. 21, 1961	Jan. 6, 1971
Thomas J. Meskill (R)	Jan. 6, 1971	Jan. 8, 1975
Ella T. Grasso (D)[19]	Jan. 8, 1975	Dec. 31, 1980
William A. O'Neill (D)[20]	Dec. 31, 1980	Jan. 9, 1991
Lowell P. Weicker Jr. (I)	Jan. 9, 1991	Jan. 4, 1995
John G. Rowland (R)	Jan. 4, 1995	

Connecticut
1. Died Jan. 5, 1796.
2. Died Dec. 1, 1797.
3. Died Aug. 7, 1809.
4. Died Oct. 25, 1812.
5. Resigned in 1831 to become U.S. senator.
6. Resigned Oct. 13, 1853.
7. As lieutenant governor, he succeeded to office.
8. The 1890 election was disputed, with Democrats claiming that Luzon Morris had won a majority of the popular vote and been elected governor, and Republicans claiming that he had not and demanding an election by the legislature. Since control of the legislature was divided, the two houses could not agree on what to do, so Bulkeley remained in office for the term.
9. Died April 21, 1909.
10. As lieutenant governor, he succeeded to office.
11. Resigned Jan. 8, 1925.
12. As lieutenant governor, he succeeded to office. Subsequently elected.
13. Resigned Dec. 27, 1946.
14. As lieutenant governor, he succeeded to office.
15. Died March 7, 1948.
16. As lieutenant governor, he succeeded to office.
17. Resigned Jan. 21, 1961.
18. As lieutenant governor, he succeeded to office. Subsequently elected.
19. Resigned Dec. 31, 1980.
20. As lieutenant governor, he succeeded to office. Subsequently elected.

DELAWARE

(Ratified the Constitution Dec. 7, 1787)

Governors	Dates of Service	
Joshua Clayton (FED)[1]	June 2, 1789	Jan. 13, 1796
Gunning Bedford Sr. (FED)[2]	Jan. 13, 1796	Sept. 28, 1797
Daniel Rogers (FED)[3]	Sept. 28, 1797	Jan. 9, 1799
Richard Bassett (FED)[4]	Jan. 1799	March 1801
James Sykes (FED)[5]	March 1801	Jan. 1802
David Hall (D-R)	Jan. 1802	Jan. 1805
Nathaniel Mitchell (FED)	Jan. 1805	Jan. 1808
George Truitt (FED)	Jan. 1808	Jan. 1811
Joseph Haslet (D-R)	Jan. 1811	Jan. 1814
Daniel Rodney (FED)	Jan. 1814	Jan. 1817
John Clark (FED)	Jan. 1817	Jan. 1820
Henry Molleston[6]		
Jacob Stout (FED)[7]	Jan. 1820	Jan. 1821
John Collins (D-R)[8]	Jan. 1821	April 1822
Caleb Rodney (D-R)[9]	April 1822	Jan. 1823
Joseph Haslet (D-R)[10]	Jan. 1823	June 20, 1823
Charles Thomas (D-R)[11]	June 20, 1823	Jan. 1824
Samuel Paynter (FED)	Jan. 1824	Jan. 1827
Charles Polk (FED)	Jan. 1827	Jan. 1830
David Hazzard (D)	Jan. 1830	Jan. 1833
Caleb P. Bennett (D)[12]	Jan. 1833	April 9, 1836
Charles Polk[13]	April 9, 1836	Jan. 1837
Cornelius P. Comegys (W)	Jan. 1837	Jan. 1841
William B. Cooper (W)	Jan. 1841	Jan. 1845
Thomas Stockton (W)[14]	Jan. 1845	March 2, 1846
Joseph Maull (W)[15]	March 2, 1846	May 1, 1846

William Temple (W)[16]	May 1, 1846	Jan. 1847
William Tharp (D)	Jan. 1847	Jan. 1851
William H. Ross (D)	Jan. 1851	Jan. 1855
Peter F. Causey (AM)	Jan. 1855	Jan. 1859
William Burton (D)	Jan. 1859	Jan. 1863
William Cannon (UN)[17]	Jan. 1863	March 1, 1865
Gove Saulsbury (D)[18]	March 1, 1865	Jan. 1871
James Ponder (D)	Jan. 1871	Jan. 1875
John P. Cochran (D)	Jan. 1875	Jan. 1879
John W. Hall (D)	Jan. 1879	Jan. 1883
Charles C. Stockley (D)	Jan. 1883	Jan. 1887
Benjamin T. Biggs (D)	Jan. 1887	Jan. 1891
Robert J. Reynolds (D)	Jan. 1891	Jan. 1895
Joshua H. Marvel (R)[19]	Jan. 1895	April 8, 1895
William T. Watson (D)[20]	April 8, 1895	Jan. 19, 1897
Ebe W. Tunnell (D)	Jan. 19, 1897	Jan. 15, 1901
John Hunn (R)	Jan. 15, 1901	Jan. 17, 1905
Preston Lea (R)	Jan. 17, 1905	Jan. 19, 1909
Simeon S. Pennewill (R)	Jan. 19, 1909	Jan. 21, 1913
Charles R. Miller (R)	Jan. 21, 1913	Jan. 17, 1917
John G. Townsend Jr. (R)	Jan. 17, 1917	Jan. 18, 1921
William D. Denney (R)	Jan. 18, 1921	Jan. 20, 1925
Robert P. Robinson (R)	Jan. 20, 1925	Jan. 15, 1929
C. Douglass Buck (R)	Jan. 15, 1929	Jan. 19, 1937
Richard C. McMullen (D)	Jan. 19, 1937	Jan. 21, 1941
Walter W. Bacon (R)	Jan. 21, 1941	Jan. 18, 1949
Elbert N. Carvel (D)	Jan. 18, 1949	Jan. 20, 1953
J. Caleb Boggs (R)[21]	Jan. 20, 1953	Dec. 30, 1960
David P. Buckson (R)[22]	Dec. 30, 1960	Jan. 17, 1961
Elbert N. Carvel (D)	Jan. 17, 1961	Jan. 19, 1965
Charles L. Terry Jr. (D)	Jan. 19, 1965	Jan. 21, 1969
Russell W. Peterson (R)	Jan. 21, 1969	Jan. 16, 1973
Sherman W. Tribbitt (D)	Jan. 16, 1973	Jan. 18, 1977
Pierre duPont (R)	Jan. 18, 1977	Jan. 15, 1985
Michael N. Castle (R)[23]	Jan. 15, 1985	Dec. 31, 1992
Dale E. Wolf (R)[24]	Jan. 1, 1993	Jan. 19, 1993
Thomas R. Carper(D)	Jan. 19, 1993	

Delaware
1. Joshua Clayton was president of Delaware from 1789 to 1793 and governor from 1793 to 1796.
2. Died Sept. 28, 1797.
3. Acting governor.
4. Resigned in March 1801.
5. Acting governor.
6. Died before taking office.
7. Acting governor.
8. Died in April 1822.
9. Acting governor.
10. Died June 20, 1823.
11. Acting governor.
12. Died April 9, 1836.
13. Acting governor.
14. Died March 2, 1846.
15. Acting governor. Died May 1, 1846.
16. Acting governor.
17. Died March 1, 1865.
18. Acting governor. Subsequently elected.
19. Died April 8, 1895.
20. Acting governor.
21. Resigned Dec. 30, 1960.
22. As lieutenant governor, he succeeded to office.
23. Resigned Dec. 31, 1992, having been elected to the U.S. House.
24. As lieutenant governor, he succeeded to office.

FLORIDA

(Became a state March 3, 1845)

Governors	Dates of Service	
William D. Moseley (D)	June 25, 1845	Oct. 1, 1849
Thomas Brown (W)	Oct. 1, 1849	Oct. 3, 1853
James E. Broome (D)	Oct. 3, 1853	Oct. 5, 1857

Madison S. Perry (D)	Oct. 5, 1857	Oct. 7, 1861
John Milton (D)[1]	Oct. 7, 1861	April 1, 1865
William Marvin[2]	July 13, 1865	Dec. 20, 1865
David S. Walker (C)	Dec. 20, 1865	July 9, 1868
Harrison Reed (R)	July 9, 1868	Jan. 7, 1873
Ossian B. Hart (R)[3]	Jan. 7, 1873	March 18, 1874
Marcellus L. Stearns (R)[4]	March 18, 1874	Jan. 2, 1877
George F. Drew (D)	Jan. 2, 1877	Jan. 4, 1881
William D. Bloxham (D)	Jan. 4, 1881	Jan. 6, 1885
Edward A. Perry (D)	Jan. 6, 1885	Jan. 8, 1889
Francis P. Fleming (D)	Jan. 8, 1889	Jan. 3, 1893
Henry L. Mitchell (D)	Jan. 3, 1893	Jan. 5, 1897
William D. Bloxham (D)	Jan. 5, 1897	Jan. 8, 1901
William S. Jennings (D)	Jan. 8, 1901	Jan. 3, 1905
Napoleon B. Broward (D)	Jan. 3, 1905	Jan. 5, 1909
Albert W. Gilchrist (D)	Jan. 5, 1909	Jan. 7, 1913
Park Trammell (D)	Jan. 7, 1913	Jan. 2, 1917
Sidney J. Catts (IP)	Jan. 2, 1917	Jan. 4, 1921
Cary A. Hardee (D)	Jan. 4, 1921	Jan. 6, 1925
John W. Martin (D)	Jan. 6, 1925	Jan. 8, 1929
Doyle E. Carlton (D)	Jan. 8, 1929	Jan. 3, 1933
David Sholtz (D)	Jan. 3, 1933	Jan. 5, 1937
Frederick P. Cone (D)	Jan. 5, 1937	Jan. 7, 1941
Spessard L. Holland (D)	Jan. 7, 1941	Jan. 2, 1945
Millard F. Caldwell (D)	Jan. 2, 1945	Jan. 4, 1949
Fuller Warren (D)	Jan. 4, 1949	Jan. 6, 1953
Daniel T. McCarty (D)[5]	Jan. 6, 1953	Sept. 28, 1953
Charley E. Johns (D)[6]	Sept. 18, 1953	Jan. 4, 1955
LeRoy Collins (D)[7]	Jan. 4, 1955	Jan. 3, 1961
Farris Bryant (D)	Jan. 3, 1961	Jan. 5, 1965
Haydon Burns (D)	Jan. 5, 1965	Jan. 3, 1967
Claude R. Kirk Jr. (R)	Jan. 3, 1967	Jan. 5, 1971
Reubin Askew (D)	Jan. 5, 1971	Jan. 2, 1979
Robert Graham (D)[8]	Jan. 2, 1979	Jan. 3, 1987
John W. Mixon (D)[9]	Jan. 3, 1987	Jan. 6, 1987
Bob Martinez (R)	Jan. 6, 1987	Jan. 8, 1991
Lawton Chiles (D)	Jan. 8, 1991	

Florida

1. Died April 1, 1865.
2. Acting governor, appointed by president.
3. Died March 18, 1874.
4. As lieutenant governor, he succeeded to office.
5. Died Sept. 28, 1953.
6. As president of the state Senate, he succeeded to office for the remainder of the first half of McCarty's term.
7. Elected in a special election to serve the last two years of McCarty's term. Subsequently re-elected.
8. Resigned Jan. 3, 1987, having been elected to the U.S. Senate.
9. As lieutenant governor, he succeeded to office.

GEORGIA

(Ratified the Constitution Jan. 2, 1788)

Governors	**Dates of Service**	
George Handley	Jan. 26, 1788	Jan. 7, 1789
George Walton (D-R)	Jan. 7, 1789	Nov. 9, 1789
Edward Telfair (D-R)	Nov. 9, 1789	Nov. 7, 1793
George Mathews (D-R)	Nov. 7, 1793	Jan. 15, 1796
Jared Irwin (D-R)	Jan. 15, 1796	Jan. 12, 1798
James Jackson (D-R)	Jan. 12, 1798	March 3, 1801
David Emanuel (D-R)	March 3, 1801	Nov. 7, 1801
Josiah Tattnall Jr. (D-R)	Nov. 7, 1801	Nov. 4, 1802
John Milledge (D-R)	Nov. 4, 1802	Sept. 23, 1806
Jared Irwin (D-R)	Sept. 23, 1806	Nov. 10, 1809
David B. Mitchell (D-R)	Nov. 10, 1809	Nov. 5, 1813
Peter Early (D-R)	Nov. 5, 1813	Nov. 10, 1815
David B. Mitchell (D-R)	Nov. 10, 1815	March 4, 1817
William Rabun (D-R)	March 4, 1817	Oct. 24, 1819
Matthew Talbot (D-R)	Oct. 24, 1819	Nov. 5, 1819
John Clark (D-R)	Nov. 5, 1819	Nov. 7, 1823

George M. Troup (D-R)	Nov. 7, 1823	Nov. 7, 1827
John Forsyth (D-R)	Nov. 7, 1827	Nov. 4, 1829
George R. Gilmer (D)	Nov. 4, 1829	Nov. 9, 1831
Wilson Lumpkin (UN D)	Nov. 9, 1831	Nov. 4, 1835
William Schley (D)	Nov. 4, 1835	Nov. 8, 1837
George R. Gilmer (W)	Nov. 8, 1837	Nov. 6, 1839
Charles J. McDonald (D)	Nov. 6, 1839	Nov. 8, 1843
George W. Crawford (W)	Nov. 8, 1843	Nov. 3, 1847
George W. Towns (D)	Nov. 3, 1847	Nov. 5, 1851
Howell Cobb (UN D)	Nov. 5, 1851	Nov. 9, 1853
Herschel V. Johnson (D)	Nov. 9, 1853	Nov. 6, 1857
Joseph E. Brown (D)	Nov. 6, 1857	June 17, 1865
James Johnson (D)	June 17, 1865	Dec. 14, 1865
Charles J. Jenkins (D)	Dec. 14, 1865	Jan. 13, 1868
Gen. Thomas H. Ruger[1]	Jan. 13, 1868	July 4, 1868
Rufus Brown Bullock (R)[2]	July 4, 1868	Oct. 23, 1871
Benjamin Conley (R)[3]	Oct. 30, 1871	Jan. 12, 1872
James M. Smith (LR)	Jan. 12, 1872	Jan. 12, 1877
Alfred Holt Colquitt (D)	Jan. 12, 1877	Nov. 4, 1882
Alexander H. Stephens (D)[4]	Nov. 4, 1882	March 4, 1883
James H. Boynton (D)[5]	March 5, 1883	May 10, 1883
Henry D. McDaniel (D)	May 10, 1883	Nov. 9, 1886
John B. Gordon (D)	Nov. 9, 1886	Nov. 8, 1890
William J. Northen (D)	Nov. 8, 1890	Oct. 27, 1894
William Y. Atkinson (D)	Oct. 27, 1894	Oct. 29, 1898
Allen D. Candler (D)	Oct. 29, 1898	Oct. 25, 1902
Joseph M. Terrell (D)	Oct. 25, 1902	June 29, 1907
Hoke Smith (D)	June 29, 1907	June 26, 1909
Joseph M. Brown (D)	June 26, 1909	July 1, 1911
Hoke Smith (D)[6]	July 1, 1911	Nov. 16, 1911
John M. Slaton (D)[7]	Nov. 16, 1911	Jan. 25, 1912
Joseph M. Brown (D)	Jan. 25, 1912	June 28, 1913
John M. Slaton (D)	June 28, 1913	June 26, 1915
Nathaniel E. Harris (D)	June 26, 1915	June 30, 1917
Hugh M. Dorsey (D)	June 30, 1917	June 25, 1921
Thomas W. Hardwick (D)	June 25, 1921	June 30, 1923
Clifford M. Walker (D)	June 30, 1923	June 25, 1927
Lamartine G. Hardman (D)	June 25, 1927	June 27, 1931
Richard B. Russell (D)[8]	June 27, 1931	Jan. 10, 1933
Eugene Talmadge (D)	Jan. 10, 1933	Jan. 12, 1937
Eurith D. Rivers (D)	Jan. 12, 1937	Jan. 14, 1941
Eugene Talmadge (D)	Jan. 14, 1941	Jan. 12, 1943
Ellis G. Arnall (D)	Jan. 12, 1943	Jan. 14, 1947
Eugene Talmadge (D)[9]		
Herman E. Talmadge (D)[10]	Jan. 14, 1947	March 18, 1947
Melvin E. Thompson (D)	March 18, 1947	Nov. 17, 1948
Herman E. Talmadge (D)	Nov. 17, 1948	Jan. 11, 1955
S. Marvin Griffin (D)	Jan. 11, 1955	Jan. 13, 1959
S. Ernest Vandiver Jr. (D)	Jan. 13, 1959	Jan. 15, 1963
Carl Edward Sanders (D)	Jan. 15, 1963	Jan. 10, 1967
Lester G. Maddox (D)[11]	Jan. 10, 1967	Jan. 12, 1971
Jimmy Carter (D)	Jan. 12, 1971	Jan. 14, 1975
George Busbee (D)	Jan. 14, 1975	Jan. 11, 1983
Joe Frank Harris (D)	Jan. 11, 1983	Jan. 14, 1991
Zell Miller (D)	Jan. 14, 1991	

Georgia

1. Military governor.
2. Resigned Oct. 23, 1871.
3. As president of the state Senate, he succeeded to office.
4. Died March 4, 1883.
5. As president of the state Senate, he succeeded to office.
6. Resigned Nov. 16, 1911.
7. As president of the state Senate, he succeeded to office.
8. Resigned Jan. 10, 1933.
9. Died Dec. 21, 1946, before his inauguration.
10. Eugene Talmadge's death led to a famous controversy that lasted several months, during which three different men claimed office as governor. The Talmadge-dominated Legislature elected Herman Talmadge, Eugene's son, to serve out his term, but this action was disputed by outgoing governor Ellis Arnall and Lieutenant Governor-elect Melvin E. Thompson. Herman Talmadge seized the governor's mansion by force, but was thrown out after 67 days in office by the Georgia Supreme Court, which ruled his election by the Legislature unconstitutional. Thompson then assumed office as governor until 1948, when a special election was held. He lost the Democratic Georgia

nomination to Talmadge, who then won the special election for the remaining two years of the term. Talmadge was re-elected in 1950.

11. Republican candidate Howard Callaway led in the popular vote, but failed to win a majority because of write-in votes cast for former governor Ellis Arnall, who had lost the Democratic primary to Lester Maddox. The Legislature elected Maddox as governor.

HAWAII

(Became a state Aug. 21, 1959)

Governors	Dates of Service	
William F. Quinn (R)	Aug. 21, 1959	Dec. 3, 1962
John A. Burns (D)	Dec. 3, 1962	Dec. 2, 1974
George R. Ariyoshi (D)	Dec. 2, 1974	Dec. 1, 1986
John Waihee (D)	Dec. 1, 1986	Dec. 5, 1994
Benjamin J. Cayetano (D)	Dec. 5, 1994	

IDAHO

(Became a state July 3, 1890)

Governors	Dates of Service	
George L. Shoup (R)[1]	Oct. 1, 1890	Dec. 1890
N. B. Willey (R)[2]	Dec. 19, 1890	Jan. 1, 1893
William J. McConnell (R)	Jan. 1893	Jan. 4, 1897
Frank Steunenberg (D)	Jan. 4, 1897	Jan. 7, 1901
Frank W. Hunt (D-FUS)	Jan. 7, 1901	Jan. 5, 1903
John T. Morrison (R)	Jan. 5, 1903	Jan. 2, 1905
Frank R. Gooding (R)	Jan. 2, 1905	Jan. 4, 1909
James H. Brady (R)	Jan. 4, 1909	Jan. 2, 1911
James H. Hawley (D)	Jan. 2, 1911	Jan. 6, 1913
John M. Haines (R)	Jan. 6, 1913	Jan. 4, 1915
Moses Alexander (D)	Jan. 4, 1915	Jan. 6, 1919
David W. Davis (R)	Jan. 6, 1919	Jan. 1, 1923
Charles C. Moore (R)	Jan. 1, 1923	Jan. 3, 1927
H. Clarence Baldridge (R)	Jan. 3, 1927	Jan. 5, 1931
C. Ben Ross (D)	Jan. 5, 1931	Jan. 4, 1937
Barzilla W. Clark (D)	Jan. 4, 1937	Jan. 2, 1939
Clarence A. Bottolfsen (R)	Jan. 2, 1939	Jan. 6, 1941
Chase A. Clark (D)	Jan. 6, 1941	Jan. 4, 1943
Clarence A. Bottolfsen (R)	Jan. 4, 1943	Jan. 1, 1945
Charles C. Gossett (D)[3]	Jan. 1, 1945	Nov. 17, 1945
Arnold Williams (D)[4]	Nov. 17, 1945	Jan. 6, 1947
Charles A. Robins (R)	Jan. 6, 1947	Jan. 1, 1951
Len B. Jordan (R)	Jan. 1, 1951	Jan. 3, 1955
Robert E. Smylie (R)	Jan. 3, 1955	Jan. 2, 1967
Don Samuelson (R)	Jan. 2, 1967	Jan. 4, 1971
Cecil D. Andrus (D)[5]	Jan. 4, 1971	Jan. 24, 1977
John V. Evans (D)[6]	Jan. 24, 1977	Jan. 5, 1987
Cecil D. Andrus (D)	Jan. 5, 1987	Jan. 2, 1995
Philip E. Batt (R)	Jan. 2, 1995	

Idaho

1. Resigned in December 1890.
2. As lieutenant governor, he succeeded to office.
3. Resigned Nov. 17, 1945.
4. As lieutenant governor, he succeeded to office.
5. Resigned Jan. 24, 1977.
6. As lieutenant governor, he succeeded to office. Subsequently elected.

ILLINOIS

(Became a state Dec. 3, 1818)

Governors	Dates of Service	
Edward Coles (D-R)	Dec. 5, 1822	Dec. 6, 1826
Ninian Edwards (NR)	Dec. 6, 1826	Dec. 6, 1830
John Reynolds (NR)[1]	Dec. 6, 1830	Nov. 17, 1834
William L. D. Ewing[2]	Nov. 17, 1834	Dec. 3, 1834
Joseph Duncan (W)	Dec. 3, 1834	Dec. 7, 1838
Thomas Carlin (D)	Dec. 7, 1838	Dec. 8, 1842
Thomas Ford (D)	Dec. 8, 1842	Dec. 9, 1846
Augustus C. French (D)	Dec. 9, 1846	Jan. 10, 1853
Joel A. Matteson (D)	Jan. 10, 1853	Jan. 12, 1857
William H. Bissell (R)[3]	Jan. 12, 1857	March 18, 1860
John Wood (R)[4]	March 21, 1860	Jan. 14, 1861
Richard Yates (R)	Jan. 14, 1861	Jan. 16, 1865
Richard J. Oglesby (R)	Jan. 16, 1865	Jan. 11, 1869
John M. Palmer (R)	Jan. 11, 1869	Jan. 13, 1873
Richard J. Oglesby (R)[5]	Jan. 13, 1873	Jan. 23, 1873
John L. Beveridge (R)[6]	Jan. 23, 1873	Jan. 8, 1877
Shelby M. Cullom (R)[7]	Jan. 8, 1877	Feb. 8, 1883
John M. Hamilton (R)[8]	Feb. 16, 1883	Jan. 30, 1885
Richard J. Oglesby (R)	Jan. 30, 1885	Jan. 14, 1889
Joseph W. Fifer (R)	Jan. 14, 1889	Jan. 10, 1893
John P. Altgeld (D)	Jan. 10, 1893	Jan. 11, 1897
John R. Tanner (R)	Jan. 11, 1897	Jan. 14, 1901
Richard Yates (R)	Jan. 14, 1901	Jan. 9, 1905
Charles S. Deneen (R)	Jan. 9, 1905	Feb. 3, 1913
Edward F. Dunne (D)	Feb. 3, 1913	Jan. 8, 1917
Frank O. Lowden (R)	Jan. 8, 1917	Jan. 10, 1921
Len Small (R)	Jan. 10, 1921	Jan. 14, 1929
Louis L. Emmerson (R)	Jan. 14, 1929	Jan. 9, 1933
Henry Horner (D)[9]	Jan. 9, 1933	Oct. 6, 1940
John H. Stelle (D)[10]	Oct. 6, 1940	Jan. 13, 1941
Dwight H. Green (R)	Jan. 13, 1941	Jan. 10, 1949
Adlai E. Stevenson (D)	Jan. 10, 1949	Jan. 12, 1953
William G. Stratton (R)	Jan. 12, 1953	Jan. 9, 1961
Otto Kerner (D)[11]	Jan. 9, 1961	May 22, 1968
Samuel H. Shapiro (D)[12]	May 22, 1968	Jan. 13, 1969
Richard B. Ogilvie (R)	Jan. 13, 1969	Jan. 8, 1973
Daniel Walker (D)	Jan. 8, 1973	Jan. 10, 1977
James R. Thompson (R)	Jan. 10, 1977	Jan. 14, 1991
Jim Edgar (R)	Jan. 14, 1991	

Illinois

1. Resigned Nov. 17, 1834.
2. Ewing was acting lieutenant governor and succeeded to office as governor following Reynolds' resignation.
3. Died March 18, 1860.
4. As lieutenant governor, he succeeded to office.
5. Resigned Jan. 23, 1873.
6. As lieutenant governor, he succeeded to office.
7. Resigned Feb. 8, 1883.
8. As lieutenant governor, he succeeded to office.
9. Died Oct. 6, 1940.
10. As lieutenant governor, he succeeded to office.
11. Resigned May 22, 1968.
12. As lieutenant governor, he succeeded to office.

INDIANA

(Became a state Dec. 11, 1816)

Governors	Dates of Service	
Jonathan Jennings (D-R)[1]	Nov. 7, 1816	Sept. 12, 1822
Ratliff Boon (D-R)[2]	Sept. 12, 1822	Dec. 4, 1822
William Hendricks (D-R)[3]	Dec. 5, 1822	Feb. 12, 1825
James B. Ray (CLAY R)[4]	Feb. 12, 1825	Dec. 7, 1831
Noah Noble (NR, W)	Dec. 7, 1831	Dec. 6, 1837
David Wallace (W)	Dec. 6, 1837	Dec. 9, 1840

Samuel Bigger (W)	Dec. 9, 1840	Dec. 6, 1843
James Whitcomb (D)[5]	Dec. 6, 1843	Dec. 27, 1848
Paris C. Dunning (D)[6]	Dec. 27, 1848	Dec. 5, 1849
Joseph A. Wright (D)	Dec. 5, 1849	Jan. 12, 1857
Ashbel P. Willard (D)[7]	Jan. 12, 1857	Oct. 4, 1860
Abraham A. Hammond (D)[8]	Oct. 4, 1860	Jan. 14, 1861
Henry S. Lane (R)[9]	Jan. 14, 1861	Jan. 16, 1861
Oliver P. Morton (R)[10]	Jan. 16, 1861	Jan. 23, 1867
Conrad Baker (R)[11]	Jan. 24, 1867	Jan. 13, 1873
Thomas A. Hendricks (D)	Jan. 13, 1873	Jan. 8, 1877
James D. Williams (D)[12]	Jan. 8, 1877	Nov. 20, 1880
Isaac P. Gray (D)[13]	Nov. 20, 1880	Jan. 10, 1881
Albert G. Porter (R)	Jan. 10, 1881	Jan. 12, 1885
Isaac P. Gray (D)	Jan. 12, 1885	Jan. 14, 1889
Alvin P. Hovey (R)[14]	Jan. 14, 1889	Nov. 21, 1891
Ira Joy Chase (R)[15]	Nov. 21, 1891	Jan. 9, 1893
Claude Matthews (D)	Jan. 1893	Jan. 11, 1897
James A. Mount (R)	Jan. 11, 1897	Jan. 14, 1901
Winfield T. Durbin (R)	Jan. 14, 1901	Jan. 9, 1905
J. Frank Hanly (R)	Jan. 9, 1905	Jan. 11, 1909
Thomas R. Marshall (D)	Jan. 11, 1909	Jan. 13, 1913
Samuel M. Ralston (D)	Jan. 13, 1913	Jan. 8, 1917
James Putnam Goodrich (R)	Jan. 8, 1917	Jan. 10, 1921
Warren T. McCray (R)[16]	Jan. 10, 1921	April 30, 1924
Emmett F. Branch (R)[17]	April 30, 1924	Jan. 12, 1925
Edward Jackson (R)	Jan. 12, 1925	Jan. 14, 1929
Harry G. Leslie (R)	Jan. 14, 1929	Jan. 9, 1933
Paul V. McNutt (D)	Jan. 9, 1933	Jan. 11, 1937
M. Clifford Townsend (D)	Jan. 11, 1937	Jan. 13, 1941
Henry F. Schricker (D)	Jan. 13, 1941	Jan. 8, 1945
Ralph F. Gates (R)	Jan. 8, 1945	Jan. 10, 1949
Henry F. Schricker (D)	Jan. 10, 1949	Jan. 12, 1953
George N. Craig (R)	Jan. 12, 1953	Jan. 14, 1957
Harold W. Handley (R)	Jan. 14, 1957	Jan. 9, 1961
Matthew E. Welsh (D)	Jan. 9, 1961	Jan. 11, 1965
Roger D. Branigin (D)	Jan. 11, 1965	Jan. 13, 1969
Edgar D. Whitcomb (R)	Jan. 13, 1969	Jan. 8, 1973
Otis R. Bowen (R)	Jan. 8, 1973	Jan. 12, 1981
Robert D. Orr (R)	Jan. 12, 1981	Jan. 9, 1989
Evan Bayh (D)	Jan. 9, 1989	Jan. 13,1997
Frank L. O'Bannon (D)	Jan. 13, 1997	

Indiana
1. Resigned Sept. 12, 1822.
2. Acting governor.
3. Resigned Feb. 12, 1825.
4. Acting governor. Subsequently elected.
5. Resigned Dec. 27, 1848.
6. Acting governor.
7. Died Oct. 4, 1860.
8. Acting governor.
9. Resigned Jan. 16, 1861.
10 Acting governor. Subsequently elected. Resigned in 1867.
11. Acting governor. Subsequently elected.
12. Died Nov. 20, 1880.
13. Acting governor.
14. Died Nov. 21, 1891.
15. Acting governor.
16. Resigned April 30, 1924.
17. As lieutenant governor, he succeeded to office.

IOWA

(Became a state Dec. 28, 1846)

Governors	Dates of Service	
Ansel Briggs (D)	Dec. 3, 1846	Dec. 4, 1850
Stephen P. Hempstead (D)	Dec. 4, 1850	Dec. 9, 1854
James W. Grimes (R)	Dec. 9, 1854	Jan. 13, 1858
Ralph P. Lowe (R)	Jan. 13, 1858	Jan. 11, 1860
Samuel J. Kirkwood (R)	Jan. 11, 1860	Jan. 14, 1864
William M. Stone (UN R)	Jan. 14, 1864	Jan. 16, 1868
Samuel Merrill (R)	Jan. 16, 1868	Jan. 11, 1872
Cyrus C. Carpenter (R)	Jan. 11, 1872	Jan. 13, 1876
Samuel J. Kirkwood (R)[1]	Jan. 13, 1876	Feb. 1, 1877
Joshua G. Newbold (R)[2]	Feb. 1, 1877	Jan. 17, 1878
John H. Gear (R)	Jan. 17, 1878	Jan. 12, 1882
Buren R. Sherman (R)	Jan. 12, 1882	Jan. 14, 1886
William Larrabee (R)	Jan. 14, 1886	Feb. 26, 1890
Horace Boies (D)	Feb. 27, 1890	Jan. 11, 1894
Frank D. Jackson (R)	Jan. 11, 1894	Jan. 16, 1896
Francis M. Drake (R)	Jan. 16, 1896	Jan. 13, 1898
Leslie M. Shaw (R)	Jan. 13, 1898	Jan. 16, 1902
Albert B. Cummins (R)[3]	Jan. 16, 1902	Nov. 24, 1908
Warren Garst (R)[4]	Nov. 24, 1908	Jan. 14, 1909
Beryl F. Carroll (R)	Jan. 14, 1909	Jan. 16, 1913
George W. Clarke (R)	Jan. 16, 1913	Jan. 11, 1917
William L. Harding (R)	Jan. 11, 1917	Jan. 13, 1921
Nathan E. Kendall (R)	Jan. 13, 1921	Jan. 15, 1925
John Hammill (R)	Jan. 15, 1925	Jan. 15, 1931
Daniel W. Turner (R)	Jan. 15, 1931	Jan. 12, 1933
Clyde L. Herring (D)	Jan. 12, 1933	Jan. 14, 1937
Nelson G. Kraschel (D)	Jan. 14, 1937	Jan. 12, 1939
George A. Wilson (R)	Jan. 12, 1939	Jan. 14, 1943
Bourke B. Hickenlooper (R)	Jan. 14, 1943	Jan. 11, 1945
Robert D. Blue (R)	Jan. 11, 1945	Jan. 13, 1949
William S. Beardsley (R)[5]	Jan. 13, 1949	Nov. 21, 1954
Leo Elthon (R)[6]	Nov. 22, 1954	Jan. 13, 1955
Leo Arthur Hoegh (R)	Jan. 13, 1955	Jan. 17, 1957
Herschel C. Loveless (D)	Jan. 17, 1957	Jan. 12, 1961
Norman A. Erbe (R)	Jan. 12, 1961	Jan. 17, 1963
Harold E. Hughes (D)[7]	Jan. 17, 1963	Jan. 1, 1969
Robert D. Fulton (D)[8]	Jan. 1, 1969	Jan. 16, 1969
Robert D. Ray (R)	Jan. 16, 1969	Jan. 14, 1983
Terry E. Branstad (R)	Jan. 14, 1983	

Iowa
1. Resigned Feb. 1, 1877.
2. As lieutenant governor, he succeeded to office.
3. Resigned Nov. 24, 1908.
4. As lieutenant governor, he succeeded to office.
5. Died Nov. 21, 1954.
6. As lieutenant governor, he succeeded to office.
7. Resigned Jan. 1, 1969.
8. As lieutenant governor, he succeeded to office.

KANSAS

(Became a state Jan. 29, 1861)

Governors	Dates of Service	
Charles Robinson (R)	Feb. 9, 1861	Jan. 12, 1863
Thomas Carney (R)	Jan. 12, 1863	Jan. 9, 1865
Samuel J. Crawford (R)[1]	Jan. 9, 1865	Nov. 4, 1868
Nehemiah Green (R)[2]	Nov. 4, 1868	Jan. 11, 1869
James Madison Harvey (R)	Jan. 11, 1869	Jan. 13, 1873
Thomas A. Osborn (R)	Jan. 13, 1873	Jan. 18, 1877
George T. Anthony (R)	Jan. 18, 1877	Jan. 13, 1879
John P. St. John (R)	Jan. 13, 1879	Jan. 8, 1883
George Washington Glick (D)	Jan. 8, 1883	Jan. 13, 1885
John A. Martin (R)	Jan. 13, 1885	Jan. 14, 1889
Lyman U. Humphrey (R)	Jan. 14, 1889	Jan. 9, 1893
Lorenzo D. Lewelling (POP)	Jan. 9, 1893	Jan. 14, 1895
Edmund N. Morrill (R)	Jan. 14, 1895	Jan. 11, 1897
John W. Leedy (D-PP)	Jan. 11, 1897	Jan. 9, 1899
William E. Stanley (R)	Jan. 9, 1899	Jan. 12, 1903
Willis J. Bailey (R)	Jan. 12, 1903	Jan. 9, 1905
Edward W. Hoch (R)	Jan. 9, 1905	Jan. 11, 1909
Walter R. Stubbs (R)	Jan. 11, 1909	Jan. 13, 1913
George H. Hodges (D)	Jan. 13, 1913	Jan. 11, 1915
Arthur Capper (R)	Jan. 11, 1915	Jan. 13, 1919
Henry J. Allen (R)	Jan. 13, 1919	Jan. 8, 1923
Jonathan McM. Davis (D)	Jan. 8, 1923	Jan. 12, 1925
Ben S. Paulen (R)	Jan. 12, 1925	Jan. 14, 1929
Clyde M. Reed (R)	Jan. 14, 1929	Jan. 12, 1931

Harry W. Woodring (D)	Jan. 12, 1931	Jan. 9, 1933
Alfred M. Landon (R)	Jan. 9, 1933	Jan. 11, 1937
Walter A. Huxman (D)	Jan. 11, 1937	Jan. 9, 1939
Payne H. Ratner (R)	Jan. 9, 1939	Jan. 11, 1943
Andrew F. Schoeppel (R)	Jan. 11, 1943	Jan. 13, 1947
Frank Carlson (R)[3]	Jan. 13, 1947	Nov. 28, 1950
Frank L. Hagaman (R)[4]	Nov. 28, 1950	Jan. 8, 1951
Edward F. Arn (R)	Jan. 8, 1951	Jan. 10, 1955
Frederick L. Hall (R)[5]	Jan. 10, 1955	Jan. 3, 1957
John McCuish (R)[6]	Jan. 3, 1957	Jan. 14, 1957
George Docking (D)	Jan. 14, 1957	Jan. 9, 1961
John Anderson Jr. (R)	Jan. 9, 1961	Jan. 11, 1965
William H. Avery (R)	Jan. 11, 1965	Jan. 9, 1967
Robert B. Docking (D)	Jan. 9, 1967	Jan. 13, 1975
Robert F. Bennett (R)	Jan. 13, 1975	Jan. 8, 1979
John Carlin (D)	Jan. 8, 1979	Jan. 12, 1987
Mike Hayden (R)	Jan. 12, 1987	Jan. 14, 1991
Joan Finney (D)	Jan. 14, 1991	Jan. 9, 1995
Bill Graves (R)	Jan. 9, 1995	

Kansas
1. Resigned Nov. 4, 1868.
2. Succeeded to office.
3. Resigned Nov. 28, 1950.
4. As lieutenant governor, he succeeded to office.
5. Resigned Jan. 3, 1957.
6. As lieutenant governor, he succeeded to office.

KENTUCKY

(Became a state June 1, 1792)

Governors	Dates of Service	
Isaac Shelby (D-R)	June 4, 1792	June 7, 1796
James Garrard (D-R)	June 7, 1796	June 1, 1804
Christopher Greenup (D-R)	June 1, 1804	June 1, 1808
Charles Scott (D-R)	June 1, 1808	June 1, 1812
Isaac Shelby (D-R)	June 1, 1812	June 1, 1816
George Madison (D-R)[1]	June 1, 1816	Oct. 21, 1816
Gabriel Slaughter (D-R)[2]	Oct. 21, 1816	June 1, 1820
John Adair (D-R)	June 1, 1820	June 1, 1824
Joseph Desha (D-R)	June 1, 1824	June 1, 1828
Thomas Metcalfe (NR)	June 1, 1828	June 1, 1832
John Breathitt (D)[3]	June 1, 1832	Feb. 22, 1834
James Morehead (NR)[4]	Feb. 22, 1834	June 1, 1836
James Clark (W)[5]	June 1, 1836	Oct. 5, 1839
Charles A. Wickliffe (W)[6]	Oct. 5, 1839	June 1, 1840
Robert P. Letcher (W)	June 1, 1840	June 1, 1844
William Owsley (W)	June 1, 1844	June 1, 1848
John J. Crittenden (W)[7]	June 1, 1848	July 31, 1850
John L. Helm (W)[8]	July 31, 1850	Sept. 2, 1851
Lazarus W. Powell (D)	Sept. 1851	Sept. 2, 1855
Charles S. Morehead (AM)	Sept. 1855	Sept. 1859
Beriah Magoffin (D)[9]	Sept. 1859	Aug. 18, 1862
James F. Robinson (UN)[10]	Aug. 18, 1862	Sept. 1863
Thomas E. Bramlette (UN)	Sept. 1863	Sept. 1867
John L. Helm (D)[11]	Sept. 3, 1867	Sept. 13, 1867
John W. Stevenson (D)[12]	Sept. 13, 1867	March 4, 1871
Preston H. Leslie (D)[13]	March 4, 1871	Sept. 1875
James B. McCreary (D)	Sept. 1875	Sept. 1879
Luke P. Blackburn (D)	Sept. 1879	Sept. 1883
J. Procter Knott (D)	Sept. 1883	Sept. 1887
Simon B. Buckner (D)	Sept. 1887	Sept. 1891
John Y. Brown (D)	Sept. 1891	Dec. 1895
William O. Bradley (R)	Dec. 1895	Dec. 12, 1899
William S. Taylor (R)[14]	Dec. 12, 1899	Jan. 31, 1900
William Goebel (D)[15]	Jan. 31, 1900	Feb. 3, 1900
John C. W. Beckham (D)[16]	Feb. 3, 1900	Dec. 10, 1907
August E. Willson (R)	Dec. 10, 1907	Dec. 12, 1911
James B. McCreary (D)	Dec. 12, 1911	Dec. 7, 1915
Augustus O. Stanley (D)[17]	Dec. 7, 1915	May 19, 1919

James D. Black (D)[18]	May 19, 1919	Dec. 9, 1919
Edwin P. Morrow (R)	Dec. 9, 1919	Dec. 11, 1923
William J. Fields (D)	Dec. 11, 1923	Dec. 13, 1927
Flem D. Sampson (R)	Dec. 13, 1927	Dec. 8, 1931
Ruby Lafoon (D)	Dec. 8, 1931	Dec. 10, 1935
Albert "Happy" Chandler (D)[19]	Dec. 10, 1935	Oct. 9, 1939
Keen Johnson (D)[20]	Oct. 9, 1939	Dec. 7, 1943
Simeon S. Willis (R)	Dec. 7, 1943	Dec. 9, 1947
Earle C. Clements (D)[21]	Dec. 9, 1947	Nov. 27, 1950
Lawrence W. Wetherby (D)[22]	Nov. 27, 1950	Dec. 13, 1955
Albert B. "Happy" Chandler (D)	Dec. 13, 1955	Dec. 9, 1959
Bert T. Combs (D)	Dec. 9, 1959	Dec. 10, 1963
Edward T. Breathitt (D)	Dec. 10, 1963	Dec. 12, 1967
Louie B. Nunn (R)	Dec. 12, 1967	Dec. 7, 1971
Wendell H. Ford (D)[23]	Dec. 7, 1971	Dec. 28, 1974
Julian Carroll (D)[24]	Dec. 28, 1974	Dec. 11, 1979
John Y. Brown Jr. (D)	Dec. 11, 1979	Dec. 13, 1983
Martha Layne Collins (D)	Dec. 13, 1983	Dec. 8, 1987
Wallace G. Wilkinson (D)	Dec. 8, 1987	Dec. 10, 1991
Brereton C. Jones (D)	Dec. 10, 1991	Dec. 12, 1995
Paul E. Patton (D)	Dec. 12, 1995	

Kentucky
1. Died Oct. 1, 1816.
2. As lieutenant governor, he succeeded to office.
3. Died Feb. 22, 1834.
4. As lieutenant governor, he succeeded to office.
5. Died Oct. 5, 1839.
6. As lieutenant governor, he succeeded to office.
7. Resigned July 31, 1850.
8. As lieutenant governor, he succeeded to office.
9. Resigned Aug. 18, 1862.
10. As president of the state Senate, he succeeded to office.
11. Died Sept. 13, 1867.
12. As lieutenant governor, he succeeded to office. Subsequently elected. Resigned March 4, 1871.
13. As president of the state Senate, he succeeded to office. Subsequently elected.
14. Taylor was removed by the Legislature following an election challenge by his Democratic opponent, William Goebel.
15. Successfully challenged the election of William S. Taylor. Died Feb. 3, 1900.
16. As lieutenant governor, he succeeded to office. Subsequently elected.
17. Resigned May 19, 1919.
18. As lieutenant governor, he succeeded to office.
19. Resigned Oct. 9, 1939.
20. As lieutenant governor, he succeeded to office. Subsequently elected.
21. Resigned Nov. 27, 1950.
22. As lieutenant governor, he succeeded to office. Subsequently elected.
23. Resigned Dec. 28, 1974.
24. As lieutenant governor, he succeeded to office. Subsequently elected.

LOUISIANA

(Became a state April 30, 1812)

Governors	Dates of Service	
William C. C. Claiborne	July 30, 1812	Dec. 16, 1816
Jacques Philippe Villere	Dec. 17, 1816	Dec. 17, 1820
Thomas B. Robertson[1]	Dec. 18, 1820	Nov. 15, 1824
Henry S. Thibodeaux[2]	Nov. 15, 1824	Dec. 13, 1824
Henry S. Johnson (AM FAC)	Dec. 13, 1824	Dec. 15, 1828
Pierre Derbigny (NR)[3]	Dec. 15, 1828	Oct. 6, 1829
Armand Beauvais[4]	Oct. 6, 1829	Jan. 14, 1830
Jacques Dupre	Jan. 14, 1830	Jan. 31, 1831
Andre B. Roman (NR)	Jan. 31, 1831	Feb. 4, 1835
Edward E. White (W)	Feb. 4, 1835	Feb. 4, 1839
Andre B. Roman (W)	Feb. 4, 1839	Jan. 30, 1843
Alexander Mouton (D)	Jan. 30, 1843	Feb. 11, 1846
Isaac Johnson (D)	Feb. 12, 1846	Jan. 27, 1850
Joseph M. Walker (D)	Jan. 28, 1850	Jan. 17, 1853
Paul O. Hebert (D)	Jan. 18, 1853	Jan. 21, 1856
Robert C. Wickliffe (D)	Jan. 22, 1856	Jan. 22, 1860
Thomas O. Moore (D)	Jan. 23, 1860	Jan. 25, 1864

George F. Shepley[5]	July 2, 1862	March 4, 1864
Henry W. Allen[6]	Jan. 25, 1864	June 2, 1865
Michael Hahn[7]	March 4, 1864	March 4, 1865
James M. Wells (D)[8]	March 4, 1865	June 3, 1867
Benjamin F. Flanders[9]	June 3, 1867	Jan. 8, 1868
Joshua Baker[10]	Jan. 8, 1868	June 27, 1868
Henry C. Warmoth (R)	June 27, 1868	Dec. 9, 1872
Pinckney B. S. Pinchback[11]	Dec. 9, 1872	Jan. 13, 1873
William P. Kellogg (R)[12]	Jan. 13, 1873	Jan. 5, 1877
Francis T. Nicholls (D)[13]	Jan. 8, 1877	Jan. 13, 1880
Louis A. Wiltz (D)[14]	Jan. 14, 1880	Oct. 16, 1881
Samuel D. McEnery (D)[15]	Oct. 16, 1881	May 20, 1888
Francis T. Nicholls (D)	May 21, 1888	May 10, 1892
Murphy J. Foster (A-LOT D, D)	May 10, 1892	May 8, 1900
William W. Heard (D)	May 8, 1900	May 10, 1904
Newton C. Blanchard (D)	May 10, 1904	May 12, 1908
Jared Y. Sanders (D)	May 12, 1908	May 14, 1912
Luther E. Hall (D)	May 14, 1912	May 9, 1916
Ruffin G. Pleasant (D)	May 9, 1916	May 11, 1920
John M Parker (D)	May 11, 1920	May 13, 1924
Henry L. Fuqua (D)[16]	May 13, 1924	Oct. 11, 1926
Oramel H. Simpson(D)[17]	Oct. 11, 1926	May 21, 1928
Huey P. Long Jr. (D)[18]	May 21, 1928	Jan. 25, 1932
Alvin O. King (D)[19]	Jan. 25, 1932	May 10, 1932
Oscar K. Allen (D)[20]	May 10, 1932	Jan. 28, 1936
James A. Noe (D)[21]	Jan. 28, 1936	May 12, 1936
Richard W. Leche (D)[22]	May 12, 1936	June 26, 1939
Earl K. Long (D)[23]	June 26, 1939	May 14, 1940
Sam H. Jones (D)	May 14, 1940	May 9, 1944
James H. Davis (D)	May 9, 1944	May 11, 1948
Earl K. Long (D)	May 11, 1948	May 13, 1952
Robert F. Kennon (D)	May 13, 1952	May 8, 1956
Earl K. Long (D)	May 8, 1956	May 10, 1960
James H. Davis (D)	May 10, 1960	May 12, 1964
John J. McKeithen (D)	May 12, 1964	May 9, 1972
Edwin W. Edwards (D)	May 9, 1972	March 10, 1980
David C. Treen (R)	March 10, 1980	March 12, 1984
Edwin W. Edwards (D)	March 12, 1984	March 14, 1988
Charles Roemer (D, R)[24]	March 14, 1988	Jan. 8, 1992
Edwin W. Edwards (D)	Jan. 8, 1992	Jan. 8, 1996
Mike Foster (R)	Jan. 8, 1996	

Louisiana

1. *Resigned Nov. 15, 1824.*
2. *As president of the state Senate, he succeeded to office.*
3. *Died Oct. 1, 1829.*
4. *As president of the state Senate, he succeeded to office.*
5. *Military governor within Union lines.*
6. *Last elected Confederate governor.*
7. *Elected within Union lines. Resigned March 4, 1865.*
8. *As lieutenant governor, he succeeded to office. Subsequently elected. Removed June 3, 1867.*
9. *Under military authority.*
10. *Under military authority.*
11. *Acting governor.*
12. *The 1872 gubernatorial election in Louisiana set off a bitter dispute between Republicans backing Kellogg and Democrats supporting his opponent, John McEnery. Each side organized its own boards to canvass the vote, resulting in two separate sets of election returns, one showing Kellogg the winner, the other McEnery. To add to the confusion, two rival legislatures assumed office, each claiming legitimacy, and Kellogg and McEnery were both inaugurated as governor by their respective factions. President Ulysses S. Grant (R) finally stepped in and recognized Kellogg as the legitimate governor on May 22, 1873.*
13. *The 1876 election set off a dispute similar to that of 1872. Nicholls, the Democrat, and Packard, the Republican, each had election returns showing him the winner. There were also two legislatures, each controlled by a different party. Nicholls set up a de facto state government and was recognized by federal authorities.*
14. *Died in October 1881.*
15. *As lieutenant governor, he succeeded to office. Subsequently elected.*
16. *Died Oct. 11, 1926.*
17. *As lieutenant governor, he succeeded to office.*
18. *Resigned Jan. 25, 1932.*
19. *As lieutenant governor, he succeeded to office.*
20. *Died Jan. 28, 1936.*
21. *As lieutenant governor, he succeeded to office.*

22. *Resigned June 26, 1939.*
23. *As lieutenant governor, he succeeded to office.*
24. *Elected in 1987 as a Democrat. Became a Republican in March 1991.*

MAINE

(Became a state March 15, 1820)

Governors	Dates of Service	
William King (D-R)[1]	May 31, 1820	May 28, 1821
William D. Williamson (D-R)[2]	May 29, 1821	Dec. 25, 1821
Benjamin Ames (D-R)[3]	Dec. 25, 1821	Jan. 2, 1821
Daniel Rose (D-R)[4]	Jan. 2, 1822	Jan. 4, 1822
Albion K. Parris (D-R)	Jan. 5, 1822	Jan. 3, 1827
Enoch Lincoln (D-R)[5]	Jan. 3, 1827	Oct. 8, 1829
Nathan Cutler (D)[6]	Oct. 12, 1829	Feb. 5, 1830
Joshua Hall (D)[7]	Feb. 5, 1830	Feb. 10, 1830
Jonathan G. Hunton (NR)	Feb. 10, 1830	Jan. 5, 1831
Samuel E. Smith (JAC D)	Jan. 5, 1831	Jan. 1, 1834
Robert P. Dunlap (D)	Jan. 1, 1834	Jan. 3, 1838
Edward Kent (W)	Jan. 3, 1838	Jan. 2, 1839
John Fairfield (D)	Jan. 2, 1839	Jan. 6, 1841
Richard H. Vose[8]	Jan. 12, 1841	Jan. 13, 1841
Edward Kent (W)	Jan. 13, 1841	Jan. 5, 1842
John Fairfield (D)[9]	Jan. 5, 1842	March 7, 1843
Edward Kavanagh (D)[10]	March 7, 1843	Jan. 1, 1844
David Dunn (D)	Jan. 2, 1844	Jan. 3, 1844
John W. Dana (D)	Jan. 3, 1844	Jan. 5, 1844
Hugh J. Anderson (D)	Jan. 5, 1844	May 12, 1847
John W. Dana (D)	May 13, 1847	May 8, 1850
John Hubbard (D)	May 9, 1850	Jan. 5, 1853
William G. Crosby (W)	Jan. 5, 1853	Jan. 3, 1855
Anson P. Morrill (R)	Jan. 3, 1855	Jan. 2, 1856
Samuel Wells (D)	Jan. 2, 1856	Jan. 8, 1857
Hannibal Hamlin (R)[11]	Jan. 8, 1857	Feb. 25, 1857
Joseph H. Williams (R)[12]	Feb. 26, 1857	Jan. 8, 1858
Lot M. Morrill (R)	Jan. 8, 1858	Jan. 2, 1861
Israel Washburn Jr. (R)	Jan. 2, 1861	Jan. 7, 1863
Abner Coburn (R)	Jan. 7, 1863	Jan. 6, 1864
Samuel Cony (UN R)	Jan. 6, 1864	Jan. 2, 1867
Joshua L. Chamberlain (R)	Jan. 2, 1867	Jan. 4, 1871
Sidney Perham (R)	Jan. 4, 1871	Jan. 7, 1874
Nelson Dingley Jr. (R)	Jan. 7, 1874	Jan. 5, 1876
Selden Connor (R)	Jan. 5, 1876	Jan. 8, 1879
Alonzo Garcelon (D)	Jan. 8, 1879	Jan. 1880
Daniel F. Davis (R)	Jan. 17, 1880	Jan. 1881
Harris M. Plaisted (D)	Jan. 13, 1881	Jan. 3, 1883
Frederick Robie (R)	Jan. 3, 1883	Jan. 5, 1887
Joseph R. Bodwell (R)[13]	Jan. 5, 1887	Dec. 15, 1887
Sebastian S. Marble (R)[14]	Dec. 16, 1887	Jan. 2, 1889
Edwin C. Burleigh (R)	Jan. 2, 1889	Jan. 4, 1893
Henry B. Cleaves (R)	Jan. 4, 1893	Jan. 6, 1897
Llewellyn Powers (R)	Jan. 6, 1897	Jan. 2, 1901
John F. Hill (R)	Jan. 2, 1901	Jan. 4, 1905
William T. Cobb (R)	Jan. 4, 1905	Jan. 6, 1909
Bert M. Fernald (R)	Jan. 6, 1909	Jan. 4, 1911
Frederick W. Plaisted (D)	Jan. 4, 1911	Jan. 1, 1913
William T. Haines (R)	Jan. 1, 1913	Jan. 6, 1915
Oakley C. Curtis (D)	Jan. 6, 1915	Jan. 3, 1917
Carl E. Milliken (R)	Jan. 3, 1917	Jan. 5, 1921
Frederic H. Parkhurst (R)[15]	Jan. 5, 1921	Jan. 31, 1921
Percival P. Baxter (R)[16]	Jan. 31, 1921	Jan. 8, 1925
Ralph O. Brewster (R)	Jan. 8, 1925	Jan. 2, 1929
William T. Gardiner (R)	Jan. 2, 1929	Jan. 4, 1933
Louis J. Brann (D)	Jan. 4, 1933	Jan. 6, 1937
Lewis O. Barrows (R)	Jan. 6, 1937	Jan. 1, 1941
Sumner Sewall (R)	Jan. 1, 1941	Jan. 3, 1945
Horace A. Hildreth (R)	Jan. 3, 1945	Jan. 5, 1949
Frederick G. Payne (R)[17]	Jan. 5, 1949	Dec. 25, 1952
Burton M. Cross (R)[18]	Dec. 26, 1952	Jan. 5, 1955
Edmund S. Muskie (D)[19]	Jan. 5, 1955	Jan. 3, 1959

Robert N. Haskell (R)[20]	Jan. 3, 1959	Jan. 8, 1959
Clinton A. Clauson (D)[21]	Jan. 8, 1959	Dec. 30, 1959
John H. Reed (R)[22]	Dec. 30, 1959	Jan. 5, 1967
Kenneth M. Curtis (D)	Jan. 5, 1967	Jan. 1, 1975
James B. Longley (I)	Jan. 2, 1975	Jan. 3, 1979
Joseph E. Brennan (D)	Jan. 3, 1979	Jan. 7, 1987
John R. McKernan Jr. (R)	Jan. 7, 1987	Jan. 1995
Angus King Jr. (I)	Jan. 5, 1995	

Maine

1. *Resigned May 28, 1821.*
2. *Acting governor. Resigned Dec. 25, 1821.*
3. *Acting governor.*
4. *Acting governor.*
5. *Died Oct. 8, 1829.*
6. *Acting governor.*
7. *Acting governor.*
8. *As president of the state Senate, acted as governor while an inconclusive popular election result was being resolved in the Legislature.*
9. *Resigned March 7, 1843.*
10. *Acting governor.*
11. *Resigned Feb. 25, 1857.*
12. *Acting governor.*
13. *Died Dec. 15, 1887.*
14. *Acting governor.*
15. *Died Jan. 31, 1921.*
16. *As president of the state Senate, he succeeded to office. Subsequently elected.*
17. *Resigned Dec. 25, 1952.*
18. *As president of the state Senate, he succeeded to office. Had previously been elected for a two-year term beginning January 1953.*
19. *Resigned Jan. 3, 1959.*
20. *As president of the state Senate, he succeeded to office.*
21. *Died Dec. 30, 1959.*
22. *As president of the state Senate, he succeeded to office. Subsequently elected in a special election for the remainder of Clauson's term. Re-elected in 1962.*

MARYLAND

(Ratified the Constitution April 28, 1788)

Governors	Dates of Service	
John Eager Howard (FED)	Nov. 24, 1788	Nov. 14, 1791
George Plater (FED)[1]	Nov. 14, 1791	Feb. 10, 1792
James Brice (FED)[2]	Feb. 13, 1792	April 5, 1792
Thomas Sim Lee (FED)	April 5, 1792	Nov. 14, 1794
John H. Stone (FED)	Nov. 14, 1794	Nov. 17, 1797
John Henry (FED)	Nov. 17, 1797	Nov. 14, 1798
Benjamin Ogle (FED)	Nov. 14, 1798	Nov. 10, 1801
John Francis Mercer (D-R)	Nov. 10, 1801	Nov. 15, 1803
Robert Bowie (D-R)	Nov. 15, 1803	Nov. 10, 1806
Robert Wright (D-R)[3]	Nov. 12, 1806	May 6, 1809
James Butcher (D-R)[4]	May 6, 1809	June 9, 1809
Edward Lloyd (D-R)	June 9, 1809	Nov. 16, 1811
Robert Bowie (D-R)	Nov. 16, 1811	Nov. 25, 1812
Levin Winder (FED)	Nov. 25, 1812	Jan. 2, 1816
Charles Ridgely (FED)	Jan. 2, 1816	Jan. 8, 1819
Charles Goldsborough (FED)	Jan. 8, 1819	Dec. 20, 1819
Samuel Sprigg (D-R)	Dec. 20, 1819	Dec. 16, 1822
Samuel Stevens Jr. (D-R)	Dec. 16, 1822	Jan. 9, 1826
Joseph Kent (D-R)	Jan. 9, 1826	Jan. 15, 1829
Daniel Martin (A-JAC D)	Jan. 15, 1829	Jan. 15, 1830
Thomas King Carroll (D)	Jan. 15, 1830	Jan. 13, 1831
Daniel Martin (A-JAC D)[5]	Jan. 13, 1831	July 11, 1831
George Howard (A-JAC D)[6]	July 11, 1831	Jan. 17, 1833
James Thomas (A-JAC D)	Jan. 17, 1833	Jan. 14, 1836
Thomas W. Veazey (W)	Jan. 14, 1836	Jan. 7, 1839
William Grason (D)	Jan. 7, 1839	Jan. 3, 1842
Francis Thomas (D)	Jan. 3, 1842	Jan. 6, 1845
Thomas G. Pratt (W)	Jan. 6, 1845	Jan. 3, 1848
Philip Francis Thomas (D)	Jan. 3, 1848	Jan. 6, 1851
Enoch L. Lowe (D)	Jan. 6, 1851	Jan. 11, 1854

Thomas W. Ligon (D)	Jan. 11, 1854	Jan. 13, 1858
Thomas H. Hicks (AM)	Jan. 13, 1858	Jan. 8, 1862
Augustus W. Bradford (UN R)	Jan. 8, 1862	Jan. 10, 1866
Thomas Swann (UN R)	Jan. 10, 1866	Jan. 13, 1869
Oden Bowie (D)	Jan. 13, 1869	Jan. 10, 1872
William P. Whyte (D)[7]	Jan. 10, 1872	March 4, 1874
James B. Groome (D)[8]	March 4, 1874	Jan. 12, 1876
John Lee Carroll (D)	Jan. 12, 1876	Jan. 14, 1880
William T. Hamilton (D)	Jan. 14, 1880	Jan. 9, 1884
Robert M. McLane (D)[9]	Jan. 9, 1884	March 27, 1885
Henry Lloyd (D)[10]	March 27, 1885	Jan. 11, 1888
Elihu E. Jackson (D)	Jan. 11, 1888	Jan. 13, 1892
Frank Brown (D)	Jan. 13, 1892	Jan. 8, 1896
Lloyd Lowndes (R)	Jan. 8, 1896	Jan. 10, 1900
John W. Smith (D)	Jan. 10, 1900	Jan. 13, 1904
Edwin Warfield (D)	Jan. 1, 1904	Jan. 8, 1908
Austin L. Crothers (D)	Jan. 8, 1908	Jan. 10, 1912
Phillips L. Goldsborough (R)	Jan. 10, 1912	Jan. 12, 1916
Emerson C. Harrington (D)	Jan. 12, 1916	Jan. 14, 1920
Albert C. Ritchie (D)	Jan. 14, 1920	Jan. 9, 1935
Harry W. Nice (R)	Jan. 9, 1935	Jan. 11, 1939
Herbert R. O'Conor (D)[11]	Jan. 11, 1939	Jan. 3, 1947
William P. Lane Jr. (D)[12]	Jan. 3, 1947	Jan. 10, 1951
Theodore R. McKeldin (R)	Jan. 10, 1951	Jan. 14, 1959
J. Millard Tawes (D)	Jan. 14, 1959	Jan. 25, 1967
Spiro T. Agnew (R)[13]	Jan. 25, 1967	Jan. 7, 1969
Marvin Mandel (D)[14]	Jan. 7, 1969	Jan. 15, 1979
Blair Lee (D)[15]	Oct. 7, 1977	Jan. 15, 1979
Harry Hughes (D)	Jan. 17, 1979	Jan. 20, 1987
William D. Schaefer (D)	Jan. 21, 1987	Jan. 18, 1995
Parris N. Glendening (D)	Jan. 18, 1995	

Maryland

1. *Died Feb. 10, 1792.*
2. *Acting governor.*
3. *Resigned May 6, 1809.*
4. *Acting governor.*
5. *Died July 11, 1831.*
6. *Acting governor. Subsequently elected by the Legislature.*
7. *Resigned March 4, 1874.*
8. *Acting governor. Subsequently elected by the Legislature.*
9. *Resigned March 27, 1885.*
10. *Acting governor. Subsequently elected by the Legislature.*
11. *Resigned Jan. 3, 1947.*
12. *Elected by the Legislature to complete the remaining five days of O'Conor's term. Had previously been elected for a four-year term beginning January 8, 1947.*
13. *Resigned Jan. 7, 1969.*
14. *Elected by the Legislature to complete Agnew's term. Subsequently re-elected in 1970 and 1974. Suspended from office Oct. 7, 1977 to Jan. 15, 1979.*
15. *As lieutenant governor, served as acting governor.*

MASSACHUSETTS

(Ratified the Constitution Feb. 6, 1788)

Governors	Dates of Service	
John Hancock	May 30, 1787	Oct. 8, 1793
Samuel Adams	Oct. 8, 1793	June 2, 1797
Increase Sumner (FED)	June 2, 1797	June 7, 1799
Moses Gill (FED)[1]	June 7, 1799	May 30, 1800
Caleb Strong (FED)	May 30, 1800	May 29, 1807
James Sullivan (D-R)	May 29, 1807	Dec. 10, 1808
Levi Lincoln (D-R)[2]	Dec. 10, 1808	May 1, 1809
Christopher Gore (FED)	May 1809	June 1810
Elbridge Gerry (D-R)	June 1810	June 1812
Caleb Strong (FED)	June 1812	May 30, 1816
John Brooks (FED)	May 30, 1816	May 31, 1823
William Eustis (D-R)	May 31, 1823	Feb. 6, 1825
Marcus Morton (D-R)[3]	Feb. 6, 1825	May 26, 1825
Levi Lincoln (AR, NR)[4]	May 26, 1825	Jan. 9, 1834
John Davis (NR, W)	Jan. 9, 1834	March 1, 1835

Samuel T. Armstrong (W)[5]	March 1, 1835	Jan. 13, 1836
Edward Everett (W)	Jan. 13, 1836	Jan. 18, 1840
Marcus Morton (D)	Jan. 18, 1840	Jan. 7, 1841
John Davis (W)	Jan. 7, 1841	Jan. 17, 1843
Marcus Morton (D)	Jan. 17, 1843	Jan. 1844
George N. Briggs (W)	Jan. 1844	Jan. 11, 1851
George S. Boutwell (D)	Jan. 11, 1851	Jan. 14, 1853
John H. Clifford (W)	Jan. 14, 1853	Jan. 12, 1854
Emory Washburn (W)	Jan. 12, 1854	Jan. 4, 1855
Henry J. Gardner (AM)	Jan. 4, 1855	Jan. 7, 1858
Nathaniel P. Banks (R)	Jan. 7, 1858	Jan. 3, 1861
John A. Andrew (R)	Jan. 3, 1861	Jan. 4, 1866
Alexander H. Bullock (UN)	Jan. 4, 1866	Jan. 7, 1869
William Claflin (R)	Jan. 7, 1869	Jan. 4, 1872
William B. Washburn (R)[6]	Jan. 4, 1872	April 29, 1874
Thomas Talbot (R)[7]	April 29, 1874	Jan. 7, 1875
William Gaston (D)	Jan. 7, 1875	Jan. 6, 1876
Alexander H. Rice (R)	Jan. 6, 1876	Jan. 2, 1879
Thomas Talbot (R)	Jan. 2, 1879	Jan. 8, 1880
John Davis Long (R)	Jan. 8, 1880	Jan. 4, 1883
Benjamin F. Butler (D)	Jan. 4, 1883	Jan. 3, 1884
George D. Robinson (R)	Jan. 3, 1884	Jan. 6, 1887
Oliver Ames (R)	Jan. 6, 1887	Jan. 7, 1890
John Q. A. Brackett (R)	Jan. 7, 1890	Jan. 8, 1891
William E. Russell (D)	Jan. 8, 1891	Jan. 4, 1894
Frederic T. Greenhalge (R)[8]	Jan. 4, 1894	March 5, 1896
Roger Wolcott (R)[9]	March 5, 1896	Jan. 4, 1900
Winthrop M. Crane (R)	Jan. 4, 1900	Jan. 8, 1903
John L. Bates (R)	Jan. 8, 1903	Jan. 5, 1905
William L. Douglas (D)	Jan. 5, 1905	Jan. 4, 1906
Curtis Guild Jr. (R)	Jan. 4, 1906	Jan. 7, 1909
Eban Sumner Draper (R)	Jan. 7, 1909	Jan. 5, 1911
Eugene N. Foss (D)	Jan. 5, 1911	Jan. 8, 1914
David I. Walsh (D)	Jan. 8, 1914	Jan. 6, 1916
Samuel W. McCall (R)	Jan. 6, 1916	Jan. 2, 1919
Calvin Coolidge (R)	Jan. 2, 1919	Jan. 6, 1921
Channing H. Cox (R)	Jan. 6, 1921	Jan. 8, 1925
Alvan T. Fuller (R)	Jan. 8, 1925	Jan. 3, 1929
Frank G. Allen (R)	Jan. 3, 1929	Jan. 8, 1931
Joseph B. Ely (D)	Jan. 8, 1931	Jan. 3, 1935
James M. Curley (D)	Jan. 3, 1935	Jan. 7, 1937
Charles F. Hurley (D)	Jan. 7, 1937	Jan. 5, 1939
Leverett Saltonstall (R)	Jan. 5, 1939	Jan. 3, 1945
Maurice J. Tobin (D)	Jan. 3, 1945	Jan. 2, 1947
Robert F. Bradford (R)	Jan. 2, 1947	Jan. 6, 1949
Paul A. Dever (D)	Jan. 6, 1949	Jan. 8, 1953
Christian A. Herter (R)	Jan. 8, 1953	Jan. 3, 1957
Foster J. Furcolo (D)	Jan. 3, 1957	Jan. 5, 1961
John A. Volpe (R)	Jan. 5, 1961	Jan. 3, 1963
Endicott Peabody (D)	Jan. 3, 1963	Jan. 7, 1965
John A. Volpe (R)[10]	Jan. 7, 1965	Jan. 22, 1969
Francis W. Sargent (R)[11]	Jan. 22, 1969	Jan. 2, 1975
Michael S. Dukakis (D)	Jan. 2, 1975	Jan. 4, 1979
Edward J. King (D)	Jan. 4, 1979	Jan. 6, 1983
Michael S. Dukakis (D)	Jan. 6, 1983	Jan. 3, 1991
William F. Weld (R)[12]	Jan. 3, 1991	July, 29, 1997
Argeo Paul Cellucci (R)[13]	July 29, 1997	

Massachusetts

1. *Acting governor.*
2. *Acting governor.*
3. *Acting governor.*
4. *ICPSR data shows that there were two elections for governor in Massachusetts in 1831 and returns for both have been provided. The winner both times was incumbent Levi Lincoln. An explanation was obtained from Albert Bushnell Hart's Commonwealth of Massachusetts, vol. 4 (New York: States History Company, 1930), p. 82. Massachusetts had a one-year term for its governors during this period. Apparently the state decided in 1831 to move its gubernatorial election from April to November to coincide with presidential elections in 1832 and succeeding years. As a consequence, Lincoln was required to run twice within the same year to make the adjustment.*
5. *Acting governor.*
6. *Resigned May 1, 1874.*
7. *Acting governor.*
8. *Died March 5, 1896.*

9. *As lieutenant governor, he succeeded to office. Subsequently elected.*
10. *Resigned Jan. 22, 1969.*
11. *As lieutenant governor, he succeeded to office. Subsequently elected.*
12. *Resigned July 29, 1997.*
13. *As lieutenant governor, he succeeded to office.*

MICHIGAN

(Became a state Jan. 26, 1837)

Governors	Dates of Service	
Stevens T. Mason (D)	Nov. 3, 1835	Jan. 7, 1840
Edward Mundy (D)[1]	April 3, 1838	June 12, 1838
William Woodbridge (W)[2]	Jan. 7, 1840	Feb. 23, 1841
James W. Gordon (W)[3]	Feb. 23, 1841	Jan. 3, 1842
John S. Barry (D)	Jan. 3, 1842	Jan. 5, 1846
Alpheus Felch (D)[4]	Jan. 5, 1846	March 3, 1847
William L. Greenly (D)[5]	March 3, 1847	Jan. 3, 1848
Epaphroditus Ransom (D)	Jan. 3, 1848	Jan. 7, 1850
John S. Barry (D)	Jan. 7, 1850	Jan. 1, 1851
Robert McClelland (D)[6]	Jan. 1, 1851	March 7, 1853
Andrew Parsons (D)[7]	March 7, 1853	Jan. 3, 1855
Kinsley S. Bingham (R)	Jan. 3, 1855	Jan. 5, 1859
Moses Wisner (R)	Jan. 5, 1859	Jan. 2, 1861
Austin Blair (R)	Jan. 2, 1861	Jan. 4, 1865
Henry H. Crapo (UN R)	Jan. 4, 1865	Jan. 6, 1869
Henry P. Baldwin (R)	Jan. 6, 1869	Jan. 1, 1873
John J. Bagley (R)	Jan. 1, 1873	Jan. 3, 1877
Charles M. Croswell (R)	Jan. 3, 1877	Jan. 1, 1881
David H. Jerome (R)	Jan. 1, 1881	Jan. 1, 1883
Josiah W. Begole (D)	Jan. 1, 1883	Jan. 1, 1885
Russell A. Alger (R)	Jan. 1, 1885	Jan. 1, 1887
Cyrus G. Luce (R)	Jan. 1, 1887	Jan. 1, 1891
Edward B. Winans (D)	Jan. 1, 1891	Jan. 1, 1893
John T. Rich (R)	Jan. 1, 1893	Jan. 1, 1897
Hazen S. Pingree (R)	Jan. 1, 1897	Jan. 1, 1901
Aaron T. Bliss (R)	Jan. 1, 1901	Jan. 1, 1905
Fred M. Warner (R)	Jan. 1, 1905	Jan. 1, 1911
Chase S. Osborn (R)	Jan. 1, 1911	Jan. 1, 1913
Woodbridge N. Ferris (D)	Jan. 1, 1913	Jan. 1, 1917
Albert E. Sleeper (R)	Jan. 1, 1917	Jan. 1, 1921
Alexander J. Groesbeck (R)	Jan. 1, 1921	Jan. 1, 1927
Fred W. Green (R)	Jan. 1, 1927	Jan. 1, 1931
Wilber M. Brucker (R)	Jan. 1, 1931	Jan. 1, 1933
William A. Comstock (D)	Jan. 1, 1933	Jan. 1, 1935
Frank D. Fitzgerald (R)	Jan. 1, 1935	Jan. 1, 1937
Frank Murphy (D)	Jan. 1, 1937	Jan. 1, 1939
Frank D. Fitzgerald (R)[8]	Jan. 1, 1939	March 16, 1939
Luren D. Dickinson (R)[9]	March 16, 1939	Jan. 1, 1941
Murray D. Van Wagoner (D)	Jan. 1, 1941	Jan. 1, 1943
Harry F. Kelly (R)	Jan. 1, 1943	Jan. 1, 1947
Kim Sigler (R)	Jan. 1, 1947	Jan. 1, 1949
G. Mennen Williams (D)	Jan. 1, 1949	Jan. 1, 1961
John B. Swainson (D)	Jan. 1, 1961	Jan. 1, 1963
George W. Romney (R)[10]	Jan. 1, 1963	Jan. 22, 1969
William G. Milliken (R)[11]	Jan. 22, 1969	Jan. 1, 1983
James J. Blanchard (D)	Jan. 1, 1983	Jan. 1, 1991
John Engler (R)	Jan. 1, 1991	

Michigan

1. *Lieutenant governor, serving as acting governor for several months in 1838.*
2. *Resigned Feb. 23, 1841.*
3. *As lieutenant governor, he succeeded to office.*
4. *Resigned March 3, 1847.*
5. *As lieutenant governor, he succeeded to office.*
6. *Resigned March 7, 1853.*
7. *As lieutenant governor, he succeeded to office.*
8. *Died March 16, 1939.*
9. *As lieutenant governor, he succeeded to office.*
10. *Resigned Jan. 22, 1969.*
11. *As lieutenant governor, he succeeded to office. Subsequently elected.*

MINNESOTA

(Became a state May 11, 1858)

Governors	Dates of Service	
Henry H. Sibley (D)	May 24, 1858	Jan. 2, 1860
Alexander Ramsey (R)[1]	Jan. 2, 1860	July 10, 1863
Henry A. Swift (R)[2]	July 10, 1863	Jan. 11, 1864
Stephen Miller (UN)	Jan. 11, 1864	Jan. 8, 1866
William R. Marshall (R)	Jan. 8, 1866	Jan. 9, 1870
Horace Austin (R)	Jan. 9, 1870	Jan. 7, 1874
Cushman K. Davis (R)	Jan. 7, 1874	Jan. 7, 1876
John S. Pillsbury (R)	Jan. 7, 1876	Jan. 10, 1882
Lucius F. Hubbard (R)	Jan. 10, 1882	Jan. 5, 1887
Andrew R. McGill (R)	Jan. 5, 1887	Jan. 9, 1889
William R. Merriam (R)	Jan. 9, 1889	Jan. 4, 1893
Knute Nelson (R)	Jan. 4, 1893	Jan. 31, 1895
David M. Clough (R)	Jan. 31, 1895	Jan. 2, 1899
John Lind (D & POP)	Jan. 2, 1899	Jan. 7, 1901
Samuel R. Van Sant (R)	Jan. 7, 1901	Jan. 4, 1905
John A. Johnson (D)[3]	Jan. 4, 1905	Sept. 21, 1909
Adolph O. Eberhart (R)[4]	Sept. 21, 1909	Jan. 5, 1915
Winfield S. Hammond (D)[5]	Jan. 5, 1915	Dec. 30, 1915
Joseph A. A. Burnquist (R)[6]	Dec. 30, 1915	Jan. 5, 1921
Jacob A. O. Preus (R)	Jan. 5, 1921	Jan. 6, 1925
Theodore Christianson (R)	Jan. 6, 1925	Jan. 6, 1931
Floyd B. Olson (F-LAB)[7]	Jan. 6, 1931	Aug. 22, 1936
Hjalmar Petersen (F-LAB)[8]	Aug. 22, 1936	Jan. 4, 1937
Elmer A. Benson (F-LAB)	Jan. 4, 1937	Jan. 2, 1939
Harold E. Stassen (R)[9]	Jan. 2, 1939	April 27, 1943
Edward J. Thye (R)[10]	April 27, 1943	Jan. 8, 1947
Luther W. Youngdahl (R)[11]	Jan. 8, 1947	Sept. 27, 1951
C. Elmer Anderson (R)[12]	Sept. 27, 1951	Jan. 5, 1955
Orville L. Freeman (DFL)	Jan. 5, 1955	Jan. 2, 1961
Elmer L. Andersen (R)[13]	Jan. 2, 1961	March 25, 1963
Karl F. Rolvaag (DFL)[14]	March 25, 1963	Jan. 2, 1967
Harold LeVander (R)	Jan. 2, 1967	Jan. 4, 1971
Wendell R. Anderson (DFL)[15]	Jan. 4, 1971	Dec. 29, 1976
Rudy Perpich (DFL)[16]	Dec. 29, 1976	Jan. 1, 1979
Albert H. Quie (I-R)	Jan. 1, 1979	Jan. 3, 1983
Rudy Perpich (DFL)	Jan. 3, 1983	Jan. 7, 1991
Arne H. Carlson (I-R)	Jan. 7, 1991	

Minnesota

  1. *Resigned July 10, 1863.*
  2. *As lieutenant governor, he succeeded to office.*
  3. *Died Sept. 21, 1909.*
  4. *As lieutenant governor, he succeeded to office. Subsequently elected.*
  5. *Died Dec. 30, 1915.*
  6. *As lieutenant governor, he succeeded to office. Subsequently elected.*
  7. *Died Aug. 22, 1936.*
  8. *As lieutenant governor, he succeeded to office.*
  9. *Resigned April 27, 1943.*
  10. *As lieutenant governor, he succeeded to office. Subsequently elected.*
  11. *Resigned Sept. 27, 1951.*
  12. *As lieutenant governor, he succeeded to office. Subsequently elected.*
  13. *The 1962 election between incumbent Governor Andersen (R) and Lieutenant Governor Karl Rolvaag (DFL) was disputed. Andersen served for almost three months of the term before the Minnesota Supreme Court ruled that Rolvaag had won by 91 votes.*
  14. *Served the remainder of the four-year term after the removal of Governor Andersen.*
  15. *Resigned Dec. 29, 1976, having been appointed to the Senate.*
  16. *As lieutenant governor, he succeeded to office.*

MISSISSIPPI

(Became a state Dec. 10, 1817)

Governors	Dates of Service	
David Holmes (D-R)	Dec. 10, 1817	Jan. 5, 1820
George Poindexter (D-R)	Jan. 5, 1820	Jan. 7, 1822
Walter Leake (D-R)[1]	Jan. 7, 1822	Nov. 17, 1825
Gerard C. Brandon (D-R)[2]	Nov. 17, 1825	Jan. 7, 1826
David Holmes (D-R)[3]	Jan. 7, 1826	July 25, 1826
Gerard C. Brandon (D)[4]	July 25, 1826	Jan. 9, 1832
Abram M. Scott (NR)[5]	Jan. 9, 1832	June 12, 1833
Charles Lynch (NR)[6]	June 12, 1833	Nov. 20, 1833
Hiram G. Runnels (D)[7]	Nov. 20, 1833	Nov. 20, 1835
John A. Quitman (W)[8]	Dec. 3, 1835	Jan. 7, 1836
Charles Lynch (W)	Jan. 7, 1836	Jan. 8, 1838
Alexander G. McNutt (D)	Jan. 8, 1838	Jan. 10, 1842
Tilgham M. Tucker (D)	Jan. 10, 1842	Jan. 10, 1844
Albert G. Brown (D)	Jan. 10, 1844	Jan. 10, 1848
Joseph M. Matthews (D)	Jan. 10, 1848	Jan. 10, 1850
John A. Quitman (D)[9]	Jan. 10, 1850	Feb. 3, 1851
John I. Guion (D)[10]	Feb. 3, 1851	Nov. 4, 1851
James Whitfield (D)[11]	Nov. 24, 1851	Jan. 10, 1852
Henry S. Foote (UN)[12]	Jan. 10, 1852	Jan. 5, 1854
John J. Pettus (D)[13]	Jan. 5, 1854	Jan. 10, 1854
John J. McRae (D)	Jan. 10, 1854	Nov. 16, 1857
William McWillie (D)	Nov. 16, 1857	Nov. 21, 1859
John J. Pettus (D)	Nov. 21, 1859	Nov. 16, 1863
Charles Clark (D)[14]	Nov. 16, 1863	May 22, 1865
William L. Sharkey	June 13, 1865	Oct. 16, 1865
Benjamin G. Humphreys[15]	Oct. 16, 1865	June 15, 1868
Adelbert Ames	June 15, 1868	March 10, 1870
James L. Alcorn (R)[16]	March 10, 1870	Nov. 30, 1871
Ridgley C. Powers (R)[17]	Nov. 30, 1871	Jan. 4, 1874
Adelbert Ames (R)[18]	Jan. 4, 1874	March 29, 1876
John M. Stone (D)[19]	March 29, 1876	Jan. 29, 1882
Robert Lowry (D)	Jan. 29, 1882	Jan. 13, 1890
John M. Stone (D)	Jan. 13, 1890	Jan. 20, 1896
Anselm J. McLaurin (D)	Jan. 20, 1896	Jan. 16, 1900
Andrew H. Longino (D)	Jan. 16, 1900	Jan. 19, 1904
James Kimble Vardaman (D)	Jan. 19, 1904	Jan. 21, 1908
Edmond Favor Noel (D)	Jan. 21, 1908	Jan. 16, 1912
Earl LeRoy Brewer (D)	Jan. 16, 1912	Jan. 18, 1916
Theodore Gilmore Bilbo (D)	Jan. 18, 1916	Jan. 20, 1920
Lee Maurice Russell (D)	Jan. 20, 1920	Jan. 22, 1924
Henry Lewis Whitfield (D)[20]	Jan. 22, 1924	March 18, 1927
Dennis Murphree (D)[21]	March 18, 1927	Jan. 17, 1928
Theodore Gilmore Bilbo (D)	Jan. 17, 1928	Jan. 19, 1932
Martin Sennett Conner (D)	Jan. 19, 1932	Jan. 21, 1936
Hugh L. White (D)	Jan. 21, 1936	Jan. 16, 1940
Paul B. Johnson (D)[22]	Jan. 16, 1940	Dec. 26, 1943
Dennis Murphree (D)[23]	Dec. 26, 1943	Jan. 18, 1944
Thomas L. Bailey (D)[24]	Jan. 18, 1944	Nov. 2, 1946
Fielding L. Wright (D)[25]	Nov. 2, 1946	Jan. 22, 1952
Hugh L. White (D)	Jan. 22, 1952	Jan. 17, 1956
J. P. Coleman (D)	Jan. 17, 1956	Jan. 19, 1960
Ross R. Barnett (D)	Jan. 19, 1960	Jan. 21, 1964
Paul B. Johnson Jr. (D)	Jan. 21, 1964	Jan. 16, 1968
John Bell Williams (D)	Jan. 16, 1968	Jan. 18, 1972
William Lowe Waller (D)	Jan. 18, 1972	Jan. 20, 1976
Cliff Finch (D)	Jan. 20, 1976	Jan. 22, 1980
William Winter (D)	Jan. 22, 1980	Jan. 10, 1984
Bill Allain (D)	Jan. 10, 1984	Jan. 12, 1988
Ray Mabus (D)	Jan. 12, 1988	Jan. 14, 1992
Kirk Fordice (R)	Jan. 14, 1992	

Mississippi

  1. *Died Nov. 17, 1825.*
  2. *As lieutenant governor, he succeeded to office.*
  3. *Resigned July 25, 1826.*
  4. *As lieutenant governor, he succeeded to office. Subsequently elected.*
  5. *Died June 12, 1833.*
  6. *As president of the state Senate, he succeeded to office.*

7. Resigned Nov. 20, 1835.
8. As president of the state Senate, he succeeded to office.
9. Resigned Feb. 3, 1851.
10 As president of the state Senate, he succeeded to office.
11. As president of the state Senate, he succeeded to office.
12. Resigned Jan. 5, 1854.
13. As president of the state Senate, he succeeded to office.
14. Removed from office May 22, 1865.
15. Removed from office June 15, 1868.
16. Resigned Nov. 30, 1871.
17. As lieutenant governor, he succeeded to office.
18. Resigned March 29, 1876.
19. As president of the state Senate, he succeeded to office. Subsequently elected.
20. Died March 18, 1927.
21. As lieutenant governor, he succeeded to office.
22. Died Dec. 26, 1943.
23. As lieutenant governor, he succeeded to office.
24. Died Nov. 2, 1946.
25. As lieutenant governor, he succeeded to office. Subsequently elected.

MISSOURI

(Became a state Aug. 10, 1821)

Governors	Dates of Service	
Alexander McNair (D-R)	Aug. 10, 1821	Nov. 15, 1824
Frederick Bates (AR)[1]	Nov. 15, 1824	Aug. 4, 1825
Abraham J. Williams (D-R)[2]	Aug. 4, 1825	Jan. 20, 1826
John Miller (JAC D)	Jan. 20, 1826	Nov. 14, 1832
Daniel Dunklin (D)	Nov. 14, 1832	Sept. 13, 1836
Lilburn W. Boggs (D)	Sept. 13, 1836	Nov. 16, 1840
Thomas Reynolds (D)[3]	Nov. 16, 1840	Feb. 9, 1844
Meredith M. Marmaduke (D)[4]	Feb. 9, 1844	Nov. 20, 1844
John C. Edwards (D)	Nov. 20, 1844	Dec. 27, 1848
Austin A. King (D)	Dec. 27, 1848	Jan. 3, 1853
Sterling Price (D)	Jan. 3, 1853	Jan. 5, 1857
Trusten Polk (D)[5]	Jan. 5, 1857	Feb. 27, 1857
Hancock Lee Jackson (D)[6]	Feb. 27, 1857	Oct. 22, 1857
Robert Marcellus Stewart (D)	Oct. 22, 1857	Jan. 3, 1861
Claiborne Fox Jackson (D)[7]	Jan. 31, 1861	July 30, 1861
Hamilton R. Gamble (UN)[8]	July 31, 1861	Jan. 31, 1864
Willard Preble Hall (UN)[9]	Jan. 31, 1864	Jan. 2, 1865
Thomas C. Fletcher (UN R)	Jan. 2, 1865	Jan. 12, 1869
Joseph W. McClurg (R)	Jan. 12, 1869	Jan. 9, 1871
Benjamin G. Brown (R)	Jan. 9, 1871	Jan. 8, 1873
Silas Woodson (D)	Jan. 8, 1873	Jan. 12, 1875
Charles Henry Hardin (D)	Jan. 12, 1875	Jan. 8, 1877
John S. Phelps (D)	Jan. 8, 1877	Jan. 10, 1881
Thomas T. Crittenden (D)	Jan. 10, 1881	Jan. 12, 1885
John S. Marmaduke (D)[10]	Jan. 12, 1885	Dec. 28, 1887
Albert P. Morehouse (D)[11]	Dec. 28, 1887	Jan. 14, 1889
David R. Francis (D)	Jan. 14, 1889	Jan. 9, 1893
William J. Stone (D)	Jan. 9, 1893	Jan. 11, 1897
Lawrence Vest Stephens (D)	Jan. 11, 1897	Jan. 14, 1901
Alexander M. Dockery (D)	Jan. 14, 1901	Jan. 9, 1905
Joseph W. Folk (D)	Jan. 9, 1905	Jan. 11, 1909
Herbert S. Hadley (R)	Jan. 11, 1909	Jan. 13, 1913
Elliot W. Major (D)	Jan. 13, 1913	Jan. 8, 1917
Frederick D. Gardner (D)	Jan. 8, 1917	Jan. 10, 1921
Arthur M. Hyde (R)	Jan. 10, 1921	Jan. 12, 1925
Samuel A. Baker (R)	Jan. 12, 1925	Jan. 14, 1929
Henry S. Caulfield (R)	Jan. 14, 1929	Jan. 9, 1933
Guy B. Park (D)	Jan. 9, 1933	Jan. 11, 1937
Lloyd C. Stark (D)	Jan. 11, 1937	Jan. 13, 1941
Forrest C. Donnell (R)	Jan. 13, 1941	Jan. 8, 1945
Phil M. Donnelly (D)	Jan. 8, 1945	Jan. 10, 1949
Forrest Smith (D)	Jan. 10, 1949	Jan. 12, 1953
Phil M. Donnelly (D)	Jan. 12, 1953	Jan. 14, 1957
James T. Blair Jr. (D)	Jan. 14, 1957	Jan. 9, 1961
John M. Dalton (D)	Jan. 9, 1961	Jan. 11, 1965
Warren E. Hearnes (D)	Jan. 11, 1965	Jan. 8, 1973
Christopher S. Bond (R)	Jan. 8, 1973	Jan. 10, 1977
Joseph P. Teasdale (D)	Jan. 10, 1977	Jan. 12, 1981
Christopher S. Bond (R)	Jan. 12, 1981	Jan. 14, 1985
John Ashcroft (R)	Jan. 14, 1985	Jan. 11, 1993
Mel Carnahan (D)	Jan. 11, 1993	

Missouri
1. Died Aug. 4, 1825.
2. Acting governor.
3. Died in 1844.
4. Acting governor.
5. Resigned Feb. 27, 1857.
6. Acting governor.
7. Removed from office in 1861 by convention.
8. Appointed governor by convention. Died Jan. 31, 1864.
9. Acting governor.
10. Died Dec. 28, 1887.
11. Acting governor.

MONTANA

(Became a state Nov. 8, 1889)

Governors	Dates of Service	
Joseph K. Toole (D)	Nov. 8, 1889	Jan. 1, 1893
John E. Rickards (R)	Jan. 2, 1893	Jan. 3, 1897
Robert B. Smith (PP & D)	Jan. 4, 1897	Jan. 7, 1901
Joseph K. Toole (D)[1]	Jan. 7, 1901	April 1, 1908
Edwin L. Norris (D)[2]	April 1, 1908	Jan. 5, 1913
Samuel V. Stewart (D)	Jan. 6, 1913	Jan. 2, 1921
Joseph M. Dixon (R)	Jan. 3, 1921	Jan. 4, 1925
John E. Erickson (D)[3]	Jan. 4, 1925	March 13, 1933
Frank H. Cooney (D)[4]	March 13, 1933	Dec. 15, 1935
William E. Holt (D)[5]	Dec. 16, 1935	Jan. 4, 1937
Roy E. Ayers (D)	Jan. 4, 1937	Jan. 6, 1942
Samuel C. Ford (R)	Jan. 6, 1941	Jan. 3, 1949
John W. Bonner (D)	Jan. 3, 1949	Jan. 4, 1953
J. Hugo Aronson (R)	Jan. 4, 1953	Jan. 4, 1961
Donald G. Nutter (R)[6]	Jan. 4, 1961	Jan. 25, 1962
Tim M. Babcock (R)[7]	Jan. 26, 1962	Jan. 6, 1969
Forrest H. Anderson (D)	Jan. 6, 1969	Jan. 1, 1973
Thomas L. Judge (D)	Jan. 1, 1973	Jan. 5, 1981
Ted Schwinden (D)	Jan. 5, 1981	Jan. 2, 1989
Stan Stephens (R)	Jan. 2, 1989	Jan. 4, 1993
Marc Racicot (R)	Jan. 4, 1993	

Montana
1. Resigned April 1, 1908.
2. As lieutenant governor, he succeeded to office. Subsequently elected.
3. Resigned March 13, 1933.
4. As lieutenant governor, he succeeded to office. Died Dec. 15, 1935.
5. As president of the state Senate, he succeeded to office.
6. Died Jan. 25, 1962.
7. As lieutenant governor, he succeeded to office. Subsequently elected.

NEBRASKA

(Became a state March 1, 1867)

Governors	Dates of Service	
David Butler (R)[1]	March 27, 1867	June 2, 1871
William H. James (R)[2]	June 2, 1871	Jan. 13, 1873
Robert W. Furnas (R)	Jan. 13, 1873	Jan. 1875
Silas Garber (R)	Jan. 1875	Jan. 1879
Albinus Nance (R)	Jan. 1879	Jan. 1883
James W. Dawes (R)	Jan. 1883	Jan. 15, 1887
John M. Thayer (R)	Jan. 15, 1887	Jan. 15, 1891
James E. Boyd (D)[3]	Jan. 15, 1891	May 5, 1891
John M. Thayer (R)[4]	May 5, 1891	Feb. 8, 1892
James E. Boyd (D)[5]	Feb. 8, 1892	Jan. 1893
Lorenzo Crounse (R)	Jan. 1893	Jan. 1895

Silas A. Holcomb (D & PPI)	Jan. 1895	Jan. 5, 1899
William A. Poynter (FUS)[6]	Jan. 5, 1899	Jan. 3, 1901
Charles H. Dietrich (R)[7]	Jan. 3, 1901	May 1, 1901
Ezra P. Savage (R)[8]	May 1, 1901	Jan. 8, 1903
John H. Mickey (R)	Jan. 8, 1903	Jan. 3, 1907
George L. Sheldon (R)	Jan. 3, 1907	Jan. 7, 1909
Ashton C. Shallenberger (D)	Jan. 7, 1909	Jan. 5, 1911
Chester H. Aldrich (R)	Jan. 5, 1911	Jan. 9, 1913
John H. Morehead (D)	Jan. 9, 1913	Jan. 4, 1917
Keith Neville (D)	Jan. 4, 1917	Jan. 9, 1919
Samuel R. McKelvie (R)	Jan. 9, 1919	Jan. 3, 1923
Charles W. Bryan (D)	Jan. 4, 1923	Jan. 8, 1925
Adam McMullen (R)	Jan. 8, 1925	Jan. 3, 1929
Arthur J. Weaver (R)	Jan. 3, 1929	Jan. 8, 1931
Charles W. Bryan (D)	Jan. 8, 1931	Jan. 3, 1935
Robert L. Cochran (D)	Jan. 3, 1935	Jan. 9, 1941
Dwight P. Griswold (R)	Jan. 9, 1941	Jan. 9, 1947
Val Peterson (R)	Jan. 9, 1947	Jan. 8, 1953
Robert Berkey Crosby (R)	Jan. 8, 1953	Jan. 6, 1955
Victor E. Anderson (R)	Jan. 6, 1955	Jan. 8, 1959
Ralph G. Brooks (D)[9]	Jan. 8, 1959	Sept. 9, 1960
Dwight W. Burney (R)[10]	Sept. 9, 1960	Jan. 5, 1961
Frank B. Morrison (D)	Jan. 5, 1961	Jan. 5, 1967
Norbert T. Tiemann (R)	Jan. 5, 1967	Jan. 7, 1971
J. James Exon (D)	Jan. 7, 1971	Jan. 3, 1979
Charles Thone (R)	Jan. 4, 1979	Jan. 6, 1983
Bob Kerrey (D)	Jan. 6, 1983	Jan. 9, 1987
Kay A. Orr (R)	Jan. 9, 1987	Jan. 9, 1991
Ben Nelson (D)	Jan. 9, 1991	

Nebraska

1. *Impeached. Removed from office June 2, 1871.*
2. *As lieutenant governor, he succeeded to office.*
3. *The election of Boyd was challenged by Governor Thayer on the grounds that Boyd had been born in Ireland and was not an American citizen, and was thus ineligible to be governor. Boyd was removed by the Nebraska Supreme Court May 5, 1891.*
4. *Following the removal of Boyd, Thayer returned to office.*
5. *U.S. Supreme Court declared that Boyd was a citizen, and he returned to office Feb. 18, 1892, and served out the remainder of his term.*
6. *Fusion composed of Democrats and Populists.*
7. *Resigned May 1, 1901.*
8. *As lieutenant governor, he succeeded to office.*
9. *Died Sept. 9, 1960.*
10. *As lieutenant governor, he succeeded to office.*

NEVADA

(Became a state Oct. 31, 1864)

Governors	**Dates of Service**	
H. G. Blasdel (UN R)	Dec. 5, 1864	Jan. 2, 1871
L. R. Bradley (D)	Jan. 3, 1871	Jan. 6, 1879
John H. Kinkead (R)	Jan. 7, 1879	Jan. 1, 1883
Jewett W. Adams (D)	Jan. 2, 1883	Jan. 3, 1887
C. C. Stevenson (R)[1]	Jan. 4, 1887	Sept. 2, 1890
Frank Bell (R)[2]	Sept. 21, 1890	Jan. 5, 1891
R. K. Colcord (R)	Jan. 6, 1891	Jan. 7, 1895
John S. Jones (D SIL)[3]	Jan. 8, 1895	April 10, 1896
Reinhold Sadler (SIL R)[4]	April 10, 1896	Jan. 1, 1903
John Sparks (D & SILVER)[5]	Jan. 1, 1903	May 22, 1908
Denver S. Dickerson (D)[6]	May 22, 1908	Jan. 2, 1911
Tasker L. Oddie (R)	Jan. 2, 1911	Jan. 4, 1915
Emmet D. Boyle (D)	Jan. 4, 1915	Jan. 1, 1923
James G. Scrugham (D)	Jan. 1, 1923	Jan. 3, 1927
Frederick B. Balzar (R)[7]	Jan. 3, 1927	March 21, 1934
Morley I. Griswold (R)[8]	March 21, 1934	Jan. 7, 1935
Richard Kirman Sr. (D)	Jan. 7, 1935	Jan. 2, 1939
Edward P. Carville (D)[9]	Jan. 2, 1939	July 24, 1945
Vail M. Pittman (D)[10]	July 24, 1945	Jan. 1, 1951
Charles H. Russell (R)	Jan. 1, 1951	Jan. 5, 1959
Grant Sawyer (D)	Jan. 5, 1959	Jan. 2, 1967
Paul D. Laxalt (R)	Jan. 2, 1967	Jan. 4, 1971
Mike O'Callaghan (D)	Jan. 4, 1971	Jan. 1, 1979
Robert F. List (R)	Jan. 1, 1979	Jan. 3, 1983
Richard H. Bryan (D)[11]	Jan. 3, 1983	Jan. 3, 1989
Bob J. Miller (D)[12]	Jan. 3, 1989	

Nevada

1. *Left office due to disability, Sept. 1, 1890. Died Sept. 21, 1890.*
2. *As lieutenant governor, he succeeded to office.*
3. *Died April 10, 1896.*
4. *As lieutenant governor, he succeeded to office. Subsequently elected.*
5. *Died May 22, 1908.*
6. *As lieutenant governor, he succeeded to office.*
7. *Died March 21, 1934.*
8. *As lieutenant governor, he succeeded to office.*
9. *Resigned July 24, 1945.*
10. *As lieutenant governor, he succeeded to office. Subsequently elected.*
11. *Resigned Jan. 3, 1989, having been elected to the U.S. Senate.*
12. *As lieutenant governor, he succeeded to office. Subsequently elected.*

NEW HAMPSHIRE

(Ratified the Constitution June 21, 1788)

Governors	**Dates of Service**	
John Sullivan (FED)	June 6, 1789	June 5, 1790
Josiah Bartlett (D-R)	June 5, 1790	June 5, 1794
Joseph T. Gilman (FED)	June 5, 1794	June 6, 1805
John Langdon (D-R)	June 6, 1805	June 8, 1809
Jeremiah Smith (FED)	June 8, 1809	June 7, 1810
John Langdon (D-R)	June 7, 1810	June 5, 1812
William Plumer (D-R)	June 5, 1812	June 3, 1813
John T. Gilman (FED)	June 13, 1813	June 6, 1816
William Plumer (D-R)	June 6, 1816	June 3, 1819
Samuel Bell (D-R)	June 3, 1819	June 5, 1823
Levi Woodbury (D-R)	June 5, 1823	June 2, 1824
David L. Morrill (D-R)	June 3, 1824	June 7, 1827
Benjamin Pierce (D-R)	June 7, 1827	June 5, 1828
John Bell (NR)	June 5, 1828	June 4, 1829
Benjamin Pierce (JAC D)	June 4, 1829	June 3, 1830
Matthew Harvey (JAC D)[1]	June 3, 1830	Feb. 28, 1831
Joseph M. Harper (D)[2]	Feb. 28, 1831	June 2, 1831
Samuel Dinsmoor (JAC D)	June 2, 1831	June 5, 1834
William Badger (D)	June 5, 1834	June 2, 1836
Isaac Hill (D)	June 2, 1836	June 5, 1839
John Page (D)	June 5, 1839	June 2, 1842
Henry Hubbard (D)	June 2, 1842	June 6, 1844
John H. Steele (D)	June 6, 1844	June 4, 1846
Anthony Colby (W)	June 4, 1846	June 3, 1847
Jared W. Williams (D)	June 3, 1847	June 7, 1849
Samuel Dinsmoor (D)	June 7, 1849	June 3, 1852
Noah Martin (D)	June 3, 1852	June 8, 1854
Nathaniel B. Baker (D)	June 8, 1854	June 7, 1855
Ralph Metcalf (AM)	June 7, 1855	June 4, 1857
William Haile (R)	June 4, 1857	June 2, 1859
Ichabod Goodwin (R)	June 2, 1859	June 6, 1861
Nathaniel S. Berry (R)	June 6, 1861	June 3, 1863
Joseph A. Gilmore (R)	June 3, 1863	June 8, 1865
Frederick Smyth (UN)	June 8, 1865	June 6, 1867
Walter Harriman (R)	June 6, 1867	June 2, 1869
Onslow Stearns (R)	June 3, 1869	June 8, 1871
James A. Weston (D)	June 14, 1871	June 6, 1872
Ezekiel A. Straw (R)	June 6, 1872	June 3, 1874
James A. Weston (D)	June 3, 1874	June 10, 1875
Person C. Cheney (R)	June 10, 1875	June 6, 1877
Benjamin F. Prescott (R)	June 7, 1877	June 5, 1879
Natt Head (R)	June 5, 1879	June 2, 1881
Charles H. Bell (R)	June 2, 1881	June 7, 1883
Samuel W. Hale (R)	June 7, 1883	June 4, 1885
Moody Currier (R)	June 4, 1885	June 2, 1887
Charles H. Sawyer (R)	June 2, 1887	June 6, 1889
David H. Goodell (R)	June 6, 1889	Jan. 8, 1891

Hiram A. Tuttle (R)	Jan. 8, 1891	Jan. 5, 1893
John B. Smith (R)	Jan. 5, 1893	Jan. 3, 1895
Charles A. Busiel (R)	Jan. 3, 1895	Jan. 7, 1897
George A. Ramsdell (R)	Jan. 7, 1897	Jan. 5, 1899
Frank W. Rollins (R)	Jan. 5, 1899	Jan. 3, 1901
Chester B. Jordan (R)	Jan. 3, 1901	Jan. 1, 1903
Nahum J. Batchelder (R)	Jan. 1, 1903	Jan. 5, 1905
John McLane (R)	Jan. 5, 1905	Jan. 3, 1907
Charles M. Floyd (R)	Jan. 3, 1907	Jan. 7, 1909
Henry B. Quinby (R)	Jan. 7, 1909	Jan. 5, 1911
Robert P. Bass (R)	Jan. 5, 1911	Jan. 2, 1913
Samuel D. Felker (D)	Jan. 2, 1913	Jan. 7, 1915
Rolland H. Spaulding (R)	Jan. 7, 1915	Jan. 3, 1917
Henry Wilder Keyes (R)[3]	Jan. 3, 1917	Jan. 2, 1919
John H. Bartlett (R)	Jan. 2, 1919	Jan. 6, 1921
Albert O. Brown (R)	Jan. 6, 1921	Jan. 4, 1923
Fred H. Brown (D)	Jan. 4, 1923	Jan. 1, 1925
John G. Winant (R)	Jan. 1, 1925	Jan. 6, 1927
Huntley N. Spaulding (R)	Jan. 6, 1927	Jan. 3, 1929
Charles W. Tobey (R)	Jan. 3, 1929	Jan. 1, 1931
John G. Winant (R)	Jan. 1, 1931	Jan. 3, 1935
H. Styles Bridges (R)	Jan. 3, 1935	Jan. 7, 1937
Francis P. Murphy (R)	Jan. 7, 1937	Jan. 2, 1941
Robert O. Blood (R)	Jan. 2, 1941	Jan. 4, 1945
Charles M. Dale (R)	Jan. 4, 1945	Jan. 6, 1949
Sherman Adams (R)	Jan. 6, 1949	Jan. 1, 1953
Hugh Gregg (R)	Jan. 1, 1953	Jan. 6, 1955
Lane Dwinell (R)	Jan. 6, 1955	Jan. 1, 1959
Wesley Powell (R)	Jan. 1, 1959	Jan. 3, 1963
John W. King (D)	Jan. 3, 1963	Jan. 2, 1969
Walter Peterson (R)	Jan. 2, 1969	Jan. 4, 1973
Meldrim Thomson Jr. (R)	Jan. 4, 1973	Jan. 4, 1979
Hugh J. Gallen (D)[4]	Jan. 4, 1979	Nov. 11, 1982
Robert B. Monier (D)[5]	Nov. 11, 1982	Nov. 30, 1982
William M. Gardner (D)[6]	Nov. 30, 1982	Dec. 1, 1982
Vesta M. Roy (D)[7]	Dec. 1, 1982	Jan. 6, 1983
John H. Sununu (R)	Jan. 6, 1983	Jan. 4, 1989
Judd Gregg (R)	Jan. 4, 1989	Jan. 7, 1993
Steve Merrill (R)	Jan. 7, 1993	Jan. 9, 1997
Jeanne Shaheen (D)	Jan. 9, 1997	

New Hampshire
1. *Resigned Feb. 8, 1831.*
2. *Acting governor in 1831.*
3. *Keyes was disqualified at the end of his term by illness and Jesse M. Barton, president of the state Senate, became acting governor.*
4. *Hospitalized Nov. 20, 1982. Died Dec. 29, 1982.*
5. *As president of the state Senate, served as acting governor until the Legislature dissolved on Nov. 30, 1982.*
6. *As secretary of state, served as acting governor until new members of the Legislature were sworn in.*
7. *As new president of the state Senate, served as acting governor.*

NEW JERSEY

(Ratified the Constitution Dec. 18, 1787)

Governors	Dates of Service	
William Livingston (FED)[1]	Aug. 27, 1776	July 25, 1790
Elisha Lawrence (FED)[2]	July 25, 1790	Oct. 30, 1790
William Paterson (FED)[3]	Oct. 30, 1790	March 4, 1793
Thomas Henderson (FED)	March 30, 1793	June 3, 1793
Richard Howell (FED)	June 3, 1793	Oct. 31, 1801
Joseph Bloomfield (D-R)	Oct. 31, 1801	Oct. 28, 1802
John Lambert (D-R)[4]	Nov. 15, 1802	Oct. 29, 1803
Joseph Bloomfield (D-R)	Oct. 29, 1803	Oct. 29, 1812
Aaron Ogden (FED)	Oct. 29, 1812	Oct. 29, 1813
William S. Pennington (D-R)[5]	Oct. 29, 1813	June 19, 1815
William Kennedy (D-R)[6]	June 19, 1815	Oct. 25, 1815
Mahlon Dickerson (D-R)[7]	Oct. 26, 1815	Feb. 1, 1817
Isaac H. Williamson (FED)	Feb. 6, 1817	Oct. 30, 1829
Peter D. Vroom (D)	Nov. 6, 1829	Oct. 26, 1832

Samuel L. Southard (W)	Oct. 26, 1832	Feb. 1833
Elias P. Seeley (W)	Feb. 27, 1833	Oct. 23, 1833
Peter D. Vroom (D)	Oct. 25, 1833	Oct. 28, 1836
Philemon Dickerson (D)	Nov. 3, 1836	Oct. 27, 1837
William Pennington (W)	Oct. 27, 1837	Oct. 27, 1843
Daniel Haines (D)	Oct. 27, 1843	Jan. 21, 1845
Charles C. Stratton (W)	Jan. 21, 1845	Jan. 18, 1848
Daniel Haines (D)	Jan. 18, 1848	Jan. 20, 1851
George F. Fort (D)	Jan. 21, 1851	Jan. 17, 1854
Rodman M. Price (D)	Jan. 17, 1854	Jan. 20, 1857
William A. Newell (FUS)	Jan. 20, 1857	Jan. 17, 1860
Charles S. Olden (R)	Jan. 17, 1860	Jan. 20, 1863
Joel Parker (D)	Jan. 20, 1863	Jan. 16, 1866
Marcus L. Ward (UN)	Jan. 16, 1866	Jan. 19, 1869
Theodore F. Randolph (D)	Jan. 19, 1869	Jan. 16, 1872
Joel Parker (D)	Jan. 16, 1872	Jan. 19, 1875
Joseph D. Bedle (D)	Jan. 19, 1875	Jan. 15, 1878
George B. McClellan (D)	Jan. 15, 1878	Jan. 18, 1881
George C. Ludlow (D)	Jan. 18, 1881	Jan. 15, 1884
Leon Abbett (D)	Jan. 15, 1884	Jan. 18, 1887
Robert S. Green (D)	Jan. 18, 1887	Jan. 21, 1890
Leon Abbett (D)	Jan. 21, 1890	Jan. 17, 1893
George T. Werts (D)	Jan. 17, 1893	Jan. 21, 1896
John W. Griggs (R)[8]	Jan. 21, 1896	Jan. 31, 1898
Foster M. Voorhees (R)[9]	Feb. 1, 1898	Oct. 18, 1898
David O. Watkins (R)[10]	Oct. 18, 1898	Jan. 17, 1899
Foster M. Voorhees (R)	Jan. 17, 1899	Jan. 21, 1902
Franklin Murphy (R)	Jan. 21, 1902	Jan. 17, 1905
Edward C. Stokes (R)	Jan. 17, 1905	Jan. 21, 1908
John F. Fort (R)	Jan. 21, 1908	Jan. 17, 1911
Woodrow Wilson (D)[11]	Jan. 17, 1911	March 1, 1913
James F. Fielder (D)[12]	March 1, 1913	Oct. 28, 1913
Leon R. Taylor (D)[13]	Oct. 28, 1913	Jan. 20, 1914
James F. Fielder (D)	Jan. 20, 1914	Jan. 15, 1917
Walter E. Edge (R)[14]	Jan. 15, 1917	May 16, 1919
William N. Runyon (R)[15]	May 16, 1919	Jan. 13, 1920
Clarence E. Case (R)[16]	Jan. 13, 1920	Jan. 20, 1920
Edward I. Edwards (D)	Jan. 20, 1920	Jan. 15, 1923
George S. Silzer (D)	Jan. 15, 1923	Jan. 19, 1926
Arthur Harry Moore (D)	Jan. 19, 1926	Jan. 15, 1929
Morgan F. Larson (R)	Jan. 15, 1929	Jan. 19, 1932
Arthur Harry Moore (D)[17]	Jan. 19, 1932	Jan. 3, 1935
Clifford R. Powell (R)[18]	Jan. 3, 1935	Jan. 8, 1935
Horace G. Prall (R)[19]	Jan. 8, 1935	Jan. 15, 1935
Harold G. Hoffman (R)	Jan. 15, 1935	Jan. 18, 1938
Arthur Harry Moore (D)	Jan. 18, 1938	Jan. 21, 1941
Charles Edison (D)	Jan. 21, 1941	Jan. 18, 1944
Walter E. Edge (R)	Jan. 18, 1944	Jan. 21, 1947
Alfred E. Driscoll (R)	Jan. 21, 1947	Jan. 19, 1954
Robert B. Meyner (D)	Jan. 19, 1954	Jan. 16, 1962
Richard J. Hughes (D)	Jan. 16, 1962	Jan. 20, 1970
William T. Cahill (R)	Jan. 20, 1970	Jan. 15, 1974
Brendan T. Byrne (D)	Jan. 15, 1974	Jan. 19, 1982
Thomas H. Kean (R)	Jan. 19, 1982	Jan. 16, 1990
James J. Florio (D)	Jan. 16, 1990	Jan. 18, 1994
Christine Todd Whitman (R)	Jan. 18, 1994	

New Jersey
1. *Died in office.*
2. *As vice president of the Legislative Council, he succeeded to office.*
3. *Resigned March 4, 1793.*
4. *Acting governor.*
5. *Resigned June 19, 1815.*
6. *As vice president of the Legislative Council, he succeeded to office.*
7. *Resigned Feb. 1, 1817.*
8. *Resigned Jan. 31, 1898.*
9. *Acting governor.*
10. *Acting governor.*
11. *Resigned March 1, 1913, having been elected president of the United States.*
12. *As president of the state Senate, he succeeded to office. Resigned Oct. 28, 1913.*
13. *Acting governor.*
14. *Resigned May 16, 1919*

15. As president of the state Senate, he succeeded to office. Service ended Jan. 13, 1920.
16. Acting governor.
17. Resigned Jan. 3, 1935.
18. As president of the state Senate, he succeeded to office. Service ended Jan. 8, 1935.
19. Acting governor.

NEW MEXICO

(Became a state Jan. 6, 1912)

Governors	Dates of Service	
William C. McDonald (D)	Jan. 6, 1912	Jan. 1, 1917
Ezequiel C. de Baca (D)[1]	Jan. 1, 1917	Feb. 18, 1917
Washington E. Lindsey (R)[2]	Feb. 19, 1917	Jan. 1, 1919
Octaviano A. Larrazolo (R)	Jan. 1, 1919	Jan. 1, 1921
Merritt C. Mechem (R)	Jan. 1, 1921	Jan. 1, 1923
James F. Hinkle (D)	Jan. 1, 1923	Jan. 1, 1925
Arthur T. Hannett (D)	Jan. 1, 1925	Jan. 1, 1927
Richard C. Dillon (R)	Jan. 1, 1927	Jan. 1, 1931
Arthur Seligman (D)[3]	Jan. 1, 1931	Sept. 25, 1933
Andrew W. Hockenhull (D)[4]	Sept. 25, 1933	Jan. 1, 1935
Clyde Tingley (D)	Jan. 1, 1935	Jan. 1, 1939
John E. Miles (D)	Jan. 1, 1939	Jan. 1, 1943
John J. Dempsey (D)	Jan. 1, 1943	Jan. 1, 1947
Thomas J. Mabry (D)	Jan. 1, 1947	Jan. 1, 1951
Edwin L. Mechem (R)	Jan. 1, 1951	Jan. 1, 1955
John F. Simms (D)	Jan. 1, 1955	Jan. 1, 1957
Edwin L. Mechem (R)	Jan. 1, 1957	Jan. 1, 1959
John Burroughs (D)	Jan. 1, 1959	Jan. 1, 1961
Edwin L. Mechem (R)[5]	Jan. 1, 1961	Nov. 30, 1962
Tom Bolack (R)[6]	Nov. 30, 1962	Jan. 1, 1963
Jack M. Campbell (D)	Jan. 1, 1963	Jan. 1, 1967
David F. Cargo (R)	Jan. 1, 1967	Jan. 1, 1971
Bruce King (D)	Jan. 1, 1971	Jan. 1, 1975
Jerry Apodaca (D)	Jan. 1, 1975	Jan. 1, 1979
Bruce King (D)	Jan. 1, 1979	Jan. 1, 1983
Toney Anaya (D)	Jan. 1, 1983	Jan. 1, 1987
Garrey E. Carruthers (R)	Jan. 1, 1987	Jan. 1, 1991
Bruce King (D)	Jan. 1, 1991	Jan. 1, 1995
Gary E. Johnson (R)	Jan. 1, 1995	

New Mexico
1. Died Feb. 18, 1917.
2. As lietuenant governor, he succeeded to office.
3. Died Sept. 25, 1933.
4. As lieutenant governor, he succeeded to office.
5. Resigned Nov. 30, 1962.
6. As lieutenant governor, he succeeded to office.

NEW YORK

(Ratified the Constitution July 26, 1788)

Governors	Dates of Service	
George Clinton (D-R)	July 9, 1777	July 1, 1795
John Jay (FED)	July 1, 1795	July 1, 1801
George Clinton (D-R)	July 1, 1801	July 1, 1804
Morgan Lewis (D-R)	July 1, 1804	July 1, 1807
Daniel D. Tompkins (D-R)[1]	July 1, 1807	Feb. 24, 1817
John Tayler (D-R)[2]	Feb. 24, 1817	July 1, 1817
De Witt Clinton (D-R)	July 1, 1817	Jan. 1, 1823
Joseph C. Yates (D-R)	Jan. 1, 1823	Jan. 1, 1825
De Witt Clinton (CLINT R)[3]	Jan. 1, 1825	Feb. 11, 1828
Nathaniel Pitcher (D-R)[4]	Feb. 11, 1828	Jan. 1, 1829
Martin Van Buren (JAC D)[5]	Jan. 1, 1829	March 12, 1829
Enos T. Throop (JAC D)[6]	March 12, 1829	Jan. 1, 1833
William L. Marcy (D)	Jan. 1, 1833	Jan. 1, 1839
William H. Seward (W)	Jan. 1, 1839	Jan. 1, 1843
William C. Bouck (D)	Jan. 1, 1843	Jan. 1, 1845
Silas Wright (D)	Jan. 1, 1845	Jan. 1, 1847
John Young (W)	Jan. 1, 1847	Jan. 1, 1849
Hamilton Fish (W)	Jan. 1, 1849	Jan. 1, 1851
Washington Hunt (W-A-RENT)	Jan. 1, 1851	Jan. 1, 1853
Horatio Seymour (D)	Jan. 1, 1853	Jan. 1, 1855
Myron H. Clark (FUS R)	Jan. 1, 1855	Jan. 1, 1857
John A. King (R)	Jan. 1, 1857	Jan. 1, 1859
Edwin D. Morgan (R)	Jan. 1, 1859	Jan. 1, 1863
Horatio Seymour (D)	Jan. 1, 1863	Jan. 1, 1865
Reuben E. Fenton (UN)	Jan. 1, 1865	Jan. 1, 1869
John T. Hoffman (D)	Jan. 1, 1869	Jan. 1, 1873
John A. Dix (R)	Jan. 1, 1873	Jan. 1, 1875
Samuel J. Tilden (D)	Jan. 1, 1875	Jan. 1, 1877
Lucius Robinson (D)[7]	Jan. 1, 1877	Jan. 1, 1880
Alonzo B. Cornell (R)	Jan. 1, 1880	Jan. 1, 1883
Grover Cleveland (D)[8]	Jan. 1, 1883	Jan. 6, 1885
David B. Hill (D)[9]	Jan. 6, 1885	Jan. 1, 1892
Roswell P. Flower (D)	Jan. 1, 1892	Jan. 1, 1895
Levi P. Morton (R)[10]	Jan. 1, 1895	Jan. 1, 1897
Frank S. Black (R)	Jan. 1, 1897	Jan. 1, 1899
Theodore Roosevelt (R)	Jan. 1, 1899	Jan. 1, 1901
Benjamin B. Odell Jr. (R)	Jan. 1, 1901	Jan. 1, 1905
Frank W. Higgins (R)	Jan. 1, 1905	Jan. 1, 1907
Charles Evans Hughes (R)[11]	Jan. 1, 1907	Oct. 6, 1910
Horace White (R)[12]	Oct. 6, 1910	Jan. 1, 1911
John A. Dix (D)	Jan. 1, 1911	Jan. 1, 1913
William Sulzer (D)[13]	Jan. 1, 1913	Oct. 17, 1913
Martin H. Glynn (D)[14]	Oct. 17, 1913	Jan. 1, 1915
Charles S. Whitman (R)	Jan. 1, 1915	Jan. 1, 1919
Alfred E. Smith (D)	Jan. 1, 1919	Jan. 1, 1921
Nathan L. Miller (R)	Jan. 1, 1921	Jan. 1, 1923
Alfred E. Smith (D)	Jan. 1, 1923	Jan. 1, 1929
Franklin D. Roosevelt (D)	Jan. 1, 1929	Jan. 1, 1933
Herbert H. Lehman (D)[15]	Jan. 1, 1933	Dec. 3, 1942
Charles Poletti (D)[16]	Dec. 3, 1942	Jan. 1, 1943
Thomas E. Dewey (R)	Jan. 1, 1943	Jan. 1, 1955
W. Averell Harriman (D)	Jan. 1, 1955	Jan. 1, 1959
Nelson A. Rockefeller (R)[17]	Jan. 1, 1959	Dec. 18, 1973
Malcolm Wilson (R)[18]	Dec. 18, 1973	Jan. 1, 1975
Hugh Carey (D)	Jan. 1, 1975	Jan. 1, 1983
Mario M. Cuomo (D)	Jan. 1, 1983	Jan. 1, 1995
George E. Pataki (R)	Jan. 1, 1995	

New York
1. Resigned Feb. 24, 1817, having been elected vice president of the United States.
2. As lieutenant governor, he succeeded to office.
3. Died Feb. 11, 1828.
4. As lieutenant governor, he succeeded to office.
5. Resigned March 12, 1829.
6. As lieutenant governor, he succeeded to office. Subsequently elected.
7. Term of office changed from two years to three years.
8. Resigned Jan. 6, 1885, having been elected president of the United States.
9. As lieutenant governor, he succeeded to office. Subsequently elected.
10. Term of office changed from three years to two years.
11. Resigned Oct. 6, 1910.
12. As lieutenant governor, he succeeded to office.
13. Impeached; removed from office Oct. 17, 1913.
14. As lieutenant governor, he succeeded to office.
15. First governor elected to a four-year term (in 1938). Resigned Dec. 3, 1942.
16. As lieutenant governor, he succeeded to office.
17. Resigned Dec. 18, 1973.
18. As lieutenant governor, he succeeded to office.

NORTH CAROLINA

(Ratified the Constitution Nov. 21, 1789)

Governors	Dates of Service	
Samuel Johnston	Dec. 20, 1787	Dec. 17, 1789
Alexander Martin (FED)	Dec. 17, 1789	Dec. 14, 1792
Richard D. Spaight (D-R)	Dec. 14, 1792	Nov. 19, 1795
Samuel Ashe (D-R)	Nov. 19, 1795	Dec. 7, 1798
William R. Davie (FED)	Dec. 7, 1798	Nov. 23, 1799
Benjamin Williams (D-R)	Nov. 23, 1799	Dec. 6, 1802
James Turner (D-R)	Dec. 6, 1802	Dec. 10, 1805
Nathaniel Alexander (D-R)	Dec. 10, 1805	Dec. 1, 1807
Benjamin Wiliams (D-R)	Dec. 1, 1807	Dec. 12, 1808
David Stone (D-R)	Dec. 12, 1808	Dec. 5, 1810
Benjamin Smith (D-R)	Dec. 5, 1810	Dec. 9, 1811
William Hawkins (D-R)	Dec. 9, 1811	Nov. 29, 1814
William Miller (D-R)	Dec. 7, 1814	Dec. 3, 1817
John Branch (D-R)	Dec. 6, 1817	Dec. 7, 1820
Jesse Franklin (D-R)	Dec. 7, 1820	Dec. 7, 1821
Gabriel Holmes (D-R)	Dec. 7, 1821	Dec. 7, 1824
Hutchins G. Burton (D-R)	Dec. 7, 1824	Dec. 8, 1827
James Iredell (D-R)	Dec. 8, 1827	Dec. 12, 1828
John Owen (D)	Dec. 12, 1828	Dec. 18, 1830
Montfort Stokes (D)	Dec. 18, 1830	Dec. 6, 1832
David L. Swain (D)	Dec. 6, 1832	Dec. 10, 1835
Richard D. Spaight Jr. (D)	Dec. 10, 1835	Dec. 31, 1836
Edward B. Dudley (W)	Dec. 31, 1836	Jan. 1, 1841
John M. Morehead (W)	Jan. 1, 1841	Jan. 1, 1845
William A. Graham (W)	Jan. 1, 1845	Jan. 1, 1849
Charles Manly (W)	Jan. 1, 1849	Jan. 1, 1851
David S. Reid (D)[1]	Jan. 1, 1851	Dec. 6, 1854
Warren Winslow (D)[2]	Dec. 6, 1854	Jan. 1, 1855
Thomas Bragg (D)	Jan. 1, 1855	Jan. 1, 1859
John W. Ellis (D)[3]	Jan. 1, 1859	July 7, 1861
Henry T. Clark (D)[4]	July 7, 1861	Sept. 8, 1862
Zebulon B. Vance (C)[5]	Sept. 8, 1862	May 29, 1865
William W. Holden[6]	May 29, 1865	Dec. 15, 1865
Jonathan Worth (C)[7]	Dec. 15, 1865	July 1, 1868
William W. Holden (R)[8]	July 1, 1868	Dec. 15, 1870
Tod R. Caldwell (R)[9]	Dec. 15, 1870	July 11, 1874
Curtis H. Brogden (R)[10]	July 11, 1874	Jan. 1, 1877
Zebulon B. Vance (D)[11]	Jan. 1, 1877	Feb. 5, 1879
Thomas J. Jarvis (D)[12]	Feb. 5, 1879	Jan. 21, 1885
Alfred M. Scales (D)	Jan. 21, 1885	Jan. 17, 1889
Daniel G. Fowle (D)[13]	Jan. 17, 1889	April 8, 1891
Thomas M. Holt (D)[14]	April 8, 1891	Jan. 18, 1893
Elias Carr (D)	Jan. 18, 1893	Jan. 12, 1897
Daniel L. Russell (D)	Jan. 12, 1897	Jan. 15, 1901
Charles B. Aycock (D)	Jan. 15, 1901	Jan. 11, 1905
R. B. Glenn (D)	Jan. 11, 1905	Jan. 12, 1909
W. W. Kitchin (D)	Jan. 12, 1909	Jan. 15, 1913
Locke Craig (D)	Jan. 15, 1913	Jan. 11, 1917
Thomas W. Bickett (D)	Jan. 11, 1917	Jan. 12, 1921
Carmeron Morrison (D)	Jan. 12, 1921	Jan. 14, 1925
Angus Wilton McLean (D)	Jan. 14, 1925	Jan. 11, 1929
O. Max Gardner (D)	Jan. 11, 1929	Jan. 5, 1933
John C. B. Ehringhaus (D)	Jan. 5, 1933	Jan. 7, 1937
Clyde R. Hoey (D)	Jan. 7, 1937	Jan. 9, 1941
J. Melville Broughton (D)	Jan. 9, 1941	Jan. 4, 1945
R. Gregg Cherry (D)	Jan. 4, 1945	Jan. 6, 1949
W. Kerr Scott (D)	Jan. 6, 1949	Jan. 8, 1953
William B. Umstead (D)[15]	Jan. 8, 1953	Nov. 7, 1954
Luther H. Hodges (D)[16]	Nov. 7, 1954	Jan. 5, 1961
Terry Sanford (D)	Jan. 5, 1961	Jan. 8, 1965
Dan K. Moore (D)	Jan. 8, 1965	Jan. 3, 1969
Robert W. Scott (D)	Jan. 3, 1969	Jan. 5, 1973
James E. Holshouser Jr. (R)	Jan. 5, 1973	Jan. 8, 1977
James B. Hunt Jr. (D)	Jan. 8, 1977	Jan. 5, 1985
James G. Martin (R)	Jan. 5, 1985	Jan. 9, 1993
James B. Hunt Jr. (D)	Jan. 9, 1993	

North Carolina

1. Resigned Dec. 6, 1854.
2. Acting governor.
3. Died July 7, 1861.
4. Acting governor.
5. Removed from office. Last Confederate governor.
6. Provisional governor appointed by President Johnson.
7. Removed July 1, 1868.
8. Impeached. Removed from office Dec. 15, 1870.
9. As lieutenant governor, he succeeded to office. Subsequently elected. Died July 11, 1874.
10. As lieutenant governor, he succeeded to office.
11. Resigned Feb. 5, 1879.
12. As lieutenant governor, he succeeded to office. Subsequently elected.
13. Died April 8, 1891.
14. As lieutenant governor, he succeeded to office.
15. Died Nov. 7, 1954.
16. As lieutenant governor, he succeeded to office. Subsequently elected.

NORTH DAKOTA

(Became a state Nov. 2, 1889)

Governors	Dates of Service	
John Miller (R)	Nov. 4, 1889	Jan. 6, 1891
Andrew H. Burke (R)	Jan. 7, 1891	Jan. 4, 1893
Eli C. D. Shortridge (FUS)	Jan. 4, 1893	Jan. 7, 1895
Roger Allin (R)	Jan. 7, 1895	Jan. 5, 1897
Frank A. Briggs (R)[1]	Jan. 5, 1897	Aug. 9, 1898
Joseph M. Devine (R)[2]	Aug. 9, 1898	Jan. 3, 1899
Frederick B. Fancher (R)	Jan. 3, 1899	Jan. 10, 1901
Frank White (R)	Jan. 10, 1901	Jan. 4, 1905
Elmore Y. Sarles (R)	Jan. 5, 1905	Jan. 9, 1907
John Burke (D)	Jan. 9, 1907	Jan. 8, 1913
Louis B. Hanna (R)	Jan. 8, 1913	Jan. 3, 1917
Lynn J. Frazier (R)[3]	Jan. 3, 1917	Nov. 23, 1921
Ragnvald A. Nestos (R)[4]	Nov. 23, 1921	Jan. 5, 1925
Arthur G. Sorlie (R)[5]	Jan. 7, 1925	Aug. 28, 1928
Walter J. Maddock (R)[6]	Aug. 28, 1928	Jan. 9, 1929
George F. Shafer (R)	Jan. 9, 1929	Dec. 31, 1932
William Langer (R)[7]	Dec. 31, 1932	July 17, 1934
Ole H. Olson (R)[8]	July 17, 1934	Jan. 7, 1935
Thomas H. Moodie (D)[9]	Jan. 7,1935	Feb. 2, 1935
Walter Welford (R)[10]	Feb. 2, 1935	Jan. 6, 1937
William Langer (I)	Jan. 6, 1937	Jan. 5, 1939
John Moses (D)	Jan. 5, 1939	Jan. 4, 1945
Fred G. Aandahl (R)	Jan. 4, 1945	Jan. 3, 1951
C. Norman Brunsdale (R)	Jan. 3, 1951	Jan. 9, 1957
John E. Davis (R)	Jan. 9, 1957	Jan. 4, 1961
William L. Guy (D)	Jan. 4, 1961	Jan. 2, 1973
Arthur A. Link (D)	Jan. 2, 1973	Jan. 7, 1981
Allen I. Olson (R)[11]	Jan. 7, 1981	Jan. 8, 1985
George Sinner (D)[11]	Jan. 8, 1985	Jan. 5, 1993
Edward T. Schafer (R)	Jan. 5, 1993	

North Dakota

1. Died in 1898.
2. As lieutenant governor, he succeeded to office.
3. Recalled in election of Oct. 28, 1921; removed Nov. 23, 1921.
4. Elected in recall election of 1921, which removed Governor Frazier. Subsequently elected for a full two-year term.
5. Died Aug. 28, 1928.
6. As lieutenant governor, he succeeded to office.
7. Removed by North Dakota Supreme Court July 17, 1934.
8. As lieutenant governor, he succeeded to office.
9. Disqualified by North Dakota Supreme Court Feb. 2, 1935.
10. As lieutenant governor, he succeeded to office.
11. Although Olson relinquished his office on Jan. 5 and Sinner assumed it Jan. 8, the North Dakota Supreme Court held that Sinner's term began Jan. 1.

OHIO

(Became a state March 1, 1803)

Governors	Dates of Service	
Edward Tiffin (D-R)[1]	March 3, 1803	March 4, 1807
Thomas Kirker (D-R)[2]	March 4, 1807	Dec. 12, 1808
Samuel Huntington (D-R)	Dec. 12, 1808	Dec. 8, 1810
Return Jonathan Meigs (D-R)[3]	Dec. 8, 1810	March 24, 1814
Othneil Looker (D-R)[4]	March 24, 1814	Dec. 8, 1814
Thomas Worthington (D-R)	Dec. 8, 1814	Dec. 14, 1818
Ethan Allen Brown (D-R)[5]	Dec. 14, 1818	Jan. 4, 1822
Allen Trimble (D-R)[6]	Jan. 4, 1822	Dec. 28, 1822
Jeremiah Morrow (JAC D)	Dec. 28, 1822	Dec. 19, 1826
Allen Trimble (NR)	Dec. 19, 1826	Dec. 18, 1830
Duncan McArthur (NR)	Dec. 18, 1830	Dec. 7, 1832
Robert Lucas (D)	Dec. 7, 1832	Dec. 12, 1836
Joseph Vance (W)	Dec. 12, 1836	Dec. 13, 1838
Wilson Shannon (D)	Dec. 13, 1838	Dec. 16, 1840
Thomas Corwin (W)	Dec. 16, 1840	Dec. 14, 1842
Wilson Shannon (D)[7]	Dec. 14, 1842	April 15, 1844
Thomas W. Bartley (D)[8]	April 15, 1844	Dec. 3, 1844
Mordecai Bartley (W)	Dec. 3, 1844	Dec. 12, 1846
William Bebb (W)	Dec. 12, 1846	Jan. 22, 1849
Seabury Ford (W)[9]	Jan. 22, 1849	Dec. 12, 1850
Reuben Wood (D)[10]	Dec. 12, 1850	July 13, 1853
William Medill (D)[11]	July 13, 1853	Jan. 14, 1856
Salmon P. Chase (R)	Jan. 14, 1856	Jan. 9, 1860
William Dennison Jr. (R)	Jan. 9, 1860	Jan. 13, 1862
David Tod (UN)	Jan. 13, 1862	Jan. 11, 1864
John Brough (UN)[12]	Jan. 11, 1864	Aug. 29, 1865
Charles Anderson (UN)[13]	Aug. 29, 1865	Jan. 8, 1866
Jacob D. Cox (UN)	Jan. 8, 1866	Jan. 13, 1868
Rutherford B. Hayes (R)	Jan. 13, 1868	Jan. 8, 1872
Edward F. Noyes (R)	Jan. 8, 1872	Jan. 12, 1874
William Allen (D)	Jan. 12, 1874	Jan. 10, 1876
Rutherford B. Hayes (R)[14]	Jan. 10, 1876	March 2, 1877
Thomas L. Young (R)[15]	March 2, 1877	Jan. 14, 1878
Richard M. Bishop (D)	Jan. 14, 1878	Jan. 12, 1880
Charles Foster (R)	Jan. 12, 1880	Jan. 14, 1884
George Hoadly (D)	Jan. 14, 1884	Jan. 11, 1886
Joseph B. Foraker (R)	Jan. 11, 1886	Jan. 13, 1890
James E. Campbell (D)	Jan. 13, 1890	Jan. 11, 1892
William McKinley Jr. (R)	Jan. 11, 1892	Jan. 13, 1896
Asa S. Bushnell (R)	Jan. 13, 1896	Jan. 8, 1900
George K. Nash (R)	Jan. 8, 1900	Jan. 11, 1904
Myron T. Herrick (R)	Jan. 11, 1904	Jan. 8, 1906
John M. Pattison (D)[16]	Jan. 8, 1906	June 18, 1906
Andrew L. Harris (R)[17]	June 18, 1906	Jan. 11, 1909
Judson Harmon (D)	Jan. 11, 1909	Jan. 13, 1913
James M. Cox (D)	Jan. 13, 1913	Jan. 11, 1915
Frank B. Willis (R)	Jan. 11, 1915	Jan. 8, 1917
James M. Cox (D)	Jan. 8, 1917	Jan. 10, 1921
Harry L. Davis (R)	Jan. 10, 1921	Jan. 8, 1923
Alvin Victor Donahey (D)	Jan. 8, 1923	Jan. 14, 1929
Myers Y. Cooper (R)	Jan. 14, 1929	Jan. 12, 1931
George White (D)	Jan. 12, 1931	Jan. 14, 1935
Martin L. Davey (D)	Jan. 14, 1935	Jan. 9, 1939
John W. Bricker (R)	Jan. 9, 1939	Jan. 8, 1945
Frank J. Lausche (D)	Jan. 8, 1945	Jan. 13, 1947
Thomas J. Herbert (R)	Jan. 13, 1947	Jan. 10, 1949
Frank J. Lausche (D)[18]	Jan. 10, 1949	Jan. 3, 1957
John W. Brown (R)[19]	Jan. 3, 1957	Jan. 14, 1957
C. William O'Neill (R)	Jan. 14, 1957	Jan. 12, 1959
Michael V. DiSalle (D)	Jan. 12, 1959	Jan. 14, 1963
James A. Rhodes (R)	Jan. 14, 1963	Jan. 11, 1971
John J. Gilligan (D)	Jan. 11, 1971	Jan. 13, 1975
James A. Rhodes (R)	Jan. 13, 1975	Jan. 10, 1983
Richard F. Celeste (D)	Jan. 10, 1983	Jan. 14, 1991
George V. Voinovich (R)	Jan. 14, 1991	

Ohio

1. *Resigned March 4, 1807.*
2. *As Speaker of the state Senate, he succeeded to office.*
3. *Resigned March 24, 1814.*
4. *As Speaker of the state Senate, he succeeded to office.*
5. *Resigned Jan. 4, 1822.*
6. *As Speaker of the state Senate, he succeeded to office.*
7. *Resigned April 15, 1844.*
8. *As Speaker of the state Senate, he succeeded to office.*
9. *The election of 1848 was disputed, and Ford's election was delayed until Jan. 22, 1849.*
10. *Resigned July 13, 1853.*
11. *As lieutenant governor, he succeeded to office. Subsequently elected.*
12. *Died Aug. 29, 1865.*
13. *As lieutenant governor, he succeeded to office.*
14. *Resigned March 2, 1877, having been elected president of the United States.*
15. *As lieutenant governor, he succeeded to office.*
16. *Died June 18, 1906.*
17. *As lieutenant governor, he succeeded to office.*
18. *Resigned Jan. 3, 1957.*
19. *As lieutenant governor, he succeeded to office.*

OKLAHOMA

(Became a state Nov. 16, 1907)

Governors	Dates of Service	
Charles N. Haskell (D)	Nov. 16, 1907	Jan. 9, 1911
Lee Cruce (D)	Jan. 9, 1911	Jan. 11, 1915
Robert L. Williams (D)	Jan. 11, 1915	Jan. 13, 1919
James B. A. Robertson (D)	Jan. 13, 1919	Jan. 8, 1923
John C. Walton (D)[1]	Jan. 8, 1923	Nov. 19, 1923
Martin E. Trapp (D)[2]	Nov. 19, 1923	Jan. 10, 1927
Henry S. Johnston (D)[3]	Jan. 10, 1927	March 20, 1929
William J. Holloway (D)[4]	March 20, 1929	Jan. 12, 1931
William H. Murray (D)	Jan. 12, 1931	Jan. 14, 1935
Ernest W. Marland (D)	Jan. 14, 1935	Jan. 9, 1939
Leon C. Phillips (D)	Jan. 9, 1939	Jan. 11, 1943
Robert S. Kerr (D)	Jan. 11, 1943	Jan. 13, 1947
Roy J. Turner (D)	Jan. 13, 1947	Jan. 8, 1951
Johnston Murray (D)	Jan. 8, 1951	Jan. 10, 1955
Raymond D. Gary (D)	Jan. 10, 1955	Jan. 12, 1959
J. Howard Edmondson (D)[5]	Jan. 12, 1959	Jan. 6, 1963
George P. Nigh (D)[6]	Jan. 6, 1963	Jan. 14, 1963
Henry L. Bellmon (R)	Jan. 14, 1963	Jan. 9, 1967
Dewey F. Bartlett (R)	Jan. 9, 1967	Jan. 11, 1971
David Hall (D)	Jan. 11, 1971	Jan. 13, 1975
David L. Boren (D)	Jan. 13, 1975	Jan. 3, 1979
George Nigh (D)	Jan. 3, 1979	Jan. 12, 1987
Henry L. Bellmon (R)	Jan. 12, 1987	Jan. 14, 1991
David Walters (D)	Jan. 14, 1991	Jan. 9, 1995
Frank Keating (R)	Jan. 9, 1995	

Oklahoma

1. *Impeached; removed from office, Nov. 19, 1923.*
2. *As lieutenant governor, he succeeded to office.*
3. *Impeached; removed from office, March 20, 1929.*
4. *As lieutenant governor, he succeeded to office.*
5. *Resigned Jan. 6, 1963.*
6. *As lieutenant governor, he succeeded to office.*

OREGON

(Became a state Feb. 14, 1859)

Governors	Dates of Service	
John Whiteaker (D)	March 3, 1859	Sept. 10, 1862
Addison C. Gibbs (UN R)	Sept. 10, 1862	Sept. 12, 1866
George L. Woods (R)	Sept. 12, 1866	Sept. 14, 1870

La Fayette Grover (D)[1]	Sept. 14, 1870	Feb. 1, 1877
Stephen F. Chadwick (D)[2]	Feb. 1, 1877	Sept. 11, 1878
William Wallace Thayer (D)	Sept. 11, 1878	Sept. 13, 1882
Zenas F. Moody (R)	Sept. 13, 1882	Jan. 12, 1887
Sylvester Pennoyer (D)	Jan. 12, 1887	Jan. 14, 1895
William P. Lord (R)	Jan. 14, 1895	Jan. 9, 1899
Theodore T. Geer (R)	Jan. 9, 1899	Jan. 14, 1903
George E. Chamberlain (D)[3]	Jan. 15, 1903	March 1, 1909
Frank W. Benson (R)[4]	March 1, 1909	June 16, 1910
Jay Bowerman (R)[5]	June 16, 1910	Jan. 8, 1911
Oswald West (D)	Jan. 11, 1911	Jan. 12, 1915
James Withycombe (R)[6]	Jan. 12, 1915	March 3, 1919
Ben W. Olcott (R)[7]	March 3, 1919	Jan. 8, 1923
Walter M. Pierce (D)	Jan. 8, 1923	Jan. 10, 1927
Isaac L. Patterson (R)[8]	Jan. 10, 1927	Dec. 21, 1929
A. W. Norblad (R)[9]	Dec. 22, 1929	Jan. 12, 1931
Julius L. Meier (I)	Jan. 12, 1931	Jan. 14, 1935
Charles H. Martin (D)	Jan. 14, 1935	Jan. 9, 1939
Charles A. Sprague (R)	Jan. 9, 1939	Jan. 11, 1943
Earl Snell (R)[10]	Jan. 11, 1943	Oct. 28, 1947
John H. Hall (R)[11]	Oct. 30, 1947	Jan. 10, 1949
Douglas McKay (R)[12]	Jan. 10, 1949	Dec. 27, 1952
Paul L. Patterson (R)[13]	Dec. 27, 1952	Jan. 31, 1956
Elmo Smith (R)[14]	Feb. 1, 1956	Jan. 14, 1957
Robert D. Holmes (D)[15]	Jan. 14, 1957	Jan. 12, 1959
Mark O. Hatfield (R)	Jan. 12, 1959	Jan. 9, 1967
Tom McCall (R)	Jan. 9, 1967	Jan. 13, 1975
Robert W. Straub (D)	Jan. 13, 1975	Jan. 8, 1979
Victor Atiyeh (R)	Jan. 8, 1979	Jan. 12, 1987
Neil Goldschmidt (D)	Jan. 12, 1987	Jan. 14, 1991
Barbara Roberts (D)	Jan. 14, 1991	Jan. 9, 1995
John Kitzhaber (D)	Jan. 9, 1995	

Oregon

1. *Resigned Feb. 1, 1877.*
2. *As secretary of state, he succeeded to office.*
3. *Resigned March 1, 1909.*
4. *As secretary of state, he succeeded to office. Resigned June 17, 1910.*
5. *As president of the state Senate, he succeeded to office.*
6. *Died March 3, 1919.*
7. *As secretary of state, he succeeded to office.*
8. *Died Dec. 21, 1929.*
9. *As president of the state Senate, he succeeded to office.*
10. *Died Oct. 28, 1947.*
11. *As speaker of the House, he succeeded to office for the remainder of the first two years of Snell's term.*
12. *Elected for the last two years of Snell's term in a special election. Subsequently re-elected. Resigned Dec. 27, 1952.*
13. *As president of the state senate, he succeeded to office. Subsequently elected. Died Jan. 31, 1956.*
14. *As president of the state Senate, he succeeded to office for the remainder of the first two years of Patterson's term.*
15. *Elected in a special election for the last two years of Patterson's term.*

PENNSYLVANIA

(Ratified the Constitution Dec. 12, 1787)

Governors	Dates of Service	
Peter Mulhenberg	Oct. 31, 1787	Oct. 14, 1788
David Redick	Oct. 14, 1788	Nov. 5, 1788
George Ross	Nov. 5, 1788	Dec. 21, 1790
Thomas Mifflin	Dec. 21, 1790	Dec. 17, 1799
Thomas McKean (D-R)	Dec. 17, 1799	Dec. 20, 1808
Simon Snyder (D-R)	Dec. 20, 1808	Dec. 16, 1817
William Findlay (D-R)	Dec. 16, 1817	Dec. 19, 1820
Joseph Hiester (D-R)	Dec. 19, 1820	Dec. 16, 1823
John A. Shulze (JAC D)	Dec. 16, 1823	Dec. 15, 1829
George Wolfe (JAC D)	Dec. 15, 1829	Dec. 15, 1835
Joseph Ritner (D)	Dec. 15, 1835	Jan. 15, 1839
David R. Porter (D)	Jan. 15, 1839	Jan. 21, 1845
Francis R. Shunk (D)[1]	Jan. 21, 1845	July 9, 1848

William F. Johnston (W)[2]	July 26, 1848	Jan. 20, 1852
William Bigler (D)	Jan. 20, 1852	Jan. 16, 1855
James Pollock (W)	Jan. 16, 1855	Jan. 19, 1858
William F. Packer (D)	Jan. 19, 1858	Jan. 15, 1861
Andrew G. Curtin (R)	Jan. 15, 1861	Jan. 15, 1867
John W. Geary (R)	Jan. 15, 1867	Jan. 21, 1873
John F. Hartranft (R)	Jan. 21, 1873	Jan. 18, 1879
Henry M. Hoyt (R)	Jan. 21, 1879	Jan. 16, 1883
Robert E. Pattison (D)	Jan. 16, 1883	Jan. 18, 1887
James A. Beaver (R)	Jan. 18, 1887	Jan. 20, 1891
Robert E. Pattison (D)	Jan. 20, 1891	Jan. 15, 1895
Daniel H. Hastings (R)	Jan. 15, 1895	Jan. 17, 1899
William A. Stone (R)	Jan. 17, 1899	Jan. 20, 1903
Samuel W. Pennypacker (R)	Jan. 20, 1903	Jan. 15, 1907
Edwin S. Stuart (R)	Jan. 15, 1907	Jan. 17, 1911
John K. Tener (R)	Jan. 17, 1911	Jan. 19, 1915
Martin G. Brumbaugh (R)	Jan. 19, 1915	Jan. 21, 1919
William C. Sproul (R)	Jan. 21, 1919	Jan. 16, 1923
Gifford Pinchot (R)	Jan. 16, 1923	Jan. 18, 1927
John S. Fisher (R)	Jan. 18, 1927	Jan. 20, 1931
Gifford Pinchot (R, PROG)	Jan. 20, 1931	Jan. 15, 1935
George H. Earle (D)	Jan. 15, 1935	Jan. 17, 1939
Arthur H. James (R)	Jan. 17, 1939	Jan. 19, 1943
Edward Martin (R)[3]	Jan. 19, 1943	Jan. 2, 1947
John C. Bell Jr. (R)[4]	Jan. 2, 1947	Jan. 21, 1947
James H. Duff (R)	Jan. 21, 1947	Jan. 16, 1951
John S. Fine (R)	Jan. 16, 1951	Jan. 18, 1955
George M. Leader (D)	Jan. 18, 1955	Jan. 20, 1959
David L. Lawrence (D)	Jan. 20, 1959	Jan. 15, 1963
William W. Scranton (R)	Jan. 15, 1963	Jan. 17, 1967
Raymond P. Shafer (R)	Jan. 17, 1967	Jan. 19, 1971
Milton J. Shapp (D)	Jan. 19, 1971	Jan. 16, 1979
Richard L. Thornburgh (R)	Jan. 16, 1979	Jan. 20, 1987
Robert P. Casey (D)	Jan. 20, 1987	Jan. 17, 1995
Tom Ridge (R)	Jan. 17, 1995	

Pennsylvania

1. *Resigned July 9, 1848.*
2. *Interregnum from July 9 to July 26, 1848. Johnston became acting governor. Subsequently elected.*
3. *Resigned Jan. 2, 1947.*
4. *As lieutenant governor, he succeeded to office.*

RHODE ISLAND

(Ratified the Constitution May 29, 1790)

Governors	Dates of Service	
Arthur Fenner (D-R)[1]	May 5, 1790	Oct. 15, 1805
Henry Smith (D-R)[2]	Oct. 15, 1805	May 7, 1806
Isaac Wilbur (D-R)[3]	May 7, 1806	May 6, 1807
James Fenner	May 6, 1807	May 1, 1811
William Jones (FED)	May 1, 1811	May 7, 1817
Nehemiah R. Knight (D-R)[4]	May 7, 1817	Jan. 9, 1821
Edward Wilcox (D-R)[5]	Jan. 9, 1821	May 2, 1821
William C. Gibbs (D-R)	May 2, 1821	May 5, 1824
James Fenner (D-R)	May 5, 1824	May 4, 1831
Lemuel H. Arnold (D)[6]	May 4, 1831	May 1, 1833
John Brown Francis (D)	May 1, 1833	May 2, 1838
William Sprague (W)	May 2, 1838	May 1, 1839
Samuel Ward King (W)[7]	May 2, 1839	May 2, 1843
James Fenner (L & O W)	May 2, 1843	May 6, 1845
Charles Jackson (LIBER W)	May 6, 1845	May 6, 1846
Byron Diman (L & O W)	May 6, 1846	May 4, 1847
Elisha Harris (W)	May 4, 1847	May 1, 1849
Henry B. Anthony (W)	May 1, 1849	May 6, 1851
Philip Allen (D)[8]	May 6, 1851	July 20, 1853
Francis M. Dimond (D)[9]	July 20, 1853	May 2, 1854
William W. Hoppin (W, R)	May 2, 1854	May 26, 1857
Elisha Dyer (R)	May 26, 1857	May 31, 1859
Thomas G. Turner	May 31, 1859	May 29, 1860

William Sprague (FUS, UN)[10]	May 29, 1860	March 3, 1863
William C. Cozzens[11]	March 3, 1863	May 26, 1863
James Y. Smith (UN R)	May 26, 1863	May 29, 1866
Ambrose E. Burnside (R)	May 29, 1866	May 25, 1869
Seth Padelford (R)	May 25, 1869	May 27, 1873
Henry Howard (R)	May 27, 1873	May 25, 1875
Henry Lippitt (R)	May 25, 1875	May 29, 1877
Charles Van Zandt (R & TEMP)	May 29, 1877	May 25, 1880
Alfred H. Littlefield (R)	May 25, 1880	May 29, 1883
Augustus O. Bourn (R)	May 29, 1883	May 26, 1885
George P. Wetmore (R)	May 26, 1885	May 31, 1887
John W. Davis (D)	May 31, 1887	May 29, 1888
Royal C. Taft (R)	May 29, 1888	May 28, 1889
Herbert W. Ladd (R)	May 28, 1889	May 27, 1890
John W. Davis (D)	May 27, 1890	May 26, 1891
Herbert W. Ladd (R)	May 26, 1891	May 31, 1892
D. Russell Brown (R)[12]	May 31, 1892	May 29, 1895
Charles W. Lippitt (R)	May 29, 1895	May 25, 1897
Elisha Dyer (R)	May 25, 1897	May 29, 1900
William Gregory (R)[13]	May 29, 1900	Dec. 16, 1901
Charles D. Kimball (R)[14]	Dec. 16, 1901	Jan. 6, 1903
Lucius F. C. Garvin (D)	Jan. 6, 1903	Jan. 3, 1905
George H. Utter (R)	Jan. 3, 1905	Jan. 1, 1907
James H. Higgins (D)	Jan. 1, 1907	Jan. 5, 1909
Aram J. Pothier (R)	Jan. 5, 1909	Jan. 5, 1915
R. Livingston Beeckman (R)	Jan. 5, 1915	Jan. 4, 1921
Emery J. San Souci (R)	Jan. 4, 1921	Jan. 2, 1923
William S. Flynn (D)	Jan. 2, 1923	Jan. 6, 1925
Aram J. Pothier (R)[15]	Jan. 6, 1925	Feb. 4, 1928
Norman S. Case (R)[16]	Feb. 4, 1928	Jan. 3, 1933
Theodore F. Green (D)	Jan. 3, 1933	Jan. 5, 1937
Robert E. Quinn (D)	Jan. 5, 1937	Jan. 3, 1939
William H. Vanderbilt (R)	Jan. 3, 1939	Jan. 7, 1941
J. Howard McGrath (D)[17]	Jan. 7, 1941	Oct. 6, 1945
John O. Pastore (D)[18]	Oct. 6, 1945	Dec. 19, 1950
John S. McKiernan (D)[19]	Dec. 19, 1950	Jan. 2, 1951
Dennis J. Roberts (D)	Jan. 2, 1951	Jan. 6, 1959
Christopher Del Sesto (R)	Jan. 6, 1959	Jan. 3, 1961
John A. Notte Jr. (D)	Jan. 3, 1961	Jan. 1, 1963
John H. Chafee (R)	Jan. 1, 1963	Jan. 7, 1969
Frank Licht (D)	Jan. 7, 1969	Jan. 2, 1973
Philip W. Noel (D)	Jan. 2, 1973	Jan. 4, 1977
Joseph J. Garrahy (D)	Jan. 4, 1977	Jan. 1, 1985
Edward D. DiPrete (R)	Jan. 1, 1985	Jan. 1, 1991
Bruce Sundlun (D)	Jan. 1, 1991	Jan. 3, 1995
Lincoln C. Almond (R)	Jan. 3, 1995	

Rhode Island

1. *Died Oct. 15, 1805.*

2. *Smith, as first senator, served as governor.*

3. *No governor was elected in 1806. Wilbur, the lieutenant governor, served as acting governor.*

4. *Resigned Jan. 9, 1821.*

5. *As lieutenant governor, he succeeded to office.*

6. *In the 1832 election, no candidate for governor received the majority of the total vote cast which was required for election. Elections were held four more times—on May 16, July 18, August 28 and Nov. 21—each one resulting without choice. Arnold was continued in office until 1833. (The returns for this election, p. 524, show only the first election.)*

7. *No governor was elected in 1839, no candidate having received a majority of the vote. In addition, no lieutenant governor was elected. King, as first senator, became acting governor for the term. Subsequently re-elected three times.*

8. *Resigned July 20, 1853.*

9. *As lieutenant governor, he succeeded to office.*

10. *Resigned March 3, 1863.*

11. *As president of the state Senate, he succeeded to office.*

12. *No candidate received a majority of the vote in the election of 1893, and under the law the Legislature was required to elect the governor. However, because of a dispute between the two houses no choice was made. Governor Brown continued in office for the term. He was re-elected in 1894. The controversy over the election resulted in repeal of the majority-vote requirement in 1893.*

13. *Died Dec. 16, 1901.*

14. *As lieutenant governor, he succeeded to office.*

15. *Died Feb. 4, 1928.*

16. *As lieutenant governor, he succeeded to office. Subsequently elected.*

17. *Resigned Oct. 6, 1945.*

18. *As lieutenant governor, he succeeded to office. Subsequently elected. Resigned Dec. 19, 1950.*

19. *As lieutenant governor, he succeeded to office.*

SOUTH CAROLINA

(Ratified the Constitution May 23, 1788)

Governors	Dates of Service	
Charles Pinckney	Jan. 26, 1789	Dec. 5, 1792
William Moultrie (FED)	Dec. 5, 1792	Dec. 1794
Arnoldus Vander Horst (FED)	Dec. 1794	Dec. 1796
Charles Pinckney (D-R)	Dec. 1796	Dec. 6, 1798
Edward Rutledge (FED)[1]	Dec. 18, 1798	Jan. 23, 1800
John Drayton (D-R)[2]	Jan. 23, 1800	Dec. 1802
James B. Richardson (D-R)	Dec. 1802	Dec. 1804
Paul Hamilton (D-R)	Dec. 1804	Dec. 1806
Charles Pinckney (D-R)	Dec. 1806	Dec. 10, 1808
John Drayton (D-R)	Dec. 10, 1808	Dec. 1810
Henry Middleton (D-R)	Dec. 10, 1810	Dec. 1812
Joseph Alston (D-R)	Dec. 1812	Dec. 1814
David R. Williams (D-R)	Dec. 1814	Dec. 1816
Andrew Pickens (D-R)	Dec. 1816	Dec. 1818
John Geddes (D-R)	Dec. 1818	Dec. 1820
Thomas Bennett (D-R)	Dec. 1820	Dec. 1822
John Lyde Wilson (D-R)	Dec. 1822	Dec. 1824
Richard I. Manning (D-R)	Dec. 1824	Dec. 1826
John Taylor (D-R)	Dec. 1826	Dec. 1828
Stephen D. Miller (D)	Dec. 1828	Dec. 1830
James Hamilton Jr. (D)	Dec. 1830	Dec. 13, 1832
Robert Y. Hayne (D)	Dec. 13, 1832	Dec. 11, 1834
George McDuffie (D)	Dec. 11, 1834	Dec. 1836
Pierce M. Butler (D)	Dec. 1836	Dec. 10, 1838
Patrick Noble (D)[3]	Dec. 10, 1838	April 7, 1840
B. K. Henagan (D)[4]	April 7, 1840	Dec. 10, 1840
John P. Richardson (D)	Dec. 10, 1840	Dec. 1842
James H. Hammond (D)	Dec. 1842	Dec. 1844
William Aiken (D)	Dec. 1844	Dec. 1846
David Johnson (D)	Dec. 1846	Dec. 1848
Whitmarsh B. Seabrook (D)	Dec. 1848	Dec. 1850
John Hugh Means (D)	Dec. 16, 1850	Dec. 1852
John Laurence Manning (D)	Dec. 1852	Dec. 1854
James H. Adams (D)	Dec. 1854	Dec. 1856
Robert F. W. Alston (D)	Dec. 1856	Dec. 1858
William H. Gist (D)	Dec. 1858	Dec. 1860
Francis W. Pickens (D)	Dec. 1860	Dec. 1862
Milledge L. Bonham (D)	Dec. 1862	Dec. 1864
Andrew G. Magrath (D)[5]	Dec. 20, 1864	May 25, 1865
Benjamin F. Perry[6]	June 30, 1865	Nov. 29, 1865
James L. Orr (C)[7]	Nov. 29, 1865	July 6, 1868
Robert K. Scott (R)	July 9, 1868	Dec. 7, 1872
Franklin J. Moses Jr. (R)	Dec. 7, 1872	Dec. 1, 1874
Daniel H. Chamberlain (R)[8]	Dec. 1, 1874	April 10, 1877
Wade Hampton (D)[9]	Dec. 14, 1876	Feb. 26, 1879
William D. Simpson (D)[10]	Feb. 26, 1879	Sept. 1, 1880
Thomas B. Jeter (D)[11]	Sept. 1, 1880	Nov. 30, 1880
Johnson Hagood (D)	Nov. 30, 1880	Dec. 1882
Hugh Smith Thompson (D)[12]	Dec. 1882	July 10, 1886
John C. Sheppard (D)[13]	July 10, 1886	Nov. 30, 1886
John P. Richardson (D)	Nov. 30, 1886	Dec. 4, 1890
Benjamin Ryan Tillman (D)	Dec. 4, 1890	Dec. 1894
John Gary Evans (D)	Dec. 4, 1894	Jan. 18, 1897
William H. Ellerbe (D)[14]	Jan. 18, 1897	June 2, 1899
Miles B. McSweeney (D)[15]	June 2, 1899	Jan. 20, 1903
Duncan C. Heyward (D)	Jan. 20, 1903	Jan. 15, 1907

Martin F. Ansel (D)	Jan. 15, 1907	Jan. 17, 1911
Coleman L. Blease (D)[16]	Jan. 17, 1911	Jan. 14, 1915
Charles A. Smith (D)[17]	Jan. 14, 1915	Jan. 19, 1915
Richard I. Manning (D)	Jan. 19, 1915	Jan. 21, 1919
Robert A. Cooper (D)[18]	Jan. 21, 1919	May 20, 1922
Wilson G. Harvey (D)[19]	May 20, 1922	Jan. 16, 1923
Thomas G. McLeod (D)	Jan. 16, 1923	Jan. 18, 1927
John G. Richards (D)	Jan. 18, 1927	Jan. 20, 1931
Ibra C. Blackwood (D)	Jan. 20, 1931	Jan. 15, 1935
Olin D. Johnston (D)	Jan. 15, 1935	Jan. 17, 1939
Burnet R. Maybank (D)[20]	Jan. 17, 1939	Nov. 4, 1941
Joseph E. Harley (D)[21]	Nov. 4, 1941	Feb. 27, 1942
Richard M. Jeffries (D)[22]	March 2, 1942	Jan. 19, 1943
Olin D. Johnston (D)[23]	Jan. 19, 1943	Jan. 2, 1945
Ransome J. Williams (D)[24]	Jan. 2, 1945	Jan. 21, 1947
J. Strom Thurmond (D)	Jan. 21, 1947	Jan. 16, 1951
James F. Byrnes (D)	Jan. 16, 1951	Jan. 18, 1955
George Bell Timmerman Jr. (D)	Jan. 18, 1955	Jan. 20, 1959
Ernest F. Hollings (D)	Jan. 20, 1959	Jan. 15, 1963
Donald S. Russell (D)[25]	Jan. 15, 1963	April 22, 1965
Robert E. McNair (D)[26]	April 22, 1965	Jan. 19, 1971
John C. West (D)	Jan. 19, 1971	Jan. 21, 1975
James Edwards (R)	Jan. 21, 1975	Jan. 10, 1979
Richard Riley (D)	Jan. 10, 1979	Jan. 14, 1987
Carroll Campbell (R)	Jan. 14, 1987	Jan. 11, 1995
David Beasley (R)	Jan. 11, 1995	

South Carolina
1. *Died Jan. 23, 1800.*
2. *As lieutenant governor, he succeeded to office. Subsequently elected.*
3. *Died April 7, 1840.*
4. *As lieutenant governor, he succeeded to office.*
5. *Last Confederate governor. Removed by federal authorities.*
6. *Provisional governor appointed by President Johnson.*
7. *Deposed by act of Congress.*
8. *There was a dispute between two factions in the House of Representatives over the elections and seating of eight of its members following the 1876 election. The pro-Chamberlain (R) faction declared Chamberlain to have been re-elected and he was re-inaugurated on December 7. The pro-Hampton (D) faction also organized as the House of Representatives and on December 14 declared Hampton to have been elected. He was inaugurated on the same day. For a time there were two rival state governments. In several cases arising later, raising the question of Hampton's authority to act as governor, the Supreme Court of the state declared him to be the lawfully elected chief executive of the state. Chamberlain dropped his claim to the office on April 10, 1877, following the withdrawal of federal troops from the state in March 1877 by President Hayes.*
9. *Resigned Feb. 26, 1879.*
10. *As lieutenant governor, he succeeded to office. Resigned in September 1880.*
11. *As president of the state Senate, he succeeded to office.*
12. *Resigned July 10, 1886.*
13. *As lieutenant governor, he succeeded to office.*
14. *Died June 2, 1899.*
15. *As lieutenant governor, he succeeded to office. Subsequently elected.*
16. *Resigned Jan. 14, 1915.*
17. *As lieutenant governor, he succeeded to office.*
18. *Resigned May 20, 1922.*
19. *As lieutenant governor, he succeeded to office.*
20. *Resigned Nov. 4, 1941.*
21. *As lieutenant governor, he succeeded to office. Died Feb. 27, 1942.*
22. *As president of the state Senate, he succeeded to office.*
23. *Resigned Jan. 2, 1945.*
24. *As lieutenant governor, he succeeded to office.*
25. *Resigned April 22, 1965.*
26. *As lieutenant governor, he succeeded to office. Subsequently elected.*

SOUTH DAKOTA

(Became a state Nov. 2, 1889)

Governors	**Dates of Service**	
Arthur C. Melette (R)	Nov. 2, 1889	Jan. 1893
Charles H. Sheldon (R)	Jan. 1893	Jan. 1, 1897
Andrew E. Lee (PP, FUS)	Jan. 1, 1897	Jan. 8, 1901

Charles N. Herreid (R)	Jan. 8, 1901	Jan. 3, 1905
Samuel H. Elrod (R)	Jan. 3, 1905	Jan. 8, 1907
Coe I. Crawford (R)	Jan. 8, 1907	Jan. 5, 1909
Robert S. Vessey (R)	Jan. 5, 1909	Jan. 7, 1913
Frank M. Byrne (R)	Jan. 7, 1913	Jan. 2, 1917
Peter Norbeck (R)	Jan. 2, 1917	Jan. 4, 1921
William H. McMaster (R)	Jan. 4, 1921	Jan. 6, 1925
Carl Gunderson (R)	Jan. 6, 1925	Jan. 4, 1927
William J. Bulow (D)	Jan. 4, 1927	Jan. 6, 1931
Warren E. Green (R)	Jan. 6, 1931	Jan. 3, 1933
Tom Berry (D)	Jan. 3, 1933	Jan. 5, 1937
Leslie Jensen (R)	Jan. 5, 1937	Jan. 3, 1939
Harlan J. Bushfield (R)	Jan. 3, 1939	Jan. 5, 1943
Merrell Q. Sharpe (R)	Jan. 5, 1943	Jan. 7, 1947
George T. Mickelson (R)	Jan. 7, 1947	Jan. 2, 1951
Sigurd Anderson (R)	Jan. 2, 1951	Jan. 4, 1955
Joe Foss (R)	Jan. 4, 1955	Jan. 6, 1959
Ralph E. Herseth (D)	Jan. 6, 1959	Jan. 3, 1961
Archie M. Gubbrud (R)	Jan. 3, 1961	Jan. 5, 1965
Nils A. Boe (R)	Jan. 5, 1965	Jan. 7, 1969
Frank L. Farrar (R)	Jan. 7, 1969	Jan. 5, 1971
Richard F. Kneip (D)[1]	Jan. 5, 1971	July 24, 1978
Harvey L. Wollman (D)[2]	July 24, 1978	Jan. 1, 1979
William J. Janklow (R)	Jan. 1, 1979	Jan. 6, 1987
George S. Mickelson (R)[3]	Jan. 6, 1987	April 19, 1993
Walter D. Miller (R)[4]	April 20, 1993	Jan. 7, 1995
William J. Janklow (R)	Jan. 7, 1995	

South Dakota
1. *Resigned July 24, 1978.*
2. *As lieutenant governor, he succeeded to office.*
3. *Died April 19, 1993.*
4. *As lieutenant governor, he succeeded to office.*

TENNESSEE

(Became a state June 1, 1796)

Governors	**Dates of Service**	
John Sevier (D-R)	March 30, 1796	Sept. 23, 1801
Archibald Roane (D-R)	Sept. 23, 1801	Sept. 23, 1803
John Sevier (D-R)	Sept. 23, 1803	Sept. 20, 1809
Willie Blount (D-R)	Sept. 20, 1809	Sept. 27, 1815
Joseph McMinn (D-R)	Sept. 27, 1815	Oct. 1, 1821
William Carroll (D-R)	Oct. 1, 1821	Oct. 1, 1827
Sam Houston (D-R)[1]	Oct. 1, 1827	April 16, 1829
William Hall (D-R)[2]	April 16, 1829	Oct. 1, 1829
William Carroll (D)	Oct. 1, 1829	Oct. 12, 1835
Newton Cannon (W)	Oct. 12, 1835	Oct. 14, 1839
James K. Polk (D)	Oct. 14, 1839	Oct. 15, 1841
James C. Jones (W)	Oct. 15, 1841	Oct. 14, 1845
Aaron V. Brown (D)	Oct. 14, 1845	Oct. 17, 1847
Neill S. Brown (W)	Oct. 17, 1847	Oct. 16, 1849
William Trousdale (D)	Oct. 16, 1849	Oct. 16, 1851
William B. Campbell	Oct. 16, 1851	Oct. 17, 1853
Andrew Johnson (D)	Oct. 17, 1853	Nov. 3, 1857
Isham G. Harris (D)	Nov. 3, 1857	March 12, 1862
Andrew Johnson[3]	March 12, 1862	March 4, 1865
William G. Brownlow (W, R)[4]	April 5, 1865	Oct. 1867
DeWitt Clinton Senter (CR)[5]	Oct. 11, 1867	Oct. 10, 1871
John C. Brown (D, LR)	Oct. 10, 1871	Jan. 18, 1875
James D. Porter Jr. (D)	Jan. 18, 1875	Feb. 16, 1879
Albert S. Marks (D)	Feb. 16, 1879	Jan. 17, 1881
Alvin Hawkins (R)	Jan. 17, 1881	Jan. 15, 1883
William B. Bate (LOWTAX D, D)	Jan. 15, 1883	Jan. 17, 1887
Robert L. Taylor (D)	Jan. 17, 1887	Jan. 19, 1891
John P. Buchanan (D)	Jan. 19, 1891	Jan. 16, 1893
Peter Turney (D)[6]	Jan. 16, 1893	Jan. 21, 1897
Robert L. Taylor (D)	Jan. 21, 1897	Jan. 16, 1899
Benton McMillin (D)	Jan. 16, 1899	Jan. 19, 1903
James B. Frazier (D)[7]	Jan. 19, 1903	March 21, 1905

John I. Cox (D)[8]	March 21, 1905	Jan. 17, 1907
Malcolm R. Patterson (D)	Jan. 17, 1907	Jan. 26, 1911
Ben W. Hooper (R)	Jan. 26, 1911	Jan. 17, 1915
Thomas C. Rye (D)	Jan. 17, 1915	Jan. 15, 1919
Albert H. Roberts (D)	Jan. 15, 1919	Jan. 15, 1921
Alfred A. Taylor (R)	Jan. 15, 1921	Jan. 16, 1923
Austin Peay (D)[9]	Jan. 16, 1923	Oct. 2, 1927
Henry H. Horton (D)[10]	Oct. 3, 1927	Jan. 17, 1933
Hill McAlister (D)	Jan. 17, 1933	Jan. 15, 1937
Gordon Browning (D)	Jan. 15, 1937	Jan. 16, 1939
Prentice Cooper (D)	Jan. 16, 1939	Jan. 16, 1945
James N. McCord (D)	Jan. 16, 1945	Jan. 17, 1949
Gordon Browning (D)	Jan. 17, 1949	Jan. 15, 1953
Frank G. Clement (D)	Jan. 15, 1953	Jan. 19, 1959
Buford Ellington (D)	Jan. 19, 1959	Jan. 15, 1963
Frank G. Clement (D)	Jan. 15, 1963	Jan. 16, 1967
Buford Ellington (D)	Jan. 16, 1967	Jan. 16, 1971
Winfield Dunn (R)	Jan. 16, 1971	Jan. 18, 1975
Ray Blanton (D)	Jan. 18, 1975	Jan. 17, 1979
Lamar Alexander (R)	Jan. 17, 1979	Jan. 17, 1987
Ned R. McWherter (D)	Jan. 17, 1987	Jan. 21, 1995
Don Sundquist (R)	Jan. 21, 1995	

Tennessee

1. *Resigned April 16, 1829.*
2. *As Speaker of the state Senate, he succeeded to office.*
3. *Appointed military governor by President Lincoln.*
4. *Resigned in October 1867.*
5. *As Speaker of the state Senate, he succeeded to office. Subsequently elected.*
6. *Governor Turney ran for re-election in 1894, but his Republican opponent, H. Clay Evans, appeared to have won a narrow victory. There were allegations of fraud, however, resulting in a recount of the votes by the Legislature. The Legislature's count made Turney the winner, and he took office for a second term.*
7. *Resigned March 21, 1905.*
8. *As Speaker of the state Senate, he succeeded to office.*
9. *Died Oct. 2, 1927.*
10. *As Speaker of the state Senate, he succeeded to office. Subsequently elected.*

James E. Ferguson (D)[11]	Jan. 19, 1915	Aug. 25, 1917
William P. Hobby (D)[12]	Aug. 25, 1917	Jan. 18, 1921
Pat M. Neff (D)	Jan. 18, 1921	Jan. 20, 1925
Miriam A. Ferguson (D)	Jan. 20, 1925	Jan. 18, 1927
Dan Moody (D)	Jan. 18, 1927	Jan. 20, 1931
Ross M. Sterling (D)	Jan. 20, 1931	Jan. 17, 1933
Miriam A. Ferguson (D)	Jan. 17, 1933	Jan. 15, 1935
James V. Allred (D)	Jan. 15, 1935	Jan. 17, 1939
W. Lee O'Daniel (D)[13]	Jan. 17, 1939	Aug. 4, 1941
Coke R. Stevenson (D)[14]	Aug. 4, 1941	Jan. 21, 1947
Beauford H. Jester (D)[15]	Jan. 21, 1947	July 11, 1949
Allan Shivers (D)[16]	July 11, 1949	Jan. 15, 1957
Price Daniel (D)	Jan. 15, 1957	Jan. 15, 1963
John B. Connally (D)	Jan. 15, 1963	Jan. 21, 1969
Preston Smith (D)	Jan. 21, 1969	Jan. 16, 1973
Dolph Briscoe (D)	Jan. 16, 1973	Jan. 16, 1979
William P. Clements (R)	Jan. 16, 1979	Jan. 18, 1983
Mark White (D)	Jan. 18, 1983	Jan. 20, 1987
William P. Clements (R)	Jan. 20, 1987	Jan. 15, 1991
Ann W. Richards (D)	Jan. 15, 1991	Jan. 17, 1995
George W. Bush (R)	Jan. 17, 1995	

Texas

1. *Resigned Nov. 23, 1853.*
2. *As lieutenant governor, he succeeded to office.*
3. *Resigned March 16, 1861.*
4. *As lieutenant governor, he succeeded to office.*
5. *Resigned Nov. 5, 1863.*
6. *Administration terminated June 17, 1865, due to fall of the Confederacy.*
7. *Provisional governor appointed by the president.*
8. *Appointed under martial law. Vacated office Sept. 30, 1869. Governorship is considered to have remained vacant until inauguration of Edmund J. Davis.*
9. *Resigned Dec. 1, 1876.*
10. *As lieutenant governor, he succeeded to office.*
11. *Impeached. Removed from office August 25, 1917.*
12. *As lieutenant governor, he succeeded to office. Subsequently elected.*
13. *Resigned Aug. 4, 1941.*
14. *As lieutenant governor, he succeeded to office. Subsequently elected.*
15. *Died July 11, 1949.*
16. *As lieutenant governor, he succeeded to office. Subsequently elected.*

TEXAS

(Became a state Dec. 29, 1845)

Governors	Dates of Service	
Jones (D)	Dec. 9, 1844	Feb. 19, 1846
J. Pinckney Henderson (D)	Feb. 19, 1846	Dec. 21, 1847
George T. Wood (D)	Dec. 21, 1847	Dec. 21, 1849
P. Hansbrough Bell (D)[1]	Dec. 21, 1849	Nov. 23, 1853
J. W. Henderson (D)[2]	Nov. 23, 1853	Dec. 21, 1853
Elisha M. Pease (D)	Dec. 21, 1853	Dec. 21, 1857
Hardin R. Runnels (D)	Dec. 21, 1857	Dec. 21, 1859
Sam Houston (ID)[3]	Dec. 21, 1859	March 16, 1861
Edward Clark (D)[4]	March 16, 1861	Nov. 7, 1861
Francis R. Lubbock[5]	Nov. 7, 1861	Nov. 5, 1863
Pendleton Murrah[6]	Nov. 5, 1863	June 17, 1865
Andrew J. Hamilton[7]	June 17, 1865	Aug. 9, 1866
J. W. Throckmorton (C)	Aug. 9, 1866	Aug. 8, 1867
Elisha M. Pease[8]	Aug. 8, 1867	Sept. 30, 1869
Edmund J. Davis (R)	Jan. 8, 1870	Jan. 15, 1874
Richard Coke (D)[9]	Jan. 15, 1874	Dec. 1, 1876
Richard B. Hubbard (D)[10]	Dec. 1, 1876	Jan. 21, 1879
Oran M. Roberts (D)	Jan. 21, 1879	Jan. 16, 1883
John Ireland (D)	Jan. 16, 1883	Jan. 18, 1887
Lawrence S. Ross (D)	Jan. 18, 1887	Jan. 20, 1891
James S. Hogg (D)	Jan. 20, 1891	Jan. 15, 1895
Charles A. Culberson (D)	Jan. 15, 1895	Jan. 17, 1899
Joseph D. Sayers (D)	Jan. 17, 1899	Jan. 20, 1903
Samuel W. T. Lanham (D)	Jan. 20, 1903	Jan. 15, 1907
Thomas M. Campbell (D)	Jan. 15, 1907	Jan. 17, 1911
Oscar B. Colquitt (D)	Jan. 17, 1911	Jan. 19, 1915

UTAH

(Became a state Jan. 4, 1896)

Governors	Dates of Service	
Heber Manning Wells (R)	Jan. 6, 1896	Jan. 2, 1905
John C. Cutler (R)	Jan. 2, 1905	Jan. 4, 1909
William Spry (R)	Jan. 4, 1909	Jan. 1, 1917
Simon Bamberger (D)	Jan. 1, 1917	Jan. 3, 1921
Charles R. Mabey (R)	Jan. 3, 1921	Jan. 5, 1925
George H. Dern (D)	Jan. 5, 1925	Jan. 2, 1933
Henry H. Blood (D)	Jan. 2, 1933	Jan. 6, 1941
Herbert B. Maw (D)	Jan. 6, 1941	Jan. 3, 1949
J. Bracken Lee (R)	Jan. 3, 1949	Jan. 7, 1957
George Dewey Clyde (R)	Jan. 7, 1957	Jan. 4, 1965
Calvin L. Rampton (D)	Jan. 4, 1965	Jan. 3, 1977
Scott M. Matheson (D)	Jan. 3, 1977	Jan. 7, 1985
Norman H. Bangerter (R)	Jan. 7, 1985	Jan. 3, 1993
Mike Leavitt (R)	Jan. 3, 1993	

VERMONT

(Became a state March 4, 1791)

Governors	Dates of Service	
Chittenden[1]	March 4, 1791	Aug. 25, 1797
Paul Brigham[2]	Aug. 25, 1797	Oct. 16, 1797
Isaac Tichenor (FED)	Oct. 16, 1797	Oct. 9, 1807

Israel Smith (D-R)	Oct. 9, 1807	Oct. 14, 1808
Isaac Tichenor (FED)	Oct. 14, 1808	Oct. 14, 1809
Jonas Galusha (D-R)	Oct. 14, 1809	Oct. 23, 1813
Martin Chittenden (FED)	Oct. 23, 1813	Oct. 14, 1815
Jonas Galusha (D-R)	Oct. 14, 1815	Oct. 13, 1820
Richard Skinner (D-R)	Oct. 13, 1820	Oct. 10, 1823
Cornelius P. Van Ness (D-R)	Oct. 10, 1823	Oct. 13, 1826
Ezra Butler (D-R)	Oct. 13, 1826	Oct. 10, 1828
Samuel C. Crafts (NR)	Oct. 10, 1828	Oct. 18, 1831
William A. Palmer (A-MAS)	Oct. 18, 1831	Nov. 2, 1835
Silas H. Jennison (W)[3]	Nov. 2, 1835	Oct. 15, 1841
Charles Paine (W)	Oct. 15, 1841	Oct. 13, 1843
John Mattocks (W)	Oct. 13, 1843	Oct. 11, 1844
William Slade (W)	Oct. 11, 1844	Oct. 9, 1846
Horace Eaton (W)	Oct. 9, 1846	Oct. 1848
Carlos Coolidge (W)	Oct. 1848	Oct. 11, 1850
Charles K. Williams (W)	Oct. 11, 1850	Oct. 1852
Erastus Fairbanks (W)	Oct. 1852	Oct. 1853
John S. Robinson (D)	Oct. 1853	Oct. 13, 1854
Stephen Royce (W, R)	Oct. 13, 1854	Oct. 10, 1856
Ryland Fletcher (R)	Oct. 10, 1856	Oct. 10, 1858
Hiland Hall (R)	Oct. 10, 1858	Oct. 12, 1860
Erastus Fairbanks (R)	Oct. 12, 1860	Oct. 11, 1861
Frederick Holbrook (R)	Oct. 11, 1861	Oct. 9, 1863
John Gregory Smith (R)	Oct. 9, 1863	Oct. 13, 1865
Paul Dillingham (R)	Oct. 13, 1865	Oct. 13, 1867
John B. Page (R)	Oct. 13, 1867	Oct. 15, 1869
Peter T. Washburn (R)[4]	Oct. 15, 1869	Feb. 7, 1870
George W. Hendee (R)[5]	Feb. 7, 1870	Oct. 6, 1870
John W. Stewart (R)	Oct. 6, 1870	Oct. 3, 1872
Julius Converse (R)	Oct. 3, 1872	Oct. 8, 1874
Asahel Peck (R)	Oct. 8, 1874	Oct. 5, 1876
Horace Fairbanks (R)	Oct. 5, 1876	Oct. 3, 1878
Redfield Proctor (R)	Oct. 3, 1878	Oct. 7, 1880
Roswell Farnham (R)	Oct. 7, 1880	Oct. 5, 1882
John L. Barstow (R)	Oct. 5, 1882	Oct. 2, 1884
Samuel E. Pingree (R)	Oct. 2, 1884	Oct. 7, 1886
Ebenezer J. Ormsbee (R)	Oct. 7, 1886	Oct. 4, 1888
William P. Dillingham (R)	Oct. 4, 1888	Oct. 2, 1890
Carroll S. Page (R)	Oct. 2, 1890	Oct. 6, 1892
Levi K. Fuller (R)	Oct. 6, 1892	Oct. 4, 1894
Urban A. Woodbury (R)	Oct. 4, 1894	Oct. 8, 1896
Josiah Grout (R)	Oct. 8, 1896	Oct. 6, 1898
Edward C. Smith (R)	Oct. 6, 1898	Oct. 4, 1900
William W. Stickney (R)	Oct. 4, 1900	Oct. 3, 1902
John G. McCullough (R)	Oct. 3, 1902	Oct. 6, 1904
Charles J. Bell (R)	Oct. 6, 1904	Oct. 4, 1906
Fletcher D. Proctor (R)	Oct. 4, 1906	Oct. 8, 1908
George H. Prouty (R)	Oct. 8, 1908	Oct. 5, 1910
John A. Mead (R)	Oct. 5, 1910	Oct. 3, 1912
Allen M. Fletcher (R)	Oct. 3, 1912	Jan. 7, 1915
Charles W. Gates (R)	Jan. 7, 1915	Jan. 4, 1917
Horace F. Graham (R)	Jan. 4, 1917	Jan. 9, 1919
Percival W. Clement (R)	Jan. 9, 1919	Jan. 6, 1921
James Hartness (R)	Jan. 6, 1921	Jan. 4, 1923
Redfield Proctor (R)	Jan. 4, 1923	Jan. 8, 1925
Franklin S. Billings (R)	Jan. 8, 1925	Jan. 6, 1927
John E. Weeks (R)	Jan. 6, 1927	Jan. 8, 1931
Stanley C. Wilson (R)	Jan. 8, 1931	Jan. 10, 1935
Charles M. Smith (R)	Jan. 10, 1935	Jan. 7, 1937
George D. Aiken (R)	Jan. 7, 1937	Jan. 9, 1941
William H. Wills (R)	Jan. 9, 1941	Jan. 4, 1945
Mortimer R. Proctor (R)	Jan. 4, 1945	Jan. 9, 1947
Ernest W. Gibson (R)[6]	Jan. 9, 1947	Jan. 16, 1950
Harold J. Arthur (R)[7]	Jan. 16, 1950	Jan. 4, 1951
Lee E. Emerson (R)	Jan. 4, 1951	Jan. 6, 1955
Joseph B. Johnson (R)	Jan. 6, 1955	Jan. 8, 1959
Robert T. Stafford (R)	Jan. 8, 1959	Jan. 5, 1961
Frank Ray Keyser Jr. (R)	Jan. 5, 1961	Jan. 10, 1963
Philip H. Hoff (D)	Jan. 10, 1963	Jan. 9, 1969
Deane C. Davis (R)	Jan. 9, 1969	Jan. 4, 1973
Thomas P. Salmon (D)	Jan. 4, 1973	Jan. 6, 1977
Richard A. Snelling (R)	Jan. 6, 1977	Jan. 10, 1985
Madeleine M. Kunin (D)	Jan. 10, 1985	Jan. 10, 1991
Richard A. Snelling (R)[8]	Jan. 10, 1991	Aug. 14, 1991
Howard Dean (D)[9]	Aug. 14, 1991	

Vermont
1. *Died Aug. 25, 1797.*
2. *As lieutenant governor, he succeeded to office.*
3. *No candidate received a majority of the vote and the Legislature failed to elect a governor in 1835. Silas H. Jennison, the lieutenant governor, served as governor for the term and was subsequently elected.*
4. *Died Feb. 7, 1870.*
5. *As lieutenant governor, he succeeded to office.*
6. *Resigned Jan. 16, 1950.*
7. *As lieutenant governor, he succeeded to office.*
8. *Died Aug. 14, 1991.*
9. *As lieutenant governor, he succeeded to office. Subsequently elected.*

VIRGINIA

(Ratified the Constitution June 25, 1788)

Governors	Dates of Service	
Beverley Randolph	Dec. 3, 1788	Dec. 1, 1791
Henry Lee	Dec. 1, 1791	Dec. 1, 1794
Robert Brooke	Dec. 1, 1794	Dec. 1, 1796
James Wood (D-R)	Dec. 1, 1796	Dec. 1, 1799
James Monroe (D-R)	Dec. 1, 1799	Dec. 1, 1802
John Page (D-R)	Dec. 1, 1802	Dec. 1, 1805
William H. Cabell (D-R)	Dec. 7, 1805	Dec. 1, 1808
John Tyler Sr. (D-R)	Dec. 1, 1808	Jan. 1811
James Monroe (D-R)[1]	Jan. 16, 1811	April 5, 1811
George William Smith (D-R)[2]	April 6, 1811	Dec. 26, 1811
Peyton Randolph (D-R)[3]	Dec. 27, 1811	Jan. 3, 1812
James Barbour(D-R)	Jan. 3, 1812	Dec. 1, 1814
Wilson Carey Nicholas (D-R)	Dec. 1, 1814	Dec. 1, 1816
James P. Preston (D-R)	Dec. 1, 1816	Dec. 1, 1819
Thomas M. Randolph (D-R)	Dec. 1, 1819	Dec. 1, 1822
James Pleasants (D-R)	Dec. 1, 1822	Dec. 1825
John Tyler Jr. (D-R)	Dec. 10, 1825	March 4, 1827
William B. Giles (D)	March 4, 1827	March 4, 1830
John Floyd (D)	March 4, 1830	March 31, 1834
Littleton W. Tazewell (D)[4]	March 31, 1834	April 30, 1836
Wyndham Robertson (D)[5]	April 30, 1836	March 31, 1837
David Campbell (D)	March 31, 1837	March 31, 1840
Thomas W. Gilmer (W)[6]	March 31, 1840	March 1841
John Mercer Patton (W)[7]	March 18, 1841	March 31, 1841
John Rutherford (W)[8]	March 31, 1841	March 31, 1842
John M. Gregory (W)[9]	March 31, 1842	Jan. 1, 1843
James McDowell (W)	Jan. 1, 1843	Jan. 1, 1846
William Smith (D)	Jan. 1, 1846	Jan. 1, 1849
John B. Floyd (D)	Jan. 1, 1849	Jan. 16, 1852
Joseph Johnson (D)	Jan. 16, 1852	Dec. 31, 1855
Henry A. Wise (D)	Jan. 1, 1856	Dec. 31, 1859
John Letcher (D)	Jan. 1, 1860	Dec. 31, 1863
William Smith (D)[10]	Jan. 1, 1864	April 1865
Francis H. Peirpoint[11]	June 20, 1861	April 4, 1868
Henry H. Wells[12]	April 4, 1868	Sept. 21, 1869
Gilbert C. Walker (C)[13]	Sept. 21, 1869	Jan. 1, 1874
James Lawson Kemper (D)	Jan. 1, 1874	Jan. 1, 1878
Frederick W. M. Holliday (D)	Jan. 1, 1878	Jan. 1, 1882
William E. Cameron (READJ)	Jan. 1, 1882	Jan. 1, 1886
Fitzhugh Lee (D)	Jan. 1, 1886	Jan. 1, 1890
Philip W. McKinney (D)	Jan. 1, 1890	Jan. 1, 1894
Charles T. O'Ferrall (D)	Jan. 1, 1894	Jan. 1, 1898
James Hoge Tyler (D)	Jan. 1, 1898	Jan. 1, 1902
Andrew J. Montague (D)	Jan. 1, 1902	Feb. 1, 1906
Claude A. Swanson (D)	Feb. 1, 1906	Feb. 1, 1910
William H. Mann (D)	Feb. 1, 1910	Feb. 1, 1914
Henry C. Stuart (D)	Feb. 1, 1914	Feb. 1, 1918
Westmoreland Davis (D)	Feb. 1, 1918	Feb. 1, 1922
E. Lee Trinkle (D)	Feb. 1, 1922	Feb. 1, 1926

Harry F. Byrd (D)	Feb. 1, 1926	Jan. 15, 1930
John G. Pollard (D)	Jan. 15, 1930	Jan. 17, 1934
George C. Peery (D)	Jan. 17, 1934	Jan. 19, 1938
James H. Price (D)	Jan. 19, 1938	Jan. 21, 1942
Colgate W. Darden Jr. (D)	Jan. 21, 1942	Jan. 16, 1946
William M. Tuck (D)	Jan. 16, 1946	Jan. 18, 1950
John S. Battle (D)	Jan. 18, 1950	Jan. 20, 1954
Thomas B. Stanley (D)	Jan. 20, 1954	Jan. 11, 1958
James Lindsay Almond Jr. (D)	Jan. 11, 1958	Jan. 13, 1962
Albertis S. Harrison Jr. (D)	Jan. 13, 1962	Jan. 15, 1966
Mills E. Godwin Jr. (D)	Jan. 16, 1966	Jan. 17, 1970
Linwood Holton (R)	Jan. 17, 1970	Jan. 12, 1974
Mills E. Godwin Jr. (R)	Jan. 12, 1974	Jan. 14, 1978
John Dalton (R)	Jan. 14, 1978	Jan. 16, 1982
Charles S. Robb (D)	Jan. 16, 1982	Jan. 18, 1986
Gerald L. Baliles (D)	Jan. 18, 1986	Jan. 14, 1990
L. Douglas Wilder (D)	Jan. 14, 1990	Jan. 15, 1994
George F. Allen (R)	Jan. 15, 1994	Jan. 17, 1998
James S. Gilmore III (R)	Jan. 17, 1998	

Virginia
1. *Resigned April 5, 1811.*
2. *As senior member of the Council of State, became acting governor. Died Dec. 1811.*
3. *As senior member of the Council of State, became acting governor.*
4. *Resigned April 30, 1836.*
5. *As senior member of the Council of State, became acting governor.*
6. *Resigned in March 1841.*
7. *As senior member of the Council of State, became acting governor. Following Gilmer's resignation, the Legislature did not elect a new governor for 21 months. Patton, Rutherford and Gregory took turns as acting governor.*
8. *As senior member of the Council of State, became acting governor.*
9. *As senior member of the Council of State, became acting governor.*
10. *Last Confederate governor.*
11. *Became Union governor June 20, 1861. Appointed provisional governor May 9, 1865.*
12. *Provisional governor.*
13. *Provisional governor from September 1869 to Jan. 1, 1870. Elected to four-year term beginning Jan. 1, 1870.*

WASHINGTON

(Became a state Nov. 11, 1889)

Governors	Dates of Service	
Elisha P. Ferry (R)	Nov. 11, 1889	Jan. 9, 1893
John H. McGraw (R)	Jan. 9, 1893	Jan. 11, 1897
John R. Rogers (PP, D)[1]	Jan. 11, 1897	Dec. 26, 1901
Henry McBride (R)[2]	Dec. 26, 1901	Jan. 9, 1905
Albert E. Mead (R)	Jan. 9, 1905	Jan. 27, 1909
Samuel G. Cosgrove (R)[3]	Jan. 27, 1909	March 28, 1909
Marion E. Hay (R)[4]	March 29, 1909	Jan. 11, 1913
Ernest Lister (D)[5]	Jan. 11, 1913	June 14, 1919
Louis F. Hart (R)[6]	June 14, 1919	Jan. 12, 1925
Roland H. Hartley (R)	Jan. 12, 1925	Jan. 9, 1933
Clarence D. Martin (D)	Jan. 9, 1933	Jan. 13, 1941
Arthur B. Langlie (R)	Jan. 13, 1941	Jan. 8, 1945
Monrad C. Wallgren (D)	Jan. 8, 1945	Jan. 10, 1949
Arthur B. Langlie (R)	Jan. 10, 1949	Jan. 14, 1957
Albert D. Rosellini (D)	Jan. 14, 1957	Jan. 11, 1965
Daniel J. Evans (R)	Jan. 11, 1965	Jan. 12, 1977
Dixy Lee Ray (D)	Jan. 12, 1977	Jan. 14, 1981
John D. Spellman (R)	Jan. 14, 1981	Jan. 16, 1985
Booth Gardner (D)	Jan. 16, 1985	Jan. 13, 1993
Mike Lowry (D)	Jan. 13, 1993	Jan. 15, 1997
Gary Locke (D)	Jan. 15, 1997	

Washington
1. *Elected as a Populist in 1896. Elected as a Democrat in 1900. Died Dec. 26, 1901.*
2. *As lieutenant governor, he succeeded to office.*
3. *Died March 28, 1909.*
4. *As lieutenant governor, he succeeded to office.*

5. *Died June 14, 1919.*
6. *As lieutenant governor, he succeeded to office. Subsequently elected.*

WEST VIRGINIA

(Became a state June 19, 1863)

Governors	Dates of Service	
Arthur I. Boreman (UN R, R)[1]	June 20, 1863	Feb. 26, 1869
Daniel D. T. Farnsworth (R)[2]	Feb. 27, 1869	March 3, 1869
William E. Stevenson (R)	March 4, 1869	March 3, 1871
John Jeremiah Jacob (D, I)	March 4, 1871	March 3, 1877
Henry Mason Mathews (D)	March 4, 1877	March 3, 1881
Jacob B. Jackson (D)	March 4, 1881	March 3, 1885
Emanuel Willis Wilson (D)[3]	March 4, 1885	Feb. 5, 1890
Aretas Brooks Fleming (D)[4]	Feb. 6, 1890	March 3, 1893
William A. MacCorkle (D)	March 4, 1893	March 3, 1897
George W. Atkinson (R)	March 4, 1897	March 4, 1901
Albert B. White (R)	March 4, 1901	March 4, 1905
William M. O. Dawson (R)	March 4, 1905	March 4, 1909
William E. Glasscock (R)	March 4, 1909	March 4, 1913
Henry D. Hatfield (R)	March 4, 1913	March 4, 1917
John J. Cornwell (D)	March 4, 1917	March 4, 1921
Ephraim F. Morgan (R)	March 4, 1921	March 4, 1925
Howard M. Gore (R)	March 4, 1925	March 4, 1929
William G. Conley (R)	March 4, 1929	March 4, 1933
Herman G. Kump (D)	March 4, 1933	Jan. 18, 1937
Homer A. Holt (D)	Jan. 18, 1937	Jan. 13, 1941
Matthew M. Neely (D)	Jan. 13, 1941	Jan. 15, 1945
Clarence W. Meadows (D)	Jan. 15, 1945	Jan. 17, 1949
Okey L. Patteson (D)	Jan. 17, 1949	Jan. 19, 1953
William C. Marland (D)	Jan. 19, 1953	Jan. 14, 1957
Cecil H. Underwood (R)	Jan. 14, 1957	Jan. 16, 1961
William W. Barron (D)	Jan. 16, 1961	Jan. 18, 1965
Hulett C. Smith (D)	Jan. 18, 1965	Jan. 13, 1969
Arch A. Moore Jr. (R)	Jan. 13, 1969	Jan. 17, 1977
John D. Rockefeller (D)	Jan. 17, 1977	Jan. 14, 1985
Arch A. Moore Jr. (R)	Jan. 14, 1985	Jan. 16, 1989
Gaston Caperton (D)	Jan. 16, 1989	Jan. 13, 1997
Cecil H. Underwood (R)	Jan. 13, 1997	

West Virginia
1. *Resigned Feb. 26, 1869.*
2. *As president of the state Senate, he succeeded to office.*
3. *Wilson continued in office for almost one year beyond the expiration of his term pending a settlement of the disputed election of 1888.*
4. *The 1888 election between Democrat Aretas Brooks Fleming and Republican Nathan Goff was very close, and the final outcome was in dispute. After almost one year of investigation, the West Virginia Legislature declared Fleming the winner, and he took office Feb. 6, 1890.*

WISCONSIN

(Became a state May 29, 1848)

Governors	Dates of Service	
Nelson Dewey (D)	June 7, 1848	Jan. 5, 1852
Leonard J. Farwell (W)	Jan. 5, 1852	Jan. 2, 1854
William A. Barstow (D)[1]	Jan. 2, 1854	March 21, 1856
Arthur MacArthur (D)[2]	March 21, 1856	March 25, 1856
Coles Bashford (R)[3]	March 25, 1856	Jan. 4, 1858
Alexander W. Randall (R)	Jan. 4, 1858	Jan. 6, 1862
Louis P. Harvey (R)[4]	Jan. 6, 1862	April 19, 1862
Edward Salomon (R)[5]	April 19, 1862	Jan. 4, 1864
James T. Lewis (R)	Jan. 4, 1864	Jan. 1, 1866
Lucius Fairchild (R)	Jan. 1, 1866	Jan. 1, 1872
Cadwallader C. Washburn (R)	Jan. 1, 1872	Jan. 5, 1874
William R. Taylor (D)	Jan. 5, 1874	Jan. 3, 1876

Harrison Ludington (R)	Jan. 3, 1876	Jan. 7, 1878
William E. Smith (R)	Jan. 7, 1878	Jan. 2, 1882
Jeremiah M. Rusk (R)	Jan. 2, 1882	Jan. 7, 1889
William D. Hoard (R)	Jan. 7, 1889	Jan. 5, 1891
George W. Peck (D)	Jan. 5, 1891	Jan. 7, 1895
William H. Upham (R)	Jan. 7, 1895	Jan. 4, 1897
Edward Scofield (R)	Jan. 4, 1897	Jan. 7, 1901
Robert M. La Follette (R)[6]	Jan. 7, 1901	Jan. 1, 1906
James O. Davidson (R)[7]	Jan. 1, 1906	Jan. 2, 1911
Francis E. McGovern (R)	Jan. 2, 1911	Jan. 4, 1915
Emanuel L. Philipp (R)	Jan. 4, 1915	Jan. 3, 1921
John J. Blaine (R)	Jan. 3, 1921	Jan. 3, 1927
Fred R. Zimmerman (R)	Jan. 3, 1927	Jan. 7, 1929
Walter J. Kohler Sr. (R)	Jan. 7, 1929	Jan. 5, 1931
Philip F. La Follette (R)	Jan. 5, 1931	Jan. 2, 1933
Albert G. Schmedeman (D)	Jan. 2, 1933	Jan. 7, 1935
Philip F. La Follette (PROG)	Jan. 7, 1935	Jan. 2, 1939
Julius P. Heil (R)	Jan. 2, 1939	Jan. 4, 1943
Orland S. Loomis (PROG)[8]		
Walter S. Goodland (R)[9]	Jan. 4, 1943	March 12, 1947
Oscar Rennebohm (R)[10]	March 12, 1947	Jan. 1, 1951
Walter J. Kohler Jr. (R)	Jan. 1, 1951	Jan. 7, 1957
Vernon W. Thomson (R)	Jan. 7, 1957	Jan. 5, 1959
Gaylord A. Nelson (D)	Jan. 5, 1959	Jan. 7, 1963
John W. Reynolds (D)	Jan. 7, 1963	Jan. 4, 1965
Warren P. Knowles (R)	Jan. 4, 1965	Jan. 4, 1971
Patrick J. Lucey (D)[11]	Jan. 4, 1971	July 7, 1977
M. J. Schreiber (D)[12]	July 7, 1977	Jan. 1, 1979
Lee S. Dreyfus (R)	Jan. 1, 1979	Jan. 3, 1983
Anthony S. Earl (D)	Jan. 3, 1983	Jan. 5, 1987
Tommy G. Thompson (R)	Jan. 5, 1987	

Wisconsin

1. Barstow's election to a second term in 1855 was disputed by his opponent, Coles Bashford, who charged fraud. Barstow took office, but resigned while the case was pending in court. The office was awarded to Bashford several days later.
2. Acting governor.
3. Successfully contested the election of William Augustus Barstow and served out the remainder of the term.
4. Died April 19, 1862.
5. Acting governor.
6. Resigned Jan. 1, 1906.
7. As lieutenant governor, he succeeded to office. Subsequently elected.
8. Elected in 1942 for a two-year term, but died Dec. 7, 1942, before inauguration.
9. As lieutenant governor, he succeeded to office. Subsequently elected. Died March 12, 1947.
10. As lieutenant governor, he succeeded to office. Subsequently elected.
11. Resigned July 7, 1977.
12. As lieutenant governor, he succeeded to office.

WYOMING

(Became a state July 10, 1890)

Governors	**Dates of Service**	
Francis E. Warren (R)[1]	Oct. 11, 1890	Nov. 24, 1890
Amos W. Barber (R)[2]	Nov. 24, 1890	Jan. 2, 1893
John E. Osborne (D)[3]	Jan. 2, 1893	Jan. 7, 1895

William A. Richards (R)	Jan. 7, 1895	Jan. 2, 1899
DeForest Richards (R)[4]	Jan. 2, 1899	April 28, 1903
Fenimore C. Chatterton (R)[5]	April 28, 1903	Jan. 2, 1905
Bryant B. Brooks (R)[6]	Jan. 2, 1905	Jan. 2, 1911
Joseph M. Carey (D)	Jan. 2, 1911	Jan. 4, 1915
John B. Kendrick (D)[7]	Jan. 4, 1915	Feb. 26, 1917
Frank L. Houx (D)[8]	Feb. 26, 1917	Jan. 6, 1919
Robert D. Carey (R)	Jan. 6, 1919	Jan. 1, 1923
William B. Ross (D)[9]	Jan. 1, 1923	Oct. 2, 1924
Frank E. Lucas (R)[10]	Oct. 2, 1924	Jan. 5, 1925
Nellie T. Ross (D)[11]	Jan. 5, 1925	Jan. 3, 1927
Frank C. Emerson (R)[12]	Jan. 3, 1927	Feb. 18, 1931
Alonzo M. Clark (R)[13]	Feb. 18, 1931	Jan. 2, 1933
Leslie A. Miller (D)[14]	Jan. 2, 1933	Jan. 2, 1939
Nels H. Smith (R)	Jan. 2, 1939	Jan. 4, 1943
Lester C. Hunt (D)[15]	Jan. 4, 1943	Jan. 3, 1949
Arthur G. Crane (R)[16]	Jan. 3, 1949	Jan. 1, 1951
Frank A. Barrett (R)[17]	Jan. 1, 1951	Jan. 3, 1953
Clifford Joy Rogers (R)[18]	Jan. 3, 1953	Jan. 3, 1955
Milward L. Simpson (R)	Jan. 3, 1955	Jan. 5, 1959
John J. Hickey (D)[19]	Jna. 5, 1959	Jan. 2, 1961
Jack R. Gage (D)[20]	Jan. 2, 1961	Jan. 6, 1963
Clifford P. Hansen (R)	Jan. 7, 1963	Jan. 2, 1967
Stanley K. Hathaway (R)	Jan. 2, 1967	Jan. 6, 1975
Ed Herschler (D)	Jan. 6, 1975	Jan. 5, 1987
Michael J. Sullivan (D)	Jan. 5, 1987	Jan. 2, 1995
Jim Geringer (R)	Jan. 2, 1995	

Wyoming

1. Resigned Nov. 24, 1890.
2. As secretary of state, he succeeded to office for the remainder of the first half of Gov. Warren's term.
3. Elected in a special election for the second half of Warren's term.
4. Died April 28, 1903.
5. As secretary of state, he succeeded to office for the remainder of the first half of Richards' term.
6. Elected in a special election for second half of Richards' term. Subsequently re-elected.
7. Resigned Feb. 26, 1917.
8. As secretary of state, he succeeded to office.
9. Died Oct. 2, 1924.
10. As secretary of state, he succeeded to office for the remainder of the first half of Ross's term.
11. Elected in a special election for the second half of Ross' (her husband's) term.
12. Died Feb. 18, 1931.
13. As secretary of state, he succeeded to office for the remainder of the first half of Gov. Emerson's term.
14. Elected in a special election for the second half of Emerson's term. Subsequently re-elected.
15. Resigned Jan. 3, 1949.
16. As secretary of state, he succeeded to office.
17. Resigned Jan. 3, 1953.
18. As secretary of state, he succeeded to office.
19. Resigned Jan. 2, 1961.
20. As secretary of state, he succeeded to office.

Political Party Abbreviations

The following political party abbreviations are used in the list of governors.

A-JAC D	Anti-Jackson Democrat	IP	Independent Party
ALI	Alaskan Independent	I-R	Independent Republican
A-LOT D	Anti-Lottery Democrat	JAC D	Jackson Democrat
AM	American	LIBER W	Liberation Whig
A-MAS	Anti-Mason	L & O W	Law and Order Whig
AM FAC	American Faction	LOW TAX D	Low Tax Democrat
AR	Adams Republican	LR	Liberal Republican
C	Conservative	NR	National Republican
CLAY R	Clay Republican	POP	Populist
CLINTON R	Clinton Republican	POP & SL D	Populist and Silver Democrat
CR	Conservative Republican	PP	People's
D	Democrat	PP & D	People's and Democrat
DFL	Democrat Farmer-Labor	PROG	Progressive
D-FUS	Democrat-Fusion	R	Republican
D & POP	Democrat and Populist	READJ	Readjuster
D-PP	Democrat-Peoples	RP & PROG	Republican, Prohibition,
D & PPI	Democrat and People's Independent		and Progressive
D-R	Democratic- Republican	R & TEMP	Republican and Temperance
D SIL	Democrat (Silver)	R & UL	Republican and Union Labor
D & SILVER	Democrat and Silver	SIL R	Silver Republican
FED	Federalist	UN	Union
F-LAB	Farmer-Labor	UN D	Union Democrat
FUS	Fusion	UN R	Union Republican
FUS R	Fusion Republican	W	Whig
I	Independent	W-A-RENT	Whig Anti-Rent
ID	Independent Democrat		

General Election Returns, 1787-1997

Sources for General Election Returns

The gubernatorial general election returns presented in this section *(pp. 39-88)* for the years 1787 through 1823 were obtained from *American State Governors, 1776-1976,* by Joseph E. Kallenbach and Jessamine S. Kallenbach (Dobbs Ferry, N.Y.: Oceana Publishing, 1977). Those for 1824 through 1973 were obtained from the Inter-University Consortium for Political and Social Research (ICPSR) at the University of Michigan. Major sources for returns from 1974 to 1997 were Congressional Quarterly, which obtained them from the state secretaries of state, and the biennial *America Votes* series published by Congressional Quarterly: Richard M. Scammon and Alice V. McGillivray, *America Votes,* vols. 11-21 (Washington, D.C.: Congressional Quarterly, 1975-1995) and Richard M. Scammon, Alice V. McGillivray and Rhodes Cook *America Votes,* vol. 22 (Washington, D.C.: Congressional Quarterly, 1998).

The symbol # next to returns before 1974 indicates that Congressional Quarterly obtained the returns from a source other than Kallenbach or the ICPSR. A complete list of other sources used appears on page 89. A General Election Candidates Index" is located on pages 159 to 174.

While complete source annotations for the ICPSR collection are too extensive to publish here, information on the sources for returns from specific elections can be obtained through the ICPSR: Inter-Univeristy Consortium for Political and Social Research, Box 1248, Ann Arbor, Mich. 48106.

Presentation of Returns

The gubernatorial returns are arranged alphabetically by state and in chronological order of election within each state listing. The candidate receiving the greatest number of popular votes is listed first with his or her vote total and percentage of the total vote cast, followed in descending order of votes received by all other candidates receiving *at least 5 percent* of the total vote cast.

Special elections to fill vacancies are designated in the returns.

Vote Totals and Percentages

The ICPSR collection includes all candidates receiving popular votes. In the *Gubernatorial Elections 1787-1997,* only gubernatorial candidates receiving *at least 5 percent of the total vote* for that election are included. For example, the ICPSR data collection for the 1908 Illinois gubernatorial election shows that 1,154,612 votes were cast, with Republican Charles S. Deneen receiving 550,076 votes (47.64 percent), Democrat Adlai E. Stevenson receiving 526,912 votes (45.64 percent) and four other candidates receiving the remaining 77,624 votes (6.72 percent). These four candidates do not appear on page 49 of this book because none of them received 5 percent or more of the vote.

The percentages used in this section were calculated to two decimal places on the basis of the total number of votes cast in the election and rounded to one place. Thus, on page 49, for the 1908 Illinois election, Deneen's percentage of the total vote is listed as 47.6 percent and Stevenson's as 45.6 percent. The percentages are rounded to one decimal place and do not add to 100 percent because of the scattered votes for the other four candidates.

Names and Party Designations

Names are listed as they were recorded in the official returns or other source documentation. In some instances, particularly in the 19th century, candidate names in the ICPSR file are incomplete. First names were the most commonly missing elements in the original sources consulted by the scholars and archivists who gathered the ICPSR returns. Congressional Quarterly has added full names when they could be determined and has corrected obvious misspellings.

In the ICPSR returns, the distinct—and in many cases, *multiple*—party designations appearing in the original sources are preserved. In many cases party labels represent combinations of multi-party support received by individual candidates. If, for example, on the ballot and official returns more than one party name was listed next to a candidate's name, then the party designation appearing in the election returns for that candidate will be a unique abbreviation for that combination of parties. *(For a list of party abbreviations used in this section, see pp. 90-91.)*

In the special case of a candidate's name listed separately on the original ballot under more than one party—where returns were reported *separately* for each party—Congressional Quarterly has summed the votes recorded under the several parties and that figure appears as the candidate's total vote. Whenever separate party totals have been summed, a *comma* separates the abbreviations of the parties contributing the largest and second largest share of the total vote.

Most cases of this special situation occurred in New York and Pennsylvania during this century. For example, in the original ICPSR returns for New York's 1946 gubernatorial election, James M. Mead received 1,532,161 votes as Democratic Party candidate, 428,903 votes as American Labor Party candidate and 177,418 votes as Liberal Party candidate for a total of 2,138,482 votes.

In organizing the ICPSR data for publication, Congressional Quarterly has summed all votes Mead received from these three parties. Thus, on page 70 only Mead's total vote of 2,138,482 appears.

Congressional Quarterly has also included party abbreviations for the two parties that contributed the most votes to Mead's total—separated by a comma. Thus, immediately following his name appear the abbreviations—D, AM LAB—indicating that Mead was a candidate of at least two parties and that the greatest number of votes he received was as a Democrat.

General Election
Returns, 1787-1997

ALABAMA

(Became a state Dec. 14, 1819)

	Candidates	Votes	%
1819	William Wyatt Bibb (D-R)	8,342	53.9
	M. D. Williams	7,140	46.1
1821	Israel Pickens (D-R)	9,616	57.4
	Dr. Henry Chambers	7,129	42.6
1823	Israel Pickens (D-R)	10,534	56.7
	Dr. Henry Chambers	8,035	43.3
1825	John Murphy (JAC D)	12,184	100.0
1827	John Murphy (JAC D)	8,334	99.2
1829	Gabriel Moore (JAC D)	10,956	100.0
1831	John Gayle (D)	15,309	55.5
	Nicholas Davis (NR)	8,923	32.4
	Samuel B. Moore	3,354	12.2
1833	John Gayle (D)	9,750	100.0
1835	Clement Comer Clay (D)	25,491	64.8
	Enoch Parsons (SR W)	13,760	35.0
1837	Arthur P. Bagby (D)	23,902	53.7
	Samuel W. Oliver (A-VB D)	20,605	46.3
1839	Arthur P. Bagby (D)	22,681	89.9
	Arthur F. Hopkins (W)	2,532	10.0
1841	Benjamin Fitzpatrick (D)	31,808	58.3
	James W. McClung (IW)	22,777	41.7
1843	Benjamin Fitzpatrick (D)	✔	
1845	Joshua L. Martin (I)	29,261	52.1
	Nathaniel Terry (D)	25,473	45.3
1847	Reuben Chapman (D)	35,880	55.7
	Nicholas Davis (W)	28,565	44.3
1849	Henry Watkins Collier (D)	37,221	98.1
1851	Henry Watkins Collier (D)	38,517	85.5
	James Shields (W)	5,760	12.8
1853	John A. Winston (D)	30,862	65.0
	Earnest (W)	9,499	20.0
	Nicks (UN D)	7,096	15.0
1855	John A. Winston (D)	43,936	57.2
	Shortridge (AM)	31,864	41.5
1857	Andrew B. Moore (D)	41,871	94.5
1859	Andrew B. Moore (D)	47,293	72.4
	William F. Samford (SO RTS D)	18,070	27.7
1861	John Gill Shorter (D)	38,221	57.5
	Thomas Hill Watts (W)	28,117	42.3
1863	Thomas Hill Watts (W)	28,201	71.7
	John Gill Shorter (D)	9,664	24.6
1865	Robert Miller Patton (W)	20,611	45.2
	Michael J. Bulger (D)	16,380	35.9
	William R. Smith (UN)	8,557	18.8
1868	William Hugh Smith (R)	62,067	100.0
1870	Robert B. Lindsay (D)	77,723	50.5
	William Hugh Smith (R)	76,282	49.5
1872	David P. Lewis (R)	89,868	52.5
	Hendon (LR)	81,371	47.5

	Candidates	Votes	%
1874	George S. Houston (D)	107,118	53.3
	David P. Lewis (R)	93,928	46.7
1876	George S. Houston (D)	96,401	63.4
	Woodruff (R)	55,682	36.6
1878	Rufus W. Cobb (D)	88,255	100.0
1880	Rufus W. Cobb (D)	134,905	76.1
	Pickens (G)	42,363	23.9
1882	Edward A. O'Neal (D)	102,617	68.7
	J. L. Sheffield (R)	46,742	31.3
1884	Edward A. O'Neal (D)	143,229	99.7

Explanation of Symbols

In the returns for gubernatorial elections, symbols are used to denote special circumstances. Where no symbol is used, the candidate who received the most votes won the election on the basis of the popular vote and served as governor. The following is a key to the symbols used:

✔ Elected and served as governor, but the number of votes and the percentage of the total received were not available.

† Elected governor by the state legislature because no candidate received a majority of the popular vote as required by state law at the time of the election. *(See p. 3 for an explanation of the election of governors by state legislatures.)*

* Symbol used for two types of situations: (1) the candidate who won the election did not serve as governor because he died before assuming office; (2) none of the candidates running qualified to become governor on the basis of the election returns or action by the state legislature. *(For an explanation of a specific case, consult the appropriate state listed in the section, "Governors of the States, 1787-1998," pp. 11-35.)*

‡ Disputed election. The symbol is used in a variety of circumstances such as an election dispute resulting in the unseating of a governor after he assumed office or resulting in rival governors each claiming to have been legitimately elected. *(For an explanation of a specific case, consult the appropriate state listed in the selection, "Governors of the States, 1787-1998," pp. 11-35.)*

Information was obtained from a source other than Congressional Quarterly's basic sources for this volume. *(For a list of the other sources used, see p. 89.)*

	Candidates	Votes	%
1886	Thomas Seay (D)	145,095	*79.4*
	Arthur Bingham (R)	36,793	*20.1*
1888	Thomas Seay (D)	155,973	*77.6*
	W. T. Ewing (R)	44,707	*22.2*
1890	Thomas G. Jones (D)	139,912	*76.1*
	Benjamin M. Long (R)	42,391	*23.1*
1892	Thomas G. Jones (D)	126,955	*52.2*
	R. F. Kolb (ID)	115,732	*47.5*
1894	W. C. Oates (D)	110,875	*57.1*
	R. F. Kolb (POP)	83,292	*42.9*
1896	Joseph F. Johnston (D)	128,549	*59.0*
	Albert T. Goodwyn (POP)	89,290	*41.0*
1898	Joseph F. Johnston (D)	110,551	*67.0*
	Gilbert B. Dean (POP)	50,052	*30.3*
1900	William J. Samford (D)	115,167	*71.0*
	John A. Steele (R)	28,305	*17.5*
	G. B. Crowe (POP)	17,444	*10.8*
1902	William D. Jelks (D)	67,748	*73.7*
	John A. W. Smith (R)	24,150	*26.3*
1906	B. B. Comer (D)	61,223	*85.5*
	Asa E. Stratton (R)	9,981	*13.9*
1910	Emmet O'Neal (D)	77,694	*78.7*
	Joseph O. Thompson (R)	19,210	*19.5*
1914	Charles Henderson (D)	61,307	*78.7*
	John B. Shields (R)	11,773	*15.1*
1918	Thomas E. Kilby (D)	54,746	*80.2*
	Smith	13,497	*19.8*
1922	William W. Brandon (D)	113,605	*77.6*
	O. D. Street (R)	31,175	*21.3*
1926	Bibb Graves (D)	93,432	*81.2*
	J. A. Bingham (R)	21,605	*18.8*
1930	B. M. Miller (D)	155,034	*61.8*
	Hugh A. Locke (I)	95,745	*38.2*
1934	Bibb Graves (D)	155,197	*86.9*
	Edmund H. Dryer (R)	22,621	*12.7*
1938	Frank Dixon (D)	115,761	*87.4*
	W. A. Clardy (R)	16,513	*12.5*
1942	Chauncey Sparks (D)	69,048	*89.0*
	Hugh McEniry (R)	8,167	*10.5*
1946	James E. Folsom (D)	174,959	*88.7*
	Lyman Ward (R)	22,362	*11.3*
1950	Gordon Persons (D)	155,414	*91.1*
	John S. Crowder (R)	15,177	*8.9*
1954	James E. Folsom (D)	244,401	*73.4*
	Tom Abernethy (R)	88,688	*26.6*
1958	John Patterson (D)	239,633	*88.4*
	William L. Longshore Jr. (R)	30,415	*11.2*
1962	George C. Wallace (D)	303,987	*96.3*
1966	Lurleen B. Wallace (D)	537,505	*63.4*
	James Martin (R)	262,943	*31.0*
	C. R. Robinson (I)	47,653	*5.6*
1970	George C. Wallace (D)	637,046	*74.5*
	John Logan Cashin (NDPA)	125,491	*14.7*
	A. C. Shelton (I)	75,679	*8.9*
1974	George C. Wallace (D)	497,574	*83.2*
	Elvin McCary (R)	88,381	*14.8*
1978	Forrest H. "Fob" James Jr. (D)	551,886	*72.6*
	Guy Hunt (R)	196,963	*25.9*
1982	George C. Wallace (D)	650,538	*57.6*
	Emory Folmar (R)	440,815	*39.1*
1986	Guy Hunt (R)	696,203	*56.4*
	Bill Baxley (D)	537,163	*43.5*
1990	Guy Hunt (R)	633,520	*52.1*
	Paul Hubbert (D)	582,106	*47.9*
1994	Forrest H. "Fob" James Jr. (R)	604,926	*50.3*
	James E. Folsom Jr. (D)	594,169	*49.4*

ALASKA

(Became a state Jan. 3, 1959)

	Candidates	Votes	%
1958	William A. Egan (D)	29,189	*59.6*
	John Butrovich Jr. (R)	19,299	*39.4*
1962	William A. Egan (D)	29,627	*52.3*
	Mike Stepovich (R)	27,054	*47.7*
1966	Walter J. Hickel (R)	33,145	*50.0*
	William A. Egan (D)	32,065	*48.4*
1970	William A. Egan (D)	42,309	*52.4*
	Keith H. Miller (R)	37,264	*46.1*
1974	Jay S. Hammond (R)	45,840	*47.7*
	William A. Egan (D)	45,553	*47.4*
	Joseph E. Vogler (ALI)	4,770	*5.0*
1978	Jay S. Hammond (R)	49,580	*39.1*
	Walter J. Hickel (WRITE IN)	33,555	*26.4*
	Chancy Croft (D)	25,656	*20.2*
	Tom Kelly (I)	15,656	*12.3*
1982	Bill Sheffield (D)	89,918	*46.1*
	Tom Fink (R)	72,291	*37.1*
	Richard L. Randolph (LIBERT)	29,067	*14.9*
1986	Steve C. Cowper (D)	84,943	*47.3*
	Arliss Sturgulewski (R)	76,515	*42.6*
	Joe Vogler (ALI)	10,013	*5.6*
1990	Walter J. Hickel (ALI)	75,721	*38.9*
	Tony Knowles (D)	60,201	*30.9*
	Arliss Sturgulewski (R)	50,991	*26.2*
1994	Tony Knowles (D)	87,693	*41.1*
	James O. "Jim" Campbell (R)	87,157	*40.8*
	John B. "Jack" Coghill (ALI)	27,838	*13.0*

ARIZONA

(Became a state Feb. 14, 1912)

	Candidates	Votes	%
1911	George W. P. Hunt (D)	11,123	*51.5*
	Edward W. Wells (R)	9,166	*42.4*
	P. W. Gallentine (SOC)	1,247	*5.8*
1914	George W. P. Hunt (D)	25,226	*49.5*
	Ralph H. Cameron (R)	17,602	*34.5*
	George U. Young (PROG)	5,206	*10.2*
	J. R. Barnette (SOC)	2,973	*5.8*
1916	Thomas E. Campbell (R)	27,976‡	*48.0*
	George W. P. Hunt (D)	27,946	*47.9*
1918	Thomas E. Campbell (R)	25,927	*49.9*
	Fred T. Colter (D)	25,588	*49.3*
1920	Thomas E. Campbell (R)	37,060	*54.2*
	Mit Simms (D)	31,385	*45.9*
1922	George W. P. Hunt (D)	37,310	*54.9*
	Thomas E. Campbell (R)	30,599	*45.1*
1924	George W. P. Hunt (D)	38,372	*50.5*
	Dwight B. Heard (R)	37,571	*49.5*
1926	George W. P. Hunt (D)	39,979	*50.3*
	E. S. Clark (R)	39,580	*49.8*
1928	John C. Phillips (R)	47,829	*51.7*
	George W. P. Hunt (D)	44,553	*48.2*
1930	George W. P. Hunt (D)	48,875	*51.4*
	John C. Phillips (R)	46,231	*48.6*
1932	B. B. Moeur (D)	75,314	*63.2*
	J. C. Kinney (R)	42,202	*35.4*
1934	B. B. Moeur (D)	61,355	*59.7*
	Thomas Maddock (R)	39,242	*38.2*
1936	R. C. Stanford (D)	87,678	*70.7*
	Thomas E. Campbell (R)	36,114	*29.1*
1938	R. T. Jones (D)	80,350	*68.6*
	Jerrie W. Lee (R)	32,022	*27.3*

	Candidates	Votes	%
1940	Sidney P. Osborn (D)	97,606	65.5
	Jerrie W. Lee (R)	50,358	33.8
1942	Sidney P. Osborn (D)	63,484	72.5
	Jerrie W. Lee (R)	23,562	26.9
1944	Sidney P. Osborn (D)	100,220	77.9
	Jerrie W. Lee (R)	27,261	21.2
1946	Sidney P. Osborn (D)	73,595	60.1
	Bruce D. Brockett (R)	48,867	39.9
1948	Dan E. Garvey (D)	104,008	59.2
	Bruce D. Brockett (R)	70,419	40.1
1950	Howard Pyle (R)	99,109	50.8
	Ana Frohmiller (D)	96,118	49.2
1952	Howard Pyle (R)	156,592	60.2
	Joe C. Haldiman (D)	103,693	39.8
1954	Ernest W. McFarland (D)	128,104	52.5
	Howard Pyle (R)	115,866	47.5
1956	Ernest W. McFarland (D)	171,848	59.6
	Horace B. Griffen (R)	116,744	40.5
1958	Paul Fannin (R)	160,136	55.1
	Robert Morrison (D)	130,329	44.9
1960	Paul Fannin (R)	235,502	59.3
	Lee Ackerman (D)	161,605	40.7
1962	Paul Fannin (R)	200,578	54.8
	Sam Goddard (D)	165,263	45.2
1964	Sam Goddard (D)	252,098	53.2
	Richard Kleindienst (R)	221,404	46.8
1966	Jack Williams (R)	203,438	53.8
	Sam Goddard (D)	174,904	46.2
1968	Jack Williams (R)	279,923	57.8
	Sam Goddard (D)	204,075	42.2
1970	Jack Williams (R)	209,356	50.9
	Raul H. Castro (D)	202,053	49.1
1974	Raul H. Castro (D)	278,375	50.4
	Russell Williams (R)	273,674	49.6
1978	Bruce Babbitt (D)	282,605	52.5
	Evan Mecham (R)	241,093	44.8
1982	Bruce Babbitt (D)	453,795	62.5
	Leo Corbet (R)	235,877	32.5
	Sam Steiger (LIBERT)	36,649	5.0
1986	Evan Mecham (R)	343,913	39.7
	Carolyn Warner (D)	298,986	34.5
	Bill Schulz (I)	224,085	25.8
1990	Fife Symington (R)	523,984	49.6
	Terry Goddard (D)	519,691	49.2
1991	Fife Symington (R)	492,569	52.4
	Terry Goddard (D)	448,168	47.6
1994	Fife Symington (R)	593,492	52.5
	Eddie Basha (D)	500,702	44.3

ARKANSAS

(Became a state June 15, 1836)

	Candidates	Votes	%
1836	James S. Conway (D)	5,338	62.2
	Absalom Fowler (W)	3,222	37.5
1840	Archibald Yell (D)	✔	
1844	Thomas S. Drew (D)	8,859	47.6
	Gibson (W)	7,244	38.9
	Byrd (I)	2,507	13.5
1849	John S. Roane (D)	3,290	50.5
	Wilson (W)	3,228	49.5
1852	Elias N. Conway (D)	15,932	55.2
	Smith (W)	12,955	44.9

	Candidates	Votes	%
1856	Elias N. Conway (D)	28,159	64.6
	Yell (AM)	15,436	35.4
1860	Henry M. Rector (ID)	31,578	52.5
	R. H. Johnson (D)	28,622	47.5
1872	Elisha Baxter (R)	41,808	51.8
	Joseph Brooks (D)	38,909	48.2
1874	A. H. Garland (D)	76,552	100.0
1876	William R. Miller (D)	69,775	65.6
	Bishop (R)	36,272	34.1
1878	William R. Miller (D)	88,726	100.0
1880	Thomas J. Churchill (D)	84,185	72.8
	Parks (G)	31,424	27.2
1882	James H. Berry (D)	87,669	59.6
	W. D. Slack (R)	49,372	33.5
	R. K. Garland (G)	10,142	6.9
1884	Simon P. Hughes (D)	100,875	64.6
	Thomas Boles (R)	55,388	35.5
1886	Simon P. Hughes (D)	90,650	55.3
	S. Gregg (R)	54,063	33.0
	C. E. Cunningham (AG WHEEL)	19,169	11.7
1888	James P. Eagle (D)	99,229	54.1
	C. M. Norwood (LAB)	84,273	45.9
1890	James P. Eagle (D)	106,267	55.5
	N. B. Fizer (R)	85,181	44.5
1892	W. M. Fishback (D)	90,115	57.7
	W. G. Whipple (R)	33,634	21.5
	J. P. Carnahan (POP)	31,116	19.9
1894	J. P. Clarke (D)	74,809	59.1
	H. L. Remmel (R)	26,085	20.6
	D. E. Barker (POP)	24,181	19.1
1896	Daniel Webster Jones (D)	91,114	64.3
	H. L. Remmel (R)	35,837	25.3
	A. W. Files (POP)	13,980	9.9
1898	Daniel Webster Jones (D)	75,354	67.4
	H. F. Auten (R)	27,524	24.6
	W. S. Morgan (POP)	8,332	7.5
1900	Jefferson Davis (D)	88,636	66.7
	H. L. Remmel (R)	40,701	30.6
1902	Jefferson Davis (D)	77,354	64.6
	Harry H. Meyers (R)	29,251	24.4
	Charles D. Greaves (POP)	8,345	7.0
1904	Jefferson Davis (D)	90,263	61.0
	Harry H. Myers (R)	53,898	36.4
1906	John S. Little (D)	105,586	69.1
	John I. Worthington (R)	41,689	27.3
1908	George W. Donaghey (D)	110,418	68.1
	John I. Worthington (R)	44,863	27.7
1910	George W. Donaghey (D)	101,612	67.4
	Andrew I. Roland (R)	39,870	26.5
	Dan Hogan (SOC)	9,196	6.1
1912	Joseph T. Robinson (D)	109,825	64.7
	Andrew I. Roland (R)	46,440	27.4
	G. E. Mikel (SOC)	13,384	7.9
1913	George W. Hays (D)	53,655	64.3
	Harry H. Meyers (R)	17,040	20.4
	George W. Murphy (PROG)	8,431	10.1
	J. Emil Webber (SOC)	4,378	5.2
1914	George W. Hays (D)	94,143	69.5
	Audrey L. Kinney (R)	30,947	22.8
	Dan Hogan (SOC)	10,434	7.7
1916	Charles H. Brough (D)	122,041	69.5
	Wallace Townsend (R)	43,963	25.0
	William Davis (SOC)	9,730	5.5
1918	Charles H. Brough (D)	68,192	93.4
	Clay Fulks (SOC)	4,792	6.6
1920	Thomas C. McRae (D)	123,637	65.0
	Wallace Townsend (R)	46,350	24.4

	Candidates	Votes	%
	J. H. Blount (NEG I)	15,627	8.2
1922	Thomas C. McRae (D)	99,987	78.1
	John W. Grabiel (R)	28,055	21.9
1924	Thomas J. Terral (D)	99,598	79.8
	John W. Grabiel (R)	25,152	20.2
1926	John E. Martineau (D)	116,735	76.5
	M. D. Bowers (R)	35,969	23.6
1928	Harvey J. Parnell (D)	151,743	77.3
	M. D. Bowers (R)	44,545	22.7
1930	Harvey J. Parnell (D)	112,847	81.2
	J. O. Livesay (R)	26,162	18.8
1932	Julius M. Futrell (D)	200,096	90.4
	J. O. Livesay (R)	19,717	8.9
1934	Julius M. Futrell (D)	123,918	89.2
	C. C. Ledbetter (R)	13,083	9.4
1936	Carl E. Bailey (D)	155,152	84.9
	Osro Cobb (R)	26,875	14.7
1938	Carl E. Bailey (D)	118,696	86.3
	Charles S. Cole (I)	12,077	8.8
1940	Homer M. Adkins (D)	184,578	91.4
	H. C. Stump (R)	16,600	8.2
1942	Homer M. Adkins (D)	98,871	100.0
1944	Ben Laney (D)	186,401	86.0
	H. C. Stump (R)	30,442	14.0
1946	Ben Laney (D)	128,029	84.1
	W. T. Mills (R)	24,133	15.9
1948	Sidney S. McMath (D)	217,771	89.2
	C. R. Black (R)	26,500	10.9
1950	Sidney S. McMath (D)	266,778	84.1
	Jefferson W. Speck (R)	50,303	15.9
1952	Francis Cherry (D)	342,292	87.4
	Jefferson W. Speck (R)	49,292	12.6
1954	Orval E. Faubus (D)	208,121	62.1
	Pratt C. Remmel (R)	127,004	37.9
1956	Orval E. Faubus (D)	321,797	80.7
	Roy Mitchell (R)	77,215	19.4
1958	Orval E. Faubus (D)	236,598	82.5
	George W. Johnson (R)	50,288	17.5
1960	Orval E. Faubus (D)	292,064	69.2
	Henry M. Britt (R)	129,921	30.8
1962	Orval E. Faubus (D)	225,743	73.3
	Willis Ricketts (R)	82,349	26.7
1964	Orval E. Faubus (D)	337,489	57.0
	Winthrop Rockefeller (R)	254,561	43.0
1966	Winthrop Rockefeller (R)	306,324	54.4
	James Johnson (D)	257,203	45.6
1968	Winthrop Rockefeller (R)	322,782	52.4
	Marion Crank (D)	292,813	47.6
1970	Dale Bumpers (D)	375,648	61.7
	Winthrop Rockefeller (R)	197,418	32.4
	Walter L. Carruth (AM)	36,132	5.9
1972	Dale Bumpers (D)	488,892	75.4
	Len E. Blaylock (R)	159,177	24.6
1974	David H. Pryor (D)	358,018	65.6
	Ken Coon (R)	187,872	34.4
1976	David H. Pryor (D)	605,083	83.2
	Leon Griffith (R)	121,716	16.7
1978	Bill Clinton (D)	335,101	63.4
	A. Lynn Lowe (R)	193,746	36.6
1980	Frank D. White (R)	435,684	51.9
	Bill Clinton (D)	403,241	48.1
1982	Bill Clinton (D)	431,855	54.7
	Frank D. White (R)	357,496	45.3
1984	Bill Clinton (D)	554,561	62.6
	Woody Freeman (R)	331,987	37.4
1986	Bill Clinton (D)	439,851	63.9
	Frank White (R)	248,415	36.1
1990	Bill Clinton (D)	400,386	57.5
	Sheffield Nelson (R)	295,925	42.5
1994	Jim Guy Tucker (D)	428,936	59.8
	Sheffield Nelson (R)	287,904	40.2

CALIFORNIA

(Became a state Sept. 9, 1850)

	Candidates	Votes	%
1849	P. H. Burnett (ID)	6,783	47.4
	W. S. Sherwood	3,220	22.7
	J. A. Sutter	2,201	15.5
	J. W. Geary	1,358	9.6
1851	John Bigler (D)	23,175	50.5
	P. B. Reading (W)	22,732	49.5
1853	John Bigler (D)	38,940	51.0
	William Walde (W)	37,454	49.0
1855	J. N. Johnson (AM)	51,157	52.5
	John Bigler (D)	46,225	47.5
1857	J. B. Weller (D)	53,122	56.7
	Edward Stanly (R)	21,040	22.5
	G. W. Bowie (AM)	19,481	20.8
1859	M. S. Latham (D)	61,352	59.7
	John Currey (A-LEC D)	31,298	30.5
	Leland Stanford (R)	10,110	9.8
1861	Leland Stanford (R)	56,036	46.8
	J. R. McConnell (SEC D)	32,751	27.4
	John Conness (UN D)	30,944	25.8
1863	Frederick F. Low (UN R)	64,283	59.0
	J. G. Downey (D)	44,622	41.0
1867	H. H. Haight (D)	49,895	54.0
	George C. Gurham (R)	40,359	43.7
1871	Newton Booth (R)	62,581	52.1
	H. H. Haight (D)	57,520	47.9
1875	William Irwin (D)	61,509	50.0
	T. G. Phelps (R)	31,322	25.5
	John Bidwell (I)	29,752	24.2
1879	George C. Perkins (R)	67,965	42.4
	Hugh J. Glenn (D)	47,667	29.8
	William F. White (WMP/L)	44,482	27.8
1882	George Stoneman (D)	90,694	55.1
	Morris M. Estee (R)	67,175	40.8
1886	Washington Bartlett (D)	84,965	43.4
	John F. Swift (R)	84,316	43.1
	C. C. O'Donnell (I)	12,227	6.3
1890	H. H. Markham (R)	125,129	49.6
	E. B. Pond (D)	117,184	46.4
1894	James H. Budd (D)	111,944	39.3
	Morris M. Estee (R)	110,738	38.9
	J. V. Webster (PP)	51,304	18.0
1898	Henry T. Gage (R & UL)	148,354	51.7
	James G. Maguire (D & POP)	129,261	45.0
1902	George C. Pardee (R)	146,332	48.1
	Franklin K. Lane (D)	143,783	47.2
1906	James N. Gillett (R)	125,887	40.4
	Theodore A. Bell (D)	117,590	37.7
	W. H. Langdon (I LEAGUE)	45,008	14.4
	Austin Lewis (SOC)	16,036	5.1
1910	Hiram W. Johnson (R)	177,191	45.9
	Theodore A. Bell (D)	154,835	40.1
	J. Stitt Wilson (SOC)	47,819	12.4
1914	Hiram W. Johnson (PROG)	460,495	49.7
	John D. Fredericks (R)	271,990	29.4
	J. B. Curtin (D)	116,121	12.5
	Noble A. Richardson (SOC)	50,716	5.5
1918	William D. Stephens (RP&PROG)	387,547	56.3
	Theodore A. Bell (I)	251,189	36.5
1922	Friend William Richardson (R)	576,445	59.7
	Thomas Lee Woolwine (D)	347,530	36.0
1926	C. C. Young (R)	814,815	71.2
	Justus S. Wardell (D)	282,451	24.7
1930	James Rolph Jr. (R)	999,393	72.2
	Milton K. Young (D)	333,973	24.1

Year	Candidates	Votes	%
1934	Frank F. Merriam (R)	1,138,620	48.9
	Upton Sinclair (D)	879,537	37.8
	Raymond L. Haight (C PROG)	302,519	13.0
1938	Culbert L. Olson (D)	1,391,734	52.5
	Frank F. Merriam (R)	1,171,019	44.2
1942	Earl Warren (R)	1,275,237	57.1
	Culbert L. Olson (D)	932,995	41.8
1946	Earl Warren (R-D)	2,344,542	91.6
	Henry R. Schmidt (P)	180,579	7.1
1950	Earl Warren (R)	2,461,754	64.9
	James Roosevelt (D)	1,333,856	35.1
1954	Goodwin J. Knight (R)	2,290,519	56.8
	Richard Perrin Graves (D)	1,739,368	43.2
1958	Edmund G. Brown (D)	3,140,076	59.8
	William F. Knowland (R)	2,110,911	40.2
1962	Edmund G. Brown (D)	3,037,109	51.9
	Richard M. Nixon (R)	2,740,351	46.8
1966	Ronald Reagan (R)	3,742,913	57.6
	Edmund G. Brown (D)	2,749,174	42.3
1970	Ronald Reagan (R)	3,439,664	52.8
	Jess Unruh (D)	2,938,607	45.1
1974	Edmund G. "Jerry" Brown Jr. (D)	3,131,648	50.1
	Houston I. Flournoy (R)	2,952,954	47.3
1978	Edmund G. "Jerry" Brown Jr. (D)	3,878,812	56.0
	Evelle J. Younger (R)	2,526,534	36.5
	Ed Clark (I)	377,960	5.5
1982	George Deukmejian (R)	3,881,014	49.3
	Tom Bradley (D)	3,787,669	48.1
1986	George Deukmejian (R)	4,506,601	60.5
	Tom Bradley (D)	2,781,714	37.4
1990	Pete Wilson (R)	3,791,904	49.2
	Dianne Feinstein (D)	3,525,197	45.8
1994	Pete Wilson (R)	4,781,766	55.2
	Kathleen Brown (D)	3,519,799	40.6

COLORADO

(Became a state Aug. 1, 1876)

Year	Candidates	Votes	%
1876	John L. Routt (R)	14,154	51.5
	Hughes (D)	13,316	48.5
1878	Frederick W. Pitkin (R)	14,308	50.0
	W. A. H. Loveland (D)	11,535	40.3
	R. G. Buckingham (G)	2,783	9.7
1880	Frederick W. Pitkin (R)	28,465	53.3
	John S. Hough (D)	23,547	44.1
1882	James B. Grant (D)	31,375	51.1
	E. L. Campbell (R)	28,820	46.9
1884	Benjamin H. Eaton (R)	33,845	50.7
	Alva Adams (D)	30,743	46.1
1886	Alva Adams (D)	29,234	49.7
	William H. Meyer (R)	26,816	45.6
1888	Job A. Cooper (R)	49,490	53.8
	T. M. Patterson (D)	39,197	42.6
1890	John L. Routt (R)	41,827	50.1
	Caldwell Yeaman (D)	35,359	42.4
	John G. Coy (F ALNC)	5,199	6.2
1892	Davis H. Waite (POP & SL D)	43,342	46.7
	Joseph C. Helm (R)	38,806	41.8
	Joseph H. Maupin (D)	8,944	9.6
1894	Albert W. McIntire (R)	93,502	52.0
	Davis H. Waite (POP)	73,894	41.1
1896	Alva Adams (D)	87,387	46.2
	M. S. Bailey (N SILVER)	71,808	38.0
	G. H. Allen (R)	23,945	12.7
1898	Charles S. Thomas (FUS)	93,966	62.8
	Henry R. Wolcott (R)	51,051	34.1

Year	Candidates	Votes	%
1900	James B. Orman (FUS)	118,647	53.8
	Frank C. Goudy (R)	96,027	43.5
1902	James H. Peabody (R)	87,684	46.9
	E. C. Stimson (D)	80,727	43.2
1904	Alva Adams (D)	123,092‡	50.6
	James H. Peabody (R)	113,754	46.8
1906	Henry A. Buchtel (R)	92,602	45.6
	Alva Adams (D)	74,416	36.6
	Ben B. Lindsey (I)	18,014	8.9
	William D. Haywood (SOC)	16,015	7.9
1908	John F. Shafroth (D)	130,141	49.4
	Jesse F. McDonald (R)	118,953	45.2
1910	John F. Shafroth (D)	114,676	54.0
	John B. Stephen (R)	97,691	46.0
1912	Elias M. Ammons (D)	114,044	42.9
	Edward P. Costigan (PROG-BMR)	66,132	24.9
	C. C. Parks (R)	63,061	23.7
	Charles A. Ashelstrom (SOC)	16,189	6.1
1914	George A. Carlson (R)	129,096	48.7
	T. M. Patterson (D)	90,640	34.2
	Edward P. Costigan (PROG)	32,920	12.4
1916	Julius C. Gunter (D)	151,912	53.3
	George A. Carlson (R)	117,723	41.3
1918	Oliver H. Shoup (R)	112,693	51.1
	Tynan (D)	102,397	46.5
1920	Oliver H. Shoup (R)	174,488	59.6
	James M. Collins (D)	108,738	37.1
1922	William E. Sweet (D)	138,098	49.6
	Benjamin Griffith (R)	134,353	48.3
1924	Clarence J. Morley (R)	178,078	51.9
	William E. Sweet (D)	151,041	44.0
1926	William H. Adams (D)	183,342	59.8
	Oliver H. Shoup (R)	116,756	38.1
1928	William H. Adams (D)	240,160	61.9
	William L. Boatright (R)	144,067	37.1
1930	William H. Adams (D)	197,067	60.4
	Robert F. Rockwell (R)	124,164	38.1
1932	Edwin C. Johnson (D)	257,188	57.2
	James D. Parriott (R)	183,258	40.8
1934	Edwin C. Johnson (D)	237,026	58.1
	Nate C. Warren (R)	162,791	39.9
1936	Teller Ammons (D)	263,311	54.6
	Charles M. Armstrong (R)	210,614	43.7
1938	Ralph L. Carr (R)	255,159	55.8
	Teller Ammons (D)	199,562	43.7
1940	Ralph L. Carr (R)	296,671	54.4
	George E. Saunders (D)	245,292	45.0
1942	John C. Vivian (R)	193,501	56.2
	Homer F. Bedford (D)	149,402	43.4
1944	John C. Vivian (R)	259,862	52.4
	Roy Best (D)	236,086	47.6
1946	William Lee Knous (D)	174,604	52.1
	Leon E. Lavington (R)	160,483	47.9
1948	William Lee Knous (D)	332,752	66.3
	David A. Hamil (R)	168,928	33.7
1950	Dan Thornton (R)	236,472	52.4
	Walter W. Johnson (D)	212,976	47.2
1952	Dan Thornton (R)	349,924	57.1
	John W. Metzger (D)	260,044	42.4
1954	Edwin C. Johnson (D)	262,205	53.6
	Donald G. Brotzman (R)	227,335	46.4
1956	Stephen L. R. McNichols (D)	331,283	51.3
	Donald G. Brotzman (R)	313,950	48.7
1958	Stephen L. R. McNichols (D)	321,165	58.4
	Palmer L. Burch (R)	228,643	41.6
1962	John A. Love (R)	349,342	56.7
	Stephen L. R. McNichols (D)	262,890	42.6
1966	John A. Love (R)	356,730	54.0
	Robert L. Knous (D)	287,132	43.5
1970	John A. Love (R)	350,690	52.5
	Mark Hogan (D)	302,432	45.2

	Candidates	Votes	%
1974	Richard D. Lamm (D)	441,408	53.2
	John D. Vanderhoof (R)	378,698	45.7
1978	Richard D. Lamm (D)	483,985	58.7
	Ted Strickland (R)	317,292	38.5
1982	Richard D. Lamm (D)	627,960	65.7
	John D. Fuhr (R)	302,740	31.7
1986	Roy Romer (D)	616,325	58.2
	Ted Strickland (R)	434,420	41.0
1990	Roy Romer (D)	626,032	61.9
	John Andrews (R)	358,403	35.4
1994	Roy Romer (D)	619,205	55.5
	Bruce Benson (R)	432,042	38.7

CONNECTICUT

(Ratified the Constitution Jan. 9, 1788)

	Candidates	Votes	%
1787-1795	Samuel Huntington	✔	
1796	Oliver Wolcott Sr.	3,805†	48.8
	Jonathan Trumbull II	1,187	15.2
	Jonathan Ingersoll	937	12.0
	Oliver Ellsworth	629	8.1
	Richard Law	485	6.2
1797	Oliver Wolcott Sr.	✔	
1798-1800	Jonathan Trumbull II	✔	
1801	Jonathan Trumbull II	11,156	83.8
	Richard Law	1,056	7.9
1802	Jonathan Trumbull II (FED)	11,398	69.9
	Ephraim Kirby (D-R)	4,523	27.7
1803	Jonathan Trumbull II (FED)	14,375	64.0
	Ephraim Kirby (D-R)	7,848	35.0
1804	Jonathan Trumbull II (FED)	11,108	61.8
	William Hart (D-R)	6,871	38.2
1805	Jonathan Trumbull II (FED)	12,700	61.9
	William Hart (D-R)	7,810	38.1
1806	Jonathan Trumbull II (FED)	13,413	58.6
	William Hart (D-R)	9,460	41.4
1807	Jonathan Trumbull II (FED)	11,959	60.0
	William Hart (D-R)	7,971	40.0
1808	Jonathan Trumbull II (FED)	12,146	61.6
	William Hart (D-R)	7,566	38.4
1809	Jonathan Trumbull II (FED)	14,650	64.2
	Asa Spalding (D-R)	8,159	35.8
1810	John Treadwell (FED)	10,265†	49.5
	Asa Spalding (D-R)	7,185	34.6
	Roger Griswold (FED)	3,110	15.0
1811	Roger Griswold (FED)	✔	
	John Treadwell (FED)		
1812	Roger Griswold (FED)	11,721	86.1
	Elijah Boardman (D-R)	1,487	10.9
1813	John C. Smith (FED)	11,893	59.1
	Elijah Boardman (D-R)	7,201	35.8
1814	John C. Smith (FED)	9,415	72.9
	Elijah Boardman (D-R)	2,619	20.3
1815	John C. Smith (FED)	8,176	59.3
	Elijah Boardman (D-R)	4,876	35.3
1816	John C. Smith (FED)	11,386	52.3
	Oliver Wolcott Jr. (AM, TOL[1])	10,170	46.7
1817	Oliver Wolcott Jr. (TOL[1], REF)	13,655	50.6
	John C. Smith (FED)	13,119	48.6
1818	Oliver Wolcott Jr. (CONST, REF)	16,432	87.0
1819	Oliver Wolcott Jr. (TOL, REF)	22,539	86.8
1820	Oliver Wolcott Jr. (D-R)	15,738	78.4
1821	Oliver Wolcott Jr. (D-R)	10,064	86.6
1822	Oliver Wolcott Jr. (D-R)	8,568	85.5
1823	Oliver Wolcott Jr. (D-R)	9,090	88.9
1824	Oliver Wolcott Jr. (D-R)	6,637	92.1
	Timothy Pitkin (OPP R)	466	6.5

	Candidates	Votes	%
1825	Oliver Wolcott Jr. (D-R)	7,147	70.1
	David Daggett (FED)	1,342	13.2
	Nathan Smith (OPP R)	863	8.5
	Timothy Pitkin (OPP R)	525	5.2
1826	Oliver Wolcott Jr. (D-R)	6,780	57.8
	David Daggett (FED)	4,340	37.0
1827	Gideon Tomlinson (OLD R)	7,681	57.7
	Oliver Wolcott (OPP R)	5,295	39.8
1828	Gideon Tomlinson (NR)	9,297	97.3
1829	Gideon Tomlinson (NR)	9,612	95.8
1830	Gideon Tomlinson (NR)	12,988	95.6
1831	John S. Peters (NR)	12,819	65.4
	Zalmon Storrs (A-MASC)	4,778	24.4
1832	John S. Peters (NR)	11,971	70.3
	Calvin Willey (D)	4,463	26.2
1833	John S. Peters (NR)	9,212	42.3
	Henry W. Edwards (D)	9,030†	41.5
	Zalmon Storrs (A-MASC)	3,250	14.9
1834	Samuel A. Foot (NR)	18,411†	49.8
	Henry W. Edwards (D)	15,834	42.9
	Zalmon Storrs (A-MASC)	2,398	6.5
1835	Henry W. Edwards (D)	22,129	51.5
	Samuel A. Foot (W)	20,335	47.3
1836	Henry W. Edwards (D)	20,360	53.6
	Gideon Tomlinson (W)	17,393	45.8
1837	Henry W. Edwards (D)	23,805	52.5
	William W. Ellsworth (W)	21,508	47.5
1838	William W. Ellsworth (W)	27,115	54.1
	S. P. Beers (D)	21,489	42.9
1839	William W. Ellsworth (W)	26,581	51.4
	Niles (D)	24,047	46.5
1840	William W. Ellsworth (W)	30,360	54.0
	Niles (D)	25,782	45.8
1841	William W. Ellsworth (W)	26,078	56.0
	Nicoll (D)	20,458	44.0
1842	Chauncey F. Cleveland (D)	25,564†	49.9
	William W. Ellsworth (W)	23,700	46.2
1843	Chauncey F. Cleveland (D)	27,416	50.1
	Roger S. Baldwin (W)	25,401	46.4
1844	Roger S. Baldwin (W)	30,093†	49.4
	Chauncey F. Cleveland (D)	28,846	47.3
1845	Roger S. Baldwin (W)	29,508	51.0
	Isaac Toucey (D)	26,258	45.3
1846	Clark Bissell (W)	27,822	48.6
	Isaac Toucey (D)	27,203†	47.5
1847	Clark Bissell (W)	30,137	50.5
	Whittlesey (D)	27,402	45.9
1848	Clark Bissell (W)	30,717	50.4
	George S. Catlin (D)	28,525	46.8
1849	Joseph Trumbull (W)	27,300†	48.8
	Thomas H. Seymour (D)	25,106	44.9
	Niles (F SOIL)	3,520	6.3
1850	Thomas H. Seymour (D)	29,022†	48.3
	Foster (W)	28,200	46.9
1851	Thomas H. Seymour (D)	30,077†	49.0
	Foster (W)	28,756	46.9
1852	Thomas H. Seymour (D)	31,624	50.4
	Kendrick (W)	28,241	45.0
1853	Thomas H. Seymour (D)	30,814	51.0
	Dutton (W)	20,671	34.2
	Gillette (F SOIL)	8,926	14.8
1854	Ingham (D)	28,538	48.6
	Henry Dutton (W)	19,465†	33.2
	Chapman (TEMP)	10,672	18.2
1855	William T. Minor (AM)	28,080†	43.5
	Ingham (D)	27,291	42.3
	Henry Dutton (W)	9,162	14.2
1856	Ingham (D)	32,704	49.0
	William T. Minor (AM)	26,008†	39.0
	Wells (R)	6,740	10.1

	Candidates	Votes	%		Candidates	Votes	%
1857	Alexander H. Holley (R)	31,709	50.4	1908	George L. Lilley (R)	98,179	51.9
	Ingham (D)	31,156	49.5		A. Heaton Robertson (D)	82,260	43.5
1858	William A. Buckingham (R)	36,298	51.8	1910	Simeon E. Baldwin (D)	77,243	46.5
	Pratt (D)	33,549	47.8		Goodwin (R)	73,528	44.3
1859	William A. Buckingham (R)	40,247	51.1		Hunter (SOC)	12,179	7.3
	Pratt (D)	38,369	48.7	1912	Simeon E. Baldwin (D)	78,264	41.1
1860	William A. Buckingham (R)	44,458	50.3		Studley (R)	67,531	35.5
	Seymour (D)	43,920	49.7		Smith (PROG)	31,020	16.3
1861	William A. Buckingham (R)	43,012	51.2		Beardsley (SOC)	10,236	5.4
	Loomis (D)	40,926	48.8	1914	Marcus H. Holcomb (R)	91,262	50.4
1862	William A. Buckingham (R)	39,782	56.5		Lyman Tingier (D)	73,888	40.8
	Loomis (D)	30,634	43.5	1916	Marcus H. Holcomb (R)	109,293	51.1
1863	William A. Buckingham (R)	41,032	51.6		Morris Beardsley (D)	96,787	45.3
	Thomas H. Seymour (D)	38,395	48.3	1918	Marcus H. Holcomb (R)	84,891	50.7
1864	William A. Buckingham (UN R)	39,820	53.8		Thomas Spellacy (D)	76,773	45.9
	Origen S. Seymour (D)	34,162	46.2	1920	Everett J. Lake (R)	230,792	63.0
1865	William A. Buckingham (UN R)	42,374	57.5		Rollin U. Tyler (D)	119,912	32.8
	Origen S. Seymour (D)	31,339	42.5	1922	Charles A. Templeton (R)	170,231	52.4
1866	Joseph R. Hawley (R)	43,974	50.3		David Fitzgerald (D)	148,641	45.7
	James E. English (D)	43,433	49.7	1924	Hiram Bingham (R)	246,336	66.2
1867	James E. English (D)	47,565	50.5		Charles Morris (D)	118,676	31.9
	Joseph R. Hawley (R)	46,578	49.5	1926	John H. Trumbull (R)	192,425	63.6
1868	James E. English (D)	50,541	50.9		Charles Morris (D)	107,045	35.4
	Marshall Jewell (R)	48,777	49.1	1928	John H. Trumbull (R)	296,216	53.6
1869	Marshall Jewell (R)	45,493	50.2		Charles Morris (D)	252,209	45.6
	James E. English (D)	45,082	49.8	1930	Wilbur L. Cross (D)	215,072	49.9
1870	James E. English (D)	44,128	50.5		E. E. Rogers (R)	209,607	48.6
	Marshall Jewell (R)	43,285	49.5	1932	Wilbur L. Cross (D)	288,347	49.0
1871	Marshall Jewell (R)	47,473	50.1		John H. Trumbull (R)	277,503	47.1
	James E. English (D)	47,370	49.9	1934	Wilbur L. Cross (D)	257,996	46.7
1872	Marshall Jewell (R)	46,563	50.0		Hugh Meade Alcorn (R)	249,397	45.2
	Richard D. Hubbard (D)	44,562	47.9		Jasper McLevy (SOC)	38,438	7.0
1873	Charles R. Ingersoll (D)	45,060	51.9	1936	Wilbur L. Cross (D)	372,953#	55.3
	Haven (R)	39,245	45.2		Arthur M. Brown (R)	277,190#	41.1
1874	Charles R. Ingersoll (D)	46,755	53.9	1938	Raymond E. Baldwin (R, UN)	230,237	36.4
	Harrison (R)	39,973	46.1		Wilbur L. Cross (D)	227,549	36.0
1875	Charles R. Ingersoll (D)	53,752	53.2		Jasper McLevy (SOC)	166,253	26.3
	Greene (R)	44,272	43.9	1940	Robert A. Hurley (D)	388,361	49.5
1876	Richard D. Hubbard (D)	61,934	50.8		Raymond E. Baldwin (R, UN)	374,581	47.8
	Robinson (R)	58,514	48.0	1942	Raymond E. Baldwin (R)	281,362	48.9
1878	Charles B. Andrews (R)	48,867†	46.7		Robert A. Hurley (D)	255,166	44.4
	Richard D. Hubbard (D)	46,385	44.3		Jasper McLevy (SOC)	34,537	6.0
	Atwater (N)	8,314	7.9	1944	Raymond E. Baldwin (R)	418,289	50.5
1880	Hobart B. Bigelow (R)	67,070	50.5		Robert A. Hurley (D)	392,417	47.4
	James E. English (D)	64,293	48.4	1946	James L. McConaughy (R)	371,852	54.4
1882	Thomas M. Waller (D)	59,014	51.0		Wilbert Snow (D)	276,335	40.4
	Morgan G. Bulkeley (R)	54,853	47.4	1948	Chester Bowles (D)	431,746	49.3
1884	Thomas M. Waller (D)	67,910	49.3		James C. Shannon (R)	429,071	49.0
	Henry B. Harrison (R)	66,274†	48.1	1950	John D. Lodge (R)	436,418	49.7
1886	Cleveland (D)	58,818	47.7		Chester Bowles (D)	419,404	47.7
	Phineas C. Lounsbury (R)	56,920†	46.2	1954	Abraham A. Ribicoff (D)	463,643	49.5
1888	Luzon B. Morris (D)	75,074	48.9		John D. Lodge (R)	460,528	49.2
	Morgan G. Bulkeley (R)	73,659†	47.9	1958	Abraham A. Ribicoff (D)	607,012	62.3
1890	Luzon B. Morris (D)	67,658*	50.0		Fred R. Zeller (R)	360,644	37.0
	S. E. Merwin (R)	63,975	47.3	1962	John N. Dempsey (D)	549,027	53.2
1892	Luzon B. Morris (D)	82,787	50.3		John Alsop (R)	482,852	46.8
	S. E. Merwin (R)	76,745	46.6	1966	John N. Dempsey (D)	561,599	55.7
1894	O. Vincent Coffin (R)	83,975	54.2		E. Clayton Gengras (R)	446,536	44.3
	Cady (D)	66,287	42.8	1970	Thomas J. Meskill (R)	582,160	53.8
1896	Lorrin A. Cooke (R)	108,807	62.5		Emilio Q. Daddario (D)	500,561	46.2
	Sargent (D)	56,524	32.5	1974	Ella T. Grasso (D)	643,490	58.4
1898	George E. Lounsbury (R)	81,015	54.2		Robert H. Steele (R)	440,169	39.9
	Morgan (D)	64,227	42.9	1978	Ella T. Grasso (D)	613,109	59.1
1900	George P. McLean (R)	95,822	53.0		Ronald A. Sarasin (R)	422,316	40.7
	S. L. Bronson (D)	81,421	45.1	1982	William A. O'Neill (D)	578,264	53.3
1902	Abiram Chamberlain (R)	85,338	53.4		Lewis B. Rome (R)	497,773	45.9
	Melbert B. Cary (D)	69,330	43.4	1986	William A. O'Neill (D)	575,638	57.9
1904	Henry Roberts (R)	104,736	54.9		Julie D. Belaga (R)	408,489	41.1
	A. Heaton Robertson (D)	79,164	41.5	1990	Lowell P. Weicker Jr. (ACP)	460,576	40.4
1906	Rollin S. Woodruff (R)	88,384	54.8		John G. Rowland (R)	427,840	37.5
	Charles Thayer (D)	67,776	42.1		Bruce A. Morrison (D)	236,641	20.7

	Candidates	Votes	%
1994	John G. Rowland (R)	415,201	36.2
	Bill Curry (D)	375,133	32.7
	Eunice Strong Groark (ACP)	216,585	18.9
	Tom Scott (I)	130,128	11.3

Connecticut
1. Toleration Party.

DELAWARE

(Ratified the Constitution Dec. 7, 1787)

	Candidates	Votes	%
1792[1]	Joshua Clayton	2,209	48.3
	Thomas Montgomery	1,902	41.6
	George Mitchell	458	10.0
1795	Gunning Bedford Jr.	2,352	52.3
	Archibald Alexander	2,142	47.7
1798	Richard Bassett (FED)	2,490	52.5
	David Hall (D-R)	2,068	43.6
1801	David Hall (D-R)	3,475	50.1
	Nathanael Mitchell (FED)	3,457	49.9
1804	Nathanael Mitchell (FED)	4,391	52.0
	Joseph Hazlett (D-R)	4,050	48.0
1807	George Truitt (FED)	3,309	51.9
	Joseph Hazlett (D-R)	3,062	48.1
1810	Joseph Hazlett (D-R)	3,664	50.5
	Daniel Rodney (FED)	3,593	49.5
1813	Daniel Rodney (FED)	4,643	55.2
	James Riddle (D-R)	3,768	44.8
1816	John Clarke (FED)	3,998	53.2
	Mansen Bull (D-R)	3,517	46.8
1819	Henry Molleston (FED)	3,823*	54.6
	Mansen Bull (D-R)	3,185	45.4
1820	John Collins (D-R)	3,965	53.1
	Jesse Green (FED)	3,500	46.9
1822	Joseph Hazlett (D-R)	3,784	50.1
	James Booth (FED)	3,762	49.9
1823	Samuel Paynter (FED)	4,348	51.8
	Daniel Hazzard (D-R)	4,051	48.2
1826	Charles Polk (FED)	4,344#	50.6
	David Hazzard (D-R)	4,238#	49.4
1829	David Hazzard (AM D-R)	✔#	
	A. Thompson (JAC D)	#	
1832	Caleb P. Bennett (D)	4,220	50.3
	Arnold Naudain (NR)	4,166	49.7
1836	Cornelius P. Comegys (W)	4,693	52.3
	Nehemiah Clark (D)	4,276	47.7
1840	William B. Cooper (W)	5,855	53.8
	Warren Jefferson (D)	5,024	46.2
1844	Thomas Stockton (W)	6,140	50.2
	William Tharp (D)	6,095	49.8
1846	William Tharp (D)	6,148	50.6
	Peter F. Causey (W)	6,012	49.4
1850	William H. Ross (D)	6,001	48.3
	Peter F. Causey (W)	5,978	48.1
1854	Peter F. Causey (AM)	6,941	52.6
	Barton (D)	6,244	47.4
1858	William Burton (D)	7,758	50.7
	Buckmaster	7,554	49.3
1862	William Cannon (UN)	8,155	50.3
	Jefferson (D)	8,044	49.7
1866	Gove Saulsbury (D)	9,810	53.3
	James Riddle (R)	8,598	46.7
1870	James Ponder (D)	11,464	55.7
	Thomas B. Coursey (R)	9,130	44.3
1874	John P. Cochran (D)	12,488	52.6
	Jump (R)	11,259	47.4

	Candidates	Votes	%
1878	John W. Hall (D)	10,730	79.1
	Stewart (NG)	2,835	20.9
1882	Charles C. Stockley (D)	16,558	53.1
	Curry (R)	14,620	46.9
1886	Benjamin T. Biggs (D)	13,942	63.6
	Hoffecker (TEMP REF)	7,835	35.8
1890	Robert J. Reynolds (D)	17,801	50.4
	Richardson (R)	17,258	48.9
1894	Joshua H. Marvel (R)	19,880	50.8
	Ebe W. Tunnell (D)	18,659	47.7
1896	Ebe W. Tunnell (D)	15,507	44.2
	John H. Hoffecker (R)	11,014	31.4
	John C. Higgins (A-AK R)	7,154	20.4
1900	John Hunn (R)	22,421	53.6
	Peter J. Ford (D)	18,808	44.9
1904	Preston Lea (R)	22,532	51.4
	Caleb S. Pennewill (D)	19,780	45.1
1908	Simeon S. Pennewill (R)	24,905	52.0
	Rowland G. Paynter (D)	22,794	47.6
1912	Charles R. Miller (R & PROG)	22,745	47.0
	Thomas M. Monaghan (D)	21,460	44.3
	George B. Hynson (PROG)	3,019	6.2
1916	John G. Townsend Jr. (R)	26,664	52.1
	James H. Hughes (D)	24,053	47.0
1920	William E. Denney (R)	51,895	55.2
	Andrew J. Lynch (D)	41,038	43.7
1924	Robert P. Robinson (R)	53,046	59.6
	Joseph Bancroft (D)	34,830	39.2
1928	C. Douglass Buck (R)	63,716	61.2
	Charles M. Wharton (D)	40,346	38.8
1932	Clayton Douglass Buck (R)	60,903	54.2
	L. Layton (D)	50,401	44.9
1936	Richard C. McMullen (D)	65,437	51.6
	Harry L. Cannon (R)	52,782	41.6
	Isaac Dolphus Short (IR)	8,400	6.6
1940	Walter W. Bacon (R)	70,629	52.4
	Josiah Marvel Jr. (D)	61,237	45.4
1944	Walter W. Bacon (R)	63,829	50.5
	Isaac J. MacCollum (D)	62,156	49.2
1948	Elbert N. Carvel (D)	75,339	53.7
	Hyland P. George (R)	64,996	46.3
1952	J. Caleb Boggs (R)	88,977	52.1
	Elbert N. Carvel (D)	81,772	47.9
1956	J. Caleb Boggs (R)	91,965	52.0
	J. H. Tyler McConnell (D)	85,047	48.1
1960	Elbert N. Carvel (D)	100,792	51.7
	John W. Rollins (R)	94,043	48.3
1964	Charles L. Terry Jr. (D)	102,797	51.4
	David P. Buckson (R)	97,374	48.7
1968	Russell W. Peterson (R)	104,474	50.5
	Charles L. Terry Jr. (D)	102,360	49.5
1972	Sherman W. Tribbitt (D)	117,274	51.3
	Russell W. Peterson (R)	109,583	47.9
1976	Pierre S. "Pete" du Pont IV (R)	130,531	56.9
	Sherman W. Tribbitt (D)	97,480	42.5
1980	Pierre S. "Pete" du Pont IV (R)	159,004	70.6
	William J. Gordy (D)	64,217	28.5
1984	Michael N. Castle (R)	132,250	55.5
	William T. Quillen (D)	108,315	44.5
1988	Michael N. Castle (R)	169,733	70.7
	Jacob Kreshtool (D)	70,236	29.3
1992	Thomas R. Carper (D)	179,365	64.7
	B. Gary Scott (R)	90,725	32.7
1996	Thomas R. Carper (D)	188,300	69.5
	Janet C. Rzewnicki (R)	82,654	30.5

Delaware
1. Before 1792 governor chosen by legislature.

FLORIDA

(Became a state March 3, 1845)

	Candidates	Votes	%
1845	William D. Moseley (D)	3,292	55.1
	R. K. McCall (W)	2,679	44.9
1848	Thomas S. Brown (W)	4,147	53.3
	W. Bailey (D)	3,636	46.7
1852	James E. Broome (D)	4,628	51.6
	George T. Ward (W)	4,336	48.4
1856	Madison S. Perry (D)	6,208	51.3
	David S. Walker (AM)	5,894	48.7
1860	John Milton (D)	6,937	57.1
	Edward Hopkins (CST U)	5,215	42.9
1865	David S. Walker (D)	5,873#	100.0
1868	Harrison Reed (R)	14,421#	59.1
	George W. Scott (D)	7,731#	31.7
	Samuel Walker (RAD R)	2,251#	9.2
1872	Ossian B. Hart (R)	17,603	52.4
	William D. Bloxham (LR)	16,004	47.6
1876	George F. Drew (D)	24,613	50.5
	Marcellus L. Stearns (R)	24,116	49.5
1880	William D. Bloxham (D)	28,372	54.9
	Simon B. Conover (R)	23,307	45.1
1884	Edward A. Perry (D)	32,096	53.5
	Pope (R)	27,865	46.5
1888	Francis P. Fleming (D)	40,195	60.4
	V. J. Shipman (R)	26,385	39.6
1892	Henry L. Mitchell (D)	32,064	78.7
	Alonzo P. Baskin (FLA PP)	8,379	20.6
1896	William D. Bloxham (D)	27,171	66.6
	E. R. Gunby (R)	8,290	20.3
	W. A. Wicks (POP)	5,370	13.2
1900	William S. Jennings (D)	29,251	82.0
	M. B. MacFarlane (R)	6,438	18.0
1904	Napoleon B. Broward (D)	28,971	79.2
	M. B. MacFarlane (R)	6,357	17.4
1908	Albert W. Gilchrist (D)	33,036	78.8
	John M. Cheney (R)	6,453	15.4
	A. J. Pettigrew (SOC)	2,427	5.8
1912	Park Trammell (D)	38,377	80.2
	Thomas W. Cox (SOC)	3,467	7.2
	William R. O'Neal (R)	2,646	5.5
1916	Sidney J. Catts (IP)	39,546#	47.7
	W. V. Knott (D)	30,343	36.6
	George W. Allen (R)	10,333	12.5
1920	Cary A. Hardee (D)	103,407	77.9
	George E. Gay (R)	23,788	17.9
1924	John W. Martin (D)	84,181	82.8
	W. O'Neal	17,499	17.2
1928	Doyle E. Carlton (D)	148,455	61.0
	W. J. Howey (R)	95,018	39.0
1932	David Sholtz (D)	186,270	66.6
	W. J. Howey (R)	93,323	33.4
1936	Fred P. Cone (D)	253,638	80.9
	E. E. Callaway (R)	59,832	19.1
1940	Spessard L. Holland (D)	334,152	100.0
1944	Millard F. Caldwell (D)	361,077	78.9
	Bert Lee Acker (R)	96,321	21.1
1948	Fuller Warren (D)	381,459	83.4
	Bert Lee Acker (R)	76,153	16.6
1952	Daniel T. McCarty (D)	624,463	74.8
	Harry S. Swan (R)	210,009	25.2

1954	Leroy Collins (D)	287,769	80.5
	J. Tom Watson (R)	69,852	19.5

1956	Leroy Collins (D)	747,753	73.7
	William A. Washburn Jr. (R)	266,980	26.3

	Candidates	Votes	%
1960	Farris Bryant (D)	849,407	59.9
	George C. Petersen (R)	569,936	40.2
1964	Haydon Burns (D)	933,554	56.1
	Charles R. Holley (R)	686,297	41.3
1966	Claude R. Kirk Jr. (R)	821,190	55.1
	Robert King High (D)	668,233	44.9
1970	Reubin Askew (D)	984,305	56.8
	Claude R. Kirk Jr. (R)	746,243	43.0
1974	Reubin Askew (D)	1,118,954	61.2
	Jerry Thomas (R)	709,438	38.8
1978	Robert Graham (D)	1,406,580	55.6
	Jack M. Eckerd (R)	1,123,888	44.4
1982	Robert Graham (D)	1,739,553	64.7
	L. A. "Skip" Bafalis (R)	949,013	35.3
1986	Bob Martinez (R)	1,847,525	54.6
	Steve Pajcic (D)	1,538,620	45.4
1990	Lawton Chiles (D)	1,995,206	56.5
	Bob Martinez (R)	1,535,068	43.5
1994	Lawton Chiles (D)	2,135,008	50.8
	Jeb Bush (R)	2,071,068	49.2

GEORGIA

(Ratified the Constitution Jan. 2, 1788)

	Candidates	Votes	%
1825[1]	George M. Troup	20,545	50.9
	John Clark	19,857	49.2
1827	John Forsyth	23,174	70.6
1829	George R. Gilmer	27,398	71.5
	Joel Crawford	10,946	28.6
1831	Wilson Lumpkin	27,224	51.7
	George R. Gilmer	25,468	48.3
1833	Wilson Lumpkin	30,868	51.4
	Joel Crawford	29,186	48.6
1835	William Schley (D)	31,190	52.3
	Dougherty (W)	28,497	47.7
1837	George R. Gilmer (W)	✔	
	William Schley (D)		
1839	Charles James McDonald (D)	34,668	51.5
	Dougherty (W)	32,715	48.6
1841	Charles James McDonald (D)	38,514	52.7
	William C. Dawson (W)	34,511	47.3
1843	George Walker Crawford (W)	38,711	52.3
	Mark A. Cooper (D)	35,273	47.7
1845	George Walker Crawford (W)	41,523	51.1
	McAllister (D)	39,753	48.9
1847	George Washington Towns (D)	43,219	50.8
	Clinch (W)	41,941	49.3
1849	George Washington Towns (D)	46,634	51.8
	Hill (W)	43,349	48.2
1851	Howell Cobb (UN)	57,414	59.7
	McDonald (SOR W)	38,824	40.3
1853	Hershel Vespasian Johnson (D)	47,638	50.3
	Jenkins (W)	47,128	49.7
1855	Hershel Vespasian Johnson (D)	54,136	52.1
	Andrews (AM)	43,358	41.8
	Overby (TEMP)	6,333	6.1
1857	Joseph Emerson Brown (D)	57,631	55.1
	Hill (AM)	46,889	44.9
1859	Joseph Emerson Brown (D)	63,806	60.2
	Akin (OPP)	42,195	39.8
1868	Rufus B. Bullock (R)	83,107	52.1
	Gordon (D)	76,539	47.9
1872	James Milton Smith (LR)	104,539	69.2
	Walker (R)	46,475	30.8
1876	Alfred Holt Colquitt (D)	110,624	76.2
	Norcross (R)	34,492	23.8

	Candidates	Votes	%
1880	Alfred Holt Colquitt (D)	117,803	64.9
	Norwood (ID)	63,631	35.1
1882	Alexander H. Stephens (D)	107,649	70.6
	Gartrell (ID)	44,893	29.4
1884	Henry D. McDaniel (D)	✔	
1886	John B. Gordon (D)	101,159	99.2
1888	John B. Gordon (D)	121,999	100.0
1890	William J. Northen (D)	105,365	100.0
1892	William J. Northen (D)	136,543	66.7
	Peck (PP)	68,093	33.3
1894	William Y. Atkinson (D)	121,249	55.6
	J. K. Hines (POP)	96,990	44.4
1896	William Y. Atkinson (D)	123,206	58.9
	Seaborn Wright (POP)	85,981	41.1
1898	Allen D. Candler (D)	118,028	69.8
	Hogan (POP)	51,191	30.3
1900	Allen D. Candler (D)	92,729	78.6
	George W. Trayler (POP)	25,285	21.4
1902	Joseph M. Terrell (D)	81,548	93.6
	Hines (POP)	5,566	6.4
1904	Joseph M. Terrell (D)	67,523	100.0
1906	Hoke Smith (D)	94,223	99.9
1908	Joseph M. Brown (D)	112,292	90.5
	Yancy Carter (I)	11,746	9.5
1910	Hoke Smith (D)	✔	
	Joseph M. Brown		
1912	John M. Slaton (D)	✔	
1914	Nathaniel E. Harris (D)	✔	
1916	Hugh M. Dorsey (D)	✔	
1918	Hugh M. Dorsey (D)	59,536	100.0
1920	Thomas W. Hardwick (D)	✔	
1922	Clifford M. Walker (D)	75,000	100.0
1924	Clifford M. Walker (D)	152,367	100.0
1926	Lamartine G. Hardman (D)	47,300	100.0
1928	Lamartine G. Hardman (D)	✔	
1930	Richard B. Russell (D)	✔	
1932	Eugene Talmadge (D)	240,242	100.0
1934	Eugene Talmadge (D)	53,101	100.0
1936	Eurith D. Rivers (D)	263,140	99.7
1938	Eurith D. Rivers (D)	66,863	94.3
1940	Eugene Talmadge (D, ID)	286,277	99.6
1942	Ellis Arnall (D)	62,220	96.3
1946	Eugene Talmadge (D)	144,067*	99.1
1948	Herman E. Talmadge (D)	354,712	97.5
1950	Herman E. Talmadge (D)	230,771	98.4
1954	S. Marvin Griffin (D)	331,899	100.0
1958	S. Ernest Vandiver (D)	168,414	100.0
1962	Carl E. Sanders (D)	311,524	100.0
1966	Howard H. Callaway (R)	453,665	47.8
	Lester Maddox (D)	450,626†	47.4
1970	Jimmy Carter (D)	620,419	59.3
	Hal Suit (R)	424,983	40.6
1974	George Busbee (D)	646,777	69.1
	Ronnie Thompson (R)	289,113	30.9
1978	George Busbee (D)	534,572	80.6
	Rodney M. Cook (R)	128,139	19.3
1982	Joe Frank Harris (D)	734,090	62.8
	Robert H. Bell (R)	434,496	37.2
1986	Joe Frank Harris (D)	828,465	70.5
	Guy Davis (R)	346,512	29.5
1990	Zell Miller (D)	766,662	52.9
	Johnny Isakson (R)	645,625	44.5
1994	Zell Miller (D)	788,926	51.1
	Guy Millner (R)	756,371	48.9

Georgia
1. *Before 1825 governor chosen by legislature.*

HAWAII

(Became a state Aug. 21, 1959)

	Candidates	Votes	%
1959	William F. Quinn (R)	86,213	51.1
	John A. Burns (D)	82,074	48.7
1962	John A. Burns (D)	114,308	58.3
	William F. Quinn (R)	81,707	41.7
1966	John A. Burns (D)	108,840	51.1
	Randolph Crossley (R)	104,324	48.9
1970	John A. Burns (D)	137,812	57.7
	Sam King (R)	101,249	42.4
1974	George R. Ariyoshi (D)	136,262	54.6
	Randolph Crossley (R)	113,388	45.4
1978	George R. Ariyoshi (D)	153,394	54.5
	John Leopold (R)	124,610	44.3
1982	George R. Ariyoshi (D)	141,043	45.2
	Frank F. Fasi (ID)	89,303	28.6
	D. G. "Andy" Anderson (R)	81,507	26.1
1986	John Waihee (D)	173,655	52.0
	D. G. "Andy" Anderson (R)	160,460	48.0
1990	John Waihee (D)	203,491	59.8
	Fred Hemmings (R)	131,310	38.6
1994	Benjamin J. Cayetano (D)	134,978	36.6
	Frank F. Fasi (BP)	113,158	30.7
	Patricia F. Saiki (R)	107,908	29.2

IDAHO

(Became a state July 3, 1890)

	Candidates	Votes	%
1890	G. L. Shoup (R)	10,262	56.4
	Wilson (D)	7,948	43.7
1892	William J. McConnell (R)	8,178	40.7
	John M. Burke (D)	6,769	33.7
	Abraham J. Crook (PP)	4,865	24.2
1894	William J. McConnell (R)	10,208	41.5
	James W. Ballantine (PP)	7,121	29.0
	Edward A. Stevenson (D)	7,057	28.7
1896	Frank Steunenberg (PP-D-S-R)	22,096	76.8
	David H. Budlong (R)	6,441	22.4
1898	Frank Steunenberg (FUS)	19,407	48.8
	A. B. Moss (R)	13,794	34.7
	J. H. Anderson (PP)	5,371	13.5
1900	Frank W. Hunt (D-FUS)	28,628	52.0
	D. W. Standrod (R)	26,468	48.0
1902	John T. Morrison (R)	31,874	52.9
	Frank W. Hunt (D)	26,021	43.2
1904	Frank R. Gooding (R)	41,877	58.7
	Henry Heitfeld (D)	24,252	34.0
	Theodore B. Shaw (SOC)	4,000	5.6
1906	Frank R. Gooding (R)	38,386	52.2
	Charles O. Stockslager (D)	29,496	40.1
	Thomas F. Kelley (SOC)	4,650	6.3
1908	James H. Brady (R)	47,864	49.6
	Moses Alexander (D)	40,145	41.6
	Ernest Untermann (SOC)	6,155	6.4
1910	James H. Hawley (D)	40,856	47.4
	James H. Brady (R)	39,961	46.4
	S. W. Motley (SOC)	5,342	6.2
1912	John M. Haines (R)	35,074	33.2
	James H. Hawley (D)	33,992	32.2
	G. H. Martin (PROG)	24,325	23.1
	L. A. Coblentz (SOC)	11,094	10.5

ILLINOIS

(Became a state Dec. 3, 1818)

	Candidates	Votes	%
1914	Moses Alexander (D)	47,618	44.1
	John M. Haines (R)	40,349	37.4
	Hugh E. McElroy (EP)	10,583	9.8
	L. A. Coblentz (SOC)	7,967	7.4
1916	Moses Alexander (D)	63,877	47.5
	David W. Davis (R)	63,305	47.1
	Annie E. Triplow (SOC)	7,321	5.4
1918	David W. Davis (R)	57,626	60.0
	H. F. Samuels (D)	38,499	40.1
1920	David W. Davis (R)	75,748	53.0
	Ted A. Walters (D)	38,509	26.9
	Sherman D. Fairchild (I)	28,752	20.1
1922	Charles C. Moore (R)	50,538	39.5
	H. F. Samuels (PROG)	40,516	31.7
	M. Alexander (D)	36,810	28.8
1924	Charles C. Moore (R)	65,408	43.9
	H. F. Samuels (PROG)	58,163	39.0
	A. L. Freehafer (D)	25,081	16.8
1926	H. C. Baldridge (R)	61,575	51.1
	W. Scott Hall (PROG)	34,208	28.4
	Asher B. Wilson (D)	24,837	20.6
1928	H. C. Baldridge (R)	87,681	57.8
	C. Ben Ross (D)	63,046	41.6
1930	C. Ben Ross (D)	73,896	56.0
	John McMurray (R)	58,002	44.0
1932	C. Ben Ross (D)	116,663	61.7
	Defenbach (R)	68,863	36.4
1934	C. Ben Ross (D)	93,313	54.6
	Frank L. Stephan (R)	75,659	44.3
1936	Barzilla W. Clark (D)	115,098	57.2
	Frank L. Stephan (R)	83,430	41.5
1938	C. A. Bottolfsen (R)	106,268	57.3
	C. Ben Ross (D)	77,697	41.9
1940	Chase A. Clark (D)	120,420	50.5
	C. A. Bottolfsen (R)	118,117	49.5
1942	C. A. Bottolfsen (R)	72,260	50.2
	Chase A. Clark (D)	71,826	49.9
1944	Charles C. Gossett (D)	109,527	52.6
	W. H. Detweiler (R)	98,532	47.4
1946	Charles A. Robins (R)	102,233	56.4
	Arnold Williams (D)	79,131	43.6
1950	Len B. Jordan (R)	107,642	52.6
	Calvin E. Wright (D)	97,150	47.4
1954	Robert E. Smylie (R)	124,038	54.2
	Clark Hamilton (D)	104,647	45.8
1958	Robert E. Smylie (R)	121,810	51.0
	A. M. Derr (D)	117,236	49.0
1962	Robert E. Smylie (R)	139,578	54.6
	Vernon K. Smith (D)	115,876	45.4
1966	Don Samuelson (R)	104,586	41.4
	Cecil D. Andrus (D)	93,744	37.1
	Perry Swisher (I)	30,913	12.2
	Philip W. Jungert (I)	23,139	9.2
1970	Cecil D. Andrus (D)	128,004	52.2
	Don Samuelson (R)	117,108	47.8
1974	Cecil D. Andrus (D)	184,142	70.9
	Jack M. Murphy (R)	68,731	26.5
1978	John V. Evans (D)	169,540	58.8
	Allan Larsen (R)	114,149	39.6
1982	John V. Evans (D)	165,365	50.6
	Philip Batt (R)	161,157	49.4
1986	Cecil D. Andrus (D)	193,429	49.9
	David H. Leroy (R)	189,794	49.0
1990	Cecil D. Andrus (D)	218,673	68.2
	Roger Fairchild (R)	101,937	31.8
1994	Phil Batt (R)	216,123	52.3
	Larry EchoHawk (D)	181,363	43.9

	Candidates	Votes	%
1818	Shadrach Bond	3,427	
1822	Edward Coles	2,854	33.2
	Joseph B. Phillips	2,687	31.2
	Thomas C. Browne	2,443	28.4
	James B. Moore	622	7.2
1826	Ninian Edwards (NR)	6,280	49.4
	Thomas Sloo Jr. (JAC D)	5,833	45.9
1830	John Reynolds (NR)	12,837	59.0
	William Kinney (JAC D)	8,938	41.1
1834	Joseph Duncan (W)	17,340	52.9
	William Kinney (D)	10,224	31.2
	Robert H. McLaughlin	4,315	13.2
1838	Thomas Carlin (D)	30,668	50.8
	Cyrus Edwards (W)	29,722	49.2
1842	Thomas Ford (D)	46,502	53.8
	Joseph Duncan (W)	39,030	45.2
1846	Augustus C. French (D)	58,660	58.2
	Thomas M. Kilpatrick (W)	37,033	36.7
	Richard Eels (LIB)	5,154	5.1
1848	Augustus C. French (D)	67,828	86.8
	W. S. D. Morison	5,659	7.2
	Charles V. Dyer	4,692	6.0
1852	Joel A. Matteson (D)	80,789	52.4
	E. B. Webb (W)	64,408	41.8
	D. A. Knowlton (F SOIL)	9,024	5.9
1856	William H. Bissell (R)	111,466	47.0
	William A. Richardson (D)	106,769	45.0
	Buckner S. Morris (AM)	19,078	8.0
1860	Richard Yates (R)	172,218	51.2
	James C. Allen (D)	159,293	47.3
1864	Richard J. Oglesby (UN R)	190,376	54.5
	James C. Robinson (D)	158,711	45.5
1868	John M. Palmer (R)	250,467	55.5
	John R. Eden (D)	200,813	44.5
1872	Richard J. Oglesby (R)	237,777	54.4
	Gust Koener (LR)	197,083	45.1
1876	Shelby M. Cullom (R)	279,263	50.6
	Lewis Steward (D & G)	272,495	49.4
1880	Shelby M. Cullom (R)	314,565	50.4
	Lyman Trumbull (D)	277,562	44.5
1884	Richard J. Oglesby (R)	334,234	49.6
	Carter H. Harrison (D)	319,645	47.5
1888	Joseph W. Fifer (R)	367,856	49.2
	John M. Palmer (D)	355,313	47.5
1892	John P. Altgeld (D)	425,498	48.7
	Joseph W. Fifer (R)	402,666	46.1
1896	John R. Tanner (R)	587,637	54.1
	John P. Altgeld (R)	474,256	43.7
1900	Richard Yates (R)	580,200	51.5
	Samuel Alschuler (D)	518,966	46.1
1904	Charles S. Deneen (R)	634,029	59.1
	Lawrence B. Stringer (D)	334,880	31.2
	John Collins (SOC)	59,062	5.5
1908	Charles S. Deneen (R)	550,076	47.6
	Adlai E. Stevenson (D)	526,912	45.6
1912	Edward F. Dunne (D)	443,120	38.1
	Charles S. Deneen (R)	318,469	27.4
	Frank H. Funk (PROG)	303,401	26.1
	John C. Kennedy (SOC)	78,679	6.8
1916	Frank O. Lowden (R)	696,535	52.7
	Edward F. Dunne (D)	556,654	42.1
1920	Len Small (R)	1,243,148	58.9
	James Hamilton Lewis (D)	731,541	34.6
1924	Len Small (R)	1,366,436	56.7
	Norman L. Jones (D)	1,021,408	42.4
1928	Louis L. Emmerson (R)	1,709,818	56.8
	Floyd E. Thompson (D)	1,284,897	42.7

	Candidates	Votes	%
1932	Henry Horner (D)	1,930,330	57.6
	Len Small (R)	1,364,043	40.7
1936	Henry Horner (D)	2,067,861	53.1
	C. Wayland Brooks (R)	1,682,674	43.2
1940	Dwight H. Green (R)	2,197,778	52.9
	Harry B. Hershey (D)	1,940,833	46.7
1944	Dwight H. Green (R)	2,013,270	50.8
	Thomas J. Courtney (D)	1,940,999	48.9
1948	Adlai E. Stevenson (D)	2,250,074	57.1
	Dwight H. Green (R)	1,678,007	42.6
1952	William G. Stratton (R)	2,317,363	52.5
	Sherwood Dixon (D)	2,089,721	47.3
1956	William G. Stratton (R)	2,171,786	50.3
	Richard B. Austin (D)	2,134,909	49.5
1960	Otto Kerner (D)	2,594,731	55.5
	William G. Stratton (R)	2,070,479	44.3
1964	Otto Kerner (D)	2,418,394	51.9
	Charles H. Percy (R)	2,239,095	48.1
1968	Richard B. Ogilvie (R)	2,307,295	51.2
	Samuel H. Shapiro (D)	2,179,501	48.4
1972	Daniel Walker (D)	2,371,303	50.7
	Richard B. Ogilvie (R)	2,293,809	49.0
1976	James R. Thompson (R)	3,000,395	64.7
	Michael J. Howlett (D)	1,610,258	34.7
1978	James R. Thompson (R)	1,859,684	59.0
	Michael Bakalis (D)	1,263,134	40.1
1982	James R. Thompson (R)	1,816,101	49.4
	Adlai E. Stevenson III (D)	1,811,027	49.3
1986	James R. Thompson (R)	1,655,945	52.7
	Adlai E. Stevenson III (IS)	1,256,725	40.0
	"Democrat" (no candidate)	208,841	6.6
1990	Jim Edgar (R)	1,653,126	50.7
	Neil F. Hartigan (D)	1,569,217	48.2
1994	Jim Edgar (R)	1,984,318	63.9
	Dawn Clark Netsch (D)	1,069,850	34.4

INDIANA

(Became a state Dec. 11, 1816)

	Candidates	Votes	%
1816	Jonathan Jennings	5,211	57.0
	Thomas Posey	3,934	43.0
1819	Jonathan Jennings	9,168	81.4
	Christopher Harrison	2,088	18.6
1822	William Hendricks	Unopposed	
1825	James Brown Ray (CLAY R)	13,852	53.2
	Isaac Blackford (NR)	12,165	46.8
1828	James Brown Ray (CLAY R)	15,131	39.5
	Israel T. Canby (JAC D)	12,251	32.0
	Harbin H. Moore (NR)	10,898	28.5
1831	Noah Noble (NR)	23,518	45.6
	James G. Read (JAC D)	21,002	40.7
	Milton Stapp (I)	6,984	13.5
1834	Noah Noble (W)	36,797	57.4
	James G. Read (D)	27,276	42.6
1837	David Wallace (W)	46,067	55.5
	John Dumont (W)	36,915	44.5
1840	Samuel Bigger (W)	62,970	53.7
	Tilghman A. Howard (D)	54,297	46.3
1843	James Whitcomb (D)	60,930	50.2
	Samuel Bigger (W)	58,809	48.4
1846	James Whitcomb (D)	64,104	50.7
	Joseph G. Marshall (W)	60,138	47.5
1849	Joseph A. Wright (D)	76,996	52.3
	John A. Matson (W)	67,218	45.6
1852	Joseph A. Wright (D)	92,959	54.7
	Nicholas McCarty (W)	73,647	43.3

	Candidates	Votes	%
1856	Ashbel P. Willard (D)	117,981	51.3
	Oliver P. Morton (R)	112,039	48.7
1860	Henry S. Lane (R)	136,725	51.9
	Thomas Andrews Hendricks (D)	126,968	48.2
1864	Oliver P. Morton (R)	152,275	53.7
	Joseph E. McDonald (D)	131,200	46.3
1868	Conrad Baker (R)	171,523	50.1
	Thomas Andrews Hendricks (D)	170,602	49.9
1872	Thomas Andrews Hendricks (D)	189,424	50.1
	Thomas McClelland Browne (R)	188,276	49.8
1876	James Douglas Williams (D)	213,164	49.1
	Benjamin Harrison (R)	208,080	47.9
1880	Albert Gallatin Porter (R)	231,405	49.2
	Franklin Landers (D)	224,452	47.7
1884	Isaac P. Gray (D)	245,130	49.5
	William H. Calkins (R)	237,748	48.0
1888	Alvin P. Hovey (R)	263,194	49.0
	Courtland C. Matson (D)	260,994	48.6
1892	Claude Matthews (D)	260,601	47.5
	Ira J. Chase (R)	253,625	46.2
1896	James A. Mount (R)	320,936	50.9
	Benjamin F. Shively (D)	294,855	46.8
1900	Winfield T. Durbin (R)	331,531	50.5
	John W. Kern (D)	306,368	46.7
1904	J. Frank Hanly (R)	359,362	53.5
	John W. Kern (D)	274,998	41.0
1908	Thomas R. Marshall (D)	348,843	49.0
	James E. Watson (R)	334,040	46.9
1912	Samuel M. Ralston (D)	275,357	43.0
	Albert J. Beveridge (PROG)	166,654	26.0
	Winfield T. Durbin (R)	141,684	22.1
	Stephen N. Reynolds (SOC)	35,464	5.5
1916	James P. Goodrich (R)	337,831	47.8
	John A. M. Adair (D)	325,060	46.0
1920	Warren T. McCray (R)	683,253	54.6
	Carleton B. McCulloch (D)	515,253	41.2
1924	Ed Jackson (R)	654,184	52.9
	Carleton B. McCulloch (D)	572,303	46.3
1928	Harry G. Leslie (R)	728,203	51.3
	Frank C. Dailey (D)	683,545	48.1
1932	Paul V. McNutt (D)	862,127	55.0
	Raymond S. Springer (R)	669,797	42.8
1936	Maurice Clifford Townsend (D)	908,494	55.4
	Raymond S. Springer (R)	727,526	44.3
1940	Henry F. Schricker (D)	889,620	49.9
	Glenn R. Hillis (R)	885,657	49.7
1944	Ralph F. Gates (R)	849,346	51.0
	Samuel D. Jackson (D)	802,765	48.2
1948	Henry F. Schricker (D)	884,995	53.6
	Hobart Creighton (R)	745,892	45.1
1952	George N. Craig (R)	1,075,685	55.7
	John A. Watkins (D)	841,984	43.6
1956	Harold W. Handley (R)	1,086,868	55.6
	Ralph Tucker (D)	859,393	44.0
1960	Matthew E. Welsh (D)	1,072,717	50.4
	Crawford F. Parker (R)	1,049,540	49.3
1964	Roger D. Branigin (D)	1,164,763	56.2
	Richard O. Ristine (R)	901,342	43.5
1968	Edgar D. Whitcomb (R)	1,080,271	52.7
	Robert L. Rock (D)	965,816	47.1
1972	Otis R. Bowen (R)	1,203,903	56.8
	Matthew E. Welsh (D)	900,489	42.5
1976	Otis R. Bowen (R)	1,236,555	56.8
	Larry A. Conrad (D)	927,243	42.6
1980	Robert D. Orr (R)	1,257,383	57.7
	John A. Hillenbrand (D)	913,116	41.9
1984	Robert D. Orr (R)	1,146,497	52.2
	W. Wayne Townsend (D)	1,036,832	47.2
1988	Evan Bayh (D)	1,138,574	53.2
	John M. Mutz (R)	1,002,207	46.8

	Candidates	Votes	%
1992	Evan Bayh (D)	1,382,151	62.0
	Linley E. Pearson (R)	822,533	36.9
1996	Frank L. O'Bannon (D)	1,087,128	51.5
	Stephen Goldsmith (R)	986,982	46.8

IOWA

(Became a state Dec. 28, 1846)

	Candidates	Votes	%
1846	Ansel Briggs (ER)	7,626	50.8
	Thomas McKnight (W)	7,379	49.2
1850	Stephen Hempstead (D)	13,486	52.9
	James L. Thompson (W)	11,403	44.8
1854	James W. Grimes (R)	23,325	52.4
	Curtis Bates (NEB)	21,202	47.6
1857	Ralph P. Lowe (R)	38,498	50.9
	Ben M. Samuels (D)	36,088	47.7
1859	Samuel J. Kirkwood (R)	56,502	51.4
	A. C. Dodge (D)	53,332	48.6
1861	Samuel J. Kirkwood (R)	60,303	55.5
	William H. Merritt (D)	43,245	39.8
1863	William M. Stone (UN)	86,118	60.5
	James M. Tuttle (D)	56,169	39.5
1865	William M. Stone (UN R)	70,461	56.4
	Thomas H. Benton (D)	54,090	43.3
1867	Samuel Merrill (R)	90,204	58.9
	Charles Mason (D)	62,966	41.1
1869	Samuel Merrill (R)	97,243	62.9
	George Gillaspie (D)	57,287	37.1
1871	Cyrus Clay Carpenter (R)	109,328	61.6
	J. C. Knapp (D)	68,199	38.4
1873	Cyrus Clay Carpenter (R)	105,132	56.0
	J. G. Vale (A-MONOP)	82,556	44.0
1875	Samuel Jordan Kirkwood (R)	124,855	57.0
	Shepherd Leffler (D)	93,270	42.6
1877	John Henry Gear (R)	121,316	49.4
	John P. Irish (D)	79,304	32.3
	Daniel P. Stubbs (G)	34,316	14.0
1879	John Henry Gear (R)	157,408	53.9
	Henry H. Trimble (D)	85,364	29.3
	Daniel Campbell (G)	45,674	15.7
1881	Buren R. Sherman (R)	133,328	56.7
	L. G. Kinne (D)	73,344	31.2
	D. M. Clark (G)	28,112	12.0
1883	Buren R. Sherman (R)	164,095	50.1
	L. G. Kinne (D)	140,012	42.8
	James B. Weaver (G)	23,089	7.1
1885	William Larrabee (R)	175,605	50.8
	Charles Whiting (D)	168,584	48.7
1887	William Larrabee (R)	169,596	50.1
	T. J. Anderson (D)	153,706	45.4
1889	Horace Boies (D)	180,106	49.9
	Joseph Hutchinson (R)	173,450	48.1
1891	Horace Boies (D)	207,594	49.4
	Herman C. Wheeler (R)	199,381	47.5
1893	Frank D. Jackson (R)	206,821	49.7
	Horace Boies (D)	174,656	42.0
	J. M. Joseph (PP)	23,980	5.8
1895	Francis M. Drake (R)	208,708	52.0
	W. I. Babb (D)	149,428	37.2
	S. B. Crane (PP)	32,189	8.0
1897	Leslie M. Shaw (R)	224,729	51.3
	Fred E. White (D)	194,853	44.5
1899	Leslie M. Shaw (R)	239,464	55.3
	Fred E. White (D)	183,301	42.3
1901	Albert B. Cummins (R)	226,902	58.1
	T. J. Phillips (D)	143,783	36.8

	Candidates	Votes	%
1903	Albert B. Cummins (R)	238,804	57.1
	J. B. Sullivan (D)	159,725	38.2
1906	Albert B. Cummins (R)	216,995	50.2
	Claude R. Porter (D)	196,123	45.4
1908	Beryl F. Carroll (R)	256,980	54.6
	Fred E. White (D)	196,929	41.8
1910	Beryl F. Carroll (R)	205,678	49.8
	Claude R. Porter (D)	187,353	45.4
1912	George W. Clarke (R)	184,150	39.9
	Edward G. Dunn (D)	182,449	39.6
	John L. Stevens (PROG)	71,879	15.6
1914	George W. Clarke (R)	207,881	49.3
	John T. Hamilton (D)	181,036	42.9
1916	William L. Harding (R)	313,586	61.0
	E. T. Meredith (D)	186,832	36.4
1918	William L. Harding (R)	192,662	50.6
	Claude R. Porter (D)	178,815	46.9
1920	Nathan E. Kendall (R)	513,118	58.7
	Clyde L. Herring (D)	338,108	38.7
1922	Nathan E. Kendall (R)	419,648	70.5
	J. R. Files (D)	175,252	29.5
1924	John Hammill (R)	604,624	72.7
	J. C. Murtagh (D)	226,850	27.3
1926	John Hammill (R)	377,330	71.3
	Alex R. Miller (D)	150,374	28.4
1928	John Hammill (R)	591,720	62.8
	L. W. Housel (D)	350,722	37.2
1930	Dan W. Turner (R)	364,036	65.7
	Fred P. Hageman (D)	186,039	33.6
1932	Clyde L. Herring (D)	508,573	52.8
	Dan W. Turner (R)	455,145	47.2
1934	Clyde L. Herring (D)	468,921	54.3
	Dan W. Turner (R)	394,634	45.7
1936	Nelson G. Kraschel (D)	524,178	48.7
	George Wilson (R)	521,747	48.4
1938	George Wilson (R)	447,061	52.7
	Nelson G. Kraschel (D)	387,779	45.7
1940	George Wilson (R)	620,480	52.7
	John Valentine (D)	553,941	47.1
1942	Bourke B. Hickenlooper (R)	438,547	62.8
	Nelson G. Kraschel (D)	258,310	37.0
1944	Robert D. Blue (R)	561,827	56.0
	R. F. Mitchell (D)	437,684	43.6
1946	Robert D. Blue (R)	362,592	57.4
	Frank Miles (D)	266,190	42.1
1948	William Beardsley (R)	553,900	55.7
	Carroll O. Switzer (D)	434,432	43.7
1950	William Beardsley (R)	506,642	59.1
	Lester S. Gillette (D)	347,176	40.5
1952	William Beardsley (R)	638,388	51.9
	Herschel C. Loveless (D)	587,671	47.8
1954	Leo A. Hoegh (R)	435,944	51.4
	Clyde E. Herring (D)	410,255	48.4
1956	Herschel C. Loveless (D)	616,852	51.2
	Leo A. Hoegh (R)	587,383	48.8
1958	Herschel C. Loveless (D)	465,024	54.1
	William G. Murray (R)	394,071	45.9
1960	Norman A. Erbe (R)	645,026	52.1
	E. J. McManus (D)	592,063	47.9
1962	Harold E. Hughes (D)	430,899	52.6
	Norman A. Erbe (R)	388,955	47.4
1964	Harold E. Hughes (D)	794,610	68.1
	Evan Hultman (R)	365,131	31.3
1966	Harold E. Hughes (D)	494,259	55.3
	William G. Murray (R)	394,518	44.2
1968	Robert D. Ray (R)	614,328	54.1
	Paul Franzenburg (D)	521,216	45.9
1970	Robert D. Ray (R)	403,394	51.0
	Robert D. Fulton (D)	368,911	46.6
1972	Robert D. Ray (R)	707,177	58.4
	Paul Franzenburg (D)	487,282	40.3

	Candidates	Votes	%
1974	Robert D. Ray (R)	534,518	58.1
	James F. Schaben (D)	377,553	41.0
1978	Robert D. Ray (R)	491,713	58.3
	Jerome D. Fitzgerald (D)	345,519	41.0
1982	Terry E. Branstad (R)	548,313	52.8
	Roxanne Conlin (D)	483,291	46.5
1986	Terry E. Branstad (R)	472,712	51.9
	Lowell L. Junkins (D)	436,987	48.0
1990	Terry E. Branstad (R)	591,852	60.6
	Donald D. Avenson (D)	379,372	38.9
1994	Terry E. Branstad (R)	566,395	56.8
	Bonnie J. Campbell (D)	414,453	41.6

KANSAS

(Became a state Jan. 29, 1861)

	Candidates	Votes	%
1862	Thomas Carney (R)	9,990	64.7
	W. R. Wagstaff (UN R)	5,456	35.3
1864	Samuel J. Crawford (R)	12,711	60.7
	Solon O. Thacher (R-UNION)	8,244	39.3
1866	Samuel J. Crawford (R)	19,370	70.4
	J. L. McDowell (N UNION)	8,151	29.6
1868	James M. Harvey (R)	29,795	68.2
	George W. Glick (D)	13,881	31.8
1870	James M. Harvey (R)	40,667	66.4
	Isaac Sharp (D)	20,496	33.5
1872	Thomas A. Osborn (R)	66,715	65.8
	Thaddeus H. Walker (LR)	34,698	34.2
1874	Thomas A. Osborn (R)	48,794	56.4
	James C. Cusey (D)	35,301	40.8
1876	George T. Anthony (R)	69,176	56.8
	John Martin (D)	46,201	37.9
1878	John P. St. John (R)	74,020	53.5
	John R. Goodin (D)	37,208	26.9
	D. P. Mitchell (G)	27,057	19.6
1880	John P. St. John (R)	115,144	57.9
	Edmund G. Ross (D)	63,557	32.0
	H. P. Vrooman (G LAB)	19,481	9.8
1882	George W. Glick (D)	83,232	46.4
	John P. St. John (R)	75,158	41.9
	Charles Robinson (G LAB)	20,933	11.7
1884	John A. Martin (R)	146,777	55.3
	George W. Glick (D)	108,284	40.8
1886	John A. Martin (R)	149,715	54.7
	Thomas Moonlight (D)	115,667	42.3
1888	L. U. Humphrey (R)	180,841	54.7
	John Martin (D)	107,582	32.5
	P. P. Elder (UN LAB)	35,847	10.8
1890	L. U. Humphrey (R)	115,024	39.1
	J. F. Willits (ALNC D)	106,945	36.3
	Charles Robinson (D & RESUB)	71,357	24.2
1892	L. D. Lewelling (POP)	162,507	50.0
	Abram W. Smith (R)	158,075	48.7
1894	E. N. Morrill (R)	148,700	49.5
	L. D. Lewelling (D-PP)	118,329	39.4
	David Overmyer (STAL D)	27,709	9.2
1896	John W. Leedy (D-PP)	167,941	50.5
	E. N. Morrill (R)	160,507	48.3
1898	W. E. Stanley (R)	149,312	51.8
	John W. Leedy (D-PP)	134,158	46.6
1900	W. E. Stanley (R)	181,897	51.9
	John W. Breidenthal (D-PP)	164,793	47.0
1902	W. J. Bailey (R)	159,242	55.5
	W. H. Craddock (D)	117,148	40.8
1904	Edward W. Hoch (R)	186,731	57.9
	David M. Dale (D)	116,991	36.3

	Candidates	Votes	%
1906	Edward W. Hoch (R)	152,147	48.2
	William A. Harris (D)	150,024	47.6
1908	W. R. Stubbs (R)	196,692	52.5
	Jeremiah D. Botkin (D)	162,385	43.3
1910	W. R. Stubbs (R)	162,181	49.8
	George H. Hodges (D)	146,014	44.8
1912	George H. Hodges (D)	167,437	46.6
	Arthur Capper (R)	167,408	46.5
	George W. Kleihege (SOC)	24,767	6.9
1914	Arthur Capper (R)	209,543	39.7
	George H. Hodges (D)	161,696	30.6
	Henry J. Allen (PROG)	84,060	15.9
	J. B. Billard (I)	47,201	8.9
1916	Arthur Capper (R)	353,169	60.8
	W. C. Lansdon (D)	192,037	33.1
1918	Henry J. Allen (R)	287,957	66.4
	W. C. Lansdon (D)	133,054	30.7
1920	Henry J. Allen (R)	319,914	58.4
	Jonathan M. Davis (D)	214,940	39.3
1922	Jonathan M. Davis (D)	271,058	50.9
	W. Y. Morgan (R)	252,602	47.4
1924	Ben S. Paulen (R)	323,402	49.0
	Jonathan M. Davis (D)	182,861	27.7
	William Allen White (I)	149,811	22.7
1926	Ben S. Paulen (R)	321,540	63.3
	Jonathan M. Davis (D)	179,308	35.3
1928	Clyde M. Reed (R)	433,395	65.6
	Chauncey B. Little (D)	219,327	33.2
1930	Harry H. Woodring (D)	217,171	35.0
	Frank Haucke (R)	216,920	34.9
	John R. Brinkley (I)	183,278	29.5
1932	Alfred M. Landon (R)	278,581	34.8
	Harry H. Woodring (D)	272,944	34.1
	John R. Brinkley (I)	244,607	30.6
1934	Alfred M. Landon (R)	422,030	53.5
	Omar B. Ketchum (D)	359,877	45.6
1936	Walter A. Huxman (D)	433,319	51.1
	Will G. West (R)	411,446	48.5
1938	Payne Ratner (R)	393,989	52.1
	Walter A. Huxman (D)	341,271	45.1
1940	Payne Ratner (R)	425,928	49.6
	William H. Burke (D)	425,498	49.6
1942	Andrew F. Schoeppel (R)	287,895	56.7
	William H. Burke (D)	212,071	41.8
1944	Andrew F. Schoeppel (R)	463,110	65.7
	Robert S. Lemon (D)	231,410	32.8
1946	Frank Carlson (R)	309,064	53.5
	Harry H. Woodring (D)	254,283	44.0
1948	Frank Carlson (R)	433,396	57.0
	Randolph Carpenter (D)	307,485	40.4
1950	Edward F. Arn (R)	333,001	53.8
	Kenneth T. Anderson (D)	275,494	44.5
1952	Edward F. Arn (R)	491,338	56.3
	Charles Rooney (D)	363,482	41.7
1954	Fred Hall (R)	329,868	53.0
	George Docking (D)	286,218	46.0
1956	George Docking (D)	479,701	55.5
	Warren W. Shaw (R)	364,340	42.1
1958	George Docking (D)	415,506	56.5
	Clyde M. Reed (R)	313,036	42.5
1960	John Anderson Jr. (R)	511,534	55.5
	George Docking (D)	402,261	43.6
1962	John Anderson Jr. (R)	341,257	53.4
	Dale E. Saffels (D)	291,285	45.6
1964	William H. Avery (R)	432,667	50.9
	Harry G. Wiles (D)	400,264	47.1
1966	Robert Docking (D)	380,030	54.8
	William H. Avery (R)	304,325	43.9
1968	Robert Docking (D)	447,269	51.9
	Rick Harman (R)	410,673	47.6

	Candidates	Votes	%
1970	Robert Docking (D)	404,611	*54.3*
	Kent Frizzell (R)	333,227	*44.7*
1972	Robert Docking (D)	571,256	*62.0*
	Morris Kay (R)	341,440	*37.1*
1974	Robert F. Bennett (R)	387,792	*49.5*
	Vern Miller (D)	384,115	*49.0*
1978	John Carlin (D)	363,835	*49.4*
	Robert F. Bennett (R)	348,015	*47.3*
1982	John Carlin (D)	405,772	*53.2*
	Sam Hardage (R)	339,356	*44.5*
1986	Mike Hayden (R)	436,267	*51.9*
	Tom Docking (D)	404,338	*48.1*
1990	Joan Finney (D)	380,609	*48.6*
	Mike Hayden (R)	333,589	*42.6*
	Christina Campbell-Cline (I)	69,127	*8.8*
1994	Bill Graves (R)	526,113	*64.1*
	Jim Slattery (D)	294,733	*35.9*

KENTUCKY

(Became a state June 1, 1792)

	Candidates	Votes	%
1800[1]	James Garrard	8,390	*39.4*
	Christopher Greenup	6,745	*31.7*
	Benjamin Logan	3,995	*18.8*
	Thomas Todd	2,166	*10.2*
1804	Christopher Greenup	25,917	
1808	Charles Scott	22,050	*61.3*
	John Allen	8,430	*23.4*
	Green Clay	5,516	*15.3*
1812	Isaac Shelby	30,362	*70.9*
	Gabriel Slaughter	12,464	*29.1*
1816	George Madison	Unopposed	
1820	John Adair	20,493	*32.8*
	William Logan	19,947	*32.0*
	Joseph Desha	12,419	*19.9*
	Anthony Butler	9,567	*15.3*
1824	Joseph Desha	38,463	*59.5*
	Christopher Tompkins	22,300	*34.5*
	William Russell	3,899	*6.0*
1828	Thomas Metcalfe (NR)	38,940	*50.5*
	William T. Barry (D)	38,231	*49.5*
1832	John Breathitt (D)	40,780	*50.9*
	Buck (NR)	39,269	*49.1*
1836	James Clark (W)	38,591	*55.8*
	M. Flournoy (D)	30,576	*44.2*
1840	Robert P. Letcher (W)	54,892	*58.4*
	French (D)	39,160	*41.6*
1844	William Owsley (W)	59,792	*52.1*
	Butler (D)	55,089	*48.0*
1848	John J. Crittenden (W)	64,982	*53.4*
	Lazarus W. Powell (D)	56,675	*46.6*
1851	Lazarus W. Powell (D)	54,821	*48.8*
	Archibald Dixon (W)	54,023	*48.1*
1855	Charles S. Morehead (AM)	69,870	*51.6*
	Clark (D)	65,570	*48.4*
1859	Beriah Magoffin (D)	76,631	*53.2*
	Joshua F. Bell (OPP)	67,504	*46.8*
1863	Thomas E. Branlette (UN)	68,422	*79.6*
	Charles A. Wickliffe (D)	17,503	*20.4*
1867	John Larue Helm (D)	90,216	*65.7*
	Sidney M. Barnes (R)	33,939	*24.7*
	William B. Kinkead (C)	13,167	*9.6*

	Candidates	Votes	%
1868	John W. Stevenson (D)	115,520	*81.3*
	R. Tarvin Baker (R)	26,610	*18.7*

	Candidates	Votes	%
1871	Preston H. Leslie (D)	126,445	*58.6*
	George M. Thomas (R)	89,298	*41.4*
1875	James B. McCreary (D)	126,976	*58.3*
	John M. Harlan (R)	90,795	*41.7*
1879	Luke P. Blackburn (D)	125,399	*55.4*
	Walter Evans (R)	81,881	*36.2*
	C. W. Cook (G)	18,954	*8.4*
1883	J. Procter Knott (D)	133,615	*60.0*
	Thomas Z. Morrow (R)	89,181	*40.0*
1887	Simon B. Buckner (D)	143,466	*50.7*
	William O. Bradley (R)	126,754	*44.8*
1891	John Young Brown (D)	144,168	*49.9*
	Andrew T. Wood (R)	116,087	*40.1*
	S. B. Erwin (POP)	25,631	*8.9*
1895	William O. Bradley (R)	172,436	*48.3*
	Hardin (D)	163,524	*45.8*
1899	William S. Taylor (R)	193,727‡	*48.1*
	William Goebel (D)	191,331	*47.5*

	Candidates	Votes	%
1900	John C. W. Beckham (D)	233,197	*49.9*
	John W. Yerkes (R)	229,468	*49.1*
1903	John C. W. Beckham (D)	229,014	*52.1*
	Belknap (R)	202,862	*46.2*
1907	August E. Willson (R)	214,478	*51.2*
	Hager (D)	196,428	*46.9*
1911	James B. McCreary (D)	226,549	*53.7*
	E. C. Orear (R)	195,672	*46.3*
1915	Augustus Owsley Stanley (D)	219,991	*49.1*
	Edwin P. Morrow (R)	219,520	*49.0*
1919	Edwin P. Morrow (R)	254,472	*53.8*
	J. D. Black (D)	214,134	*45.3*
1923	William J. Fields (D)	356,045	*53.3*
	Charles I. Dawson (R)	306,277	*45.8*
1927	Flem D. Sampson (R)	399,698	*52.1*
	John C. W. Beckham (D)	367,576	*47.9*
1931	Ruby Lafoon (D)	438,513	*54.3*
	William B. Harrison (R)	366,982	*45.4*
1935	Albert B. "Happy" Chandler (D)	556,262	*54.5*
	King Swope (R)	461,104	*45.1*
1939	Keen Johnson (D)	460,834	*56.5*
	King Swope (R)	354,704	*43.5*
1943	Simeon S. Willis (R)	279,144	*50.5*
	J. Lyter Donaldson (D)	270,525	*48.9*
1947	Earle C. Clements (D)	387,795	*57.2*
	Eldon S. Dummit (R)	287,756	*42.5*
1951	Lawrence W. Wetherby (D)	346,345	*54.6*
	Eugene Siler (R)	288,014	*45.4*
1955	Albert B. "Happy" Chandler (D)	451,647	*58.0*
	Edwin R. Denney (R)	322,671	*41.5*
1959	Bert T. Combs (D)	516,549	*60.6*
	John M. Robsion (R)	336,456	*39.4*
1963	Edward T. Breathitt (D)	449,551	*50.7*
	Louie B. Nunn (R)	436,496	*49.3*
1967	Louie B. Nunn (R)	454,123	*51.2*
	Henry Ward (D)	425,674	*48.0*
1971	Wendell H. Ford (D)	470,720	*50.6*
	Tom Emberton (R)	412,653	*44.3*
1975	Julian Carroll (D)	470,159	*62.8*
	Robert E. Gable (R)	277,998	*37.2*
1979	John Y. Brown Jr. (D)	558,088	*59.4*
	Louie B. Nunn (R)	381,278	*40.6*
1983	Martha Layne Collins (D)	561,674	*54.6*
	Jim Bunning (R)	454,650	*44.2*
1987	Wallace G. Wilkinson (D)	504,367	*64.9*
	John Harper (R)	273,035	*35.1*
1991	Brereton Jones (D)	540,468	*64.7*
	Larry J. Hopkins (R)	294,452	*35.3*

	Candidates	Votes	%
1995	Paul E. Patton (D)	500,787	50.9
	Larry E. Forgy (R)	479,227	48.7

Kentucky

1. *Governors were chosen by a specially elected body of electors in 1792 and 1796.*

LOUISIANA

(Became a state April 30, 1812)

	Candidates	Votes	%
1812[1]	W. C. C. Claiborne (AM FAC)[2]	2,757	71.2
	Jacques Villeré (CREOLE)	946	24.4
1816[1]	Jacques Villeré (CREOLE)	2,314	51.9
	Joshua Lewis (AM FAC)[2]	2,145	48.1
1820[1]	Thomas B. Robertson (AM FAC)[2]	1,903	40.1
	Pierre Derbigny (CREOLE)	1,187	25.0
	A. L. Duncan (AM FAC)[2]	1,031	21.7
	Jean Noel Destrehan (CREOLE)	627	13.2
1824[1]	Henry Johnson (AM FAC)[2]	2,649	44.9
	Jacques Villeré (CREOLE)	1,773	30.0
	Bernard Marigny (CREOLE)	1,484	25.1
1828[1]	Pierre Derbigny (NR)	3,253	44.2
	Thomas Butler (JAC D)	1,629	22.1
	Bernard Marigny (JAC D)	1,291	17.5
	Philemon Thomas (NR)	1,194	16.2
1831[1]	Andre B. Roman (NR)	3,630	43.6
	W. S. Hamilton (JAC D)	2,730	32.8
	Arnaud Beauvais (NR)	1,502	18.1
	David Randall (JAC D)	456	5.5
1834[1]	Edward D. White (W)	6,018	57.6
	Dawson (D)	4,438	42.4
1838[1]	Andre B. Roman (W)	7,588	52.8
	Prieur (D)	6,776	47.2
1842[1]	Alexander Mouton (D)	9,716	54.2
	Henry Johnson (W)	8,204	45.8
1846	Isaac Johnson (D)	13,353	53.2
	Debuys (W)	11,101	44.2
1849	Joseph Walker (D)	18,459	51.5
	Declouet (W)	17,407	48.5
1852	Paul O. Hebert (D)	17,529	53.0
	Louis Bordelon (W)	15,532	47.0
1855	Robert C. Wickliffe (D)	22,382	53.6
	Derbigny (AM)	19,417	46.5
1859	Thomas O. Moore (D)	25,434	62.0
	Wells (OPP)	15,587	38.0
1864	Henry W. Allen	7,497	87.5
	Stafford	807	9.4
1865	James Madison Wells (D)	22,532	78.2
	Henry W. Allen	6,297	21.8
1868	Henry C. Warmoth (R)	64,271	62.8
	James G. Taliaferro (D)	38,118	37.2
1872	William Pitt Kellogg (R)	72,890‡	57.4
	John McEnery (D)	54,079	42.6
1876	Francis T. Nicholls (D)	84,487‡	52.5
	Stephen B. Packard (R)	76,476	47.5
1879	Louis A. Wiltz (D)	73,623	64.6
	Taylor Beattie (R)	40,415	35.4
1884	Samuel D. McEnery (D)	88,780	67.1
	John A. Stevenson (R)	43,502	32.9
1888	Francis T. Nicholls (D)	136,747	72.5
	Henry C. Warmoth (R)	51,993	27.6
1892	Murphy J. Foster (A-LOT D)	79,407	44.5
	Samuel D. McEnery (D)	47,046	26.4
	A. H. Leonard (R)	29,648	16.6
	John E. Breaux (IR)	12,409	7.0
	R. H. Tannehill (POP)	9,792	5.5

	Candidates	Votes	%
1896	Murphy J. Foster (D)	116,116	56.9
	John N. Pharr (R POP FU)	87,698	43.0
1900	William Wright Heard (D)	60,206	78.3
	Don Caffery Jr. (R FUS, PP)	14,215	18.5
1904	Newton C. Blanchard (D)	47,745	89.0
	W. J. Behan (R)	5,877	11.0
1908	Jared Y. Sanders (D)	60,066	87.1
	Henry N. Pharr (R)	7,617	11.1
1912	Luther E. Hall (D)	50,581	89.5
	H. S. Suthon (R)	4,961	8.8
1916	Ruffin G. Pleasant (D)	80,807	62.5
	John M. Parker (PROG)	48,085	37.2
1920	John M. Parker (D)	53,792#	97.6
1924	Henry L. Fuqua (D)	66,203	97.9
1928	Huey P. Long (D)	92,941	96.1
1932	Oscar K. Allen (D)	110,193	100.0
1936	Richard W. Leche (D)	131,999	100.0
1940	Sam H. Jones (D)	225,840	99.4
1944	Jimmie H. Davis (D)	51,604	100.0
1948	Earl K. Long (D)	76,566	100.0
1952	Robert F. Kennon (D)	118,723	96.0
1956	Earl K. Long (D)	172,291	100.0
1960	Jimmie H. Davis (D)	407,907	80.5
	F. C. Grevemberg (R)	86,135	17.0
1964	John J. McKeithen (D)	469,589	60.7
	Charlton H. Lyons Sr. (R)	297,753	38.5
1968	John J. McKeithen (D)	372,762	100.0
1972	Edwin W. Edwards (D)	641,146	57.2
	David C. Treen (R)	480,424	42.8
1975	Edwin W. Edwards (D)	430,095	100.0
1979	David C. Treen (R)	690,691	50.3
	Louis Lambert (D)	681,134	49.7
1983	Edwin W. Edwards (D)	1,008,282	62.4
	David C. Treen (R)	586,643	36.3
1991[3]	Edwin W. Edwards (D)	1,057,031	61.2
	David Duke (R)	671,009	38.8
1995	M. J. "Mike" Foster (R)	984,499	63.5
	Cleo Fields (D)	565,861	36.5

Louisiana

1. *Until 1845 the governor was elected by joint vote of the two houses of the legislature, which could choose one of the two who received the most popular votes. In all nine elections under this system the candidate receiving a popular plurality was subsequently chosen by the legislature. Thereafter elections were determined by a plurality of the popular vote.*

2. *Until 1828, contests were essentially between candidates supported by the "American" and "Creole" factions of the Jeffersonian Republican party.*

3. *The 1987 election was decided in the all-party primary unique to Louisiana. The candidate who finished second withdrew. See p. 116.*

MAINE

(Became a state March 15, 1820)

	Candidates	Votes	%
1820	William King (D-R)	21,083	95.3
1821	Albion K. Parris (D-R)	12,887	52.8
	Ezekiel Whitman (FED)	6,811	27.9
	Joshua Wingate Jr. (D-R)	3,879	15.9
1822	Albion K. Parris (D-R)	15,476	69.8
	Ezekiel Whitman (FED)	5,795	26.1
1823	Albion K. Parris (D-R)	18,550	95.6
1824	Albion K. Parris (D-R)	19,759	96.8
1825	Albion K. Parris (D-R)	14,206	93.1
1826	Enoch Lincoln (D-R)	20,689	98.2
1827	Enoch Lincoln (D-R)	19,969	97.6
1828	Enoch Lincoln (D-R)	25,755	91.6
1829	Jonathan G. Hunton (NR)	23,315	50.1
	Smith (JAC D)	22,991	49.4

	Candidates	Votes	%
1830	Samuel E. Smith (JAC D)	30,215	*51.1*
	Jonathan G. Hunton (NR)	28,639	*48.5*
1831	Samuel E. Smith (D)	28,292	*56.3*
	Daniel Goodenow (NR)	21,821	*43.5*
1832	Samuel E. Smith (D)	31,987	*52.8*
	Daniel Goodenow (NR)	27,651	*45.6*
1833	Robert P. Dunlap (D)	25,731	*52.1*
	Daniel Goodenow (W)	18,112	*36.7*
	Samuel E. Smith (DISS D)	3,024	*6.1*
1834	Robert P. Dunlap (D)	38,133	*52.1*
	Peleg Sprague (W)	33,912	*46.3*
1835	Robert P. Dunlap (D)	27,733	*61.4*
	William King (W)	16,860	*37.3*
1836	Robert P. Dunlap (D)	31,837	*58.2*
	Edward Kent (W)	22,703	*41.5*
1837	Edward Kent (W)	34,358	*50.1*
	Gorham Parks (D)	33,879	*49.4*
1838	John Fairfield (D)	46,216	*51.6*
	Edward Kent (W)	42,897	*47.9*
1839	John Fairfield (D)	40,768	*53.8*
	Edward Kent (W)	34,749	*45.9*
1840	Edward Kent (W)	45,574†	*50.0*
	John Fairfield (D)	45,507	*49.9*
1841	John Fairfield (D)	47,354	*55.0*
	Edward Kent (W)	36,780	*42.7*
1842	John Fairfield (D)	40,855	*56.9*
	Edward Robinson (W)	26,745	*37.3*
	James Appleton	4,080	*5.7*
1843	Hugh J. Anderson (D)	27,631	*55.4*
	Edward Robinson (W)	17,244	*34.6*
	James Appleton (LIB & SC)	4,962	*10.0*
1844	Hugh J. Anderson (D)	40,540	*51.1*
	Edward Robinson (W)	33,342	*42.0*
	James Appleton (LIB & SC)	5,527	*7.0*
1845	Hugh J. Anderson (D)	31,353	*50.7*
	Freeman H. Morse (W)	24,880	*40.2*
1846	John W. Dana (D)	33,805†	*46.9*
	David Bronson (W)	28,986	*40.2*
	Samuel Fessenden (LIB & SC)	9,343	*13.0*
1847	John W. Dana (D)	33,461	*51.3*
	David Bronson (W)	24,304	*37.2*
	Samuel Fessenden (LIB & SC)	7,517	*11.5*
1848	John W. Dana (D)	37,310†	*47.0*
	Elijah L. Hamlin (W)	30,026	*37.9*
	Samuel Fessenden (F SOIL)	11,978	*15.1*
1849	John Hubbard (D)	37,534	*50.9*
	Elijah L. Hamlin (W)	28,260	*38.3*
	George F. Talbot (FS & SC)	8,025	*10.9*
1850	John Hubbard (D)	41,220	*51.0*
	William G. Crosby (W)	32,308	*40.0*
	George F. Talbot (F SOIL)	7,271	*9.0*
1852	John Hubbard (D)	41,616†	*44.3*
	William G. Crosby (W)	29,129	*31.0*
	Anson G. Chandler (A-MAINE)	21,589	*23.0*
1853	Albert Pillsbury (D)	36,127	*43.3*
	William G. Crosby (W)	27,259†	*32.7*
	Anson P. Morrill (WILDCAT)	11,012	*13.2*
	Ezekiel Holmes (FS & SC)	9,039	*10.8*
1854	Anson P. Morrill (R)	44,817†	*49.5*
	Albion K. Parris (D)	28,285	*31.2*
	Isaac Reed (W)	14,014	*15.5*
1855	Anson P. Morrill (R)	51,488	*46.6*
	Samuel Wells (D)	48,367†	*43.8*
	Isaac Reed (W)	10,645	*9.6*
1856	Hannibal Hamlin (R)	69,444	*57.4*
	Samuel Wells (D)	44,912	*37.1*
	George F. Patten (W)	6,664	*5.5*
1857	Lot M. Morrill (R)	54,283	*56.0*
	Manassah H. Smith (D)	42,647	*44.0*
1858	Lot M. Morrill (R)	60,599	*53.5*
	Manassah H. Smith (D)	52,697	*46.5*

	Candidates	Votes	%
1859	Lot M. Morrill (R)	57,215	*55.8*
	Manassah H. Smith (D)	45,407	*44.3*
1860	Israel Washburn Jr. (R)	70,014	*56.5*
	E. K. Smart (D)	52,167	*42.1*
1861	Israel Washburn Jr. (R)	57,475	*58.7*
	C. D. Jameson (D)	21,119	*21.6*
	John W. Dana (OPP D)	19,363	*19.8*
1862	Abner Coburn (R)	46,689	*53.3*
	Bion Bradbury (D)	33,645	*38.4*
	C. D. Jameson (D)	7,302	*8.3*
1863	Samuel Cony (UN R)	67,916	*57.4*
	Bion Bradbury (D)	50,366	*42.6*
1864	Samuel Cony (UN R)	65,583	*58.6*
	Joseph Howard (D)	46,403	*41.4*
1865	Samuel Cony (UN R)	54,430	*63.3*
	Joseph Howard (D)	31,609	*36.7*
1866	Joshua L. Chamberlain (R)	69,626	*62.4*
	Eben F. Pillsbury (D)	41,939	*37.6*
1867	Joshua L. Chamberlain (R)	57,713	*55.6*
	Eben F. Pillsbury (D)	45,990	*44.3*
1868	Joshua L. Chamberlain (R)	75,523	*57.3*
	Eben F. Pillsbury (D)	56,207	*42.7*
1869	Joshua L. Chamberlain (R)	50,784	*53.3*
	Franklin Smith (D)	39,428	*41.4*
	N. G. Hichborn (TEMP)	5,028	*5.3*
1870	Sidney Perham (R)	54,019	*54.1*
	Charles W. Roberts (D)	45,732	*45.8*
1871	Sidney Perham (R)	58,285	*55.1*
	Charles P. Kimball (D)	47,538	*44.9*
1872	Sidney Perham (R)	71,883	*56.5*
	Charles P. Kimball (D)	55,343	*43.5*
1873	Nelson Dingley Jr. (R)	45,239	*55.9*
	Joseph Titcomb (D)	32,924	*40.7*
1874	Nelson Dingley Jr. (R)	50,865	*53.4*
	Joseph Titcomb (D)	41,898	*44.0*
1875	Selden Connor (R)	57,782	*51.7*
	Charles W. Roberts (D)	53,837	*48.2*
1876	Selden Connor (R)	75,867	*55.5*
	John C. Talbot (D)	60,423	*44.2*
1877	Selden Connor (R)	53,584	*52.5*
	Joseph H. Williams (D)	42,311	*41.5*
	Henry C. Munson (G)	5,291	*5.2*
1878	Selden Connor (R)	56,559	*44.8*
	Joseph L. Smith (G)	41,371	*32.8*
	Alonzo Garcelon (D)	28,218†	*22.4*
1879	Daniel F. Davis (R)	68,527†	*49.5*
	Joseph L. Smith (NG)	47,987	*34.7*
	Alonzo Garcelon (D)	21,525	*15.6*
1880	Harris M. Plaisted (D & G)	73,713	*49.9*
	Daniel F. Davis (R)	73,544	*49.8*
1882	Frederick Robie (R)	72,481	*52.4*
	Harris M. Plaisted (FUS)	63,921	*46.2*
1884	Frederick Robie (R)	78,699	*55.4*
	John B. Redman (D)	58,983	*41.5*
1886	Joseph R. Bodwell (R)	68,850	*53.7*
	Clark S. Edwards (D)	55,289	*43.1*
1888	Edwin C. Burleigh (R)	79,401	*54.6*
	William L. Putnam (D)	61,348	*42.2*
1890	Edwin C. Burleigh (R)	64,264	*56.4*
	William P. Thompson (D)	45,370	*39.8*
1892	Henry B. Cleaves (R)	67,900	*52.1*
	Charles F. Johnson (D)	55,392	*42.5*
1894	Henry B. Cleaves (R)	69,322	*64.3*
	Charles F. Johnson (D)	30,405	*28.2*
1896	Llewellyn Powers (R)	82,596	*66.9*
	M. P. Frank (D)	34,350	*27.8*
1898	Llewellyn Powers (R)	53,900	*62.9*
	Samuel L. Lord (D)	28,485	*33.2*
1900	John F. Hill (R)	73,470	*62.3*
	Samuel L. Lord (D)	40,086	*34.0*

	Candidates	Votes	%
1902	John F. Hill (R)	65,354	59.5
	Samuel W. Gould (D)	38,107	34.7
1904	William T. Cobb (R)	76,962	58.5
	C. W. Davis (D)	50,146	38.1
1906	William T. Cobb (R)	69,427	52.0
	C. W. Davis (D)	61,363	46.0
1908	Bert M. Fernald (R)	73,537	51.6
	Obadiah Gardner (D)	66,282	46.5
1910	Frederick W. Plaisted (D)	73,304	52.0
	Bert M. Fernald (R)	64,644	45.9
1912	William T. Haines (R)	70,931	50.0
	Frederick W. Plaisted (D)	67,702	47.7
1914	Oakley C. Curtis (D)	62,076	43.8
	William T. Haines (R)	58,887	41.6
	H. P. Gardner (PROG)	18,226	12.9
1916	Carl E. Milliken (R)	81,760	54.0
	Oakley C. Curtis (D)	67,930	44.9
1918	Carl E. Milliken (R)	63,607	52.3
	Bertrand G. McIntire (D)	58,062	47.7
1920	Frederick H. Parkhurst (R)	135,393	65.9
	Bertrand G. McIntire (D)	70,047	34.1
1922	Percival P. Baxter (R)	103,713	58.0
	William R. Pattangall (D)	75,226	42.0
1924	Ralph O. Brewster (R)	145,281	57.2
	William R. Pattangall (D)	108,626	42.8
1926	Ralph O. Brewster (R)	100,776	55.5
	Ernest L. McLean (D)	80,748	44.5
1928	William Tudor Gardiner (R)	148,053	69.3
	Edward C. Moran Jr. (D)	65,572	30.7
1930	William Tudor Gardiner (R)	82,310	55.1
	Edward C. Moran Jr. (D)	67,172	44.9
1932	Louis J. Brann (D)	121,158	50.3
	Burleigh Martin (R)	118,800	49.3
1934	Louis J. Brann (D)	156,917	54.0
	Alfred K. Ames (R)	133,414	45.9
1936	Lewis O. Barrows (R)	173,716	56.0
	F. Harold Dubord (D)	130,466	42.1
1938	Lewis O. Barrows (R)	157,206	52.9
	Louis J. Brann (D)	139,745	47.0
1940	Sumner Sewall (R)	162,719	63.8
	Fulton J. Redman (D)	92,053	36.1
1942	Sumner Sewall (R)	118,047	66.8
	George W. Lane Jr. (D)	58,558	33.2
1944	Horace A. Hildreth (R)	131,849	70.3
	Paul J. Jullien (D)	55,781	29.7
1946	Horace A. Hildreth (R)	110,327	61.3
	F. Davis Clark (D)	69,624	38.7
1948	Frederick G. Payne (R)	145,956	65.6
	Louis B. Lausier (D)	76,544	34.4
1950	Frederick G. Payne (R)	145,823	60.5
	Earle S. Grant (D)	94,304	39.1
1952	Burton M. Cross (R)	128,532	52.1
	James C. Oliver (D)	82,538	33.4
	Neil Bishop (IR)	35,732	14.5
1954	Edmund S. Muskie (D)	135,673	54.5
	Burton M. Cross (R)	113,298	45.5
1956	Edmund S. Muskie (D)	180,254	59.2
	W. A. Trafton Jr. (R)	124,395	40.8
1958	Clinton A. Clauson (D)	145,673	52.0
	Horace A. Hildreth (R)	134,572	48.0
1960	John H. Reed (R)	219,768	52.7
	Frank M. Coffin (D)	197,447	47.3
1962	John H. Reed (R)	146,604	50.1
	Maynard C. Dolloff (D)	146,121	49.9
1966	Kenneth M. Curtis (D)	172,036	53.1
	John H. Reed (R)	151,802	46.9

	Candidates	Votes	%
1970	Kenneth M. Curtis (D)	163,138	50.1
	James S. Erwin (R)	162,248	49.9
1974	James B. Longley (I)	142,464	39.1
	George J. Mitchell (D)	132,219	36.3
	James S. Erwin (R)	84,176	23.1
1978	Joseph E. Brennan (D)	176,493	47.7
	Linwood E. Palmer (R)	126,862	34.3
	Herman C. Frankland (I)	65,889	17.8
1982	Joseph E. Brennan (D)	281,066	61.1
	Charles R. Cragin (R)	172,949	37.6
1986	John R. McKernan Jr. (R)	170,312	39.9
	James Tierney (D)	128,744	30.1
	Sherry E. Huber (I)	64,317	15.1
	John E. Menario (I)	63,474	14.9
1990	John R. McKernan Jr. (R)	243,766	46.7
	Joseph E. Brennan (D)	230,038	44.0
	Andrew Adam (Unenrolled)	48,377	9.3
1994	Angus King (I)	180,829	35.4
	Joseph E. Brennan (D)	172,951	33.8
	Susan M. Collins (R)	117,990	23.1
	Jonathan K. Carter (I)	32,695	6.4

MARYLAND

(Ratified the Constitution April 28, 1788)

	Candidates	Votes	%
1838 [1]	William Grayson (D)	27,722	50.3
	John L. Steele (W)	27,409	49.7
1841	Francis Thomas (D)	28,959	50.6
	Johnson (W)	28,320	49.4
1844	Thomas G. Pratt (W)	35,040	50.4
	Carroll (D)	34,495	49.6
1847	Philip Francis Thomas (D)	34,368	50.5
	Goldsborough (W)	33,730	49.5
1850	Enoch L. Lowe (D)	36,340	51.0
	Clark (W)	34,858	49.0
1853	Thomas Watkins Ligon (D)	39,087	52.8
	Richard J. Bowie (W)	34,939	47.2
1857	Thomas Holliday Hicks (AM)	47,141	54.9
	John C. Groome (D)	38,681	45.1
1861	Augustus W. Bradford (UN R)	57,498	68.8
	Howard (PEACE D)	26,086	31.2
1864	Thomas Swann (UN R)	40,579	55.9
	E. F. Chambers (D)	32,068	44.1
1867	Oden Bowie (D)	63,694	74.3
	Hugh L. Bond (R)	22,050	25.7
1871	William P. Whyte (D)	73,959	55.7
	Jacob Tome (R)	58,824	44.3
1875	John Lee Carroll (D)	85,447	54.1
	Harris (R)	72,544	45.9
1879	William T. Hamilton (D)	90,731	56.9
	Garey (R)	68,619	43.1
1883	Robert M. McLane (D)	92,694	53.5
	Holton (R)	80,712	46.6
1887	Elihu E. Jackson (D)	99,038	52.1
	Brooks (R)	86,622	45.6
1891	Frank Brown (D)	108,539	56.5
	Vannort (R)	78,388	40.8
1895	Lloyd Lowndes (R)	124,936	52.0
	John E. Hurst (D)	106,169	44.2
1899	John Walter Smith (D)	128,409	51.1
	Lloyd Lowndes (R)	116,286	46.3
1903	Edwin Warfield (D)	108,548	52.0
	S. A. Williams (R)	95,923	46.0
1907	Austin L. Crothers (D)	102,051	50.7
	Gaither (R)	94,302	46.8
1911	Phillips Lee Goldsborough (R)	106,392	49.3
	Arthur Pue Gorman (D)	103,395	47.9

	Candidates	Votes	%
1915	Emerson C. Harrington (D)	119,317	*49.6*
	Ovington E. Weller (R)	116,136	*48.2*
1919	Albert C. Ritchie (D)	112,240	*49.1*
	Harry W. Nice (R)	112,075	*49.0*
1923	Albert C. Ritchie (D)	177,871	*56.0*
	Alexander Armstrong (R)	137,471	*43.3*
1926	Albert C. Ritchie (D)	207,435	*57.9*
	Addison E. Mullikin (R)	148,145	*41.4*
1930	Albert C. Ritchie (D)	283,639	*56.0*
	William F. Broening (R)	216,864	*42.8*
1934	Harry W. Nice (R)	253,813	*49.5*
	Albert C. Ritchie (D)	247,664	*48.3*
1938	Herbert R. O'Conor (D)	308,372	*54.6*
	Harry W. Nice (R)	242,095	*42.9*
1942	Herbert R. O'Conor (D)	198,486	*52.6*
	Theodore R. McKeldin (R)	179,206	*47.5*
1946	William Preston Lane Jr. (D)	268,084	*54.7*
	Theodore R. McKeldin (R)	221,752	*45.3*
1950	Theodore R. McKeldin (R)	369,807	*57.3*
	William Preston Lane Jr. (D)	275,824	*42.7*
1954	Theodore R. McKeldin (R)	381,451	*54.5*
	Harry Clifton Byrd (D)	319,033	*45.5*
1958	J. Millard Tawes (D)	485,061	*63.6*
	James Patrick Devereux (R)	278,173	*36.5*
1962	J. Millard Tawes (D)	428,071	*55.6*
	Frank Small Jr. (R)	341,271	*44.4*
1966	Spiro T. Agnew (R)	455,318	*49.5*
	George P. Mahoney (D)	373,543	*40.6*
	Hyman A. Pressman (I)	90,899	*9.9*
1970	Marvin Mandel (D)	639,579	*65.7*
	C. Stanley Blair (R)	314,336	*32.3*
1974	Marvin Mandel (D)	602,648	*63.5*
	Louise Gore (R)	346,449	*36.5*
1978	Harry Hughes (D)	718,328	*71.0*
	J. Glenn Beall Jr. (R)	293,635	*29.0*
1982	Harry Hughes (D)	705,910	*62.0*
	Robert A. Pascal (R)	432,826	*38.0*
1986	William D. Schaefer (D)	907,301	*82.4*
	Thomas J. Mooney (R)	194,187	*17.6*
1990	William D. Schaefer (D)	664,015	*59.8*
	William S. Shepard (R)	446,980	*40.2*
1994	Parris N. Glendening (D)	708,094	*50.2*
	Ellen R. Sauerbrey (R)	702,101	*49.8*

Maryland
1. *Before 1838 governor chosen by General Assembly.*

MASSACHUSETTS

(Ratified the Constitution Feb. 6, 1788)

	Candidates	Votes	%
1788	John Hancock	17,841	*80.5*
1789	John Hancock	17,264	*80.7*
1790	John Hancock	14,283	*86.5*
1791	John Hancock	15,996	*93.9*
1792	John Hancock	14,628	*86.6*
1793	John Hancock	16,428	*89.9*
1794	Samuel Adams	14,425	*61.5*
1795	Samuel Adams	15,976	*90.2*
1796[1]	Samuel Adams	15,195	*57.4*
	Increase Sumner (FED)	11,298	*42.6*
1797[1]	Increase Sumner (FED)	14,540	*56.7*
	James Sullivan (D-R)	11,118	*43.3*
1798[1]	Increase Sumner (FED)	18,245	*75.2*
	James Sullivan (D-R)	6,014	*24.8*
1799	Increase Sumner (FED)	24,073	*72.9*

	Candidates	Votes	%
1800	Caleb Strong (FED)	19,630	*50.3*
	Elbridge Gerry (D-R)	17,019	*43.6*
1801	Caleb Strong (FED)	25,452	*55.3*
	Elbridge Gerry (D-R)	20,184	*43.9*
1802	Caleb Strong (FED)	29,983	*60.5*
	Elbridge Gerry (D-R)	19,443	*43.9*
1803	Caleb Strong (FED)	29,199	*67.3*
	Elbridge Gerry (D-R)	13,910	*32.3*
1804	Caleb Strong (FED)	30,011	*55.1*
	James Sullivan (D-R)	23,996	*44.0*
1805	Caleb Strong (FED)	35,204	*51.0*
	James Sullivan (D-R)	33,518	*48.6*
1806	Caleb Strong (FED)	37,740	*50.2*
	James Sullivan (D-R)	37,109	*49.4*
1807	James Sullivan (D-R)	41,954	*51.5*
	Caleb Strong (FED)	39,224	*48.1*
1808	James Sullivan (D-R)	41,193	*50.8*
	Christopher Gore (FED)	39,643	*48.9*
1809	Christopher Gore (FED)	47,916	*51.3*
	Levi Lincoln I (D-R)	45,118	*48.3*
1810	Elbridge Gerry (D-R)	46,541	*51.2*
	Christopher Gore (FED)	44,079	*48.5*
1811	Elbridge Gerry (D-R)	43,328	*51.6*
	Christopher Gore (FED)	40,142	*47.8*
1812	Caleb Strong (FED)	52,696	*50.6*
	Elbridge Gerry (D-R)	51,326	*49.3*
1813	Caleb Strong (FED)	56,754	*56.6*
	Joseph B. Varnum (D-R)	42,789	*42.7*
1814	Caleb Strong (FED)	56,374	*55.0*
	Lemuel Dexter (D-R)	45,953	*44.8*
1815	Caleb Strong (FED)	50,921	*53.6*
	Lemuel Dexter (D-R)	43,938	*46.2*
1816	John Brooks (FED)	49,527	*51.1*
	Lemuel Dexter (D-R)	47,321	*48.8*
1817	John Brooks (FED)	46,160	*54.6*
	Henry Dearborn (D-R)	38,129	*45.1*
1818	John Brooks (FED)	39,538	*55.7*
	Benjamin W. Crowninshield (D-R)	30,041	*42.4*
1819	John Brooks (FED)	42,875	*53.7*
	Benjamin W. Crowninshield (D-R)	35,277	*44.2*
1820	John Brooks (FED)	31,072	*58.3*
	William Eustis (D-R)	21,927	*41.1*
1821	John Brooks (FED)	28,608	*58.3*
	William Eustis (D-R)	20,268	*41.3*
1822	John Brooks (FED)	28,487	*57.1*
	William Eustis (D-R)	21,177	*42.5*
1823	William Eustis (D-R)	34,402	*52.7*
	Harrison G. Otis (FED)	30,171	*46.2*
1824	William Eustis (D-R)	38,650	*52.9*
	Samuel Lathrop (FED)	34,210	*46.8*
1825	Levi Lincoln (R-FF)	35,221	*94.1*
1826	Levi Lincoln (AR)	27,884	*68.0*
	Samuel Hubbard (FED)	9,044	*22.1*
	James Lloyd (FED)	2,212	*.5.4*
1827	Levi Lincoln (AR)	29,029	*74.2*
	William C. Jarvis (FB R)	7,130	*18.2*
1828	Levi Lincoln (AR)	27,981	*81.5*
	Marcus Morton (JAC R)	4,423	*12.9*
1829	Levi Lincoln (NR)	25,217	*71.6*
	Marcus Morton (JAC R)	6,864	*19.5*
1830	Levi Lincoln (NR)	30,908	*65.5*
	Marcus Morton (JAC R)	14,440	*30.6*
1831	Levi Lincoln (NR)	31,875	*65.2*
	Marcus Morton (JAC R)	12,694	*26.0*
1831	Levi Lincoln (NR)	28,804	*53.9*
	Samuel Lathrop (A-MAS)	13,357	*25.0*
	Marcus Morton (D)	10,975	*20.6*
1832	Levi Lincoln (NR)	33,946	*52.9*
	Marcus Morton (D)	15,197	*23.7*
	Samuel Lathrop (A-MAS)	14,755	*23.0*

Gubernatorial Elections

	Candidates	Votes	%		Candidates	Votes	%
1833	John Davis (NR)	25,149†	40.3	1858	Nathaniel P. Banks (R)	68,700	57.6
	John Quincy Adams (A-MAS)	18,274	29.3		Erasmus D. Beach (D)	38,298	32.1
	Marcus Morton (D)	15,493	24.8		Amos A. Lawrence (AM)	12,084	10.1
	Samuel L. Allen (WM)	3,459	5.5	1859	Nathaniel P. Banks (R)	58,780	54.0
1834	John Davis (W)	43,757	58.1		Benjamin F. Butler (D)	35,334	32.5
	Marcus Morton (D)	18,683	24.8		George N. Briggs (AM)	14,365	13.2
	John Bailey (A-MAS)	10,160	13.5	1860	John A. Andrew (R)	104,527	61.6
1835	Edward Everett (W)	37,555	57.9		Erasmus D. Beach (D)	35,191	20.8
	Marcus Morton (D)	25,227	38.9		Amos A. Lawrence (CST U)	23,816	14.0
1836	Edward Everett (W)	42,160	53.8	1861	John A. Andrew (R)	65,261	67.1
	Marcus Morton (D)	35,992	45.9		Isaac Davis (D)	31,266	32.1
1837	Edward Everett (W)	50,565	60.3	1862	John A. Andrew (R)	79,835	59.5
	Marcus Morton (D)	32,987	39.4		Charles Devens Jr. (PP)	54,167	40.4
1838	Edward Everett (W)	51,642	55.0	1863	John A. Andrew (UN R)	70,483	70.7
	Marcus Morton (D)	41,795	44.5		Henry W. Paine (D)	29,207	29.3
1839	Marcus Morton (D)	51,034	50.0	1864	John A. Andrew (UN)	125,281	71.8
	Edward Everett (W)	50,725	49.7		Henry W. Paine (D)	49,190	28.2
1840	John Davis (W)	70,884	55.7	1865	Alexander H. Bullock (UN)	69,912	76.6
	Marcus Morton (D)	55,169	43.3		Darius N. Couch (D)	21,245	23.3
1841	John Davis (W)	55,974	50.4	1866	Alexander H. Bullock (R)	91,980	77.5
	Marcus Morton (D)	51,367	46.3		Theodore H. Sweetser (D)	26,671	22.5
1842	Marcus Morton (D)	56,491†	47.9	1867	Alexander H. Bullock (R)	98,306	58.3
	John Davis (W)	54,939	46.6		John Quincy Adams (D)	70,360	41.7
	Samuel E. Sewall (LIB)	6,382	5.4	1868	William Claflin (R)	132,121	67.6
1843	George N. Briggs (W)	57,899†	47.7		John Quincy Adams (D)	63,266	32.4
	Marcus Morton (D)	54,242	44.7	1869	William Claflin (R)	74,106	53.5
	Samuel E. Sewall (LIB)	8,903	7.3		John Quincy Adams (D)	50,735	36.6
1844	George N. Briggs (W)	69,570	51.8		Edwin M. Chamberlain (LAB REF)	13,567	9.8
	George Bancroft (D)	54,714	40.8	1870	William Claflin (R)	79,549	53.0
	Samuel E. Sewall (LIB)	9,734	7.3		John Quincy Adams (D)	48,680	32.3
1845	George N. Briggs (W)	51,638†	48.8		Wendell Phillips (LAB REF & P)	21,946	14.6
	Isaac Davis (D)	37,427	35.3	1871	William B. Washburn (R)	75,129	54.9
	Samuel E. Sewall (LIB)	8,316	7.9		John Quincy Adams (D)	47,725	34.9
	Henry Shaw (AM R)	8,089	7.6		Edwin M. Chamberlain (LAB REF)	6,848	5.0
1846	George N. Briggs (W)	54,813	53.8	1872	William B. Washburn (R)	133,900	69.1
	Isaac Davis (D)	33,199	32.6		Francis W. Bird (LR)	59,626	30.8
	Samuel E. Sewall (LIB)	9,997	9.8	1873	William B. Washburn (R)	72,183	54.6
1847	George N. Briggs (W)	53,742	51.0		William Gaston (D)	59,360	44.9
	Caleb Cushing (D)	39,398	37.4	1874	William Gaston (D)	96,376	51.8
	Samuel E. Sewall (LIB)	9,157	8.7		Thomas Talbot (R)	89,344	48.0
1848	George N. Briggs (W)	61,640†	49.7	1875	Alexander H. Rice (R)	83,639	48.3
	Stephen C. Phillips (F SOIL)	36,011	29.0		William Gaston (D)	78,333	45.2
	Caleb Cushing (D)	25,323	20.4		John I. Baker (TEMP)	9,124	5.3
1849	George N. Briggs (W)	54,009†	49.3	1876	Alexander H. Rice (R)	137,665	53.6
	George S. Boutwell (D)	30,040	27.4		Charles Francis Adams (D)	106,850	41.6
	Stephen C. Phillips (F SOIL)	25,247	23.1	1877	Alexander H. Rice (R)	91,255	49.5
1850	George N. Briggs (W)	56,778	46.8		William Gaston (D)	73,185	39.7
	George S. Boutwell (D)	36,023†	29.7		Robert C. Pitman (P)	16,354	8.9
	Stephen C. Phillips (F SOIL)	27,636	22.8	1878	Thomas Talbot (R)	134,725	52.6
1851	Robert C. Winthrop (W)	64,279	46.9		Benjamin F. Butler (BUT D & R)	109,435	42.7
	George S. Boutwell (D)	43,889†	32.0	1879	John D. Long (R)	122,751	50.4
	John G. Palfrey (F SOIL)	28,560	20.9		Benjamin F. Butler (BUT D & R)	109,149	44.8
1852	John H. Clifford (W)	62,233†	45.0	1880	John D. Long (R)	164,926	58.4
	Henry W. Bishop (D)	38,763	28.0		Charles P. Thompson (D)	111,410	39.5
	Horace Mann (F SOIL)	36,740	26.5	1881	John D. Long (R)	96,609	61.2
1853	Emory Washburn (W)	59,224†	45.9		Charles P. Thompson (D)	54,586	34.6
	Henry W. Bishop (D)	35,086	27.2	1882	Benjamin F. Butler (D-NG LAB)	133,946	52.3
	Henry Wilson (F SOIL)	29,020	22.5		Robert R. Bishop (R)	119,997	46.8
1854	Henry J. Gardner (AM)	81,503	62.6	1883	George D. Robinson (R)	160,092	51.3
	Emory Washburn (W)	27,279	20.9		Benjamin F. Butler (D & G)	150,228	48.1
	Henry W. Bishop (D)	13,742	10.6	1884	George D. Robinson (R)	159,345	52.4
1855	Henry J. Gardner (AM)	51,497	37.7		William C. Endicott (D)	111,829	36.8
	Julius Rockwell (R)	36,715	26.9		Matthew J. McCafferty (G)	24,363	8.0
	Erasmus D. Beach (D)	34,728	25.5	1885	George D. Robinson (R)	112,243	53.5
	Samuel H. Walley (W)	13,296	9.7		Frederick O. Prince (D)	90,346	43.1
1856	Henry J. Gardner (FREM AM)	92,467	58.9	1886	Oliver Ames (R)	122,346	50.2
	Erasmus D. Beach (D)	40,077	25.5		John F. Andrew (D)	112,883	46.3
	George W. Gordon (FILL AM)	10,385	6.6	1887	Oliver Ames (R)	136,000	51.1
1857	Nathaniel P. Banks (R)	60,797	46.6		Henry B. Lovering (D)	118,394	44.5
	Henry J. Gardner (AM)	37,596	28.8	1888	Oliver Ames (R)	180,849	52.7
	Erasmus D. Beach (D)	31,760	24.3		William E. Russell (D)	152,780	44.5

	Candidates	Votes	%
1889	John Q. A. Brackett (R)	127,357	48.4
	William E. Russell (D)	120,582	45.8
	John Blackmer (P)	15,108	5.7
1890	William E. Russell (D)	140,507	49.2
	John Q. A. Brackett (R)	131,454	46.0
1891	William E. Russell (D)	157,982	49.1
	Charles H. Allen (R)	151,515	47.1
1892	William E. Russell (D)	186,377	49.0
	William H. Haile (R)	183,843	48.4
1893	Frederic T. Greenhalge (R)	192,613	52.8
	John E. Russell (D)	156,916	43.0
1894	Frederic T. Greenhalge (R)	189,307	56.5
	John E. Russell (D)	123,930	37.0
1895	Frederic T. Greenhalge (R)	186,280	56.8
	George Fred Williams (D)	121,599	37.1
1896	Roger Wolcott (R)	258,204	67.1
	George Fred Williams (D, BRYAN D)	103,662	27.0
1897	Roger Wolcott (R)	165,095	61.2
	George Fred Williams (D)	79,552	29.5
	William Everett (DN)	13,879	5.1
1898	Roger Wolcott (R)	191,146	60.2
	Alexander B. Bruce (D)	107,960	34.0
1899	Winthrop Murray Crane (R)	168,902	56.5
	Robert Treat Paine (D)	103,802	34.7
1900	Winthrop Murray Crane (R)	228,054	59.1
	Robert Treat Paine (D)	130,078	33.7
1901	Winthrop Murray Crane (R)	185,809	57.3
	Josiah Quincy (D)	114,362	35.2
1902	John L. Bates (R)	196,276	49.2
	William A. Gaston (D)	159,156	39.9
	John C. Chase (SOC)	33,629	8.4
1903	John L. Bates (R)	199,684	50.4
	William A. Gaston (D)	163,700	41.3
	John C. Chase (SOC)	25,251	6.4
1904	William L. Douglas (D)	234,670	52.1
	John L. Bates (R)	198,681	44.1
1905	Curtis Guild Jr. (R)	197,469	50.5
	Charles W. Bartlett (D)	174,911	44.7
1906	Curtis Guild Jr. (R)	222,528	52.0
	John B. Moran (D, I LEAGUE)	192,295	44.9
1907	Curtis Guild Jr. (R)	188,068	50.3
	Henry M. Whitney (D, D CIT)	84,379	22.6
	Thomas L. Hisgen (I LEAGUE)	75,499	20.2
1908	Eben S. Draper (R)	228,318	51.6
	James H. Vahey (D)	168,162	38.0
	William N. Osgood (I LEAGUE)	23,101	5.2
1909	Eben S. Draper (R)	190,186	48.6
	James H. Vahey (D)	182,252	46.6
1910	Eugene N. Foss (D, D & PROG)	229,352	52.0
	Eben S. Draper (R)	194,173	44.1
1911	Eugene N. Foss (D, D & PROG)	214,897	48.8
	Louis A. Frothingham (R)	206,795	47.0
1912	Eugene N. Foss (D)	193,184	40.6
	Joseph Walker (R)	143,597	30.2
	Charles S. Bird (PROG)	122,602	25.8
1913	David I. Walsh (D)	183,267	39.8
	Charles S. Bird (PROG)	127,755	27.7
	Augustus P. Gardner (R)	116,705	25.3
1914	David I. Walsh (D)	210,442	45.9
	Samuel W. McCall (R)	198,627	43.4
	Joseph Walker (PROG)	32,145	7.0
1915	Samuel W. McCall (R)	235,863	47.0
	David I. Walsh (D)	229,550	45.7
1916	Samuel W. McCall (R)	276,123	52.5
	Frederick W. Mansfield (D)	229,883	43.7
1917	Samuel W. McCall (R)	226,145	58.3
	Frederick W. Mansfield (D)	135,676	35.0
1918	Calvin Coolidge (R)	214,863	50.9
	Richard H. Long (D)	197,828	46.8

	Candidates	Votes	%
1919	Calvin Coolidge (R)	317,774	60.9
	Richard H. Long (D)	192,673	37.0
1920	Channing H. Cox (R)	643,869	67.0
	John J. Walsh (D)	290,350	30.2
1922	Channing H. Cox (R)	464,873	52.2
	John F. Fitzgerald (D)	404,192	45.4
1924	Alvan T. Fuller (R)	650,817	56.0
	James M. Curley (D)	490,010	42.2
1926	Alvan T. Fuller (R)	595,006	58.8
	William A. Gaston (D)	407,389	40.3
1928	Frank G. Allen (R)	769,372	50.1
	Charles H. Cole (D)	750,137	48.8
1930	Joseph B. Ely (D)	606,902	49.5
	Frank G. Allen (R)	590,238	48.2
1932	Joseph B. Ely (D)	825,479	52.8
	William Sterling Youngman (R)	704,576	45.0
1934	James M. Curley (D)	736,463	49.7
	Gaspar G. Bacon (R)	627,413	42.3
	Frank A. Goodwin (E TAX)	94,141	6.4
1936	Charles F. Hurley (D)	867,743	47.6
	John W. Haigis (R)	839,740	46.1
1938	Leverett Saltonstall (R)	941,465	53.3
	James M. Curley (D)	793,884	45.0
1940	Leverett Saltonstall (R)	999,223	49.7
	Paul A. Dever (D)	993,635	49.5
1942	Leverett Saltonstall (R)	758,402	54.1
	Roger L. Putnam (D)	630,265	45.0
1944	Maurice J. Tobin (D)	1,048,284	53.6
	Horace T. Cahill (R)	897,708	45.9
1946	Robert F. Bradford (R)	911,152	54.1
	Maurice J. Tobin (D)	762,743	45.3
1948	Paul A. Dever (D)	1,239,247	59.0
	Robert F. Bradford (R)	849,895	40.5
1950	Paul A. Dever (D)	1,074,570	56.3
	Arthur W. Coolidge (R)	824,069	43.1
1952	Christian A. Herter (R)	1,175,955	49.9
	Paul A. Dever (D)	1,161,499	49.3
1954	Christian A. Herter (R)	985,339	51.8
	Robert F. Murphy (D)	910,087	47.8
1956	Foster Furcolo (D)	1,234,618	52.8
	Sumner G. Whittier (R)	1,096,759	46.9
1958	Foster Furcolo (D)	1,067,020	56.2
	Charles Gibbons (R)	818,463	43.1
1960	John A. Volpe (R)	1,269,295	52.5
	Joseph D. Ward (D)	1,130,810	46.8
1962	Endicott Peabody (D)	1,053,322	49.9
	John A. Volpe (R)	1,047,891	49.7
1964	John A. Volpe (R)	1,176,462	50.3
	Francis X. Bellotti (D)	1,153,416	49.3
1966	John A. Volpe (R)	1,277,358	62.6
	Edward J. McCormack (D)	752,720	36.9
1970	Francis W. Sargent (R)	1,058,623	56.7
	Kevin H. White (D)	799,269	42.8
1974	Michael S. Dukakis (D)	992,284	53.5
	Francis W. Sargent (R)	784,353	42.3
1978	Edward J. King (D)	1,030,294	52.5
	Francis W. Hatch (R)	926,072	47.2
1982	Michael S. Dukakis (D)	1,219,109	59.5
	John W. Sears (R)	749,679	36.6
1986	Michael S. Dukakis (D)	1,157,786	68.7
	George Kariotis (R)	525,364	31.2
1990	William F. Weld (R)	1,175,817	50.2
	John Silber (D)	1,099,878	46.9
1994	William F. Weld (R)	1,533,430	70.9
	Mark Roosevelt (D)	611,650	28.3

Massachusetts

1. *Totals for losing candidates in these elections include some votes for other candidates.*

MICHIGAN

(Became a state Jan. 26, 1837)

	Candidates	Votes	%
1835	Stevens T. Mason (D)	7,385	89.2
	John Biddle (W)	815	9.8
1837	Stevens T. Mason (D)	15,318	50.2
	Charles C. Trowbridge (W)	14,884	48.8
1839	William Woodbridge (W)	19,069	51.9
	E. Farnsworth (D)	17,710	48.2
1841	John S. Barry (D)	21,001	55.8
	Philo C. Fuller (W)	15,449	41.1
1843	John S. Barry (D)	21,394	54.6
	Zind Pilcher (W)	15,024	38.3
	James G. Birney (LIB)	2,736	7.0
1845	Alpheus Felch (D)	20,123	50.8
	Stephen Vickery (W)	16,322	41.2
	James G. Birney (LIB)	3,048	7.7
1847	Epaphroditus Ransom (D)	24,639	53.2
	James M. Edmunds (W)	18,990	41.0
	Chester Gurney (LIB)	2,585	5.6
1849	John S. Barry (D)	27,845	54.0
	Flavius Littlejohn (W FS)	23,561	45.7
1851	Robert McClelland (D)	23,827	58.3
	Townsend E. Gidley (W FS)	16,901	41.3
1852	Robert McClelland (D)	42,791	51.4
	Zacharaiah Chandler (W)	34,662	41.6
	Isaac P. Christiancy (F SOIL)	5,880	7.1
1854	Kinsley S. Bingham (R)	43,652	53.0
	Barry (NEB D)	38,676	47.0
1856	Kinsley S. Bingham (R)	71,402	56.9
	Felch (D)	54,085	43.1
1858	Moses Wisner (R)	65,201	53.8
	Stuart (D)	56,060	46.2
1860	Austin Blair (R)	87,780	56.7
	Barry (D)	67,053	43.3
1862	Austin Blair (R)	68,716	52.5
	Stout (D)	62,102	47.5
1864	Henry H. Crapo (UN R)	91,353	55.2
	William H. Fenton (D)	74,293	44.9
1866	Henry H. Crapo (R)	97,112	58.6
	Williams (D)	68,650	41.4
1868	Henry P. Baldwin (R)	128,042	56.8
	John Moore (D)	97,290	43.2
1870	Henry P. Baldwin (R)	100,176	53.8
	Charles C. Comstock (D)	83,391	44.8
1872	John J. Bagley (R)	137,602	63.0
	Blair (L)	80,958	37.0
1874	John J. Bagley (R)	111,519	50.5
	Henry Chamberlain (D)	105,550	47.8
1876	Charles M. Croswell (R)	165,926	52.3
	Webber (D)	142,493	44.9
1878	Charles M. Croswell (R)	126,280	45.4
	Barnes (D)	78,503	28.2
	Smith (NG)	73,313	26.4
1880	David H. Jerome (R)	178,944	51.3
	Holloway (D)	137,671	39.4
	Woodman (G)	31,085	8.9
1882	Josiah W. Begole (D & G)	154,269	49.5
	David H. Jerome (R)	149,697	48.0
1884	Russell A. Alger (R)	190,840	47.7
	Josiah W. Begole (D & G)	186,884	46.7
	David Preston (P)	22,307	5.6
1886	Cyrus G. Luce (R)	181,474	47.7
	George L. Yaple (D)	174,042	45.7
	Samuel Dickie (P)	25,179	6.6
1888	Cyrus G. Luce (R)	233,595	49.2
	Wellington R. Burt (D)	216,450	45.6
1890	Edward B. Winans (D)	183,725	46.2
	James M. Turner (R)	172,205	43.3
	Azariah S. Partridge (P)	28,681	7.2
1892	John T. Rich (R)	221,228	47.2
	Allen B. Morse (D)	205,138	43.8
1894	John T. Rich (R)	237,215	56.9
	Spencer O. Fisher (D)	130,823	31.4
	Alva W. Nichols (PP)	30,008	7.2
1896	Hazen S. Pingree (R)	304,431	55.6
	Charles R. Sligh (D & POP)	225,200	41.1
1898	Hazen S. Pingree (R)	243,239	57.8
	Justin R. Whiting (DPUS)	168,142	39.9
1900	Aaron T. Bliss (R)	305,612	55.8
	William C. Maybury (D)	226,208	41.3
1902	Aaron T. Bliss (R)	211,261	52.5
	Lorenzo T. Durand (D)	174,077	43.3
1904	Fred M. Warner (R)	283,799	54.1
	Woodbridge N. Ferris (D)	223,571	42.6
1906	Fred M. Warner (R)	227,567	60.9
	Charles H. Kimmerle (D)	130,018	34.8
1908	Fred M. Warner (R)	262,141	48.4
	Lawton T. Hemans (D)	252,611	46.6
1910	Chase S. Osborn (R)	202,803	52.9
	Lawton T. Hemans (D)	159,770	41.6
1912	Woodbridge N. Ferris (D)	194,017	35.4
	Amos S. Musselman (R)	169,963	31.0
	Lucius W. Watkins (N PROG)	152,909	27.9
1914	Woodbridge N. Ferris (D)	212,063	48.2
	Chase S. Osborn (R)	176,254	40.0
	Henry R. Pattengill (N PROG)	36,747	8.3
1916	Albert E. Sleeper (R)	363,724	55.8
	Edwin F. Sweet (D)	264,440	40.6
1918	Albert E. Sleeper (R)	266,738	61.4
	John W. Bailey (D)	158,142	36.4
1920	Alexander J. Groesbeck (R)	703,180	66.4
	Woodbridge N. Ferris (D)	310,566	29.3
1922	Alexander J. Groesbeck (R)	356,933	61.2
	Alva M. Cummins (D)	218,252	37.4
1924	Alexander J. Groesbeck (R)	799,225	68.8
	Edward Frensdorf (D)	343,577	29.6
1926	Fred W. Green (R)	399,564	63.4
	William A. Comstock (D)	227,155	36.0
1928	Fred W. Green (R)	961,179	69.9
	William A. Comstock (D)	404,546	29.4
1930	Wilber M. Brucker (R)	483,990	56.9
	William A. Comstock (D)	357,664	42.0
1932	William A. Comstock (D)	887,672	54.9
	Wilber M. Brucker (R)	696,935	43.1
1934	Frank D. Fitzgerald (R)	659,743	52.4
	Arthur J. Lacy (D)	577,044	45.8
1936	Frank Murphy (D)	892,774	51.0
	Frank D. Fitzgerald (R)	843,855	48.2
1938	Frank D. Fitzgerald (R)	847,245	52.8
	Frank Murphy (D)	753,752	47.0
1940	Murray D. Van Wagoner (D)	1,077,065	53.1
	Luren D. Dickinson (R)	945,784	46.6
1942	Harry F. Kelly (R)	645,335	52.6
	Murray D. Van Wagoner (D)	573,314	46.7
1944	Harry F. Kelly (R)	1,208,859	54.7
	Edward J. Fry (D)	989,307	44.8
1946	Kim Sigler (R)	1,003,878	60.3
	Murray D. Van Wagoner (D)	644,540	38.7
1948	G. Mennen Williams (D)	1,128,664	53.4
	Kim Sigler (R)	964,810	45.7
1950	G. Mennen Williams (D)	935,152	49.8
	Harry F. Kelly (R)	933,998	49.7
1952	G. Mennen Williams (D)	1,431,893	50.0
	Fred M. Alger Jr. (R)	1,423,275	49.7
1954	G. Mennen Williams (D)	1,216,308	55.6
	Donald S. Leonard (R)	963,300	44.1
1956	G. Mennen Williams (D)	1,666,689	54.7
	Albert E. Cobo (R)	1,376,376	45.1
1958	G. Mennen Williams (D)	1,225,533	53.0
	Paul D. Bagwell (R)	1,078,089	46.6

	Candidates	Votes	%
1960	John B. Swainson (D)	1,643,634	50.5
	Paul D. Bagwell (R)	1,602,022	49.2
1962	George Romney (R)	1,420,086	51.4
	John B. Swainson (D)	1,339,513	48.5
1964	George Romney (R)	1,764,355	55.9
	Neil Staebler (D)	1,381,442	43.7
1966	George Romney (R)	1,490,430	60.5
	Zolton A. Ferency (D)	963,383	39.1
1970	William G. Milliken (R)	1,338,711	50.4
	Sander Levin (D)	1,294,600	48.7
1974	William G. Milliken (R)	1,356,865	51.1
	Sander Levin (D)	1,242,247	46.8
1978	William G. Milliken (R)	1,628,485	56.8
	William Fitzgerald (D)	1,237,256	43.2
1982	James J. Blanchard (D)	1,561,291	51.4
	Richard H. Headlee (R)	1,369,582	45.1
1986	James J. Blanchard (D)	1,632,138	68.1
	William Lucas (R)	753,647	31.4
1990	John Engler (R)	1,276,134	49.8
	James J. Blanchard (D)	1,258,539	49.1
1994	John Engler (R)	1,899,101	61.5
	Howard Wolpe (D)	1,188,438	38.5

MINNESOTA

(Became a state May 11, 1858)

	Candidates	Votes	%
1857	Henry H. Sibley (D)	17,790	50.3
	Alexander Ramsey (R)	17,550	49.7
1859	Alexander Ramsey (R)	21,335	54.8
	George L. Becker (D)	17,583	45.2
1861	Alexander Ramsey (R)	16,274#	60.9
	E. O. Hamlin (D)	10,448#	39.1
1863	Stephen Miller (UN)	19,628	60.6
	Henry T. Wells (D)	12,739	39.4
1865	William R. Marshall (R)	17,308	55.6
	H. M. Rice (D)	13,847	44.5
1867	William R. Marshall (R)	34,874	54.2
	Charles E. Flandrau (D)	29,511	45.8
1869	Horace Austin (R)	27,599	50.4
	George L. Otis (D)	25,390	46.4
1871	Horace Austin (R)	46,669	59.9
	Winthrop Young (D)	31,212	40.1
1873	Cushman K. Davis (R)	40,741#	52.9
	Ara Barton (IR & D)	35,245#	45.8
1875	John S. Pillsbury (R)	45,073#	53.6
	David L. Buell (D)	35,275#	41.9
1877	John S. Pillsbury (R)	57,071#	57.9
	W. L. Banning (D)	39,147#	39.7
1879	John S. Pillsbury (R)	57,522	54.0
	Edmund Rice (D)	41,844	39.3
1881	Lucius F. Hubbard (R)	65,025	63.6
	R. W. Johnson (D)	37,168	36.4
1883	Lucius F. Hubbard (R)	72,462	55.4
	A. Bierman (D)	58,245	44.6
1886	A. R. McGill (R)	106,966	48.5
	A. A. Ames (D)	104,483	47.4
1888	William R. Merriam (R)	134,355	51.3
	Eugene M. Wilson (D)	110,251	42.1
	Hugh Harrison (P)	17,150	6.6
1890	William R. Merriam (R)	88,111	36.6
	Thomas Wilson (D)	85,844	35.6
	Sidney M. Owen (ALNC)	58,513	24.3
1892	Knute Nelson (R)	109,220	42.7
	Daniel W. Lawler (D)	94,600	37.0
	Ignatius Donnelly (PP)	39,860	15.6
1894	Knute Nelson (R)	147,943	49.9
	Sidney M. Owen (PP)	87,898	29.7
	George L. Becker (D)	53,583	18.1

	Candidates	Votes	%
1896	David M. Clough (R)	165,906	49.2
	John Lind (PP & D)	162,254	48.1
1898	John Lind (D & POP)	131,980	52.3
	William H. Eustis (R)	111,796	44.3
1900	Samuel R. Van Sant (R)	152,905	48.7
	John Lind (PP & D)	150,651	48.0
1902	Samuel R. Van Sant (R)	155,849	57.5
	Leonard A. Rosing (D)	99,362	36.7
1904	John A. Johnson (D)	147,992	48.7
	Robert C. Dunn (R)	140,130	46.1
1906	John A. Johnson (D)	168,480	60.9
	A. L. Cole (R)	96,162	34.8
1908	John A. Johnson (D)	175,036	52.2
	Jacob F. Jacobson (R)	147,034	43.8
1910	Adolph O. Eberhart (R)	164,185	55.7
	James Gray (D)	103,779	35.2
1912	Adolph O. Eberhart (R)	129,688	40.7
	Peter M. Ringdal (D)	99,659	31.3
	P. V. Collins (PROG)	33,455	10.5
	E. E. Lobeck (P)	29,876	9.4
	David Morgan (PUB OWN)	25,769	8.1
1914	Winfield S. Hammond (D)	156,304	45.5
	William E. Lee (R)	143,730	41.9
	W. G. Calderwood (P)	18,582	5.4
	Tom J. Lewis (SOC)	17,325	5.1
1916	Joseph A. A. Burnquist (R)	245,841	62.9
	Thomas P. Dwyer (D)	93,112	23.8
	J. O. Bentall (SOC)	26,306	6.7
	Thomas J. Anderson (P)	19,884	5.1
1918	Joseph A. A. Burnquist (R)	166,615	45.1
	David H. Evans (F-LAB)	111,966	30.3
	Fred E. Wheaton (D)	76,838	20.8
1920	Jacob A. O. Preus (R)	415,805	53.1
	Henrik Shipstead (I)	281,406	35.9
	L. C. Hodgson (D)	81,291	10.4
1922	Jacob A. O. Preus (R)	309,756	45.2
	Magnus Johnson (F-LAB)	295,479	43.1
	Edward Indrehus (D)	79,903	11.7
1924	Theodore Christianson (R)	406,692	48.7
	Floyd B. Olson (F-LAB)	366,029	43.8
	Carlos Avery (D)	49,353	5.9
1926	Theodore Christianson (R)	395,779	56.5
	Magnus Johnson (F-LAB)	266,845	38.1
	Alfred Jaques (D)	38,008	5.4
1928	Theodore Christianson (R)	549,857	55.0
	Ernest Lundeen (F-LAB)	227,193	22.7
	Andrew Nelson (D)	213,734	21.4
1930	Floyd B. Olson (F-LAB)	472,354	59.3
	Ray P. Chase (R)	289,528	36.4
1932	Floyd B. Olson (F-LAB)	522,438	50.6
	Earle Brown (R)	334,081	32.3
	John E. Regan (D)	169,859	16.4
1934	Floyd B. Olson (F-LAB)	468,812	44.6
	Martin A. Nelson (R)	396,359	37.7
	John E. Regan (D)	176,928	16.8
1936	Elmer A. Benson (F-LAB)	680,342	60.7
	Martin A. Nelson (R)	431,841	38.6
1938	Harold E. Stassen (R)	678,839	59.9
	Elmer A. Benson (F-LAB)	387,263	34.2
	Thomas Gallagher (D)	65,875	5.8
1940	Harold E. Stassen (R)	654,686	52.1
	Hjalmar Petersen (F-LAB)	459,609	36.5
	Ed Murphy (D)	140,021	11.1
1942	Harold E. Stassen (R)	409,800	51.6
	Hjalmar Petersen (F-LAB)	299,917	37.8
	John D. Sullivan (D)	75,151	9.5
1944	Edward J. Thye (R)	701,185	61.1
	Byron G. Allen (DFL)	440,132	38.3
1946	Luther W. Youngdahl (R)	519,067	59.0
	Harold H. Barker (DFL)	349,565	39.7

	Candidates	Votes	%		Candidates	Votes	%
1948	Luther W. Youngdahl (R)	643,572	*53.2*	1843	Albert G. Brown (A-RPT D)	21,115	*52.9*
	Charles L. Halsted (DFL)	545,746	*45.1*		Clayton (W)	17,442	*43.7*
1950	Luther W. Youngdahl (R)	635,800	*60.8*	1845	Albert G. Brown (D)	27,669	*64.8*
	Harry H. Peterson (DFL)	400,637	*38.3*		Coopwood (W)	15,029	*35.2*
1952	C. Elmer Anderson (R)	785,125	*55.3*	1849	John A. Quitman (D)	33,117	*59.0*
	Orville L. Freeman (DFL)	624,480	*44.0*		Lea (W)	22,996	*40.9*
1954	Orville L. Freeman (DFL)	607,099	*52.7*	1851	Henry S. Foote (UN)	27,836	*51.4*
	C. Elmer Anderson (R)	538,865	*46.8*		Jefferson Davis (SO RTS)	26,301	*48.6*
1956	Orville L. Freeman (DFL)	731,180	*51.4*	1853	John J. McCrae (D)	30,460	*54.0*
	Ancher Nelsen (R)	685,196	*48.2*		Rogers (W)	25,967	*46.0*
1958	Orville L. Freeman (DFL)	658,326	*56.8*	1855	John J. McCrae (D)	32,669	*54.2*
	George Mackinnon (R)	490,731	*42.3*		C. D. Fontaine (AM)	27,578	*45.8*
1960	Elmer L. Andersen (R)	783,813	*50.6*	1857	William McWillie (D)	27,376	*66.0*
	Orville L. Freeman (DFL)	760,934	*49.1*		William Yerger (AM)	14,085	*34.0*
1962	Karl F. Rolvaag (DFL)	619,842‡	*49.7*	1859	John J. Pettus (D)	34,559	*76.8*
	Elmer L. Andersen (R)	619,751	*49.7*		H. W. Walter (OPP)	10,408	*23.1*
1966	Harold Levander (R)	680,593	*52.6*	1861	John J. Pettus	29,959	*86.9*
	Karl F. Rolvaag (DFL)	607,943	*46.9*		Jacob Thompson	3,556	*10.3*
1970	Wendell R. Anderson (DFL)	737,921	*54.3*	1863	Charles Clark	16,050	*69.8*
	Douglas M. Head (R)	621,780	*45.7*		A. M. West	4,914	*21.4*
1974	Wendell R. Anderson (DFL)	786,787	*62.8*		Reuben Davis	2,021	*8.8*
	John W. Johnson (R)	367,722	*29.3*	1865	Benjamin G. Humphreys (SEC W)	19,037	*42.2*
1978	Albert H. Quie (I-R)	830,019	*52.3*		E. S. Fisher (UN)	15,557	*34.5*
	Rudy Perpich (DFL)	718,244	*45.3*		W. S. Patton	10,519	*23.3*
1982	Rudy Perpich (DFL)	1,049,104	*58.6*	1868	Benjamin G. Humphreys (D)	62,321	*52.6*
	Wheelock Whitney (I-R)	715,796	*40.0*		Beriah B. Eggleston (R)	56,072	*47.4*
1986	Rudy Perpich (DFL)	790,138	*55.8*	1869	James L. Alcorn (R)	76,186	*66.7*
	Cal R. Ludeman (I-R)	606,755	*42.9*		Louis Dent (C)	38,097	*33.3*
1990	Arne Carlson (I-R)	895,988	*49.6*	1873	Adelbert Ames (R)	73,324	*58.1*
	Rudy Perpich (DFL)	836,218	*46.3*		James L. Alcorn (I)	52,857	*41.9*
1994	Arne H. Carlson (I-R)	1,094,165	*62.0*	1877	John M. Stone (D)	96,376	*98.8*
	John Marty (DFL)	589,344	*33.4*	1881	Robert Lowry (D)	76,805	*59.6*
					King (G & R)	51,994	*40.4*
				1885	Robert Lowry (D)	88,783	*100.0*
				1889	John M. Stone (D)	84,929	*100.0*
	MISSISSIPPI			1895	Anselm J. McLaurin (D)	46,870	*72.1*
					Frank Burkitt (PP)	18,167	*27.9*
	(Became a state Dec. 10, 1817)			1899	Andrew H. Longino (D)	42,273	*87.4*
					R. K. Prewitt (POP)	6,097	*12.6*
	Candidates	Votes	%	1903	James K. Vardaman (D)	32,191	*100.0*
				1907	Edmund F. Noel (D)	29,528	*100.0*
1817	David Holmes	4,108		1911	Earl Brewer (D)	40,471	*95.2*
1819	George Poindexter	2,721	*61.5*	1915	Theodore G. Bilbo (D)	50,541	*92.6*
	Thomas Hinds	1,702	*38.5*		J. T. Lester (SOC)	4,046	*7.4*
1821	Walter Leake	4,730	*78.8*	1919	Lee M. Russell (D)	39,239	*96.9*
	Charles B. Green	1,269	*21.2*	1923	Henry L. Whitfield (D)	29,138	*100.0*
1823	Walter Leake	4,730	*51.3*	1927	Theodore G. Bilbo (D)	31,717	*100.0*
	David Dickson	2,511	*27.2*	1931	Martin S. Conner (D)	45,942	*100.0*
	William Lattimore	1,986	*21.5*	1935	Hugh L. White (D)	45,881	*100.0*
1825	David Holmes (OLD R)	7,850	*84.0*	1939	Paul B. Johnson (D)	61,614	*100.0*
	Cowles Mead (OLD R)	1,499	*16.0*	1943	Thomas L. Bailey (D)	50,488	*100.0*
1827	Gerard C. Brandon	5,482	*51.0*	1947	Fielding L. Wright (D)	161,993	*97.5*
	Daniel Williams	3,392	*31.6*	1951	Hugh L. White (D)	43,422	*100.0*
	Beverly R. Grayson	1,866	*17.4*	1955	J. P. Coleman (D)	40,707	*100.0*
1829	Gerard C. Brandon (JAC D)	6,052	*64.6*	1959	Ross R. Barnett (D)	57,671	*100.0*
	George W. Winchester (NR)	3,310	*35.4*	1963	Paul B. Johnson Jr. (D)	225,456	*61.9*
1831	Abram M. Scott (NR)	3,953	*30.5*		Rubel L. Phillips (R)	138,605	*38.1*
	Hiram G. Runnels (JAC D)	3,711	*28.6*	1967	John Bell Williams (D)	315,318	*70.3*
	Charles Lynch (JAC D)	2,902	*22.4*		Rubel L. Phillips (R)	133,379	*29.7*
	Wiley Harris (JAC D)	1,899	*14.7*	1971	William L. Waller (D)	601,222	*77.0*
1833	Hiram G. Runnels (D)	6,614	*52.9*		James Charles Evers (I)	172,762	*22.1*
	Abram M. Scott (W)	5,900	*47.2*	1975	Cliff Finch (D)	369,568	*52.2*
1835	Charles Lynch (W)	9,877	*51.1*		Gil Carmichael (R)	319,632	*45.1*
	Hiram G. Runnels (D)	9,451	*48.9*	1979	William F. Winter (D)	413,620	*61.1*
1837	Alexander G. McNutt (D)	12,823	*46.4*		Gil Carmichael (R)	263,702	*38.9*
	Morgan	9,861	*35.7*	1983	Bill Allain (D)	409,209#	*55.1*
	Grimball (W)	4,951	*17.9*		Leon Bramlett (R)	288,764#	*38.9*
1839	Alexander G. McNutt (D)	18,880	*54.3*	1987	Ray Mabus (D)	387,346	*53.8*
	Edward Turner (W)	15,886	*45.7*		Jack Reed (R)	332,985	*46.3*
1841	Tilgham M. Tucker (D)	19,059	*53.2*	1991	Kirk Fordice (R)	361,500	*50.8*
	D. O. Shattuck (W)	16,783	*46.8*		Ray Mabus (D)	338,435	*47.6*

	Candidates	Votes	%
1995	Kirk Fordice (R)	455,261	*55.6*
	Dick Molpus (D)	364,210	*44.4*

MISSOURI

(Became a state Aug. 10, 1821)

	Candidates	Votes	%
1820	Alexander McNair (D-R)	6,576	*72.0*
	William Clark (D-R)	2,556	*28.0*
1824	Frederick Bates (AR)	6,165	*57.1*
	William H. Ashley (CLAY R)	4,636	*42.9*
1825	John Miller (JAC D)	2,801	*47.9*
	Carr (JAC D)	1,622	*27.8*
	Todd (NR)	1,423	*24.3*
1828	John Miller	11,043	*100.0*
1832	Daniel Dunklin (D)	9,141	*50.9*
	John Bull (A-JAC)	8,132	*45.2*
1836	Lilburn W. Boggs (D)	14,315	*52.3*
	Ashley (I)	13,055	*47.7*
1840	Thomas Reynolds (D)	29,656	*57.2*
	Clark (W)	22,205	*42.8*
1844	John Cummins Edwards (D)	36,978	*54.1*
	Allen (W)	31,357	*45.9*
1848	Austin A. King (D)	48,921	*59.0*
	James S. Rollins (W)	33,942	*41.0*
1852	Sterling Price (D)	46,494	*58.7*
	James Winston (W)	32,706	*41.3*
1856	Trusten Polk (D)	47,066	*40.8*
	R. C. Ewing (AM)	40,620	*35.2*
	Thomas Hart Benton (BENTON D)	27,615	*24.0*

1857	R. M. Stewart (D)	47,975	*50.2*
	J. S. Rollins (AM & EMANC)	47,619	*49.8*

1860	Claiborne Fox Jackson (D)	74,239	*47.0*
	Sample Orr (OPP)	66,400	*42.0*
	Hancock Jackson (SOC)	11,362	*7.2*
1864	Thomas C. Fletcher (UN R)	73,600	*70.3*
	Thomas L. Price (D)	31,064	*29.7*
1868	Joseph W. McClurg (R)	82,090	*56.7*
	John S. Phelps (D)	62,778	*43.3*
1870	Benjamin Gratz Brown (D)	104,374	*62.3*
	Joseph W. McClurg (R)	63,235	*37.7*
1872	Silas Woodson (D & L)	156,767	*56.3*
	John B. Henderson (R)	121,889	*43.7*
1874	Charles H. Hardin (D)	149,566	*57.2*
	William Gentry (R)	112,104	*42.8*
1876	John S. Phelps (D)	199,583	*57.0*
	Gustavus A. Finkelnburg (R)	147,684	*42.2*
1880	Thomas Theodore Crittenden (D)	207,670	*52.2*
	Dyer (R)	153,636	*38.6*
	Brown (G)	36,340	*9.1*
1884	John Sappington Marmaduke (D)	218,885	*50.1*
	Nicholas Ford (G & R)	207,939	*47.5*
1888	David Rowland Francis (D)	255,764	*49.4*
	E. E. Kimball (R)	242,531	*46.8*
1892	William Joel Stone (D)	265,044	*49.0*
	William Warner (R)	235,383	*43.5*
	L. Leonard (PP)	37,262	*6.9*
1896	Lawrence Vest Stephens (D)	351,062	*52.9*
	Robert E. Lewis (R)	307,729	*46.4*
1900	Alexander Monroe Dockery (D)	350,045	*51.2*
	Flory (R)	317,905	*46.5*
1904	Joseph Wingate Folk (D)	326,652	*50.7*
	Cyrus P. Walbridge (R)	296,552	*46.1*

	Candidates	Votes	%
1908	Herbert Spencer Hadley (R)	355,932	*49.7*
	Cowherd (D)	340,053	*47.5*
1912	Elliott Woolfolk Major (D)	337,019	*48.2*
	John C. McKinley (R)	217,819	*31.2*
	Albert D. Nortoni (PROG)	109,146	*15.6*
1916	Frederick Dozier Gardner (D)	382,355	*48.7*
	Lamm (R)	380,092	*48.4*
1920	Arthur Mastick Hyde (R)	722,020	*54.3*
	Atkinson (D)	580,726	*43.6*
1924	Samuel Aaron Baker (R)	640,135	*49.4*
	A. T. Nelson (D)	634,263	*48.9*
1928	Henry Stewart Caulfield (R)	784,311	*51.6*
	Francis M. Wilson (D)	731,783	*48.2*
1932	Guy Brasfield Park (D)	968,551	*60.2*
	Edward H. Winter (R)	629,428	*39.1*
1936	Lloyd Crow Stark (D)	1,037,133	*57.1*
	Jesse W. Barrett (R)	772,934	*42.5*
1940	Forrest C. Donnell (R)	911,530	*50.1*
	Larry McDaniel (D)	907,917	*49.9*
1944	Phil M. Donnelly (D)	793,490	*50.9*
	Jean Paul Bradshaw (R)	762,908	*49.0*
1948	Forrest Smith (D)	893,092	*57.0*
	Murray E. Thompson (R)	670,064	*42.8*
1952	Phil M. Donnelly (D)	983,169	*52.6*
	Howard Elliott (R)	886,270	*47.4*
1956	James T. Blair Jr. (D)	941,528	*52.1*
	Lon Hocker (R)	866,810	*47.9*
1960	John M. Dalton (D)	1,095,195	*58.0*
	Edward G. Farmer (R)	792,131	*42.0*
1964	Warren E. Hearnes (D)	1,110,651	*62.1*
	Ethan A. H. Shepley (R)	678,949	*37.9*
1968	Warren E. Hearnes (D)	1,063,495	*60.7*
	Lawrence K. Roos (R)	688,300	*39.3*
1972	Christopher S. Bond (R)	1,029,451	*55.2*
	Edward L. Dowd (D)	832,751	*44.6*
1976	Joseph P. Teasdale (D)	971,184	*50.2*
	Christopher S. Bond (R)	958,110	*49.6*
1980	Christopher S. Bond (R)	1,098,950	*52.6*
	Joseph P. Teasdale (D)	981,884	*47.0*
1984	John Ashcroft (R)	1,194,506	*56.7*
	Kenneth J. Rothman (D)	913,700	*43.3*
1988	John Ashcroft (R)	1,339,531	*64.2*
	Betty Hearnes (D)	724,919	*34.8*
1992	Mel Carnahan (D)	1,375,425	*58.7*
	William L. Webster (R)	968,574	*41.3*
1996	Mel Carnahan (D)	1,224,801	*57.2*
	Margaret Kelly (R)	866,268	*40.4*

MONTANA

(Became a state Nov. 8, 1889)

	Candidates	Votes	%
1889	Joseph K. Toole (D)	19,735	*51.0*
	Thomas C. Power (R)	18,991	*49.0*
1892	John E. Rickards (R)	18,187	*41.2*
	Timothy E. Collins (D)	17,650	*40.0*
	William Kennedy (PP)	7,794	*17.6*
1896	Robert B. Smith (PP & D)	36,688	*71.0*
	Alexander C. Botkin (R-SIL R)	14,993	*29.0*
1900	Joseph K. Toole (D)	31,419	*49.3*
	David S. Folsom (R)	22,691	*35.6*
	Thomas S. Hogan (ID)	9,188	*14.4*
1904	Joseph K. Toole (D-LAB-PP)	35,377	*53.8*
	William Lindsay (R)	26,957	*41.0*
	Malcolm A. O'Malley (SOC)	3,431	*5.2*

Gubernatorial Elections

	Candidates	Votes	%
1908	Edwin L. Norris (D)	32,282	47.3
	Edward Donlan (R)	30,792	45.2
	Harry Hazelton (SOC)	5,112	7.5
1912	Samuel V. Stewart (D)	25,371	31.7
	Harry L. Wilson (R)	22,950	28.7
	Frank J. Edwards (PROG)	18,881	23.6
	Lewis J. Duncan (SOC)	12,766	16.0
1916	Samuel V. Stewart (D)	85,683	49.4
	Frank J. Edwards (R)	76,556	44.1
	Lewis J. Duncan (SOC)	11,342	6.5
1920	Joseph M. Dixon (R)	111,113	59.7
	Burton K. Wheeler (D)	74,875	40.3
1924	John E. Erickson (D)	88,801	51.0
	Joseph M. Dixon (R)	74,126	42.6
	Frank J. Edwards (F-LAB)	10,576	6.1
1928	John E. Erickson (D)	114,256	58.7
	Wellington D. Rankin (R)	79,777	41.0
1932	John E. Erickson (D)	104,949	48.5
	Frank A. Hazelbaker (R)	101,105	46.7
1936	Roy E. Ayers (D)	115,310	51.0
	Frank A. Hazelbaker (R)	108,854	48.1
1940	Samuel C. Ford (R)	124,435	50.7
	Roy E. Ayers (D)	119,453	48.6
1944	Samuel C. Ford (R)	116,461	56.4
	Leif Erickson (D)	89,224	43.2
1948	John W. Bonner (D)	124,267	55.7
	Samuel C. Ford (R)	97,792	43.9
1952	John Hugo Aronson (R)	134,423	51.0
	John W. Bonner (D)	129,369	49.0
1956	John Hugo Aronson (R)	138,878	51.4
	Arnold H. Olsen (D)	131,488	48.6
1960	Donald G. Nutter (R)	154,230	55.1
	Paul Cannon (D)	125,651	44.9
1964	Tim Babcock (R)	144,113	51.3
	Roland Renne (D)	136,862	48.7
1968	Forrest H. Anderson (D)	150,481	54.1
	Tim Babcock (R)	116,432	41.9
1972	Thomas L. Judge (D)	172,523	54.1
	Ed Smith (R)	146,231	45.9
1976	Thomas L. Judge (D)	195,420	61.7
	Robert Woodahl (R)	115,848	36.6
1980	Ted Schwinden (D)	199,574	55.4
	Jack Ramirez (R)	160,892	44.6
1984	Ted Schwinden (D)	266,578	70.3
	Pat M. Goodover (R)	100,070	26.4
1988	Stan Stephens (R)	190,604	51.9
	Thomas L. Judge (D)	169,313	46.1
1992	Marc Racicot (R)	209,401	51.3
	Dorothy Bradley (D)	198,421	48.7
1996	Marc Racicot (R)	320,768	79.6
	Judy Jacobson (D)	84,407	20.4

NEBRASKA

(Became a state March 1, 1867)

	Candidates	Votes	%
1866	David Butler (R)	4,083	50.4
	J. S. Morton (D)	4,001	49.4
1868	David Butler (R)	8,576	57.5
	T. R. Porter (D)	6,349	42.5
1870	David Butler (R)	11,126	56.3
	J. H. Croxton (D)	8,648	43.7
1872	Robert W. Furnas (R)	16,543	59.6
	H. C. Lett (D)	11,227	40.4
1874	Silas Garber (R)	21,548	59.9
	Albert Tuxbury (D)	8,946	24.9
	J. F. Gardner (PP I)	4,159	11.6

	Candidates	Votes	%
1876	Silas Garber (R)	31,947	61.2
	Paren England (D)	17,219	33.0
	J. F. Gardner (G)	3,022	5.8
1878	Albinus Nance (R)	29,269	56.1
	W. H. Webster (D)	13,471	25.8
	Levi G. Todd (G)	9,484	18.2
1880	Albinus Nance (R)	55,237	63.2
	T. W. Tipton (D)	28,167	32.3
1882	James W. Dawes (R)	43,495	48.8
	J. S. Morton (D)	28,562	32.1
	E. P. Ingersoll (G)	16,991	19.1
1884	James W. Dawes (R)	72,835	54.5
	J. S. Morton (D)	57,634	43.2
1886	John M. Thayer (R)	76,456	55.2
	J. E. North (D)	52,456	37.9
	H. W. Hardy (P)	8,198	5.9
1888	John M. Thayer (R)	103,982	51.3
	J. A. McShane (D)	85,420	42.1
1890	James E. Boyd (D)	71,331‡	33.3
	J. H. Powers (PP I)	70,187	32.8
	L. D. Richards (R)	68,878	32.2
1892	Lorenzo Crounse (R)	78,426	39.7
	Charles Henry Van Wyck (PP I)	68,617	34.8
	J. S. Morton (D)	44,195	22.4
1894	Silas A. Holcomb (D & PPI)	97,825	48.0
	T. J. Majors (R)	94,613	46.4
1896	Silas A. Holcomb (D & PPI)	116,415	53.5
	J. H. McColl (R)	94,724	43.5
1898	William A. Poynter (FUS)	95,703	50.2
	M. L. Hayward (R)	92,982	48.8
1900	Charles H. Dietrich (R)	113,879	48.9
	William A. Poynter (FUS)	113,018	48.5
1902	John H. Mickey (R)	96,471	49.7
	William H. Thompson (FUS)	91,116	46.9
1904	John H. Mickey (R)	111,711	49.7
	George W. Berge (FUS)	102,568	45.6
1906	George L. Sheldon (R)	97,858	51.3
	Ashton Shallenberger (D & PPI)	84,885	44.5
1908	Ashton Shallenberger (D & PPI)	132,960	49.9
	George L. Sheldon (R)	125,967	47.3
1910	Chester H. Aldrich (R)	123,070	51.9
	James C. Dahlman (D)	107,760	45.5
1912	John H. Morehead (D & PPI)	123,997	49.3
	Chester H. Aldrich (R & PROG)	114,075	45.3
1914	John H. Morehead (D & PPI)	120,201	50.4
	R. B. Howell (R)	101,229	42.4
1916	Keith Neville (D & PPI)	143,564	49.3
	Abraham L. Sutton (R & PROG)	136,811	47.0
1918	Samuel R. McKelvie (R)	121,188	54.5
	Keith Neville (D)	97,886	44.0
1920	Samuel R. McKelvie (R)	152,863	40.4
	John H. Morehead (D)	130,433	34.5
	Arthur G. Wray (NON PL)	88,905	23.5
1922	Charles W. Bryan (D)	214,070	54.6
	Charles H. Randall (R)	164,435	42.0
1924	Adam McMullen (R)	229,067	51.1
	J. N. Norton (D)	183,709	41.0
	Dan Butler (PROG)	35,594	7.9
1926	Adam McMullen (R)	206,120	49.8
	Charles W. Bryan (D)	202,688	49.0
1928	Arthur J. Weaver (R)	308,262	57.0
	Charles W. Bryan (D)	230,640	42.6
1930	Charles W. Bryan (D)	222,161	50.8
	Arthur J. Weaver (R)	215,615	49.3
1932	Charles W. Bryan (D)	296,117	52.5
	Dwight Griswold (R)	260,888	46.3
1934	Robert L. Cochran (D)	284,095	50.8
	Dwight Griswold (R)	266,707	47.7
1936	Robert L. Cochran (D)	333,412	55.9
	Dwight Griswold (R)	257,279	43.1

Candidates	Votes	%
1938 Robert L. Cochran (D)	218,787	44.0
Charles J. Warner (R)	201,898	40.6
Charles W. Bryan	76,258	15.4
1940 Dwight Griswold (R)	365,638	60.9
Terry Carpenter (D)	235,167	39.1
1942 Dwight Griswold (R)	283,271	74.8
Charles W. Bryan (D)	95,231	25.2
1944 Dwight Griswold (R)	410,136	76.1
George W. Olsen (D)	128,760	23.9
1946 Val Peterson (R)	249,468	65.5
Frank Sorrell (D)	131,367	34.5
1948 Val Peterson (R)	286,119	60.1
Frank Sorrell (D)	190,214	39.9
1950 Val Peterson (R)	247,089	54.9
Walter R. Raecke (D)	202,638	45.1
1952 Robert B. Crosby (R)	365,409	61.4
Walter R. Raecke (D)	229,400	38.6
1954 Victor E. Anderson (R)	250,080	60.3
William Ritchie (D)	164,753	39.7
1956 Victor E. Anderson (R)	308,285	54.3
Frank Sorrell (D)	228,048	40.2
George L. Morris	31,583	5.6
1958 Ralph G. Brooks (D)	211,345	50.2
Victor E. Anderson (R)	209,705	49.8
1960 Frank B. Morrison (D)	311,344	52.0
John R. Cooper (R)	287,302	48.0
1962 Frank B. Morrison (D)	242,669	52.2
Fred A. Seaton (R)	221,885	47.8
1964 Frank B. Morrison (D)	347,026	60.0
Dwight W. Burney (R)	231,029	40.0
1966 Norbert T. Tiemann (R)	299,245	61.5
Philip C. Sorensen (D)	186,985	38.5
1970 J. James Exon (D)	248,552	53.8
Norbert T. Tiemann (R)	201,994	43.8
1974 J. James Exon (D)	267,012	59.2
Richard D. Marvel (R)	159,780	35.4
Ernest W. Chambers (I)	24,320	5.4
1978 Charles Thone (R)	275,473	55.9
Gerald T. Whelan (D)	216,754	44.0
1982 Robert Kerrey (D)	277,436	50.6
Charles Thone (R)	270,203	49.3
1986 Kay A. Orr (R)	298,325	52.9
Helen Boosalis (D)	265,156	47.0
1990 Ben Nelson (D)	292,771	49.9
Kay A. Orr (R)	288,741	49.2
1994 Ben Nelson (D)	423,270	73.0
Gene Spence (R)	148,230	25.6

NEVADA

(Became a state Oct. 31, 1864)

Candidates	Votes	%
1864 Henry G. Blasdel (UN R)	9,834	60.0
David E. Buell (D)	6,555	40.0
1866 Henry G. Blasdel (R)	5,125	55.5
John D. Winters (D)	4,105	44.5
1870 L. R. Bradley (D)	7,200	53.9
F. A. Tritte (R)	6,147	46.1
1874 L. R. Bradley (D)	10,339	57.1
Hazlett	7,754	42.9
1878 John H. Kinkead (R)	9,678	51.4
L. R. Bradley (D)	9,151	48.6
1882 Jewett W. Adams (D)	7,770	54.3
Enoch Strother (R)	6,535	45.7
1886 C. C. Stevenson (R)	6,463	52.4
Jewett W. Adams (D)	5,869	47.6
1890 R. K. Colcord (R)	6,601	53.3
Thomas Winters (D)	5,791	46.7
1894 J. S. Jones (D SIL)	5,223	49.9
A. C. Cleveland (R)	3,861	36.9
G. E. Peckham (POP)	711	6.8
Theodore Winters (D)	678	6.5
1898 Reinhold Sadler (SIL R)	3,570	35.7
William McMillan (R)	3,548	35.5
George Russell (D)	2,057	20.6
J. B. McCullough (PP)	833	8.3
1902 John Sparks (D & SILVER)	6,540	57.8
A. C. Cleveland (R)	4,778	42.2
1906 John Sparks (D & SILVER)	8,686	58.5
James F. Mitchell (R)	5,336	36.0
Thomas B. Casey (SOC)	815	5.5
1910 Tasker L. Oddie (R)	10,435	50.6
D. S. Dickerson (D)	8,798	42.7
Henry F. Gegax (SOC)	1,393	6.8
1914 Emmet D. Boyle (D)	9,623	44.7
Tasker L. Oddie (R)	8,537	39.6
W. A. Morgan (SOC)	3,391	15.7
1918 Emmet D. Boyle (D)	12,875	52.1
Tasker L. Oddie (R)	11,845	47.9
1922 James G. Scrugham (D)	15,437	53.9
John H. Miller (R)	13,215	46.1
1926 Fred B. Balzar (R)	16,374	53.0
James G. Scrugham (D)	14,521	47.0
1930 Fred B. Balzar (R)	18,442	53.3
C. L. Richards (D)	16,192	46.8
1934 Richard Kirman Sr. (D)	23,088	53.9
Morley Griswold (R)	14,778	34.5
L. C. Branson (I)	4,940	11.5
1938 Edward P. Carville (D)	28,528	61.9
John A. Fulton (R)	17,586	38.1
1942 Edward P. Carville (D)	24,505	60.3
A. V. Tallman (R)	16,164	39.8
1946 Vail Pittman (D)	28,655	57.4
Melvin E. Jepson (R)	21,247	42.6
1950 Charles H. Russell (R)	35,609	57.6
Vail Pittman (D)	26,164	42.4
1954 Charles H. Russell (R)	41,665	53.1
Vail Pittman (D)	36,797	46.9
1958 Grant Sawyer (D)	50,864	59.9
Charles H. Russell (R)	34,025	40.1
1962 Grant Sawyer (D)	64,784	66.8
Oran K. Gragson (R)	32,145	33.2
1966 Paul Laxalt (R)	71,807	52.2
Grant Sawyer (D)	65,870	47.8
1970 Mike O'Callaghan (D)	70,697	48.1
Ed Fike (R)	64,400	43.8
1974 Mike O'Callaghan (D)	114,114	67.4
Shirley Crumpler (R)	28,959	17.1
James Ray Houston (IA)	26,285	15.5
1978 Robert F. List (R)	108,097	56.2
Robert E. Rose (D)	76,361	39.7
1982 Richard H. Bryan (D)	128,132	53.4
Robert F. List (R)	100,104	41.8
1986 Richard H. Bryan (D)	187,268	71.9
Patty Cafferata (R)	65,081	25.0
1990 Bob J. Miller (D)	207,878	64.8
Jim Gallaway (R)	95,789	29.9
1994 Bob J. Miller (D)	200,026	53.9
Jim Gibbons (R)	156,875	42.3

NEW HAMPSHIRE

(Ratified the Constitution June 21, 1788)

	Candidates	Votes	%
1788	John Langdon	4,421	50.0
	John Sullivan	3,664	41.5
1789	John Sullivan	3,657†	42.9
	John Pickering	3,488	40.9
	Josiah Bartlett	968	11.3
1790	John Pickering	3,189	41.0
	Joshua Wentworth	2,369	30.4
	Josiah Bartlett	1,676†	21.5
1791	Josiah Bartlett	8,679	96.8
1792	Josiah Bartlett	8,092	96.5
1793	Josiah Bartlett	7,388	75.0
	John Langdon	1,306	13.3
	John T. Gilman	708	7.2
1794	John T. Gilman	7,629	72.9
1795	John T. Gilman	9,340	98.9
1796	John T. Gilman (FED)	7,809	72.5
1797	John T. Gilman (FED)	9,625	88.9
1798	John T. Gilman (FED)	9,397	77.3
	Oliver Peabody (D-R)	1,189	9.8
	Timothy Walker	734	6.0
1799	John T. Gilman (FED)	10,138	86.4
1800	John T. Gilman (FED)	10,362	61.8
	Timothy Walker (D-R)	6,039	36.0
1801	John T. Gilman (FED)	10,898	65.5
	Timothy Walker (D-R)	5,249	31.5
1802	John T. Gilman (FED)	10,377	54.1
	John Langdon (D-R)	8,753	45.7
1803	John T. Gilman (FED)	12,263	57.5
	John Langdon (D-R)	9,011	42.3
1804	John T. Gilman (FED)	12,246	50.4
	John Langdon (D-R)	12,009	49.5
1805	John Langdon (D-R)	16,097	56.6
	John T. Gilman (FED)	12,287	43.2
1806	John Langdon (D-R)	15,277	74.3
	Timothy Farrar (FED)	1,720	8.4
	John T. Gilman (FED)	1,553	7.5
1807	John Langdon (D-R)	13,912	82.5
1808	John Langdon (D-R)	12,641	79.5
	John T. Gilman (FED)	1,261	7.9
1809	Jeremiah Smith (FED)	15,610	50.4
	John Langdon (D-R)	15,241	49.2
1810	John Langdon (D-R)	16,325	51.7
	Jeremiah Smith (FED)	15,166	48.0
1811	John Langdon (D-R)	17,554	54.7
	Jeremiah Smith (FED)	14,477	45.1
1812	John T. Gilman (FED)	15,613	48.8
	William Plumer (D-R)	15,492†	48.4
1813	John T. Gilman (FED)	18,107	50.7
	William Plumer (D-R)	17,410	48.7
1814	John T. Gilman (FED)	19,695	51.1
	William Plumer (D-R)	18,794	48.7
1815	John T. Gilman (FED)	18,357	50.7
	William Plumer (D-R)	17,799	49.2
1816	William Plumer (D-R)	20,338	53.0
	James Sheafe (FED)	17,994	46.9
1817	William Plumer (D-R)	19,088	54.0
	James Sheafe (FED)	12,029	34.0
	Jeremiah Mason (FED)	3,607	10.2
1818	William Plumer (D-R)	18,674	59.3
	Jeremiah Mason (FED)	6,850	21.8
	William Hale (FED)	5,019	16.0
1819	Samuel Bell (D-R)	13,761	56.7
	William Hale (FED)	8,660	35.7
1820	Samuel Bell (D-R)	22,212	89.7
1821	Samuel Bell (D-R)	22,582	92.4
1822	Samuel Bell (D-R)	22,934	95.6

	Candidates	Votes	%
1823	Levi Woodbury (D-R)	16,985	56.7
	Samuel Dinsmoor Sr. (D-R)	12,718	42.5
1824	David L. Morrill	14,429†	49.7
	Levi Woodbury	11,274	38.9
	Jeremiah Smith	2,868	9.9
1825	David L. Morrill	✔	
1826	David L. Morrill	17,528	58.8
	Benjamin Pierce	12,287	41.2
1827	Benjamin Pierce	✔	
	David L. Morrill		
1828	John Bell (NR)	21,784	52.7
	Benjamin Pierce (JAC D)	19,562	47.3
1829	Benjamin Pierce (JAC D)	21,601	53.6
	John Bell (NR)	18,708	46.4
1830	Matthew Harvey (JAC D)	22,502	54.9
	Upham (NR)	18,490	45.1
1831	Samuel Dinsmoor (JAC D)	23,503	55.6
	Ichabod Bartlett (NR)	18,681	44.2
1832	Samuel Dinsmoor (D)	24,175	62.3
	Ichabod Bartlett	14,604	37.7
1833	Samuel Dinsmoor (D)	28,270	84.5
1834	William Badger (D)	✔	
1835	William Badger (D)	23,709	63.4
	Joseph Healy	13,707	36.6
1836	Isaac Hill (D)	✔	
1837	Isaac Hill (D)	✔	
1838	Isaac Hill (D)	28,741	52.7
	J. Wilson Jr. (W)	25,565	46.9
1839	John Page (D)	30,466	55.9
	J. Wilson Jr. (W)	23,925	43.9
1840	John Page (D)	29,469	58.1
	Enos Stevens (W)	20,700	40.8
1841	John Page (D)	29,453	56.7
	Enos Stevens (W)	21,178	40.8
1842	Henry Hubbard (D)	26,830	55.8
	Enos Stevens (W)	12,364	25.7
	John H. White (ID)	5,994	12.5
	Daniel Hoit (AB)	2,756	5.7
1843	Henry Hubbard (D)	23,052	51.7
	Anthony Colby (W)	12,561	28.2
	John H. White (C)	5,497	12.3
	Daniel Hoit (AB)	3,416	7.7
1844	John H. Steele (D)	26,155	53.6
	Anthony Colby (W)	14,794	30.3
	Daniel Hoit (AB)	5,737	11.8
1845	John H. Steele (D)	23,298	51.3
	Anthony Colby (FEDL)	15,591	34.4
	Daniel Hoit (AB)	5,464	12.0
1846	Jared W. Williams (D)	26,914	48.6
	Anthony Colby (W)	17,704†	32.0
	Nathaniel S. Berry (AB)	10,406	18.8
1847	Jared W. Williams (D)	30,806	50.9
	Anthony Colby (W)	21,109	34.9
	Nathaniel S. Berry (AB)	8,531	14.1
1848	Jared W. Williams (D)	32,193	52.4
	Nathaniel S. Berry (W FS)	28,819	46.9
1849	Samuel Dinsmoor Jr. (D)	30,107	53.6
	Levi Chamberlain (W)	18,764	33.4
	Nathaniel S. Berry (FS & SC)	7,162	12.8
1850	Samuel Dinsmoor Jr. (D)	30,683	55.1
	Levi Chamberlain (W)	18,387	33.0
	Nathaniel S. Berry (F SOIL)	6,556	11.8
1851	Samuel Dinsmoor Jr. (D)	27,350†	47.1
	Thomas E. Sawyer (W)	18,407	31.7
	John Atwood (F SOIL)	12,159	20.9
1852	Noah Martin (D)	30,747	51.0
	Thomas E. Sawyer (W)	19,850	32.9
	John Atwood (F SOIL)	9,483	15.7
1853	Noah Martin (D)	30,924	54.7
	James Bell (W)	17,580	31.1
	John H. White (F SOIL)	7,997	14.1

	Candidates	Votes	%
1854	Nathaniel B. Baker (D)	29,788	*51.3*
	James Bell (W)	17,028	*29.4*
	Jared Perkins (F SOIL)	11,081	*19.1*
1855	Ralph Metcalf (AM)	32,783	*50.7*
	Nathaniel B. Baker (D)	27,055	*41.8*
	James Bell (W)	3,436	*5.3*
1856	Ralph Metcalf (AM)	32,119†	*48.2*
	John S. Wells (D)	32,031	*48.0*
1857	William Haile (R)	34,214	*51.9*
	John S. Wells (D)	31,209	*47.4*
1858	William Haile (R)	36,308	*53.4*
	Asa P. Cate (D)	31,597	*46.5*
1859	Ichabod Goodwin (R)	36,296	*52.5*
	Asa P. Cate (D)	32,802	*47.5*
1860	Ichabod Goodwin (R)	38,031	*53.1*
	Asa P. Cate (D)	33,543	*46.9*
1861	Nathaniel S. Berry (R)	35,467	*52.9*
	Stark (D)	31,452	*46.9*
1862	Nathaniel S. Berry (R)	32,150	*51.5*
	Stark (D)	28,566	*45.8*
1863	Eastman (D)	32,833	*49.6*
	Joseph A. Gilmore (R)	29,035†	*43.8*
	Harriman (UN)	4,372	*6.6*
1864	Joseph A. Gilmore (UN)	37,006	*54.2*
	Edward W. Harrington (D)	31,340	*45.9*
1865	Frederick Smyth (UN)	34,145	*54.9*
	Edward W. Harrington (D)	28,017	*45.0*
1866	Frederick Smyth (R)	35,137	*53.5*
	John G. Sinclair (D)	30,481	*46.4*
1867	Walter Harriman (R)	35,809	*52.2*
	John G. Sinclair (D)	32,663	*47.6*
1868	Walter Harriman (R)	39,785	*51.6*
	John G. Sinclair (D)	37,262	*48.3*
1869	Onslow Stearns (R)	35,777	*52.8*
	John Bedell (D)	32,004	*47.2*
1870	Onslow Stearns (R)	34,912	*51.0*
	John Bedell (D)	25,023	*36.6*
1871	James A. Weston (D)	34,700†	*49.8*
	James Pike (R)	33,892	*48.6*
1872	Ezekiel A. Straw (R)	38,751	*50.8*
	James A. Weston (D)	36,584	*47.9*
1873	Ezekiel A. Straw (R)	34,023	*50.2*
	James A. Weston (D)	32,016	*47.2*
1874	James A. Weston (D)	35,608†	*49.6*
	Luther McCutchins (R)	34,143	*47.5*
1875	Person C. Cheney (R)	39,293†	*49.6*
	Hiram R. Roberts (D)	39,121	*49.4*
1876	Person C. Cheney (R)	41,761	*52.0*
	Marcy (D)	38,133	*47.5*
1877	Benjamin F. Prescott (R)	40,757	*52.3*
	Marcy (D)	36,726	*47.2*
1878	Benjamin F. Prescott (R)	39,372	*50.6*
	McKean (D)	37,860	*48.7*
1879	Natt Head (R)	38,175	*50.3*
	McKean (D)	31,135	*41.0*
	W. S. Brown (N)	6,507	*8.6*
1880	Charles H. Bell (R)	44,434	*51.6*
	Frank Jones (D)	40,815	*47.4*
1882	Samuel W. Hale (R)	38,399	*50.4*
	M. V. B. Edgerly (D)	36,879	*48.4*
1884	Moody Currier (R)	42,514	*50.3*
	Hill (D)	39,637	*46.9*
1886	Charles H. Sawyer (R)	37,819†	*48.9*
	Cogswell (D)	37,334	*48.2*
1888	David H. Goodell (R)	44,809†	*49.5*
	Charles H. Amsden (D)	44,217	*48.8*
1890	Hiram A. Tuttle (R)	42,479†	*49.3*
	Charles H. Amsden (D)	42,386	*49.2*
1892	John B. Smith (R)	43,676	*50.2*
	Luther F. McKinney (D)	41,501	*47.7*

	Candidates	Votes	%
1894	Charles A. Busiel (R)	46,491	*56.0*
	Henry O. Kent (D)	33,959	*40.9*
1896	George A. Ramsdell (R)	48,387	*61.4*
	Henry O. Kent (D)	28,333	*36.0*
1898	Frank W. Rollins (R)	44,730	*54.2*
	Charles F. Stone (D)	35,653	*43.2*
1900	Chester B. Jordan (R)	53,891	*59.4*
	Frederick E. Potter (D)	34,956	*38.5*
1902	Nahum J. Bachelder (R)	42,115	*53.2*
	Henry F. Hollis (D)	33,844	*42.8*
1904	John McLane (R)	51,171	*57.8*
	Henry F. Hollis (D)	35,437	*40.1*
1906	Charles M. Floyd (R)	40,581†	*49.8*
	Nathan C. Jameson (D)	37,672	*46.2*
1908	Henry B. Quinby (R)	44,630	*50.4*
	Clarence E. Carr (D)	41,386	*46.7*
1910	Robert P. Bass (R)	44,908	*53.4*
	Clarence E. Carr (D)	37,737	*44.8*
1912	Samuel D. Felker (D)	34,203†	*41.1*
	Franklin Worcester (R)	32,504	*39.0*
	Winston Churchill (PROG)	14,401	*17.3*
1914	Rolland H. Spaulding (R)	46,413	*55.2*
	Albert W. Noone (D)	33,674	*40.0*
1916	Henry W. Keyes (R)	45,851	*53.2*
	John C. Hutchins (D)	38,853	*45.1*
1918	John H. Bartlett (R)	38,228	*54.1*
	Martin (D)	32,383	*45.9*
1920	Albert O. Brown (R)	93,273	*59.6*
	Charles E. Tilton (D)	62,174	*39.7*
1922	Fred H. Brown (D)	70,160	*53.3*
	Windsor H. Goodnow (R)	61,526	*46.7*
1924	John G. Winant (R)	88,650	*53.9*
	Fred H. Brown (D)	75,691	*46.1*
1926	Huntley N. Spaulding (R)	77,394	*59.7*
	Eaton D. Sargent (D)	52,236	*40.3*
1928	Charles W. Tobey (R)	108,431	*57.5*
	Eaton D. Sargent (D)	79,798	*42.3*
1930	John G. Winant (R)	75,518	*58.0*
	Albert W. Noone (D)	54,441	*41.8*
1932	John G. Winant (R)	106,777	*54.2*
	Henri Ledoux (D)	89,487	*45.4*
1934	H. Styles Bridges (R)	89,481	*50.6*
	John L. Sullivan (D)	87,019	*49.2*
1936	Francis P. Murphy (R)	118,178	*56.6*
	Amos Blandin (D)	89,011	*42.6*
1938	Francis P. Murphy (R)	107,841	*57.1*
	John L. Sullivan (D)	80,847	*42.8*
1940	Robert O. Blood (R)	112,386	*50.7*
	F. Clyde Keefe (D)	109,093	*49.3*
1942	Robert O. Blood (R)	83,766	*52.2*
	William J. Neal (D)	76,782	*47.8*
1944	Charles M. Dale (R)	115,799	*53.1*
	James J. Powers (D)	102,232	*46.9*
1946	Charles M. Dale (R)	103,204	*63.1*
	F. Clyde Keefe (D)	60,247	*36.9*
1948	Sherman Adams (R)	116,212	*52.2*
	Herbert W. Hill (D)	105,207	*47.3*
1950	Sherman Adams (R)	108,907	*57.0*
	Robert P. Bingham (D)	82,258	*43.0*
1952	Hugh Gregg (R)	167,791	*63.2*
	William H. Craig (D)	97,924	*36.9*
1954	Lane Dwinell (R)	107,287	*55.1*
	John Shaw (D)	87,344	*44.9*
1956	Lane Dwinell (R)	141,578	*54.7*
	John Shaw (D)	117,117	*45.3*
1958	Wesley Powell (R)	106,790	*51.7*
	Bernard L. Boutin (D)	99,955	*48.4*
1960	Wesley Powell (R)	161,123	*55.5*
	Bernard L. Boutin (D)	129,404	*44.5*

	Candidates	Votes	%
1962	John W. King (D)	135,481	58.9
	John Pillsbury (R)	94,567	41.1
1964	John W. King (D)	190,863	66.8
	John Pillsbury (R)	94,824	33.2
1966	John W. King (D)	125,882	53.9
	Hugh Gregg (R)	107,259	45.9
1968	Walter Peterson (R)	149,902	52.5
	Emile R. Bussiere (D)	135,378	47.4
1970	Walter Peterson (R)	102,298	46.0
	Roger J. Crowley Jr. (D)	98,098	44.1
	Meldrim Thomson Jr. (AM)	22,033	9.9
1972	Meldrim Thomson Jr. (R)	133,702	41.4
	Roger J. Crowley Jr. (D)	126,107	39.0
	Malcolm McLane (I)	63,199	19.6
1974	Meldrim Thomson Jr. (R)	115,933	51.1
	Richard W. Leonard (D)	110,591	48.8
1976	Meldrim Thomson Jr. (R)	197,589	57.7
	Harry V. Spanos (D)	145,015	42.3
1978	Hugh J. Gallen (D)	133,133	49.4
	Meldrim Thomson Jr. (R)	122,464	45.4
1980	Hugh J. Gallen (D)	226,436	59.0
	Meldrim Thomson Jr. (R)	156,178	40.7
1982	John H. Sununu (R)	145,389	51.4
	Hugh J. Gallen (D)	132,317	46.8
1984	John H. Sununu (R)	256,571	66.8
	Chris Spirou (D)	127,156	33.1
1986	John H. Sununu (R)	134,824	53.7
	Paul McEachern (D)	116,142	46.3
1988	Judd Gregg (R)	267,064	60.4
	Paul McEachern (D)	172,543	39.1
1990	Judd Gregg (R)	177,611	60.2
	J. Joseph Grandmaison (D)	101,886	34.6
1992	Steve Merrill (R)	289,170	56.0
	Deborah "Arnie" Arnesen (D)	206,232	40.0
1994	Steven Merrill (R)	218,134	69.9
	Wayne D. King (D)	79,686	25.6
1996	Jeanne Shaheen (D)	284,175	57.2
	Ovide M. Lamontagne (R)	196,321	39.5

NEW JERSEY

(Ratified the Constitution Dec. 18, 1787)

	Candidates	Votes	%
1844[1]	Charles C. Stratton (W)	37,949	50.9
	Thompson (D)	36,591	49.1
1847	Daniel Haines (D)	34,765	51.9
	William Wright (W)	32,251	48.1
1850	George F. Fort (D)	39,723	53.8
	Runk (W)	34,054	46.2
1853	Rodman M. Price (D)	38,312	52.6
	Haywood (W)	34,530	47.4
1856	William A. Newell (FUS)	50,803	51.3
	Alexander (D)	48,246	48.7
1859	Charles S. Olden (R)	53,315	50.8
	Wright (D)	51,714	49.2
1862	Joel Parker (D)	61,307	56.8
	Marcus L. Ward (UN)	46,710	43.2
1865	Marcus L. Ward (UN)	67,525	51.1
	Runyon (D)	64,706	48.9
1868	Theodore F. Randolph (D)	83,955	51.4
	John I. Blair (R)	79,333	48.6
1871	Joel Parker (D)	82,362	51.9
	Cornelius Walsh (R)	76,383	48.1
1874	Joseph D. Bedle (D)	97,283	53.7
	Halsey (R)	84,050	46.4
1877	George B. McClellan (D)	97,837	51.7
	Newell (R)	85,094	44.9

	Candidates	Votes	%
1880	George C. Ludlow (D)	121,666	49.5
	Potts (R)	121,015	49.3
1883	Leon Abbett (D)	103,856	49.9
	Dixon (R)	97,047	46.7
1886	Robert S. Green (D)	109,939	47.4
	Howey (R)	101,919	44.0
	Fisk (P)	19,808	8.6
1889	Leon Abbett (D)	138,245	51.4
	Grubb (R)	123,992	46.1
1892	George T. Werts (D)	167,257	49.7
	John Kean Jr. (R)	159,632	47.4
1895	John W. Griggs (R)	162,900	52.3
	McGill (D)	136,000	43.6
1898	Foster M. Voorhees (R)	164,051	48.9
	Elvin W. Crane (D & CD)	158,552	47.3
1901	Franklin Murphy (R)	183,814	50.9
	James M. Seymour (D)	166,681	46.1
1904	Edward C. Stokes (R)	231,363	53.5
	Black (D)	179,719	41.6
1907	John Franklin Fort (R)	194,313	49.3
	Katzenbach (D)	186,300	47.3
1910	Woodrow Wilson (D)	233,682	53.9
	Vivian M. Lewis (R)	184,626	42.6
1913	James F. Fielder (D)	173,148	46.1
	Edward C. Stokes (R)	140,298	37.4
	Everett Colby (PROG)	41,132	11.0
1916	Walter E. Edge (R)	247,343	55.4
	Wittpenn (D)	177,696	39.8
1919	Edward I. Edwards (D)	217,486	49.2
	Newton A. K. Bugbee (R)	202,976	45.9
1922	George S. Silzer (D)	427,206	52.2
	Runyon (R)	383,312	46.8
1925	Arthur Harry Moore (D)	471,549	51.9
	Arthur Whitney (R)	433,121	47.6
1928	Morgan F. Larson (R)	824,005	54.9
	William L. Dill (D)	671,728	44.7
1931	Arthur Harry Moore (D)	735,504	57.8
	David Baird Jr. (R)	505,451	39.7
1934	Harold G. Hoffman (R)	686,530	49.9
	William L. Dill (D)	674,096	49.0
1937	Arthur Harry Moore (D)	746,033	50.8
	Lester H. Clee (R)	700,767	47.8
1940	Charles Edison (D)	984,407	51.4
	Robert C. Hendrickson (R)	920,512	48.0
1943	Walter E. Edge (R)	634,364	55.2
	Vincent J. Murphy (D)	506,604	44.1
1946	Alfred E. Driscoll (R)	807,378	57.1
	Lewis G. Hansen (D)	585,960	41.4
1949	Alfred E. Driscoll (R)	885,882	51.5
	Elmer H. Wene (D)	810,022	47.1
1953	Robert B. Meyner (D)	962,710	53.2
	Paul L. Troast (R)	809,068	44.7
1957	Robert B. Meyner (D)	1,101,130	54.6
	Malcolm S. Forbes (R)	897,321	44.5
1961	Richard J. Hughes (D)	1,084,194	50.4
	James P. Mitchell (R)	1,049,274	48.7
1965	Richard J. Hughes (D)	1,279,568	57.4
	Wayne Dumont Jr. (R)	915,996	41.1
1969	William T. Cahill (R)	1,411,905	59.7
	Robert B. Meyner (D)	911,003	38.5
1973	Brendan T. Byrne (D)	1,397,613	66.4
	Charles W. Sandman Jr. (R)	676,235	32.1
1977	Brendan T. Byrne (D)	1,184,564	55.7
	Raymond H. Bateman (R)	888,880	41.8
1981	Thomas H. Kean (R)	1,145,999	49.5
	James J. Florio (D)	1,144,202	49.4
1985	Thomas H. Kean (R)	1,372,631	70.3
	Peter Shapiro (D)	578,402	29.7
1989	James J. Florio (D)	1,379,937	61.2
	Jim Courter (R)	838,553	37.2

	Candidates	Votes	%
1993	Christine Todd Whitman (R)	1,236,124	*49.3*
	James J. Florio (D)	1,210,031	*48.3*
1997	Christine Todd Whitman (R)	1,133,394	*46.9*
	James McGreevey (D)	1,107,968	*45.8*

New Jersey
1. Before 1844 governor chosen by legislature.

NEW MEXICO

(Became a state Jan. 6, 1912)

	Candidates	Votes	%
1911	W. C. McDonald (D)	31,036	*51.0*
	Holm O. Bursum (R)	28,019	*46.1*
1916	Ezequiel C. deBaca (D)	32,875	*49.4*
	Holm O. Bursum (R)	31,552	*47.4*
1918	Octaviano A. Larrazolo (R)	23,752	*50.5*
	Felix Garcia (D)	22,433	*47.7*
1920	Merritt C. Mechem (R)	54,426	*51.3*
	Richard H. Hanna (D)	50,755	*47.8*
1922	James F. Hinkle (D)	60,317	*54.6*
	C. L. Hill (R)	49,363	*44.7*
1924	Arthur T. Hannett (D)	56,183	*48.8*
	Manuel B. Otero (R)	55,984	*48.6*
1926	Richard C. Dillon (R)	56,294	*51.6*
	Arthur T. Hannett (D)	52,523	*48.2*
1928	Richard C. Dillon (R)	65,967	*55.6*
	Robert C. Dow (D)	52,550	*44.3*
1930	Arthur Seligman (D)	62,789	*53.2*
	Clarence M. Botts (R)	55,026	*46.6*
1932	Arthur Seligman (D)	83,612	*54.8*
	Richard C. Dillon (R)	67,406	*44.2*
1934	Clyde Tingley (D)	78,390	*51.9*
	Jaffa Miller (R)	71,899	*47.6*
1936	Clyde Tingley (D)	97,090	*57.2*
	Jaffa Miller (R)	72,539	*42.8*
1938	John E. Miles (D)	82,344	*52.2*
	Albert K. Mitchell (R)	75,017	*47.6*
1940	John E. Miles (D)	103,035	*55.6*
	Maurice Miera (R)	82,306	*44.4*
1942	John J. Dempsey (D)	59,258	*54.6*
	Joseph F. Tondre (R)	49,380	*45.5*
1944	John J. Dempsey (D)	76,443	*51.8*
	Carroll G. Gunderson (R)	71,113	*48.2*
1946	Thomas J. Mabry (D)	70,055	*52.8*
	Edward L. Safford (R)	62,575	*47.2*
1948	Thomas J. Mabry (D)	103,969	*54.7*
	Manuel Lujan (R)	86,023	*45.3*
1950	Edwin L. Mechem (R)	96,846	*53.7*
	John E. Miles (D)	83,359	*46.3*
1952	Edwin L. Mechem (R)	129,116	*53.8*
	Everett Grantham (D)	111,034	*46.2*
1954	John F. Simms Jr. (D)	110,583	*57.0*
	Alvin Stockton (R)	83,373	*43.0*
1956	Edwin L. Mechem (R)	131,488	*52.2*
	John F. Simms Jr. (D)	120,263	*47.8*
1958	John Burroughs (D)	103,481	*50.5*
	Edwin L. Mechem (R)	101,567	*49.5*
1960	Edwin L. Mechem (R)	153,765	*50.3*
	John Burroughs (D)	151,777	*49.7*
1962	Jack M. Campbell (D)	130,933	*53.0*
	Edwin L. Mechem (R)	116,184	*47.0*
1964	Jack M. Campbell (D)	191,497	*60.2*
	Merle H. Tucker (R)	126,540	*39.8*
1966	David F. Cargo (R)	134,625	*51.7*
	T. E. Lusk (D)	125,587	*48.3*
1968	David F. Cargo (R)	160,140	*50.5*
	Fabian Chavez Jr. (D)	157,230	*49.5*

	Candidates	Votes	%
1970	Bruce King (D)	148,835	*51.3*
	Pete V. Domenici (R)	134,640	*46.4*
1974	Jerry Apodaca (D)	164,172	*49.9*
	Joseph R. Skeen (R)	160,430	*48.8*
1978	Bruce King (D)	174,631	*50.5*
	Joseph R. Skeen (R)	170,848	*49.4*
1982	Toney Anaya (D)	215,840	*53.0*
	John B. Irick (R)	191,626	*47.0*
1986	Garrey E. Carruthers (R)	209,455	*53.0*
	Ray B. Powell (D)	185,378	*47.0*
1990	Bruce King (D)	224,564	*54.6*
	Frank M. Bond (R)	185,692	*45.2*
1994	Gary E. Johnson (R)	232,945	*49.8*
	Bruce King (D)	186,686	*39.9*
	Roberto Mondragon (GREEN)	47,990	*10.3*

NEW YORK

(Ratified the Constitution July 26, 1788)

	Candidates	Votes	%
1789	George Clinton	6,391	*51.7*
	Robert Yates	5,962	*48.3*
1792	George Clinton (ANTI-FED)[1]	8,440	*50.3*
	John Jay (FED)	8,332	*49.7*
1795	John Jay (FED)	13,481	*53.1*
	Robert Yates (ANTI-FED)[1]	11,892	*46.9*
1798	John Jay (FED)	16,012	*54.0*
	Robert R. Livingston (ANTI-FED)[1]	13,632	*46.0*
1801	George Clinton (D-R)	24,808	*54.3*
	Stephen Van Rensselaer (FED)	20,843	*45.7*
1804	Morgan Lewis (FED)	30,829	*58.2*
	Aaron Burr (D-R)	22,139	*41.8*
1807	Daniel Tompkins (D-R)	35,074	*53.1*
	Morgan Lewis (ANTI-CLINT)[2]	30,989	*46.9*
1810	Daniel Tompkins (D-R)	43,094	*54.2*
	Jonas Platt (ANTI-CLINT)[2]	36,484	*45.8*
1813	Daniel Tompkins (D-R)	43,324	*52.2*
	Stephen Van Rensselaer (FED)	39,718	*47.8*
1816	Daniel Tompkins (D-R)	45,412	*54.0*
	Rufus King (FED)	38,647	*46.0*

	Candidates	Votes	%
1817	De Witt Clinton (D-R)	43,310	*96.7*

	Candidates	Votes	%
1820	De Witt Clinton (CLINT R)	47,447	*50.8*
	Daniel Tompkins (ANTI-CL R)[3]	45,990	*49.2*
1822	Joseph C. Yates (D-R)	128,493	*97.8*
1824	De Witt Clinton (CLINT R)	103,684	*54.1*
	Samuel Young (VB R)	88,037	*45.9*
1826	De Witt Clinton (CLINT R)	99,808	*51.0*
	William B. Rochester (VB R)	96,080	*49.1*
1828	Martin Van Buren (JAC D)	136,795	*49.5*
	Smith Thompson (NR)	106,415	*38.5*
	Solomon Southwick (A-MAS)	33,335	*12.1*
1830	Enos T. Throop (JAC D)	128,947	*51.7*
	Francis Granger (NR)	120,667	*48.3*
1832	William L. Marcy (JAC D)	166,410	*51.5*
	Francis Granger (NR)	156,672	*48.5*
1834	William L. Marcy (D)	181,900	*51.8*
	William H. Seward (W)	169,008	*48.2*
1836	William L. Marcy (D)	166,218	*54.9*
	Jesse Buel (W)	136,653	*45.1*
1838	William H. Seward (W)	192,882	*51.4*
	William L. Marcy (D)	182,461	*48.6*
1840	Wiliam H. Seward (W)	222,011	*50.3*
	William C. Bouck (D)	216,726	*49.1*

Gubernatorial Elections

	Candidates	Votes	%		Candidates	Votes	%
1842	William C. Bouck (D)	208,062	51.8	1912	William Sulzer (D)	649,559	41.5
	Luther Bradish (W)	186,089	46.4		Job E. Hedges (R)	444,105	28.3
1844	Silas Wright (D)	241,087	49.5		Oscar S. Straus (IL & NPR)	393,183	25.1
	Millard Fillmore (W)	231,060	47.4	1914	Charles S. Whitman (R)	686,701	47.7
1846	John Young (W)	197,627	50.7		Martin H. Glynn (D, I LEAGUE)	541,269	37.5
	Silas Wright (D)	192,361	49.3		William Sulzer (AM, P)	126,270	8.8
1848	Hamilton Fish (W)	218,280	47.9	1916	Charles S. Whitman (R, N PROG)	850,020	52.6
	John Dix (F SOIL)	123,360	27.1		Samuel Seabury (D)	686,862	42.5
	Reuben Walworth (D)	114,457	25.1	1918	Alfred E. Smith (D)	1,009,936	47.4
1850	Washington Hunt (W-A-RENT)	214,614	49.6		Charles S. Whitman (R, P)	995,094	46.6
	Horatio Seymour (D)	214,352	49.6		Charles W. Ervin (SOC)	121,705	5.7
1852	Horatio Seymour (D)	264,121	50.3	1920	Nathan L. Miller (R)	1,335,878	46.6
	Washington Hunt (W)	241,525	46.0		Alfred E. Smith (D)	1,261,812	44.0
1854	Myron H. Clark (FUS R)	156,804	33.4		Joseph D. Cannon (SOC)	159,804	5.6
	Horatio Seymour (SOFT D)	156,495	33.3	1922	Alfred E. Smith (D)	1,397,657	55.2
	Daniel Ullman (AM)	122,282	26.1		Nathan L. Miller (R)	1,011,725	40.0
	Greene C. Bronson (HARD D)	33,850	7.2	1924	Alfred E. Smith (D)	1,627,111	50.0
1856	John A. King (R)	264,400	44.5		Theodore Roosevelt Jr. (R)	1,518,552	46.6
	Amasa J. Parker (D)	198,616	33.4	1926	Alfred E. Smith (D)	1,523,813	52.3
	Erastus Brooks (AM)	130,870	22.0		Ogden L. Mills (R)	1,276,137	43.8
1858	Edwin D. Morgan (R)	247,868	45.5	1928	Franklin D. Roosevelt (D)	2,130,238	49.0
	Amasa J. Parker (D)	230,329	42.3		Albert Ottinger (R)	2,104,630	48.4
	Lorenzo Burrows (AM)	61,137	11.2	1930	Franklin D. Roosevelt (D)	1,770,342	56.1
1860	Edwin D. Morgan (R)	358,002	53.2		Charles H. Tuttle (R)	1,045,231	33.1
	William Kelly (DOUG D)	294,803	43.8		Robert P. Carroll (LAW PRES)	191,666	6.1
1862	Horatio Seymour (D)	306,649	50.9	1932	Herbert H. Lehman (D)	2,659,597	56.7
	James S. Wadsworth (UN)	295,897	49.1		William J. Donovan (R)	1,812,002	38.6
1864	Reuben E. Fenton (UN)	369,557	50.6	1934	Herbert H. Lehman (D)	2,201,727	57.8
	Horatio Seymour (D)	361,264	49.4		Robert Moses (R)	1,393,744	36.6
1866	Reuben E. Fenton (UN)	366,315	50.9	1936	Herbert H. Lehman (D, AM LAB)	2,970,595	53.5
	John T. Hoffman (D)	352,526	49.0		William F. Bleakley (R)	2,450,105	44.1
1868	John T. Hoffman (D)	439,301	51.6	1938	Herbert H. Lehman (D, AM LAB)	2,391,331	50.4
	John A. Griswold (R)	411,355	48.4		Thomas E. Dewey (R, I PROG)	2,326,892	49.0
1870	John T. Hoffman (D)	399,552	51.9	1942	Thomas E. Dewey (R)	2,148,546	52.1
	Stewart L. Woodford (R)	366,436	47.6		John J. Bennett Jr. (D)	1,501,039	36.4
1872	John A. Dix (R)	445,801	53.2		Dean Alfange (AM LAB)	403,626	9.8
	Francis Kernan (LR)	392,350	46.8	1946	Thomas E. Dewey (R)	2,825,633	56.9
1874	Samuel J. Tilden (D)	416,391	52.4		James M. Mead (D, AM LAB)	2,138,482	43.1
	John A. Dix (R)	366,074	46.1	1950	Thomas E. Dewey (R)	2,819,523	53.1
1876	Lucius Robinson (D)	519,832	51.3		Walter A. Lynch (D, L)	2,246,855	42.3
	Edwin D. Morgan (R)	489,371	48.3	1954	Averell Harriman (D, L)	2,560,738	49.6
1879	Alonzo B. Cornell (R)	418,567	46.7		Irving M. Ives (R)	2,549,613	49.4
	Lucius Robinson (D)	375,790	41.9	1958	Nelson A. Rockefeller (R)	3,126,929#	54.7
	John Kelly (TAM D)	77,566	8.7		Averell Harriman (D, L)	2,553,895#	44.7
1882	Grover Cleveland (D)	535,318	58.5	1962	Nelson A. Rockefeller (R)	3,081,587	53.1
	Charles J. Folger (R)	341,464	37.3		Robert M. Morgenthau (D, L)	2,552,418	44.0
1885	David B. Hill (D)	501,456	48.9	1966	Nelson A. Rockefeller (R)	2,690,626	44.6
	Ira Davenport (R)	490,331	47.9		Frank O'Connor (D)	2,298,363	38.1
1888	David B. Hill (D)	650,464	49.4		Paul L. Adams (C)	510,023	8.5
	Warner Miller (R)	631,303	48.0		Franklin Roosevelt Jr. (L)	507,234	8.4
1891	Roswell P. Flower (D)	582,893	50.1	1970	Nelson A. Rockefeller (R, CSI)	3,151,432	52.4
	Jacob Sloat Fassett (R)	534,956	46.0		Arthur J. Goldberg (D, L)	2,421,426	40.3
1894	Levi P. Morton (R)	673,818	53.1		Paul L. Adams (C)	422,514	7.0
	David B. Hill (D)	517,710	40.8	1974	Hugh L. Carey (D, L)	3,028,503	57.2
1896	Frank S. Black (R)	774,253	55.3		Malcolm Wilson (R, C)	2,219,667	41.9
	Wilbur E. Porter (D)	561,361	40.1	1978	Hugh L. Carey (D, L)	2,429,272	50.9
1898	Theodore Roosevelt (R)	661,707	49.0		Perry B. Duryea (R, C)	2,156,404	45.2
	Augustus Van Wyck (D)	643,921	47.7	1982	Mario M. Cuomo (D, L)	2,675,213	50.9
1900	Benjamin B. Odell Jr. (R)	804,859	52.0		Lew Lehrman (R, C)	2,494,827	47.5
	John B. Stanchfield (D)	693,733	44.8	1986	Mario M. Cuomo (D, L)	2,775,229	64.6
1902	Benjamin B. Odell Jr. (R)	665,150	48.1		Andrew P. O'Rourke (R, C)	1,363,810	31.8
	Bird S. Coler (D)	655,398	47.4	1990	Mario M. Cuomo (D, L)	2,157,087	53.2
1904	Frank W. Higgins (R)	813,264	50.3		Pierre A. Rinfret (R)	865,948	21.3
	D. Cady Herrick (D)	732,704	45.3		Herbert I. London (C)	827,614	20.4
1906	Charles Evans Hughes (R)	749,002	50.5	1994	George E. Pataki (R, C, TCN)	2,538,702	48.8
	William R. Hearst (D, I LEAGUE)	691,105	46.6		Mario M. Cuomo (D, L)	2,364,904	45.4
1908	Charles Evans Hughes (R)	804,651	49.1				
	Lewis Stuyvesant Chanler (D)	735,189	44.8				
1910	John A. Dix (D)	689,700	48.0				
	Henry L. Stimson (R)	622,299	43.3				

New York
1. Anti-Federalist Party
2. Anti-Clinton Party
3. Anti-Clinton Republican Party

70

NORTH CAROLINA

(Ratified the Constitution Nov. 21, 1789)

	Candidates	Votes	%
1836[1]	Edward B. Dudley (W)	33,993	53.2
	Richard D. Spaight (D)	29,950	46.8
1838	Edward B. Dudley (W)	38,119	64.2
	John Branch (D)	21,155	35.6
1840	John M. Morehead (W)	44,514	55.0
	Romulus M. Saunders (D)	36,428	45.0
1842	John M. Morehead (W)	39,596	53.1
	Louis D. Henry (D)	35,024	46.9
1844	William A. Graham (W)	42,586	51.9
	Michael Hoke (D)	39,433	48.1
1846	William A. Graham (W)	43,486	55.0
	James B. Shepard (D)	35,627	45.0
1848	Charles Manly (W)	42,536	50.5
	David S. Reid (D)	41,682	49.5
1850	David S. Reid (D)	45,058	51.6
	Charles Manly (W)	42,341	48.5
1852	David S. Reid (D)	48,484	53.0
	John Kerr (W)	42,993	47.0
1854	Thomas Bragg (D)	48,705	51.1
	Alfred Dockery (W)	46,644	48.9
1856	Thomas Bragg (D)	57,698	56.2
	John A. Gilmer (AM)	44,970	43.8
1858	John W. Ellis (D)	56,429	58.5
	Duncan K. McCrae (DISTRIB)	40,036	41.5
1860	John W. Ellis (D)	59,396	52.7
	John Pool (W)	53,303	47.3
1862	Zebulon B. Vance	55,282	72.7
	William J. Johnston	20,813	27.4
1864	Zebulon B. Vance	58,070	80.0
	William W. Holden	14,491	20.0
1865	Jonathan Worth	32,539	55.7
	William W. Holden	25,809	44.2
1866	Jonathan Worth (C)	34,250	75.9
	Alfred Dockery (NC R)	10,759	23.8
1868	William W. Holden (R)	92,235	55.5
	Thomas S. Ashe (C)	73,600	44.3
1872	Tod R. Caldwell (R)	98,630	50.5
	Augustus S. Merrimon (D)	96,731	49.5
1876	Zebulon B. Vance (D)	123,265	52.8
	Thomas Settle (R)	110,061	47.2
1880	Thomas J. Jarvis (D)	121,837	51.3
	Ralph P. Buxton (R)	115,559	48.7
1884	Alfred M. Scales (D)	143,249	53.8
	Tyre York (R)	122,795	46.1
1888	Daniel G. Fowle (D)	148,405	52.0
	Oliver H. Dockery (R)	134,035	46.9
1892	Elias Carr (D)	135,327	48.3
	David M. Furches (R)	94,681	33.8
	Wyatt P. Exum (PP)	47,747	17.0
1896	Daniel L. Russell (R)	154,025	46.5
	Cyrus B. Watson (D)	145,286	43.9
	William A. Guthrie (PP)	30,943	9.4
1900	Charles B. Aycock (D)	186,650	59.6
	Spencer B. Adams (R)	126,296	40.3
1904	R. B. Glenn (D)	128,761	61.7
	C. J. Harris (R)	79,505	38.1
1908	W. W. Kitchin (D)	145,102	57.3
	J. E. Cox (R)	107,760	42.6
1912	Locke Craig (D)	149,972	61.4
	Iredell Meares (PROG)	49,925	20.4
	Thomas Settle (R)	43,627	17.9
1916	Thomas W. Bickett (D)	167,664	58.1
	Frank A. Linney (R)	120,157	41.7
1920	Cameron Morrison (D)	308,151	57.2
	John J. Parker (R)	230,193	42.8
1924	Angus Wilton McLean (D)	294,441	61.3
	I. M. Meekins (R)	185,578	38.7

	Candidates	Votes	%
1928	O. Max Gardner (D)	362,009	55.6
	H. F. Seawell (R)	289,415	44.4
1932	J. C. B. Ehringhaus (D)	497,708	70.1
	Clifford Frazier (R)	212,561	29.9
1936	Clyde R. Hoey (D)	542,139	66.7
	Gilliam Grissom (R)	270,943	33.3
1940	J. Melville Broughton (D)	608,744	75.7
	Robert H. McNeill (R)	195,402	24.3
1944	R. Gregg Cherry (D)	528,995	69.6
	Frank C. Patton (R)	230,968	30.4
1948	W. Kerr Scott (D)	570,995	73.2
	George M. Pritchard (R)	206,166	26.4
1952	William B. Umstead (D)	796,306	67.5
	H. F. Seawell Jr. (R)	383,329	32.5
1956	Luther H. Hodges (D)	760,480	67.0
	Kyle Hayes (R)	375,379	33.1
1960	Terry Sanford (D)	735,248	54.5
	Robert L. Gavin (R)	613,975	45.5
1964	Dan K. Moore (D)	790,343	56.6
	Robert L. Gavin (R)	606,165	43.4
1968	Robert W. Scott (D)	821,232	52.7
	James C. Gardner (R)	737,075	47.3
1972	James C. Holshouser Jr. (R)	767,470	51.0
	Hargrove Bowles Jr. (D)	729,104	48.5
1976	James B. Hunt Jr. (D)	1,081,293	65.0
	David T. Flaherty (R)	564,102	33.9
1980	James B. Hunt Jr. (D)	1,143,145	61.9
	Beverly Lake (R)	691,449	37.4
1984	James G. Martin (R)	1,208,167	54.3
	Rufus Edmisten (D)	1,011,209	45.4
1988	James G. Martin (R)	1,222,338	56.1
	Robert B. Jordan III (D)	957,687	43.9
1992	James B. Hunt Jr. (D)	1,368,246	52.7
	Jim Gardner (R)	1,121,955	43.2
1996	James B. Hunt Jr. (D)	1,436,638	56.0
	Robin Hayes (R)	1,097,053	42.8

North Carolina

1. *Before 1836 governor chosen by General Assembly.*

NORTH DAKOTA

(Became a state Nov. 2, 1889)

	Candidates	Votes	%
1889	John Miller (R)	25,365	66.6
	William Roach (D)	12,733	33.4
1890	Andrew H. Burke (R)	19,053	52.2
	William Roach (D)	12,604	34.6
	Muir (I)	4,821	13.2
1892	Eli C. D. Shortridge (FUS)	18,943	52.4
	Andrew H. Burke (R)	17,203	47.6
1894	Roger Allin (R)	23,723	55.8
	Wallace (POP)	9,354	22.0
	Kinter (D)	8,188	19.2
1896	Frank A. Briggs (R)	25,918	55.6
	R. B. Richardson (FUS)	20,690	44.4
1898	Frederick B. Fancher (R)	27,308	58.4
	Holmes (FUS)	19,496	41.7
1900	Frank White (R)	34,052	59.2
	M. A. Wipperman (D & I)	22,275	38.7
1902	Frank White (R)	31,613	62.7
	Cronan (D)	17,576	34.9
1904	Elmore Y. Sarles (R)	48,026	70.7
	M. F. Hegge (D)	16,744	24.7
1906	John Burke (D)	34,424	53.2
	Elmore Y. Sarles (R)	29,309	45.3
1908	John Burke (D)	49,398	51.1
	C. A. Johnson (R)	46,849	48.4

	Candidates	Votes	%
1910	John Burke (D)	47,005	50.0
	C. A. Johnson (R)	44,555	47.4
1912	Louis B. Hanna (R)	39,811	45.5
	F. O. Hellstrom (D)	31,544	36.0
	W. D. Sweet (PROG)	9,406	10.7
	A. E. Bowen Jr. (SOC)	6,835	7.8
1914	Louis B. Hanna (R)	44,279	49.6
	F. O. Hellstrom (D)	34,746	38.9
	J. A. Williams (SOC)	6,019	6.7
1916	Lynn J. Frazier (R)	87,665	79.2
	D. H. McArthur (D)	20,351	18.4
1918	Lynn J. Frazier (R & NP)	54,517	59.7
	S. J. Doyle (D & I)	36,733	40.3
1920	Lynn J. Frazier (R & NP)	117,018	51.0
	J. F. T. O'Connor (D & I)	112,488	49.0

	Candidates	Votes	%
1921	Ragnvald A. Nestos (IR)	111,434	50.9
	Lynn J. Frazier (R & NP)	107,332	49.1

	Candidates	Votes	%
1922	Ragnvald A. Nestos (R)	110,321	57.7
	William Lemke (NON PART)	81,048	42.4
1924	Arthur G. Sorlie (R)	101,170	53.9
	Halvor L. Halvorson (D)	86,414	46.1
1926	Arthur G. Sorlie (R)	131,003	81.7
	D. M. Holmes (D)	24,287	15.2
1928	George F. Shafer (R)	131,193	56.5
	Walter Maddock (D)	100,205	43.2
1930	George F. Shafer (R)	133,264	73.6
	Pierce Blewett (D)	41,988	23.2
1932	William Langer (R)	134,231	54.8
	Herbert C. Depuy (D)	110,263	45.0
1934	Thomas H. Moodie (D)	145,433	53.0
	Lydia Langer (R)	127,954	46.6
1936	William Langer (I)	98,750	35.8
	Walter Welford (R)	95,697	34.7
	John Moses (D)	80,726	29.3
1938	John Moses (D)	138,270	52.5
	John N. Hagan (R)	125,246	47.5
1940	John Moses (D)	173,278	63.1
	Jack A. Patterson (R)	101,287	36.9
1942	John Moses (D)	101,390	57.6
	Oscar W. Hagen (R)	74,577	42.4
1944	Fred G. Aandahl (R)	107,863	52.0
	William T. Depuy (D)	59,961	28.9
	Alvin C. Strutz (IR)	38,997	18.8
1946	Fred G. Aandahl (R)	116,672	68.9
	Quentin Burdick (D)	52,719	31.1
1948	Fred G. Aandahl (R)	131,764	61.3
	Howard Henry (D)	80,655	37.5
1950	Norman Brunsdale (R)	121,822	66.3
	Clyde G. Byerly (D)	61,950	33.7
1952	Norman Brunsdale (R)	199,944	78.7
	Ole S. Johnson (D)	53,990	21.3
1954	Norman Brunsdale (R)	124,253	64.2
	Cornelius Bymers (D)	69,248	35.8
1956	John E. Davis (R)	147,566	58.5
	Wallace E. Warner (D)	104,869	41.5
1958	John E. Davis (R)	111,836	53.1
	John F. Lord (D)	98,763	46.9
1960	William L. Guy (D)	136,148	49.4
	C. P. Dahl (R)	122,486	44.5
	Herschel Lashkowitz (I)	16,741	6.1
1962	William L. Guy (D)	115,258	50.4
	Mark Andrews (R)	113,251	49.6
1964	William L. Guy (D)	146,414	55.7
	Don Halcrow (R)	116,247	44.3
1968	William L. Guy (D)	135,955	54.8
	Robert P. McCarney (R)	108,382	43.7

	Candidates	Votes	%
1972	Arthur A. Link (D)	143,899	51.0
	Richard Larsen (R)	138,032	49.0
1976	Arthur A. Link (D)	153,309	51.6
	Richard Elkin (R)	138,321	46.5
1980	Allen I. Olson (R)	162,230	53.6
	Arthur A. Link (D)	140,391	46.4
1984	George Sinner (D)	173,922	55.3
	Allen I. Olson (R)	140,460	44.7
1988	George Sinner (D)	179,094	59.9
	Leon Mallberg (R)	119,986	40.1
1992	Edward T. Schafer (R)	176,398	57.9
	Nicholas Spaeth (D)	123,845	40.6
1996	Edward T. Schafer (R)	174,937	66.2
	Lee Kaldor (D)	89,349	33.8

OHIO

(Became a state March 1, 1803)

	Candidates	Votes	%
1803	Edward Tiffin (D-R)	4,564	
1805	Edward Tiffin (D-R)	4,783	
1807[1]	Return J. Meigs Jr. (D-R)	5,550	53.8
	Nathanael Massie (D-R)	4,757	46.2
1808	Samuel Huntington (D-R)	7,293	44.8
	Thomas Worthington (D-R)	5,601	34.4
	Thomas Kirker (D-R)	3,397	20.9
1810	Return J. Meigs Jr. (D-R)	9,924	56.2
	Thomas Worthington (D-R)	7,731	43.8
1812	Return J. Meigs Jr. (FED)	11,859	60.0
	Thomas Scott (D-R)	7,903	40.0
1814	Thomas Worthington (D-R)	15,879	72.0
	Othniel Looker (FED)	6,171	28.0
1816	Thomas Worthington (D-R)	22,931	74.4
	James Dunlap (D-R)	6,295	20.4
	Ethan A. Brown (FED)	1,607	5.2
1818	Ethan A. Brown (D-R)	30,194	78.9
	James Dunlap (D-R)	8,075	21.1
1820	Ethan A. Brown (D-R)	34,836	71.3
	Jeremiah Morrow (D-R)	9,426	19.3
	William H. Harrison (D-R)	4,348	8.9
1822	Jeremiah Morrow (D-R)	26,059	43.4
	Allen Trimble (FED)	22,889	38.1
	William W. Irwin (D-R)	11,060	18.4
1824	Jeremiah Morrow (JAC D)	38,328	51.0
	Allen Trimble (NR)	36,869	49.0
1826	Allen Trimble (NR)	70,475	84.2
	Alex Campbell	4,765	5.7
	Benjamin Tappan	4,209	5.0
1828	Allen Trimble (NR)	53,971	51.4
	John W. Campbell (JAC D)	51,004	48.5
1830	Duncan McArthur (NR)	49,677	50.1
	Robert Lucas (JAC D)	49,186	49.6
1832	Robert Lucas (D)	71,038	52.9
	Darius Lyman (NR)	63,213	47.1
1834	Robert Lucas (D)	70,738	51.2
	James Findlay (W)	67,414	48.8
1836	Joseph Vance (W)	92,204	51.6
	Eli Baldwin (D)	86,158	48.3
1838	Wilson Shannon (D)	107,884	51.4
	Joseph Vance (W)	102,146	48.6
1840	Thomas Corwin (W)	145,444	52.9
	Wilson Shannon (D)	129,312	47.1
1842	Wilson Shannon (D)	119,774	49.3
	Thomas Corwin (W)	117,902	48.6
1844	Mordecai Bartley (W)	146,333	48.7
	David Tod (D)	145,062	48.3

	Candidates	Votes	%
1846	William Bebb (W)	118,857	48.3
	David Tod (D)	116,554	47.3
1848	Seabury Ford (W)	148,766‡	49.9
	John B. Weller (D)	148,452	49.8
1850	Reuben Wood (D)	133,093	49.7
	William Johnston (W)	121,105	45.2
	Edward Smith (F SOIL)	13,747	5.1
1851	Reuben Wood (D)	145,656	51.6
	Samuel F. Vinton (W)	119,550	42.4
	Samuel Lewis (F SOIL)	16,910	6.0
1853	William Medill (D)	147,663	52.1
	Nelson Barrere (W)	85,843	30.3
	Samuel Lewis (F SOIL)	49,846	17.6
1855	Salmon P. Chase (R)	146,720	48.6
	William Medill (D)	131,019	43.4
	Allen Trimble (W)	24,276	8.0
1857	Salmon P. Chase (R)	160,685	48.6
	H. B. Payne (D)	159,294	48.2
1859	William Dennison Jr. (R)	184,502	51.9
	Rufus P. Ranney (D)	171,266	48.1
1861	David Tod (UN)	206,997	57.7
	Hugh J. Jewett (D)	151,774	42.3
1863	John Brough (UN)	288,856	60.6
	C. L. Vallandigham (D)	187,728	39.4
1865	Jacob D. Cox (UN)	223,642	53.5
	George W. Morgan (D)	193,791	46.4
1867	Rutherford B. Hayes (R)	243,811	50.3
	A. G. Thurman (D)	240,622	49.7
1869	Rutherford B. Hayes (R)	236,092	50.7
	George H. Pendleton (D)	228,703	49.1
1871	Edward F. Noyes (R)	238,273	51.8
	George W. McCook (D)	218,105	47.4
1873	William Allen (D)	214,654	47.8
	Edward F. Noyes (R)	213,837	47.6
1875	Rutherford B. Hayes (R)	297,817	50.3
	William Allen (D)	292,279	49.3
1877	Richard M. Bishop (D)	271,642	48.9
	William H. West (R)	249,105	44.9
1879	Charles Foster (R)	336,321	50.3
	Thomas Ewing (D)	319,132	47.7
1881	Charles Foster (R)	312,785	50.1
	John W. Bookwalter (D)	288,426	46.2
1883	George Hoadly (D)	359,693	50.1
	Joseph B. Foraker (R)	347,164	48.3
1885	Joseph B. Foraker (R)	359,281	49.1
	George Hoadly (D)	341,830	46.8
1887	Joseph B. Foraker (R)	356,534	47.9
	Thomas E. Powell (D)	333,205	44.8
1889	James E. Campbell (D)	379,423	48.9
	Joseph B. Foraker (R)	368,551	47.5
1891	William McKinley Jr. (R)	386,739	48.6
	James E. Campbell (D)	365,228	45.9
1893	William McKinley Jr. (R)	433,342	52.6
	Lawrence T. Neal (D)	352,347	42.8
1895	Asa S. Bushnell (R)	427,141	51.0
	James E. Campbell (D)	334,519	40.0
	Jacob S. Coxey (PP)	52,625	6.3
1897	Asa S. Bushnell (R)	429,915	50.3
	Horace L. Chapman (D)	401,750	47.0
1899	George K. Nash (R)	417,199	45.9
	John R. McLean (D)	368,176	40.5
	Samuel M. Jones (NON PART)	106,721	11.8
1901	George K. Nash (R)	436,092	52.7
	James Kilbourne (D)	368,525	44.5
1903	Myron T. Herrick (R)	475,560	54.9
	Tom L. Johnson (D)	361,748	41.8
1905	John M. Pattison (D)	473,264	50.5
	Myron T. Herrick (R)	430,617	46.0
1908	Judson Harmon (D)	552,569	49.2
	Andrew L. Harris (R)	533,197	47.5
1910	Judson Harmon (D)	477,077	51.6
	Warren G. Harding (R)	376,700	40.8
	Tom Clifford (SOC)	60,637	6.6
1912	James M. Cox (D)	439,023	42.4
	Robert B. Brown (R)	272,500	26.3
	Arthur L. Garford (PROG)	217,903	21.0
	C. E. Ruthenberg (SOC)	87,709	8.5
1914	Frank B. Willis (R)	523,074	46.3
	James M. Cox (D)	493,804	43.7
	James R. Garfield (PROG)	60,904	5.4
1916	James M. Cox (D)	568,218	48.4
	Frank B. Willis (R)	561,602	47.8
1918	James M. Cox (D)	486,403	50.6
	Frank B. Willis (R)	474,559	49.4
1920	Harry L. Davis (R)	1,039,835	51.9
	Vic Donahey (D)	918,962	45.9
1922	Vic Donahey (D)	821,948	50.5
	Carmi A. Thompson (R)	804,200	49.4
1924	Vic Donahey (D)	1,065,981	54.0
	Harry L. Davis (R)	888,139	45.0
1926	Vic Donahey (D)	707,733	50.5
	Myers Y. Cooper (R)	685,897	49.0
1928	Myers Y. Cooper (R)	1,355,517	54.8
	Martin L. Davey (D)	1,106,739	44.7
1930	George White (D)	1,033,168	52.8
	Myers Y. Cooper (R)	923,538	47.2
1932	George White (D)	1,356,518	52.8
	David S. Ingalls (R)	1,151,933	44.9
1934	Martin L. Davey (D)	1,118,257	51.1
	Clarence J. Brown (R)	1,052,851	48.1
1936	Martin L. Davey (D)	1,539,461	52.0
	John W. Bricker (R)	1,412,773	47.7
1938	John W. Bricker (R)	1,265,548	52.5
	Charles Sawyer (D)	1,147,323	47.6
1940	John W. Bricker (R)	1,824,863	55.6
	Martin L. Davey (D)	1,460,396	44.5
1942	John W. Bricker (R)	1,086,937	60.5
	John McSweeney (D)	709,599	39.5
1944	Frank J. Lausche (D)	1,603,809	51.8
	James Garfield Stewart (R)	1,491,450	48.2
1946	Thomas J. Herbert (R)	1,166,550	50.6
	Frank J. Lausche (D)	1,125,997	48.9
1948	Frank J. Lausche (D)	1,619,775	53.7
	Thomas J. Herbert (R)	1,398,514	46.3
1950	Frank J. Lausche (D)	1,522,249	52.6
	Don H. Ebright (R)	1,370,570	47.4
1952	Frank J. Lausche (D)	2,015,110	55.9
	Charles P. Taft (R)	1,590,058	44.1
1954	Frank J. Lausche (D)	1,405,262	54.1
	James A. Rhodes (R)	1,192,528	45.9
1956	C. William O'Neill (R)	1,984,988	56.0
	Michael V. DiSalle (D)	1,557,103	44.0
1958	Michael V. DiSalle (D)	1,869,260	56.9
	C. William O'Neill (R)	1,414,874	43.1
1962	James A. Rhodes (R)	1,836,432	58.9
	Michael V. DiSalle (D)	1,280,521	41.1
1966	James A. Rhodes (R)	1,795,277	62.2
	Frazier Reams Jr. (D)	1,092,054	37.8
1970	John J. Gilligan (D)	1,725,560	54.2
	Roger Cloud (R)	1,382,659	43.4
1974	James A. Rhodes (R)	1,493,679	48.6
	John J. Gilligan (D)	1,482,191	48.2
1978	James A. Rhodes (R)	1,402,167	49.3
	Richard F. Celeste (D)	1,354,631	47.6
1982	Richard F. Celeste (D)	1,981,882	59.0
	Clarence Brown Jr. (R)	1,303,962	38.8
1986	Richard F. Celeste (D)	1,858,372	60.6
	James A. Rhodes (R)	1,207,264	39.4
1990	George V. Voinovich (R)	1,928,103	55.7
	Anthony J. Celebrezze Jr. (D)	1,539,416	44.3

OREGON

(Became a state Feb. 14, 1859)

	Candidates	Votes	%
1994	George V. Voinovich (R)	2,401,572	71.8
	Robert L. Burch Jr. (D)	835,849	25.0

Ohio

1. The election was challenged by Massie. The legislature eventually declared Meigs ineligible and arranged for a new election in 1808. Pending the outcome of that election, Speaker of the Senate Thomas Kirker was acting governor.

OKLAHOMA

(Became a state Nov. 16, 1907)

	Candidates	Votes	%
1907	Charles N. Haskell (D)	137,633	53.4
	Frank Frantz (R)	110,296	42.8
1910	Lee Cruce (D)	119,873	48.6
	J. W. McNeal (R)	99,319	40.2
	J. T. Crumbie (SOC)	24,457	9.9
1914	Robert L. Williams (D)	100,596	39.7
	John Fields (R)	95,909	37.8
	Fred W. Holt (SOC)	52,704	20.8
1918	James B. A. Robertson (D)	104,132	53.5
	Horace G. McKeever (R)	82,905	42.6
1922	John C. Walton (D)	280,207	54.5
	John Fields (R)	230,469	44.8
1926	Henry S. Johnston (D)	213,162	54.9
	Omer K. Benedict (R)	171,710	44.2
1930	William H. Murray (D)	301,921	59.1
	Ira A. Hill (R)	208,575	40.8
1934	E. W. Marland (D)	365,992	58.2
	William B. Pine (R)	243,936	38.8
1938	Leon C. Phillips (D)	355,740	70.0
	Ross Rizley (R)	148,861	29.3
1942	Robert S. Kerr (D)	196,565	51.9
	William J. Otjen (R)	180,454	47.6
1946	Roy J. Turner (D)	259,491	52.5
	Olney F. Flynn (R)	227,426	46.0
1950	Johnston Murray (D)	329,308	51.1
	Jo O. Ferguson (R)	313,205	48.6
1954	Raymond Gary (D)	357,386	58.7
	Reuben K. Sparks (R)	251,808	41.3
1958	J. Howard Edmondson (D)	399,504	74.1
	Phil Ferguson (R)	107,495	20.0
	D. A. Jelly Boyce (I)	31,840	5.9
1962	Henry L. Bellmon (R)	392,316	55.3
	W. P. Atkinson (D)	315,357	44.4
1966	Dewey F. Bartlett (R)	377,078	55.7
	Preston J. Moore (D)	296,328	43.8
1970	David Hall (D)	338,338	48.4
	Dewey F. Bartlett (R)	336,157	48.1
1974	David L. Boren (D)	514,389	63.9
	James M. Inhofe (R)	290,459	36.1
1978	George Nigh (D)	402,240	51.7
	Ron Shotts (R)	367,055	47.2
1982	George Nigh (D)	548,159	62.1
	Tom Daxon (R)	332,207	37.6
1986	Henry L. Bellmon (R)	431,762	47.5
	David Walters (D)	405,295	44.5
	Jerry Brown (I)	60,115	6.6
1990	David Walters (D)	523,196	57.4
	Bill Price (R)	297,584	32.7
	Thomas D. Ledgerwood II (I)	90,534	9.9
1994	Frank Keating (R)	466,740	46.9
	Jack Mildren (D)	294,936	29.6
	Wes Watkins (I)	233,336	23.5

OREGON

(Became a state Feb. 14, 1859)

	Candidates	Votes	%
1858	John Whiteaker (D)	5,134	54.7
	E. M. Barnum (OPP)	4,213	44.9
1862	A. C. Gibbs (UN R)	7,039	67.1
	John F. Miller (D)	3,450	32.9
1866	George L. Woods (R)	10,316	50.7
	James K. Kelly (D)	10,039	49.3
1870	La Fayette Grover (D)	11,726	51.4
	Joel Palmer (R)	11,095	48.6
1874	La Fayette Grover (D)	9,713	38.2
	J. C. Tolman (R)	9,163	36.1
	Thomas F. Campbell (I)	6,532	25.7
1878	William Wallace Thayer (D)	15,689	47.9
	C. C. Beekman (R)	15,610	47.7
1882	Zenas F. Moody (R)	21,481	51.8
	Smith (D)	20,029	48.3
1886	Sylvester Pennoyer (D)	27,901	50.9
	T. R. Cornelius (R)	24,199	44.1
1890	Sylvester Pennoyer (D)	38,920	53.6
	D. P. Thompson (R)	33,765	46.5
1894	William P. Lord (R)	41,139	47.2
	Nathan Pierce (PP)	26,125	30.0
	William Galloway (D)	17,865	20.5
1898	Theodore Thurston Geer (R)	45,094	53.2
	W. R. King (D-PP)	34,542	40.8
1902	George E. Chamberlain (D)	41,857	46.2
	W. J. Furnish (R)	41,611	45.9
1906	George E. Chamberlain (D)	46,002	47.6
	James Withycombe (R)	43,508	45.0
	C. W. Barzee (SOC)	4,468	5.0
1910	Oswald West (D)	54,853	46.6
	Jay Bowerman (R)	48,751	41.4
	W. S. Richards (SOC)	8,040	6.8
	A. E. Eaton (P)	6,046	5.1
1914	James Withycombe (R)	121,037	48.8
	C. J. Smith (D)	94,594	38.1
	W. J. Smith (SOC)	14,284	5.8
1918	James Withycombe (R)	81,067	53.0
	Walter M. Pierce (D)	65,440	42.8
1922	Walter M. Pierce (D)	133,392	57.4
	Ben W. Olcott (R)	99,164	42.6
1926	I. L. Patterson (R)	120,073	53.1
	Walter M. Pierce (D)	93,470	41.4
	H. H. Stallard (I)	12,402	5.5
1930	Julius L. Meier (I)	135,608	54.5
	Ed F. Bailey (D)	62,434	25.1
	Phil Metschan (R)	46,840	18.8
1934	Charles H. Martin (D)	116,677	38.6
	Peter Zimmerman (I)	95,519	31.6
	Joe E. Dunne (R)	86,923	28.7
1938	Charles A. Sprague (R)	214,062	57.4
	Henry L. Hess (D)	158,744	42.6
1942	Earl Snell (R)	220,188	77.9
	Lew Wallace (D)	62,561	22.1
1946	Earl Snell (R)	237,681	69.1
	Carl C. Donaugh (D)	106,474	30.9
1948	Douglas McKay (R)	271,295	53.2
	Lew Wallace (D)	226,949	44.5
1950	Douglas McKay (R)	334,160	66.1
	Austin F. Flegal (D)	171,750	34.0
1954	Paul Patterson (R)	322,522	56.9
	Joseph K. Carson Jr. (D)	244,179	43.1

	Candidates	Votes	%
1956	Robert D. Holmes (D)	369,439	50.5
	Elmo Smith (R)	361,840	49.5
1958	Mark O. Hatfield (R)	331,900	55.3
	Robert D. Holmes (D)	267,934	44.7
1962	Mark O. Hatfield (R)	345,497	54.2
	Robert Y. Thornton (D)	265,359	41.6
1966	Tom McCall (R)	377,346	55.3
	Robert W. Straub (D)	305,008	44.7
1970	Tom McCall (R)	369,964	55.6
	Robert W. Straub (D)	293,892	44.2
1974	Robert W. Straub (D)	444,812	57.7
	Victor Atiyeh (R)	324,751	42.1
1978	Victor Atiyeh (R)	498,452	54.9
	Robert W. Straub (D)	409,411	44.9
1982	Victor Atiyeh (R)	639,841	61.4
	Ted Kulongoski (D)	374,316	35.9
1986	Neil Goldschmidt (D)	549,456	51.9
	Norma Paulus (R)	506,986	47.8
1990	Barbara Roberts (D)	508,749	45.7
	Dave Frohnmayer (R)	444,646	40.0
	Al Mobley (I)	144,062	12.9
1994	John Kitzhaber (D)	622,083	50.9
	Denny Smith (R)	517,874	42.4

PENNSYLVANIA

(Ratified the Constitution Dec. 12, 1787)

	Candidates	Votes	%
1790	Thomas Mifflin	27,725	90.8
	Arthur St. Clair (FED)	2,802	9.2
1793	Thomas Mifflin (D-R)	18,590	63.5
	Frederick A. Muhlenberg (FED)	10,706	36.5
1796	Thomas Mifflin (D-R)	30,020	96.7
1799	Thomas McKean (D-R)	38,036	53.8
	James Ross (FED)	32,641	46.2
1802	Thomas McKean (D-R)	47,849	73.6
	James Ross (FED)	17,037	26.2
1805	Thomas McKean (I D-R)[1]	43,644	52.9
	Simon Snyder (D-R)	38,833	47.1
1808	Simon Snyder (D-R)	67,975	60.9
	James Ross (FED)	39,575	35.5
1811	Simon Snyder (D-R)	52,319	90.8
	William Tilghman (FED)	3,609	6.3
1814	Simon Snyder (D-R)	51,009	62.6
	Isaac Wayne (FED)	29,566	36.3
1817	William Findlay (D-R)	66,331	52.8
	Joseph Hiester (D-R/FED)	59,272	47.2
1820	Joseph Hiester (D-R)	67,905	50.6
	William Findlay (D-R)	66,300	49.4
1823	John Andrew Schulze (D-R)	89,928	58.3
	Andrew Gregg	64,211	41.7
1826	John Andrew Schulze (JAC D)	72,710	96.9
1829	George Wolf (JAC D)	78,138	60.1
	Joseph Ritner (A-MAS)	51,776	39.9
1832	George Wolf (D)	91,385	50.9
	Joseph Ritner (A-MAS)	88,115	49.1
1835	Joseph Ritner (D)	94,023	46.9
	George Wolf (W)	65,804	32.8
	Henry Muhlenburgh	40,586	20.3
1838	David R. Porter (D)	127,821	51.1
	Joseph Ritner (A-MASC)	122,325	48.9
1841	David R. Porter (D)	136,504	54.4
	John Banks (W)	113,453	45.3

	Candidates	Votes	%
1844	Francis R. Shunk (D)	160,322	50.3
	Joseph Markle (W)	156,041	48.9
1847	Francis R. Shunk (D)	146,081	50.8
	James Irwin (W)	128,148	44.6
1848	William F. Johnston (W)	168,522	50.0
	Morris Longstreth (D)	168,225	50.0
1851	William Bigler (D)	186,499	50.9
	William F. Johnston (W)	178,034	48.6
1854	James Pollock (W)	203,822	54.6
	William Bigler (D)	166,991	44.8
1857	William F. Packer (D)	188,836	52.0
	David Wilmot (R)	146,139	40.2
	Isaac Hazlehurst (AM)	28,168	7.8
1860	Andrew G. Curtin (R)	262,403	53.3
	Henry D. Foster (D)	230,269	46.7
1863	Andrew G. Curtin (R)	269,496	51.5
	George W. Woodward (D)	254,171	48.5
1866	John White Geary (R)	307,274	51.4
	Hiester Clymer (D)	290,096	48.6
1869	John White Geary (R)	290,552	50.4
	Asa Packer (D)	285,956	49.6
1872	John Frederick Hartranft (R)	353,387	52.6
	Charles B. Buckalew (D)	317,823	47.3
1875	John Frederick Hartranft (R)	304,175	49.9
	Cyrus L. Pershing (D)	292,136	47.9
1878	Henry Martyn Hoyt (R)	319,567	45.5
	Andrew H. Dill (D)	297,060	42.3
	Samuel R. Mason (G)	81,758	11.6
1882	Robert E. Pattison (D)	355,791	47.8
	James A. Beaver (R)	315,589	42.4
	John Stewart (IR)	43,743	5.9
1886	James A. Beaver (R)	412,285	50.3
	Chauncey F. Black (D)	369,634	45.1
1890	Robert E. Pattison (D)	464,209	50.0
	George W. Delamater (R)	447,655	48.2
1894	Daniel H. Hastings (R)	574,801	60.3
	William M. Singerly (D)	333,404	35.0
1898	William A. Stone (R)	476,206	49.0
	George A. Jenks (D)	358,300	36.9
	Silas C. Swallow (P, HG)	132,931	13.7
1902	Samuel W. Pennypacker (R)	592,867	54.2
	Robert E. Pattison (D)	436,451	39.9
1906	Edwin S. Stuart (R)	506,418	50.3
	Lewis Emery Jr. (D, LINCOLN)	458,064	45.5
1910	John K. Tener (R)	412,658	41.3
	William H. Berry (KEY)	382,127	38.3
	Webster Grim (D)	129,395	13.0
	John W. Slayton (SOC)	53,055	5.3
1914	Martin G. Brumbaugh (R, KEY)	588,705	53.0
	Vance C. McCormick (D, WASH)	453,880	40.8
1918	William Sproul (R, WASH)	552,537	61.1
	Eugene C. Bonniwell (D, F PLAY)	305,315	33.7
1922	Gifford Pinchot (R)	831,696	56.8
	John A. McSparran (D)	581,625	39.7
1926	John S. Fisher (R)	1,102,823	73.3
	Eugene C. Bonniwell (D, LAB)	365,280	24.3
1930	Gifford Pinchot (R, P)	1,068,874	50.8
	John M. Hemphill (D, L)	1,010,204	47.7
1934	George H. Earle (D)	1,476,377	50.0
	William A. Schnader (R)	1,410,138	47.8
1938	Arthur H. James (R)	2,036,345	53.4
	Charles Jones (D, ROYAL OAK)	1,756,280	46.1
1942	Edward Martin (R)	1,367,531	53.7
	F. Clair Ross (D)	1,149,897	45.1
1946	James H. Duff (R)	1,828,462	58.5
	John S. Rice (D)	1,270,947	40.7
1950	John S. Fine (R)	1,796,119	50.7
	Richardson Dilworth (D)	1,710,355	48.3
1954	George M. Leader (D)	1,996,266	53.7
	Lloyd H. Wood (R)	1,717,070	46.2

	Candidates	Votes	%
1958	David L. Lawrence (D)	2,024,852	50.8
	Arthur T. McGonigle (R)	1,948,769	48.9
1962	William W. Scranton (R)	2,424,918	55.4
	Richardson Dilworth (D)	1,938,627	44.3
1966	Raymond P. Shafer (R)	2,110,349	52.1
	Milton Shapp (D)	1,868,719	46.1
1970	Milton Shapp (D)	2,043,029	55.2
	Raymond J. Broderick (R)	1,542,854	41.7
1974	Milton Shapp (D)	1,878,252	53.8
	Andrew "Drew" L. Lewis Jr. (R)	1,578,917	45.2
1978	Richard L. Thornburgh (R)	1,966,042	52.5
	Peter Flaherty (D)	1,737,888	46.4
1982	Richard L. Thornburgh (R)	1,872,784	50.8
	Allen E. Ertel (D)	1,772,353	48.1
1986	Robert P. Casey (D)	1,717,484	50.7
	William W. Scranton (R)	1,638,268	48.3
1990	Robert P. Casey (D)	2,065,244	67.7
	Barbara Hafer (R)	987,516	32.3
1994	Tom J. Ridge (R)	1,627,976	45.4
	Mark S. Singel (D)	1,430,099	39.9
	Peg Luksik (CST)	460,269	12.8

Pennsylvania
1. Independent Democratic-Republican.

RHODE ISLAND

(Ratified the Constitution May 29, 1790)

	Candidates	Votes	%
1790-1796	Arthur Fenner	✔	
1797	Arthur Fenner	1,204	
1798-1800	Arthur Fenner	✔	
1801	Arthur Fenner	3,756	
1802	Arthur Fenner	3,802	66.3
	William Greene	1,934	33.7
1803-1805	Arthur Fenner	✔	
1806	Richard Jackson Jr.	1,662 *	43.1
	Henry Smith	1,097	28.4
	Peleg Arnold	1,094	28.3
1807	James Fenner	2,564	65.9
	Seth Wheaton	1,268	32.6
1808-1810	James Fenner	✔	
1811	William Jones (FED)	3,885	51.1
	James Fenner	3,651	48.1
1812	William Jones (FED)	4,122	51.5
	James Fenner	3,874	48.4
1813	William Jones	3,350	
1814	William Jones	2,713	76.6
1815	William Jones (FED)	3,372	56.6
	Peleg Arnold (D-R)	2,588	43.4
1816	William Jones (FED)	3,591	52.4
	Nehemiah R. Knight (D-R)	3,259	47.6
1817	Nehemiah R. Knight (D-R)	3,949	50.4
	William Jones (FED)	3,878	49.5
1818	Nehemiah R. Knight (D-R)	4,509	53.7
	Elisha R. Potter (FED)	3,893	46.3
1819	Nehemiah R. Knight	2,664	
1820	Nehemiah R. Knight	1,981	100.0
1821	William C. Gibbs (D-R)	3,801	57.6
	Samuel W. Bridgham	2,801¹	
1822	William C. Gibbs	2,092	100.0
1823	William C. Gibbs	1,647	100.0
1824	James Fenner	2,146	78.3
	Wheeler Martin	594	21.7
1825	James Fenner	1,731	100.0
1826	James Fenne	✔	
1827	James Fenner	2,421	100.0

	Candidates	Votes	%
1828	James Fenner	4,233	100.0
1829	James Fenner	3,584	100.0
1830	James Fenner	2,793	63.1
	Asa Messer	1,455	32.9
1831	Lemuel H. Arnold	3,780	56.8
	James Fenner	2,877	43.2
1832	Lemuel H. Arnold	2,711*	48.5
	James Fenner	2,283	40.8
	William Sprague	592	10.6
1833	John Brown Francis	4,025	55.0
	Lemuel H. Arnold	3,292	45.0
1834	John Brown Francis	3,676	51.0
	Nehemiah R. Knight	3,520	48.9
1835	John Brown Francis	3,880	50.7
	Nehemiah R. Knight	3,774	49.3
1836	John Brown Francis	4,020	56.2
	Tristam Burges	2,984	41.7
1837	John Brown Francis	2,716	73.1
	William Peckham	946	25.5
1838	William Sprague	3,984	52.5
	John Brown Francis	3,504	46.2
1839	William Sprague	2,948*	47.4
	Nathaniel Bullock	2,771	44.6
	Tristam Burges	457	7.4
1840	Samuel Ward King (W)	4,797	58.4
	Thomas F. Carpenter	3,418	41.6
1841	Samuel Ward King (W)	2,648	97.7
1842	Samuel Ward King (W)	4,866	67.9
	Thomas F. Carpenter	2,291	32.0
1843	James Fenner (L & O W)	9,140	55.3
	Thomas F. Carpenter (D)	7,393	44.7
1844	James Fenner (LAW ORD)	5,560	96.4
1845	Charles Jackson (LIBER W)	7,900	50.4
	James Fenner (L & O W)	7,699	49.2
1846	Byron Diman (L & O W)	7,477†	49.8
	Charles Jackson (D & LIBN)	7,391	49.2
1847	Elisha Harris (W)	6,300	55.3
	Olney Ballou (D)	4,350	38.2
1848	Elisha Harris (W)	5,695	58.0
	Adnah Sackett (D)	3,683	37.5
1849	Henry B. Anthony (W)	5,081	59.0
	Adnah Sackett (D)	2,964	34.4
	Edward Harris (F SOIL)	458	5.3
1850	Henry B. Anthony (W)	3,629	80.2
	Edward Harris (F SOIL)	761	16.8
1851	Philip Allen (D)	6,958	52.6
	Josiah Chapin (W)	6,071	45.9
1852	Philip Allen (D)	9,184	51.2
	Elisha Harris (W)	8,746	48.8
1853	Philip Allen (D)	10,371	54.2
	William W. Hoppin (W)	8,228	43.0
1854	William W. Hoppin (W)	9,112	58.4
	Francis M. Dimond (D)	6,484	41.6
1855	William W. Hoppin (W & AM)	10,466	81.5
	Americus V. Potter (D)	2,306	18.0
1856	William W. Hoppin (AM & R)	10,035	58.3
	Americus V. Potter (D)	7,158	41.6
1857	Elisha Dyer (R)	9,621	65.3
	Americus V. Potter (D)	5,123	34.8
1858	Elisha Dyer (R)	7,934	69.0
	Elisha R. Potter (D)	3,572	31.0
1859	Thomas G. Turner (R)	8,904	71.3
	Elisha R. Potter (D)	3,567	28.6
1860	William Sprague (FUS)	12,295	52.8
	Seth Padelford (R)	10,835	46.6
1861	William Sprague (UN)	11,844	53.7
	James Y. Smith (R)	10,200	46.3
1862	William Sprague (UN)	11,195	99.5
1863	James Y. Smith (R)	10,828	58.0
	William C. Cozzens (D & CST)	7,537	40.4

	Candidates	Votes	%
1864	James Y. Smith (UN R)	8,840	50.4
	George H. Browne (D)	7,302	41.7
	Amos C. Barstow (CONST)	1,339	7.6
1865	James Y. Smith (UN R)	10,061	93.0
1866	Ambrose E. Burnside (R)	8,197	73.3
	Lymon Pierce (D)	2,816	25.2
1867	Ambrose E. Burnside (R)	7,372	69.9
	Lymon Pierce (D)	3,178	30.1
1868	Ambrose E. Burnside (R)	10,038	63.7
	Lymon Pierce (D)	5,731	36.3
1869	Seth Padelford (R)	7,370	68.5
	Lymon Pierce (D)	3,390	31.5
1870	Seth Padelford (R)	10,493	62.5
	Lymon Pierce (D)	6,295	37.5
1871	Seth Padelford (R)	8,838	62.2
	Thomas Steere (D)	5,367	37.8
1872	Seth Padelford (R)	9,455	53.6
	Olney Arnold (D)	8,193	46.4
1873	Henry Howard (R)	9,656	71.8
	Benjamin G. Chace (D)	3,786	28.2
1874	Henry Howard (R)	12,335	87.5
	Lymon Pierce (D)	1,589	11.3
1875	Rowland Hazard (I)	8,724	39.2
	Henry Lippitt (R)	8,368†	37.6
	Charles R. Cutler (D)	5,166	23.2
1876	Henry Lippitt (R)	8,689†	45.6
	Albert C. Howard (P)	6,733	35.4
	William B. Beach (D)	3,599	18.9
1877	Charles C. Van Zandt (R & TEMP)	12,455	50.9
	Jerothmul B. Barnaby (D)	11,783	48.2
1878	Charles C. Van Zandt (R & TEMP)	11,454	58.1
	Isaac Lawrence (D)	7,639	38.8
1879	Charles C. Van Zandt (R & TEMP)	9,717	62.1
	Thomas W. Segar (D)	5,506	35.2
1880	Alfred H. Littlefield (R)	10,224†	44.8
	Horace A. Kimball (D)	7,440	32.6
	Albert C. Howard (IR & P)	5,047	22.1
1881	Alfred H. Littlefield (R)	10,849	67.0
	Horace A. Kimball (D)	4,756	29.4
1882	Alfred H. Littlefield (R)	10,056	64.8
	Horace A. Kimball (D)	5,311	34.2
1883	Augustus O. Bourn (R)	13,078	54.5
	William Sprague (D)	10,201	42.5
1884	Augustus O. Bourn (R)	15,936	62.4
	Thomas W. Segar (D)	9,592	37.6
1885	George Peabody Wetmore (R)	12,563	56.0
	Ziba O. Slocum (D)	8,674	38.6
	George H. Slade (P)	1,206	5.4
1886	George Peabody Wetmore (R)	14,340	53.4
	Amasa Sprague (D)	9,994	37.0
	George H. Slade (P)	2,585	9.6
1887	John W. Davis (D)	18,095	51.5
	George Peabody Wetmore (R)	15,111	43.0
	Thomas H. Peabody (P)	1,895	5.4
1888	Royal C. Taft (R)	20,744	52.3
	John W. Davis (D)	17,556	44.3
1889	John W. Davis (D)	21,289	49.4
	Herbert W. Ladd (R)	16,870†	39.1
	James H. Chace (LAW ENF)	3,596	8.3
1890	John W. Davis (D)	20,548†	48.8
	Herbert W. Ladd (R)	18,988	45.1
1891	John W. Davis (D)	22,249	49.0
	Herbert W. Ladd (R)	20,995†	46.2
1892	D. Russell Brown (R)	27,461	50.2
	William T. C. Wardwell (D)	25,433	46.5
1893	David S. Baker (D)	22,015*	46.7
	D. Russell Brown (R)	21,830	46.3
	Metcalf (P)	3,265	6.9
1894	D. Russell Brown (R)	29,157	53.2
	David S. Baker Jr. (D)	22,650	41.3
1895	Charles Warren Lippitt (R)	25,098	56.9
	George L. Littlefield (D)	14,289	32.4
	Smith Quimby (P)	2,624	6.0
1896	Charles Warren Lippitt (R)	28,472	56.4
	George L. Littlefield (D)	17,061	33.8
	Thomas H. Peabody (P)	2,950	5.8
1897	Elisha Dyer (R)	24,309	58.1
	Daniel T. Church (D)	13,675	32.7
	Thomas H. Peabody (P)	2,096	5.0
1898	Elisha Dyer (R)	24,743	57.7
	Daniel T. Church (D)	13,224	30.9
	James P. Reid (SOC LAB)	2,877	6.7
1899	Elisha Dyer (R)	24,308	56.4
	George W. Greene (D)	14,602	33.9
	Thomas F. Herrick (SOC LAB)	2,941	6.8
1900	William Gregory (R)	26,043	54.3
	Nathan W. Littlefield (D)	17,184	35.9
	James P. Reid (SOC LAB)	2,858	6.0
1901	William Gregory (R)	25,575	53.6
	Lucius F. C. Garvin (D)	19,038	39.9
1902	Lucius F. C. Garvin (D)	32,279	54.0
	Charles Dean Kimball (R)	24,541	41.0
1903	Lucius F. C. Garvin (D)	30,578	49.3
	Samuel Pomeroy Colt (R)	29,275	47.2
1904	George H. Utter (R)	33,821	48.9
	Lucius F. C. Garvin (D)	32,965	47.7
1905	George H. Utter (R)	31,311	53.3
	Lucius F. C. Garvin (D)	25,816	44.0
1906	James H. Higgins (D)	33,195	49.9
	George H. Utter (R)	31,877	47.9
1907	James H. Higgins (D)	33,300	50.4
	Frederick H. Jackson (R)	31,005	46.9
1908	Aram J. Pothier (R)	38,676	52.6
	Olney Arnold (D)	31,406	42.7
1909	Aram J. Pothier (R)	37,107	57.0
	Olney Arnold (D)	25,338	38.9
1910	Aram J. Pothier (R)	33,540	49.6
	Lewis A. Waterman (D)	32,400	47.9
1911	Aram J. Pothier (R)	37,969	53.4
	Lewis A. Waterman (D)	30,575	43.0
1912	Aram J. Pothier (R)	34,133	43.7
	Theodore Francis Green (D)	32,725	41.9
	Albert H. Humes (PROG)	8,457	10.8
1914	R. Livingston Beeckman (R)	41,996	53.8
	Patrick H. Quinn (D)	32,182	41.3
1916	R. Livingston Beeckman (R)	49,524	55.9
	Addison P. Munroe (D)	36,158	40.8
1918	R. Livingston Beeckman (R)	42,682	53.1
	Alberic A. Archambault (D)	36,031	44.8
1920	Emery J. San Souci (R)	109,138	64.6
	Edward M. Sullivan (D)	55,963	33.2
1922	William S. Flynn (D)	81,935	51.7
	Harold J. Gross (R)	74,724	47.2
1924	Aram J. Pothier (R)	122,749	58.6
	Felix A. Toupin (D)	85,942	41.0
1926	Aram J. Pothier (R)	89,574	53.9
	Joseph H. Gainer (D)	75,882	45.7
1928	Norman S. Case (R)	121,748	51.6
	Alberic A. Archambault (D)	113,594	48.1
1930	Norman S. Case (R)	112,070	50.5
	Theodore Francis Green (D)	108,558	48.9
1932	Theodore Francis Green (D)	146,474	55.2
	Norman S. Case (R)	115,438	43.5
1934	Theodore Francis Green (D)	140,258	56.6
	Luke H. Callan (R)	105,139	42.4
1936	Robert E. Quinn (D)	160,776	53.7
	Charles P. Sisson (R)	137,369	45.9
1938	William H. Vanderbilt (R)	167,003	53.7
	Robert E. Quinn (D)	129,603	41.6
1940	J. Howard McGrath (D)	177,937	55.8
	William H. Vanderbilt (R)	140,480	44.1

Gubernatorial Elections

	Candidates	Votes	%
1942	J. Howard McGrath (D)	139,407	58.5
	James O. McManus (R)	98,741	41.5
1944	J. Howard McGrath (D)	179,010	60.7
	Norman D. Macleod (R)	116,158	39.4
1946	John O. Pastore (D)	148,885	54.1
	John G. Murphy (R)	126,456	45.9
1948	John O. Pastore (D)	198,056	61.2
	Albert P. Ruerat (R)	124,441	38.4
1950	Dennis J. Roberts (D)	176,125	59.3
	Eugene J. Lachapelle (R)	120,683	40.7
1952	Dennis J. Roberts (D)	215,587	52.6
	Raoul Archambault Jr. (R)	194,102	47.4
1954	Dennis J. Roberts (D)	189,595	57.7
	Dean J. Lewis (R)	137,131	41.7
1956	Dennis J. Roberts (D)	192,315	50.1
	Christopher Del Sesto (R)	191,604	49.9
1958	Christopher Del Sesto (R)	176,505	50.9
	Dennis J. Roberts (D)	170,275	49.1
1960	John A. Notte Jr. (D)	227,318	56.6
	Christopher Del Sesto (R)	174,044	43.4
1962	John H. Chafee (R)	163,952	50.1
	John A. Notte Jr. (D)	163,554	49.9
1964	John H. Chafee (R)	239,501	61.2
	Edward P. Gallogly (D)	152,165	38.9
1966	John H. Chafee (R)	210,202	63.3
	Horace E. Hobbs (D)	121,862	36.7
1968	Frank Licht (D)	195,766	51.0
	John H. Chafee (R)	187,958	49.0
1970	Frank Licht (D)	173,420	50.1
	Herbert F. DeSimone (R)	171,549	49.5
1972	Philip W. Noel (D)	216,953	52.6
	Herbert F. DeSimone (R)	194,315	47.1
1974	Philip W. Noel (D)	252,436	78.5
	James W. Nugent (R)	69,224	21.5
1976	J. Joseph Garrahy (D)	218,561	54.8
	James L. Taft (R)	178,254	44.7
1978	J. Joseph Garrahy (D)	197,386	62.8
	Lincoln Almond (R)	96,596	30.7
	Joseph A. Doorley Jr. (I)	20,381	6.5
1980	J. Joseph Garrahy (D)	299,174	73.7
	Vincent A. Cianci (R)	106,729	26.3
1982	J. Joseph Garrahy (D)	247,208	73.3
	Vincent Mazullo (R)	79,602	23.6
1984	Edward D. DiPrete (R)	245,059	60.0
	Anthony J. Solomon (D)	163,311	40.0
1986	Edward D. DiPrete (R)	208,822	64.7
	Bruce Sundlun (D)	104,508	32.4
1988	Edward D. DiPrete (R)	203,550	50.8
	Bruce Sundlun (D)	196,936	49.2
1990	Bruce Sundlun (D)	264,411	74.2
	Edward D. DiPrete (R)	92,177	25.8
1992	Bruce Sundlun (D)	261,484	61.6
	Elizabeth Ann Leonard (R)	145,590	34.3
1994	Lincoln C. Almond (R)	171,194	47.4
	Myrth York (D)	157,361	43.5
	Robert J. Healey (I)	32,822	9.1

Rhode Island
1. *Includes votes for other candidates.*

SOUTH CAROLINA

(Ratified the Constitution May 23, 1788)

	Candidates	Votes	%
1865[1]	James L. Orr	9,771	51.8
	Wade Hampton	9,109	48.3
1868	Robert K. Scott (R)	69,693	75.0
	W. D. Porter	23,087	24.8
1870	Robert K. Scott (R)	85,071	62.3
	R. B. Carpenter (D)	51,537	37.7
1872	Franklin J. Moses Jr. (R)	69,838	65.4
	Reuben Tomlinson (ID)	36,553	34.2
1874	Daniel H. Chamberlain (R)	80,403	53.9
	John T. Green (I REF D)	68,818	46.1
1876	Wade Hampton	92,261	50.3
	Daniel H. Chamberlain (R)	91,127	49.7
1878	Wade Hampton (D)	119,550	99.8
1880	Johnson Hagood (D)	117,432	96.4
1882	Hugh S. Thompson (D)	67,158	79.5
	McLane (G)	17,319	20.5
1884	Hugh S. Thompson (D)	67,895	100.0
1886	John P. Richardson (D)	33,114	100.0
1888	John P. Richardson (D)	58,730	100.0
1890	Benjamin Ryan Tillman (D)	59,159	79.8
	A. C. Haskell (ID)	14,828	20.0
1892	Benjamin Ryan Tillman (D)	56,673	99.9
1894	John Gary Evans (D)	39,507	69.6
	Sampson Pope (POP)	17,278	30.4
1896	William H. Ellerbe (D)	59,424	89.1
	Sampson Pope (LW R)	4,432	6.7
1898	William H. Ellerbe (D)	28,225	100.0
1900	Miles B. McSweeney (D)	46,457	100.0
1902	Duncan C. Heyward (D)	31,817	100.0
1904	Duncan C. Heyward (D)	51,917	100.0
1906	Martin F. Ansel (D)	30,251	99.9
1908	Martin F. Ansel (D)	61,060	100.0
1910	Coleman L. Blease (D)	30,739	99.8
1912	Coleman L. Blease (D)	44,122	99.5
1914	Richard I. Manning (D)	34,600	99.8
1916	Richard I. Manning (D)	60,396	97.9
1918	Robert A. Cooper (D)	25,267	100.0
1920	Robert A. Cooper (D)	58,050	100.0
1922	Thomas G. McLeod (D)	34,065	100.0
1924	Thomas G. McLeod (D)	53,545	100.0
1926	John G. Richards (D)	16,589	100.0
1930	Ibra C. Blackwood (D)	17,790	100.0
1934	Olin D. Johnston (D)	23,177	100.0
1938	Burnet R. Maybank (D)	49,009	99.4
1942	Olin D. Johnston (D)	23,859	100.0
1946	J. Strom Thurmond (D)	26,520	100.0
1950	James F. Byrnes (D)	50,633	100.0
1954	George Bell Timmerman Jr. (D)	214,204	100.0
1958	Ernest F. Hollings (D)	77,714	100.0
1962	Donald Russell (D)	253,704	100.0
1966	Robert E. McNair (D)	255,854	58.2
	Joseph O. Rogers Jr. (R)	184,088	41.8
1970	John C. West (D)	250,551	51.7
	Albert Watson (R)	221,233	45.6
1974	James B. Edwards (R)	266,109	50.9
	W. J. Bryan Dorn (D)	248,938	47.6
1978	Richard W. Riley (D)	384,898	61.4
	Edward L. Young (R)	236,946	37.8
1982	Richard W. Riley (D)	468,819	69.8
	W. D. Workman (R)	202,806	30.2
1986	Carroll Campbell (R)	384,565	51.0
	Mike Daniel (D)	361,325	47.9
1990	Carroll Campbell (R)	528,831	69.5
	Theo Mitchell (D)	212,034	27.9
1994	David Beasley (R)	470,756	50.4
	Nick A. Theodore (D)	447,002	47.9

South Carolina
1. *Before 1865 governor chosen by legislature.*

SOUTH DAKOTA

(Became a state Nov. 2, 1889)

	Candidates	Votes	%
1889	Arthur C. Mellette (R)	53,964	69.3
	P. F. McClure (D)	23,840	30.6
1890	Arthur C. Mellette (R)	34,487	44.5
	H. L. Loucks (I)	24,591	31.7
	Maris Taylor (D)	18,484	23.8
1892	Charles H. Sheldon (R)	33,214	47.2
	A. L. Vanosdel (I)	22,323	31.7
	Peter Couchman (D)	14,872	21.1
1894	Charles H. Sheldon (R)	40,402	52.0
	Isaac Howe (I)	27,568	35.5
	James A. Ward (D)	8,756	11.3
1896	Andrew E. Lee (PP)	41,177	49.8
	A. O. Ringsrud (R)	40,869	49.4
1898	Andrew E. Lee (FUS)	37,319	49.6
	Kirk G. Phillips (R)	36,980	49.2
1900	Charles N. Herreid (R)	53,788	56.3
	Burre H. Lien (FUS)	40,091	42.0
1902	Charles N. Herreid (R)	48,195	64.7
	John W. Martin (D)	21,396	28.7
1904	Samuel H. Elrod (R)	68,561	68.3
	Louis N. Crill (D)	24,772	24.7
1906	Coe I. Crawford (R)	48,709	65.3
	John A. Stransky (D)	19,923	26.7
1908	Robert S. Vessey (R)	62,989	55.3
	Andrew E. Lee (D)	44,876	39.4
1910	Robert S. Vessey (R)	61,744	58.4
	Chauncey L. Wood (D)	37,983	35.9
1912	Frank M. Byrne (R)	57,161	48.5
	Edwin S. Johnson (D)	53,850	45.7
1914	Frank M. Byrne (R)	49,138	50.1
	J. W. McCarter (D)	34,542	35.2
	R. O. Richards (I)	9,725	9.9
1916	Peter Norbeck (R)	72,789	56.6
	Rinehart (D)	50,545	39.3
1918	Peter Norbeck (R)	51,175	53.2
	Mark P. Bates (NON PART)	25,118	26.1
	James B. Bird (D)	17,858	18.6
1920	William H. McMaster (R)	103,592	56.3
	Mark P. Bates (NON PART)	48,426	26.3
	W. W. Howes (D)	31,870	17.3
1922	William H. McMaster (R)	78,984	45.0
	Louis N. Crill (D)	50,409	28.7
	Lorraine Daly (NON PART)	46,033	26.2
1924	Carl Gunderson (R)	109,914	53.9
	William J. Bulow (D)	46,613	22.9
	A. L. Putnam (F-LAB)	27,027	13.3
	R. O. Richards (I)	20,359	10.0
1926	William J. Bulow (D)	87,076	47.4
	Carl Gunderson (R)	74,101	40.3
	Tom Ayres (F-LAB)	11,958	6.5
	John E. Hipple (I)	10,637	5.8
1928	William J. Bulow (D)	136,016	52.5
	Buell F. Jones (R)	121,643	46.9
1930	Warren E. Green (R)	107,643	53.0
	D. A. McCullough (D)	93,954	46.2
1932	Tom Berry (D)	158,058	55.6
	Warren E. Green (R)	120,473	42.4
1934	Tom Berry (D)	172,228	58.6
	William C. Allen (R)	119,477	40.7
1936	Leslie Jensen (R)	151,659	51.6
	Tom Berry (D)	142,255	48.4
1938	Harlan J. Bushfield (R)	149,362	54.0
	Oscar Fosheim (D)	127,485	46.1
1940	Harlan J. Bushfield (R)	167,686	55.1
	Lewis W. Bicknell (D)	136,428	44.9
1942	Merrell Q. Sharpe (R)	109,786	61.5
	Lewis B. Bicknell (D)	68,706	38.5

	Candidates	Votes	%
1944	Merrell Q. Sharpe (R)	148,646	65.5
	Lynn Fellows (D)	78,276	34.5
1946	George T. Mickelson (R)	108,998	67.2
	Richard Haeder (D)	53,294	32.8
1948	George T. Mickelson (R)	149,883	61.1
	Harold J. Volz (D)	95,489	38.9
1950	Sigurd Anderson (R)	154,254	60.9
	Joe Robbie (D)	99,062	39.1
1952	Sigurd Anderson (R)	203,102	70.2
	Sherman A. Iverson (D)	86,412	29.9
1954	Joe Foss (R)	133,878	56.7
	Ed C. Martin (D)	102,377	43.3
1956	Joe Foss (R)	158,819	54.4
	Ralph Herseth (D)	133,198	45.6
1958	Ralph Herseth (D)	132,761	51.4
	Phil Saunders (R)	125,520	48.6
1960	Archie M. Gubbrud (R)	154,530	50.7
	Ralph Herseth (D)	150,095	49.3
1962	Archie M. Gubbrud (R)	143,682	56.1
	Ralph Herseth (D)	112,438	43.9
1964	Nils A. Boe (R)	150,151	51.7
	John F. Lindley (D)	140,419	48.3
1966	Nils A. Boe (R)	131,710	57.7
	Robert Chamberlin (D)	96,504	42.3
1968	Frank L. Farrar (R)	159,646	57.7
	Robert Chamberlin (D)	117,260	42.4
1970	Richard F. Kneip (D)	131,616	54.9
	Frank L. Farrar (R)	108,347	45.2
1972	Richard F. Kneip (D)	185,012	60.0
	Carveth Thompson (R)	123,165	40.0
1974	Richard F. Kneip (D)	149,151	53.6
	John E. Olson (R)	129,077	46.4
1978	William J. Janklow (R)	147,116	56.6
	Roger McKellips (D)	112,679	43.4
1982	William J. Janklow (R)	197,426	70.9
	Michael J. O'Connor (D)	81,136	29.1
1986	George S. Mickelson (R)	152,543	51.8
	R. Lars Herseth (D)	141,898	48.2
1990	George S. Mickelson (R)	151,198	58.9
	Bob L. Samuelson (D)	105,525	41.1
1994	William J. Janklow (R)	172,515	55.4
	Jim Beddow (D)	126,273	40.5

TENNESSEE

(Became a state June 1, 1796)

	Candidates	Votes	%
1796[1]	John Sevier	✔	
1797	John Sevier	✔	
1799[2]	John Sevier	5,295	99.7
1801	Archibald Roane	8,438	99.9
1803	John Sevier	6,786	58.0
	Archibald Roane	4,923	42.0
1805[2]	John Sevier	10,293	63.7
	Archibald Roane	5,855	36.3
1807	John Sevier	✔	
	William Cocke		
1809	Willie Blount	✔	
	William Cocke		
1811	Willie Blount	✔	
1813	Willie Blount	21,510	
1815[2]	Joseph McMinn	14,873	42.8
	Robert Weakley	7,209	20.7
	Jesse Wharton	6,038	17.4
	Robert C. Foster	3,809	11.0
	Thomas Johnson	2,826	8.1

Gubernatorial Elections

	Candidates	Votes	%
1817	Joseph McMinn	27,802	*64.3*
	Robert C. Foster	15,450	*35.7*
1819	Joseph McMinn	35,244	
	Enoch Parsons		
1821	William Carroll	42,210	*79.0*
	Edward Ward	11,200	*21.0*
1823	William Carroll	32,597	
1825	William Carroll	14,807	*99.8*
1827	Samuel Houston	40,017	*54.7*
	Newton Cannon	31,244	*42.7*
1829	William Carroll	59,875	*99.8*
1831	William Carroll (D)	64,834	*97.3*
1833	William Carroll (D)	53,224	*97.8*
1835	Newton Cannon (W)	41,862	*50.4*
	William Carroll	33,180	*40.0*
	Humphries	7,999	*9.6*
1837	Newton Cannon (W)	53,385	*60.9*
	Armstrong (D)	34,312	*39.1*
1839	James K. Polk (D)	53,714	*51.0*
	Newton Cannon (W)	51,624	*49.0*
1841	James C. Jones (W)	53,829	*51.5*
	James K. Polk (D)	50,705	*48.5*
1843	James C. Jones (W)	52,584	*51.3*
	James K. Polk (D)	49,944	*48.7*
1845	Aaron V. Brown (D)	58,277	*50.6*
	Foster (W)	56,805	*49.4*
1847	Neill S. Brown (W)	61,450	*50.4*
	Aaron V. Brown (D)	60,454	*49.6*
1849	William Trousdale (D)	61,740	*50.6*
	Neill S. Brown (W)	60,340	*49.4*
1851	William B. Campbell (W)	63,423	*50.7*
	William Trousdale (D)	61,648	*49.3*
1853	Andrew Johnson (D)	63,413	*50.9*
	Henry (W)	61,163	*49.1*
1855	Andrew Johnson (D)	67,499	*50.8*
	Gentry (AM)	65,332	*49.2*
1857	Isham G. Harris (D)	71,539	*54.4*
	Hatton (AM)	59,867	*45.6*
1859	Isham G. Harris (D)	76,226	*52.8*
	Netherland (OPP)	68,218	*47.2*
1863	Robert L. Caruthers	7,050	*98.4*
1865	William G. Brownlow (W, R)	22,814	*99.9*
1867	William G. Brownlow (R)	74,484	*76.9*
	Emerson Etheridge (C)	22,440	*23.2*
1869	De Witt Clinton Senter (CR)	120,333	*68.6*
	William B. Stokes (RAD R)	55,036	*31.4*
1870	John C. Brown	76,666	*65.0*
	W. H. Wisener (R)	41,278	*35.0*
1872	John C. Brown (LR)	97,689	*53.7*
	Freeman (R)	84,100	*46.3*
1874	James D. Porter Jr. (D)	103,061	*64.9*
	Horace Maynard (R)	55,836	*35.1*
1876	James D. Porter Jr. (D)	123,740	*58.8*
	Thomas (I)	73,695	*35.0*
1878	Albert S. Marks (D)	89,097	*60.3*
	E. M. Wight (R)	43,175	*29.2*
	R. M. Edwards (G)	15,470	*10.5*
1880	Alvin Hawkins (R)	103,966	*42.6*
	Wright (STC D)	79,081	*32.4*
	Wilson (LOWTAX D)	57,568	*23.6*
1882	William B. Bate (LOWTAX D)	120,091	*52.9*
	Alvin Hawkins (R)	93,182	*41.0*
1884	William B. Bate (D)	132,201	*51.3*
	Reid (R)	125,276	*48.7*
1886	Robert L. Taylor (D)	126,491	*53.5*
	Alfred A. Taylor (R)	109,842	*46.5*
1888	Robert L. Taylor (D)	156,799	*51.8*
	Samuel W. Hawkins (R)	139,014	*45.9*
1890	John P. Buchanan (D)	113,536	*56.6*
	Baxter (R)	76,071	*37.9*
	Kelly (P)	11,011	*5.5*
1892	Peter Turney (D)	126,248	*47.9*
	George W. Winsted (R)	100,599	*38.1*
	John P. Buchanan (PP)	31,515	*12.0*
1894	H. Clay Evans (R)	105,164‡	*45.2*
	Peter Turney (D)	104,350	*44.9*
	Mills (POP)	23,129	*9.9*
1896	Robert L. Taylor (D)	156,227	*48.8*
	G. N. Tillman (R)	149,374	*46.6*
1898	Benton McMillin (D)	105,640	*57.9*
	Fowler (R)	72,611	*39.8*
1900	Benton McMillin (D)	145,708	*53.9*
	John E. McCall (R)	119,831	*44.3*
1902	James B. Frazier (D)	98,951	*61.8*
	Campbell (R)	59,002	*36.8*
1904	James B. Frazier (D)	131,503	*55.7*
	Littleton (R)	103,409	*43.8*
1906	Malcolm R. Patterson (D)	111,876	*54.4*
	Evans (R)	92,804	*45.2*
1908	Malcolm R. Patterson (D)	133,176	*53.7*
	G. N. Tillman (R)	113,269	*45.7*
1910	Ben W. Hooper (R)	133,076	*51.9*
	Robert L. Taylor (D)	121,694	*47.5*
1912	Ben W. Hooper (R)	124,641	*50.2*
	Benton McMillin (D)	116,610	*46.9*
1914	Tom C. Rye (D)	137,636	*53.6*
	Ben W. Hooper (R)	117,717	*45.8*
1916	Tom C. Rye (D)	146,759	*55.0*
	John W. Overall (R)	117,819	*44.2*
1918	Albert H. Roberts (D)	98,628	*62.4*
	H. B. Lindsay (R)	59,518	*37.6*
1920	Alfred A. Taylor (R)	229,133	*54.9*
	Albert H. Roberts (D)	185,890	*44.6*
1922	Austin Peay (D)	141,012	*57.9*
	Alfred A. Taylor (R)	102,586	*42.1*
1924	Austin Peay (D)	162,002	*57.2*
	T. F. Peck (R)	121,228	*42.8*
1926	Austin Peay (D)	84,979	*64.7*
	Walter White (R)	46,238	*35.2*
1928	Henry H. Horton (D)	195,546	*61.1*
	Raleigh Hopkins (R)	124,733	*39.0*
1930	Henry H. Horton (D)	153,341	*63.8*
	C. Arthur Bruce (R)	85,558	*35.6*
1932	Hill McAlister (D)	169,075	*42.8*
	John E. McCall (R)	117,797	*29.8*
	Lewis S. Pope (I)	106,990	*27.1*
1934	Hill McAlister (D)	198,743	*61.8*
	Lewis S. Pope (FUS)	122,965	*38.2*
1936	Gordon Browning (D)	332,523	*80.4*
	P. H. Thach (R)	77,392	*18.7*
1938	Prentice Cooper (D)	210,567	*71.7*
	Howard H. Baker (R)	83,031	*28.3*
1940	Prentice Cooper (D)	323,466	*72.1*
	C. Arthur Bruce (R)	125,245	*27.9*
1942	Prentice Cooper (D)	120,148	*70.2*
	C. N. Frazier (R)	51,120	*29.9*
1944	James N. McCord (D)	275,746	*62.5*
	J. W. Kilgo (R)	158,742	*36.0*
1946	James N. McCord (D)	149,937	*65.3*
	W. O. Lowe (R)	73,222	*31.9*
1948	Gordon Browning (D)	363,903	*66.9*
	Roy Acuff (R)	179,957	*33.1*
1950	Gordon Browning (D)	184,437	*78.1*
	John R. Neal (R)	51,757	*21.9*
1952	Frank G. Clement (D)	640,290	*79.4*
	R. Beecher Witt (R)	166,377	*20.6*
1954	Frank G. Clement (D)	281,291	*87.2*
	John R. Neal (I)	39,574	*12.3*
1958	Buford Ellington (D)	248,874	*57.5*
	James N. McCord (I)	136,406	*31.5*
	Thomas P. Wall (R)	35,938	*8.3*

	Candidates	Votes	%
1962	Frank G. Clement (D)	315,648	50.9
	William R. Anderson (I)	203,765	32.8
	Hubert D. Patty (R)	99,884	16.1
1966	Buford Ellington (D)	532,998	81.2
	H. L. Crowder (I)	64,602	9.8
	Charles Moffett (I)	50,221	7.7
1970	Winfield Dunn (R)	575,777	52.0
	John J. Hooker Jr. (D)	509,521	46.0
1974	Ray Blanton (D)	576,833	55.4
	Lamar Alexander (R)	455,467	43.8
1978	Lamar Alexander (R)	661,959	55.6
	Jake Butcher (D)	523,495	44.0
1982	Lamar Alexander (R)	737,963	59.6
	Randy Tyree (D)	500,937	40.4
1986	Ned R. McWherter (D)	656,602	54.3
	Winfield Dunn (R)	553,449	45.7
1990	Ned R. McWherter (D)	480,885	60.8
	Dwight Henry (R)	289,348	36.6
1994	Don Sundquist (R)	807,104	54.3
	Phil Bredesen (D)	664,252	44.7

Tennessee
1. Until the 1830s contests were essentially on a personal popularity basis among members of the Democratic-Republican Party.
2. Returns are incomplete.

TEXAS

(Became a state Dec. 29, 1845)

	Candidates	Votes	%
1845	J. Pinckney Henderson	7,853#	82.0
	James B. Miller	1,673#	17.5
1847	George T. Wood (D)	6,801	53.5
	J. B. Miller (D)	4,022	31.6
	N. H. Darnell	1,285	10.1
1849	P. Hansbrough Bell (D)	10,226	48.0
	George T. Wood	8,430	39.6
	John T. Mills	2,632	12.4
1851	P. Hansbrough Bell	12,484	47.0
	M. T. Johnson	5,029	18.9
	J. A. Green	3,941	14.8
	B. H. Epperson	2,868	10.8
	J. J. Chambers	2,148	8.1
1853	Elisha M. Pease (D)	13,099	36.2
	W. B. Ochiltree (W)	9,180	25.4
	G. T. Wood (D)	5,983	16.5
	L. D. Evans (D)	4,679	12.9
	T. J. Chambers (D)	2,449	6.8
1855	Elisha M. Pease (D)	20,136	58.4
	D. C. Dickson (KN)	13,081	37.9
1857	Hardin R. Runnels (D)	32,552	57.9
	Sam Houston (AM)	23,628	42.1
1859	Sam Houston (ID)	36,227	56.8
	Hardin R. Runnels (D)	27,500	43.2
1861	Francis R. Lubbock	21,860	38.1
	Edward Clark	21,675	37.8
	T. J. Chambers	13,759	24.0
1863	Pendleton Murrah	17,486	56.6
	T. J. Chambers	12,254	39.7
1865	J. W. Throckmorton (C)	49,277	80.3
	Elisha M. Pease (R)	12,068	19.7
1866	J. W. Throckmorton	48,631	80.1
	Elisha M. Pease (R)	12,051	19.9
1869	Edmund J. Davis (R)	39,838	50.2
	A. J. Hamilton (D)	39,046	49.2
1873	Richard Coke (D)	98,906	66.0
	Edmund J. Davis (R)	51,049	34.0
1875	Richard Coke (D)	149,974	75.0

	Candidates	Votes	%
	William Chambers (R)	49,994	25.0
1878	Oran M. Roberts (D)	158,960	67.1
	William H. Hamman (NG)	55,004	23.2
	A. B. Norton (R)	22,941	9.7
1880	Oran M. Roberts (D)	165,949	62.9
	E. J. Davis (R)	64,372	24.4
	W. H. Hamman (G)	33,699	12.8
1882	John Ireland (D)	150,811	58.0
	George W. Jones (R-G-FUS)	108,988	41.9
1884	John Ireland (D)	210,691	63.2
	George W. Jones (R)	98,031	29.4
	A. B. Norton (G)	23,464	7.0
1886	Lawrence S. Ross (D)	229,806	73.0
	A. M. Cochran (R)	66,456	21.1
	E. L. Dahoney (P)	18,556	5.9
1888	Lawrence S. Ross (D)	249,361	70.8
	Marion Martin (P & F ALNC)	102,807	29.2
1890	James S. Hogg (D)	261,998	76.7
	Webster Flanagan (R)	76,932	22.5
1892	James S. Hogg (D)	190,386	43.7
	George Clark (R)	133,434	30.7
	Thomas L. Nugent (POP)	108,483	24.9
1894	Charles A. Culberson (D)	207,171	48.9
	Thomas L. Nugent (POP)	151,595	35.8
	W. K. Makemson (R)	54,525	12.9
1896	Charles A. Culberson (D)	298,568	55.3
	Jerome C. Kearby (POP)	238,688	44.2
1898	Joseph D. Sayers (D)	291,548	71.2
	Barnett Gibbs (POP)	114,865	28.1
1900	Joseph D. Sayers (D)	303,548	67.6
	R. E. Hannay (R)	112,864	25.1
	T. J. McMinn (POP)	26,579	5.9
1902	Samuel W. T. Lanham (D)	269,076	74.9
	George W. Burkett (R)	65,706	18.3
1904	Samuel W. T. Lanham (D)	204,961	73.6
	J. G. Lowden (R)	56,499	20.3
1906	Thomas M. Campbell (D)	149,263	81.2
	C. A. Gray (R)	23,779	12.9
1908	Thomas M. Campbell (D)	220,996	72.9
	John N. Simpson (R)	73,309	24.2
1910	Oscar B. Colquitt (D)	174,578	79.8
	J. O. Terrell (R)	26,176	12.0
	Reddin Andrews (SOC)	11,536	5.3
1912	Oscar B. Colquitt (D)	233,073	77.8
	Reddin Andrews (SOC)	25,238	8.4
	C. W. Johnson (R)	22,914	7.6
	Ed C. Lasater (PROG)	15,754	5.3
1914	James E. Ferguson (D)	176,601	82.0
	E. R. Meitzen (SOC)	24,977	11.6
	John W. Philip (R)	11,405	5.3
1916	James E. Ferguson (D)	297,177	80.5
	R. B. Creager (R)	49,117	13.3
	E. R. Meitzen (SOC)	19,278	5.2
1918	William P. Hobby (D)	148,982	84.0
	Charles A. Boynton (R)	26,713	15.1
1920	Pat M. Neff (D)	290,672	60.2
	J. G. Culbertson (R)	90,102	18.7
	T. H. McGregor (AM)	69,380	14.4
	H. Capers (B & T R)	26,128	5.4
1922	Pat M. Neff (D)	332,676	81.9
	W. H. Atwell (R)	73,569	18.1
1924	Miriam A. Ferguson (D)	422,563	58.9
	George C. Butte (R)	294,920	41.1
1926	Dan Moody (D)	233,002	87.5
	H. H. Haines (R)	32,434	12.2
1928	Dan Moody (D)	582,897	82.4
	W. H. Holmes (R)	123,337	17.4
1930	Ross Sterling (D)	253,732	80.0
	W. E. Talbot (R)	62,334	19.7
1932	Miriam A. Ferguson (D)	521,395	61.6
	Orville Bullington (R)	322,589	38.1

	Candidates	Votes	%
1934	James V. Allred (D)	428,755	96.4
1936	James V. Allred (D)	780,442	92.9
	C. O. Harris (R)	58,744	7.0
1938	W. Lee O'Daniel (D)	358,943	96.8
1940	W. Lee O'Daniel (D)	1,040,358	94.7
	G. C. Hopkins (R)	57,971	5.3
1942	Coke R. Stevenson (D)	280,735	96.8
1944	Coke R. Stevenson (D)	1,006,778	90.9
	B. J. Peasley (R)	101,110	9.1
1946	Beauford H. Jester (D)	345,507	91.2
	Eugene Nolte Jr. (R)	33,277	8.8
1948	Beauford H. Jester (D)	1,024,160	84.7
	Alvin H. Lane (R)	177,399	14.7
1950	Allan Shivers (D)	367,345	90.2
	Ralph W. Currie (R)	39,793	9.8
1952	Allan Shivers (D, R)	1,853,863	99.9
1954	Allan Shivers (D)	569,533	89.4
	Tod R. Adams (R)	66,154	10.4
1956	Price Daniel (D)	1,433,051	78.4
	William R. Bryant (R)	271,088	14.8
	W. Lee O'Daniel (WRITE IN)	122,103	6.7
1958	Price Daniel (D)	695,035	88.1
	Edwin S. Mayer (R)	94,098	11.9
1960	Price Daniel (D)	1,637,755	72.8
	William M. Steger (R)	612,963	27.2
1962	John B. Connally (D)	847,036	54.0
	Jack Cox (R)	715,025	45.6
1964	John B. Connally (D)	1,877,793	73.8
	Jack Crichton (R)	661,675	26.0
1966	John B. Connally (D)	1,037,517	72.8
	T. E. Kennerly (R)	368,025	25.8
1968	Preston Smith (D)	1,662,019	57.0
	Paul Eggers (R)	1,254,333	43.0
1970	Preston Smith (D)	1,197,726	53.6
	Paul Eggers (R)	1,037,723	46.4
1972	Dolph Briscoe (D)	1,633,493	47.9
	Hank C. Grover (R)	1,533,986	45.0
	Ramsey Muniz (LRU)	214,118	6.3
1974	Dolph Briscoe (D)	1,016,334	61.4
	Jim Granberry (R)	514,725	31.1
	Ramsey Muniz (LRU)	93,295	5.6
1978	William P. Clements (R)	1,183,839	50.0
	John Hill (D)	1,166,979	49.2
1982	Mark White (D)	1,697,870	53.2
	William P. Clements (R)	1,465,937	45.9
1986	William P. Clements (R)	1,813,779	52.7
	Mark White (D)	1,584,515	46.1
1990	Ann W. Richards (D)	1,925,670	49.5
	Clayton Williams (R)	1,826,431	46.9
1994	George W. Bush (R)	2,350,994	53.5
	Ann Richards (D)	2,016,928	45.9

UTAH

(Became a state Jan. 4, 1896)

	Candidates	Votes	%
1896	Heber M. Wells (R)	20,833	50.3
	J. T. Caine (D)	18,519	44.7
1900	Heber M. Wells (R)	47,600	51.7
	James H. Moyle (D)	44,447	48.3
1904	John C. Cutler (R)	50,837	50.0
	James H. Moyle (D)	38,047	37.4
	William M. Ferry (AM)	7,959	7.8
1908	William Spry (R)	52,913	47.5
	Jesse William Knight (D)	43,266	38.8
	James A. Street (AM)	11,404	10.2

	Candidates	Votes	%
1912	William Spry (R)	42,552	38.2
	John F. Tolton (D)	36,076	32.4
	Nephi L. Morris (PROG)	23,590	21.2
	Homer P. Burt (SOC)	8,797	7.9
1916	Simon Bamberger (D)	78,298	55.0
	Nephi L. Morris (R)	59,522	41.8
1920	Charles R. Mabey (R)	83,518	58.2
	T. N. Taylor (D)	54,913	38.3
1924	George H. Dern (D)	81,308	53.0
	Charles R. Mabey (R)	72,127	47.0
1928	George H. Dern (D)	102,953	58.5
	William H. Wattis (R)	72,306	41.1
1932	Henry H. Blood (D)	116,031	56.4
	William W. Seegmiller (R)	85,913	41.8
1936	Henry H. Blood (D)	109,656	51.0
	Ray E. Dillman (R)	80,118	37.2
	Harman W. Peery	24,754	11.5
1940	Herbert B. Maw (D)	128,519	52.1
	Don B. Colton (R)	117,713	47.7
1944	Herbert B. Maw (D)	123,907	50.2
	J. Bracken Lee (R)	122,851	49.8
1948	J. Bracken Lee (R)	151,253	55.0
	Herbert B. Maw (D)	123,814	45.0
1952	J. Bracken Lee (R)	180,516	55.1
	Earl J. Glade (D)	147,188	44.9
1956	George Dewey Clyde (R)	127,164	38.2
	L. C. Romney (D)	111,297	33.4
	J. Bracken Lee (I)	94,428	28.4
1960	George Dewey Clyde (R)	195,634	52.7
	William A. Barlocker (D)	175,855	47.3
1964	Calvin L. Rampton (D)	226,956	57.0
	Mitchell Melich (R)	171,300	43.0
1968	Calvin L. Rampton (D)	289,283	68.7
	Carl W. Buehner (R)	131,729	31.3
1972	Calvin L. Rampton (D)	331,998	69.7
	Nicholas L. Strike (R)	144,449	30.3
1976	Scott M. Matheson (D)	280,706	52.0
	Vernon B. Romney (R)	248,027	46.0
1980	Scott M. Matheson (D)	330,974	55.2
	Bob Wright (R)	266,578	44.4
1984	Norman H. Bangerter (R)	351,792	55.9
	Wayne Owens (D)	275,669	43.8
1988	Norman H. Bangerter (R)	260,462	40.1
	Ted Wilson (D)	249,321	38.4
	Merrill Cook (I)	136,651	21.0
1992	Michael O. Leavitt (R)	321,713	42.2
	Merrill Cook (IP)	255,753	33.5
	Stewart Hanson (D)	177,181	23.2
1996	Michael O. Leavitt (R)	503,693	75.0
	Jim Bradley (D)	156,616	23.3

VERMONT

(Became a state March 4, 1791)

	Candidates	Votes	%
1791	Thomas Chittenden	✔	
1792	Thomas Chittenden	✔	
1793	Thomas Chittenden	3,184	51.7
	Isaac Tichenor	2,712	44.1
1794	Thomas Chittenden	2,643	52.1
	Isaac Tichenor	2,000	39.4
1795	Thomas Chittenden	4,260	60.7
	Isaac Tichenor	2,038	29.1
1796	Thomas Chittenden	✔	
1797	Isaac Tichenor (FED)	†	
1798	Isaac Tichenor (FED)	6,211	66.4
	Moses Robinson (D-R)	2,805	30.0

	Candidates	Votes	%
1799	Isaac Tichenor (FED)	✔	
1800	Isaac Tichenor (FED)	6,444	64.0
	Israel Smith (D-R)	3,239	32.2
1801	Isaac Tichenor (FED)	✔	
1802	Isaac Tichenor (FED)	7,823	60.5
	Israel Smith (D-R)	5,085	39.3
1803	Isaac Tichenor (FED)	✔	
1804	Isaac Tichenor (FED)	8,075	56.6
	Jonathan Robinson (D-R)	6,184	43.4
1805	Isaac Tichenor (FED)	8,682	60.9
	Jonathan Robinson (D-R)	5,056	35.5
1806	Isaac Tichenor (FED)	8,551	54.1
	Israel Smith (D-R)	6,930	43.9
1807	Israel Smith (D-R)	9,983	53.2
	Isaac Tichenor (FED)	8,571	45.7
1808	Isaac Tichenor (FED)	13,634	50.8
	Israel Smith (D-R)	12,775	47.6
1809	Jonas Galusha (D-R)	14,583	51.1
	Isaac Tichenor (FED)	13,467	47.2
1810	Jonas Galusha (D-R)	13,810	57.3
	Isaac Tichenor (FED)	9,912	41.2
1811	Jonas Galusha (D-R)	13,828	54.0
	Martin Chittenden (FED)	11,214	43.8
1812	Jonas Galusha (D-R)	19,158	53.6
	Martin Chittenden (FED)	15,950	44.6
1813	Jonas Galusha (D-R)	16,828	49.5
	Martin Chittenden (FED)	16,532†	48.7
1814	Martin Chittenden (FED)	17,466†	49.4
	Jonas Galusha (D-R)	17,411	49.3
1815	Jonas Galusha (D-R)	18,055	52.1
	Martin Chittenden (FED)	16,032	46.3
1816	Jonas Galusha (D-R)	17,262	55.2
	Samuel Strong (FED)	13,888	44.4
1817	Jonas Galusha (D-R)	13,756	64.3
	Isaac Tichenor (FED)	7,430	34.7
1818	Jonas Galusha (D-R)	15,243	95.3
1819	Jonas Galusha (D-R)	12,268	81.5
	William C. Bradley (D-R)	1,035	6.9
1820	Richard Skinner (D-R)	13,152	93.4
1821	Richard Skinner (D-R)	12,434	98.7
1822	Richard Skinner (D-R)	✔	
1823	Cornelius P. Van Ness (D-R)	11,479	85.6
	Dudley Chase	1,088	8.1
1824	Cornelius P. Van Ness (D-R)	13,428	85.8
	Joel Doolittle	1,882	12.0
1825	Cornelius P. Van Ness (D-R)	12,229	98.4
1826	Ezra Butler (D-R)	8,966	63.3
	Joel Doolittle	3,157	22.3
1827	Ezra Butler (D-R)	13,699	85.2
	Joel Doolittle	1,951	12.1
1828	Samuel C. Crafts (NR)	16,285	91.8
	Joel Doolittle	933	5.3
1829	Samuel C. Crafts (NR)	14,325#	55.7
	Heman Allen (A-MASC)	7,376#	28.7
	Joel Doolittle (JAC)	3,973#	15.4
1830	Samuel C. Crafts (OPP)-	13,476#	43.9
	William A. Palmer (A-MAS)	10,923#	35.6
	Ezra Meech (JAC)	6,285#	20.5
1831	William A. Palmer (A-MAS)-	15,258#	44.0
	Heman Allen (NR)	12,990#	37.5
	Ezra Meech (JAC)	6,158#	17.8
1832	William A. Palmer (A-MAS)	17,318†	42.2
	Samuel C. Crafts (NR)	15,499	37.7
	Ezra Meech (D)	8,210	20.0
1833	William A. Palmer (A-MAS)	20,565	52.9
	Ezra Meech (FUS)	15,683	40.3
1834	William A. Palmer (A-MAS)	17,131†	45.4
	William C. Bradley (D)	10,385	27.5
	Horatio Seymour (W)	10,159	26.9
1835	William A. Palmer (A-MAS)	16,210*	46.4
	William C. Bradley (D)	13,254	37.9
	Charles Paine (W)	5,435	15.6
1836	Silas H. Jennison (W & A-MASC)	20,371	55.8
	William C. Bradley (D)	16,134	44.2
1837	Silas H. Jennison (W)	22,257	55.7
	William C. Bradley (D)	17,722	44.3
1838	Silas H. Jennison (W)	22,169	56.0
	William C. Bradley (D)	17,416	44.0
1839	Silas H. Jennison (W)	24,621	52.5
	Nathan Smilie (D)	22,256	47.5
1840	Silas H. Jennison (W)	33,653	59.4
	Paul Dillingham Jr. (D)	23,000	40.6
1841	Charles Paine (W)	23,582†	48.5
	Nathan Smilie (D)	21,693	44.6
	Titus Hutchinson (LIB)	3,091	6.4
1842	Charles Paine (W)	27,167	50.9
	Nathan Smilie (D)	24,130	45.2
1843	John Mattocks (W)	24,465†	48.7
	Daniel Kellogg (D)	21,982	43.8
	Charles K. Williams (LIB)	3,766	7.5
1844	William Slade (W)	28,265	51.5
	Daniel Kellogg (D)	20,930	38.2
	William R. Shafter (LIB)	5,618	10.2
1845	William Slade (W)	22,770†	47.2
	Daniel Kellogg (D)	18,591	38.5
	William R. Shafter (LIB)	6,534	13.5
1846	Horace Eaton (W)	23,638†	48.5
	John Smith (D)	17,877	36.7
	Lawrence Brainerd (F SOIL)	7,118	14.6
1847	Horace Eaton (W)	22,455†	46.7
	Paul Dillingham Jr. (D)	18,661	38.8
	Lawrence Brainerd (F SOIL)	6,926	14.4
1848	Carlos Coolidge (W)	22,132†	43.7
	Oscar L. Shafter (F SOIL D)	15,018	29.6
	Paul Dillingham (CASS D)	13,477	26.6
1849	Carlos Coolidge (W)	26,443†	49.6
	Horatio Needham (F SOIL D)	23,492	44.1
	Jonas Clark (D)	3,357	6.3
1850	Charles K. Williams (W)	24,809	51.3
	Lucius B. Peck (F SOIL D)	19,189	39.6
	John Roberts (HUNKER D)	4,379	9.1
1851	Charles K. Williams (W)	22,864	51.0
	Timothy B. Redfield (F SOIL)	15,121	33.7
	John S. Robinson (HUNKER D)	6,790	15.2
1852	Erastus Fairbanks (W)	23,795†	49.3
	John S. Robinson (D)	15,001	31.1
	Lawrence Brainerd (F SOIL)	9,445	19.6
1853	Erastus Fairbanks (W)	21,118	44.1
	John S. Robinson (D)	18,287†	38.2
	Lawrence Brainerd (F SOIL)	8,370	17.5
1854	Stephen Royce (W)	27,811	62.4
	Merritt Clark (D)	15,130	33.9
1855	Stephen Royce (R)	25,699#	59.0
	Merritt Clark (D)	12,800#	29.4
	James M. Slade (AM)	3,631#	8.3
1856	Ryland Fletcher (R)	34,757	74.3
	Henry Keyes (D)	11,747	25.1
1857	Ryland Fletcher (R)	27,065	67.1
	Henry Keyes (D)	12,984	32.2
1858	Hiland Hall (R)	29,460	68.5
	Henry Keyes (D)	13,538	31.5
1859	Hiland Hall (R)	31,367	68.4
	John G. Saxe (D)	14,499	31.6
1860	Erastus Fairbanks (R)	34,260	71.0
	John G. Saxe (DOUG D)	11,890	24.6
1861	Frederick Holbrook (UN R)	33,155	78.8
	Andrew Tracy (UN D)	5,722	13.6
	B. H. Smalley (BRECK D)	3,190	7.6
1862	Frederick Holbrook (R)	30,032	88.5
	B. H. Smalley (D)	3,724	11.0

Gubernatorial Elections

	Candidates	Votes	%
1863	John Gregory Smith (R)	29,613	71.2
	Timothy P. Redfield (D)	11,962	22.8
1864	John Gregory Smith (UN)	31,260	71.8
	Timothy P. Redfield (D)	12,283	28.2
1865	Paul Dillingham (R)	27,586	75.7
	Charles N. Davenport (D)	8,857	24.3
1866	Paul Dillingham (R)	34,117	75.1
	Charles N. Davenport (D)	11,292	24.9
1867	John B. Page (R)	31,694	73.3
	John L. Edwards (D)	11,510	26.6
1868	John B. Page (R)	42,615	73.6
	John L. Edwards (D)	15,289	26.4
1869	Peter T. Washburn (R)	31,834	73.5
	Homer W. Heaton (D)	11,455	26.5
1870	John W. Stewart (R)	33,367	73.5
	Homer W. Heaton (D)	12,058	26.5
1872	Julius Converse (R)	41,946	71.6
	A. B. Gardner (LR)	16,613	28.4
1874	Asahel Peck (R)	33,582	71.7
	W. H. H. Bingham (D)	13,257	28.3
1876	Horace Fairbanks (R)	44,723	68.0
	W. H. H. Bingham (D)	20,988	31.9
1878	Redfield Proctor (R)	37,312	64.3
	W. H. H. Bingham (D)	17,274	29.8
1880	Roswell Farnham (R)	47,848	67.7
	Edward J. Phelps (D)	21,245	30.1
1882	John L. Barstow (R)	35,839	69.1
	George E. Eaton (D)	14,466	27.9
1884	Samuel E. Pingree (R)	42,524	67.3
	Lyman W. Redington (D)	19,820	31.4
1886	Ebenezer J. Ormsbee (R)	37,709	66.0
	Stephen C. Shurtleff (D)	17,187	30.1
1888	William P. Dillingham (R)	48,522	69.9
	Stephen C. Shurtleff (D)	19,527	28.1
1890	Carroll S. Page (R)	33,462	62.1
	Herbert F. Brigham (D)	19,299	35.8
1892	Levi K. Fuller (R)	38,918	65.2
	B. B. Smalley (D)	19,216	32.2
1894	Urban A. Woodbury (R)	42,663	73.6
	George W. Smith (D)	14,142	24.4
1896	Josiah Grout (R)	53,426	76.4
	J. Henry Jackson (D)	14,855	21.3
1898	Edward C. Smith (R)	38,555	71.0
	Thomas W. Moloney (D)	14,686	27.0
1900	William W. Stickney (R)	48,441	72.2
	John H. Center (D)	17,129	25.5
1902	John G. McCullough (R)	31,864†	45.6
	Percival W. Clement (H LIC)	28,201	40.3
	Felix W. McGettrick (D)	7,364	10.5
1904	Charles J. Bell (R)	48,115	72.2
	Eli H. Porter (D)	16,556	24.9
1906	Fletcher D. Proctor (R)	42,332	60.1
	Percival W. Clement (ID)	26,912	38.2
1908	George H. Prouty (R)	45,598	70.8
	James E. Burke (D)	15,953	24.8
1910	John A. Mead (R)	35,263	64.2
	Charles D. Watson (D)	17,425	31.7
1912	Allen M. Fletcher (R)	26,237†	40.5
	Harland B. Howe (D)	20,001	30.9
	Frazer Metzger (PROG)	15,629	24.1
1914	Charles W. Gates (R)	36,972	59.5
	Harland B. Howe (D)	16,191	26.1
	Walter J. Aldrich (PROG)	6,929	11.2
1916	Horace F. Graham (R)	43,265	71.1
	William B. Mayo (D)	15,789	26.0
1918	Percival W. Clement (R)	28,358	67.2
	William B. Mayo (D, P)	13,859	32.8
1920	James Hartness (R, P)	67,674	78.0
	Fred C. Martin (D)	18,917	21.8
1922	Redfield Proctor (R, P)	51,104	74.8
	J. Holmes Jackson (D)	17,059	25.0

	Candidates	Votes	%
1924	Franklin S. Billings (R)	75,510	79.3
	Fred C. Martin (D)	18,263	19.2
1926	John E. Weeks (R)	44,564	60.9
	Herbert C. Comings (D, P)	28,651	39.1
1928	John E. Weeks (R)	94,974	73.5
	Harry C. Shurtleff (D)	33,563	26.0
1930	Stanley C. Wilson (R)	52,836	71.0
	Park H. Pollard (D)	21,540	28.9
1932	Stanley C. Wilson (R)	81,656	61.7
	James P. Leamy (D)	49,247	37.2
1934	Charles M. Smith (R)	73,620	57.3
	James P. Leamy (D)	54,159	42.1
1936	George D. Aiken (R)	83,602	60.9
	Alfred H. Heininger (D)	53,218	38.8
1938	George D. Aiken (R)	75,098	66.8
	Fred C. Martin (D)	37,404	33.3
1940	William H. Wills (R)	87,346	64.0
	John McGrath (D)	49,068	36.0
1942	William H. Wills (R)	44,804	77.9
	Park H. Pollard (D)	12,708	22.1
1944	Mortimer R. Proctor (R)	78,907	65.9
	Ernest H. Bailey (D)	40,835	34.1
1946	Ernest W. Gibson (R)	57,849	80.3
	Berthold C. Coburn (D)	14,096	19.6
1948	Ernest W. Gibson (R)	86,394	71.9
	Charles F. Ryan (D)	33,588	28.0
1950	Lee E. Emerson (R)	64,915	74.5
	J. Edward Moran (D)	22,227	25.5
1952	Lee E. Emerson (R)	78,338	51.9
	Robert W. Larrow (D)	60,051	39.8
	Henry W. Vail (IR)	12,447	8.3
1954	Joseph B. Johnson (R)	59,778	52.3
	E. Frank Branon (D)	54,554	47.7
1956	Joseph B. Johnson (R)	88,379	57.5
	E. Frank Branon (D)	65,420	42.5
1958	Robert T. Stafford (R)	62,222	50.3
	Bernard J. Leddy (D)	61,503	49.7
1960	F. Ray Keyser Jr. (R)	92,861	56.4
	Russell F. Niquette (D)	71,755	43.6
1962	Philip H. Hoff (D, I)	61,383	50.6
	F. Ray Keyser Jr. (R)	60,035	49.4
1964	Philip H. Hoff (D)	106,611	64.9
	Ralph A. Foote (R, I)	57,576	35.1
1966	Philip H. Hoff (D)	78,669	57.7
	Richard A. Snelling (R)	57,577	42.3
1968	Deane C. Davis (R)	89,387	55.5
	John J. Daley (D)	71,656	44.5
1970	Deane C. Davis (R)	87,458	57.0
	Leo O'Brien Jr. (D)	66,028	43.0
1972	Thomas P. Salmon (D, I VT)	104,533	55.2
	Luther F. Hackett (R)	82,491	43.6
1974	Thomas P. Salmon (D, I VT)	79,842	56.6
	Walter L. Kennedy (R)	53,672	38.0
	Martha Abbott (LU)	7,629	5.4
1976	Richard A. Snelling (R)	99,268	53.4
	Stella B. Hackel (D)	75,262	40.5
	Bernard J. Sanders (LU)	11,317	6.1
1978	Richard A. Snelling (R)	78,181	62.8
	Edwin C. Granai (D)	42,482	34.1
1980	Richard A. Snelling (R)	123,229	58.6
	J. Jerome Diamond (D)	77,363	36.8
1982	Richard A. Snelling (R)	93,111	55.0
	Madeleine M. Kunin (D)	74,394	44.0
1984	Madeleine M. Kunin (D)	116,938	50.0
	John J. Easton (R)	113,264	48.5
1986	Madeleine M. Kunin[1] (D)	92,379	47.0
	Peter Smith (R)	75,162	38.2
	Bernard Sanders (I)	28,430	14.5
1988	Madeleine M. Kunin (D)	134,438	55.4
	Michael Bernhardt (R)	105,191	43.3

	Candidates	Votes	%
1990	Richard A. Snelling (R)	109,540	*51.8*
	Peter Welch (D)	97,321	*46.0*
1992	Howard Dean (D)	213,523	*74.7*
	John McClaughry (R)	65,837	*23.0*
1994	Howard Dean (D)	145,661	*68.7*
	David Kelley (R)	40,292	*19.0*
	Thomas J. Morse (I)	15,000	*7.1*
1996	Howard Dean (D)	179,544	*70.5*
	John L. Gropper (R)	57,161	*22.4*

Vermont

1. *Since no candidate won a clear majority of the total vote cast for governor, the election passed to the state legislature. Sitting in joint assembly in January 1987, the legislature elected Kunin with 139 votes to 39 for Smith and 1 for Sanders.*

VIRGINIA

(Ratified the Constitution June 25, 1788)

	Candidates	Votes	%
1851[1]	Joseph Johnson (D)	67,074	*53.0*
	Summers (W)	59,476	*47.0*
1855	Henry A. Wise (D)	83,224	*53.2*
	Flournoy (AM)	73,244	*46.8*
1859	John Letcher (D)	77,112	*51.9*
	Goggin (OPP)	71,543	*48.1*
1861	John Letcher	✔	
1863	William Smith	✔	
	Munford		
	Flournoy		
1869	Gilbert C. Walker (C)	119,535	*54.2*
	H. H. Wells (RAD)	101,204	*45.9*
1873	James L. Kemper (D)	119,672	*56.2*
	Robert W. Hughes (R)	93,413	*43.8*
1877	Frederick W. M. Holliday (D)	101,873	*95.9*
1881	William E. Cameron (READJ)	113,464	*53.0*
	John W. Daniel (D)	100,757	*47.0*
1885	Fitzhugh Lee (D)	152,547	*52.8*
	John S. Wise (R)	136,508	*47.2*
1889	Philip W. McKinney (D)	163,180	*57.2*
	William Mahone (R)	121,240	*42.5*
1893	Charles T. O'Ferrall (D)	128,144	*59.7*
	Edmund R. Cocke (POP)	79,653	*37.1*
1897	James Hoge Tyler (D)	110,253	*64.6*
	Patrick H. McCaull (R)	56,739	*33.2*
1901	A. J. Montague (D)	116,691	*58.2*
	J. Hampton Hoge (R)	81,366	*40.6*
1905	Claude A. Swanson (D)	84,235	*64.5*
	Lunsford L. Lewis (R)	45,815	*35.1*
1909	William Hodges Mann (D)	70,759	*63.4*
	William P. Kent (R)	40,357	*36.1*
1913	Henry C. Stuart (D)	66,518	*91.9*
	C. Campbell (SOC)	3,789	*5.2*
1917	Westmoreland Davis (D)	64,226	*71.5*
	T. J. Muncy (R)	24,957	*27.8*
1921	Elbert Lee Trinkle (D)	139,416	*66.2*
	Henry W. Anderson (R)	65,833	*31.2*
1925	Harry F. Byrd (D)	107,378	*74.1*
	S. Harris Hoge (R)	37,592	*25.9*
1929	John Garland Pollard (D)	169,329	*62.8*
	William Moseley Brown (R)	99,650	*36.9*
1933	George C. Peery (D)	122,820	*73.7*
	Fred W. McWane (R)	40,377	*24.2*
1937	James H. Price (D)	124,145	*82.8*
	J. Powell Royall	23,670	*15.8*
1941	Colgate W. Darden Jr. (D)	98,680	*80.6*
	Muse	21,896	*17.9*
1945	William M. Tuck (D)	112,355	*66.6*
	S. Lloyd Landreth	52,386	*31.0*

	Candidates	Votes	%
1949	John S. Battle (D)	184,772	*70.4*
	Walter Johnson (R)	71,991	*27.4*
1953	Thomas B. Stanley (D)	226,998	*54.8*
	Ted Dalton (R)	183,328	*44.3*
1957	J. Lindsay Almond Jr. (D)	326,921	*63.2*
	Ted Dalton (R)	188,628	*36.4*
1961	Albertis S. Harrison Jr. (D)	251,861	*63.8*
	H. Clyde Pearson (R)	142,567	*36.1*
1965	Mills E. Godwin Jr. (D)	269,526	*47.9*
	Linwood Holton (R)	212,207	*37.7*
	William J. Story Jr. (C)	75,307	*13.4*
1969	Linwood Holton (R)	480,869	*52.5*
	William C. Battle (D)	415,695	*45.4*
1973	Mills E. Godwin Jr. (R)	525,075	*50.7*
	Henry Howell (I)	510,103	*49.3*
1977	John Dalton (R)	699,302	*55.9*
	Henry Howell (D)	541,319	*43.3*
1981	Charles S. Robb (D)	760,357	*53.5*
	J. Marshall Coleman (R)	659,398	*46.4*
1985	Gerald L. Baliles (D)	741,438	*55.2*
	Wyatt B. Durrette (R)	601,652	*44.8*
1989	L. Douglas Wilder (D)	896,936	*50.1*
	J. Marshall Coleman (R)	890,195	*49.8*
1993	George F. Allen (R)	1,045,319	*58.3*
	Mary Sue Terry (D)	733,527	*40.9*
1997	James S. Gilmore (R)	969,062	*55.8*
	Donald. S. Breyer (D)	738,971	*42.6*

Virginia

1. *Before 1851 governor was elected by General Assembly.*

WASHINGTON

(Became a state Nov. 11, 1889)

	Candidates	Votes	%
1889	Elisha P. Ferry (R)	33,711	*57.7*
	Eugene Scruple (D)	24,732	*42.3*
1892	John H. McGraw (R)	33,281	*37.0*
	Henry J. Snively (D)	28,959	*32.2*
	C. W. Young (PP)	23,750	*26.4*
1896	John R. Rogers (PP)	50,849	*55.6*
	P. C. Sullivan (R)	38,154	*41.7*
1900	John R. Rogers (D)	52,048	*48.9*
	J. M. Frink (R)	49,860	*46.8*
1904	Albert E. Mead (R)	74,278	*51.3*
	George Turner (D)	59,119	*40.9*
	D. Burgess (SOC)	7,421	*5.1*
1908	Samuel G. Cosgrove (R)	110,190	*62.6*
	John Pattison (D)	58,126	*33.0*
1912	Ernest Lister (D)	97,251	*30.6*
	M. E. Hay (R)	96,629	*30.4*
	Robert T. Hodge (PROG)	77,731	*24.4*
	Anna A. Maley (SOC)	37,155	*11.7*
1916	Ernest Lister (D)	181,745	*48.1*
	Henry McBride (R)	167,809	*44.4*
	L. E. Katterfeld (SOC)	21,117	*5.6*
1920	Louis F. Hart (R)	210,662	*52.7*
	Robert Bridges (F-LAB)	121,371	*30.4*
	W. W. Black (D)	66,079	*16.5*
1924	Roland H. Hartley (R)	220,162	*56.4*
	Ben F. Hill (D)	126,447	*32.4*
	J. R. Oman (F-LAB)	40,073	*10.3*
1928	Roland H. Hartley (R)	281,991	*56.2*
	Scott Bullitt (D)	214,334	*42.7*
1932	Clarence D. Martin (D)	352,215	*57.3*
	John A. Gellatly (R)	207,497	*33.8*
	L. C. Hicks (LIB)	41,710	*6.8*
1936	Clarence D. Martin (D)	466,550	*69.4*
	Roland H. Hartley (R)	189,141	*28.1*

	Candidates	Votes	%
1940	Arthur B. Langlie (R)	392,522	50.2
	C. C. Dill (D)	386,706	49.5
1944	Monrad C. Wallgren (D)	428,834	51.5
	Arthur B. Langlie (R)	400,604	48.1
1948	Arthur B. Langlie (R)	445,958	50.5
	Monrad C. Wallgren (D)	417,035	47.2
1952	Arthur B. Langlie (R)	567,822	52.7
	Hugh B. Mitchell (D)	510,675	47.4
1956	Albert D. Rosellini (D)	616,773	54.6
	Emmett T. Anderson (R)	508,041	45.0
1960	Albert D. Rosellini (D)	611,987	50.3
	Lloyd Andrews (R)	594,122	48.9
1964	Daniel J. Evans (R)	697,256	55.8
	Albert D. Rosellini (D)	548,692	43.9
1968	Daniel J. Evans (R)	692,378	54.7
	John J. O'Connell (D)	560,262	44.3
1972	Daniel J. Evans (R)	747,825	50.8
	Albert D. Rosellini (D)	630,613	42.8
	Vick Gould (TPCT)	86,843	5.9
1976	Dixy Lee Ray (D)	821,797	53.1
	John D. Spellman (R)	687,039	44.4
1980	John D. Spellman (R)	981,083	56.7
	James A. McDermott (D)	749,813	43.3
1984	Booth Gardner (D)	1,006,993	53.3
	John D. Spellman (R)	881,994	46.7
1988	Booth Gardner (D)	1,166,448	62.2
	Bob Williams (R)	708,481	37.8
1992	Mike Lowry (D)	1,184,315	52.2
	Ken Eikenberry (R)	1,086,216	47.8
1996	Gary Locke (D)	1,296,492	58.0
	Ellen Craswell (R)	940,538	42.0

WEST VIRGINIA

(Became a state June 19, 1863)

	Candidates	Votes	%
1863	Arthur I. Boreman (UN R)	25,797	100.0
1864	Arthur I. Boreman (UN R)	19,353	100.0
1866	Arthur I. Boreman (R)	23,802	58.1
	Benjamin H. Smith (D)	17,158	41.9
1868	William E. Stevenson (R)	26,935	54.6
	James M. Camden (D)	22,358	45.4
1870	John J. Jacob (D)	29,097	51.9
	William E. Stevenson (R)	26,924	48.1
1872	John J. Jacob (I)	42,888	51.6
	Johnson N. Camden (D)	40,305	48.5
1876	Henry M. Mathews (D)	56,206	56.2
	Nathan Goff (R)	43,477	43.5
1880	Jacob B. Jackson (D)	60,991	51.3
	George C. Sturgiss (R)	44,855	37.7
	N. B. French (G)	13,027	11.0
1884	E. Willis Wilson (D)	71,408	52.0
	Edwin Maxwell (R)	66,059	48.1
1888	Nathan Goff (R)	78,904‡	50.0
	A. Brooks Fleming (D)	78,798	50.0
1892	William A. MacCorkle (D)	84,585	49.4
	Thomas E. Davis (R)	80,658	47.1
1896	George W. Atkinson (R)	105,588	52.4
	Cornelius C. Watts (D)	93,558	46.4
1900	A. B. White (R)	118,798	53.8
	John H. Holt (D)	100,233	45.4
1904	William M. O. Dawson (R)	121,540	50.8
	John J. Cornwell (D)	112,538	47.0
1908	William E. Glasscock (R)	130,807	50.7
	Bennett (D)	118,909	46.1
1912	H. D. Hatfield (R)	128,062	47.7
	W. R. Thompson (D)	119,292	44.5
	Walter B. Hilton (SOC)	15,048	5.6

	Candidates	Votes	%
1916	John J. Cornwell (D)	143,324	49.5
	Robinson (R)	140,558	48.6
1920	Ephraim F. Morgan (R)	242,237	47.3
	Arthur B. Koontz (D)	185,662	36.3
	S. B. Montgomery (NON PART)	81,330	15.9
1924	Howard M. Gore (R)	302,987	53.0
	Jake Fisher (D)	261,846	45.8
1928	William G. Conley (R)	345,729	53.7
	J. Alfred Taylor (D)	296,637	46.1
1932	Herman G. Kump (D)	402,316	53.8
	T. C. Townsend (R)	342,660	45.8
1936	Homer A. Holt (D)	492,333	59.2
	Summers H. Sharp (R)	339,890	40.8
1940	Matthew M. Neely (D)	496,028	56.4
	Daniel Boone Dawson (R)	383,698	43.6
1944	Clarence W. Meadows (D)	395,122	54.4
	Daniel Boone Dawson (R)	330,649	45.6
1948	Okey L. Patteson (D)	438,752	57.1
	Herbert S. Boreman (R)	329,309	42.9
1952	William C. Marland (D)	454,898	51.5
	Rush D. Holt (R)	427,629	48.5
1956	Cecil H. Underwood (R)	440,502	53.9
	Robert H. Mollohan (D)	377,121	46.1
1960	W. W. Barron (D)	446,755	54.0
	Harold E. Neely (R)	380,665	46.0
1964	Hulett Smith (D)	433,023	54.9
	Cecil H. Underwood (R)	355,559	45.1
1968	Arch A. Moore Jr. (R)	378,315	50.9
	James M. Sprouse (D)	365,530	49.1
1972	Arch A. Moore Jr. (R)	423,817	54.7
	John D. Rockefeller IV (D)	350,462	45.3
1976	John D. Rockefeller IV (D)	495,661	66.2
	Cecil H. Underwood (R)	253,420	33.8
1980	John D. Rockefeller IV (D)	401,863	54.1
	Arch A. Moore Jr. (R)	337,240	45.4
1984	Arch A. Moore Jr. (R)	394,937	53.3
	Clyde M. See Jr. (D)	346,565	46.7
1988	Gaston Caperton (D)	382,421	58.9
	Arch A. Moore Jr. (R)	267,172	41.1
1992	Gaston Caperton (D)	368,302	56.0
	Cleve Benedict (R)	240,390	36.6
	Charlotte Jean Pritt (WRITE IN)	48,501	7.4
1996	Cecil H. Underwood (R)	324,518	51.6
	Charlotte Jean Pritt (D)	287,870	45.8

WISCONSIN

(Became a state May 29, 1848)

	Candidates	Votes	%
1848	Nelson Dewey (D)	19,875	57.6
	Tweedy (W)	14,621	42.4
1849	Nelson Dewey (D)	16,701	52.6
	Collins (W)	11,317	35.6
	Chase (F SOIL)	3,761	11.8
1851	Leonard J. Farwell (W)	22,319	50.6
	Upham (D)	21,812	49.4
1853	William Augustus Barstow (D)	30,455	54.7
	Holton (W)	21,886	39.3
	Baird (W)	3,318	6.0
1855	William Augustus Barstow (D)	36,387‡	50.1
	Coles Bashford (R)	36,197	49.9
1857	Alexander W. Randall (R)	44,693	50.3
	Cross (D)	44,239	49.7
1859	Alexander W. Randall (R)	63,466	51.6
	Harrison C. Hobart (D)	59,525	48.4
1861	Louis P. Harvey (R)	53,777	54.2
	Ferguson (D)	45,456	45.8

	Candidates	Votes	%
1863	James T. Lewis (R)	78,470	58.8
	Henry L. Palmer (D)	55,049	41.2
1865	Lucius Fairchild (R)	58,332	54.7
	Harrison C. Hobart (D)	48,330	45.3
1867	Lucius Fairchild (R)	73,637	51.7
	John J. Tallmadge (D)	68,873	48.3
1869	Lucius Fairchild (R)	69,502	53.2
	Charles D. Robinson (D)	61,239	46.8
1871	Cadwallader C. Washburn (R)	78,301	53.2
	James R. Doolittle (D)	68,920	46.8
1873	William R. Taylor (D)	81,599	55.2
	Cadwallader C. Washburn (R)	66,224	44.8
1875	Harrison Ludington (R)	85,165	50.2
	William R. Taylor (D)	84,374	49.8
1877	William E. Smith (R)	78,750	44.9
	Mallory (D)	70,486	40.2
	Edward P. Allis (G)	26,116	14.9
1879	William E. Smith (R)	100,537	53.2
	Jenkins (D)	75,030	39.7
	May (G)	12,996	6.9
1881	Jeremiah M. Rusk (R)	81,754	47.6
	Nicholas D. Fratt (D)	69,797	40.6
	Theodore D. Kanouse (P)	13,225	7.7
1884	Jeremiah M. Rusk (R)	163,210	51.0
	Nicholas D. Fratt (D)	143,943	45.0
1886	Jeremiah M. Rusk (R)	133,247	46.5
	Gilbert M. Woodward (D)	114,525	40.0
	John Cochrane (LAB)	21,467	7.5
	John M. Olin (P)	17,089	6.0
1888	William D. Hoard (R)	175,696	49.5
	James Morgan (D)	155,423	43.8
1890	George W. Peck (D)	160,388	51.9
	William D. Hoard (R)	132,074	42.7
1892	George W. Peck (D)	178,135	47.9
	John C. Spooner (R)	170,538	45.9
1894	William H. Upham (R)	196,151	52.3
	George W. Peck (D)	142,250	37.9
	D. Frank Powell (PP)	25,604	6.8
1896	Edward Scofield (R)	264,981	59.7
	Willis C. Silverthorn (D)	169,257	38.1
1898	Edward Scofield (R)	173,137	52.6
	Hiram Wilson Sawyer (D)	135,353	41.1
1900	Robert M. La Follette (R)	264,419	59.8
	Louis G. Bomrich (D)	160,674	36.4
1902	Robert M. La Follette (R)	193,407	52.9
	David S. Rose (D)	145,820	39.9
1904	Robert M. La Follette (R)	227,253	50.6
	George W. Peck (D)	176,301	39.2
	Arnold (SOCIAL D)	24,857	5.5
1906	James O. Davidson (R)	183,526	57.4
	John A. Aylward (D)	103,114	32.3
	Winfield R. Gaylord (SOCIAL D)	24,435	7.6
1908	James O. Davidson (R)	242,963	54.0
	John A. Aylward (D)	165,977	36.9
	Harvey D. Brown (SOCIAL D)	28,583	6.4
1910	Francis E. McGovern (R)	161,559	50.6
	Schmitz (D)	110,446	34.6
	Jacobs (SOCIAL D)	39,539	12.4
1912	Francis E. McGovern (R)	179,317	45.6
	John C. Karel (D)	167,298	42.5
	Carl D. Thompson (SOCIAL D)	34,385	8.7
1914	Emanuel L. Philipp (R)	140,835	43.3
	John C. Karel (D)	119,567	36.7
	John J. Blaine (I)	32,543	10.0
	Oscar Ameringer (SOCIAL D)	25,940	8.0
1916	Emanuel L. Philipp (R)	227,896	52.7
	Burt Williams (D)	164,633	38.1
	Rae Weaver (SOC)	30,813	7.1
1918	Emanuel L. Philipp (R)	155,799	47.0
	Moehlenpah (D)	112,576	34.0
	Seidel (SOC)	57,532	17.4

	Candidates	Votes	%
1920	John J. Blaine (R)	366,247	53.0
	McCoy (D)	247,746	35.8
	Coleman (SOC)	71,103	10.3
1922	John J. Blaine (R)	367,929	76.4
	Arthur A. Bentley (ID)	51,061	10.6
	Louis A. Arnold (SOC)	39,570	8.2
1924	John J. Blaine (R)	412,255	51.8
	Martin L. Lueck (D)	317,550	39.9
	William F. Quick (SOC)	45,268	5.7
1926	Fred R. Zimmerman (R)	350,927	63.5
	Charles B. Perry (I)	76,507	13.8
	Virgil H. Cady (D)	72,627	13.1
	Herman O. Kent (SOC)	40,293	7.3
1928	Walter J. Kohler Sr. (R)	547,738	55.4
	Albert G. Schmedeman (D)	394,368	39.9
1930	Philip F. La Follette (R)	392,958	64.8
	Hammersley (D)	170,020	28.0
1932	Albert G. Schmedeman (D)	590,114	52.5
	Walter J. Kohler Sr. (R)	470,805	41.9
	Metcalfe (SOC)	56,965	5.1
1934	Philip F. La Follette (PROG)	373,083	39.1
	Albert G. Schmedeman (D)	359,467	37.7
	Greene (R)	172,980	18.1
1936	Philip F. La Follette (PROG)	573,724	46.4
	Alexander Wiley (R)	363,973	29.4
	William L. Lueck (D)	268,530	21.7
1938	Julius P. Heil (R)	543,675	55.4
	Philip F. La Follette (PROG)	353,381	36.0
	Bolens (D)	78,446	8.0
1940	Julius P. Heil (R)	558,678	40.7
	Orland S. Loomis (PROG)	546,436	39.8
	McGovern (D)	264,985	19.3
1942	Orland S. Loomis (PROG)	397,664*	49.7
	Julius P. Heil (R)	291,945	36.5
	Sullivan (D)	98,153	12.3
1944	Walter S. Goodland (R)	697,740	52.8
	Daniel W. Hoan (D)	536,357	40.6
	Benz (PROG)	76,028	5.8
1946	Walter S. Goodland (R)	621,970	59.8
	Daniel W. Hoan (D)	406,499	39.1
1948	Oscar Rennebohm (R)	684,839	54.1
	Carl W. Thompson (D)	558,497	44.1
1950	Walter J. Kohler Jr. (R)	605,649	53.2
	Carl W. Thompson (D)	525,319	46.2
1952	Walter J. Kohler Jr. (R)	1,009,171	62.5
	William Proxmire (D)	601,844	37.3
1954	Walter J. Kohler Jr. (R)	596,158	51.5
	William Proxmire (D)	560,747	48.4
1956	Vernon W. Thomson (R)	808,273	51.9
	William Proxmire (D)	749,421	48.1
1958	Gaylord A. Nelson (D)	644,296	53.6
	Vernon W. Thomson (R)	556,391	46.3
1960	Gaylord A. Nelson (D)	890,868	51.6
	Philip G. Kuehn (R)	837,123	48.4
1962	John W. Reynolds (D)	637,491	50.4
	Philip G. Kuehn (R)	625,536	49.4
1964	Warren P. Knowles (R)	856,779	50.6
	John W. Reynolds (D)	837,901	49.4
1966	Warren P. Knowles (R)	626,041	53.5
	Patrick J. Lucey (D)	539,258	46.1
1968	Warren P. Knowles (R)	893,463	52.9
	Bronson C. La Follette (D)	791,100	46.8
1970	Patrick J. Lucey (D)	728,403	54.2
	Jack B. Olson (R)	602,617	44.9
1974	Patrick J. Lucey (D)	628,639	53.2
	William D. Dyke (R)	497,195	42.1
1978	Lee S. Dreyfus (R)	816,056	54.4
	Martin J. Schreiber (D)	673,813	44.9
1982	Anthony S. Earl (D)	896,812	56.7
	Terry J. Kohler (R)	662,838	41.9

	Candidates	Votes	%
1986	Tommy G. Thompson (R)	805,090	52.7
	Anthony S. Earl (D)	705,578	46.2
1990	Tommy G. Thompson (R)	802,321	58.2
	Thomas Loftus (D)	576,280	41.8
1994	Tommy G. Thompson (R)	1,051,326	67.2
	Chuck Chvala (D)	482,850	30.9

WYOMING

(Became a state July 10, 1890)

	Candidates	Votes	%
1890	Francis E. Warren (R)	8,879	55.4
	George W. Baxter (D)	7,153	44.6
1892	John E. Osborne (D)	9,290	53.8
	Edward Ivinson (R)	7,509	43.5
1894	William A. Richards (R)	10,149	52.6
	William H. Holliday (D)	6,965	36.1
	Lewis C. Tidball (POP)	2,176	11.3
1898	DeForest Richards (R)	10,383	52.4
	Horace C. Alger (D)	8,989	45.4
1902	DeForest Richards (R)	14,483	57.8
	George T. Beck (D)	10,017	40.0
1904	Bryant B. Brooks (R)	17,765	57.5
	John E. Osborne (D)	12,137	39.3
1906	Bryant B. Brooks (R)	16,317	60.2
	Stephen A. D. Keister (D)	9,444	34.8
1910	Joseph M. Carey (D)	21,086	55.6
	W. E. Mullen (R)	15,235	40.2
1914	John B. Kendrick (D)	22,387	51.6
	Hilliard S. Ridgely (R)	19,174	44.2
1918	Robert D. Carey (R)	23,825	56.1
	Frank L. Houx (D)	18,640	43.9
1922	William B. Ross (D)	31,110	50.6
	John W. Hay (R)	30,387	49.4

	Candidates	Votes	%
1924	Nellie T. Ross (D)	43,323	55.1
	E. J. Sullivan (R)	35,275	44.9
1926	Frank C. Emerson (R)	35,651	50.9
	Nellie T. Ross (D)	34,286	49.0
1930	Frank C. Emerson (R)	38,058	50.6
	Leslie A. Miller (D)	37,188	49.4
1932	Leslie A. Miller (D)	48,130	50.9
	Harry R. Weston (R)	44,692	47.2
1934	Leslie A. Miller (D)	54,305	57.9
	A. M. Clark (R)	38,792	41.4
1938	Nels H. Smith (R)	57,288	59.8
	Leslie A. Miller (D)	38,501	40.2
1942	Lester C. Hunt (D)	39,599	51.3
	Nels H. Smith (R)	37,568	48.7
1946	Lester C. Hunt (D)	43,020	52.9
	Earl Wright (R)	38,333	47.1
1950	Frank A. Barrett (R)	54,441	56.2
	John J. McIntyre (D)	42,518	43.9
1954	Milward L. Simpson (R)	56,275	50.5
	William Jack (D)	55,163	49.5
1958	J. J. Hickey (D)	55,070	48.9
	Milward L. Simpson (R)	52,488	46.6
1962	Clifford P. Hansen (R)	64,970	54.5
	Jack R. Gage (D)	54,298	45.5
1966	Stanley K. Hathaway (R)	65,624	54.3
	Ernest Wilkerson (D)	55,249	45.7
1970	Stanley K. Hathaway (R)	74,249	62.8
	John J. Rooney (D)	44,008	37.2
1974	Ed Herschler (D)	71,741	55.9
	Dick Jones (R)	56,645	44.1
1978	Ed Herschler (D)	69,972	50.9
	John C. Ostlund (R)	67,595	49.1
1982	Ed Herschler (D)	106,427	63.1
	Warren A. Morton (R)	62,128	36.9
1986	Michael J. Sullivan (D)	88,879	54.0
	Pete Simpson (R)	75,841	46.0
1990	Michael J. Sullivan (D)	104,638	65.4
	Mary Mead (R)	55,471	34.6
1994	Jim Geringer (R)	118,016	58.7
	Kathy Karpan (D)	80,747	40.2

Governor Returns: Other Sources

In the preceding section *(pp. 39-88)*, the symbol # is used to denote returns taken from a source other than Congressional Quarterly's principal sources of historical gubernatorial popular election returns: the Inter-University Consortium for Political and Social Research (ICPSR) for 1824-1974 returns; Joseph E. Kallenbach and Jessamine S. Kallenbach, *American State Governors,* *1776-1976,* vol. 1 (Dobbs Ferry, N.Y.: Oceana Publications, 1977) for pre-1824 returns; and Congressional Quarterly's biennial series *America Votes* (Washington, D.C.: Congressional Quarterly) for elections since 1975. This page lists the source for elections where the symbol # appears. *(For a description of the ICPSR collection, see p. 38.)*

Delaware 1826, 1829:
Secretary of State of Delaware.

Florida 1865, 1868:
Morris, Allen, *The Florida Handbook 1975-76* (Tallahassee, Fla.: Peninsular Publishing, 1975), p. 532.

Florida 1916:
Governors of the States 1900-1974 (Lexington, Ky.: Council of State Governments), p. 16.

Louisiana 1920:
Secretary of State of Louisiana.

Minnesota 1861, 1873, 1875, 1877:
The Minnesota Legislative Manual 1973-1974 (St. Paul, Minn.: State of Minnesota), pp. 507-508.

Mississippi 1983:
Secretary of State of Mississippi.

New York 1958:
Scammon, Richard M., *America Votes 3* (Pittsburgh: University of Pittsburgh, 1959), p. 272.

Texas 1845:
Kallenbach, Joseph E., and Jessamine S. Kallenbach, *American State Governors, 1776-1976,* vol. 1 (Dobbs Ferry, N.Y.: Oceana Publications, 1977), p. 572.

Vermont 1829, 1830, 1831, 1855:
Vermont State Manual and Legislative Directory, pp. 314-315.

Political Party Abbreviations

The following political party abbreviations are used in the general elections returns.

A-AK R	Anti-Addicks Republican	D-NG LAB	Democratic-National Green Labor
AB	Abolition	DOUG D	Douglas Democrat
ACP	A Connecticut Party	D & POP	Democrat and Populist
AG WHEEL	Agricultural Wheeler	D-PP	Democrat-Peoples
A-JAC	Anti-Jackson	D & PPI	Democrat and People's Independent
A-LEC D	Anti-Lecompton Democrat	D & PROG	Democrat and Progressive
ALI	Alaskan Independent	DPUS	D.P.U.S.
ALNC	Alliance	D-R	Democratic Republican
ALNC D	Alliance Democrat	D & RESUB	Democrat and Resubmission
A-LOT D	Anti-Lottery Democrat	D-R/FED	Democrat-Republican/Federalist
AM	American	D SIL	Democrat (Silver)
A-MAINE	Anti-Maine Law	D & SILVER	Democrat and Silver
A-MAS	Anti-Mason	EP	Elec. Prog.
A-MASC	Anti-Masonic	EQ	Equal Right
AM D-R	American Democratic-Republican	E TAX	Equal Tax
AM & EMANC	American and Emancipationist	F ALNC	Farmers' Alliance
AM FAC	American Faction	FB R	'Free Bridge' Republican
AM LAB	American Labor	FED	Federalist
A-MONOP	Anti-Monopoly	FEDL	Federal
AM R	American Republican	FILL AM	Fillmore American
AM & R	American and Republican	F-LAB	Farmer-Labor
ANTI-CLINT	Anti-Clinton	FLA PP	Florida People's Party
ANTI-CL R	Anti-Clinton Republican	F PLAY	Fair Play
ANTI-FED	Anti-Federalist	FREM AM	Fremont American
AR	Adams Republican	F SOIL	Free Soil
A-RPT D	Anti-Redemption Democrat	F SOIL D	Free Soil Democrat
A-VB D	Anti-Van Buren Democrat	FS & SC	Free Soil and Scattering
BENTON D	Benton Democrat	FUS	Fusion
BP	Best Party	FUS R	Fusion Republican
BRECK D	Breckinridge Democrat	G	Greenback
BRYAN D	Bryan Democrat	G LAB	Greenback Labor
B & T R	Brindle-Tail Republican	G & R	Greenback and Republican
BUT D & R	Butler Democrat and Republican	GREEN	Green
C	Conservative	HARD D	Hard Democratic
CASS D	Cass Democrat	HG	Honest Government
CLAY R	Clay Republican	H LIC	High License
CLINTON R	Clinton Republican	HUNKER D	Hunker Democrat
CONST	Constitution	I	Independent
C PROG	Conservative Progressive	IA	Independent American
CR	Conservative Republican	ID	Independent Democrat
CREOLE	Creole Faction	I D-R	Independent Democratic Republican
CSI	Civil Service Independents	I LEAGUE	Independence League
CST	Constitutional	IL & NPR	Independent League and National Progressive
CST U	Constitutional Union		
D	Democrat	IP	Independent Party
D CIT	Democratic Citizen	I PROG	Independent Progressive
D & CD	Democrat and Co. Democrat	IR, I-R	Independent Republican
D & CST	Democrat and Constitution	IR & D	Independent Republican and Democrat
DFL	Democrat Farmer- Labor		
D-FUS	Democrat-Fusion	I REF D	Independent Reform Democrat
D & G	Democrat and Greenback	IS	Illinois Solidarity
D & I	Democrat and Independent	I VT	Independent Vermonters
DISS D	Dissident Democrat	IW	Independent Whig
DISTRIB	Distributionist Candidate	JAC	Jackson
D & L	Democrat and Liberal	JAC D	Jackson Democrat
D-LAB-PP	Democrat-Labor Peoples	JAC R	Jackson Republican
D & LIBN	Democrat and Liberation	KEY	Keystone
DN	Democratic National	KN	Know-Nothing

L	Liberal	R-D	Republican-Democrat
LAB	Labor	READJ	Readjuster
LAB REF	Labor Reform	REF	Reform
LAB REF & P	Labor Reform and Prohibition	R-FF	Republican-Federalist Fusion
LAW ENF	Law Enforcement	R FUS	Republican Fusion
LAW ORD	Law and Order	R-G-FUS	Republican-Greenback-Fusion
LAW PRES	Law Preservation	R & NP	Republican and Nonpartisan
LIB	Liberty	ROYAL OAK	Royal Oak
LIBERT	Libertarian	R POP FU	Republican Populist Fusion
LIBER W	Liberation Whig	RP & PROG	Republican, Prohibition, and Progressive
LIB & SC	Liberty and Scattering		
LINCOLN	Lincoln	R & PROG	Republican and Progressive
L & O W	Law and Order Whig	R-SIL R	Republican-Silver Republican
LOW TAX D	Low Tax Democrat	R & UL	Republican and Union Labor
LR	Liberal Republican	R-UNION	Republican Union
LRU	La Raza Unida	SEC D	Secession Democrat
LU	Liberty Union	SEC W	Secessionist Whig
LW R	Lily-White Republican	SIL R	Silver Republican
N	National Party	SOC	Socialist
NC R	North Carolina Republican	SOCIAL D	Social Democrat
NEB	Nebraska	SOC LAB	Socialist Labor
NEB D	Nebraska Democrat	SOFT D	Soft Democrat
NG	National Greenback	SO RTS	Southern Rights
NON PART	Non Partisan	SO RTS D	Southern Rights Democrat
NON PL	Nonpartisan League	SOR W	Southern Rights Whig
N PROG	National Progressive	SR W	State Rights Whig
NR	National Republican	STAL D	Stalwart Democrat
N SILVER	National Silver	STC D	State Credit Democrat
N UNION	National Union	TAM D	Tammany Democrat
OLD R	Old Republican	TCN	Tax Cut Now
OPP	Opposition	TEMP	Temperance
OPP D	Opposition Democrat	TEMP REF	Temperance Reform
OPP R	Opposition Republican	TOL	Toleration
P	Prohibition	TPCT	Taxpayers Party to Cut Taxes
PEACE D	Peace Democrat	UN	Union
P & F ALNC	Prohibition and Farmer's Alliance	UN D	Union Democrat
POP	Populist	UN LAB	Union Labor
POP & SL D	Populist and Silver Democrat	UN R	Union Republican
PP	People's	VB R	Van Buren Republican
PP & D	People's and Democrat	W	Whig
PP-D-S-R	Peoples-Democrat Silver-Republican	W & AM	Whig and American
		W & A-MASC	Whig and Anti-Masonic
PP I	People's Independent	W-A-RENT	Whig Anti-Rent
PROG	Progressive	WASH	Washington
PROG-BMR	Progressive-Bull Moose-Roosevelt	W FS	Whig Free Soil
PUB OWN	Public Ownership	WILDCAT	Wildcat
R	Republican	WM	Workingmen
RAD	Radical	WMP/L	Workingman's Party or League
RAD R	Radical Republican	WRITE IN	Write in

Primary Election
Returns, 1919-1997

Sources for Primary Election Returns

Gubernatorial primary election returns for all 50 states are presented in this section *(pp. 95-154)*. Returns for most states go back to 1956. Primary returns for 11 Southern states (Alabama, Arkansas, Florida, Georgia, Louisiana, Mississippi, North Carolina, South Carolina, Tennessee, Texas and Virginia) go back to 1919 where available *(for a discussion of the importance of Southern primaries, see pp. 5-8)*.

The major source for primary election returns for all non-Southern states was the *America Votes* series, compiled biennially by the Elections Research Center, Washington, D.C., and published by Congressional Quarterly: Richard M. Scammon and Alice V. McGillivray, *America Votes*, vols. 11-21 (Washington, D.C.: Congressional Quarterly, 1975-1995); and Richard M. Scammon, Alice V. McGillivray and Rhodes Cook *America Votes*, vol. 22 (Washington, D.C.: Congressional Quarterly, 1998). Other sources were the returns obtained by Congressional Quarterly after each federal and gubernatorial election from the state secretaries of state. In cases of discrepancies, *Gubernatorial Elections 1787-1997*, accepted the *America Votes* figure. The first year for which *America Votes* reported primary returns, 1956, was chosen as the starting point because gubernatorial primary votes for earlier years are not readily available.

For the 11 Southern states that were members of the Civil War Confederacy (Alabama, Arkansas, Florida, Georgia, Louisiana, Mississippi, North Carolina, South Carolina, Tennessee, Texas and Virginia), the primary election returns presented for the years 1919 through 1973 were obtained, except where indicted by a footnote, from the Inter-University Consortium for Political and Social Research (ICPSR) at the University of Michigan. Major sources for returns since 1973 were Congressional Quarterly, which obtained them from the state secretaries of state and the *America Votes* series.

The vast majority of Southern primaries during the period of 1919 to 1973 were held to nominate candidates of the dominant Democratic Party. In many cases, the winner of the Democratic primary went into the general election facing no Republican opponent.

Compilation of ICPSR Data File

Statewide candidate totals for Southern primary elections for governor were prepared by the ICPSR staff from several sources. Election returns for the years prior to 1949 were obtained from *Southern Primaries and Elections* (University: University of Alabama Press, 1950), edited by Alexander Heard and Donald S. Strong. It should be noted that, although they transcribed their data from official returns, Professors Heard and Strong found that many of the returns contained errors and discrepancies between the sum of county totals and the state total, or returns published as final in newspapers and secretary of state reports. No attempt was made by Heard and Strong to correct these discrepancies because the source of the error could not be determined.

For the period from 1949 to 1973, candidate totals

were acquired from two sources. The first was a collection of Southern primary electoral statistics prepared from official returns by Hugh Davis Graham, chairman, division of social sciences, University of Maryland (Baltimore County), and Numan V. Bartley, department of history, University of Georgia (Athens). In addition, reference was made to official returns supplied to ICPSR by the various secretaries of state in conjunction with the ICPSR effort to maintain its continuing collection of election materials. The returns obtained from Bartley and Graham, and the secretary of state offices, were compared with published reports of the election outcomes (notably state manuals and the *America Votes* series) to verify the completeness and accuracy of the returns.

Presentation of Returns

The gubernatorial primary returns are arranged alphabetically by state and in chronological order of election within each state listing.

Candidates are listed in descending order, with the candidate receiving the greatest number of popular votes listed first. Percentage of the total vote is listed for each candidate who received *at least 5 percent* of the total vote cast.

Primaries for special elections to fill vacancies and runoff primaries are designated in the returns. For Southern states prior to 1974, Republican primary results have been included, whenever available.

Names, Vote Totals and Percentages

The names of gubernatorial primary candidates are listed as they appeared in the source materials. In a few cases, first names are not known.

For pre-1976 Southern primary elections included in this section, the ICPSR computed statewide vote totals for each candidate.

Percentages of the total vote were calculated on the basis of each candidate's proportion of the *total number of votes cast* for all candidates. Percentages have been calculated to two decimal places and rounded to one place. Due to rounding and the scattered votes of minor candidates, percentages in individual primary races may not add up to 100.

If no vote is shown for a candidate but the percentage of total vote is listed as 100 percent, in most cases the candidates in question ran unopposed and state election officials either did not bother to put the candidate's name on the ballot or simply did not make an effort to record the total number of votes.

When gubernatorial primary elections were held under a preferential voting system and the use of second choice votes was required to determine a winner, the symbol appears next to the winner's name. *(Explanation of preferential voting, p. 6.)*

Where no primary is indicated for a year in which a state elected a governor, it generally means that party conventions chose the nominees. Notes at the end of a state's listing explain other unusual circumstances.

Primary Election
Returns, 1919-1997

ALABAMA

Candidates	Votes	%
1922		
Democratic Primary		
William W. Brandon (D)	163,217	78.7
Bibb Graves (D)	44,151	21.3
1926		
Democratic Primary		
Bibb Graves (D)	61,493 ✔	27.6
McDowell (D)	59,699	26.8
Carmichael (D)	54,072	24.3
Patterson (D)	47,411	21.3
Democratic Second Choice		
Bibb Graves (D)	21,978	31.0
Patterson (D)	20,893	29.5
Carmichael (D)	20,061	28.3
McDowell (D)	7,943	11.2
1930		
Democratic Primary		
B. M. Miller (D)	77,066 ✔	39.2
W. C. Davis (D)	70,966	36.1
W. Finnell (D)	19,320	9.8
Charles C. McCall (D)	19,004	9.7
Democratic Second Choice		
W. C. Davis (D)	10,673	25.8
B. M. Miller (D)	9,994	24.2
W. Finnell (D)	9,867	23.9
Charles C. McCall (D)	6,467	15.7
J. A. Carnley (D)	2,819	6.8
1934		
Democratic Primary		
Bibb Graves (D)	132,462	43.4
Frank M. Dixon (D)	97,508	32.0
Leon McCord (D)	75,208	24.6
Democratic Runoff		
Bibb Graves (D)	157,140	53.7
Frank M. Dixon (D)	135,309	46.3
1938		
Democratic Primary		
Frank M. Dixon (D)	152,860	48.6
Chauncey Sparks (D)[1]	74,554	23.7
R. J. Goode (D)	70,287	22.4

	Candidates	Votes	%
1942			
	Democratic Primary		
	Chauncey Sparks (D)	145,798	52.2
	James E. Folsom (D)	73,306	26.2
	Chris J. Sherlock (D)	53,448	19.1
1946	**Democratic Primary**		
	James E. Folsom (D)	104,152	28.5
	Handy Ellis (D)	88,459	24.2
	Joe N. Poole (D)	70,925	19.4
	Elbert Boozer (D)	58,134	15.9
	Gordon Persons (D)	43,843	12.0
	Democratic Runoff		
	James E. Folsom (D)	205,168	58.7
	Handy Ellis (D)	144,126	41.3
1950	**Democratic Primary**		
	Gordon Persons (D)	137,055	34.1
	Philip J. Hamm (D)[2]	56,395	14.0
	Elbert Boozer (D)	48,021	11.9
	J. Bruce Henderson (D)	38,867	9.7
	Chauncey Sparks (D)	27,404	6.8
	Eugene "Bull" Connor (D)	20,629	5.1
	Robert K. "Buster" Bell (D)	20,171	5.0
1954	**Democratic Primary**		
	James E. Folsom (D)	305,384	51.4
	Jimmy Faulkner (D)	151,925	25.6
	Jim Allen (D)	61,530	10.4
	J. Bruce Henderson (D)	47,969	8.1
1958	**Democratic Primary**		
	John Patterson (D)	196,859	31.8
	George C. Wallace (D)	162,435	26.3
	Jimmy Faulkner (D)	91,512	14.8
	A. W. Todd (D)	59,240	9.6
	Laurie C. Battle (D)	38,955	6.3
	Democratic Runoff		
	John Patterson (D)	315,353	55.7
	George C. Wallace (D)	250,451	44.3
1962	**Democratic Primary**		
	George C. Wallace (D)	207,062	32.5
	Ryan deGraffenried (D)	160,704	25.2
	James E. Folsom (D)	159,640	25.1
	Macdonald Gallion (D)	80,374	12.6

Gubernatorial Elections

Candidates	Votes	%
Democratic Runoff		
George C. Wallace (D)	340,730	55.9
Ryan deGraffenried (D)	269,122	44.1
1966 **Democratic Primary**		
Lurleen B. Wallace (D)	480,841	54.1
Richmond M. Flowers (D)	172,386	19.4
Carl Elliott (D)	71,972	8.1
Bob Gilchrist (D)	49,502	5.6
1970 **Democratic Primary**		
Albert Brewer (D)	428,146	42.0
George C. Wallace (D)	416,443	40.8
Charles Woods (D)	149,887	14.7
Democratic Runoff		
George C. Wallace (D)	559,832	51.6
Albert Brewer (D)	525,951	48.4
1974 **Republican Primary**		
Elvin McCary (R)		100.0
Democratic Primary		
George C. Wallace (D)	536,235	64.7
Gene McLain (D)	249,695	30.1
1978 **Republican Primary**		
Guy Hunt (R)	21,499	83.2
Bert Hayes (R)	2,817	10.9
Julian Elgin (R)	1,534	5.9
Democratic Primary		
Forrest H. "Fob" James Jr. (D)	256,196	28.5
Bill Baxley (D)	210,089	23.3
Albert Brewer (D)	193,479	21.5
Sid McDonald (D)	143,930	16.0
Jere Beasley (D)	77,202	8.6
Democratic Runoff		
Forrest H. "Fob" James Jr. (D)	515,520	55.2
Bill Baxley (D)	418,932	44.8
1982 **Republican Primary**		
Emory Folmar (R)		100.0
Democratic Primary		
George C. Wallace (D)	425,469	42.5
George McMillan (D)	296,262	29.6
Joe C. McCorquodale (D)	250,614	25.1
Democratic Runoff		
George C. Wallace (D)	512,203	51.2
George McMillan (D)	488,444	48.8
1986 **Republican Primary**		
Guy Hunt (R)	20,823	71.3
Doug Carter (R)	8,371	28.7

Candidates	Votes	%
Democratic Primary		
Bill Baxley (D)	345,985	36.8
Charles Graddick (D)	275,714	29.3
Forrest H. James (D)	195,844	20.8
George McMillan (D)	117,258	12.5
Democratic Runoff[3]		
Charles Graddick (D)	470,051	50.5
Bill Baxley (D)	461,295	49.5
1990 **Republican Primary**		
Guy Hunt (R)	119,877	95.8
Democratic Primary		
Paul R. Hubbert (D)	233,808	31.5
Don Siegelman (D)	184,635	24.9
Forrest H. "Fob" James Jr. (D)	160,121	21.6
Ronnie G. Flippo (D)	128,105	17.3
Democratic Runoff		
Paul R. Hubbert (D)	309,609	53.6
Don Siegelman (D)	267,588	46.4
1994 **Republican Primary**		
Forrest H. "Fob" James Jr. (R)	84,019	39.5
Ann Bedsole (R)	54,449	25.6
Winton Blount (R)	51,785	24.4
Mickey Kirkland (R)	18,538	8.7
Democratic Primary		
James E. Folsom Jr. (D)	380,227	54.0
Paul R. Hubbert (D)	285,554	40.6
Republican Runoff		
Forrest H. "Fob" James Jr. (R)	130,233	62.4
Ann Bedsole (R)	78,338	37.6

Alabama

1. Sparks withdrew from the race May 11, 1938, declining a runoff with Dixon, who became the Democratic nominee.

2. Hamm withdrew May 12, 1950, declining a runoff with Persons, who became the Democratic nominee.

3. After the Democratic runoff primary a subcommittee of Alabama's Democratic party declared Baxley the nominee, deciding that voters who voted in the Republican primary had crossed over and voted in the Democratic runoff primary for Graddick, against party rules. This decision was contested through the courts, but the Democratic party decision was upheld.

ALASKA[1]

Candidates	Votes	%
1958 **Republican Primary**		
John Butrovich (R)		100.0
Democratic Primary		
William A. Egan (D)	22,735	61.1
Victor Rivers (D)	8,845	23.7
J. G. Williams (D)	5,656	15.2

	Candidates	Votes	%
1962	**Republican Primary**		
	Mike Stepovich (R)	6,415	*38.1*
	Howard W. Pollock (R)	5,247	*31.2*
	John B. Coghill (R)	2,295	*13.6*
	Verne O. Martin (R)	1,504	*8.9*
	Milo H. Fritz (R)	1,371	*8.1*
	Democratic Primary		
	William A. Egan (D)	13,698	*62.3*
	George H. Byer (D)	5,275	*24.0*
	Warren A. Taylor (D)	2,386	*10.8*
1966	**Republican Primary**		
	Walter J. Hickel (R)	10,580	*55.3*
	Bruce Kendall (R)	4,511	*23.6*
	Mike Stepovich (R)	4,039	*21.1*
	Democratic Primary		
	William A. Egan (D)	19,801	*61.0*
	Wendell P. Kay (D)	12,660	*39.0*
1970	**Republican Primary**		
	Keith Miller (R)	19,153	*53.4*
	Howard W. Pollock (R)	16,691	*46.5*
	Democratic Primary		
	William A. Egan (D)	23,973	*67.5*
	Larry Carr (D)	11,350	*31.9*
1974	**Republican Primary**		
	Jay S. Hammond (R)	28,602	*47.2*
	Walter J. Hickel (R)	20,728	*34.2*
	Keith Miller (R)	10,864	*17.9*
	Democratic Primary		
	William A. Egan (D)	20,356	*91.0*
1978[2]	**Republican Primary**		
	Jay S. Hammond (R)	31,896	*39.1*
	Walter J. Hickel (R)	31,798	*38.9*
	Tom Fink (R)	17,487	*21.4*
	Democratic Primary		
	Chancy Croft (D)	8,911	*36.1*
	Edward A. Merdes (D)	8,639	*35.0*
	Jalmar M. Kerttula (D)	7,125	*28.9*
1982	**Republican Primary**		
	Tom Fink (R)	41,911	*51.3*
	Terry Miller (R)	36,594	*44.8*
	Democratic Primary		
	Bill Sheffield (D)	21,940	*39.7*
	Steve Cowper (D)	21,680	*39.2*
	H. A. Boucher (D)	8,584	*15.5*

	Candidates	Votes	%
1986	**Republican Primary**		
	Arliss Sturgulewski (R)	25,740	*30.6*
	Walter J. Hickel (R)	23,733	*28.3*
	Richard Randolph (R)	18,164	*21.6*
	Joe L. Hayes (R)	7,989	*9.5*
	Bob Richards (R)	4,973	*5.9*
	Democratic Primary		
	Steve Cowper (D)	36,233	*54.5*
	Bill Sheffield (D)	29,935	*45.0*
	Alaskan Independence Primary		
	Joe Vogler (ALI)		*100.0*
	Libertarian Primary		
	Mary O'Brannon (LIBERT)	205	*53.5*
	Ed Hoch (LIBERT)	178	*46.5*
1990	**Republican Primary[3]**		
	Arliss Sturgulewski (R)	26,906	*36.4*
	James O. Campbell (R)	23,442	*31.7*
	Rick Halford (R)	22,466	*30.4*
	Democratic Primary		
	Tony Knowles (D)	36,019	*56.1*
	Stephen McAlpine (D)	27,656	*43.0*
	Alaskan Independence Primary		
	John Lindauer (ALI)[4]	3,505	*87.7*
	William DeRushe (ALI)	492	*12.3*
1994	**Republican Primary**		
	James O. "Jim" Campbell (R)	24,854	*49.8*
	Tom Fink (R)	23,586	*47.2*
	Democratic Primary		
	Tony Knowles (D)	24,727	*43.6*
	Stephen McAlpine (D)	17,482	*30.9*
	Sam Cotten (D)	13,899	*24.5*
	Alaskan Independence Primary		
	John B. "Jack" Coghill (ALI)	4,213	*80.1*
	Jude Henzler (ALI)	465	*8.8*
	Al Rowe (ALI)	348	*6.6*
	Green Primary		
	Jim Sykes (GREEN)	2,505	*100.0*

Alaska

1. In Alaska's so-called "jungle" primaries, all candidates for an office appeared together on the same ballot with their parties designated. Nominations went to the Republican and Democrat receiving the most votes for the office. Percentages were calculated here as if candidates had run in separate party primaries.

2. There were recounts of the votes received by the two top finishers in both primaries. In the Republican recount, Hammond's vote was 31,921 (50.0 percent) and Hickel's was 31,823 (49.9 percent). In the Democratic recount, Croft's vote was 8,910 (50.7 percent) and Merdes' was 8,655 (49.3 percent).

3. The Republican primary ballot was a single-ballot and only registered Republican, Non Partisan, and Undeclared voters could participate in the pri-

mary. All other parties ran on a multiparty ballot and the primary was open to all registered voters except Republicans.

4. Lindauer withdrew after the primary and Walter J. Hickel was substituted by the party committee.

ARIZONA

	Candidates	Votes	%
1956	**Republican Primary**		
	Horace B. Griffen (R)	20,471	46.0
	O. D. Miller (R)	17,858	40.1
	Fred Trump (R)	6,199	13.9
	Democratic Primary		
	Ernest W. McFarland (D)		100.0
1958	**Republican Primary**		
	Paul Fannin (R)		100.0
	Democratic Primary		
	Robert Morrison (D)	77,931	50.4
	Dick Searles (D)	58,699	37.9
	Marvin L. Burton (D)	18,122	11.7
1960	**Republican Primary**		
	Paul Fannin (R)		100.0
	Democratic Primary		
	Lee Ackerman (D)		100.0
1962	**Republican Primary**		
	Paul Fannin (R)		100.0
	Democratic Primary		
	Sam Goddard (D)	91,661	59.8
	Joe Haldiman (D)	41,645	27.2
	J. M. Morris (D)	19,850	13.0
1964	**Republican Primary**		
	Richard Kleindienst (R)	64,310	62.8
	Evan Mecham (R)	38,131	37.2
	Democratic Primary		
	Sam Goddard (D)	114,377	60.0
	Art Brock (D)	57,067	30.0
	J. M. Morris (D)	11,303	5.9
1966	**Republican Primary**		
	John R. Williams (R)	37,409	44.3
	John Haugh (R)	25,905	30.6
	Robert W. Pickrell (R)	21,192	25.1
	Democratic Primary		
	Sam Goddard (D)	63,180	45.5
	Norman Green (D)	53,921	38.9
	Andrew J. Gilbert (D)	23,637	17.0

	Candidates	Votes	%
1968	**Republican Primary**		
	John R. Williams (R)		100.0
	Democratic Primary		
	Sam Goddard (D)	112,948	73.4
	Currin V. Shields (D)	30,337	19.7
	Jack DeVault (D)	10,613	6.9
1970	**Republican Primary**		
	John R. Williams (R)		100.0
	Democratic Primary		
	Raul H. Castro (D)	63,294	52.0
	Jack Ross (D)	30,921	25.4
	George Nader (D)	27,534	22.6
1974	**Republican Primary**		
	Russell Williams (R)	53,132	35.6
	Evan Mecham (R)	30,266	20.3
	William C. Jacquin (R)	27,138	18.2
	John R. Driggs (R)	23,519	15.7
	Milton H. Graham (R)	15,315	10.2
	Democratic Primary		
	Raul H. Castro (D)	115,268	67.2
	Jack Ross (D)	31,250	18.2
	David R. Moss (D)	19,143	11.2
1978	**Republican Primary**		
	Evan Mecham (R)	50,713	44.1
	Jack Londen (R)	40,116	34.9
	Democratic Primary		
	Bruce Babbitt (D)	108,548	76.8
	David R. Moss (D)	32,785	23.2
	Libertarian Primary		
	V. Gene Lewter (LIBERT)		100.0
	Socialist Worker Primary		
	Jessica Sampson (SOC WORK)		100.0
1982	**Republican Primary**		
	Leo Corbet (R)	108,766	61.7
	Evan Mecham (R)	67,456	38.3
	Democratic Primary		
	Bruce Babbitt (D)	142,559	85.8
	Steve Jancek (D)[1]	23,492	14.1
	Libertarian Primary		
	Sam Stelger (LIBERT)		100.0
1986	**Republican Primary**		
	Evan Mecham (R)	121,614	53.7
	Burton S. Barr (R)	104,682	46.3

Candidates	Votes	%
Democratic Primary		
Carolyn Warner (D)	106,687	*50.6*
Tony Mason (D)	92,413	*43.9*
Dave Moss (D)	11,588	*5.5*
1990 Republican Primary		
Fife Symington (R)	163,010	*43.8*
Evan Mecham (R)	91,136	*24.5*
Fred Koory (R)	61,487	*16.5*
Sam Steiger (R)	49,019	*13.2*
Democratic Primary		
Terry Goddard (D)	212,579	*84.0*
Dave Moss (D)	40,478	*16.0*
1994 Republican Primary		
Fife Symington (R)	202,588	*68.1*
Barbara Barrett (R)	94,740	*31.9*
Democratic Primary		
Eddie Basha (D)	96,613	*36.8*
Terry Goddard (D)	92,239	*35.2*
Paul Johnson (D)	73,512	*16.0*
Libertarian Primary		
John Buttrick (LIBERT)	5,052	*100.0*

Arizona
1. *Jancek died before the primary, but his name remained on the ballot.*

ARKANSAS

Candidates	Votes	%
1920 Democratic Primary		
Thomas C. McRae (D)	41,907	*26.9*
Smead Powell (D)	32,263	*20.7*
Thomas J. Terral (D)	29,303	*18.8*
J. C. Floyd (D)	21,596	*13.9*
G. R. Haynie (D)	16,747	*10.8*
1922 Democratic Primary		
Thomas C. McRae (D)	127,728	*70.5*
E. P. Toney (D)	53,572	*29.6*
1924 Democratic Primary		
Thomas J. Terral (D)	54,533	*26.3*
Lee Cazort (D)	43,466	*21.0*
John E. Martineau (D)	35,438	*17.1*
Jim G. Ferguson (D)	27,155	*13.1*
Hamp Williams (D)	23,785	*11.5*
Jacob R. Willson (D)	22,626	*10.9*
1926 Democratic Primary		
John E. Martineau (D)	117,232	*53.5*
Thomas J. Terral (D)	101,981	*46.5*

	Candidates	Votes	%
1928	**Democratic Primary**		
	Harvey J. Parnell (D)	94,207	*41.7*
	Brooks Hays (D)	57,497	*25.4*
	Thomas J. Terral (D)	34,476	*15.2*
	J. Carrol Cone (D)	31,786	*14.1*
1930	**Democratic Primary**		
	Harvey J. Parnell (D)	133,870	*54.2*
	Brooks Hays (D)	88,541	*35.8*
	J. C. Sheffield (D)	20,133	*8.2*
1932	**Democratic Primary**		
	J. Marion Futrell (D)	124,239	*44.0*
	Thomas J. Terral (D)	59,066	*21.0*
	A. B. Priddy (D)	37,134	*13.2*
	D. H. Blackwood (D)	33,147	*11.8*
1934	**Democratic Primary**		
	J. Marion Futrell (D)	167,917	*65.9*
	Howard Reed (D)	86,894	*34.1*
1936	**Democratic Primary**		
	Carl E. Bailey (D)	76,014	*32.0*
	Ed F. McDonald (D)	72,075	*30.3*
	R. A. Cook (D)	60,768	*25.6*
	Thomas J. Terral (D)	23,663	*10.0*
1938	**Democratic Primary**		
	Carl E. Bailey (D)	146,472	*51.5*
	R. A. Cook (D)	131,791	*46.3*
1940	**Democratic Primary**		
	Homer M. Adkins (D)	142,247	*56.2*
	Carl E. Bailey (D)	110,613	*43.7*
1942	**Democratic Primary**		
	Homer M. Adkins (D)	120,811	*71.8*
	Fred Keller (D)	44,304	*26.3*
1944	**Democratic Primary**		
	Ben Laney (D)	70,965	*38.6*
	J. Bryan Sims (D)[1]	63,454	*34.5*
	David L. Terry (D)	49,685	*27.0*
1946	**Democratic Primary**		
	Ben Laney (D)	125,444	*64.6*
	J. M. Malone (D)	63,601	*32.8*
1948	**Democratic Primary**		
	Sidney S. McMath (D)	87,829	*34.1*
	Jack Holt (D)	60,313	*23.4*
	James McKrell (D)	57,030	*22.1*
	Horace Thompson (D)	48,674	*18.9*
	Democratic Runoff		
	Sidney S. McMath (D)	157,137	*51.7*
	Jack Holt (D)	146,880	*48.3*

Gubernatorial Elections

	Candidates	Votes	%
1950	**Democratic Primary**		
	Sidney S. McMath (D)	209,559	*64.0*
	Ben T. Laney (D)	112,651	*34.4*
1952	**Democratic Primary**		
	Sidney S. McMath (D)	100,858	*30.7*
	Francis Cherry (D)	91,195	*27.7*
	Tackett (D)	63,827	*19.4*
	Jack Holt (D)	45,233	*13.8*
	Murry (D)	27,937	*8.5*
	Democratic Runoff		
	Francis Cherry (D)	237,448	*63.1*
	Sidney S. McMath (D)	139,052	*36.9*
1954	**Democratic Primary**		
	Francis Cherry (D)	154,879	*47.7*
	Orval E. Faubus (D)	109,614	*33.8*
	Guy Jones (D)	41,249	*12.7*
	McMillan (D)	18,857	*5.8*
	Democratic Runoff		
	Orval E. Faubus (D)	191,328	*50.9*
	Francis Cherry (D)	184,509	*49.1*
1956	**Democratic Primary**		
	Orval E. Faubus (D)	180,760	*58.1*
	James Johnson (D)	83,856	*26.9*
	Jim Snoddy (D)	43,630	*14.0*
1958	**Republican Primary**		
	George W. Johnson (R)	3,147	*72.7*
	Donald D. Layne (R)	1,273	*28.8*
	Democratic Primary		
	Orval E. Faubus (D)	264,346	*68.9*
	Chris Finkbeiner (D)	60,173	*15.7*
	Lee Ward (D)	59,385	*15.5*
1960	**Republican Primary**		
	Henry M. Britt (R)		*100.0*
	Democratic Primary		
	Orval E. Faubus (D)	238,997	*58.8*
	Joe C. Hardin (D)	66,499	*16.4*
	Bruce Bennett (D)	58,400	*14.4*
	H. E. Williams (D)	33,374	*8.2*
1962	**Republican Primary**		
	Willis Ricketts (R)		*100.0*
	Democratic Primary		
	Orval E. Faubus (D)	208,996	*51.6*
	Sidney S. McMath (D)	83,473	*20.6*
	Dale Alford (D)	82,815	*20.4*
	Vernon H. Whitten (D)	22,377	*5.5*

	Candidates	Votes	%
1964	**Republican Primary**		
	Winthrop Rockefeller (R)		*100.0*
	Democratic Primary		
	Orval E. Faubus (D)	239,890	*65.7*
	Ervin Odell Dorsey (D)	69,638	*19.1*
	Joe Hubbard (D)	39,199	*10.7*
1966	**Republican Primary**		
	Winthrop Rockefeller (R)	19,646	*98.5*
	Democratic Primary		
	James Johnson (D)	105,607	*25.1*
	Frank Holt (D)	92,711	*22.1*
	Brooks Hays (D)	64,814	*15.4*
	Dale Alford (D)	53,531	*12.7*
	Sam Boyce (D)	49,744	*11.8*
	Raymond Rebsamen (D)	35,607	*8.5*
	Democratic Runoff		
	James Johnson (D)	210,543	*51.9*
	Frank Holt (D)	195,442	*48.1*
1968	**Republican Primary**		
	Winthrop Rockefeller (R)	27,913	*95.5*
	Democratic Primary		
	Marion Crank (D)	106,092	*25.6*
	Virginia Johnson (D)	86,038	*20.7*
	Ted Boswell (D)	85,629	*20.6*
	Bruce Bennett (D)	65,095	*15.7*
	Frank Whitbeck (D)	61,758	*14.9*
	Democratic Runoff		
	Marion Crank (D)	215,087	*63.3*
	Virginia Johnson (D)	124,880	*36.7*
1970	**Republican Primary**		
	Winthrop Rockefeller (R)	58,197	*96.8*
	Democratic Primary		
	Orval E. Faubus (D)	156,578	*36.4*
	Dale Bumpers (D)	86,156	*20.0*
	Joe Purcell (D)	81,566	*18.9*
	Hayes C. McClerkin (D)	45,011	*10.5*
	Bill Wells (D)	32,543	*7.6*
	Democratic Runoff		
	Dale Bumpers (D)	259,780	*58.7*
	Orval E. Faubus (D)	182,732	*41.3*
1972	**Republican Primary**		
	Len E. Blaylock (R)		*100.0*

Candidates	Votes	%
Democratic Primary		
Dale Bumpers (D)	330,088	66.7
Q. Byrum Hurst (D)	81,239	16.4
Mack Harbour (D)	55,172	11.2

1974 | **Republican Primary**

Candidates	Votes	%
Ken Coon (R)	3,698	81.9
Joseph Weston (R)	815	18.1
Democratic Primary		
David Pryor (D)	297,673	51.0
Orval E. Faubus (D)	193,105	33.1
Bob Riley (D)	92,612	15.9

1976 | **Republican Primary**

Candidates	Votes	%
Leon Griffith (R)	13,044	57.2
Joseph Weston (R)	9,753	42.8
Democratic Primary		
David Pryor (D)	312,865	59.5
Jim Lindsey (D)	171,031	32.5
Frank Lady (D)	36,832	7.0

1978 | **Republican Primary**

Candidates	Votes	%
A. Lynn Lowe (R)		100.0
Democratic Primary		
Bill Clinton (D)	341,118	59.7
Joe D. Woodward (D)	123,674	21.6
Frank Lady (D)	76,026	13.1

1980 | **Republican Primary**

Candidates	Votes	%
Frank D. White (R)	5,867	71.8
Marshall Chrisman (R)	2,310	28.2
Democratic Primary		
Bill Clinton (D)	306,735	68.9
Monroe A. Schwarzlose (D)	138,660	31.1

1982 | **Republican Primary**

Candidates	Votes	%
Frank D. White (R)	11,111	83.2
Marshall Chrisman (R)	1,410	10.6
Connie Voll (R)	826	6.2
Democratic Primary		
Bill Clinton (D)	236,961	41.8
Joe Purcell (D)	166,066	29.3
Jim Guy Tucker (D)	129,362	22.8
Democratic Runoff		
Bill Clinton (D)	239,209	53.7
Joe Purcell (D)	206,358	46.3

1984 | **Republican Primary**

Candidates	Votes	%
Woody Freeman (R)	13,030	68.4
Erwin Davis (R)	6,010	31.2

Candidates	Votes	%
Democratic Primary		
Bill Clinton (D)	317,577	64.4
Lonnie Turner (D)	119,266	24.2
Kermit Moss (D)	31,727	6.4

1986 | **Republican Primary**

Candidates	Votes	%
Frank D. White (R)	13,831	61.9
Wayne Lanier (R)	4,576	20.5
Maurice Britt (R)	3,116	13.9
Democratic Primary		
Bill Clinton (D)	315,397	60.6
Orval E. Faubus (D)	174,402	33.5
Dean Goldsby (D)	30,829	5.9

1990 | **Republican Primary**

Candidates	Votes	%
Sheffield Nelson (R)	47,246	54.3
Tommy F. Robinson (R)	39,731	45.7
Democratic Primary		
Bill Clinton (D)	269,329	54.8
Tom McRae (D)	190,887	38.9

1994 | **Republican Primary**

Candidates	Votes	%
Sheffield Nelson (R)	24,054	50.8
Steve Luelf (R)	20,953	44.2
William L. Jones (R)	2,346	5.0

Arkansas
1. Sims withdrew from a runoff, and Laney became the Democratic nominee.

CALIFORNIA

Candidates	Votes	%
1958	**Republican Primary**	
William F. Knowland (R)	1,290,106	77.5
Edmund G. Brown (D)	374,879	22.5
Democratic Primary		
Edmund G. Brown (D)	1,890,622	82.6
William F. Knowland (R)	313,385	13.7
1962	**Republican Primary**	
Richard M. Nixon (R)	1,285,151	65.4
Joseph C. Shell (R)	656,542	33.4
Democratic Primary		
Edmund G. Brown (D)	1,739,792	81.4
Prohibition Primary		
Robert L. Wyckoff		100.0
1966	**Republican Primary**	
Ronald Reagan (R)	1,417,623	64.7
George Christopher (R)	675,683	30.8

Gubernatorial Elections

Candidates	Votes	%
Democratic Primary		
Edmund G. Brown (D)	1,355,262	*51.9*
Samuel W. Yorty (D)	981,088	*37.6*

1970

Candidates	Votes	%
Republican Primary		
Ronald Reagan (R)		*100.0*
Democratic Primary		
Jess Unruh (D)	1,602,690	*64.0*
Samuel W. Yorty (D)	659,494	*26.3*
American Independent Primary		
William K. Shearer (AMI)	14,069	*61.4*
Keith H. Greene (AMI)	8,827	*38.5*
Peace and Freedom Primary		
Ricardo Romo (PFP)	6,214	*63.5*
Warren A. Nielsen (PFP)	3,569	*36.5*

1974

Candidates	Votes	%
Republican Primary		
Houston I. Flournoy (R)	1,164,015	*63.0*
Ed Reinecke (R)	556,259	*30.1*
Democratic Primary		
Edmund G. Brown Jr. (D)	1,085,752	*37.7*
Joseph L. Alioto (D)	544,007	*18.9*
Robert Moretti (D)	478,469	*16.6*
William M. Roth (D)	293,686	*10.2*
Jerome R. Waldie (D)	227,489	*7.9*
American Independent Primary		
Edmon V. Kaiser (AMI)		*100.0*
Peace and Freedom Primary		
Elizabeth Keathley (PFP)	2,111	*28.1*
Lester H. Higby (PFP)	1,855	*24.7*
C. T. Weber (PFP)	1,822	*24.2*
Trudy Saposhnek (PFP)	1,417	*18.8*

1978

Candidates	Votes	%
Republican Primary		
Evelle J. Younger (R)	1,008,087	*40.0*
Ed Davis (R)	738,741	*29.3*
Ken Maddy (R)	484,583	*19.2*
Pete Wilson (R)	230,146	*9.1*
Democratic Primary		
Edmund G. Brown Jr. (D)	2,567,067	*77.5*
American Independent Primary		
Theresa F. Dietrich (AMI)	12,278	*57.4*
Laszlo Kecskemethy (AMI)	9,112	*42.6*
Peace and Freedom Primary		
Marilyn Seals (PFP)		*100.0*

1982

Candidates	Votes	%
Republican Primary		
George Deukmejian (R)	1,165,266	*51.1*
Mike Curb (R)	1,020,935	*44.8*
Democratic Primary		
Tom Bradley (D)	1,726,985	*61.1*
John Garamendi (D)	712,161	*25.2*
American Independent Primary		
James C. Griffin (AMI)		*100.0*
Peace and Freedom Primary		
Elizabeth Martinez (PFP)	4,353	*55.1*
Jan B. Tucker (PFP)	3,552	*44.9*
Libertarian Primary		
Dan P. Dougherty (LIBERT)		*100.0*

1986

Candidates	Votes	%
Republican Primary		
George Deukmejian (R)	1,927,288	*93.6*
William H. R. Clark (R)	132,125	*6.4*
Democratic Primary		
Tom Bradley (D)	1,768,042	*81.5*
Hugh G. Bagley (D)	141,217	*6.5*
Charles Pineda (D)	109,001	*5.0*
American Independent Primary		
Gary V. Miller (AMI)		*100.0*
Peace and Freedom Primary		
Maria E. Munoz (PFP)	3,508	*69.8*
Cheryl Zuur (PFP)	1,519	*30.2*
Libertarian Primary		
Joseph Fuhrig (LIBERT)		*100.0*

1990

Candidates	Votes	%
Republican Primary		
Pete Wilson (R)	1,856,613	*87.5*
David M. Williams (R)	107,397	*5.1*
Democratic Primary		
Dianne Feinstein (D)	1,361,361	*52.3*
John Van de Kamp (D)	1,067,899	*41.0*
American Independent Primary		
Jerome McCready (AMI)	8,921	*54.1*
Chuck Morsa (AMI)	7,563	*45.9*
Libertarian Primary		
Dennis Thompson (LIBERT)		*100.0*
Peace and Freedom Primary		
Maria E. Munoz (PFP)	3,461	*56.7*
Merle Woo (PFP)	2,647	*43.3*

	Candidates	Votes	%
1994	**Republican Primary**		
	Pete Wilson (R)	1,266,832	61.4
	Ron K. Unz (R)	707,431	34.3
	Democratic Primary		
	Kathleen Brown (D)	1,110,372	48.4
	John Garamendi (D)	755,876	32.9
	Tom Hayden (D)	318,777	13.9
	American Independent Primary		
	Jerome McCready (AMI)	18,984	100.0
	Libertarian Primary		
	Richard Rider (LIBERT)	13,757	81.1
	Peace and Freedom Primary		
	Gloria Estela La Riva (PFP)	4,633	62.3
	Green Primary		
	John T. Selawsky (GREEN)	3,688	16.6
	James Ogle (GREEN)	2,930	13.2
	John Lewallen (GREEN)	2,923	13.1

COLORADO

	Candidates	Votes	%
1956	**Republican Primary**		
	Donald G. Brotzman (R)		100.0
	Democratic Primary		
	Stephen McNichols (D)		100.0
1958	**Republican Primary**		
	Palmer L. Burch (R)		100.0
	Democratic Primary		
	Stephen McNichols (D)		100.0
1962	**Republican Primary**		
	John A. Love (R)	66,027	59.6
	David A. Hamil (R)	44,693	40.4
	Democratic Primary		
	Stephen McNichols (D)		100.0
1966	**Republican Primary**		
	John A. Love (R)		100.0
	Democratic Primary		
	Robert L. Knous (D)		100.0
1970	**Republican Primary**		
	John A. Love (R)		100.0

	Candidates	Votes	%
	Democratic Primary		
	Mark Hogan (D)		100.0
1974	**Republican Primary**		
	John D. Vanderhoof (R)	94,334	60.5
	Robert W. Daniels (R)	61,691	39.5
	Democratic Primary		
	Richard D. Lamm (D)	120,452	58.7
	Thomas Farley (D)	84,796	41.3
1978	**Republican Primary**		
	Ted Strickland (R)	87,248	59.0
	Richard Plock (R)	60,597	41.0
	Democratic Primary		
	Richard D. Lamm (D)		100.0
1982	**Republican Primary**		
	John D. Fuhr (R)		100.0
	Democratic Primary		
	Richard D. Lamm (D)		100.0
1986	**Republican Primary**		
	Ted Strickland (R)	66,796	35.6
	Steve Schuck (R)	64,245	34.2
	Bob Kirscht (R)	56,779	30.2
	Democratic Primary		
	Roy Romer (D)		100.0
1990	**Republican Primary**		
	John Andrews (R)		100.0
	Democratic Primary		
	Roy Romer (D)		100.0
1994	**Republican Primary**		
	Bruce Benson (R)	109,462	61.2
	Michael C. Bird (R)	38,571	21.6
	Dick Sargent (R)	30,326	17.0
	Democratic Primary		
	Roy Romer (D)	61,686	100.0

CONNECTICUT[1]

	Candidates	Votes	%
1970	**Republican Primary**		
	Thomas J. Meskill (R)	93,419	71.4
	Wallace Barnes (R)	37,383	28.6

	Candidates	Votes	%
1978	**Democratic Primary**		
	Ella T. Grasso (D)	137,904	*67.3*
	Robert K. Killian (D)	66,924	*32.7*
1986	**Republican Primary**		
	Julie D. Belaga (R)	39,074	*41.3*
	Richard C. Bozzuto (R)	33,852	*35.8*
	Gerald Labriola (R)	21,610	*22.9*
1990	**Democratic Primary**		
	Bruce A. Morrison (D)	84,771	*64.7*
	William J. Cibes (D)	46,294	*35.3*
1994	**Republican Primary**		
	John G. Rowland (R)	78,051	*67.8*
	Pauline R. Kezer (R)	37,010	*32.2*
	Democratic Primary		
	Bill Curry (D)	93,241	*54.7*
	John B. Larson (D)	77,165	*45.3*

Connecticut

1. In Connecticut, party conventions nominated candidates subject to a system of "challenge" primaries that allowed defeated candidates to petition for a popular vote if they received at least 20 percent of the convention vote. Returns are given here for challenge primaries held for the governorship nomination between 1956 and 1990.

DELAWARE[1]

	Candidates	Votes	%
1972	**Republican Primary**		
	Russell W. Peterson (R)	23,929	*54.3*
	David P. Buckson (R)	20,138	*45.7*
1980	**Republican Primary**		
	Pierre S. "Pete" du Pont IV (R)		*100.0*
	Democratic Primary		
	William J. Gordy (D)		*100.0*
1984	**Republican Primary**		
	Michael N. Castle (R)		*100.0*
	Democratic Primary		
	William T. Quillen (D)	20,473	*59.1*
	Sherman W. Tribbitt (D)	14,185	*40.9*
1988	**Republican Primary**		
	Michael N. Castle (R)		*100.0*
	Democratic Primary		
	Jacob Kreshtool (D)		*100.0*
1992	**Republican Primary**		
	B. Gary Scott (R)	23,994	*81.8*
	Wilfred Plomis (R)	5,346	*18.2*

	Candidates	Votes	%
	Democratic Primary		
	Thomas R. Carper (D)	36,600	*89.2*
	Daniel D. Rappa (D)	4,434	*10.8*
1996	**Republican Primary**		
	Janet C. Rzewnicki (R)		*100.0*
	Democratic Primary		
	Thomas R. Carper (D)		*100.0*

Delaware

1. From 1972 through 1992 Delaware used a system of "challenge" primaries, in which a candidate for statewide office who received at least 35 percent of the convention vote could challenge the endorsed candidate in a primary.

FLORIDA

	Candidates	Votes	%
1920	**Democratic Primary**		
	Cary E. Hardee (D)	52,591	*59.5*
	V. C. Swearingen (D)	30,240	*34.2*
	Lincoln Hulley (D)	5,591	*6.3*
	Democratic Second Choice		
	Cary A. Hardee (D)	1,559	*51.7*
	V. C. Swearingen (D)	1,459	*48.3*
1924	**Democratic Primary**		
	John W. Martin (D)	55,715	✔ *38.0*
	Sidney J. Catts (D)	43,230	*29.5*
	Frank E. Jennings (D)	37,962	*25.9*
	Worth W. Trammell (D)	8,381	*5.7*
	Democratic Second Choice		
	John W. Martin (D)	17,339	*74.1*
	Sidney J. Catts (D)	6,067	*25.9*
1928	**Democratic Primary**		
	Doyle E. Carlton (D)	77,569	✔ *30.4*
	Sidney J. Catts (D)	68,984	*27.1*
	Fons A. Hathaway (D)	67,849	*26.6*
	John S. Taylor (D)	37,304	*14.6*
	Democratic Second Choice		
	Doyle E. Carlton (D)	28,471	*75.9*
	Sidney J. Catts (D)	9,066	*24.2*
1932	**Democratic Primary**		
	John W. Martin (D)	66,940	*24.2*
	David Sholtz (D)	55,406	*20.0*
	Cary A. Hardee (D)	50,427	*18.2*
	Stafford Caldwell (D)	44,938	*16.2*
	Charles M. Durrance (D)	36,291	*13.1*
	Democratic Runoff		
	David Sholtz (D)	173,540	*62.8*
	John W. Martin (D)	102,805	*37.2*

	Candidates	Votes	%
1936	**Democratic Primary**		
	Raleigh Pettaway (D)	51,705	*15.7*
	Fred P. Cone (D)	46,842	*14.3*
	William C. Hodges (D)	46,471	*14.1*
	Jerry W. Carter (D)	35,578	*10.8*
	B. F. Paty (D)	34,153	*10.4*
	Dan Chappell (D)	29,494	*9.0*
	Grady Burton (D)	24,985	*7.6*
	Peter Thomasello Jr. (D)	22,355	*6.8*
	Stafford Caldwell (D)	19,789	*6.0*
	Democratic Runoff		
	Fred P. Cone (D)	184,540	*58.8*
	Raleigh Pettaway (D)	129,150	*41.2*
1940	**Democratic Primary**		
	Spessard L. Holland (D)	118,962	*24.7*
	Francis P. Whitehair (D)	95,431	*19.8*
	Fuller Warren (D)	83,316	*17.3*
	B. F. Paty (D)	75,608	*15.7*
	W. B. Fraser (D)	36,855	*7.7*
	James Barbee (D)	33,699	*7.0*
	Democratic Runoff		
	Spessard L. Holland (D)	272,718	*57.0*
	Francis P. Whitehair (D)	206,158	*43.1*
1944	**Republican Primary**		
	Bert L. Acker (R)	5,954	*61.3*
	Edward T. Keenan (R)	3,766	*38.7*
	Democratic Primary		
	Millard F. Caldwell (D)	116,111	*28.6*
	Robert A. "Lex" Green (D)	113,300	*27.9*
	E. R. Graham (D)	91,174	*22.5*
	F. D. Upchurch (D)	30,524	*7.5*
	Raymond Sheldon (D)	27,940	*6.9*
	J. Edwin Baker (D)	27,028	*6.6*
	Democratic Runoff		
	Millard F. Caldwell (D)	215,485	*55.3*
	Robert A. "Lex" Green (D)	174,100	*44.7*
1948	**Republican Primary**		
	Bert L. Acker (R)	10,807	*64.0*
	John L. Cogdill (R)	6,079	*36.0*
	Democratic Primary		
	Fuller Warren (D)	183,326	*32.7*
	Daniel T. McCarty (D)	161,788	*28.9*
	Colin English (D)	85,158	*15.2*
	W. A. Shands (D)	62,358	*11.1*
	J. Tom Watson (D)	51,505	*9.2*
	Democratic Runoff		
	Fuller Warren (D)	299,641	*52.0*
	Daniel T. McCarty (D)	276,425	*48.0*

	Candidates	Votes	%
1952	**Republican Primary[1]**		
	Harry S. Swan (R)	11,148	*43.0*
	Bert L. Acker (R)	9,728	*37.5*
	Elmore F. Kitzmiller (R)	5,050	*19.5*
	Republican Runoff		
	Harry S. Swan (R)	10,217	*63.0*
	Bert L. Acker (R)	5,995	*37.0*
	Democratic Primary		
	Daniel T. McCarty (D)	316,427	*48.9*
	Brailey Odham (D)	232,565	*31.5*
	Alto Adams (D)	126,426	*17.1*
	Democratic Runoff		
	Daniel T. McCarty (D)	384,200	*53.3*
	Brailey Odham (D)	336,716	*46.7*
1954[1]	**Republican Special Primary**		
	J. Tom Watson (R)	24,429	*68.0*
	Charles E. Compton (R)	11,552	*32.0*
	Democratic Special Primary		
	Charley E. Johns (D)	255,787	*38.4*
	Leroy Collins (D)	222,791	*33.4*
	Brailey Odham (D)	187,782	*28.2*
	Democratic Special Runoff		
	Leroy Collins (D)	380,323	*54.8*
	Charley E. Johns (D)	314,198	*45.2*
1956	**Republican Primary**		
	W. A. Washburn Jr. (R)		*100.0*
	Democratic Primary		
	Leroy Collins (D)	434,274	*51.7*
	Sumter L. Lowery (D)	179,019	*21.3*
	Farris Bryant (D)	110,469	*13.2*
	Fuller Warren (D)	107,990	*12.9*
1960	**Republican Primary**		
	George C. Peterson (R)	65,202	*72.7*
	Emerson H. Rupert (R)	24,484	*27.3*
	Democratic Primary		
	Farris Bryant (D)	193,507	*20.7*
	Doyle E. Carlton Jr. (D)	186,228	*19.9*
	Haydon Burns (D)	166,352	*17.8*
	John M. McCarty (D)	144,750	*15.5*
	Fred Dickinson (D)	115,520	*12.3*
	Thomas E. David (D)	80,057	*8.5*

Gubernatorial Elections

	Candidates	Votes	%
	Democratic Runoff		
	Farris Bryant (D)	512,757	55.2
	Doyle E. Carlton Jr. (D)	416,052	44.8
1964	**Republican Primary**		
	Charles R. Holley (R)	70,573	53.9
	H. B. Foster (R)	33,563	25.6
	Ken Folks (R)	26,815	20.5
	Democratic Primary		
	Haydon Burns (D)	312,453	27.5
	Robert King High (D)	207,280	18.3
	Scott Kelly (D)	205,078	18.1
	Fred Dickinson (D)	184,865	16.3
	John E. Mathews (D)	140,210	12.3
	Frederick B. Karl (D)	85,953	7.6
	Democratic Runoff		
	Haydon Burns (D)	648,093	58.2
	Robert King High (D)	465,547	41.8
1966	**Republican Primary**		
	Claude R. Kirk Jr. (R)	100,838	80.8
	Richard B. Muldrew (R)	23,953	19.2
	Democratic Primary		
	Haydon Burns (D)	372,451	35.4
	Robert King High (D)	338,281	32.1
	Scott Kelly (D)	331,580	31.5
	Democratic Runoff		
	Robert King High (D)	596,471	53.9
	Haydon Burns (D)	509,271	46.1
1970	**Republican Primary**		
	Claude R. Kirk Jr. (R)	172,888	48.1
	Jack M. Eckerd (R)	137,731	38.4
	L. A. "Skip" Bafalis (R)	48,378	13.5
	Republican Runoff		
	Claude R. Kirk Jr. (R)	199,943	56.8
	Jack M. Eckerd (R)	152,327	43.2
	Democratic Primary		
	Earl Faircloth (D)	227,413	30.0
	Reubin Askew (D)	206,333	27.2
	John E. Matthews (D)	186,053	24.5
	Chuck Hall (D)	139,384	18.4
	Democratic Runoff		
	Reubin Askew (D)	447,025	57.7
	Earl Faircloth (D)	328,038	42.3
1974	**Republican Primary**		
	Jerry Thomas (R)		100.0

	Candidates	Votes	%
	Democratic Primary		
	Reubin Askew (D)	597,137	68.8
	Ben Hill Griffin (D)	137,008	16.3
	Tom Adams (D)	85,557	10.2
1978	**Republican Primary**		
	Jack M. Eckerd (R)	244,394	63.8
	Louis Frey (R)	138,437	36.2
	Democratic Primary		
	Robert L. Shevin (D)	364,732	35.2
	Bob Graham (D)	261,972	25.2
	Hans G. Tanzler (D)	124,706	12.0
	Jim Williams (D)	124,427	12.0
	Bruce A. Smathers (D)	85,298	8.2
	Claude R. Kirk Jr. (D)	62,534	6.0
	Democratic Runoff		
	Bob Graham (D)	482,535	53.5
	Robert L. Shevin (D)	418,636	46.5
1982	**Republican Primary**		
	L. A. "Skip" Bafalis (R)	325,108	86.4
	Vernon Davids (R)	51,340	13.6
	Democratic Primary		
	Bob Graham (D)	839,320	84.5
	Fred Kuhn (D)	93,078	9.4
	Robert P. Kunst (D)	61,136	6.2
1986	**Republican Primary**		
	Bob Martinez (R)	244,499	44.1
	Louis Frey (R)	138,017	24.9
	Tom Gallagher (R)	127,709	23.0
	Chester Clem (R)	44,438	8.0
	Republican Runoff		
	Bob Martinez (R)	259,333	66.3
	Louis Frey (R)	131,652	33.7
	Democratic Primary		
	Steve Pajcic (D)	361,359	35.9
	Jim Smith (D)	310,479	30.8
	Harry Johnston (D)	258,038	25.6
	Mark K. Goldstein (D)	54,077	5.4
	Democratic Runoff		
	Steve Pajcic (D)	429,427	50.6
	Jim Smith (D)	418,614	49.4
1990	**Republican Primary**		
	Bob Martinez (R)	460,718	69.0
	Marlene Howard (R)	132,565	19.8
	John Davis (R)	34,720	5.2

Candidates	Votes	%
Democratic Primary		
Lawton Chiles (D)	746,325	69.5
Bill Nelson (D)	327,731	30.5
1994 **Republican Primary**		
Jeb Bush (R)	411,680	45.7
Jim Smith (R)	165,869	18.4
Tom Gallagher (R)	117,067	13.0
Ander Crenshaw (R)	109,148	12.1
Kenneth L. Connor (R)	83,945	9.3
Democratic Primary		
Lawton Chiles (D)	603,657	72.2
Jack Gargan (D)	232,757	27.8

Florida
1. Returns from Florida Handbook, 1975-76, p. 534.

GEORGIA

Candidates	Votes	%
1920 **Democratic Primary**		
Thomas W. Hardwick (D)	99,210	42.9
Clifford M. Walker (D)	90,738	39.2
John N. Holder (D)	37,957	16.4
Democratic Runoff[1]		
Thomas W. Hardwick (D)	84,257	55.3
Clifford M. Walker (D)	68,234	44.8
1922 **Democratic Primary**		
Clifford M. Walker (D)	123,784	58.1
Thomas W. Hardwick (D)	86,389	40.6
1924 **Democratic Primary**		
Clifford M. Walker (D)		100.0
1926 **Democratic Primary**		
John N. Holder (D)	71,976	37.3
Lamartine G. Hardman (D)	67,708	35.1
George H. Carswell (D)	32,484	16.8
J. O. Wood (D)	20,857	10.8
Democratic Runoff[1]		
Lamartine G. Hardman (D)	80,868	57.3
John N. Holder (D)	60,197	42.7
1928 **Democratic Primary**		
Lamartine G. Hardman (D)	137,430	58.5
Eurith D. Rivers (D)	97,339	41.5
1930 **Democratic Primary**		
Richard B. Russell (D)	56,177	27.3
George H. Carswell (D)	51,851	25.2
Eurith D. Rivers (D)	47,121	22.9
John N. Holder (D)	44,318	21.5

Candidates	Votes	%
Democratic Runoff[1]		
Richard B. Russell (D)	99,505	67.9
George H. Carswell (D)	47,157	32.2
1932 **Democratic Primary**		
Eugene Talmadge (D)	116,381	42.0
Abit Nix (D)	78,588	28.4
Thomas W. Hardwick (D)	35,252	12.7
John N. Holder (D)	19,697	7.1
1934 **Democratic Primary**		
Eugene Talmadge (D)	178,409	66.0
Claude Pittman (D)	87,049	32.2
1936 **Democratic Primary**		
Eurith D. Rivers (D)	233,503	60.0
Charles D. Redwine (D)	123,095	31.6
Blanton Fortson (D)	32,715	8.4
1938 **Democratic Primary**		
Eurith D. Rivers (D)	160,459	51.1
Hugh Howell (D)	134,121	42.7
J. J. Mangham (D)	19,537	6.2
1940 **Democratic Primary**		
Eugene Talmadge (D)	183,133	51.6
Columbus Roberts (D)	127,653	36.0
Abit Nix (D)	44,282	12.5
1942 **Democratic Primary**		
Ellis Arnall (D)	174,757	57.7
Eugene Talmadge (D)	128,394	42.4
1946 **Democratic Primary**		
J. V. Carmichael (D)	313,389	45.3
Eugene Talmadge (D)[2]	297,245	43.0
Eurith D. Rivers (D)	69,489	10.0
1948 **Democratic Special Primary**		
Herman E. Talmadge (D)	357,865	51.8
M. E. Thompson (D)	312,035	45.1
1950 **Democratic Primary**		
Herman E. Talmadge (D)	287,637	49.3
M. E. Thompson (D)	279,137	47.9
1954 **Democratic Primary**		
S. Marvin Griffin (D)	234,690	36.3
M. E. Thompson (D)	162,007	25.1
Tom Linder (D)	87,204	13.5
Fred Hand (D)	78,125	12.1
Charlie Gowen (D)	73,809	11.4
1958 **Democratic Primary**		
S. Ernest Vandiver (D)	499,477	80.5
William T. Bodenhamer (D)	87,830	14.2
Lee Roy Abernathy (D)	33,099	5.3

Gubernatorial Elections

	Candidates	Votes	%
1962	**Democratic Primary**		
	Carl E. Sanders (D)	494,978	58.1
	S. Marvin Griffin (D)	332,746	39.0
1966	**Democratic Primary**		
	Ellis Arnall (D)	231,480	29.4
	Lester Maddox (D)	185,672	23.6
	Jimmy Carter (D)	164,562	20.9
	James H. Gray (D)	152,973	19.4
	Garland T. Byrd (D)	39,994	5.1
	Democratic Runoff		
	Lester Maddox (D)	443,055	54.3
	Ellis Arnall (D)	373,004	45.7
1970	**Republican Primary**		
	Hal Suit (R)	62,868	58.5
	James L. Bentley (R)	40,251	37.4
	Democratic Primary		
	Jimmy Carter (D)	388,280	48.6
	Carl E. Sanders (D)	301,659	37.8
	C. B. King (D)	70,424	8.8
	Democratic Runoff		
	Jimmy Carter (D)	506,462	59.4
	Carl E. Sanders (D)	345,906	40.6
1974	**Republican Primary**		
	Ronnie Thompson (R)	19,691	41.0
	Harold Dye (R)	10,912	22.7
	George Lankford (R)	8,618	17.9
	Harry Geisinger (R)	6,078	12.7
	W. M. "Bill" Coolidge (R)	2,723	5.7
	Republican Runoff		
	Ronnie Thompson (R)	22,211	50.6
	Harold Dye (R)	21,669	49.4
	Democratic Primary		
	Lester Maddox (D)	310,384	36.3
	George Busbee (D)	177,997	20.8
	Bert Lance (D)	147,026	17.2
	David H. Gambrell (D)	66,000	7.7
	George T. Smith (D)	43,196	5.1
	Democratic Runoff		
	George Busbee (D)	551,106	59.9
	Lester Maddox (D)	369,608	40.1
1978	**Republican Primary**		
	Rodney M. Cook (R)	23,231	87.3
	Bud Herrin (R)	3,374	12.7
	Democratic Primary		
	George Busbee (D)	503,875	72.4
	Roscoe Emory Dean (D)	111,901	16.1
	J. B. Stoner (D)	37,654	5.4

	Candidates	Votes	%
1982	**Republican Primary**		
	Bob Bell (R)	36,347	59.2
	Ben Blackburn (R)	25,063	40.8
	Democratic Primary		
	Bo Ginn (D)	316,019	35.1
	Joe Frank Harris (D)	223,445	24.8
	Norman Underwood (D)	147,536	16.4
	Jack Watson (D)	114,533	12.7
	Billy Lovett (D)	62,341	6.9
	Democratic Runoff		
	Joe Frank Harris (D)	500,765	55.0
	Bo Ginn (D)	410,259	45.0
1986	**Republican Primary**		
	Guy Davis (R)		100.0
	Democratic Primary		
	Joe Frank Harris (D)	521,704	85.3
	Kenneth B. Quarterman (D)	89,759	14.7
1990	**Republican Primary**		
	Johnny Isakson (R)	87,795	74.3
	Bob Wood (R)	14,496	12.3
	Greeley Ellis (R)	13,062	11.1
	Democratic Primary		
	Zell Miller (D)	434,405	41.3
	Andrew Young (D)	303,159	28.8
	Roy E. Barnes (D)	219,136	20.8
	Lauren McDonald (D)	64,212	6.1
	Democratic Runoff		
	Zell Miller (D)	591,166	61.8
	Andrew Young (D)	364,861	38.2
1994	**Republican Primary**		
	Guy W. Millner (R)	142,263	47.9
	John Knox (R)	84,563	28.5
	Paul Heard (R)	46,761	15.7
	Nimrod McNair (R)	20,042	6.7
	Democratic Primary		
	Zell Miller (D)	321,963	70.0
	Jim Boyd (D)	78,444	17.1
	Mark Tate (D)	30,749	6.7
	Charles Poag (D)	28,623	6.2

Georgia

1. In the Georgia primaries for the Democratic nomination for governor in 1920, 1926, 1930 and 1948, no candidate received a majority of the county unit votes. Thus, runoffs were necessary in each case between the two candidates who received the most county unit votes; these also happened to be the candidates who had the most popular votes.

In the runoffs, the candidate who achieved a county unit majority was the winner, regardless of whether he had a popular vote majority; but the county unit winner also finished first in the popular vote in each case. (For an explanation of the Georgia county unit system, see p. 7.)

2. Under Georgia's county unit system, Talmadge actually won the primary easily even though he finished in second place in the popular vote. He

received 244 county unit votes, 59.5 percent, to Carmichael's 144 votes, 35.1 percent. (Explanation of county unit system, p. 7)

Talmadge later won the general election but died before his term was to begin, precipitating a famous crisis in Georgia's gubernatorial succession. (Footnote, p. 15)

HAWAII

	Candidates	Votes	%
1959	**Republican Primary**		
	William F. Quinn (R)		100.0
	Democratic Primary		
	John A. Burns (D)	69,152	89.8
	E. D. Hitchcock (D)	7,828	10.2
	Commonwealth Primary		
	David Kihei (CP)	65	64.4
	Epifanio Taok (CP)	36	35.6
1962	**Republican Primary**		
	William F. Quinn (R)	44,205	57.1
	James K. Kealoha (R)	33,272	49.9
	Democratic Primary		
	John A. Burns (D)	71,540	90.2
	Hyman Greenstein (D)	7,781	9.8
1966	**Republican Primary**		
	Randolph Crossley (R)	35,311	98.1
	Democratic Primary		
	John A. Burns (D)	86,825	79.5
	G. J. Fontes (D)	22,401	20.5
1970	**Republican Primary**		
	Samuel P. King (R)	20,605	49.3
	Hebden Porteus (R)	17,880	42.8
	David Watumull (R)	3,318	7.9
	Democratic Primary		
	John A. Burns (D)	82,441	53.2
	Thomas P. Gill (D)	69,209	44.7
1974	**Republican Primary**		
	Randolph Crossley (R)	25,425	82.5
	Joseph K. Hao (R)	5,405	17.5
	Democratic Primary		
	George R. Ariyoshi (D)	71,319	36.2
	Frank F. Fasi (D)	62,023	31.5
	Thomas P. Gill (D)	59,280	30.1
1978	**Republican Primary**		
	John Leopold (R)	20,524	91.6

	Candidates	Votes	%
	Democratic Primary		
	George R. Ariyoshi (D)	130,527	50.3
	Frank F. Fasi (D)	126,903	48.9
	Aloha Democrat Primary		
	John Moore (A-D)		100.0
	Libertarian Primary		
	Gregory Reeser (LIBERT)		100.0
	Non Partisan Primary		
	Alema Leota (NON PART)	236	58.9
	Frank Pore (NON PART)	165	41.1
1982	**Republican Primary**		
	D. G. Anderson (R)	11,997	96.8
	Democratic Primary		
	George R. Ariyoshi (D)	128,993	53.9
	Jean King (D)	106,935	44.7
	Independent Democratic Primary		
	Frank F. Fasi (ID)		100.0
	Non Partisan Primary		
	BraDa Ji Price (NON PART)[1]		100.0
1986	**Republican Primary**		
	D. G. Anderson (R)	38,790	94.6
	Democratic Primary		
	John Waihee (D)	105,579	45.6
	Cecil Heftel (D)	83,939	36.2
	Patsy T. Mink (D)	37,998	16.4
1990	**Republican Primary**		
	Fred Hemmings (R)	38,827	90.1
	Democratic Primary		
	John Waihee (D)	179,383	88.5
	Libertarian Primary		
	Triaka-Don Smith (LIBERT)		100.0
1994	**Republican Primary**		
	Patricia F. Saiki (R)	49,953	85.7
	Democratic Primary		
	Benjamin J. Cayetano (D)	110,782	52.2
	John Lewin (D)	76,666	36.1
	Libertarian Primary		
	George Peabody (LIBERT)	312	63.2

Candidates	Votes	%
Green Primary		
Michael Kioni Dudley (GREEN)	753	30.5
Edwina A. Wong (GREEN)	637	25.8
Gregory Goodwin (GREEN)	391	15.9
Best Primary		
Frank F. Fasi (BP)	30,879	95.3

Hawaii

1. Price withdrew and no substitution was made.

IDAHO

	Candidates	Votes	%
1958	**Republican Primary**		
	Robert E. Smylie (R)		100.0
	Democratic Primary		
	A. M. Derr (D)	25,599	34.5
	H. Max Hanson (D)	25,477	34.3
	John Glasby (D)	21,207	28.6
1962	**Republican Primary**		
	Robert E. Smylie (R)	37,761	57.2
	Elvin A. Lindquist (R)	16,565	25.1
	George L. Crookham (R)	11,669	17.7
	Democratic Primary		
	Vernon K. Smith (D)	35,574	43.1
	Charles Herndon (D)	18,072	21.9
	John G. Walters (D)	13,186	16.0
	Howard D. Hechtner (D)	7,952	9.6
	Conley Ward (D)	5,427	6.6
1966	**Republican Primary**		
	Don Samuelson (R)	52,891	61.0
	Robert E. Smylie (R)	33,753	39.0
	Democratic Primary		
	Charles Herndon (D)[1]	28,926	40.7
	Cecil D. Andrus (D)	27,649	39.0
	William J. Dee (D)	14,409	20.3
1970	**Republican Primary**		
	Don Samuelson (R)	46,719	58.4
	Dick Smith (R)	33,339	41.6
	Democratic Primary		
	Cecil D. Andrus (D)	29,036	46.0
	Vernon Ravenscroft (D)	23,369	37.1
	Lloyd Walker (D)	10,664	16.9
1974	**Republican Primary**		
	Jack M. Murphy (R)		100.0
	Democratic Primary		
	Cecil D. Andrus (D)		100.0

	Candidates	Votes	%
1978	**Republican Primary**		
	Allan Larsen (R)	33,778	28.7
	Vernon Ravenscroft (D)	32,455	27.6
	C. L. Otter (R)	30,523	26.0
	Larry Jackson (R)	13,510	11.5
	Democratic Primary		
	John V. Evans (D)		100.0
	American Primary		
	Wayne L. Loveless (AM)		100.0
1982	**Republican Primary**		
	Phillip Batt (R)	63,622	63.9
	Ralph Olmstead (R)	35,932	36.1
	Democratic Primary		
	John V. Evans (D)		100.0
1986	**Republican Primary**		
	David H. Leroy (R)		100.0
	Democratic Primary		
	Cecil D. Andrus (D)		100.0
1990	**Republican Primary**		
	Roger Fairchild (R)	37,728	37.1
	Rachel S. Gilbert (R)	33,483	32.9
	Milton E. Erhart (R)	30,514	30.0
	Democratic Primary		
	Cecil D. Andrus (D)		100.0
1994	**Republican Primary**		
	Phil Batt (R)	57,066	48.0
	Larry Eastland (R)	38,664	32.5
	Charles L. Winder (R)	16,063	13.5
	Doug Dorn (R)	7,098	6.0
	Democratic Primary		
	Larry EchoHawk (D)	42,661	73.8
	Ron Beitelspacher (D)	12,377	21.4

Idaho

1. Herndon died after the primary and the Democratic state central committee substituted Andrus as the nominee.

ILLINOIS

	Candidates	Votes	%
1956	**Republican Primary**		
	William G. Stratton (R)	556,909	69.8
	Warren E. Wright (R)	187,645	23.5

Candidates	Votes	%
Democratic Primary		
Herbert C. Paschen (D)[1]	475,813	57.8
Morris B. Sachs (D)	347,458	42.2
1960 **Republican Primary**		
William G. Stratton (R)	499,365	59.1
Hayes Robertson (R)	345,340	40.9
Democratic Primary		
Otto Kerner (D)	649,253	60.9
Joseph D. Lohman (D)	232,345	21.8
Stephen A. Mitchell (D)	184,651	17.3
1964 **Republican Primary**		
Charles H. Percy (R)	626,111	60.3
William J. Scott (R)	388,903	37.4
Democratic Primary		
Otto Kerner (D)		100.0
1968 **Republican Primary**		
Richard B. Ogilvie (R)	335,727	47.5
John H. Altofer (R)	288,904	40.9
William G. Stratton (R)	50,041	7.1
Democratic Primary		
Samuel H. Shapiro (D)		100.0
1972 **Republican Primary**		
Richard B. Ogilvie (R)	442,323	75.5
John Mathis (D)	143,053	24.4
Democratic Primary		
Daniel Walker (D)	735,193	51.4
Paul Simon (D)	694,900	48.6
1976 **Republican Primary**		
James R. Thompson (R)	625,457	86.4
Richard H. Cooper (R)	97,937	13.5
Democratic Primary		
Michael J. Howlett (D)	811,721	53.8
Daniel Walker (D)	696,380	46.2
1978 **Republican Primary**		
James R. Thompson (R)		100.0
Democratic Primary		
Michael Bakalis (D)	601,045	82.8
W. Dakin Williams (D)	124,406	17.2
1982 **Republican Primary**		
James R. Thompson (R)	507,893	83.7
John E. Roche (R)	54,858	9.0
V. A. Kelley (R)	43,627	7.2

Candidates	Votes	%
Democratic Primary		
Adlai E. Stevenson III (D)		100.0
1986 **Republican Primary**		
James R. Thompson (R)	452,685	90.9
Peter Bowen (R)	45,236	9.1
Democratic Primary		
Adlai E. Stevenson III (D)[2]	735,249	92.9
Larry Burgess (D)	55,930	7.1
1990 **Republican Primary**		
Jim Edgar (R)	482,441	62.8
Steven Baer (R)	256,889	33.5
Democratic Primary		
Neil F. Hartigan (D)		100.0
1994 **Republican Primary**		
Jim Edgar (R)	521,590	75.0
Jack Roeser (R)	173,742	25.0
Democratic Primary		
Dawn C. Netsch (D)	487,364	44.3
Roland W. Burris (D)	401,142	36.5
Richard Phelan (D)	160,576	14.6

Illinois
1. Paschen withdrew after the primary and the Democratic state committee substituted Richard B. Austin as the party's nominee.
2. Stevenson withdrew after the primary on the ground that the nominated candidate for lieutenant governor was a known supporter of Lyndon LaRouche, whose views were so different from Stevenson's as to make a joint candidacy impossible. No replacement candidate was named by the Democratic party. A new party, Illinois Solidarity, was formed with Stevenson as its gubernatorial candidate.

INDIANA

Candidates	Votes	%
1976[1] **Republican Primary**		
Otis R. Bowen (R)		100.0
Democratic Primary		
Larry A. Conrad (D)	358,421	64.5
Jack L. New (D)	105,965	19.1
Robert J. Fair (D)	91,606	16.5
1980 **Republican Primary**		
Robert D. Orr (R)		100.0
Democratic Primary		
John A. Hillenbrand (D)	284,182	52.4
W. Wayne Townsend (D)	257,779	47.6
1984 **Republican Primary**		
Robert D. Orr (R)	319,889	71.6
John Snyder (R)	126,778	28.4

Gubernatorial Elections

Candidates	Votes	%
Democratic Primary		
W. Wayne Townsend (D)	347,948	56.9
Virginia Dill McCarty (D)	219,806	35.9
Donald W. Mantooth (D)	43,507	7.1
1988 Republican Primary		
John M. Mutz (R)		100.0
Democratic Primary		
Evan Bayh (D)	493,198	83.1
Stephen J. Daily (D)	66,242	11.2
Frank L. O'Bannon (D)	34,360	5.8
1992 Republican Primary		
Linley E. Pearson (R)	223,373	48.9
H. Dean Evans (R)	153,089	33.5
John A. Johnson (R)	80,784	17.7
Democratic Primary		
Evan Bayh (D)	390,938	100.0
1996 Republican Primary		
Stephen Goldsmith (R)	298,532	54.1
Rex Early (R)	204,301	37.0
George Witwer (R)	48,749	8.8
Democratic Primary		
Frank O'Bannon (D)	305,589	100.0

Indiana

1. *Until 1976 all nominations for statewide office in Indiana were made by state party conventions.*

IOWA

Candidates	Votes	%
1956 Republican Primary		
Leo A. Hoegh (R)		100.0
Democratic Primary		
Herschel C. Loveless (D)	77,206	70.0
Lawrence E. Plummer (D)	33,103	30.0
1958 Republican Primary		
William G. Murray (R)	112,496	56.6
W. H. Nicholas (R)	86,154	43.4
Democratic Primary		
Herschel C. Loveless (D)		100.0
1960 Republican Primary		
Norman A. Erbe (R)	81,869	36.3
Jack Schroeder (R)	75,599	33.5
W. H. Nicholas (R)	68,037	30.2

Candidates	Votes	%
Democratic Primary		
E. J. McManus (D)	74,990	61.7
Harold E. Hughes (D)	46,542	38.3
1962 Republican Primary		
Norman A. Erbe (R)	134,010	67.7
W. H. Nicholas (R)	63,966	32.3
Democratic Primary		
Harold E. Hughes (D)	66,624	78.9
Lewis E. Lint (D)	17,770	21.1
1964 Republican Primary		
Evan Hultman (R)		100.0
Democratic Primary		
Harold E. Hughes (D)		100.0
1966 Republican Primary		
William G. Murray (R)	87,371	50.5
Robert K. Beck (R)	85,733	49.5
Democratic Primary		
Harold E. Hughes (D)		100.0
1968 Republican Primary		
Robert Ray (R)	108,744	43.2
Donald E. Johnson (R)	77,715	30.8
Robert K. Beck (R)	65,439	26.0
Democratic Primary		
Paul Franzenburg		100.0
1970 Republican Primary		
Robert Ray (R)		100.0
Democratic Primary		
Robert Fulton (D)	48,459	46.7
William Gannon (D)	46,524	44.8
Robert L. Nereim (D)	8,796	8.5
1972 Republican Primary		
Robert Ray (R)		100.0
Democratic Primary		
Paul Franzenburg (D)	85,807	57.5
John Tapscott (D)	63,284	42.4
American Independent Primary		
Robert D. Dilley (AMI)		100.0
1974 Republican Primary		
Robert Ray (R)		100.0

Candidates	Votes	%
Democratic Primary		
James F. Schaben (D)	59,840	44.8
William Gannon (D)	52,420	39.3
Clark Rasmussen (D)	21,240	15.9
1978 Republican Primary		
Robert Ray (R)	136,517	87.5
Donovan D. Nelson (R)	19,486	12.5
Democratic Primary		
Jerome D. Fitzgerald (D)	58,039	55.5
Tom Whitney (D)	37,132	35.5
Warren D. Strait (D)	9,443	9.0
1982 Republican Primary		
Terry Branstad (R)		100.0
Democratic Primary		
Roxanne Conlin (D)	94,481	48.2
Jerome D. Fitzgerald (D)	61,340	31.3
Edward L. Campbell (D)	40,233	20.5
1986 Republican Primary		
Terry E. Branstad (R)		100.0
Democratic Primary		
Lowell L. Junkins (D)	70,605	52.6
Bob Anderson (D)	44,550	33.2
George R. Kinley (D)	15,473	11.5
1990 Republican Primary		
Terry E. Branstad (R)		100.0
Democratic Primary		
Donald D. Avenson (D)	79,022	39.5
Tom Miller (D)	63,364	31.6
John Chrystal (D)	52,170	26.0
1994 Republican Primary		
Terry E. Branstad (R)	161,228	51.8
Fred Grandy (R)	149,809	48.1
Democratic Primary		
Bonnie J. Campbell (D)	99,718	77.7
William J. Reichardt (D)	24,630	19.2

KANSAS

Candidates	Votes	%
1956 Republican Primary		
Warren W. Shaw (R)	156,476	52.7
Fred Hall (R)	123,398	41.5

	Candidates	Votes	%
	Democratic Primary		
	George Docking (D)	76,544	50.3
	Harry H. Woodring (D)	75,548	49.7
1958	**Republican Primary**		
	Clyde M. Reed (R)	142,247	72.6
	Fred Hall (R)	35,632	18.2
	Democratic Primary		
	George Docking (D)		100.0
1960	**Republican Primary**		
	John Anderson (R)	128,081	48.7
	McDill Boyd (R)	116,725	44.4
	William H. Addington (R)	18,169	6.9
	Democratic Primary		
	George Docking (D)		100.0
1962	**Republican Primary**		
	John Anderson (R)	164,888	84.1
	Harvey F. Crouch (R)	31,221	15.9
	Democratic Primary		
	Dale E. Saffels (D)	69,728	59.7
	George Hart (D)	47,055	40.3
1964	**Republican Primary**		
	William H. Avery (R)	85,746	30.4
	McDill Boyd (R)	75,451	26.7
	Paul R. Wunsch (R)	71,601	25.4
	William M. Ferguson (R)	36,622	13.0
	Democratic Primary		
	Harry G. Wiles (D)	50,590	32.4
	Jules V. Doty (D)	37,305	23.9
	George Hart (D)	30,973	19.8
	Joseph W. Henkle (D)	21,304	13.6
	J. Donald Coffin (D)	9,140	5.9
1966	**Republican Primary**		
	William H. Avery (R)	144,842	75.1
	Dell Crozier (R)	48,051	24.9
	Democratic Primary		
	Robert Docking (D)	96,414	85.5
	George Hart (D)	16,385	14.5
1968	**Republican Primary**		
	Rick Harman (R)	133,454	48.9
	John Crutcher (R)	128,635	47.1
	Democratic Primary		
	Robert Docking (D)		100.0

Gubernatorial Elections

	Candidates	Votes	%
1970	**Republican Primary**		
	Kent Frizzell (R)	141,298	60.5
	Rick Harman (R)	78,086	33.4
	Democratic Primary		
	Robert Docking (D)		100.0
1972	**Republican Primary**		
	Morris Kay (R)	138,815	46.6
	John Anderson (R)	88,088	29.6
	Ray E. Frisbie (R)	46,125	15.5
	Reynolds Shultz (R)	24,911	8.4
	Democratic Primary		
	Robert Docking (D)		100.0
1974	**Republican Primary**		
	Robert F. Bennett (R)	67,347	32.4
	Donald O. Concannon (R)	66,817	32.1
	Forrest J. Robinson (R)	56,440	27.2
	Robert W. Clack (R)	17,333	8.3
	Democratic Primary		
	Vern Miller (D)		100.0
1978	**Republican Primary**		
	Robert F. Bennett (R)	142,239	69.2
	Robert R. Sanders (R)	40,542	19.7
	Harold Knight (R)	22,671	11.1
	Democratic Primary		
	John Carlin (D)	71,366	55.2
	Bert Chaney (D)	34,132	26.4
	Harry G. Wiles (D)	23,762	18.4
1982	**Republican Primary**		
	Sam Hardage (R)	86,692	36.8
	Dave Owen (R)	79,770	33.8
	Wendell Lady (R)	61,419	26.0
	Democratic Primary		
	John Carlin (D)	103,780	78.9
	Jimmy D. Montgomery (D)	27,785	21.1
1986	**Republican Primary**		
	Mike Hayden (R)	99,669	36.1
	Larry Jones (R)	85,989	31.1
	Jack H. Brier (R)	37,410	13.6
	Gene Bicknell (R)	25,733	9.3
	Richard J. Peckham (R)	18,876	6.8
	Democratic Primary		
	Thomas R. Docking (D)		100.0
1990	**Republican Primary**		
	Mike Hayden (R)	138,467	44.7
	Nestor Weigand (R)	130,816	42.3
	Richard Peckham (R)	29,033	9.4

	Candidates	Votes	%
	Democratic Primary		
	Joan Finney (D)	81,250	47.2
	John Carlin (D)	79,406	46.1
	Fred Phelps (D)	11,572	6.7
1994	**Republican Primary**		
	Bill Graves (R)	115,608	40.9
	Gene Bicknell (R)	79,816	28.2
	Fred Kerr (R)	63,495	22.5
	Democratic Primary		
	Jim Slattery (D)	84,389	53.0
	Joan Wagnon (D)	42,115	26.5
	James L. Francisco (D)	16,048	10.1
	Leslie Kitchenmaster (D)	11,253	7.1

KENTUCKY

	Candidates	Votes	%
1959	**Republican Primary**		
	John M. Robsion (R)	63,130	86.3
	Thurman J. Hamlin (R)	6,019	8.2
	Granville Thomas (R)	3,991	5.5
	Democratic Primary		
	Bert T. Combs (D)	292,462	53.0
	Harry Lee Waterfield (D)	259,461	45.6
1963	**Republican Primary**		
	Louie B. Nunn (R)	77,455	88.5
	J. N. R. Cecil (R)	10,039	11.5
	Democratic Primary		
	Edward T. Breathitt (D)	318,858	53.8
	Albert B. Chandler (D)	256,451	43.2
1967	**Republican Primary**		
	Louie B. Nunn (R)	90,216	50.4
	Marlow W. Cook (R)	86,397	48.3
	Democratic Primary		
	Henry Ward (D)	207,797	52.4
	Albert B. Chandler (D)	111,782	28.2
	Harry Lee Waterfield (D)	42,583	10.7
1971	**Republican Primary**		
	Thomas Emberton (R)	84,863	84.1
	Ried Martin (R)	6,379	6.3
	Thurman J. Hamlin (R)	5,469	5.4
	Democratic Primary		
	Wendell H. Ford (D)	237,815	53.0
	Bert T. Combs (D)	195,678	43.6

	Candidates	Votes	%
1975	**Republican Primary**		
	Robert E. Gable (R)	38,113	*51.3*
	Elmer Begley (R)	16,885	*22.7*
	T. William Klein (R)	10,844	*14.6*
	Granville Thomas (R)	8,426	*11.3*
	Democratic Primary		
	Julian Carroll (D)	263,965	*66.3*
	Todd Hollenbach (D)	113,285	*28.5*
1979	**Republican Primary**		
	Louie B. Nunn (R)	106,006	*79.6*
	Ray B. White (R)	18,514	*13.9*
	Democratic Primary		
	John Y. Brown Jr. (D)	165,158	*29.1*
	Harvey Sloane (D)	139,713	*24.6*
	Terry McBrayer (D)	131,530	*23.2*
	Carroll Hubbard (D)	68,577	*12.1*
	Thelma L. Stovall (D)	47,633	*8.4*
1983	**Republican Primary**		
	Jim Bunning (R)	72,808	*74.4*
	Lester Burns (R)	7,340	*7.5*
	Donald Wiggins (R)	5,464	*5.6*
	Elizabeth Wickham (R)	5,174	*5.3*
	Democratic Primary		
	Martha Layne Collins (D)	223,692	*34.0*
	Harvey Sloane (D)	219,160	*33.3*
	Grady Strumbo (D)	199,795	*30.3*
1987	**Republican Primary**		
	John Harper (R)	37,432	*41.4*
	Joseph E. Johnson (R)	22,396	*24.8*
	Leonard W. Beasley (R)	21,067	*23.3*
	Thurman J. Hamlin (R)	9,475	*10.5*
	Democratic Primary		
	Wallace G. Wilkinson (D)	221,138	*34.9*
	John Y. Brown, Jr. (D)	163,204	*25.8*
	Steven L. Beshear (D)	114,439	*18.1*
	Grady Stumbo (D)	84,613	*13.4*
	Julian Carroll (D)	42,137	*6.6*
1991	**Republican Primary**		
	Larry J. Hopkins (R)	81,526	*50.6*
	Larry E. Forgy (R)	79,581	*49.4*
	Democratic Primary		
	Brereton C. Jones (D)	184,703	*37.5*
	Scott Baesler (D)	149,352	*30.4*
	Floyd G. Poore (D)	132,060	*26.8*
	Gatewood Galbraith (D)	25,834	*5.3*
1995	**Republican Primary**		
	Larry E. Forgy (R)	97,099	*82.4*
	Robert E. Gable (R)	17,054	*14.5*

	Candidates	Votes	%
	Democratic Primary		
	Paul E. Patton (D)	152,203	*44.9*
	Bob Babbage (D)	81,352	*24.0*
	John "Eck" Rose (D)	71,740	*21.2*
	Gatewood Galbraith (D)	29,039	*8.6*

LOUISIANA

	Candidates	Votes	%
1920	**Democratic Primary**		
	John M. Parker (D)	77,868	*54.2*
	Frank P. Stubbs (D)	65,685	*45.8*
1924	**Democratic Primary**		
	Hewitt Bouanchaud (D)	84,162	*35.1*
	Henry L. Fuqua (D)	81,382	*34.0*
	Huey P. Long (D)	73,985	*30.9*
	Democratic Runoff		
	Henry L. Fuqua (D)	125,880	*57.8*
	Hewitt Bouanchaud (D)	92,006	*42.2*
1928	**Democratic Primary**		
	Huey P. Long (D)	126,842	*43.9*
	Riley J. Wilson (D)[1]	81,747	*28.3*
	O. H. Simpson (D)	80,326	*27.8*
1932	**Democratic Primary**		
	Oscar K. Allen (D)	214,699	*56.5*
	Dudley J. LeBlanc (D)	110,048	*29.0*
	George Seth Guion (D)	53,756	*14.2*
1936	**Democratic Primary**		
	Richard W. Leche (D)	362,502	*67.1*
	Cleveland Dear (D)	176,150	*32.6*
1940	**Democratic Primary**		
	Earl K. Long (D)	226,385	*40.9*
	Sam H. Jones (D)	154,936	*28.0*
	J. A. Noe (D)	116,564	*21.1*
	James H. Morrison (D)	48,243	*8.7*
	Democratic Runoff		
	Sam H. Jones (D)	284,437	*51.7*
	Earl K. Long (D)	265,403	*48.3*
1944	**Democratic Primary**		
	Jimmie H. Davis (D)	167,434	*34.9*
	Lewis L. Morgan (D)	131,682	*27.5*
	James H. Morrison (D)	76,081	*15.9*
	Dudley J. LeBlanc (D)	40,392	*8.4*
	Sam S. Caldwell (D)	34,335	*7.2*
	Democratic Runoff		
	Jimmie H. Davis (D)	251,228	*53.6*
	Lewis L. Morgan (D)	217,915	*46.5*

	Candidates	Votes	%
1948	**Democratic Primary**		
	Earl K. Long (D)	267,253	*41.5*
	Sam H. Jones (D)	147,329	*22.9*
	Robert F. Kennon (D)	127,569	*19.8*
	James H. Morrison (D)	101,754	*15.8*
	Democratic Runoff		
	Earl K. Long (D)	432,528	*65.9*
	Sam H. Jones (D)	223,971	*34.1*
1952	**Democratic Primary**		
	Carlos G. Spaht (D)	173,987	*22.8*
	Robert F. Kennon (D)	163,434	*21.5*
	Hale Boggs (D)	142,542	*18.7*
	James M. McLemore (D)	116,405	*15.3*
	William J. Dodd (D)	90,925	*11.9*
	Dudley J. LeBlanc (D)	62,906	*8.3*
	Democratic Runoff		
	Robert F. Kennon (D)	482,302	*61.4*
	Carlos G. Spaht (D)	302,743	*38.6*
1956	**Democratic Primary**		
	Earl K. Long (D)	421,681	*51.4*
	deLesseps S. Morrison (D)	191,576	*23.4*
	Frederick T. Preaus (D)	95,955	*11.7*
	Francis C. Grevemberg (D)	62,309	*7.6*
	James M. McLemore (D)	48,188	*5.9*
1959[2]	**Republican Primary**		
	F. C. Grevemberg (R)		*100.0*
	Democratic Primary		
	deLesseps S. Morrison (D)	278,956	*33.1*
	Jimmie H. Davis (D)	213,551	*25.3*
	William M. Rainach (D)	143,095	*17.0*
	James A. Noe (D)	97,654	*11.6*
	William J. Dodd (D)	85,436	*10.1*
	Democratic Runoff		
	Jimmie H. Davis (R)	487,681	*54.1*
	deLesseps S. Morrison (D)	414,110	*45.9*
1963[3]	**Republican Primary**		
	Charlton H. Lyons Sr. (R)		*100.0*
	Democratic Primary		
	deLesseps S. Morrison (D)	299,702	*33.1*
	John J. McKeithen (D)	157,304	*17.4*
	Gillis W. Long (D)	137,778	*15.2*
	Robert F. Kennon (D)	127,870	*14.1*
	Shelby M. Jackson (D)	103,949	*11.5*
	Democratic Runoff		
	John J. McKeithen (D)	492,905	*52.2*
	deLesseps S. Morrison (D)	451,161	*47.8*

	Candidates	Votes	%
1967	**Democratic Primary**		
	John J. McKeithen (D)	836,304	*80.6*
	John R. Rarick (D)	179,846	*17.3*
1971	**Republican Primary**		
	David C. Treen (R)	9,732	*92.1*
	Robert Ross (R)	839	*7.9*
	Democratic Primary		
	Edwin W. Edwards (D)	276,397	*23.5*
	J. Bennett Johnston (D)	208,830	*17.8*
	Gillis W. Long (D)	164,276	*14.0*
	Jimmie H. Davis (D)	138,756	*11.8*
	John G. Schwegmann (D)	92,072	*7.8*
	A. A. Aycock (D)	88,465	*7.5*
	Samuel Bell (D)	72,486	*6.2*
	Speedy O. Long (D)	61,359	*5.2*
	Democratic Runoff		
	Edwin W. Edwards (D)	584,262	*50.2*
	J. Bennett Johnston (D)	579,774	*49.8*
1975[4]	**Open Primary**		
	Edwin W. Edwards (D)	750,107	*62.3*
	Robert C. Jones (D)	292,220	*24.3*
	Wade O. Martin (D)	146,368	*12.2*
1979[5]	**Open Primary**		
	David C. Treen (R)	297,674	*21.8*
	Louis Lambert (D)	283,266	*20.7*
	James E. Fitzmorris (D)	280,760	*20.6*
	Paul Hardy (D)	227,026	*16.6*
	E. L. Henry (D)	135,769	*9.9*
	Edgar G. Mouton (D)	124,333	*9.1*
1987	**Open Primary**		
	Charles "Buddy" Roemer (D)	516,078	*33.1*
	Edwin W. Edwards (D)[6]	437,801	*28.0*
	Bob Livingston (R)	287,780	*18.5*
	W. J. Tauzin (D)	154,079	*9.9*
	James H. Brown (D)	138,223	*8.8*
1991	**Open Primary**		
	Edwin W. Edwards (D)	523,195	*33.8*
	David E. Duke (R)	491,342	*31.7*
	Charles "Buddy" Roemer (R)	410,690	*26.5*
	Clyde C. Holloway (R)	82,683	*5.3*
1995	**Open Primary**		
	M. J. "Mike" Foster (R)	385,267	*26.1*
	Cleo Fields (D)	280,921	*19.0*
	Mary L. Landrieu (D)	271,938	*18.4*
	Charles "Buddy" Roemer (R)	263,330	*17.8*
	Phil Preis (D)	133,271	*9.0*

Louisiana

1. Wilson declined a runoff with Long, who became the Democratic nominee.

2. The Democratic and Republican primaries were held Dec. 5, 1959; the Democratic runoff was held Jan. 9, 1960.

3. The Democratic and Republican primaries were held Dec. 7, 1963; the Democratic runoff was held Jan. 11, 1964.

4. In 1975 Louisiana eliminated the partisan primary for governor and instituted an open primary with candidates from all parties running on the same ballot. Any candidate who received a majority appeared in the general election unopposed. If no candidate received 50 percent, a runoff was held between the two top finishers.

5. In 1979 there was a court-ordered recount of the votes for the top three candidates. Results were as follows: Treen: 297,469 votes, 34.6%; Lambert: 282,708, 32.8%; and Fitzmorris: 280,412, 32.6%.

6. Edwards withdrew and no runoff election was held in November.

MAINE

	Candidates	Votes	%
1956	**Republican Primary**		
	Willis A Trafton (R)	42,901	51.0
	Philip F. Chapman (R)	24,787	29.4
	Alexander A. LaFleur (R)	16,479	19.6
	Democratic Primary		
	Edmund S. Muskie (D)		100.0
1958	**Republican Primary**		
	Horace A. Hildreth (R)	63,424	62.0
	Philip F. Chapman (R)	38,865	38.0
	Democratic Primary		
	Clinton A. Clauson (D)	20,736	51.8
	Maynard C. Dolloff (D)	19,301	48.2
1960	**Republican Primary**		
	John H. Reed (R)		100.0
	Democratic Primary		
	Frank M. Coffin (D)		100.0
1962	**Republican Primary**		
	John H. Reed (R)		100.0
	Democratic Primary		
	Maynard C. Dolloff (D)	18,234	50.3
	Richard J. Dubord (D)	18,007	49.7
1966	**Republican Primary**		
	John H. Reed (R)	55,924	59.7
	James S. Erwin (R)	37,765	40.3
	Democratic Primary		
	Kenneth M. Curtis (D)	30,879	55.6
	Carlton D. Reed (D)	13,839	24.9
	Dana W. Childs (D)	10,793	19.4
1970	**Republican Primary**		
	James S. Erwin (R)	72,760	89.1
	Calvin F. Grass (R)	8,898	10.9
	Democratic Primary		
	Kenneth M. Curtis (D)	33,052	63.2
	Plato Truman (D)	19,266	36.8

	Candidates	Votes	%
1974	**Republican Primary**		
	James S. Erwin (R)	38,044	39.3
	Harrison L. Richardson (R)	36,693	37.9
	Wakine G. Tanous (R)	18,786	19.4
	Democratic Primary		
	George J. Mitchell (D)	33,312	37.5
	Joseph E. Brennan (D)	23,443	26.4
	Peter S. Kelley (D)	21,358	24.1
	Lloyd P. LaFountain (D)	7,954	9.0
1978	**Republican Primary**		
	Linwood E. Palmer (R)	35,976	48.7
	Charles L. Cragin (R)	28,244	38.3
	Jerrold B. Speers (R)	9,603	13.0
	Democratic Primary		
	Joseph E. Brennan (D)	38,361	52.0
	Philip L. Merrill (D)	26,803	36.3
	Richard J. Carey (D)	8,588	11.6
1982	**Republican Primary**		
	Charles L. Cragin (R)	32,235	38.0
	Sherry F. Huber (R)	27,739	32.7
	Richard H. Pierce (R)	24,820	29.3
	Democratic Primary		
	Joseph E. Brennan (D)	56,990	76.8
	Georgette B. Berube (D)	17,219	23.2
1986	**Republican Primary**		
	John R. McKernan (R)	79,393	68.4
	Porter D. Leighton (R)	36,705	31.6
	Democratic Primary		
	James Tierney (D)	44,087	37.2
	Severin M. Beliveau (D)	27,991	23.6
	G. William Diamond (D)	24,693	20.8
	David E. Redmond (D)	17,598	14.9
1990	**Republican Primary**		
	John R. McKernan (R)		100.0
	Democratic Primary		
	Joseph E. Brennan (D)		100.0
1994	**Republican Primary**		
	Susan M. Collins (R)	19,477	21.5
	Sumner H. Lipman (R)	15,282	16.9
	Jasper S. Wyman (R)	14,418	15.9
	Judith C. Foss (R)	11,780	13.0
	Paul R. Young (R)	10,119	11.2
	Mary Adams (R)	7,854	8.7
	Charles M. Webster (R)	6,239	6.9
	Pamela A. Cahill (R)	5,218	5.8

Candidates	Votes	%
Democratic Primary		
Joseph E. Brennan (D)	56,932	56.3
Thomas H. Allen (D)	24,095	23.8
Richard E. Barringer (D)	9,191	9.1
Robert L. Woodbury (D)	8,243	8.1

MARYLAND

Candidates	Votes	%
1958 Republican Primary		
James Devereux (R)		100.0
Democratic Primary		
J. Millard Tawes (D)	261,594	82.0
Bruce S. Campbell (D)	24,953	7.8
Morgan L. Amaimo (D)	16,459	5.2
Joseph A. Phillips (D)	15,836	5.0
1962 Republican Primary		
Frank Small (R)	71,791	77.8
Karla Balentine (R)	11,504	12.5
Joseph L. Pavlock (R)	8,972	9.7
Democratic Primary		
J. Millard Tawes (D)	178,792	40.4
George P. Mahoney (D)	125,966	28.5
David Hume (D)	118,295	26.7
1966 Republican Primary		
Spiro T. Agnew (R)	98,531	83.2
Andrew J. Groszer (R)	9,987	8.4
Democratic Primary		
George P. Mahoney (D)	148,446	30.2
Carlton R. Sickles (D)	146,507	29.8
Thomas B. Finan (D)	134,216	27.3
Clarence W. Miles (D)	42,304	8.6
1970 Republican Primary		
C. Stanley Blair (R)	101,541	81.5
Peter James (R)	15,790	12.8
John C. Webb (R)	7,194	5.7
Democratic Primary		
Marvin Mandel (D)	414,160	89.1
1974 Republican Primary		
Louise Gore (R)	57,626	53.6
Lawrence J. Hogan (R)	49,887	46.4
Democratic Primary		
Marvin Mandel (D)	254,509	65.7
Wilson K. Barnes (D)	96,902	25.0

Candidates	Votes	%
1978 Republican Primary		
J. Glenn Beall Jr. (R)	76,011	57.7
Carlton Beall (R)	30,119	22.8
Louise Gore (R)	20,690	15.7
Democratic Primary		
Harry R. Hughes (D)	213,457	37.2
Blair Lee (D)	194,236	33.9
Theodore G. Venetoulis (D)	140,486	24.5
1982 Republican Primary		
Robert A. Pascal (R)	113,425	84.3
Ross Z. Pierpont (R)	21,165	15.7
Democratic Primary		
Harry R. Hughes (D)	393,244	59.8
Harry J. McGuirk (D)	129,049	26.3
Harry W. Kelley (D)	61,271	12.5
1986 Republican Primary		
Thomas J. Mooney (R)		100.0
Democratic Primary		
William D. Schaefer (D)	395,170	61.7
Stephen H. Sachs (D)	224,755	35.1
1990 Republican Primary		
William S. Shepard (R)	66,966	52.7
Ross Z. Pierpont (R)	60,065	47.3
Democratic Primary		
William D. Schaefer (D)	358,534	78.1
Frederick M. Griisser (D)	100,816	21.9
1994 Republican Primary		
Ellen R. Sauerbrey (R)	123,676	52.2
Helen D. Bentley (R)	89,821	37.9
William S. Shepard (R)	23,505	9.9
Democratic Primary		
Parris N. Glendening (D)	293,314	53.6
American Joe Miedusiewski (D)	100,326	18.3
Melvin A. Steinberg (D)	82,308	15.0
Don Allensworth (D)	46,888	8.6

MASSACHUSETTS

Candidates	Votes	%
1956 Republican Primary		
Sumner G. Whittier (R)		100.0
Democratic Primary		
Foster Furcolo (D)	358,051	73.1
Thomas H. Buckley (D)	131,496	26.9

	Candidates	Votes	%
1958[1]	**Republican Primary**		
	Charles Gibbons (R)	158,944	84.3
	George Fingold (R)	23,031	12.2
	Democratic Primary		
	Foster Furcolo (D)		100.0
1960	**Republican Primary**		
	John A. Volpe (R)		100.0
	Democratic Primary		
	Joseph D. Ward (D)	180,848	30.2
	Endicott Peabody (D)	152,762	25.5
	Francis E. Kelly (D)	98,107	16.4
	Robert F. Murphy (D)	76,577	12.8
	John F. Kennedy (D)[2]	52,972	8.8
1962	**Republican Primary**		
	John A. Volpe (R)		100.0
	Democratic Primary		
	Endicott Peabody (D)	596,553	80.0
	Clement A. Riley (D)	149,499	20.0
1964	**Republican Primary**		
	John A. Volpe (R)		100.0
	Democratic Primary		
	Francis X. Bellotti (D)	363,675	49.6
	Endicott Peabody (D)	336,780	45.9
1966	**Republican Primary**		
	John A. Volpe (R)		100.0
	Democratic Primary		
	Edward J. McCormack (D)	343,381	55.1
	Kenneth P. O'Donnell (D)	279,541	44.9
1970	**Republican Primary**		
	Francis W. Sargent (R)		100.0
	Democratic Primary		
	Kevin H. White (D)	231,605	34.3
	Maurice A. Donahue (D)	218,665	32.4
	Francis X. Bellotti (D)	164,313	24.4
	Kenneth P. O'Donnell (D)	59,970	8.9
1974	**Republican Primary**		
	Francis W. Sargent (R)	124,250	63.3
	Carroll P. Sheehan (R)	71,936	36.7
	Democratic Primary		
	Michael S. Dukakis (D)	444,590	57.7
	Robert H. Quinn (D)	326,385	42.3
1978	**Republican Primary**		
	Francis W. Hatch (R)	141,070	56.0
	Edward F. King (R)	110,932	44.0

	Candidates	Votes	%
	Democratic Primary		
	Edward J. King (D)	442,174	51.1
	Michael S. Dukakis (D)	365,417	42.2
	Barbara Ackermann (D)	58,220	6.7
1982	**Republican Primary**		
	John W. Sears (R)	90,617	50.7
	John R. Lakian (R)	46,675	26.1
	Andrew H. Card (R)	40,899	22.9
	Democratic Primary		
	Michael S. Dukakis (D)	631,911	53.5
	Edward J. King (D)	549,335	46.5
1986	**Republican Primary**		
	Gregory S. Hyatt (R)[3]	31,021	48.2
	Royall H. Switzler (R)	20,802	32.3
	George Kariotis (R)	11,787	18.3
	Democratic Primary		
	Michael S. Dukakis (D)		100.0
1990	**Republican Primary**		
	William F. Weld (R)	270,455	60.5
	Steven D. Pierce (R)	176,184	39.4
	Democratic Primary		
	John Silber (D)	562,222	53.4
	Francis X. Bellotti (D)	459,128	43.6
1994	**Republican Primary**		
	William F. Weld (R)	211,325	99.7
	Democratic Primary		
	Mark Roosevelt (D)	215,061	47.9
	George A. Bachrach (D)	120,567	26.9
	Michael J. Barrett (D)	111,199	24.8

Massachusetts

1. *Fingold died a few days before the primary. Charles Gibbons, supported by the Republican state committee, polled 158,944 sticker and write-in votes, followed by 23,031 for Fingold, whose name remained on the ballot, and 6,535 other write-ins.*

2. *John F. Kennedy of Canton, Mass.; not to be confused with Sen. John F. Kennedy, D-Mass., then a candidate for president.*

3. *Hyatt withdrew after the primary, and Kariotis was substituted by the Republican state central committee.*

MICHIGAN

	Candidates	Votes	%
1956	**Republican Primary**		
	Albert E. Cobo (R)	348,652	69.0
	Donald S. Leonard (R)	156,822	31.0
	Democratic Primary		
	G. Mennen Williams (D)		100.0

Gubernatorial Elections

1958	Republican Primary		
	Paul D. Bagwell (R)		100.0
	Democratic Primary		
	G. Mennen Williams (D)	385,864	85.5
	W. L. Johnson (D)	65,614	14.5
1960	**Republican Primary**		
	Paul D. Bagwell (R)		100.0
	Democratic Primary		
	John B. Swainson (D)	274,743	50.8
	James M. Hare (D)	205,086	37.9
	Edward Connor (D)	60,895	11.3
1962	**Republican Primary**		
	George W. Romney (R)		100.0
	Democratic Primary		
	John B. Swainson (D)		100.0
1964	**Republican Primary**		
	George W. Romney (R)	583,356	87.9
	George N. Higgins (R)	80,608	12.1
	Democratic Primary		
	Neil Staebler (D)		100.0
1966	**Republican Primary**		
	George W. Romney (R)		100.0
	Democratic Primary		
	Zoltan A. Ferency (D)		100.0
1970	**Republican Primary**		
	William G. Milliken (R)	416,491	77.8
	James C. Turner (R)	119,140	22.2
	Democratic Primary		
	Sander Levin (D)	304,343	54.1
	Zolton A. Ferency (D)	167,442	29.8
	George N. Parris (D)	49,559	8.8
	George F. Montgomery (D)	41,218	7.3
	American Independent Primary		
	James L. McCormick (WRITE IN)		
1974	**Republican Primary**		
	William G. Milliken (R)		100.0
	Democratic Primary		
	Sander M. Levin (D)	445,273	61.3
	Jerome P. Cavanagh (D)	199,361	27.4
	James E. Wells (D)	81,844	11.3

	Candidates	Votes	%
1978	**Republican Primary**		
	William G. Milliken (R)		100.0
	Democratic Primary		
	William Fitzgerald (D)	240,641	39.8
	Zolton A. Ferency (D)	151,062	25.0
	Patrick McCullough (D)	108,742	18.0
	William Ralls (D)	104,364	17.2
1982	**Republican Primary**		
	Richard H. Headlee (R)	220,378	34.4
	James H. Brickley (R)	194,429	30.3
	L. Brooks Patterson (R)	180,065	28.1
	Jack Welborn (R)	46,505	7.2
	Democratic Primary		
	James J. Blanchard (D)	406,941	50.2
	William Fitzgerald (D)	138,453	17.1
	David A. Plawecki (D)	95,805	11.8
	Zolton A. Ferency (D)	85,088	10.5
	Edward C. Pierce (D)	44,894	5.5
1986	**Republican Primary**		
	William Lucas (R)	259,153	44.5
	Dick Chrysler (R)	198,174	34.0
	Colleen Engler (R)	63,927	11.0
	Dan Murphy (R)	61,073	10.5
	Democratic Primary		
	James J. Blanchard (D)	428,125	93.7
	Henry Wilson (D)	28,940	6.3
1990	**Republican Primary**		
	John Engler (R)	409,747	86.6
	John Lauve (R)	63,457	13.4
	Democratic Primary		
	James J. Blanchard (D)		100.0
1994	**Republican Primary**		
	John Engler (R)	549,565	99.8
	Democratic Primary		
	Howard Wolpe (D)	242,847	35.2
	Debbie Stabenow (D)	209,641	30.4
	Larry Owen (D)	176,675	25.6
	Lynn Jondahl (D)	59,127	8.6

MINNESOTA[1]

	Candidates	Votes	%
1956	**Republican Primary**		
	Ancher Nelsen (R)	283,844	94.4

Candidates	Votes	%
Democratic Primary		
Orville L. Freeman (DFL)	269,740	*89.5*
1958 Republican Primary		
George MacKinnon (R)	202,833	*85.3*
Glenn B. Brown (R)	34,878	*14.7*
Democratic Primary		
Orville L. Freeman (DFL)	331,822	*87.6*
Harold Strom (DFL)	47,041	*12.4*
1960 Republican Primary		
Elmer L. Andersen (R)		*100.0*
Democratic Primary		
Orville L. Freeman (DFL)	264,571	*88.8*
Belmont Tudisco (DFL)	33,452	*11.2*
1962 Republican Primary		
Elmer L. Andersen (R)		*100.0*
Democratic Primary		
Karl F. Rolvaag (DFL)	271,818	*92.5*
Belmont Tudisco (DFL)	22,042	*7.5*
1966 Republican Primary		
Harold LeVander (R)	276,403	*97.9*
Democratic Primary		
Karl F. Rolvaag (DFL)	336,656	*66.3*
A. M. Keith (DFL)	157,661	*31.0*
1970 Republican Primary		
Douglas M. Head (R)	210,621	*87.5*
John C. Peterson (R)	19,737	*8.2*
Democratic Primary		
Wendell R. Anderson (DFL)		*100.0*
1974 Republican Primary		
John W. Johnson (R)		*100.0*
Democratic Primary		
Wendell R. Anderson (DFL)	254,671	*78.2*
Thomas E. McDonald (DFL)	70,871	*21.8*
1978 Republican Primary		
Albert H. Quie (I-R)	174,799	*83.6*
Robert W. Johnson (I-R)	34,406	*16.4*
Democratic Primary		
Rudy Perpich (DFL)	390,069	*80.0*
Alice Tripp (DFL)	97,247	*20.0*
American Primary		
Richard Pedersen (AM)		*100.0*

	Candidates	Votes	%
1982	**Republican Primary**		
	Wheelock Whitney (I-R)	185,801	*60.1*
	Lou Wangberg (I-R)	105,696	*34.2*
	Harold E. Stassen (I-R)	17,795	*5.7*
	Democratic Primary		
	Rudy Perpich (DFL)	275,920	*51.2*
	Warren Spannaus (DFL)	248,218	*46.1*
1986	**Republican Primary**		
	Cal R. Ludeman (I-R)	147,674	*76.9*
	James H. Lindau (I-R)	30,768	*16.0*
	Democratic Primary		
	Rudy Perpich (DFL)	293,426	*57.5*
	George Latimer (DFL)	207,198	*40.6*
1990	**Republican Primary**		
	Jon Grunseth (I-R)[2]	169,451	*49.4*
	Arne Carlson (I-R)	108,446	*31.6*
	Doug Kelley (I-R)	57,872	*16.9*
	Democratic Primary		
	Rudy Perpich (DFL)	218,410	*55.5*
	Mike Hatch (DFL)	166,183	*42.2*
1994	**Republican Primary**		
	Arne Carlson (I-R)	321,084	*66.5*
	Allen Quist (I-R)	161,670	*33.5*
	Democratic Primary		
	John Marty (DFL)	144,462	*37.8*
	Mike Hatch (DFL)	139,109	*36.4*
	Tony Bouza (DFL)	93,841	*24.6*

Minnesota

1. In Minnesota, the Democratic Party is known as the Democratic-Farmer-Labor Party (DFL). From 1976 to 1994, Republican Party was known as the Independent Republican Party (I-R).

2. Grunseth withdrew after the primary and Carlson was substituted by the state party committee.

MISSISSIPPI

	Candidates	Votes	%
1919	**Democratic Primary**		
	Lee M. Russell (D)	48,348	*32.6*
	Oscar Johnston (D)	39,206	*26.4*
	A. H. Longino (D)	30,831	*20.8*
	Ross A. Collins (D)	30,026	*20.2*
	Democratic Runoff		
	Lee M. Russell (D)	77,427	*52.7*
	Oscar Johnston (D)	69,565	*47.3*

Gubernatorial Elections

	Candidates	Votes	%
1923	**Democratic Primary**		
	Henry L. Whitfield (D)	85,328	33.6
	Theodore G. Bilbo (D)	65,105	25.6
	Martin S. Conner (D)	48,739	19.2
	L. C. Franklin (D)	37,245	14.7
	Percey Bell (D)	17,724	7.0
	Democratic Runoff		
	Henry L. Whitfield (D)	134,715	53.3
	Theodore G. Bilbo (D)	118,143	46.7
1927	**Democratic Primary**		
	Theodore G. Bilbo (D)	135,065	46.9
	Dennis Murphree (D)	71,836	25.0
	Martin S. Conner (D)	57,402	19.9
	A. C. Anderson (D)	23,528	8.2
	Democratic Runoff		
	Theodore G. Bilbo (D)	153,669	52.8
	Dennis Murphree (D)	137,130	47.2
1931	**Democratic Primary**		
	Hugh L. White (D)	108,022	34.5
	Martin S. Conner (D)	92,089	29.4
	Paul B. Johnson (D)	58,668	18.7
	Mitchell (D)	54,202	17.3
	Democratic Runoff		
	Martin S. Conner (D)	170,690	54.1
	Hugh L. White (D)	144,918	45.9
1935	**Democratic Primary**		
	Paul B. Johnson (D)	111,523	31.5
	Hugh L. White (D)	110,825	31.3
	Dennis Murphree (D)	92,997	26.2
	Franklin (D)	34,700	9.8
	Democratic Runoff		
	Hugh L. White (D)	182,771	51.7
	Paul B. Johnson (D)	170,705	48.3
1939	**Democratic Primary**		
	Paul B. Johnson (D)	103,099	33.5
	Martin S. Conner (D)	79,305	25.8
	Thomas L. Bailey (D)	58,987	19.2
	Franklin (D)	31,845	10.4
	Snider (D)	24,244	7.9
	Democratic Runoff		
	Paul B. Johnson (D)	163,620	54.7
	Martin S. Conner (D)	135,724	45.3
1943	**Democratic Primary**		
	Martin S. Conner (D)	110,917	38.8
	Thomas L. Bailey (D)	68,963	24.1
	Dennis Murphree (D)	68,510	24.0
	Franklin (D)	37,240	13.0

	Candidates	Votes	%
	Democratic Runoff		
	Thomas L. Bailey (D)	143,153	53.2
	Martin S. Conner (D)	125,882	46.8
1947	**Democratic Primary**		
	Fielding L. Wright (D)	202,014	55.3
	Paul B. Johnson Jr. (D)	112,123	30.7
	Jesse M. Byrd (D)	37,997	10.4
1951	**Democratic Primary**		
	Hugh L. White (D)	94,820	23.3
	Paul B. Johnson Jr. (D)	86,150	21.1
	Sam Lumpkin (D)	84,451	20.7
	Ross R. Barnett (D)	81,674	20.0
	Mary D. Cain (D)	24,756	6.1
	Jesse M. Byrd (D)	22,783	5.6
	Democratic Runoff		
	Hugh L. White (D)	201,222	51.2
	Paul B. Johnson Jr. (D)	191,966	48.8
1955	**Democratic Primary**		
	Paul B. Johnson Jr. (D)	122,423	28.1
	James P. Coleman (D)	104,140	23.9
	Fielding L. Wright (D)	94,410	21.6
	Ross R. Barnett (D)	92,785	21.3
	Mary D. Cain (D)	22,469	5.2
	Democratic Runoff		
	James P. Coleman (D)	233,237	55.6
	Paul B. Johnson Jr. (D)	185,924	44.4
1959	**Democratic Primary**		
	Ross R. Barnett (D)	155,508	35.3
	Carroll Gartin (D)	151,043	34.3
	Charles L. Sullivan (D)	131,792	29.9
	Democratic Runoff		
	Ross R. Barnett (D)	230,557	54.3
	Carroll Gartin (D)	193,706	45.7
1963	**Republican Primary**		
	Rubel L. Phillips (R)		100.0
	Democratic Primary		
	Paul B. Johnson Jr. (D)	182,540	38.5
	James P. Coleman (D)	156,296	33.0
	Charles L. Sullivan (D)	132,321	27.9
	Democratic Runoff		
	Paul B. Johnson Jr. (D)	261,493	57.3
	James P. Coleman (D)	194,958	42.7
1967	**Republican Primary**		
	Rubel L. Phillips (R)		100.0

Candidates	Votes	%
Democratic Primary		
William Winter (D)	222,001	*32.5*
John Bell Williams (D)	197,778	*28.9*
James E. "Jimmy" Swan (D)	124,361	*18.2*
Ross R. Barnett (D)	76,053	*11.1*
William L. Waller (D)	60,090	*8.8*
Democratic Runoff		
John Bell Williams (D)	371,815	*54.5*
William Winter (D)	310,527	*45.5*

1971 Democratic Primary

Candidates	Votes	%
Charles L. Sullivan (D)	288,219	*37.8*
William L. Waller (D)	227,424	*29.8*
James E. "Jimmy" Swan (D)	128,946	*16.9*
Roy C. Adams (D)	45,445	*6.0*
Ed Pittman (D)	38,170	*5.0*
Democratic Runoff		
William L. Waller (D)	389,952	*54.2*
Charles L. Sullivan (D)	329,236	*45.8*

1975 Democratic Primary

Candidates	Votes	%
William Winter (D)	286,652	*36.3*
Cliff Finch (D)	253,829	*32.1*
Maurice Dantin (D)	179,472	*22.7*
John Arthur Eaves (D)	50,606	*6.4*
Democratic Runoff		
Cliff Finch (D)	442,865	*57.7*
William Winter (D)	324,749	*42.3*

1979 Republican Primary

Candidates	Votes	%
Gil Carmichael (R)	17,216	*53.1*
Leon Bramlett (R)	15,236	*46.9*
Democratic Primary		
Evelyn Gandy (D)	224,746	*30.5*
William Winter (D)	183,944	*25.0*
John A. Eaves (D)	143,411	*19.5*
Jim Herring (D)	135,812	*18.4*
Democratic Runoff		
William Winter (D)	386,174	*56.6*
Evelyn Gandy (D)	295,835	*43.4*

1983 Republican Primary

Candidates	Votes	%
Leon Bramlett (R)		*100.0*
Democratic Primary		
Evelyn Gandy (D)	316,304	*38.2*
William A. Allain (D)	293,348	*35.4*
Mike P. Sturdivant (D)	172,526	*21.0*
Democratic Runoff		
William A. Allain (D)	405,348	*52.4*
Evelyn Gandy (D)	367,953	*47.5*

1987 Republican Primary

Candidates	Votes	%
Jack Reed (R)	14,798	*78.5*
Doug Lemon (R)	4,057	*21.5*
Democratic Primary		
Ray Mabus (D)	304,559	*35.7*
Mike P. Sturdivant (D)	131,180	*16.2*
William L. Waller (D)	105,056	*13.0*
John A. Eaves (D)	98,517	*12.2*
Maurice Dantin (D)	83,603	*10.3*
Ed Pittman (D)	73,667	*9.1*
Democratic Runoff		
Ray Mabus (D)	428,883	*64.3*
Mike P. Sturdivant (D)	238,039	*35.7*

1991 Republican Primary

Candidates	Votes	%
Kirk Fordice (R)	28,411	*44.7*
Pete Johnson (R)	27,561	*43.4*
Bobby Clanton (R)	7,589	*11.9*
Republican Runoff		
Kirk Fordice (R)	31,753	*60.6*
Pete Johnson (R)	20,622	*39.4*
Democratic Primary		
Ray Mabus (D)	368,679	*50.7*
Wayne Dowdy (D)	299,172	*41.2*
George Blair (D)	58,614	*8.1*

1995 Republican Primary

Candidates	Votes	%
Kirk Fordice (R)	117,907	*93.7*
Democratic Primary		
Dick Molpus (D)	396,816	*77.1*
Shawn O'Hara (D)	117,833	*22.9*

MISSOURI

Candidates	Votes	%
1956 Republican Primary		
Lon Hocker (R)	136,388	*66.9*
Joseph M. Whealen (R)	53,811	*26.4*
Winford Sidebotham (R)	13,710	*6.7*
Democratic Primary		
James T. Blair (D)	387,330	*88.1*
Charles A. Lee (D)	34,107	*7.7*
1960 Republican Primary		
Edward G. Farmer (R)	107,637	*54.1*
William B. Ewald (R)	57,953	*29.1*
Harry C. Timmerman (R)	33,388	*16.8*

Gubernatorial Elections

Candidates	Votes	%
Democratic Primary		
John M. Dalton (D)	466,984	86.4
1964 **Republican Primary**		
Ethan Shepley (R)	161,327	75.7
Harry C. Timmerman (R)	17,510	8.2
William B. Ewald (R)	17,170	8.1
Joseph M. Badgett (R)	17,156	8.0
Democratic Primary		
Warren E. Hearnes (D)	334,708	51.9
Hilary A. Bush (D)	283,640	44.0
1968 **Republican Primary**		
Lawrence K. Roos (R)	170,428	76.4
Harry C. Timmerman (R)	41,549	18.6
Harvey F. Euge (R)	10,994	5.0
Democratic Primary		
Warren E. Hearnes (D)	497,056	85.5
Robert B. Curtis (D)	42,971	7.4
Milton Morris (D)	41,506	7.1
1972 **Republican Primary**		
Christopher S. "Kit" Bond (R)	265,467	75.1
Gene McNary (R)	56,652	16.0
R. J. King (R)	21,422	6.1
Democratic Primary		
Edward L. Dowd (D)	265,011	40.8
William S. Morris (D)	152,055	23.4
Joseph P. Teasdale (D)	135,965	20.9
Earl R. Blackwell (D)	72,212	11.1
Non Partisan Primary		
Paul J. Leonard (NON PART)	606	55.4
Charles S. Miller (NON PART)	487	44.6
1976 **Republican Primary**		
Christopher S. "Kit" Bond (R)	286,377	92.0
Harvey F. Euge (R)	24,975	8.0
Democratic Primary		
Joseph P. Teasdale (D)	419,656	48.6
William Cason (D)	340,208	39.4
1980 **Republican Primary**		
Christopher S. "Kit" Bond (R)	223,678	63.5
William Phelps (R)	122,867	34.9
Democratic Primary		
Joseph P. Teasdale (D)	359,263	54.0
James I. Spainhower (D)	294,917	44.3

	Candidates	Votes	%
1984	**Republican Primary**		
	John Ashcroft (R)	245,308	67.4
	Gene McNary (R)	115,516	31.8
	Democratic Primary		
	Kenneth J. Rothman (D)	288,543	56.0
	Mel Carnahan (D)	104,368	20.3
	Norman L. Merrell (D)	97,973	19.0
1988	**Republican Primary**		
	John Ashcroft (R)		100.0
	Democratic Primary		
	Betty C. Hearnes (D)	375,564	81.5
	Lavoy Reed (D)	85,409	18.5
1992	**Republican Primary**		
	William L. Webster (R)	183,968	43.8
	Roy D. Blunt (R)	163,719	39.0
	Wendell Bailey (R)	63,481	15.1
	Democratic Primary		
	Mel Carnahan (D)	388,098	55.4
	Vince Schoemehl (D)	235,652	33.6
	Sharon Rogers (D)	35,104	5.0
1996	**Republican Primary**		
	Margaret Kelly (R)	219,435	77.7
	John M. Swenson (R)	29,675	10.5
	David Andrew Brown (R)	18,755	6.6
	Lester W. "Les" Duggan Jr. (R)	14,448	5.1
	Democratic Primary		
	Mel Carnahan (D)	347,488	81.6
	Ruth Redel (D)	33,452	7.9
	Edwin W. Howald (D)	29,890	7.0
	Libertarian Primary		
	J Mark Ogelsby (LIBERT)	1,627	63.7
	Martin Lindstedt (LIBERT)	926	36.3

MONTANA

	Candidates	Votes	%
1956	**Republican Primary**		
	J. Hugo Aronson (R)		100.0
	Democratic Primary		
	Arnold H. Olsen (D)	55,269	44.9
	John W. Bonner (D)	51,306	41.7
	Danny O'Neill (D)	14,777	12.0

	Candidates	Votes	%
1960	**Republican Primary**		
	Donald G. Nutter (R)	33,099	*50.4*
	Wesley A. D'Ewart (R)	32,538	*49.6*
	Democratic Primary		
	Paul Cannon (D)	44,690	*34.9*
	Jack Toole (D)	40,537	*31.6*
	Mike Kuchera (D)	33,216	*25.9*
	Willard E. Fraser (D)	6,505	*5.1*
1964	**Republican Primary**		
	Tim M. Babcock (R)		*100.0*
	Democratic Primary		
	Roland Renne (D)	71,967	*55.9*
	Mike Kuchera (D)	56,710	*44.1*
1968	**Republican Primary**		
	Tim M. Babcock (R)	50,369	*55.1*
	Ted James (R)	36,664	*40.1*
	Democratic Primary		
	Forrest H. Anderson (D)	39,057	*38.3*
	Eugene H. Mahoney (D)	35,562	*34.9*
	LeRoy Anderson (D)	16,476	*16.2*
	Willard E. Fraser (D)	8,525	*8.3*
1972	**Republican Primary**		
	Ed Smith (R)	39,552	*40.6*
	Frank Dunkle (R)	37,375	*38.4*
	Tom A. Selstad (R)	18,046	*18.5*
	Democratic Primary		
	Thomas L. Judge (D)	75,917	*59.9*
	Dick Dzivi (D)	38,639	*30.5*
1976	**Republican Primary**		
	Robert Woodahl (R)	47,629	*56.7*
	John K. McDonald (R)	36,420	*43.3*
	Democratic Primary		
	Thomas L. Judge (D)		*100.0*
1980	**Republican Primary**		
	Jack Ramirez (R)	48,926	*68.4*
	Al Bishop (R)	14,522	*20.3*
	Florence Haegen (R)	8,118	*11.3*
	Democratic Primary		
	Ted Schwinden (D)	69,051	*50.6*
	Thomas L. Judge (D)	57,946	*42.5*
1984	**Republican Primary**		
	Pat M. Goodover (R)	56,199	*100.0*

	Candidates	Votes	%
	Democratic Primary		
	Ted Schwinden (D)	80,633	*81.4*
	Robert Carlson Kelleher (D)	18,423	*18.6*
1988	**Republican Primary**		
	Stan Stephens (R)	44,022	*50.1*
	Cal Winslow (R)	37,875	*43.1*
	Jim Waltermire (R)[1]	6,024	*6.9*
	Democratic Primary		
	Thomas L. Judge (D)	46,412	*39.3*
	Frank Morrison (D)	32,124	*27.2*
	Mike Greely (D)	26,827	*22.7*
	Ted Neuman (D)	7,297	*6.2*
1992	**Republican Primary**		
	Marc Racicot (R)	68,013	*68.7*
	Andrea Bennett (R)	31,038	*31.3*
	Democratic Primary		
	Dorothy Bradley (D)	54,453	*41.2*
	Mike McGrath (D)	44,323	*33.5*
	Frank Morrison (D)	23,883	*18.1*
1996	**Republican Primary**		
	Marc Racicot (R)	92,644	*76.4*
	Rob Natelson (R)	28,672	*23.6*
	Democratic Primary		
	Chet Blaylock (D)[2]	55,120	*74.6*
	Bob Kelleher (D)	18,761	*25.4*

Montana
1. *Waltermire died two months before the primary.*
2. *Blaylock died Oct. 23 and was succeeded as the party's gubernatorial candidate by Judy Jacobson.*

NEBRASKA

	Candidates	Votes	%
1956	**Republican Primary**		
	Victor E. Anderson (R)	86,168	*82.6*
	Edwin L. Hart (R)	18,202	*17.4*
	Democratic Primary		
	Frank Sorrell (D)	43,301	*69.9*
	Ted Baum (D)	18,667	*30.1*
1958	**Republican Primary**		
	Victor E. Anderson (R)	90,150	*76.4*
	Louis H. Hector (R)	27,768	*23.5*
	Democratic Primary		
	Ralph G. Brooks (D)	37,816	*54.8*
	Edward A. Dosek (D)	31,221	*45.2*

Gubernatorial Elections

	Candidates	Votes	%
1960	**Republican Primary**		
	John R. Cooper (R)	61,286	*37.7*
	Hazel Abel (R)	39,109	*24.1*
	Terry Carpenter (R)	25,659	*15.8*
	Dwain Williams (R)	23,545	*14.5*
	Del Lienemann (R)	9,390	*5.8*
	Democratic Primary		
	Frank B. Morrison (D)	51,335	*48.0*
	Robert Conrad (D)	44,486	*41.6*
	Charles A. Bates (D)	5,477	*5.1*
1962	**Republican Primary**		
	Fred A. Seaton (R)	130,816	*85.3*
	George A. Clarke (R)	17,368	*11.3*
	Democratic Primary		
	Frank B. Morrison (D)	78,817	*76.6*
	Mrs. Ralph G. Brooks (D)	15,565	*15.1*
	Tony Mangiamelli (D)	8,464	*8.3*
1964	**Republican Primary**		
	Dwight W. Burney (R)	82,256	*58.8*
	Jack Romans (R)	44,102	*31.5*
	Democratic Primary		
	Frank B. Morrison (D)	83,362	*88.8*
	Charles A. Bates (D)	6,543	*7.0*
1966	**Republican Primary**		
	Norbert T. Tiemann (R)	78,338	*44.0*
	Val Peterson (R)	63,589	*35.7*
	Bruce Hagemeister (R)	22,574	*12.7*
	Henry E. Kuhlmann (R)	12,052	*6.8*
	Democratic Primary		
	Philip C. Sorensen (D)	65,051	*56.8*
	J. W. Burbach (D)	35,439	*30.9*
	Henry E. Ley (D)	13,819	*12.1*
1970	**Republican Primary**		
	Norbert T. Tiemann (R)	97,616	*50.5*
	Clifton B. Batchelder (R)	89,355	*46.2*
	Democratic Primary		
	J. James Exon (D)	54,783	*44.6*
	J. W. Burbach (D)	51,760	*42.2*
	Richard R. Larsen (D)	15,602	*12.7*
1974	**Republican Primary**		
	Richard D. Marvel (R)		*100.0*
	Democratic Primary		
	J. James Exon (D)	125,690	*87.4*
	Richard D. Schmitz (D)	17,889	*12.4*
1978	**Republican Primary**		
	Charles Thone (R)	89,378	*45.3*
	Robert A. Phares (R)	48,402	*24.5*

	Candidates	Votes	%
	Stanley R. Juelfs (R)	43,828	*22.2*
	Vance D. Rogers (R)	14,076	*7.1*
	Democratic Primary		
	Gerald T. Whelan (D)	104,178	*79.4*
	Robert V. Hansen (D)	26,509	*20.2*
1982	**Republican Primary**		
	Charles Thone (R)	115,750	*62.5*
	Stan DeBoer (R)	55,983	*30.2*
	Barton E. Chandler (R)	13,086	*7.1*
	Democratic Primary		
	Bob Kerrey (D)	87,913	*71.0*
	George Burrows (D)	35,426	*28.6*
1986	**Republican Primary**		
	Kay Orr (R)	75,914	*39.4*
	Kermit Brashear (R)	60,308	*31.3*
	Nancy Hoch (R)	42,649	*22.1*
	Democratic Primary		
	Helen Boosalis (D)	63,833	*44.0*
	David A. Domina (D)	37,975	*26.2*
	Chris Beutler (D)	31,605	*21.8*
1990	**Republican Primary**		
	Kay Orr (R)	130,045	*68.1*
	Mort Sullivan (R)	59,048	*30.9*
	Democratic Primary[1]		
	Ben Nelson (D)	44,721	*26.8*
	Bill Hoppner (D)	44,679	*26.7*
	Mike Boyle (D)	41,227	*24.7*
	Bill Harris (D)	31,527	*18.9*
1994	**Republican Primary**		
	Gene Spence (R)	69,529	*38.1*
	Ralph Knobel (R)	57,719	*31.6*
	Alan Jacobsen (R)	27,374	*15.0*
	John DeCamp (R)	24,414	*13.4*
	Democratic Primary		
	Ben Nelson (D)	101,422	*88.1*
	Robert F. Winingar (D)	6,993	*6.1*
	Robb Nimic (D)	6,373	*5.5*

Nebraska

1. The figures for Nelson and Hoppner are for the recount.

NEVADA

	Candidates	Votes	%
1958	**Republican Primary**		
	Charles H. Russell (R)		*100.0*
	Democratic Primary		
	Grant Sawyer (D)	20,711	*46.3*
	Harvey Dickerson (D)	13,372	*29.9*
	George E. Franklin (D)	10,175	*22.7*

	Candidates	Votes	%
1962	**Republican Primary**		
	Oran K. Gragson (R)	16,538	64.3
	H. M. Greenspun (R)	9,176	35.7
	Democratic Primary		
	Grant Sawyer (D)	40,168	81.4
	Gene Austin (D)	5,017	10.2
1966	**Republican Primary**		
	Paul Laxalt (R)	32,768	94.7
	John P. Screen (R)	1,834	5.3
	Democratic Primary		
	Grant Sawyer (D)	40,982	58.6
	Edward G. Marshall (D)	13,858	19.8
	Charles E. Springer (D)	13,270	19.0
1970	**Republican Primary**		
	Ed Fike (R)	31,931	88.2
	Margie Dyer (R)	4,281	11.8
	Democratic Primary		
	Mike O'Callaghan (D)	41,185	68.8
	Hank Thornley (D)	16,107	26.9
1974	**Republican Primary**		
	Shirley Crumpler (R)	17,076	49.4
	William Bickerstaff (R)	13,632	39.5
	Gilbert D. Buck (R)	2,405	7.0
	Democratic Primary		
	Mike O'Callaghan (D)	69,089	90.8
1978	**Republican Primary**		
	Robert F. List (R)	39,997	82.4
	William C. Allen (R)	3,038	6.3
	"None of these candidates"[1]	3,570	7.3
	Democratic Primary		
	Robert E. Rose (D)	41,672	48.1
	John Foley (D)	20,186	23.3
	Jack Schofield (D)	18,414	21.3
1982	**Republican Primary**		
	Robert F. List (R)	39,319	57.0
	Mike Moody (R)	13,849	20.1
	"None of these candidates"[1]	13,252	19.2
	Democratic Primary		
	Richard H. Bryan (D)	55,261	51.1
	Myron E. Leavitt (D)	34,783	32.1
	Stan Colton (D)	10,830	10.0

	Candidates	Votes	%
1986	**Republican Primary**		
	Patty Cafferata (R)	31,430	46.1
	Jim Stone (R)	12,296	18.0
	Marcia J. Wines (R)	5,599	8.2
	"None of these candidates"[1]	15,116	22.2
	Democratic Primary		
	Richard H. Bryan (D)	71,920	79.9
	Herb Tobman (D)	13,776	15.3
1990	**Republican Primary**		
	Jim Gallaway (R)	37,467	49.3
	"None of these candidates"[1]	16,565	21.8
	Charlie Brown (R)	16,067	21.1
	Democratic Primary		
	Robert J. Miller (D)	71,537	81.0
	"None of these candidates"[1]	7,394	8.4
1994	**Republican Primary**		
	Jim Gibbons (R)	59,705	51.2
	Cheryl A. Lau (R)	37,749	32.3
	"None of these candidates"[1]	10,391	8.9
	Democratic Primary		
	Robert J. Miller (D)	75,311	62.7
	Jan L. Jones (D)	33,566	27.9
	"None of these candidates"[1]	6,917	5.8

Nevada
1. *Nevada provided space on the ballot for a vote against the candidates listed.*

NEW HAMPSHIRE

	Candidates	Votes	%
1956	**Republican Primary**		
	Lane Dwinell (R)	38,734	53.1
	Wesley Powell (R)	33,408	45.8
	Democratic Primary		
	John Shaw (D)		100.0
1958	**Republican Primary**		
	Wesley Powell (R)	39,761	47.5
	Hugh Gregg (R)	39,365	47.1
	Democratic Primary		
	Bernard L. Boutin (D)	16,646	47.0
	John Shaw (D)	12,783	36.1
	Alfred J. Champagne (D)	4,586	13.0
1960	**Republican Primary**		
	Wesley Powell (R)	49,119	49.9
	Hugh Gregg (R)	48,108	48.8

Gubernatorial Elections

Candidates	Votes	%
Democratic Primary		
Bernard L. Boutin (D)	31,650	77.6
John Shaw (D)	7,151	17.5
1962 Republican Primary		
John Pillsbury (R)	55,784	56.4
Wesley Powell (R)	42,005	42.4
Democratic Primary		
John W. King (D)	27,933	93.2
Elmer E. Bussey (D)	2,039	6.8
1964 Republican Primary		
John Pillsbury (R)	32,200	51.4
Wesley Powell (R)	21,764	34.7
John W. King (WRITE IN)	3,608	5.8
John C. Mongan (R)	3,532	5.6
Democratic Primary		
John W. King (D)		100.0
1966 Republican Primary		
Hugh Gregg (R)	33,946	44.9
James J. Barry (R)	20,791	27.5
Alexander M. Taft (R)	14,845	19.6
Democratic Primary		
John W. King (D)		100.0
1968 Republican Primary		
Walter R. Peterson (R)	29,262	34.1
Wesley Powell (R)	26,498	30.9
Meldrim Thomson (R)	25,275	29.5
Democratic Primary		
Emile R. Bussiere (D)	12,021	32.7
Henry P. Sullivan (D)	10,895	29.6
Vincent P. Dunn (D)	10,412	28.3
1970 Republican Primary		
Walter R. Peterson (R)	43,667	50.9
Meldrim Thomson Jr. (R)	41,392	48.2
Democratic Primary		
Roger J. Crowley (D)	17,089	47.5
Charles F. Whittemore (D)	13,354	37.1
Dennis J. Sullivan (D)	4,747	13.2
1972 Republican Primary		
Meldrim Thomson Jr. (R)	43,611	47.9
Walter R. Peterson (R)	41,252	45.3
Democratic Primary		
Roger J. Crowley (D)	29,326	61.4
Robert E. Raiche (D)	16,216	33.9

	Candidates	Votes	%
1974	**Republican Primary**		
	Meldrim Thomson Jr. (R)	47,244	54.9
	David L. Nixon (R)	37,286	43.3
	Democratic Primary		
	Richard W. Leonard (D)	16,503	37.8
	Harry V. Spanos (D)	14,149	32.4
	Hugh Gallen (D)	13,030	29.8
1976	**Republican Primary**		
	Meldrim Thomson Jr. (R)	52,968	64.6
	Gerald J. Zeiller (R)	26,728	32.6
	Democratic Primary		
	Harry V. Spanos (D)	21,589	41.3
	James A. Connor (D)	15,758	30.2
	Hugh Gallen (D)	13,629	26.1
1978	**Republican Primary**		
	Meldrim Thomson Jr. (R)	45,069	59.7
	Wesley Powell (R)	28,286	37.4
	Democratic Primary		
	Hugh Gallen (D)	26,217	73.0
	Delbert F. Downing (D)	9,688	27.0
1980	**Republican Primary**		
	Meldrim Thomson Jr. (R)	55,554	56.4
	Louis C. D'Allesandro (R)	40,060	40.7
	Democratic Primary		
	Hugh Gallen (D)	37,786	81.3
	Thomas B. Wingate (D)	8,689	18.7
1982	**Republican Primary**		
	John H. Sununu (R)	26,617	31.9
	Robert B. Monier (R)	24,823	29.7
	Louis C. D'Allesandro (R)	24,163	29.0
	Democratic Primary		
	Hugh Gallen (D)		100.0
1984	**Republican Primary**		
	John H. Sununu (R)	52,737	84.1
	James F. Fallon (R)	8,994	14.3
	Democratic Primary		
	Chris Spirou (D)	22,835	49.5
	Paul McEachern (D)	18,460	40.0
	Robert L. Dupay (D)	4,060	8.8
1986	**Republican Primary**		
	John H. Sununu (R)	44,906	77.3
	Roger L. Easton (R)	12,702	21.9

Candidates	Votes	%
Democratic Primary		
Paul McEachern (D)	19,731	*54.6*
Paul M. Gagnon (D)	9,790	*27.1*
Bruce Anderson (D)	5,816	*16.1*
1988 Republican Primary		
Judd Gregg (R)	65,777	*79.0*
Robert F. Shaw (R)	15,133	*18.2*
Democratic Primary		
Paul McEachern (D)		*100.0*
1990 Republican Primary		
Judd Gregg (R)	67,934	*80.8*
Robert A. Bonser (R)	15,207	*18.1*
Democratic Primary		
J. Joseph Grandmaison (D)	22,246	*45.7*
Robert F. Preston (D)	21,653	*44.5*
Paul Blacketor (D)	3,923	*8.1*
1992 Republican Primary		
Steve Merrill (R)	60,809	*52.7*
Edward C. du Pont (R)	25,530	*22.1*
Elizabeth Hager (R)	24,433	*21.2*
Democratic Primary		
Deborah A. Arnesen (D)	41,770	*47.7*
Norman E. D'Amours (D)	23,919	*27.3*
Ned Helms (D)	19,792	*22.6*
1994 Republican Primary		
Steve Merrill (R)	68,340	*87.9*
Fred Bramante (R)	6,623	*8.5*
Democratic Primary		
Wayne D. King (D)	24,867	*89.5*
Libertarian Primary		
Steve Winter (LIBERT)	773	*76.7*
Calvin Warburton (LIBERT)	235	*23.3*
1996 Republican Primary		
Ovide M. Lamontagne (R)	47,628	*46.7*
Bill Zeliff (R)	43,407	*42.5*
Al Rubega (R)	6,062	*5.9*
Democratic Primary		
Jeanne Shaheen (D)	52,293	*85.7*
Sid Lovett (D)	4,289	*7.0*
Libertarian Primary		
Robert Kingsbury (LIBERT)	325	*46.0*
Clarence G. Blevens (LIBERT)	222	*31.4*
Finlay Rotthaus (LIBERT)	159	*22.5*

NEW JERSEY

Candidates	Votes	%
1957 Republican Primary		
Malcolm S. Forbes (R)	216,677	*63.7*
Wayne Dumont (R)	123,350	*36.3*
Democratic Primary		
Robert B. Meyner (D)		*100.0*
1961 Republican Primary		
James P. Mitchell (R)	202,188	*43.7*
Walter H. Jones (R)	160,553	*34.7*
Wayne Dumont (R)	95,761	*20.7*
Democratic Primary		
Richard J. Hughes (D)	222,789	*84.2*
Weldon R. Sheets (D)	21,285	*8.0*
Eugene E. Demarest (D)	20,487	*7.7*
1965 Republican Primary		
Wayne Dumont (R)	167,402	*50.3*
Charles W. Sandman (R)	154,491	*46.5*
Democratic Primary		
Richard J. Hughes (D)	236,518	*90.9*
William J. Clark (D)	23,722	*9.1*
1969 Republican Primary		
William T. Cahill (R)	158,980	*39.3*
Charles W. Sandman (R)	144,877	*35.8*
Harry L. Sears (R)	46,778	*11.6*
Francis X. McDermott (R)	35,503	*8.8*
Democratic Primary		
Robert B. Meyner (D)	173,801	*44.8*
William F. Kelly (D)	87,888	*22.6*
Henry Hellstoski (D)	60,483	*15.6*
D. Louis Tonti (D)	34,810	*9.0*
Ned J. Parsekian (D)	24,908	*6.4*
1973 Republican Primary		
Charles W. Sandman (R)	209,657	*57.5*
William T. Cahill (R)	148,034	*40.6*
Democratic Primary		
Brendan T. Byrne (D)	193,120	*45.3*
Ann Klein (D)	116,705	*27.4*
Ralph C. DeRose (D)	95,085	*22.3*
1977 Republican Primary		
Raymond H. Bateman (R)	196,592	*54.7*
Thomas H. Kean (R)	129,982	*36.2*
C. Robert Sarcone (R)	20,861	*5.8*

	Candidates	Votes	%
	Democratic Primary		
	Brendan T. Byrne (D)	175,448	30.3
	Robert A. Roe (D)	134,116	23.2
	Ralph C. DeRose (D)	99,948	17.3
	James J. Florio (D)	87,743	15.1
	Joseph A. Hoffman (D)	58,835	10.2
1981	**Republican Primary**		
	Thomas H. Kean (R)	122,512	30.7
	Lawrence F. Kramer (R)	83,565	21.0
	Joseph Sullivan (R)	67,651	17.0
	Jim Wallwork (R)	61,816	15.5
	Barry T. Parker (R)	26,040	6.5
	Democratic Primary		
	James J. Florio (D)	164,179	25.9
	Robert A. Roe (D)	98,660	15.6
	Kenneth A. Gibson (D)	95,212	15.0
	Joseph P. Merlino (D)	70,910	11.2
	John J. Degnan (D)	65,844	10.4
	Thomas F. X. Smith (D)	57,479	9.1
1985	**Republican Primary**		
	Thomas H. Kean (R)		100.0
	Democratic Primary		
	Peter Shapiro (D)	101,243	31.0
	John F. Russo (D)	86,827	26.6
	Kenneth A. Gibson (D)	85,293	26.1
	Stephen B. Wiley (D)	27,914	8.6
	Robert J. Del Tufo (D)	19,742	6.0
1989	**Republican Primary**		
	James A. Courter (R)	112,326	29.0
	Cary Edwards (R)	85,313	22.0
	Chuck Hardwick (R)	82,392	21.3
	Bill Gormley (R)	66,430	17.2
	Gerald Cardinale (R)	32,250	8.3
	Democratic Primary		
	James J. Florio (D)	251,979	68.2
	Barbara Boggs Sigmund (D)	61,033	16.5
	Alan J. Karcher (D)	56,311	15.2
1993	**Republican Primary**		
	Christine Todd Whitman (R)	159,765	40.0
	Cary Edwards (R)	131,578	32.9
	Bill Wallwork (R)	96,034	24.0
	Democratic Primary		
	James J. Florio (D)		100.0
1997	**Republican Primary**		
	Christine Todd Whitman (R)	147,731	100.0
	Democratic Primary		
	James McGreevey (D)	148,153	39.9
	Robert E. Andrews (D)	138,160	37.2
	Michael Murphy (D)	79,172	21.3

NEW MEXICO

	Candidates	Votes	%
1956	**Republican Primary**		
	Edwin L. Mechem (R)		100.0
	Democratic Primary		
	John F. Simms (D)	46,722	48.3
	Ingram B. Pickett (D)	43,937	45.4
	Robert F. Stephens (D)	6,067	6.3
1958	**Republican Primary**		
	Edwin L. Mechem (R)		100.0
	Democratic Primary		
	John Burroughs (D)	46,344	43.8
	Joseph A. Bursey (D)	33,623	31.7
	Ingram B. Pickett (D)	18,150	17.1
	Robert C. Dow (D)	5,569	5.2
1960	**Republican Primary**		
	Edwin L. Mechem (R)	29,486	76.0
	Paul W. Robinson (R)	9,331	24.0
	Democratic Primary		
	John Burroughs (D)	66,541	53.7
	Joseph A. Bursey (D)	48,841	39.4
	Thomas E. Holland (D)	8,413	6.8
1962	**Republican Primary**		
	Edwin L. Mechem (R)		100.0
	Democratic Primary		
	Jack M. Campbell (D)	47,873	38.7
	Ed V. Mead (D)	44,385	35.9
	Leo T. Murphy (D)	28,755	23.3
1964	**Republican Primary**		
	Merle H. Tucker (R)		100.0
	Democratic Primary		
	Jack M. Campbell (D)		100.0
1966	**Republican Primary**		
	David F. Cargo (R)	17,836	51.8
	Clifford J. Hawley (R)	16,588	48.2
	Democratic Primary		
	Thomas E. Lusk (D)	85,211	59.9
	John Burroughs (D)	57,143	40.1
1968	**Republican Primary**		
	David F. Cargo (R)	28,014	54.9
	Clifford J. Hawley (R)	23,052	45.1

Candidates	Votes	%
Democratic Primary		
Fabian Chavez (D)	41,348	30.9
Bruce King (D)	24,658	18.4
Calvin Horn (D)	24,376	18.2
Mack Easley (D)	21,436	16.0
Bobby M. Mayfield (D)	19,528	14.6

1970

Candidates	Votes	%
Republican Primary		
Pete V. Domenici (R)	25,881	46.0
Stephen C. Helbing (R)	13,265	23.6
Edward M. Hartman (R)	5,309	9.4
Tom Clear (R)	5,262	9.3
Junio Lopez (R)	4,272	7.6
Democratic Primary		
Bruce King (D)	62,718	48.9
Jack Daniels (D)	47,523	37.1
Alexander F. Sceresse (D)	17,918	14.0

1974

Candidates	Votes	%
Republican Primary		
Joe Skeen (R)	28,227	55.4
John P. Eastham (R)	15,003	29.5
James L. Hughes (R)	4,758	9.3
Walter E. Bruce (R)	2,913	5.7
Democratic Primary		
Jerry Apodaca (D)	45,447	30.6
Tibo J. Chavez (D)	35,090	23.6
Odis Echols (D)	25,760	17.3
Bobby M. Mayfield (D)	22,806	15.3
Drew Cloud (D)	12,707	8.6

1978

Candidates	Votes	%
Republican Primary		
Joe Skeen (R)	38,638	81.2
Philip R. Grant (R)	8,966	18.8
Democratic Primary		
Bruce King (D)	92,432	61.3
Robert E. Ferguson (D)	58,334	38.7

1982

Candidates	Votes	%
Republican Primary		
John B. Irick (R)	35,789	54.5
William A. Sego (R)	27,220	41.5
Democratic Primary		
Toney Anaya (D)	101,077	56.9
Aubrey L. Dunn (D)	60,866	34.3
Fabian Chavez (D)	11,874	6.7

1986

Candidates	Votes	%
Republican Primary		
Garrey E. Carruthers (R)	27,671	31.1
Joseph H. Mercer (R)	23,560	26.4
Colin R. McMillan (R)	19,807	22.2
Frank M. Bond (R)	10,619	11.9
Paul F. Becht (R)	6,566	7.4
Democratic Primary		
Ray B. Pohwell (D)		100.0

1990

Candidates	Votes	%
Republican Primary		
Frank M. Bond (R)	44,928	55.5
Les Houston (R)	27,073	33.4
James A. Caudell (R)	4,681	5.8
Harry F. Kinney (R)	4,289	5.3
Democratic Primary		
Bruce King (D)	95,884	52.9
Paul Bardacke (D)	70,169	38.7

1994

Candidates	Votes	%
Republican Primary		
Gary E. Johnson (R)	32,091	34.5
Dick Cheney (R)	30,811	33.1
John Dendahl (R)	18,007	19.3
David F. Cargo (R)	12,105	13.0
Democratic Primary		
Bruce King (D)	76,039	38.8
Casey E. Luna (D)	71,364	36.4
Jim Baca (D)	48,401	24.7

NEW YORK

Candidates	Votes	%
1970[1] **Republican Primary**		
Nelson A. Rockefeller (R)		100.0
Democratic Primary		
Arthur J. Goldberg (D)	493,295	52.2
Howard J. Samuels (D)	451,703	47.8
Conservative Primary		
Paul L. Adams (C)		100.0
Liberal Primary		
Arthur J. Goldberg (L)		100.0
1974 **Republican Primary**		
Malcolm Wilson (R)		100.0
Democratic Primary		
Hugh L. Carey (D)	600,283	60.8
Howard J. Samuels (D)	387,369	39.2
Conservative Primary		
Malcolm Wilson (C)		100.0
Liberal Primary		
Edward Morrison (L)[2]		100.0
1978 **Republican Primary**		
Perry B. Duryea (R)		100.0

Candidates	Votes	%
Democratic Primary		
Hugh L. Carey (D)	376,457	*52.0*
Mary Anne Krupsak (D)	244,252	*33.7*
Jeremiah B. Bloom (D)	103,479	*14.3*
Conservative Primary		
Perry B. Duryea (C)		*100.0*
Liberal Primary		
Hugh L. Carey (L)		*100.0*
1982 Republican Primary		
Lew Lehrman (R)	464,231	*80.6*
Paul J. Curran (R)	111,814	*19.4*
Democratic Primary		
Mario M. Cuomo (D)	678,900	*52.3*
Edward I. Koch (D)	618,356	*47.7*
Conservative Primary		
Lew Lehrman (R)		*100.0*
Liberal Primary		
Mario M. Cuomo (L)		*100.0*
Right to Life Primary		
Robert J. Bohner (RTL)		*100.0*
1986 Republican Primary		
Andrew P. O'Rouke (R)		*100.0*
Democratic Primary		
Mario M. Cuomo (D)		*100.0*
Conservative Primary		
Andrew P. O'Rouke (C)		*100.0*
Liberal Primary		
Mario M. Cuomo (L)		*100.0*
Right to Life Primary		
Denis E. Dillon (RTL)		*100.0*
1990 Republican Primary		
Pierre A. Rinfret (R)		*100.0*
Democratic Primary		
Mario M. Cuomo (D)		*100.0*
Conservative Primary		
Herbert I. London (C)		*100.0*
Liberal Primary		
Mario M. Cuomo (L)		*100.0*

Candidates	Votes	%
Right to Life Primary		
Louis P. Wein (RTL)		*100.0*
1994 Republican Primary		
George E. Pataki (R)	273,620	*75.6*
Richard M. Rosenbaum (R)	88,302	*24.4*
Democratic Primary		
Mario M. Cuomo (D)	548,762	*79.5*
Lenora B. Fulani (D)	141,918	*20.5*
Conservative Primary		
George E. Pataki (C)	17,649	*78.4*
Robert G. Relph (C)	4,862	*21.6*

New York

1. Until 1970, candidates for state office in New York were nominated by state party conventions or central committees.

2. Morrison withdrew after the primary and the Liberal state committee substituted Hugh L. Carey as the party's nominee.

NORTH CAROLINA

	Candidates	Votes	%
1920	**Democratic Primary**		
	Cameron Morrison (D)	49,070	*38.3*
	O. Max Gardner (D)	48,983	*38.2*
	R. N. Page (D)	30,180	*23.5*
	Democratic Runoff		
	Cameron Morrison (D)	70,332	*53.5*
	O. Max Gardner (D)	61,073	*46.5*
1924	**Democratic Primary**		
	Angus Wilton McLean (D)	151,197	*64.4*
	Josiah W. Bailey (D)	83,573	*35.6*
1928	**Democratic Primary**		
	O. Max Gardner (D)		*100.0*
1932	**Democratic Primary**		
	J. C. B. Ehringhaus (D)	162,498	*42.8*
	R. T. Fountain (D)	115,127	*30.3*
	Allen J. Maxwell (D)	102,032	*26.9*
	Democratic Runoff		
	J. C. B. Ehringhaus (D)	182,005	*51.9*
	R. T. Fountain (D)	168,971	*48.1*
1936	**Democratic Primary**		
	Clyde R. Hoey (D)	193,972	*37.5*
	Ralph McDonald (D)	189,504	*36.7*
	A. H. Graham (D)	126,782	*24.5*

Candidates	Votes	%
Democratic Runoff		
Clyde R. Hoey (D)	266,354	55.4
Ralph McDonald (D)	214,414	44.6
1940 Republican Primary		
Robert H. McNeill (R)	13,190	47.3
Pritchard (R)	11,847	42.7
Hoffman (R)	2,773	10.0
Democratic Primary		
J. Melville Broughton (D)	147,386	31.4
W. P. Horton (D)[1]	105,916	22.6
A. J. Maxwell (D)	102,095	21.8
Lee Gravely (D)	63,030	13.4
Thomas E. Cooper (D)	33,176	7.1
1944 Democratic Primary		
R. Gregg Cherry (D)	185,027	57.5
Ralph McDonald (D)	134,661	41.9
1948 Democratic Primary		
Charles M. Johnson (D)	170,141	40.2
W. Kerr Scott (D)	161,293	38.1
R. Mayne Albright (D)	76,281	18.0
Democratic Runoff		
W. Kerr Scott (D)	217,620	54.4
Charles M. Johnson (D)	182,684	45.6
1952 Democratic Primary		
William B. Umstead (D)	294,170	52.1
Hubert E. Olive (D)	265,675	47.1
1956 Republican Primary		
Kyle Hayes (R)		100.0
Democratic Primary		
Luther H. Hodges (D)	401,082	86.0
Tom Sawyer (D)	29,248	6.3
Harry P. Stokely (D)	24,416	5.2
1960 Republican Primary		
Robert L. Gavin (R)		100.0
Democratic Primary		
Terry Sanford (D)	269,463	41.3
I. Beverly Lake (D)	181,692	27.8
Malcolm B. Seawell (D)	101,148	15.5
John D. Larkins (D)	100,757	15.4
Democratic Runoff		
Terry Sanford (D)	352,133	56.1
I. Beverly Lake (D)	275,905	43.9
1964 Republican Primary		
Robert L. Gavin (R)	53,145	83.3
Charles W. Strong (R)	8,652	13.6

Candidates	Votes	%
Democratic Primary		
Richardson Preyer (D)	281,430	36.6
Dan K. Moore (D)	257,872	33.5
I. Beverly Lake (D)	217,172	28.2
Democratic Runoff		
Dan K. Moore (D)	480,431	62.1
Richardson Preyer (D)	293,863	38.0
1968 Republican Primary		
James C. Gardner (R)	113,584	72.7
John L. Stikley (R)	42,483	27.3
Democratic Primary		
Robert W. Scott (D)	337,368	48.1
J. Melville Broughton Jr. (D)[2]	233,924	33.4
Reginald A. Hawkins (D)	129,808	18.5
1972 Republican Primary		
James C. Gardner (R)	84,906	49.8
James E. Holshouser Jr. (R)	83,637	49.0
Republican Runoff		
James E. Holshouser Jr. (R)	69,916	50.6
James C. Gardner (R)	68,134	49.4
Democratic Primary		
Hargrove "Skipper" Bowles Jr. (D)	367,433	45.5
H. P. "Pat" Taylor (D)	304,910	37.7
Reginald A. Hawkins (D)	65,950	8.2
Wilbur Hobby (D)	58,990	7.3
Democratic Runoff		
Hargrove "Skipper" Bowles Jr. (D)	336,034	54.3
H. P. "Pat" Taylor (D)	282,345	45.7
1976 Republican Primary		
David T. Flaherty (R)	57,663	49.8
Coy C. Privette (R)	37,573	32.4
J. F. Alexander (R)	16,149	13.9
Republican Runoff		
David T. Flaherty (R)	45,661	60.5
Coy C. Privette (R)	29,810	39.5
Democratic Primary		
James B. "Jim" Hunt Jr. (D)	362,102	53.4
Edward M. O'Herron (D)	157,815	23.2
George Wood (D)	121,673	17.9
1980 Republican Primary		
I. Beverly Lake Jr. (R)	119,255	80.8
C. J. Carstens (R)	28,354	19.2
Democratic Primary		
James B. "Jim" Hunt Jr. (D)	524,844	69.6
Robert W. Scott (D)	217,289	28.8

	Candidates	Votes	%
1984	**Republican Primary**		
	James G. Martin (R)	128,714	*91.7*
	Ruby T. Hooper (R)	11,640	*8.3*
	Democratic Primary		
	Rufus Edmisten (D)	295,051	*30.9*
	H. Edward Knox (D)	249,286	*26.1*
	D. M. Faircloth (D)	153,210	*16.0*
	Thomas O. Gilmore (D)	82,299	*8.6*
	James C. Green (D)	80,775	*8.4*
	John Ingram (D)	75,248	*7.9*
	Democratic Runoff		
	Rufus Edmisten (D)	352,351	*51.9*
	H. Edward Knox (D)	326,278	*48.1*
1988	**Republican Primary**		
	James G. Martin (R)		*100.0*
	Democratic Primary		
	Robert B. Jordan (D)	403,145	*79.7*
	Billy Martin (D)	60,770	*12.0*
1992	**Republican Primary**		
	James C. Gardner (R)	215,528	*82.0*
	Ruby T. Hooper (R)	26,179	*10.0*
	Gary M. Dunn (R)	21,256	*8.1*
	Democratic Primary		
	James B. "Jim" Hunt Jr. (D)	459,300	*65.5*
	Lacy H. Thornburg (D)	188,806	*26.9*
1996	**Republican Primary**		
	Robin Hayes (R)	140,351	*50.2*
	Richard Vinroot (R)	127,916	*45.7*
	Democratic Primary		
	James B. "Jim" Hunt Jr. (D)		*100.0*

North Carolina

1. *Horton declined a runoff with Broughton, who became the Democratic nominee.*

2. *J. Melville Broughton Jr. declined a runoff with Scott, who became the Democratic nominee.*

NORTH DAKOTA

	Candidates	Votes	%
1956	**Republican Primary**		
	John E. Davis (R)	55,149	*53.3*
	Ray Schnell (R)	48,296	*46.7*
	Democratic Primary		
	Wallace E. Warner (D)		*100.0*
1958	**Republican Primary**		
	John E. Davis (R)		*100.0*

	Candidates	Votes	%
	Democratic Primary		
	John F. Lord (D)	26,447	*55.4*
	Art Ford (D)	21,271	*44.6*
1960	**Republican Primary**		
	C. P. Dahl (R)	86,900	*77.6*
	Orris G. Nordhougen (R)	25,132	*22.4*
	Democratic Primary		
	William L. Guy (D)		*100.0*
1962	**Republican Primary**		
	Mark Andrews (R)		*100.0*
	Democratic Primary		
	William L. Guy (D)		*100.0*
1964	**Republican Primary**		
	Donald M. Halcrow (R)	43,089	*55.0*
	Robert P. McCarney (R)	35,269	*45.0*
	Democratic Primary		
	William L. Guy (D)		*100.0*
1968	**Republican Primary**		
	Robert P. McCarney (R)	47,324	*52.5*
	Edward W. Doherty (R)	42,845	*47.5*
	Democratic Primary		
	William L. Guy (D)		*100.0*
1972	**Republican Primary**		
	Richard Larsen (R)	66,045	*67.8*
	Robert P. McCarney (R)	31,377	*32.2*
	Democratic Primary		
	Arthur A. Link (D)	29,979	*93.1*
	Edward P. Burns (D)	2,231	*6.9*
1976	**Republican Primary**		
	Richard Elkin (R)	54,427	*81.9*
	Herb Geving (R)	12,013	*18.1*
	Democratic Primary		
	Arthur A. Link (D)		*100.0*
	American Primary		
	Martin Vaaler (AM)		*100.0*
1980	**Republican Primary**		
	Allen I. Olson (R)	60,016	*75.7*
	Orville W. Hagen (R)	19,306	*24.3*
	Democratic Primary		
	Arthur A. Link (D)		*100.0*

	Candidates	Votes	%
1984	**Republican Primary**		
	Allen I. Olson (R)	41,191	*100.0*
	Democratic Primary		
	George A. Sinner (D)	36,461	*87.6*
	Anna Belle Bourgois (D)	5,180	*12.4*
1988	**Republican Primary**		
	Leon L. Mallberg (R)		*100.0*
	Democratic Primary		
	George A. Sinner (D)		*100.0*
1992	**Republican Primary**		
	Edward T. Schafer (R)	47,300	*100.0*
	Democratic Primary		
	Nicholas Spaeth (D)	50,607	*65.1*
	Bill Heigaard (D)	27,161	*34.9*
1996	**Republican Primary**		
	Edward T. Schafer (R)	48,412	*100.0*
	Democratic Primary		
	Lee Kaldor (D)	46,049	*100.0*

OHIO

	Candidates	Votes	%
1956	**Republican Primary**		
	C. William O'Neill (R)	425,947	*72.5*
	John W. Brown (R)	161,826	*27.5*
	Democratic Primary		
	Michael V. DiSalle (D)	279,831	*57.4*
	John E. Sweeney (D)	106,071	*21.8*
	Robert W. Reider (D)	41,224	*8.5*
	Frank X. Kryzan (D)	37,290	*7.6*
1958	**Republican Primary**		
	C. William O'Neill (R)	346,660	*63.6*
	Charles P. Taft (R)	198,173	*36.4*
	Democratic Primary		
	Michael V. DiSalle (D)	242,830	*37.7*
	Anthony J. Celebrezze (D)	140,453	*21.8*
	Albert S. Porter (D)	108,498	*16.8*
	Robert N. Gorman (D)	57,694	*9.0*
	M. E. Sensenbrenner (D)	52,350	*8.1*
	Clingan Jackson (D)	35,175	*5.5*
1962	**Republican Primary**		
	James A. Rhodes (R)	520,868	*89.6*
	William L. White (R)	59,916	*10.3*

	Candidates	Votes	%
	Democratic Primary		
	Michael V. DiSalle (D)	331,463	*50.3*
	Mark McElroy (D)	299,207	*45.4*
1966	**Republican Primary**		
	James A. Rhodes (R)	577,827	*88.7*
	William L. White (R)	73,428	*11.3*
	Democratic Primary		
	Frazier Reams Jr. (D)	326,419	*58.5*
	Harry H. McIlwain (D)	231,406	*41.5*
1970	**Republican Primary**		
	Roger Cloud (R)	468,369	*50.5*
	Donald E. Lukens (R)	283,257	*30.5*
	Paul W. Brown (R)	164,672	*17.7*
	Democratic Primary		
	John J. Gilligan (D)	547,675	*59.7*
	Robert E. Sweeney (D)	216,195	*23.6*
	Mark McElroy (D)	153,702	*16.7*
	American Independent Primary		
	Edwin G. Lawton (AMI)	3,463	*64.9*
	Robert W. Annable (AMI)	1,870	*35.1*
1974	**Republican Primary**		
	James A. Rhodes (R)	385,669	*62.8*
	Charles E. Fry (R)	183,899	*29.9*
	Bert Dawson (R)	44,938	*7.3*
	Democratic Primary		
	John J. Gilligan (D)	713,488	*70.6*
	James D. Nolan (D)	297,244	*29.4*
1978	**Republican Primary**		
	James A. Rhodes (R)	393,632	*67.7*
	Charles F. Kurfess (R)	187,544	*32.3*
	Democratic Primary		
	Richard F. Celeste (D)	491,524	*84.6*
	Dale Reusch (D)	88,314	*15.2*
1982	**Republican Primary**		
	Clarence Brown Jr. (R)	347,176	*51.5*
	Seth Taft (R)	153,806	*22.8*
	Thomas A. Van Meter (R)	136,761	*20.3*
	Robert W. Teater (R)	35,821	*5.3*
	Democratic Primary		
	Richard F. Celeste (D)	436,887	*42.4*
	William J. Brown (D)	383,007	*37.2*
	Jerry Springer (D)	210,524	*20.4*
	Libertarian Primary		
	Phyllis Goetz (LIBERT)		*100.0*

	Candidates	Votes	%
1986	**Republican Primary**		
	James A. Rhodes (R)	352,261	*48.2*
	Paul E. Gillmor (R)	281,737	*38.5*
	Paul E. Pfeifer (R)	96,948	*13.3*
	Democratic Primary		
	Richard F. Celeste (D)		*100.0*
1990	**Republican Primary**		
	George Voinovich (R)		*100.0*
	Democratic Primary		
	Anthony J. Celebrezze (D)	683,932	*83.9*
	Michael H. Lord (D)	131,564	*16.1*
1994	**Republican Primary**		
	George Voinovich (R)	750,779	*100.0*
	Democratic Primary		
	Robert L. Burch (D)	408,159	*58.8*
	Peter M. Schuller (D)	286,275	*41.2*

OKLAHOMA

	Candidates	Votes	%
1958	**Republican Primary**		
	Phil Ferguson (R)	31,602	*51.4*
	Clarence E. Barnes (R)	21,075	*34.3*
	Carmon C. Harris (R)	5,941	*9.7*
	Democratic Primary		
	J. Howard Edmondson (D)	108,358	*21.1*
	W. P. Atkinson (D)	107,616	*20.9*
	George Miskovsky (D)	87,766	*17.1*
	William O. Coe (D)	72,763	*14.2*
	Bill Doenges (D)	57,990	*11.3*
	Jim A. Rinehart (D)	39,279	*7.6*
	Democratic Runoff		
	J. Howard Edmondson (D)	363,742	*69.6*
	W. P. Atkinson (D)	158,780	*30.4*
1962	**Republican Primary**		
	Henry L. Bellmon (R)	56,560	*91.4*
	Leslie C. Skoien (R)	5,313	*8.6*
	Democratic Primary		
	Raymond Gary (D)	176,525	*33.0*
	W. P. Atkinson (D)	91,182	*17.1*
	Preston J. Moore (D)	85,248	*16.0*
	George Nigh (D)	84,404	*15.8*
	Fred R. Harris (D)	78,476	*14.7*

	Candidates	Votes	%
	Democratic Runoff		
	W. P. Atkinson (D)	231,994	*50.0*
	Raymond Gary (D)	231,545	*49.9*
1966	**Republican Primary**		
	Dewey F. Bartlett (R)	46,053	*49.0*
	John N. H. Camp (R)	45,185	*48.1*
	Democratic Primary		
	Raymond Gary (D)	160,825	*31.6*
	Preston J. Moore (D)	104,081	*20.4*
	David Hall (D)	94,309	*18.5*
	Cleeta J. Rogers (D)	71,248	*14.0*
	Charles Nesbitt (D)	26,546	*5.2*
	Republican Runoff		
	Dewey F. Bartlett (R)	46,916	*55.2*
	John N. H. Camp (R)	38,043	*44.8*
	Democratic Runoff		
	Preston J. Moore (D)	228,625	*53.7*
	Raymond Gary (D)	196,835	*46.3*
1970	**Republican Primary**		
	Dewey F. Bartlett (R)		*100.0*
	Democratic Primary		
	David Hall (D)	198,976	*49.5*
	Bryce Baggett (D)	96,069	*23.9*
	Joe Cannon (D)	56,842	*14.1*
	Wilburn Cartwright (D)	50,396	*12.5*
	Democratic Runoff		
	David Hall (D)	179,902	*57.5*
	Bryce Baggett (D)	132,952	*42.5*
1974	**Republican Primary**		
	James M. Inhofe (R)	88,594	*58.8*
	Denzil D. Garrison (R)	62,188	*41.2*
	Democratic Primary		
	Clem R. McSpadden (D)	238,534	*37.7*
	David L. Boren (D)	225,321	*35.6*
	David Hall (D)	169,290	*26.7*
	Democratic Runoff		
	David L. Boren (D)	286,171	*53.5*
	Clem R. McSpadden (D)	248,623	*46.5*
1978	**Republican Primary**		
	Ron Shotts (R)	82,895	*76.8*
	Jerry L. Mash (R)	13,145	*12.2*
	Jim Head (R)	11,826	*11.0*
	Democratic Primary		
	George Nigh (D)	276,910	*49.9*
	Larry Derryberry (D)	208,055	*37.5*
	Bob Funston (D)	69,475	*12.5*

Candidates	Votes	%
Democratic Runoff		
George Nigh (D)	269,681	*57.7*
Larry Derryberry (D)	197,457	*42.3*

1982

Candidates	Votes	%
Republican Primary		
Tom Daxon (R)	73,677	*64.7*
Neal A. McCaleb (R)	35,379	*31.1*
Democratic Primary		
George Nigh (D)	379,301	*82.6*
Howard L. Bell (D)	79,735	*17.4*

1986

Candidates	Votes	%
Republican Primary		
Henry L. Bellmon (R)	111,665	*70.3*
Mike Fair (R)	33,266	*20.9*
Democratic Primary		
David Walters (D)	238,165	*46.0*
Mike Turpen (D)	207,357	*40.0*
Leslie Fisher (D)	33,639	*6.5*
Democratic Runoff		
David Walters (D)	235,373	*50.4*
Mike Turpen (D)	231,390	*49.6*

1990

Candidates	Votes	%
Republican Primary		
Vince Orza (R)	75,992	*40.1*
Bill Price (R)	51,355	*27.1*
Burns Hargis (R)	33,641	*17.8*
Jerry Brown (R)	25,670	*13.5*
Republican Runoff		
Bill Price (R)	94,682	*50.8*
Vince Orza (R)	91,599	*49.2*
Democratic Primary		
Wes Watkins (D)	175,568	*32.3*
David Walters (D)	171,730	*31.6*
Steve Lewis (D)	160,455	*29.5*
Democratic Runoff		
David Walters (D)	243,252	*50.7*
Wes Watkins (D)	236,597	*49.3*

1994

Candidates	Votes	%
Republican Primary		
Frank Keating (R)	117,265	*56.9*
Jerry Pierce (R)	60,280	*29.3*
Virginia Hale (R)	15,229	*7.4*
Democratic Primary		
Jack Mildren (D)	214,765	*48.6*
Bernice Shedrick (D)	165,066	*37.3*
Danny Williams (D)	46,571	*10.5*

OREGON

	Candidates	Votes	%
1956	**Republican Primary**		
	Elmo E. Smith (R)	225,748	*91.0*
	Earl L. Dickson (R)	22,306	*9.0*
	Democratic Primary		
	Robert D. Holmes (D)	112,307	*50.8*
	Lew Wallace (D)	108,822	*49.2*
1958	**Republican Primary**		
	Mark O. Hatfield (R)	106,687	*47.9*
	Sig Unander (R)	65,180	*29.2*
	Warren Gill (R)	40,489	*18.2*
	Democratic Primary		
	Robert D. Holmes (D)	129,491	*62.0*
	Lew Wallace (D)	59,992	*28.7*
	Wiley W. Smith (D)	18,484	*8.8*
1962	**Republican Primary**		
	Mark O. Hatfield (R)	174,811	*82.2*
	George Altvater (R)	37,306	*17.5*
	Democratic Primary		
	Robert Y. Thornton (D)	149,000	*66.2*
	Walter J. Pearson (D)	62,331	*27.7*
1966	**Republican Primary**		
	Tom McCall (R)	215,959	*91.4*
	John L. Reynolds (R)	20,286	*8.6*
	Democratic Primary		
	Robert W. Straub (D)	182,697	*72.5*
	Ben Musa (D)	41,610	*16.5*
	Emmet T. Rogers (D)	17,618	*7.0*
1970	**Republican Primary**		
	Tom McCall (R)	183,298	*74.4*
	Robert H. Wampler (R)	38,322	*15.6*
	Andrew R. Gigler (R)	24,797	*10.1*
	Democratic Primary		
	Robert W. Straub (D)	182,683	*65.9*
	Art Pearl (D)	33,716	*12.2*
	Gracie Hansen (D)	20,329	*7.3*
	Al Holdiman (D)	18,180	*6.6*
1974	**Republican Primary**		
	Victor G. Atiyeh (R)	144,454	*60.7*
	Clay Myers (R)	79,003	*33.2*
	Democratic Primary		
	Robert W. Straub (D)	107,205	*33.6*
	Betty Roberts (D)	98,654	*30.9*
	Jim Redden (D)	88,795	*27.8*

	Candidates	Votes	%
1978	**Republican Primary**		
	Victor G. Atiyeh (R)	115,593	*46.4*
	Tom McCall (R)	83,568	*33.5*
	Roger Martin (R)	42,644	*17.1*
	Democratic Primary		
	Robert W. Straub (D)	144,761	*51.0*
	Marvin J. Hollingsworth (D)	52,901	*18.7*
	Emily Ashworth (D)	49,201	*17.3*
1982	**Republican Primary**		
	Victor G. Atiyeh (R)	208,333	*82.4*
	Clif Everett (R)	17,741	*7.0*
	Walter Huss (R)	16,892	*6.7*
	Democratic Primary		
	Ted Kulongoski (D)	186,580	*59.5*
	Don Clark (D)	60,850	*19.4*
	Jerry Rust (D)	22,962	*7.3*
1986	**Republican Primary**		
	Norma Paulus (R)	219,505	*77.0*
	Betty Freauf (R)	36,384	*12.8*
	Democratic Primary		
	Neil Goldschmidt (D)	214,148	*67.4*
	Edward N. Fadeley (D)	81,300	*25.6*
1990	**Republican Primary**		
	Dave Frohnmayer (R)	227,867	*79.1*
	John K. Lim (R)	32,397	*11.2*
	Democratic Primary		
	Barbara Roberts (D)		*100.0*
1994	**Republican Primary**		
	Denny Smith (R)	135,330	*49.5*
	Craig Berkman (R)	110,821	*40.5*
	Jack Feder (R)	15,055	*5.5*
	Democratic Primary		
	John Kitzhaber (D)	250,514	*88.5*
	Paul D. Wells (D)	30,052	*10.6*

PENNSYLVANIA

	Candidates	Votes	%
1958	**Republican Primary**		
	A. T. McGonigle (R)	578,286	*53.3*
	Harold E. Stassen (R)	344,043	*31.7*
	William S. Livengood (R)	138,284	*12.7*
	Democratic Primary		
	David Lawrence (D)	730,229	*74.4*
	Roy E. Furman (D)	194,464	*19.8*
	Edward P. Lavelle (D)	56,188	*5.7*

	Candidates	Votes	%
1962	**Republican Primary**		
	William W. Scranton (R)	743,785	*78.0*
	J. Collins McSparran (R)	209,041	*21.9*
	Democratic Primary		
	Richardson Dilworth (D)	651,096	*72.9*
	Harvey F. Johnston (D)	143,243	*16.0*
	Charles J. Schmitt (D)	96,899	*10.9*
1966	**Republican Primary**		
	Raymond P. Shafer (R)	835,768	*78.0*
	Harold E. Stassen (R)	172,150	*16.1*
	George J. Brett (R)	63,366	*5.9*
	Democratic Primary		
	Milton Shapp (D)	543,057	*48.6*
	Robert P. Casey (D)	493,886	*44.2*
	Erwin L. Murray (D)	80,803	*7.2*
1970	**Republican Primary**		
	Raymond Broderick (R)		*100.0*
	Democratic Primary		
	Milton Shapp (D)	519,161	*49.1*
	Robert P. Casey (D)	480,944	*45.5*
	American Independent Primary		
	Francis T. McGeever (AMI)		*100.0*
	Constitutional Primary		
	Andrew J. Watson (CST)		*100.0*
1974	**Republican Primary**		
	Andrew L. Lewis (R)	534,637	*76.9*
	Alvin J. Jacobson (R)	97,072	*14.0*
	Leonard M. Strunk (R)	63,868	*9.2*
	Democratic Primary		
	Milton Shapp (D)	729,201	*70.4*
	Martin P. Mullen (D)	199,613	*19.3*
	Harvey F. Johnston (D)	106,474	*10.3*
	Constitutional Primary		
	Stephen Depue (CST)	1,006	*52.8*
	Norah M. Cope (CST)	898	*47.2*
1978	**Republican Primary**		
	Richard L. Thornburgh (R)	325,376	*32.6*
	Arlen Specter (R)	206,802	*20.7*
	Bob Butera (R)	190,653	*19.1*
	David W. Marston (R)	161,813	*16.2*
	Henry Hager (R)	57,119	*5.7*
	Democratic Primary		
	Peter Flaherty (D)	574,889	*44.9*
	Robert P. Casey (D)	445,146	*34.7*
	Ernest P. Kline (D)	223,811	*17.5*

	Candidates	Votes	%
1982	**Republican Primary**		
	Richard L. Thornburgh (R)		100.0
	Democratic Primary		
	Allen E. Ertel (D)	436,251	57.6
	Steve Douglas (D)	143,762	19.0
	Earl S. McDowell (D)	116,880	15.4
	Eugene Knox (D)	59,925	7.9
1986	**Republican Primary**		
	William W. Scranton (R)		100.0
	Democratic Primary		
	Robert Casey (D)	549,376	56.4
	Edward G. Rendell (D)	385,539	39.6
1990	**Republican Primary**		
	Barbara Hafer (R)	321,026	54.4
	Marguerite A. Luksik (R)	268,773	45.6
	Democratic Primary		
	Robert Casey (D)	636,594	77.5
	Philip J. Berg (D)	184,365	22.5
1994	**Republican Primary**		
	Tom J. Ridge (R)	344,708	34.6
	Ernie Preate (R)	287,400	28.8
	Sam Katz (R)	156,895	15.7
	Mike Fisher (R)	139,712	14.0
	John F. Perry (R)	68,069	6.8
	Democratic Primary		
	Mark S. Singel (D)	346,334	31.2
	Dwight Evans (D)	234,285	21.1
	Catherine B. Knoll (D)	217,267	19.6
	Lynn Yeakel (D)	153,966	13.9
	Charles Vope (D)	122,627	11.0

RHODE ISLAND

	Candidates	Votes	%
1956	**Republican Primary**		
	Christopher Del Sesto (R)		100.0
	Democratic Primary		
	Dennis J. Roberts (D)		100.0
1958	**Republican Primary**		
	Christopher Del Sesto (R)		100.0
	Democratic Primary		
	Dennis J. Roberts (D)	53,121	56.1
	Armand H. Coté (D)	41,536	43.9

	Candidates	Votes	%
1960	**Republican Primary**		
	Christopher Del Sesto (R)		100.0
	Democratic Primary		
	John A. Notte (D)	73,607	56.3
	Armand H. Coté (D)	57,200	43.7
1962	**Republican Primary**		
	John H. Chafee (R)	17,756	62.5
	Louis Jackvony (R)	10,459	36.8
	Democratic Primary		
	John A. Notte (D)	49,204	53.1
	Kevin Coleman (D)	41,658	45.0
1964	**Republican Primary**		
	John H. Chafee (R)		100.0
	Democratic Primary		
	Edward P. Gallogly (D)	55,282	56.7
	Alexander R. Walsh (D)	25,457	26.1
	John L. Rego (D)	16,715	17.2
1966	**Republican Primary**		
	John H. Chafee (R)		100.0
	Democratic Primary		
	Horace E. Hobbs (D)		100.0
1968	**Republican Primary**		
	John H. Chafee (R)		100.0
	Democratic Primary		
	Frank Licht (D)		100.0
1970	**Republican Primary**		
	Herbert F. DeSimone (R)	11,826	96.0
	Democratic Primary		
	Frank Licht (D)		100.0
1972	**Republican Primary**		
	Herbert F. DeSimone (R)		100.0
	Democratic Primary		
	Philip W. Noel (D)		100.0
1974	**Republican Primary**		
	James W. Nugent (R)		100.0
	Democratic Primary		
	Philip W. Noel (D)		100.0
1976	**Republican Primary**		
	James L. Taft (R)		100.0

139

	Candidates	Votes	%
	Democratic Primary		
	J. Joseph Garrahy (D)	113,625	*82.4*
	Giovani Folcarelli (D)	24,314	*17.6*
1978	**Republican Primary**		
	Lincoln Almond (R)		*100.0*
	Democratic Primary		
	J. Joseph Garrahy (D)		*100.0*
1982	**Republican Primary**		
	Vincent Marzullo (R)		*100.0*
	Democratic Primary		
	J. Joseph Garrahy (D)		*100.0*
1984	**Republican Primary**		
	Edward D. DiPrete (R)	245,059	*100.0*
	Democratic Primary		
	Anthony J. Solomon (D)	73,090	*57.9*
	Joseph W. Walsh (D)	53,041	*42.0*
1986	**Republican Primary**		
	Edward D. DiPrete (R)		*100.0*
	Democratic Primary		
	Bruce G. Sundlun (D)	43,120	*75.3*
	Steve White (D)	14,124	*24.7*
1988	**Republican Primary**		
	Edward D. DiPrete (R)		*100.0*
	Democratic Primary		
	Bruce G. Sundlun (D)	68,065	*90.3*
	Peter Van Daam (D)	7,328	*9.7*
1990	**Republican Primary**		
	Edward D. DiPrete (R)	7,644	*70.8*
	Steve White (R)	3,157	*29.2*
	Democratic Primary		
	Bruce G. Sundlun (D)	68,021	*40.5*
	Francis X. Flaherty (D)	53,821	*32.1*
	Joseph R. Paolino (D)	46,074	*27.4*
1992	**Republican Primary**		
	Elizabeth Ann Leonard (R)	7,534	*52.1*
	J. Michael Levesque (R)	6,926	*47.9*
	Democratic Primary		
	Bruce G. Sundlun (D)	78,735	*52.2*
	Francis X. Flaherty (D)	72,011	*47.8*
1994	**Republican Primary**		
	Lincoln C. Almond (R)	24,873	*57.8*
	Ronald K. Machtley (R)	18,150	*42.2*

Candidates	Votes	%
Democratic Primary		
Myrth York (D)	56,719	*57.2*
Bruce G. Sundlun (D)	27,432	*27.7*
Louise Durfee (D)	11,914	*12.0*

SOUTH CAROLINA

	Candidates	Votes	%
1920	**Democratic Primary**		
	Robert A. Cooper (D)		*100.0*
1922	**Democratic Primary**		
	Coleman L. Blease (D)	77,798	*44.8*
	Thomas G. McLeod (D)	65,768	*37.9*
	George K. Laney (D)	23,164	*13.4*
	Democratic Runoff		
	Thomas G. McLeod (D)	100,114	*53.8*
	Coleman L. Blease (D)	85,834	*46.2*
1924[1]	**Democratic Primary**		
	Thomas G. McLeod (D)	107,356	*61.2*
	J. T. Duncan (D)	68,155	*38.8*
1926	**Democratic Primary**		
	John G. Richards (D)	44,806	*25.8*
	Ibra C. Blackwood (D)	34,870	*20.1*
	Edmund B. Jackson (D)	33,804	*19.5*
	Carroll D. Nance (D)	16,970	*9.8*
	George K. Laney (D)	13,386	*7.7*
	Thomas H. Peeples (D)	10,636	*6.1*
	D. A. G. Ouzts (D)	10,570	*6.1*
	Democratic Runoff		
	John G. Richards (D)	95,007	*58.2*
	Ibra C. Blackwood (D)	68,224	*41.8*
1930	**Democratic Primary**		
	Olin D. Johnston (D)	58,653	*24.9*
	Ibra C. Blackwood (D)	43,859	*18.6*
	Lever (D)	39,477	*16.8*
	Williams (D)	36,488	*15.5*
	Keith (D)	28,780	*12.2*
	Herbert (D)	17,102	*7.3*
	Democratic Runoff		
	Ibra C. Blackwood (D)	118,721	*50.2*
	Olin D. Johnston (D)	117,752	*49.8*
1934	**Democratic Primary**		
	Olin D. Johnston (D)	104,799	*35.2*
	Coleman L. Blease (D)	85,795	*28.9*
	Wyndham Manning (D)	55,767	*18.8*
	Pearce (D)	36,328	*12.2*

Candidates	Votes	%
Democratic Runoff		
Olin D. Johnston (D)	157,673	*56.2*
Coleman L. Blease (D)	122,876	*43.8*

1938   **Democratic Primary**

Candidates	Votes	%
Burnet R. Maybank (D)	177,900	*44.9*
Wyndham Manning (D)	74,356	*18.8*
Coleman L. Blease (D)	60,823	*15.4*
Bennett (D)	47,882	*12.1*
Adams (D)	26,376	*6.7*

Democratic Runoff

Candidates	Votes	%
Burnet R. Maybank (D)	163,947	*52.3*
Wyndham Manning (D)	149,368	*47.7*

1942   **Democratic Primary**

Candidates	Votes	%
Olin D. Johnston (D)	121,465	*51.8*
Wyndham Manning (D)	113,014	*48.2*

1946   **Democratic Primary**

Candidates	Votes	%
Strom Thurmond (D)	96,691	*33.4*
James C. McLeod (D)	83,464	*28.9*
Williams (D)	35,813	*12.4*
Taylor (D)	22,447	*7.8*
O'Neal (D)	16,574	*5.7*
Long (D)	16,503	*5.7*

Democratic Runoff

Candidates	Votes	%
Strom Thurmond (D)	144,420	*57.0*
James C. McLeod (D)	109,169	*43.1*

1950   **Democratic Primary**

Candidates	Votes	%
James F. Byrnes (D)	248,069	*71.6*
Bates (D)	63,143	*18.2*
Pope (D)	29,622	*8.6*

1954   **Democratic Primary**

Candidates	Votes	%
George Bell Timmerman Jr. (D)	185,541	*61.3*
Bates (D)	116,942	*38.7*

1958   **Democratic Primary**

Candidates	Votes	%
Ernest F. Hollings (D)	158,159	*41.9*
Donald S. Russell (D)	132,099	*35.0*
William C. Johnston (D)	86,981	*23.1*

Democratic Runoff

Candidates	Votes	%
Ernest F. Hollings (D)	190,691	*56.8*
Donald S. Russell (D)	145,162	*43.2*

1962   **Democratic Primary**

Candidates	Votes	%
Donald S. Russell (D)	199,619	*60.8*
Burnet R. Maybank (D)	103,015	*31.4*
A. W. Bethea (D)	17,251	*5.3*

1966   **Democratic Primary**

Candidates	Votes	%
Robert E. McNair (D)		*100.0*

1970   **Democratic Primary**

Candidates	Votes	%
John C. West (D)		*100.0*

1974   **Republican Primary**

Candidates	Votes	%
James B. Edwards (R)	20,177	*57.7*
William C. Westmoreland (R)	14,777	*42.3*

Democratic Primary

Candidates	Votes	%
Charles D. Ravenel (D)	107,345	*33.6*
William Jennings Bryan Dorn (D)	105,734	*33.1*
Earle E. Morris Jr. (D)	80,292	*25.2*

Democratic Runoff

Candidates	Votes	%
Charles D. Ravenel (D)[2]	186,985	*54.8*
William Jennings Bryan Dorn (D)	154,187	*45.2*

1978   **Republican Primary**

Candidates	Votes	%
Edward L. Young (R)	12,172	*51.4*
Raymond Finch (R)	11,499	*48.6*

Democratic Primary

Candidates	Votes	%
W. Brantley Harvey (D)	142,785	*37.5*
Richard Riley (D)	125,185	*32.9*
William Jennings Bryan Dorn (D)	112,793	*29.6*

Democratic Runoff

Candidates	Votes	%
Richard Riley (D)	180,882	*53.3*
W. Brantley Harvey (D)	158,665	*46.7*

1982   **Republican Primary**

Candidates	Votes	%
W. D. Workman (R)	17,128	*81.8*
Roddy T. Martin (R)	3,816	*18.2*

Democratic Primary

Candidates	Votes	%
Richard Riley (D)		*100.0*

1986   **Republican Primary**

Candidates	Votes	%
Carroll Campbell (R)		*100.0*

Democratic Primary[3]

Candidates	Votes	%
Mike Daniel (D)	156,077	*47.4*
Phil Lader (D)	86,136	*26.1*
Frank Eppes (D)	59,125	*17.9*
Hugh Leatherman (D)	28,158	*8.5*

1990   **Republican Primary**

Candidates	Votes	%
Carroll Campbell (R)		*100.0*

Democratic Primary

Candidates	Votes	%
Theo Mitchell (D)	116,471	*60.1*
Ernie Passailaigue (D)	77,429	*39.9*

1994   **Republican Primary**

Candidates	Votes	%
David Beasley (R)	119,724	*47.2*
Arthur Ravenel (R)	81,129	*32.0*
Thomas F. Hartnett (R)	52,866	*20.8*

Candidates	Votes	%
Democratic Primary		
Nick A. Theodore (D)	129,572	*49.6*
Joe Riley (D)	99,967	*38.2*
T. Travis Medlock (D)	22,468	*8.6*
Republican Runoff		
David Beasley (R)	134,297	*57.6*
Arthur Ravenel (R)	98,915	*42.4*
Democratic Runoff		
Nick A. Theodore (D)	113,127	*50.4*
Joe Riley (D)	111,517	*49.6*

South Carolina

1. The New York Times of Aug. 28, 1924, provided the returns given for McLeod and Duncan. Gov. McLeod was renominated and subsequently re-elected to a second term.

2. Charles D. Ravenel was ruled ineligible by the state Supreme Court because he did not meet the state's residency requirement for gubernatorial candidates. At a special state party convention, Dorn was designated to replace Ravenel as the Democratic candidate.

3. Neither Lader nor the other two candidates requested a runoff primary, and Daniel was declared the nominee.

SOUTH DAKOTA

	Candidates	Votes	%
1956	**Republican Primary**		
	Joe J. Foss (R)		*100.0*
	Democratic Primary		
	Ralph Herseth (D)		*100.0*
1958	**Republican Primary**		
	Phil Saunders (R)	49,746	*61.6*
	L. R. Houck (R)	21,621	*26.8*
	Charles Lacey (R)	9,384	*11.6*
	Democratic Primary		
	Ralph Herseth (D)		*100.0*
1960	**Republican Primary**		
	Archie M. Gubbrud (R)		*100.0*
	Democratic Primary		
	Ralph Herseth (D)		*100.0*
1962	**Republican Primary**		
	Archie M. Gubbrud (R)		*100.0*
	Democratic Primary		
	Ralph Herseth (D)		*100.0*
1964	**Republican Primary**		
	Nils A. Boe (R)	50,335	*53.5*
	Sigurd Anderson (R)	43,809	*46.5*

	Candidates	Votes	%
	Democratic Primary		
	John F. Lindley (D)	27,071	*65.8*
	Merton B. Tice (D)	14,051	*34.2*
1966	**Republican Primary**		
	Nils A. Boe (R)		*100.0*
	Democratic Primary		
	Robert Chamberlin (D)		*100.0*
1968	**Republican Primary**		
	Frank Farrar (R)		*100.0*
	Democratic Primary		
	Robert Chamberlin (D)		*100.0*
1970	**Republican Primary**		
	Frank Farrar (R)	48,520	*58.2*
	Frank E. Henderson (R)	34,893	*41.8*
	Democratic Primary		
	Richard F. Kneip (D)		*100.0*
1972	**Republican Primary**		
	Carveth Thompson (R)	65,538	*72.4*
	Simon W. Chance (R)	24,975	*27.6*
	Democratic Primary		
	Richard K. Kneip (D)		*100.0*
1974	**Republican Primary**		
	John E. Olson (R)	49,973	*55.6*
	Ronald F. Williamson (R)	25,509	*28.4*
	Oscar W. Hagen (R)	14,444	*16.1*
	Democratic Primary		
	Richard F. Kneip (D)	45,932	*66.2*
	Bill Dougherty (D)	23,467	*33.8*
1978	**Republican Primary**		
	William J. Janklow (R)	46,423	*50.9*
	LeRoy G. Hoffman (R)	30,026	*32.9*
	Clint Roberts (R)	14,774	*16.2*
	Democratic Primary		
	Roger McKellips (D)	34,160	*49.1*
	Harvey Wollman (D)	32,690	*47.0*
1982	**Republican Primary**		
	William J. Janklow (R)		*100.0*
	Democratic Primary		
	Michael J. O'Connor (D)	24,101	*58.8*
	Elvern R. Varilek (D)	16,916	*41.2*

	Candidates	Votes	%
1986	**Republican Primary**		
	George S. Mickelson (R)	40,979	35.3
	Clint Roberts (R)	37,250	32.1
	Lowell Hansen (R)	21,884	18.8
	Alice Kundert (R)	15,985	13.8
	Democratic Primary		
	R. Lars Herseth (D)	30,801	42.8
	Richard F. Kneip (D)	27,811	38.7
	Kenneth D. Stofferahn (D)	13,332	18.5
1990	**Republican Primary**		
	George S. Mickelson (R)		100.0
	Democratic Primary		
	Bob L. Samuelson (D)		100.0
1994	**Republican Primary**		
	William J. Janklow (R)	57,221	54.0
	Walter D. Miller (R)	48,754	46.0
	Democratic Primary		
	Jim Beddow (D)	29,082	55.5
	Carrol V. "Red" Allen (D)	12,184	23.2
	Jim Burg (D)	11,181	21.3

TENNESSEE

	Candidates	Votes	%
1920	**Democratic Primary**		
	Albert H. Roberts (D)	67,886	59.6
	W. R. Crabtree (D)	44,853	39.4
1922	**Democratic Primary**		
	Austin Peay (D)	63,940	39.2
	Benton McMillin (D)	59,922	36.8
	Harvey Hannah (D)	24,062	14.8
	L. E. Gwinn (D)	15,137	9.3
1924	**Democratic Primary**		
	Austin Peay (D)	125,031	79.0
	John R. Neal (D)	33,199	21.0
1926	**Democratic Primary**		
	Austin Peay (D)	96,545	51.6
	Hill McAlister (D)	88,488	47.3
1928	**Democratic Primary**		
	Henry H. Horton (D)	97,333	44.7
	Hill McAlister (D)	92,017	42.3
	Lewis S. Pope (D)	27,779	12.8
1930	**Democratic Primary**		
	Henry H. Horton (D)	144,990	58.9
	L. E. Gwinn (D)	101,285	41.1

	Candidates	Votes	%
1932	**Democratic Primary**		
	Hill McAlister (D)	116,020	40.9
	Lewis S. Pope (D)	106,450	37.5
	M. R. Patterson (D)	58,915	20.8
1934	**Democratic Primary**		
	Hill McAlister (D)	191,460	58.3
	Lewis S. Pope (D)	137,253	41.8
1936	**Democratic Primary**		
	Gordon Browning (D)	243,463	68.0
	Burgin E. Dossett (D)	109,170	30.5
1938	**Democratic Primary**		
	Prentice Cooper (D)	237,853	59.5
	Gordon Browning (D)	158,854	39.7
1940	**Democratic Primary**		
	Prentice Cooper (D)	240,427	83.6
	Dempster (D)	44,122	15.3
1942	**Democratic Primary**		
	Prentice Cooper (D)	171,259	57.6
	J. Ridley Mitchell (D)	124,037	41.7
1944	**Republican Primary**		
	John W. Kilgo (R)	33,979	63.9
	W. O. Lowe (R)	13,425	25.2
	H. C. Lowery (R)	3,681	6.9
	Democratic Primary		
	James N. McCord (D)	132,466	87.4
	John R. Neal (D)	11,659	7.7
1946	**Republican Primary**		
	W. O. Lowe (R)	33,269	100.0
	Democratic Primary		
	James N. McCord (D)	187,119	59.8
	Gordon Browning (D)	120,535	38.5
1948	**Republican Primary**		
	Roy Acuff (R)	90,140	80.6
	Robert M. McMurry (R)	21,765	19.5
	Democratic Primary		
	Gordon Browning (D)	240,676	55.8
	James N. McCord (D)	183,948	42.6
1950	**Democratic Primary**		
	Gordon Browning (D)	267,855	55.7
	Clifford R. Allen (D)	208,634	43.4
1952	**Democratic Primary**		
	Frank G. Clement (D)	302,491	46.7
	Gordon Browning (D)	245,166	37.9
	Clifford R. Allen (D)	75,269	11.6

Gubernatorial Elections

	Candidates	Votes	%
1954	**Democratic Primary**		
	Frank G. Clement (D)	481,808	68.2
	Gordon Browning (D)	195,156	27.6
1958	**Republican Primary**		
	Robert L. Peters (R)	18,323	59.3
	Hansell Proffitt (R)	12,565	40.7
	Democratic Primary		
	Buford Ellington (D)	213,415	31.1
	Andrew T. Taylor (D)	204,629	29.9
	Edmund Orgill (D)	204,382	29.8
	Clifford R. Allen (D)	56,854	8.3
1962	**Republican Primary**		
	Hubert D. Patty		100.0
	Democratic Primary		
	Frank G. Clement (D)	309,333	42.5
	P. R. Olgiati (D)	211,812	29.1
	William W. Farris (D)	202,813	27.9
1966	**Democratic Primary**		
	Buford Ellington (D)	413,950	53.5
	John J. Hooker (D)	360,105	46.5
1970	**Republican Primary**		
	Winfield Dunn (R)	81,475	33.2
	Maxey Jarman (R)	70,420	28.7
	William Jenkins (R)	50,910	20.8
	Claude Robertson (R)	40,547	16.5
	Democratic Primary		
	John J. Hooker (D)	261,580	44.3
	Stanley Snodgrass (D)	193,199	32.7
	Robert L. Taylor (D)	90,009	15.3
1974	**Republican Primary**		
	Lamar Alexander (R)	120,773	48.5
	Nat Winston (R)	90,980	36.5
	Dortch Oldham (R)	35,683	14.3
	Democratic Primary		
	Ray Blanton (D)	148,062	22.7
	Jake Butcher (D)	131,412	20.2
	Tom Wiseman (D)	89,061	13.7
	Hudley Crockett (D)	86,852	13.2
	Franklin Haney (D)	84,155	12.9
	Stanley Snodgrass (D)	40,211	6.2
1978	**Republican Primary**		
	Lamar Alexander (R)	230,922	86.0
	Harold Sterling (R)	34,037	12.7
	Democratic Primary		
	Jake Butcher (D)	320,329	40.9
	Bob Clement (D)	288,577	36.9
	Richard Fulton (D)	122,101	15.6
	Roger Murray (D)	40,871	5.2

	Candidates	Votes	%
1982	**Republican Primary**		
	Lamar Alexander (R)		100.0
	Democratic Primary		
	Randy Tyree (D)	318,205	50.0
	Anna Belle Clement O'Brien (D)	254,500	40.0
1986	**Republican Primary**		
	Winfield Dunn (R)	222,458	94.2
	Democratic Primary		
	Ned McWherter (D)	314,449	42.5
	Jane Eskind (D)	225,551	30.5
	Richard Fulton (D)	190,016	25.7
1990	**Republican Primary**		
	Dwight Henry (R)	92,100	53.5
	Charles R. Moffett (R)	26,363	15.3
	Terry A. Williams (R)	18,153	10.6
	Carroll Turner (R)	16,293	9.5
	Hubert D. Patty (R)	10,097	5.9
	Robert O. Watson (R)	8,893	5.2
	Democratic Primary		
	Ned McWherter (D)		100.0
1994	**Republican Primary**		
	Don Sunquist (R)	386,696	83.3
	David Y. Copeland (R)	69,773	15.0
	Democratic Primary		
	Phil Bredesen (D)	284,803	53.0
	Bill Morris (D)	103,869	19.3
	Steve Hewlett (D)	43,478	8.1
	Frank Cochran (D)	41,097	7.7

TEXAS

	Candidates	Votes	%
1920	**Democratic Primary**		
	Joseph W. Bailey (D)	152,340	33.9
	Pat M. Neff (D)	149,818	33.3
	Robert E. Thomason (D)	99,002	22.0
	Ben F. Looney (D)	48,640	10.8
	Democratic Runoff		
	Pat M. Neff (D)	264,075	58.8
	Joseph W. Bailey (D)	184,702	41.2
1922	**Democratic Primary**		
	Pat M. Neff (D)	318,000	53.9
	Fred S. Rogers (D)	195,941	33.2
	Harry T. Warner (D)	57,617	9.8

	Candidates	Votes	%
1924	**Democratic Primary**		
	F. D. Robertson (D)	193,508	*27.5*
	Miriam A. Ferguson (D)	146,424	*20.8*
	Lynch Davidson (D)	141,208	*20.1*
	T. W. Davidson (D)	125,011	*17.8*
	Democratic Runoff		
	Miriam A. Ferguson (D)	413,751	*56.7*
	F. D. Robertson (D)	316,019	*43.3*
1926	**Republican Primary**		
	H. H. Haines (R)	11,215	*73.4*
	E. P. Scott (R)	4,074	*26.7*
	Democratic Primary		
	Dan Moody (D)	409,732	*49.9*
	Miriam A. Ferguson (D)	283,482	*34.5*
	Lynch Davidson (D)	122,449	*14.9*
	Democratic Runoff		
	Dan Moody (D)	495,723	*64.7*
	Miriam A. Ferguson (D)	270,595	*35.3*
1928	**Democratic Primary**		
	Dan Moody (D)	442,080	*59.9*
	Louis J. Wardlaw (D)	245,508	*33.3*
1930	**Republican Primary**		
	George C. Butte (R)	5,001	*51.2*
	H. E. Exum (R)	2,773	*28.4*
	John F. Grant (R)	1,800	*18.4*
	Democratic Primary		
	Miriam A. Ferguson (D)	242,959	*29.2*
	Ross S. Sterling (D)	170,754	*20.5*
	Clint C. Small (D)	138,934	*16.7*
	T. B. Love (D)	87,068	*10.5*
	James Young (D)	73,385	*8.8*
	Barry Miller (D)	54,652	*6.6*
	E. B. Mayfield (D)	54,459	*6.5*
	Democratic Runoff		
	Ross S. Sterling (D)	473,371	*55.2*
	Miriam A. Ferguson (D)	384,402	*44.8*
1932	**Democratic Primary**		
	Miriam A. Ferguson (D)	402,238	*41.8*
	Ross S. Sterling (D)	296,383	*30.8*
	Tom F. Hunter (D)	220,391	*22.9*
	Democratic Runoff		
	Miriam A. Ferguson (D)	477,644	*50.2*
	Ross S. Sterling (D)	473,846	*49.8*
1934	**Republican Primary**		
	D. E. Waggoner (R)	13,043	*100.0*

	Candidates	Votes	%
	Democratic Primary		
	James V. Allred (D)	298,903	*29.9*
	Tom F. Hunter (D)	243,254	*24.3*
	C. C. McDonald (D)	207,200	*20.7*
	Clint C. Small (D)	125,324	*12.5*
	Edgar E. Witt (D)	62,476	*6.2*
	Maury Hughes (D)	58,815	*5.9*
	Democratic Runoff		
	James V. Allred (D)	499,343	*52.1*
	Tom F. Hunter (D)	459,106	*47.9*
1936	**Democratic Primary**		
	James V. Allred (D)	553,219	*52.5*
	Tom F. Hunter (D)	239,460	*22.7*
	F. W. Fischer (D)	145,877	*13.9*
	Roy Sanderford (D)	81,170	*7.7*
1938	**Democratic Primary**		
	W. Lee O'Daniel (D)	573,166	*51.4*
	Ernest O. Thompson (D)	231,630	*20.8*
	William McCraw (D)	152,278	*13.7*
	Tom F. Hunter (D)	117,634	*10.6*
1940	**Democratic Primary**		
	W. Lee O'Daniel (D)	645,646	*54.3*
	Ernest O. Thompson (D)	256,923	*21.6*
	Harry Hines (D)	119,121	*10.0*
	Miriam A. Ferguson (D)	100,578	*8.5*
	Jerry Sadler (D)	61,396	*5.2*
1942	**Democratic Primary**		
	Coke R. Stevenson (D)	651,218	*68.5*
	Hal H. Collins (D)	272,469	*28.6*
1944	**Democratic Primary**		
	Coke R. Stevenson (D)	696,586	*84.6*
	Minnie F. Cunningham (D)	48,039	*5.8*
1946	**Democratic Primary**		
	Beauford H. Jester (D)	443,804	*38.2*
	Homer P. Rainey (D)	291,282	*25.0*
	Grover Sellers (D)	162,431	*14.0*
	Jerry Sadler (D)	103,120	*8.9*
	John Lee Smith (D)	102,941	*8.9*
	Democratic Runoff		
	Beauford H. Jester (D)	701,018	*66.3*
	Homer P. Rainey (D)	355,654	*33.7*
1948	**Democratic Primary**		
	Beauford H. Jester (D)	642,025	*53.1*
	Roger Q. Evans (D)	279,602	*23.1*
	Caso March (D)	187,658	*15.5*
1950	**Democratic Primary**		
	Allan Shivers (D)	829,730	*76.4*
	Caso March (D)	195,997	*18.0*

Gubernatorial Elections

	Candidates	Votes	%
1952	**Democratic Primary**		
	Allan Shivers (D)	833,861	61.5
	Ralph Yarborough (D)	488,345	36.0
1954	**Democratic Primary**		
	Allan Shivers (D)	668,913	49.5
	Ralph Yarborough (D)	645,994	47.8
	Democratic Runoff		
	Allan Shivers (D)	775,088	53.2
	Ralph Yarborough (D)	683,132	46.9
1956	**Democratic Primary**		
	Price Daniel (D)	628,914	39.9
	Ralph Yarborough (D)	463,416	29.4
	W. Lee O'Daniel (D)	347,757	22.1
	J. Evetts Haley (D)	88,772	5.6
	Democratic Runoff		
	Price Daniel (D)	698,001	50.1
	Ralph Yarborough (D)	694,830	49.9
1958	**Republican Primary**		
	Edwin S. Mayer (R)		100.0
	Democratic Primary		
	Price Daniel (D)	799,107	60.7
	Henry B. Gonzalez (D)	245,969	18.7
	W. Lee O'Daniel (D)	238,767	18.1
1960	**Democratic Primary**		
	Price Daniel (D)	908,992	59.5
	Jack Cox (D)	619,834	40.5
1962	**Republican Primary**		
	Jack Cox (R)	99,138	86.0
	Roy Whittenbury (R)	16,112	14.0
	Democratic Primary		
	John B. Connally (D)	431,498	29.8
	Don Yarborough (D)	317,986	22.0
	Price Daniel (D)	248,524	17.2
	Will Wilson (D)	171,617	11.9
	Marshall Formby (D)	139,094	9.6
	Edwin A. Walker (D)	138,387	9.6
	Democratic Runoff		
	John B. Connally (D)	565,174	51.2
	Don Yarborough (D)	538,924	48.8
1964	**Republican Primary**		
	Jack Crichton (R)		100.0
	Democratic Primary		
	John B. Connally (D)	1,125,884	69.1
	Don Yarborough (D)	471,411	28.9

	Candidates	Votes	%
1966	**Republican Primary**		
	T. E. Kennerly (R)		100.0
	Democratic Primary		
	John B. Connally (D)	932,641	74.3
	Stanley C. Woods (D)	291,651	23.2
1968	**Republican Primary**		
	Paul W. Eggers (R)	65,501	62.5
	John R. Trice (R)	28,849	27.5
	Wallace Sisk (R)	10,415	10.0
	Democratic Primary		
	Don Yarborough (D)	419,003	23.9
	Preston Smith (D)	389,564	22.3
	Waggoner Carr (D)	257,535	14.7
	Dolph Briscoe (D)	225,686	12.9
	Eugene Locke (D)	218,118	12.5
	John Hill (D)	154,908	8.9
	Democratic Runoff		
	Preston Smith (D)	767,490	55.3
	Don Yarborough (D)	621,226	44.7
1970	**Republican Primary**		
	Paul W. Eggers (R)	101,875	93.4
	Roger Martin (R)	7,146	6.6
	Democratic Primary		
	Preston Smith (D)		100.0
1972	**Republican Primary**		
	Henry C. Grover (R)	37,118	32.6
	Albert B. Fay (R)	24,329	21.3
	David Reagan (R)	20,119	17.6
	Tom McElroy (R)	19,559	17.2
	John Hall (R)	4,864	7.0
	Republican Runoff		
	Henry C. Grover (R)	37,842	66.4
	Albert B. Fay (R)	19,166	33.6
	Democratic Primary		
	Dolph Briscoe (D)	963,397	43.9
	Frances Farenthold (D)	612,051	27.9
	Ben Barnes (D)	392,356	17.9
	Preston Smith (D)	190,709	8.7
	Democratic Runoff		
	Dolph Briscoe (D)	1,100,601	55.3
	Frances Farenthold (D)	889,544	44.7
1974	**Republican Primary**		
	Jim Granberry (R)	53,617	77.6
	Odell McBrayer (R)	15,484	22.4

UTAH

Candidates	Votes	%
Democratic Primary		
Dolph Briscoe (D)	1,025,632	67.4
Frances Farenthold (D)	437,287	28.7
1978 Republican Primary		
William P. Clements (R)	115,345	72.8
Ray Hutchison (R)	38,268	24.2
Democratic Primary		
John Hill (D)	932,338	51.4
Dolph Briscoe (D)	753,305	41.6
Preston Smith (D)	92,088	5.1
1982 Republican Primary		
William P. Clements (R)	246,120	92.6
Lowell D. Embs (R)	19,731	7.4
Democratic Primary		
Mark White (D)	592,210	44.9
Buddy Temple[1] (D)	402,567	30.5
Bob Armstrong (D)	261,940	19.9
1986 Republican Primary		
William P. Clements (R)	318,808	58.5
Tom Loeffler (R)	117,673	21.6
Kent Hance (R)	108,238	19.8
Democratic Primary		
Mark White (D)	589,536	53.8
Andrew C. Briscoe (D)	248,850	22.7
A. Don Crowder (D)	120,999	11.0
Bobby Locke (D)	58,936	5.4
1990 Republican Primary		
Clayton Williams (R)	520,014	60.8
Kent Hance (R)	132,142	15.5
Tom Luce (R)	115,835	13.5
Jack Rains (R)	82,461	9.6
Democratic Primary		
Ann Richards (D)	580,191	39.0
Jim Mattox (D)	546,103	36.7
Mark White (D)	286,161	19.2
Democratic Runoff		
Ann Richards (D)	640,995	57.1
Jim Mattox (D)	481,739	42.9
1994 Republican Primary		
George W. Bush (R)	520,130	93.3
Ray Hollis (R)	37,210	6.7
Democratic Primary		
Ann Richards (D)	806,607	77.8
Gary Espinosa (D)	230,337	22.2

Texas
1. Temple withdrew and no runoff was held.

	Candidates	Votes	%
1956	**Republican Primary**		
	George D. Clyde (R)	62,811	53.5
	J. Bracken Lee (R)	54,544	46.5
	Democratic Primary		
	L. C. Romney (D)	40,908	52.0
	John S. Boyden (D)	37,798	48.0
1960	**Republican Primary**		
	George D. Clyde (R)	50,592	57.8
	Lamont B. Gundersen (R)	37,002	42.2
	Democratic Primary		
	W. A. Barlocker (D)	74,424	70.6
	Ira A. Huggins (D)	31,045	29.4
1964	**Republican Primary**		
	Mitchell Melich (R)	63,108	53.0
	D. James Cannon (R)	55,938	47.0
	Democratic Primary		
	Calvin L. Rampton (D)	57,848	62.7
	Ernest Howard Dean (D)	34,470	37.3
1968	**Republican Primary**		
	Carl W. Buehner (R)	93,635	70.1
	Lamar A. Rawlings (R)	39,907	29.9
	Democratic Primary		
	Calvin L. Rampton (D)		100.0
1972	**Republican Primary**		
	Nicholas L. Strike (R)		100.0
	Democratic Primary		
	Calvin L. Rampton (D)		100.0
1976	**Republican Primary**		
	Vernon B. Romney (R)	87,251	53.4
	Dixie L. Leavitt (R)	76,139	46.6
	Democratic Primary		
	Scott M. Matheson (D)	50,505	59.0
	John P. Creer (D)	35,154	41.0
1984	**Republican Primary**		
	Norman H. Bangerter (R)	94,347	56.4
	Dan Marriott (R)	72,940	43.6
	Democratic Primary		
	Wayne Owens (D)	51,302	62.0
	Kem C. Gardner (D)	31,421	38.0

	Candidates	Votes	%
1992	**Republican Primary**		
	Mike Leavitt (R)	143,514	56.0
	Richard M. Eyre (R)	112,881	44.0
	Democratic Primary		
	Stewart Hanson (D)	64,084	56.8
	Patrick Shea (D)	48,758	43.2

VERMONT

	Candidates	Votes	%
1956	**Republican Primary**		
	Joseph B. Johnson (R)		100.0
	Democratic Primary		
	E. Frank Branon (D)		100.0
1958	**Republican Primary**		
	Robert T. Stafford (R)		100.0
	Democratic Primary		
	Bernard J. Leddy (D)		100.0
1960	**Republican Primary**		
	F. Ray Keyser (R)	17,491	29.6
	Robert S. Babcock (R)	16,762	28.4
	A. Luke Crispe (R)	14,874	25.2
	W. A. Simpson (R)	9,916	16.8
	Democratic Primary		
	Russell F. Niquette (D)		100.0
1962	**Republican Primary**		
	F. Ray Keyser (R)		100.0
	Democratic Primary		
	Philip H. Hoff (D)		100.0
1964	**Republican Primary**		
	Ralph A. Foote (R)	19,121	42.8
	Robert S. Babcock (R)	16,225	36.3
	Roger MacBride (R)	9,265	20.7
	Democratic Primary		
	Philip H. Hoff (D)		100.0
1966	**Republican Primary**		
	Richard A. Snelling (R)	22,069	59.0
	Thomas L. Hayes (R)	15,286	40.9
	Democratic Primary		
	Philip H. Hoff (D)		100.0

	Candidates	Votes	%
1968	**Republican Primary**		
	Deane C. Davis (R)	36,719	62.7
	James L. Oakes (R)	21,791	37.2
	Democratic Primary		
	John J. Daley (D)		100.0
1970	**Republican Primary**		
	Deane C. Davis (R)	31,549	79.3
	Thomas L. Hayes (R)	8,048	20.2
	Democratic Primary		
	Leo O'Brien (D)	18,058	54.7
	John J. Daley (D)	14,795	44.8
1972	**Republican Primary**		
	Luther F. Hackett (R)	33,323	54.4
	James M. Jeffords (R)	27,902	45.5
	Democratic Primary		
	Thomas P. Salmon (D)		100.0
1974	**Republican Primary**		
	Walter L. Kennedy (R)	23,738	55.5
	Harry R. Montague (R)	13,901	32.5
	T. James Lannon (R)	4,667	10.9
	Democratic Primary		
	Thomas P. Salmon (D)	18,498	83.6
	John F. Reilly (D)	3,537	16.0
1976	**Republican Primary**		
	Richard Snelling (R)	24,279	70.8
	William G. Craig (R)	9,429	27.5
	Democratic Primary		
	Stella B. Hackel (D)	18,522	44.0
	Brian D. Burns (D)	14,725	34.9
	Robert O'Brien (D)	8,809	20.9
	Liberty Union Primary		
	Bernard Sanders (LU)		100.0
1978	**Republican Primary**		
	Richard A. Snelling (R)		100.0
	Democratic Primary		
	Edwin C. Granai (D)	8,572	64.6
	Bernard G. O'Shea (D)	4,570	34.4
	Liberty Union Primary		
	Earl S. Gardner (LU)		100.0
1980	**Republican Primary**		
	Richard A. Snelling (R)	38,228	85.0
	Clifford Thompson (R)	3,432	7.6
	Kirk E. Faryniasz (R)	2,273	5.0

Candidates	Votes	%
Democratic Primary		
M. Jerome Diamond (D)	15,738	50.3
Timothy J. O'Connor (D)	14,857	47.5
1982 Republican Primary		
Richard A. Snelling (R)		100.0
Democratic Primary		
Madeleine M. Kunin (D)	16,002	90.7
Clifford Thompson (D)	1,433	8.1
Liberty Union Primary		
Richard F. Gottlieb (LU)		100.0
1984 Republican Primary		
John J. Easton (R)	30,436	61.3
Hilton Wick (R)	19,170	38.2
Democratic Primary		
Madeleine M. Kunin (D)	17,138	100.0
Liberty Union Primary		
Richard F. Gottlieb (LU)		100.0
1986 Republican Primary		
Peter Smith (R)		100.0
Democratic Primary		
Madeleine M. Kunin (D)		100.0
Liberty Union Primary		
Richard F. Gottlieb (LU)		100.0
1988 Republican Primary		
Michael Bernhardt (R)		100.0
Democratic Primary		
Madeleine M. Kunin (D)		100.0
Liberty Union Primary		
Richard F. Gottlieb (LU)		100.0
1990 Republican Primary		
Richard A. Snelling (R)	38,881	86.7
Richard F. Gottlieb (R)	5,503	12.3
Democratic Primary		
Peter Welch (D)	14,656	86.6
William Gwin (D)	1,719	10.2
Libertarian Primary		
David Atkinson (LIBERT)		100.0
1992 Republican Primary		
John McClaughry (R)	28,026	92.5

Candidates	Votes	%
Democratic Primary		
Howard B. Dean (D)	25,504	98.5
Liberty Union Primary		
Richard F. Gottlieb (LU)		100.0
1994 Republican Primary		
David F. Kelley (R)	9,864	33.5
Thomas J. Morse (R)	8,508	28.9
John L. Gropper (R)	7,675	26.1
August Jaccaci (R)	1,626	5.5
Democratic Primary		
Howard B. Dean (D)	25,544	95.6
Liberty Union Primary		
Richard F. Gottlieb (LU)	278	91.0
1996 Republican Primary		
John L. Gropper (R)	12,626	62.2
Thomas J. Morse (LIBERT)	6,710	33.1
Democratic Primary		
Howard B. Dean (D)	18,112	97.8
Liberty Union Primary		
Mary Alice Herbert (LU)	237	92.2

VIRGINIA[1]

Candidates	Votes	%
1921 Democratic Primary		
Elbert Lee Trinkle (D)	86,812	57.5
Henry St. George Tucker (D)	64,286	42.6
1925 Democratic Primary		
Harry F. Byrd (D)	107,317	61.4
G. Walter Mapp (D)	67,579	38.6
1929 Democratic Primary		
John Garland Pollard (D)	104,310	75.5
G. Walter Mapp (D)	29,386	21.3
1933 Democratic Primary		
George C. Peery (D)	116,837	61.6
J. T. Deal (D)	40,268	21.2
W. Worth Smith (D)	32,518	17.2
1937 Democratic Primary		
James H. Price (D)	166,319	86.1
Vivian L. Page (D)	26,955	14.0

	Candidates	Votes	%
1941	**Democratic Primary**		
	Colgate W. Darden Jr. (D)	105,655	76.6
	Vivian L. Page (D)	19,526	14.2
	Hudson Cary (D)	12,793	9.3
1945	**Democratic Primary**		
	William M. Tuck (D)	97,304	70.1
	Moss A. Plunkett (D)	41,484	29.9
1949	**Democratic Primary**		
	John S. Battle (D)	135,426	42.8
	Francis P. Miller (D)	111,697	35.3
	Horace H. Edwards (D)	47,435	15.0
	Remmie L. Arnold (D)	22,054	7.0
1953	**Democratic Primary**		
	Thomas B. Stanley (D)	150,499	65.9
	Charles R. Fenwick (D)	77,715	34.1
1957	**Democratic Primary**		
	J. Lindsay Almond Jr. (D)	119,307	79.5
	Howard H. Carwile (D)	30,794	20.5
1961	**Democratic Primary**		
	Albertis S. Harrison Jr. (D)	199,519	56.7
	A. E. S. Stephens (D)	152,639	43.3
1965	**Democratic Primary**		
	Mills E. Godwin Jr. (D)		100.0
1969	**Democratic Primary**		
	William C. Battle (D)	158,956	38.9
	Henry Howell (D)	154,617	37.8
	Fred G. Pollard (D)	95,057	23.3
	Democratic Runoff		
	William C. Battle (D)	226,108	52.5
	Henry Howell (D)	207,505	47.9
1977	**Democratic Primary**		
	Henry Howell (D)	253,373	51.4
	Andrew P. Miller (D)	239,735	48.6
1989	**Republican Primary**		
	J. Marshall Coleman (R)	147,941	36.8
	Paul S. Trible (R)	141,120	35.1
	Stanford E. Parris (R)	112,826	28.1

Virginia

1. *After 1977, candidates were chosen by convention rather than through primaries, except for the Republican nomination in 1989.*

WASHINGTON[1]

	Candidates	Votes	%
1956	**Republican Primary**		
	Emmett T. Anderson (R)	192,500	59.6
	Don Eastvold (R)	99,020	30.7

	Candidates	Votes	%
	Democratic Primary		
	Albert D. Rosellini (D)	236,291	55.7
	Earl S. Coe (D)	140,882	33.2
	Roderick Lindsay (D)	39,072	9.2
1960	**Republican Primary**		
	Lloyd J. Andrews (R)	263,897	64.6
	Newman Clark (R)	144,440	35.4
	Democratic Primary		
	Albert D. Rosellini (D)	244,579	82.2
	John Patric (D)	28,970	9.7
	Bruce M. Sigman (D)	24,031	8.1
1964	**Republican Primary**		
	Daniel J. Evans (R)	323,152	59.9
	Richard G. Christensen (R)	213,217	39.5
	Democratic Primary		
	Albert D. Rosellini (D)	243,220	84.9
	Jessop McDonnell (D)	17,262	6.0
1968	**Republican Primary**		
	Daniel J. Evans (R)	305,897	89.4
	Democratic Primary		
	John J. O'Connell (D)	182,969	50.5
	Martin J. Durkan (D)	162,382	44.8
1972	**Republican Primary**		
	Daniel J. Evans (R)	224,953	67.9
	Perry B. Woodall (R)	100,372	30.3
	Democratic Primary		
	Albert D. Rosellini (D)	276,121	47.5
	Martin J. Durkan (D)	195,931	33.7
	James A. McDermott (D)	99,155	17.1
1976	**Republican Primary**		
	John Spellman (R)	185,439	60.5
	Harley Hoppe (R)	111,957	36.5
	Democratic Primary		
	Dixy Lee Ray (D)	205,232	37.6
	Wes Uhlman (D)	198,336	36.4
	Marvin Durning (D)	136,290	25.0
1980	**Republican Primary**		
	John Spellman (R)	162,426	40.6
	Duane Berentson (R)	154,724	38.7
	Bruce Chapman (R)	70,875	17.7
	Democratic Primary		
	James A. McDermott (D)	321,256	56.4
	Dixy Lee Ray (D)	234,252	41.1

	Candidates	Votes	%
1984	**Republican Primary**		
	John Spellman (R)	239,463	*95.5*
	Democratic Primary		
	Booth Gardner (D)	421,087	*64.4*
	Jim McDermott (D)	209,435	*32.0*
1988	**Republican Primary**		
	Bob Williams (R)	187,797	*56.4*
	Norm Maleng (R)	139,274	*41.4*
	Democratic Primary		
	Booth Gardner (D)	539,243	*90.6*
	Jeanne Dixon (D)	31,917	*5.4*
1992	**Republican Primary**		
	Ken Eikenberry (R)	258,553	*39.1*
	Sid Morrison (R)	250,418	*37.9*
	Dan McDonald (R)	144,050	*21.8*
	Democratic Primary		
	Mike Lowry (D)	337,783	*70.1*
	Joe King (D)	96,480	*20.0*
	Sally McQuown (D)	31,175	*6.5*
1996	**Republican Primary**		
	Ellen Craswell (R)	185,680	*31.9*
	Dale Foreman (R)	162,615	*28.0*
	Norm Maleng (R)	109,088	*18.8*
	Jim Waldo (R)	63,854	*11.0*
	Pam Roach (R)	29,533	*5.1*
	Democratic Primary		
	Gary Locke (D)	287,762	*45.6*
	Norman Rice (D)	212,888	*33.7*
	Jay Inslee (D)	118,571	*18.8*

Washington

1. *In Washington's so-called "jungle" primaries, all candidates for an office appeared together on the same ballot with their parties designated. Nominations went to the Republican and Democrat receiving the most votes for the office. Independents and minor party candidates gained a place on the general election ballot by obtaining at least 1 percent of the total vote cast in the primary. Percentages were calculated here as if candidates had run in separate party primaries.*

WEST VIRGINIA

	Candidates	Votes	%
1956	**Republican Primary**		
	Cecil H. Underwood (R)	98,344	*50.5*
	John T. Copenhaver (R)	91,088	*46.8*
	Democratic Primary		
	Robert H. Mollohan (D)	148,557	*42.6*
	Milton J. Ferguson (D)	95,869	*27.5*
	J. Howard Myers (D)	75,606	*21.7*
	Joe F. Burdett (D)	24,913	*7.1*

	Candidates	Votes	%
1960	**Republican Primary**		
	Harold E. Neely (R)	102,618	*55.3*
	Chapman Revercomb (R)	83,028	*44.7*
	Democratic Primary		
	W. W. Barron (D)	187,501	*51.0*
	Hulett C. Smith (D)	140,079	*38.1*
	Orel J. Skeen (D)	39,907	*10.9*
1964	**Republican Primary**		
	Cecil H. Underwood (R)	152,573	*89.7*
	Harry H. Cupp (R)	11,325	*6.7*
	Democratic Primary		
	Hulett C. Smith (D)	186,273	*53.3*
	Bonn Brown (D)	85,527	*24.4*
	Julius W. Singleton (D)	47,845	*13.7*
	Harold G. Cutright (D)	30,119	*8.6*
1968	**Republican Primary**		
	Arch A. Moore Jr. (R)	106,299	*57.0*
	Cecil H. Underwood (R)	76,659	*41.1*
	Democratic Primary		
	James M. Sprouse (D)	123,181	*37.6*
	C. Donald Robertson (D)	118,637	*36.2*
	Paul J. Kaufman (D)	72,917	*22.3*
1972	**Republican Primary**		
	Arch A. Moore Jr. (R)		*100.0*
	Democratic Primary		
	John D. "Jay" Rockefeller IV (D)	262,613	*72.2*
	Lee M. Kenna (D)	63,514	*17.5*
	Robert Myers (D)	37,616	*10.3*
1976	**Republican Primary**		
	Cecil H. Underwood (R)	97,671	*64.4*
	Ralph D. Albertazzie (R)	44,393	*29.3*
	Democratic Primary		
	John D. "Jay" Rockefeller IV (D)	206,732	*49.7*
	James M. Sprouse (D)	118,707	*28.5*
	Ken Hechler (D)	52,791	*12.7*
	John G. Hutchinson (D)	26,222	*6.3*
1980	**Republican Primary**		
	Arch A. Moore Jr. (R)		*100.0*
	Democratic Primary		
	John D. "Jay" Rockefeller IV (D)	250,550	*78.0*
	H. John Rogers (D)	70,452	*21.9*
1984	**Republican Primary**		
	Arch A. Moore Jr. (R)	135,887	*100.0*

Candidates	Votes	%
Democratic Primary		
Clyde M. See (D)	148,049	*39.8*
Warren R. McGraw (D)	104,138	*28.0*
Chauncey H. Browning (D)	101,712	*27.4*

1988

Candidates	Votes	%
Republican Primary		
Arch A. Moore Jr. (R)	78,495	*53.2*
John R. Raese (R)	68,973	*46.8*
Democratic Primary		
Gaston Caperton (D)	132,435	*38.0*
Clyde M. See (D)	94,364	*27.0*
Mario J. Palumbo (D)	51,722	*14.8*
Gus R. Douglass (D)	48,748	*14.0*

1992

Candidates	Votes	%
Republican Primary		
Cleveland K. Benedict (R)	104,169	*86.4*
Vernon Criss (R)	16,350	*13.6*
Democratic Primary		
Gaston Caperton (D)	142,261	*42.7*
Charlotte Pritt (D)	115,498	*34.7*
Mario J. Palumbo (D)	66,984	*20.1*

1996

Candidates	Votes	%
Republican Primary		
Cecil H. Underwood (R)	54,628	*40.8*
Jon McBride (R)	44,255	*33.0*
David McKinley (R)	35,089	*26.2*
Democratic Primary		
Charlotte Pritt (D)	130,107	*39.5*
Joe Manchin III (D)	107,124	*32.6*
Jim Lees (D)	64,100	*19.5*

WISCONSIN

Candidates	Votes	%
1956 **Republican Primary**		
Vernon W. Thomson (R)		*100.0*
Democratic Primary		
William Proxmire (D)		*100.0*
1958 **Republican Primary**		
Vernon W. Thomson (R)		*100.0*
Democratic Primary		
Gaylord Nelson (D)		*100.0*
1960 **Republican Primary**		
Philip G. Kuehn (R)		*100.0*
Democratic Primary		
Gaylord Nelson (D)		*100.0*

	Candidates	Votes	%
1962	**Republican Primary**		
	Philip G. Kuehn (R)	250,539	*53.8*
	Wilbur N. Renk (R)	199,616	*42.9*
	Democratic Primary		
	John W. Reynolds (D)		*100.0*
1964	**Republican Primary**		
	Warren P. Knowles (R)	246,760	*71.9*
	Milo G. Knutson (R)	96,421	*28.1*
	Democratic Primary		
	John W. Reynolds (D)	241,170	*70.3*
	Dominic H. Frinzi (D)	102,066	*29.7*
1966	**Republican Primary**		
	Warren P. Knowles (R)		*100.0*
	Democratic Primary		
	Patrick J. Lucey (D)	128,359	*45.2*
	David Carley (D)	95,803	*33.7*
	Dominic H. Frinzi (D)	44,344	*15.6*
	Abe L. Swed (D)	15,362	*5.4*
1968	**Republican Primary**		
	Warren P. Knowles (R)		*100.0*
	Democratic Primary		
	Bronson C. LaFollette (D)	173,458	*84.4*
	Floyd L. Wille (D)	31,778	*15.5*
1970	**Republican Primary**		
	Jack B. Olson (R)	203,434	*91.4*
	Roman R. Blenski (R)	19,061	*8.6*
	Democratic Primary		
	Patrick J. Lucey (D)	177,584	*60.6*
	Donald O. Peterson (D)	105,849	*36.1*
	American Primary		
	Leo J. McDonald (AM)		*100.0*
1974	**Republican Primary**		
	William D. Dyke (R)		*100.0*
	Democratic Primary		
	Patrick J. Lucey (D)	259,001	*78.2*
	Edmond E. Hou-Seye (D)	72,113	*21.8*
	American Primary		
	William H. Upham (AM)		*100.0*
1978	**Republican Primary**		
	Lee Sherman Dreyfus (R)	197,279	*57.9*
	Bob Kasten (R)	143,361	*42.1*

Candidates	Votes	%
Democratic Primary		
Martin J. Schreiber (D)	217,572	60.4
David Carley (D)	132,901	36.9
Conservative Primary		
Eugene R. Zimmerman (C)		100.0

1982 **Republican Primary**

Candidates	Votes	%
Terry J. Kohler (R)	227,844	68.2
Lowell B. Jackson (R)	106,413	31.8
Democratic Primary		
Anthony S. Earl (D)	268,857	45.9
Martin J. Schreiber (D)	245,952	42.0
James B. Wood (D)	71,282	12.2
Libertarian Primary		
Larry Smiley (LIBERT)		100.0
Constitution Primary		
James P. Wickstrom (CONST)		100.0
Socialist Workers Primary		
Peter Seidman (SOC WORK)		100.0

1986 **Republican Primary**

Candidates	Votes	%
Tommy G. Thompson (R)	156,875	52.1
Jonathan B. Barry (R)	67,114	22.3
George Watts (R)	58,424	19.4
Albert L. Wiley (R)	15,233	5.1
Democratic Primary		
Anthony S. Earl (D)	215,183	80.2
Edmond Hou-Seye (D)	52,784	19.7
Labor-Farm Primary		
Kathryn A. Christensen (LAB F)		100.0

1990 **Republican Primary**

Candidates	Votes	%
Tommy G. Thompson (R)	201,467	92.5
Bennett A. Masel (R)	11,230	5.2
Democratic Primary		
Thomas Loftus (D)		100.0

1994 **Republican Primary**

Candidates	Votes	%
Tommy G. Thompson (R)	321,487	99.8
Democratic Primary		
Chuck Chvala (D)	121,916	99.8
Libertarian Primary		
David S. Harmon (LIBERT)	1,109	99.6

Candidates	Votes	%
U.S. Taxpayers Primary		
Edward J. Frami (USTAX)	856	99.3
Independent Primary		
Michael J. Mangan (I)	554	100.0

WYOMING

Candidates	Votes	%

1958 **Republican Primary**

Candidates	Votes	%
Milward L. Simpson (R)	28,749	77.6
Stanley Edwards (R)	8,294	22.4
Democratic Primary		
J. J. Hickey (D)		100.0

1962 **Republican Primary**

Candidates	Votes	%
Clifford P. Hansen (R)	28,494	57.0
Charles M. Crowell (R)	16,906	33.8
R. E. Cheever (R)	4,575	9.1
Democratic Primary		
Jack R. Gage (D)	21,051	55.5
William Jack (D)	16,875	44.5

1966 **Republican Primary**

Candidates	Votes	%
Stan Hathaway (R)	26,110	55.2
Joe Burke (R)	19,815	41.9
Democratic Primary		
Ernest Wilkerson (D)	13,145	31.1
Bill Nation (D)	9,834	23.2
Jack R. Gage (D)	8,661	20.5
Raymond B. Whitaker (D)	6,238	14.7
Howard L. Burke (D)	4,426	10.5

1970 **Republican Primary**

Candidates	Votes	%
Stan Hathaway (R)		100.0
Democratic Primary		
John J. Rooney (D)		100.0

1974 **Republican Primary**

Candidates	Votes	%
Dick Jones (R)	15,502	26.5
Malcolm Wallop (R)	14,688	25.1
Roy Peck (R)	14,217	24.3
Clarence Brimmer (R)	14,014	24.0
Democratic Primary		
Ed Herschler (D)	19,997	46.6
Harry E. Leimback (D)	15,255	35.5
John J. Rooney (D)	7,674	17.9

	Candidates	Votes	%
1978	**Republican Primary**		
	John C. Ostlund (R)	40,251	*58.9*
	Gus Fleischli (R)	24,824	*36.4*
	Democratic Primary		
	Ed Herschler (D)	28,406	*65.3*
	Margaret McKinstry (D)	15,111	*34.7*
1982	**Republican Primary**		
	Warren A. Morton (R)	52,536	*74.3*
	Rex G. Welty (R)	9,106	*12.9*
	Carl A. Johnson (R)	9,025	*12.8*
	Democratic Primary		
	Ed Herschler (D)	44,396	*85.2*
	Pat McGuire (D)	7,720	*14.8*
1986	**Republican Primary**		
	Peter Simpson (R)	25,948	*27.6*
	Bill Budd (R)	25,495	*27.1*
	Fred Schroeder (R)	15,013	*16.0*
	Russ Donley (R)	12,979	*13.8*
	David R. Nicholas (R)	11,092	*11.8*

	Candidates	Votes	%
	Democratic Primary		
	Mike Sullivan (D)	29,266	*70.9*
	Pat McGuire (D)	5,406	*13.1*
	Keith B. Goodenough (D)	4,039	*9.8*
	Al Hamburg (D)	2,554	*6.2*
1990	**Republican Primary**		
	Mary Mead (R)	51,160	*67.3*
	Nyla Murphy (R)	24,916	*32.7*
	Democratic Primary		
	Mike Sullivan (D)	38,447	*88.4*
	Ron Clingman (D)	5,026	*11.6*
1994	**Republican Primary**		
	Jim Geringer (R)	37,847	*42.7*
	John Perry (R)	28,019	*31.6*
	Charles K. Scott (R)	19,305	*21.8*
	Democratic Primary		
	Kathy Karpan (D)	39,824	*100.0*

Political Party Abbreviations

The following political party abbreviations are used in the primary election returns.

A-D	Aloha Democrat	ID	Independent Democrat
ALI	Alaskan Independent	I-R	Independent Republican
AM	American	L	Liberal
AMI	American Independent	LAB F	Labor Farm
BP	Best Party	LIBERT	Libertarian
C	Conservative	LU	Liberty Union
CONST	Constitution	NON PART	Non Partisan
CP	Commonwealth	PFP	Peace and Freedom
CST	Constitutional	R	Republican
D	Democrat	RTL	Right to Life
DFL	Democrat Farmer-Labor	SOC WORK	Socialist Workers
GREEN	Green	USTAX	U.S. Taxpayers
I	Independent	WRITE IN	Write in

Political Party Abbreviations

The following list provides a key to the political party abbreviations used in *Gubernatorial Elections 1787-1997*. This list was developed by Congressional Quarterly from three sources for party designations: the Inter-University Consortium for Political and Social Research (ICPSR), for most election returns up to 1973; and Richard M. Scammon and Alice V. McGillivray's *America Votes* series, for most election returns from 1974 to 1990; and the *Congressional Quarterly Weekly Report* for most returns from 1992 to 1997. In cases of discrepancy, the ICPSR party designation was used.

The election data obtained from the ICPSR contain hundreds of different party labels. In many cases the party labels represent combinations of multi-party support received by individual candidates. However, in preparing the returns for publication, many of the party labels were eliminated because the candidate(s) did not receive at least 5 percent of the votes cast. The names of the parties appear below in the form they were obtained from ICPSR, Scammon, and the *Congressional Quarterly Weekly Report*.

A-AK R	Anti-Addicks Republican	D & CD	Democrat and Co. Democrat
AB	Abolition	D CIT	Democratic Citizen
ACP	A Connecticut Party	D & CST	Democrat and Constitution
A-D	Aloha Democrat	DFL	Democrat Farmer-Labor
AG WHEEL	Agricultural Wheeler	D-FUS	Democrat-Fusion
A-JAC	Anti-Jackson	D & G	Democrat and Greenback
A-JAC D	Anti-Jackson Democrat	D & I	Democrat and Independent
A-LEC D	Anti-Lecompton Democrat	DISS D	Dissident Democrat
ALI	Alaskan Independent	DISTRIB	Distributionist Candidate
ALNC	Alliance	D & L	Democrat and Liberal
ALNC D	Alliance Democrat	D-LAB-PP	Democrat-Labor-Peoples
A-LOT D	Anti-Lottery Democrat	D & LIBN	Democrat and Liberation
AM	American	DN	Democratic National
A-MAINE	Anti-Maine Law	D-NG LAB	Democratic-National Green Labor
A-MAS	Anti-Mason	DOUG D	Douglas Democrat
A-MASC	Anti-Masonic	D & POP	Democrat and Populist
AM D-R	American Democratic-Republican	D-PP	Democrat-Peoples
AM & EMANC	American and Emancipationist	D & PPI	Democrat and People's Independent
AM FAC	American Faction	D & PROG	Democrat and Progressive
AMI	American Independent	DPUS	D.P.U.S.
AM LAB	American Labor	D-R	Democratic-Republican
A-MONOP	Anti-Monopoly	D & RESUB	Democrat and Resubmission
AM R	American Republican	D-R/FED	Democrat-Republican/Federalist
AM & R	American and Republican	D SIL	Democrat (Silver)
ANTI-CLINT	Anti-Clinton	D & SILVER	Democrat and Silver
ANTI-CL R	Anti-Clinton Republican	EP	Elec. Prog.
ANTI-FED	Anti-Federalist	EQ	Equal Right
AR	Adams Republican	E TAX	Equal Tax
A-RPT D	Anti-Redemption Democrat	F ALNC	Farmers' Alliance
A-VB D	Anti-Van Buren Democrat	FB R	'Free Bridge' Republican
BENTON D	Benton Democrat	FED	Federalist
BP	Best Party	FEDL	Federal
BRECK D	Breckinridge Democrat	FILL AM	Fillmore American
BRYAN D	Bryan Democrat	F-LAB	Farmer-Labor
B & T R	Brindle-Tail Republican	FLA PP	Florida People's Party
BUT D & R	Butler Democrat and Republican	F PLAY	Fair Play
C	Conservative	FREM AM	Fremont American
CASS D	Cass Democrat	F SOIL	Free Soil
CLAY R	Clay Republican	F SOIL D	Free Soil Democrat
CLINTON R	Clinton Republican	FS & SC	Free Soil and Scattering
CONST	Constitution	FUS	Fusion
CP	Commonwealth	FUS R	Fusion Republican
C PROG	Conservative Progressive	G	Greenback
CR	Conservative Republican	G LAB	Greenback Labor
CREOLE	Creole Faction	G & R	Greenback and Republican
CSI	Civil Service Independents	GREEN	Green
CST	Constitutional	HARD D	Hard Democratic
CST U	Constitutional Union	HG	Honest Government
D	Democrat	H LIC	High License

HUNKER D	Hunker Democrat	PP & D	People's and Democrat
I	Independent	PP-D-S-R	Peoples-Democrat-Silver-Republican
IA	Independent American	PP I	People's Independent
ID	Independent Democrat	PROG	Progressive
I D-R	Independent Democratic Republican	PROG-BMR	Progressive-Bull Moose-Roosevelt
I LEAGUE	Independence League	PUB OWN	Public Ownership
IL & NPR	Independent League and National Progressive	R	Republican
IP	Independent Party	RAD	Radical
I PROG	Independent Progressive	RAD R	Radical Republican
IR, I-R	Independent Republican	R-D	Republican-Democrat
IR & D	Independent Republican and Democrat	READJ	Readjuster
I REF D	Independent Reform Democrat	REF	Reform
IS	Illinois Solidarity	R-FF	Republican-Federalist Fusion
I VT	Independent Vermonters	R FUS	Republican Fusion
IW	Independent Whig	R-G-FUS	Republican-Greenback-Fusion
JAC	Jackson	R & NP	Republican and Nonpartisan
JAC D	Jackson Democrat	ROYAL OAK	Royal Oak
JAC R	Jackson Republican	R POP FU	Republican Populist Fusion
KEY	Keystone	RP & PROG	Republican, Prohibition, and Progressive
KN	Know-Nothing	R & PROG	Republican and Progressive
L	Liberal	R-SIL R	Republican-Silver Republican
LAB	Labor	R & TEMP	Republican and Temperance
LAB F	Labor Farm	RTL	Right to Life
LAB REF	Labor Reform	R & UL	Republican and Union Labor
LAB REF & P	Labor Reform and Prohibition	R-UNION	Republican Union
LAW ENF	Law Enforcement	SEC D	Secession Democrat
LAW ORD	Law and Order	SEC W	Secessionist Whig
LAW PRES	Law Preservation	SIL R	Silver Republican
LIB	Liberty	SOC	Socialist
LIBERT	Libertarian	SOCIAL D	Social Democrat
LIBER W	Liberation Whig	SOC LAB	Socialist Labor
LIB & SC	Liberty and Scattering	SOC WORK	Socialist Workers
LINCOLN	Lincoln	SOFT D	Soft Democrat
L & O W	Law and Order Whig	SO RTS	Southern Rights
LOW TAX D	Low Tax Democrat	SO RTS D	Southern Rights Democrat
LR	Liberal Republican	SOR W	Southern Rights Whig
LRU	La Raza Unida	SR W	State Rights Whig
LU	Liberty Union	STAL D	Stalwart Democrat
LW R	Lily-White Republican	STC D	State Credit Democrat
N	National Party	TAM D	Tammany Democrat
NC R	North Carolina Republican	TCN	Tax Cut Now
NEB	Nebraska	TEMP	Temperance
NEB D	Nebraska Democrat	TEMP REF	Temperance Reform
NG	National Greenback	TOL	Toleration
NON PART	Non Partisan	TPCT	Taxpayers Party to Cut Taxes
NON PL	Nonpartisan League	UN	Union
N PROG	National Progressive	UN D	Union Democrat
NR	National Republican	UN LAB	Union Labor
N SILVER	National Silver	UN R	Union Republican
N UNION	National Union	USTAX	U.S. Taxpayers
OLD R	Old Republican	VB R	Van Buren Republican
OPP	Opposition	W	Whig
OPP D	Opposition Democrat	W & AM	Whig and American
OPP R	Opposition Republican	W & A-MASC	Whig and Anti-Masonic
P	Prohibition	W-A-RENT	Whig Anti-Rent
PEACE D	Peace Democrat	WASH	Washington
P & F ALNC	Prohibition and Farmer's Alliance	W FS	Whig Free Soil
PFP	Peace and Freedom	WILDCAT	Wildcat
POP	Populist	WM	Workingmen
POP & SL D	Populist and Silver Democrat	WMP/L	Workingman's Party or League
PP	People's	WRITE IN	Write in

Bibliography

Books

Barone, Michael, and Grant Ujifusa. *The Almanac of American Politics, 1998*. Rev. ed. Washington, D.C.: National Journal, 1997.

Bartley, Numan V. *From Thurmond to Wallace: Political Tendencies in Georgia 1948-1968*. Baltimore: Johns Hopkins Press, 1970.

—, and Hugh D. Graham. *Southern Elections: County and Precinct Data, 1950-1972*. Baton Rouge: Louisiana State University Press, 1977.

Bass, Jack, and Walter DeVries. *Transformation of Southern Politics: Social Change and Political Consequence Since 1945*. Athens: University of Georgia Press, 1995

Bryce, James. *The American Commonwealth*. 1922. Reprint. New York: AMS Press, 1973.

Ceaser, James, and Andrew Busch. *Upside Down and Inside Out: The 1992 Elections and American Politics*. Lanham, Md.: Rowman and Littlefield, 1993.

Congressional Quarterly. *Politics in America 1998*. Washington, D.C.: Congressional Quarterly, 1997.

—. *American Leaders 1789-1994* Washington, D.C.: Congressional Quarterly, 1994.

Council of State Governments. *State Elective Officials and the Legislatures 1991-1992*. Lexington, Ky.: Council of State Governments, 1991.

—. *Book of the States, 1996-1997*. Vol. 31. Lexington, Ky.: Council of State Governments, 1996.

Ewing, Cortez A. *Primary Elections in the South: Study in Uniparty Politics*. 1953. Reprint. Westport, Conn.: Greenwood Press, 1980.

Germond, Jack W., and Jules Witcover. *Mad as Hell: Revolt at the Ballot Box, 1992*. New York: Warner Books, 1993.

Glashan, Roy R. *American Governors and Gubernatorial Elections, 1775-1978*. Westport, Conn.: Meckler Publishing, 1979.

Grantham, Dewey W. *Democratic South*. 1963. Reprint. New York: W. W. Norton, 1965.

Haider, Donald H. *When Governments Come to Washington: Governors, Mayors, and Intergovernmental Lobbying*. New York: Free Press, 1974.

Heard, Alexander, and Donald S. Strong. *Southern Primaries and Elections 1920-1949*. 1950. Reprint. Salem, N.H.: Ayers, 1970.

Jacob, Herbert. *Politics in the American States*. 3rd ed. Boston: Little, Brown, 1976.

Jacobstein, Helen L. *The Segregation Factor in the Florida Democratic Gubernatorial Primary Election of 1956*. Gainesville: University of Florida Press, 1972.

Jewell, Malcolm E. *Parties and Primaries: Nominating State Governors*. New York: Praeger, 1984.

Kallenbach, Joseph E., and Jessamine S. Kallenbach. *American State Governors, 1776-1976*. 3 vols. Dobbs Ferry, N.Y.: Oceana Publishing, 1977.

Key, V. O. Jr. *Southern Politics in State and Nation*. Knoxville: University of Tennessee Press, 1984.

Kousser, J. Morgan. *The Shaping of Southern Politics: Suffrage Restrictions and the Establishment of the One Party South, 1880-1910*. New Haven, Conn.: Yale University Press, 1974.

Kurland, Gerald. *George Wallace: Southern Governor and Presidential Candidate*. Charlotteville, N.Y.: SamHar Press, 1972.

Lamis, Alexander P. *The Two-Party South*. 2nd ed. New York: Oxford University Press, 1990.

Lipson, Leslie. *The American Governor from Figurehead to Leader*. 1939. Reprint. Westport, Conn.: Greenwood Press, 1969.

McGillivray, Alice V. *Congressional and Gubernatorial Primaries: 1993-1994: A Handbook of Election Statistics*. Washington, D.C.: Congressional Quarterly, 1995.

Mullaney, Marie M. *Biographical Directory of the Governors of the United States 1983-1988*. Westport, Conn.: Meckler Publishing, 1989.

—. *Biographical Directory of the Governors of the United States 1988-1994*. Westport, Conn.: Greenwood Press, 1994.

Raimo, John, ed. *Biographical Directory of the Governors of the United States, 1978-1983*. Westport, Conn.: Meckler Publishing, 1985.

Ransone, Coleman B., Jr. *The American Governorship*. Westport, Conn.: Greenwood Press, 1982.

—. *The Office of the Governor in the United States*. 1956. Reprint. Salem, N.C.: Ayer.

Reichley, A. James, ed. *Elections American Style*. Washington, D.C.: Brookings, 1987.

Sabato, Larry. *Goodbye to Good-time Charlie: The American Governorship Transformed*. Washington, D.C.: CQ Press, 1983.

Sale, Kirkpatrick. *Power Shift: The Rise of the Southern Rim and Its Challenge to the Eastern Establishment*. New York: Random House, 1975.

Scammon, Richard M. *America Votes: A Handbook of Contemporary Election Statistics*. vols. 1 and 2. New York: Macmillan, 1956, 1958. *America Votes*. vols. 3-5. Pittsburgh: University of Pittsburgh, 1959, 1962, and 1964. *America Votes*. Vols. 6-11. Washington, D.C.: Congressional Quarterly, 1966-1975.

—, and Alice V. McGillivray. *America Votes*. Vols. 12-21. Washington, D.C.: Congressional Quarterly, 1977-1995.

—, Alice V. McGillivray and Rhodes Cook. *America Votes*. Vol. 22. Washington, D.C.: Congressional Quarterly, 1998.

Sindler, Allan P., ed. *Huey Long's Louisiana: State Politics 1920-1952*. 1956. Reprint. Baltimore: Johns Hopkins University Press, 1980.

Sobel, Robert, ed. *Biographical Directory of the Governors of the United States, 1789-1978*. 4 vols. Westport, Conn.: Meckler Publishing, 1978.

Spence, James R. *The Making of a Governor: The Moore-Preyer-Lake Primaries of 1964*. Winston-Salem, N.C.: John H. Blair, 1968.

Stanley, Harold W., and Richard G. Niemi. *Vital Statistics on American Politics 1997-1998*. Washington, D.C.: Congressional Quarterly, 1998.

Steed, Robert P., and Laurence W. Moreland, eds. *Party Politics in the South*. New York: Praeger, 1980.

Tindale, George B. *The Disruption of the Solid South*. New York: W. W. Norton, 1972.

Woodward, C. Vann. *Origins of the New South, 1877-1913*. Baton Rouge: Louisiana State University Press, 1971.

Articles

Abrams, Burton A. "Political Power and the Market for Governors." *Public Choice* 37 (1981): 521-529.

Bibby, John F. "Political Parties and Federalism: The Republican National Committee Involvement in Gubernatorial and Legislative Elections." *Publius* 9 (Winter 1979): 229-236.

Black, Merle, and Earl Black. "Republican Party Development in the South: The Rise of the Contested Primary." *Social Science Quarterly* (December 1976): 566-578.

Bryan, Richard J. "Legislative Election of a Governor." *North Carolina Law Review* (December 1967): 128-142.

Cosman, Bernard. "Republican in the South: Goldwater's Impact Upon Voting Alignment in Congressional, Gubernatorial and Senatorial Races." *Southwestern Social Science Quarterly* (June 1967): 13-23.

Eismeier, Theodore J. "Votes and Taxes: The Political Economy of the American Governorship." *Polity* 15 (Spring 1983): 368-379.

Ferejohn, John A., and Randall L. Calvert. "Presidential Coattails in Historical Perspective." *American Journal of Political Science* 28 (February 1984): 127-146.

Jewell, Malcolm E. "Voting Turnout in State Gubernatorial Primaries." *Western Political Quarterly* 30 (June 1977): 236-254.

McCrary, Peyton, Clark Miller and Dale Baum. "Class and Party in Secession Crisis: Voting Behavior in the Deep South." *Journal of Interdisciplinary History* 8 (Winter 1977): 429-457.

Patterson, Samuel C. "Campaign Spending in Contests for Governor." *Western Political Quarterly* 35 (December 1982): 457-477.

Penning, James M., and Corwin E. Smidt. "Public Funding of Gubernatorial Elections: The Views of State Legislatures." *American Politics Quarterly* 10 (July 1982): 315-332.

Pettigrew, Thomas F. "Faubus and Segregation: An Analysis of Arkansas Voting." *Public Opinion Quarterly* (Fall 1960): 346-347.

Piereson, James E. "Sources of Candidate Success in Gubernatorial Elections, 1910-1970." *Journal of Politics* 39 (November 1977): 939-958.

"Post-Mortem of a Georgia Primary." *New South* (Summer 1969): 80-88.

Reiter, Howard L. "Who Voted for Longley? Maine Elects an Independent Governor." *Polity* 10 (Fall 1977): 65-85.

Worsnop, Richard L. "Changing Southern Politics." *Editorial Research Reports* 1 (Jan. 19, 1966): 43-59.

General Election Candidates Index

The General Election Candidates Index includes all candidates appearing in General Election Returns, 1787-1997. The index includes candidates' names followed by state abbreviations and the years of candidacy. To locate a candidate's returns, turn to pages 39 to 89 where the returns are arranged alphabetically by state *(State Abbreviations below)* and in chronological order of election for each state.

A

Aandahl, Fred G. (ND) - 1944, 1946, 1948
Abbett, Leon (NJ) - 1883, 1889
Abbott, Martha (VT) - 1974
Abernethy, Tom (AL) - 1954
Acker, Bert Lee (FL) - 1944, 1948
Ackerman, Lee (AZ) - 1960
Acuff, Roy (TN) - 1948
Adair, John (KY) - 1820
Adair, John A. M. (IN) - 1916
Adam, Andrew (ME) - 1990
Adams, Alva (CO) - 1884, 1886, 1896, 1904, 1906
Adams, Charles Francis (MA) - 1876
Adams, Jewett W. (NV) - 1882, 1886
Adams, John Quincy (MA) - 1833, 1867, 1868, 1869, 1870, 1871
Adams, Paul L. (NY) - 1966, 1970
Adams, Samuel (MA) - 1794, 1795, 1796
Adams, Sherman (NH) - 1948, 1950
Adams, Spencer B. (NC) - 1900
Adams, Tod R. (TX) - 1954
Adams, William H. (CO) - 1926, 1928, 1930
Adkins, Homer M. (AR) - 1940, 1942
Agnew, Spiro T. (MD) - 1966
Aiken, George D. (VT) - 1936, 1938
Akin (GA) - 1859
Alcorn, Hugh Meade (CT) - 1934
Alcorn, James L. (MS) - 1869, 1873
Aldrich, Chester H. (NE) - 1910, 1912
Aldrich, Walter J. (VT) - 1914
Alexander (NJ) - 1856
Alexander, Archibald (DE) - 1795

Alexander, Lamar (TN) - 1974, 1978, 1982
Alexander, Moses (ID) - 1908, 1914, 1916, 1922
Alfange, Dean (NY) - 1942
Alger, Fred M. Jr. (MI) - 1952
Alger, Horace C. (WY) - 1898
Alger, Russell A. (MI) - 1884
Allain, Bill (MS) - 1983
Allen (MO) - 1844
Allen, Byron G. (MN) - 1944
Allen, Charles H. (MA) - 1891
Allen, Frank G. (MA) - 1928, 1930
Allen, G. H. (CO) - 1896
Allen, George W. (FL) - 1916
Allen, George F. (VA) - 1993
Allen, Heman (VT) - 1829, 1831
Allen, Henry J. (KS) - 1914, 1918, 1920
Allen, Henry W. (LA) - 1864, 1865
Allen, James C. (IL) - 1860
Allen, John (KY) - 1808
Allen, Oscar K. (LA) - 1932
Allen, Philip (RI) - 1851, 1852, 1853
Allen, Samuel L. (MA) - 1833
Allen, William (OH) - 1873, 1875
Allen, William C. (SD) - 1934
Allin, Roger (ND) - 1894
Allis, Edward P. (WI) - 1877
Allred, James V. (TX) - 1934, 1936
Almond, J. Lindsay Jr. (VA) - 1957
Almond, Lincoln (RI) - 1978, 1994
Alschuler, Samuel (IL) - 1900
Alsop, John P. (IL) - 1892, 1896
Altgeld, John P. (IL) - 1892, 1896
Ameringer, Oscar (WI) - 1914
Ames, A. A. (MN) - 1886
Ames, Adelbert (MS) - 1873
Ames, Alfred K. (ME) - 1934

Ames, Oliver (MA) - 1886, 1887, 1888
Ammons, Elias M. (CO) - 1912
Ammons, Teller (CO) - 1936, 1938
Amsden, Charles H. (NH) - 1888, 1890
Anaya, Toney (NM) - 1982
Andersen, Elmer L. (MN) - 1960, 1962
Anderson, C. Elmer (MN) - 1952, 1954
Anderson, D. G. "Andy" (HI) - 1982, 1986
Anderson, Emmett T. (WA) - 1956
Anderson, Forrest H. (MT) - 1968
Anderson, Henry W. (VA) - 1921
Anderson, Hugh J. (ME) - 1843, 1844, 1845
Anderson, J. H. (ID) - 1898
Anderson, John Jr. (KS) - 1960, 1962
Anderson, Kenneth T. (KS) - 1950
Anderson, Sigurd (SD) - 1950, 1952
Anderson, T. J. (IA) - 1887
Anderson, Thomas J. (MN) - 1916
Anderson, Victor E. (NE) - 1954, 1956, 1958
Anderson, Wendell R. (MN) - 1970, 1974
Anderson, William R. (TN) - 1962
Andrew, John A. (MA) - 1860, 1861, 1862, 1863, 1864
Andrew, John F. (MA) - 1886
Andrews (GA) - 1855
Andrews, Charles B. (CT) - 1878
Andrews, John (CO) - 1990
Andrews, Lloyd (WA) - 1960
Andrews, Mark (ND) - 1962
Andrews, Reddin (TX) - 1910, 1912

Andrus, Cecil D. (ID) - 1966, 1970, 1974, 1986, 1990
Ansel, Martin F. (SC) - 1906, 1908
Anthony, George T. (KS) - 1876
Anthony, Henry B. (RI) - 1849, 1850
Apodaca, Jerry (NM) - 1974
Appleton, James (ME) - 1842, 1843, 1844
Archambault, Alberic A. (RI) - 1918, 1928
Archambault, Raoul Jr. (RI) - 1952
Ariyoshi, George R. (HI) - 1974, 1978, 1982
Armstrong (TN) - 1837
Armstrong, Alexander (MD) - 1923
Armstrong, Charles M. (CO) - 1936
Arn, Edward F. (KS) - 1950, 1952
Arnall, Ellis (GA) - 1942
Arnesen, Deborah Arnie (NH) - 1992
Arnold (WI) - 1904
Arnold, Lemuel H. (RI) - 1831, 1832, 1833
Arnold, Louis A. (WI) - 1922
Arnold, Olney (RI) - 1872, 1908, 1909
Arnold, Peleg (RI) - 1806, 1815
Aronson, John Hugo (MT) - 1952, 1956
Ashcroft, John (MO) - 1984, 1988
Ashe, Thomas S. (NC) - 1868
Ashelstrom, Charles A. (CO) - 1912
Ashley (MO) - 1836
Ashley, William H. (MO) - 1824
Askew, Reubin (FL) - 1970, 1974
Atiyeh, Victor G. (OR) - 1974, 1978, 1982
Atkinson (MO) - 1920
Atkinson, George W. (WV) - 1896
Atkinson, W. P. (OK) - 1962

State Abbreviations

Alabama	AL	Illinois	IL	Montana	MT	Rhode Island	RI
Alaska	AK	Indiana	IN	Nebraska	NE	South Carolina	SC
Arizona	AZ	Iowa	IA	Nevada	NV	South Dakota	SD
Arkansas	AR	Kansas	KS	New Hampshire	NH	Tennessee	TN
California	CA	Kentucky	KY	New Jersey	NJ	Texas	TX
Colorado	CO	Louisiana	LA	New Mexico	NM	Utah	UT
Connecticut	CT	Maine	ME	New York	NY	Vermont	VT
Delaware	DE	Maryland	MD	North Carolina	NC	Virginia	VA
Florida	FL	Massachusetts	MA	North Dakota	ND	Washington	WA
Georgia	GA	Michigan	MI	Ohio	OH	West Virginia	WV
Hawaii	HI	Minnesota	MN	Oklahoma	OK	Wisconsin	WI
Idaho	ID	Mississippi	MS	Oregon	OR	Wyoming	WY
		Missouri	MO	Pennsylvania	PA		

Atkinson, William Y. (GA) - 1894, 1896
Atwater (CT) - 1878
Atwell, W. H. (TX) - 1922
Atwood, John (NH) - 1851, 1852
Austin, Horace (MN) - 1869, 1871
Austin, Richard B. (IL) - 1956
Auten, H. F. (AR) - 1898
Avenson, Donald D. (IA) - 1990
Avery, Carlos (MN) - 1924
Avery, William H. (KS) - 1964, 1966
Aycock, Charles B. (NC) - 1900
Ayers, Roy E. (MT) - 1936, 1940
Aylward, John A. (WI) - 1906, 1908
Ayres, Tom (SD) - 1926

B

Babb, W. I. (IA) - 1895
Babbitt, Bruce (AZ) - 1978, 1980
Babcock, Tim (MT) - 1964, 1968
Bachelder, Nahum J. (NH) - 1902
Bacon, Gaspar G. (MA) - 1934
Bacon, Waler W. (DE) - 1940, 1944
Badger, William (NH) - 1834, 1835
Bafalis, L. A. "Skip" (FL) - 1982
Bagby, Arthur P. (AL) - 1837, 1839
Bagley, John J. (MI) - 1872, 1874
Bagwell, Paul D. (MI) - 1958, 1960
Bailey, Carl E. (AR) - 1936, 1938
Bailey, Ed F. (OR) - 1930
Bailey, Ernest H. (VT) - 1944
Bailey, John (MA) - 1834
Bailey, John W. (MI) - 1918
Bailey, M. S. (CO) - 1896
Bailey, Thomas L. (MS) - 1943
Bailey, W. (FL) - 1848
Bailey, W. J. (KS) - 1902
Baird (WI) - 1853
Baird, David Jr. (NJ) - 1931
Bakalis, Michael (IL) - 1978
Baker, Conrad (IN) - 1868
Baker, Davis S. Jr. (RI) - 1893, 1894
Baker, Howard H. (TN) - 1938
Baker, John I. (MA) - 1875
Baker, Nathaniel B. (NH) - 1854, 1855
Baker, R. Tarvin (KY) - 1868
Baker, Samuel Aaron (MO) - 1924
Baldridge, H. C. (ID) - 1926, 1928
Baldwin, Eli (OH) - 1836
Baldwin, Henry P. (MI) - 1868, 1870
Baldwin, Raymond E. (CT) - 1938, 1940, 1942, 1944
Baldwin, Roger S. (CT) - 1843, 1844, 1845
Baldwin, Simeon E. (CT) - 1910, 1912
Baliles, Gerald L. (VA) - 1985
Ballantine, James W. (ID) - 1894
Ballou, Olney (RI) - 1847
Balzar, Fred B. (NV) - 1926, 1930
Bamberger, Simon (UT) - 1916
Bancroft, George (MA) - 1844
Bancroft, Joseph (DE) - 1924
Bangerter, Norman H. (UT) - 1984, 1988
Banks, John (PA) - 1841
Banks, Nathaniel P. (MA) - 1857, 1858, 1859
Banning, W. L. (MN) - 1877
Barker, D. E. (AR) - 1894
Barker, Harold H. (MN) - 1946
Barlocker, William A. (UT) - 1960
Barnaby, Jerothmul B. (RI) - 1877
Barnes (MI) - 1878
Barnes, Sidney M. (KY) - 1867
Barnett, Ross R. (MS) - 1959
Barnette, J. R. (AZ) - 1914
Barnum, E. M. (OR) - 1858
Barrere, Nelson (OH) - 1853

Barrett, Frank A. (WY) - 1950
Barrett, Jesse W. (MO) - 1936
Barron, W. W. (WV) - 1960
Barrows, Lewis O. (ME) - 1936, 1938
Barry (MI) - 1854, 1860
Barry, John S. (MI) - 1841, 1843, 1849
Barry, William T. (KY) - 1828
Barstow, Amos C. (RI) - 1864
Barstow, John L. (VT) - 1882
Barstow, William Augustus (WI) - 1853, 1855
Bartlett, Charles W. (MA) - 1905
Bartlett, Dewey F. (OK) - 1966, 1970
Bartlett, Ichabod (NH) - 1831, 1832
Bartlett, John H. (NH) - 1918
Bartlett, Josiah (NH) - 1789, 1790, 1791, 1792, 1793
Bartlett, Washington (CA) - 1886
Bartley, Mordecai (OH) - 1844
Barton (DE) - 1854
Barton, Ara (MN) - 1873
Barzee, C. W. (OR) - 1906
Basha, Eddie (AZ) - 1994
Bashford, Coles (WI) - 1855
Baskin, Alonzo P. (FL) - 1892
Bass, Robert P. (NH) - 1910
Bassett, Richard (DE) - 1798
Bate, William B. (TN) - 1882, 1884
Bateman, Raymond H. (NJ) - 1977
Bates, Curtis (IA) - 1854
Bates, Frederick (MO) - 1824
Bates, John L. (MA) - 1902, 1903, 1904
Bates, Mark P. (SD) - 1918, 1920
Batt, Philip (ID) - 1982, 1994
Battle, John S. (VA) - 1949
Battle, William C. (VA) - 1969
Baxley, Bill (AL) - 1986
Baxter (TN) - 1890
Baxter, Elisha (AR) - 1872
Baxter, George W. (WY) - 1890
Baxter, Percival P. (ME) - 1922
Bayh, Evan (IN) - 1988, 1992
Beach, Erasmus D. (MA) - 1855, 1856, 1857, 1858, 1860
Beach, William B. (RI) - 1876
Beall, J. Glenn (MD) - 1978
Beardsley (CT) - 1912
Beardsley, Morris (CT) - 1916
Beardsley, William (IA) - 1948, 1950, 1952
Beasley, David (SC) - 1994
Beattie, Taylor (LA) - 1879
Beauvais, Arnaud (LA) - 1831
Beaver, James A. (PA) - 1882, 1886
Bebb, William (OH) - 1846
Beck, George T. (WY) - 1902
Becker, George L. (MN) - 1859, 1894
Beckham, John C. W. (KY) - 1900, 1903, 1927
Beddow, Jim (SD) - 1994
Bedell, John (NH) - 1869, 1870
Bedford, Gunning Jr. (DE) - 1795
Bedford, Homer F. - (CO) - 1942
Bedle, Joseph D. (NJ) - 1874
Beeckman, R. Livingston (RI) - 1914, 1916, 1918
Beekman, C. C. (OR) - 1878
Beers, S. P. (CT) - 1838
Begole, Josiah W. (MI) - 1882, 1884
Behan, W. J. (LA) - 1904
Belaga, Julie D. (CT) - 1986
Belknap (KY) - 1903
Bell, Bob (GA) - 1982
Bell, Charles H. (NH) - 1880
Bell, Charles J. (VT) - 1904
Bell, James (NH) - 1853, 1854, 1855
Bell, John (NH) - 1828, 1829
Bell, Joshua F. (KY) - 1859
Bell, P. Hansbrough (TX) - 1849, 1851

Bell, Samuel (NH) - 1819, 1820, 1821, 1822
Bell, Theodore A. (CA) - 1906, 1910, 1918
Bellmon, Henry L. (OK) - 1962, 1986
Bellotti, Francis X. (MA) - 1964
Benedict, Cleve (WV) - 1992
Benedict, Omer K. (OK) - 1926
Bennett (WV) - 1908
Bennett, Caleb P. (DE) - 1832
Bennett, John J. Jr. (NY) - 1942
Bennett, Robert F. (KS) - 1974, 1978
Benson, Bruce (CO) - 1994
Benson, Elmer A. (MN) - 1936, 1938
Bentall, J. O. (MN) - 1916
Bentley, Arthur A. (WI) - 1922
Benton, Thomas H. (IA) - 1865
Benton, Thomas Hart (MO) - 1856
Benz (WI) - 1944
Berge, George W. (NE) - 1904
Bernhardt, Michael (VT) - 1988
Berry, James H. (AR) - 1882
Berry, Nathaniel S. (NH) - 1846, 1847, 1848, 1849, 1850, 1861, 1862
Berry, Tom (SD) - 1932, 1934, 1936
Berry, William H. (PA) - 1910
Best, Roy (CT) - 1944
Beveridge, Albert J. (IN) - 1912
Bibb, William Wyatt (AL) - 1819
Bickett, Thomas W. (NC) - 1916
Bicknell, Lewis W. (SD) - 1940, 1942
Biddle, John (MI) - 1835
Bidwell, John (CA) - 1875
Bierman, A. (MN) - 1883
Bigelow, Hobart B. (CT) - 1880
Bigger, Samuel (IN) - 1840, 1843
Biggs, Benjamin T. (DE) - 1886
Bigler, John (CA) - 1851, 1853, 1855
Bigler, William (PA) - 1851, 1854
Bilbo, Theodore G. (MS) - 1915, 1927
Billard, J. B. (KS) - 1914
Billings, Franklin S. (VT) - 1924
Bingham, Arthur (AL) - 1886
Bingham, Hiram (CT) - 1924
Bingham, J. A. (AL) - 1926
Bingham, Kinsley S. (MI) - 1854, 1856
Bingham, Robert P. (NH) - 1950
Bingham, W. H. H. (VT) - 1874, 1876, 1878
Bird, Charles Sumner (MA) - 1912, 1913
Bird, Francis W. (MA) - 1872
Bird, James B. (SD) - 1918
Birney, James G. (MI) - 1843, 1845
Bishop (AR) - 1876
Bishop, Henry W. (MA) - 1852, 1853, 1854
Bishop, Neil (ME) - 1952
Bishop, Richard M. (OH) - 1877
Bishop, Robert R. (MA) - 1882
Bissell, Clark (CT) - 1846, 1847, 1848
Bissell, William H. (IL) - 1856
Black (NJ) - 1904
Black, C. R. (AR) - 1948
Black, Chauncey F. (PA) - 1886
Black, Frank S. (NY) - 1896
Black, J. D. (KY) - 1919
Black, W. W. (WA) - 1920
Blackburn, Luke P. (KY) - 1879
Blackford, Isaac (IN) - 1825
Blackmer, John (MA) - 1889
Blackwood, Ibra C. (SC) - 1930
Blaine, John J. (WI) - 1914, 1920, 1922, 1924
Blair (MI) - 1872
Blair, Austin (MI) - 1860, 1862
Blair, C. Stanley (MD) - 1970
Blair, James T. Jr. (MO) - 1956

Blair, John I. (NJ) - 1868
Blanchard, James J. (MI) - 1982, 1986, 1990
Blanchard, Newton C. (LA) - 1904
Blandin, Amos (NH) - 1936
Blanton, Ray (TN) - 1974
Blasdel, Henry G. (NV) - 1864, 1866
Blaylock, Len E. (AR) - 1972
Bleakley, William F. (NY) - 1936
Blease, Coleman L. (SC) - 1910, 1912
Blewett, Pierce (ND) - 1930
Bliss, Aaron T. (MI) - 1900, 1902
Blood, Henry H. (UT) - 1932, 1936
Blood, Robert O. (NH) - 1940, 1942
Blount, J. H. (AR) - 1920
Blount, Willie (TN) - 1809, 1811, 1813
Bloxham, William D. (FL) - 1872, 1880, 1896
Blue, Robert D. (IA) - 1944, 1946
Boardman, Elijah (CT) - 1812, 1813, 1814, 1815
Boatright, William L. (CO) - 1928
Bodwell, Joseph R. (ME) - 1886
Boe, Nils A. (SD) - 1964, 1966
Boggs, J. Caleb (DE) - 1952, 1956
Boggs, Lilburn W. (MO) - 1836
Bolens (WI) - 1938
Boles, Horace (IA) - 1889, 1891, 1893
Boles, Thomas (AR) - 1884
Bomrich, Louis G. (WI) - 1900
Bond, Christopher S. (MO) - 1972, 1976, 1980
Bond, Frank M. (NM) - 1990
Bond, Hugh L. (MD) - 1867
Bond, Shadrach (IL) - 1818
Bonner, John W. (MT) - 1948, 1952
Bonniwell, Eugene C. (PA) - 1918, 1926
Bookwalter, John W. (OH) - 1881
Boosalis, Helen (NE) - 1986
Booth, Gardner (WA) - 1988
Booth, James (DE) - 1822
Booth, Newton (CA) - 1871
Bordelon, Louis (LA) - 1852
Boreman, Arthur I. (WV) - 1863, 1864, 1866
Boreman, Herbert S. (WV) - 1948
Boren, David L. (OK) - 1974
Botkin, Alexander C. (MT) - 1896
Botkin, Jeremiah D. (KS) - 1908
Bottolfsen, C. A. (ID) - 1938, 1940, 1942
Botts, Clarence M. (NM) - 1930
Bouck, William C. (NY) - 1840, 1842
Bourn, Augustus O. (RI) - 1883, 1884
Boutin, Bernard L. (NH) - 1958, 1960
Boutwell, George S. (MA) - 1849, 1850, 1851
Bowen, A. E. Jr. (ND) - 1912
Bowen, Otis R. (IN) - 1972, 1976
Bowerman, Jay (OR) - 1910
Bowers, M. D. (AR) - 1926, 1928
Bowie, G. W. (CA) - 1857
Bowie, Oden (MD) - 1867
Bowie, Richard J. (MD) - 1853
Bowles, Chester (CT) - 1948, 1950
Bowles, Hargrove Jr. (NC) - 1972
Boyce, D. A. Jelly (OK) - 1958
Boyd, James E. (NE) - 1890
Boyle, Emmet D. (NV) - 1914, 1918
Boynton, Charles A. (TX) - 1918
Brackett, John Q. A. (MA) - 1889, 1890
Bradbury, Bion (ME) - 1862, 1863
Bradford, Augustus W. (MD) - 1861
Bradford, Robert F. (MA) - 1946, 1948
Bradish, Luther (NY) - 1842

Bradley, Dorothy (MT) - 1992
Bradley, Jim (UT) - 1996
Bradley, L. R. (NV) - 1870, 1874, 1878
Bradley, Tom (CA) - 1982, 1986
Bradley, William C. (VT) - 1819, 1834, 1835, 1836, 1837, 1838
Bradley, William O. (KY) - 1887, 1895
Bradshaw, John Paul (MO) - 1944
Brady, James H. (ID) - 1908, 1910
Bragg, Thomas (NC) - 1854, 1856
Brainard, Lawrence (VT) - 1846, 1847, 1852, 1853
Bramlett, Leon (MS) - 1983
Bramlette, Thomas E. (KY) - 1863
Branch, John (NC) - 1838
Brandon, Gerald C. (MS) - 1827, 1829
Brandon, William W. (AL) - 1922
Branigin, Roger D. (IN) - 1964
Brann, Louis J. (ME) - 1932, 1934, 1938
Branon, E. Frank (VT) - 1954, 1956
Branson, L. C. (NV) - 1934
Branstad, Terry E. (IA) - 1982, 1986, 1990, 1994
Breathitt, Edward T. (KY) - 1963
Breathitt, John (KY) - 1832
Breaux, John E. (LA) - 1892
Bredesen, Phil (TN) - 1994
Breidenthal, John W. (KS) - 1900
Brennan, Joseph E. (ME) - 1978, 1982, 1990, 1994
Brewer, Earl (MS) - 1911
Brewster, Ralph O. (ME) - 1924, 1926
Breyer, Donald. S. (VA) - 1997
Bricker, John W. (OH) - 1936, 1938, 1940, 1942
Bridges, H. Styles (NH) - 1934
Bridges, Robert (WA) - 1920
Bridgham, Samuel W. (RI) - 1821
Briggs, Ansel (IA) - 1846
Briggs, Frank A. (ND) - 1896
Briggs, George N. (MA) - 1843, 1844, 1845, 1846, 1847, 1848, 1849, 1850, 1859
Brigham, Herbert F. (VT) - 1890
Brinkley, John R. (KS) - 1930, 1932
Briscoe, Dolph (TX) - 1972, 1974
Britt, Henry M. (AR) - 1960
Brockett, Bruce D. (AZ) - 1946, 1948
Broderick, Raymond J. (PA) - 1970
Broening, William F. (MD) - 1930
Bronson, David (ME) - 1846, 1847
Bronson, Greene C. (NY) - 1854
Bronson, S. L. (CT) - 1900
Brooks (MD) - 1887
Brooks, Bryant B. (WY) - 1904, 1906
Brooks, C. Wayland (IL) - 1936
Brooks, Erastus (NY) - 1856
Brooks, John (MA) - 1816, 1817, 1818, 1819, 1820, 1821, 1822
Brooks, Joseph (AR) - 1872
Brooks, Ralph G. (NE) - 1958
Broome, James E. (FL) - 1852
Brotzman, Donald G. (CO) - 1954, 1956
Brough, Charles H. (AR) - 1916, 1918
Brough, John (OH) - 1863
Broughton, J. Melville (NC) - 1940
Broward, Napoleon Bonaparte (FL) - 1904
Brown (MO) - 1880
Brown, Aaron V. (TN) - 1845, 1847
Brown, Albert G. (MS) - 1843, 1845
Brown, Albert O. (NH) - 1920
Brown, Arthur M. (CT) - 1936
Brown, Benjamin Gratz (MO) - 1870
Brown, Clarence J. (OH) - 1934
Brown, Clarence Jr. (OH) - 1982

Brown, D. Russell (RI) - 1892, 1893, 1894
Brown, Earl (MN) - 1932
Brown, Edmund G. (CA) - 1958, 1962, 1966
Brown, Edmund G. "Jerry" Jr. (CA) - 1974, 1978
Brown, Ethan A. (OH) - 1816, 1818, 1820
Brown, Frank (MD) - 1891
Brown, Fred H. (NH) - 1922, 1924
Brown, Harvey D. (WI) - 1908
Brown, Jerry (OK) - 1986
Brown, John C. (TN) - 1870, 1872
Brown, John Y. Jr. (KY) - 1979
Brown, John Young (KY) - 1891
Brown, Joseph Emerson (GA) - 1857, 1859
Brown, Joseph M. (GA) - 1908, 1910
Brown, Kathleen (CA) - 1994
Brown, Neill S. (TN) - 1847, 1849
Brown, Robert B. (OH) - 1912
Brown, Thomas S. (FL) - 1848
Brown, W. S. (NH) - 1879
Brown, William Moseley (VA) - 1929
Browne, George H. (RI) - 1864
Browne, Thomas C. (IL) - 1822
Browne, Thomas McClelland (IN) - 1872
Browning, Gordon (TN) - 1936, 1948, 1950
Brownlow, William G. (TN) - 1865, 1867
Bruce, Alexander B. (MA) - 1898
Bruce, C. Arthur (TN) - 1930, 1940
Brucker, Wilber M. (MI) - 1930, 1932
Brumbaugh, Martin G. (PA) - 1914
Brunsdale, Norman (ND) - 1950, 1952, 1954
Bryan, Charles W. (NE) - 1922, 1926, 1928, 1930, 1932, 1938, 1942
Bryan, Richard H. (NV) - 1982, 1986
Bryant, Farris (FL) - 1960
Bryant, William H. (TX) - 1956
Buchanan, John P. (TN) - 1890, 1892
Buchtel, Henry A. (CO) - 1906
Buck (KY) - 1832
Buck, Clayton Douglass (DE) - 1928, 1932
Buckalew, Charles B. (PA) - 1872
Buckingham, R. G. (CO) - 1878
Buckingham, William A. (CT) - 1858, 1859, 1860, 1861, 1862, 1863, 1864, 1865
Buckmaster (DE) - 1858
Buckner, Simon B. (KY) - 1887
Buckson, David P. (DE) - 1964
Budd, James H. (CA) - 1894
Budlong, David H. (ID) - 1896
Buehner, Carl W. (UT) - 1968
Buel, Jesse (NY) - 1836
Buell, David E. (NV) - 1864
Buell, David L. (MN) - 1875
Bugbee, Newton A. K. (NJ) - 1919
Bulger, Michael J. (AL) - 1865
Bulkeley, Morgan G. (CT) - 1882, 1888
Bull, John (MO) - 1832
Bull, Mansen (DE) - 1816, 1819
Bullington, Orville (TX) - 1932
Bullitt, Scott (WA) - 1928
Bullock, Alexander H. (MA) - 1865, 1866, 1867
Bullock, Nathaniel (RI) - 1839
Bullock, Rufus B. (GA) - 1868
Bulow, William J. (SD) - 1924, 1926, 1928
Bumpers, Dale L. (AR) - 1970, 1972
Bunning, Jim (KY) - 1983
Burch, Palmer L. (CO) - 1958
Burch, Robert L. Jr. (OH) - 1994
Burdick, Quentin (ND) - 1946

Burges, Tristam (RI) - 1836, 1839
Burgess, D. (WA) - 1904
Burke, Andrew H. (ND) - 1890, 1892
Burke, James E. (VT) - 1908
Burke, John (ND) - 1906, 1908, 1910
Burke, John M. (ID) - 1892
Burke, William H. (KS) - 1940, 1942
Burkett, George W. (TX) - 1902
Burkitt, Frank (MS) - 1895
Burleigh, Edwin C. (ME) - 1888, 1890
Burnett, P. H. (CA) - 1849
Burney, Dwight W. (NE) - 1964
Burnquist, Joseph A. A. (MN) - 1916, 1918
Burns, Haydon (FL) - 1964
Burns, John A. (HI) - 1959, 1962, 1966, 1970
Burnside, Ambrose E. (RI) - 1866, 1867, 1868
Burr, Aaron (NY) - 1804
Burroughs, John (NM) - 1958, 1960
Burrows, Lorenzo (NY) - 1858
Bursum, Holm O. (NM) - 1911, 1916
Burt, Homer P. (UT) - 1912
Burt, Wellington R. (MI) - 1888
Burton, William (DE) - 1858
Busbee, George (GA) - 1974, 1978
Bush, George W. (TX) - 1994
Bush, Jeb (FL) - 1994
Bushfield, Harlan J. (SD) - 1938, 1940
Bushnell, Asa S. (OH) - 1895, 1897
Busiel, Charles A. (NH) - 1894
Bussiere, Emile R. (NH) - 1968
Butcher, Jake (TN) - 1978
Butler (KY) - 1844
Butler, Anthony (KY) - 1820
Butler, Benjamin F. (MA) - 1859, 1878, 1879, 1882, 1883
Butler, Dan (NE) - 1924
Butler, David (NE) - 1866, 1868, 1870
Butler, Ezra (VT) - 1826, 1827
Butler, Thomas (LA) - 1828
Butovich, John Jr. (AK) - 1958
Butte, George C. (TX) - 1924
Buxton, Ralph P. (NC) - 1880
Byerly, Clyde G. (ND) - 1950
Bymers, Cornelius (ND) - 1954
Byrd (AR) - 1844
Byrd, Harry Clifton (MD) - 1954
Byrd, Harry F. (VA) - 1925
Byrne, Brendan T. (NJ) - 1973, 1977
Byrne, Frank M. (SD) - 1912, 1914
Byrnes, James F. (SC) - 1950

C

Cady (CT) - 1894
Cady, Virgil H. (WI) - 1926
Cafferata, Patty (NV) - 1986
Caffery, Don Jr. (LA) - 1900
Cahill, Horace T. (MA) - 1944
Cahill, William T. (NJ) - 1969
Caine, J. T. (UT) - 1896
Calderwood, W. G. (MN) - 1914
Caldwell, Millard F. (FL) - 1944
Caldwell, Tod R. (NC) - 1872
Calkins, William H. (IN) - 1884
Callan, Luke H. (RI) - 1934
Callaway, E. E. (FL) - 1936
Callaway, Howard H. (GA) - 1966
Camden, James M. (WV) - 1868
Camden, Johnson N. (WV) - 1872
Cameron, Ralph H. (AZ) - 1914
Cameron, William E. (VA) - 1881
Campbell (TN) - 1902
Campbell, Alex (OH) - 1826
Campbell, Bonnie J. (IA) - 1994
Campbell, C. (VA) - 1913

Campbell, Carroll (SC) - 1986, 1990
Campbell, Daniel (IA) - 1879
Campbell, E. L. (CO) - 1882
Campbell, Jack M. (NM) - 1962, 1964
Campbell, James E. (OH) - 1889, 1891, 1895
Campbell, James O. "Jim" (AK) - 1994
Campbell, John W. (OH) - 1828
Campbell, Thomas E. (AZ) - 1916, 1918, 1920, 1922, 1936
Campbell, Thomas F. (OR) - 1874
Campbell, Thomas M. (TX) - 1906, 1908
Campbell, William B. (TN) - 1851
Campbell-Cline, Christina (KS) - 1990
Canby, Israel T. (IN) - 1828
Candler, Allen D. (GA) - 1898, 1900
Cannon, Harry L. (DE) - 1936
Cannon, Joseph D. (NY) - 1920
Cannon, Newton (TN) - 1827, 1835, 1837, 1839
Cannon, Paul (MT) - 1960
Cannon, William (DE) - 1862
Capers, H. (TX) - 1920
Caperton, Gaston (WV) - 1988, 1992
Capper, Arthur (KS) - 1912, 1914, 1916
Carey, Hugh L. (NY) - 1974, 1978
Carey, Joseph M. (WY) - 1910
Carey, Robert D. (WY) - 1918
Cargo, David F. (NM) - 1966, 1968
Carlin, John (KS) - 1978, 1982
Carlin, Thomas (IL) - 1838
Carlson, Arne (MN) - 1990, 1994
Carlson, Frank (KS) - 1946, 1948
Carlson, George A. (CO) - 1914, 1916
Carlton, Doyle E. (FL) - 1928
Carmichael, Gil (MS) - 1975, 1979
Carnahan, J. P. (AR) - 1892
Carnahan, Mel (MO) - 1992, 1996
Carney, Thomas (KS) - 1862
Carpenter, Cyrus Clay (IA) - 1871, 1873
Carpenter, R. B. (SC) - 1870
Carpenter, Randolph (KS) - 1948
Carpenter, Terry (NE) - 1940
Carpenter, Thomas F. (RI) - 1840, 1842, 1843
Carper, Thomas R. (DE) - 1992, 1996
Carr (MO) - 1825
Carr, Clarence E. (NH) - 1908, 1910
Carr, Elias (NC) - 1892
Carr, Ralph L. (CO) - 1938, 1940
Carroll (MD) - 1844
Carroll, Beryl F. (IA) - 1908, 1910
Carroll, John Lee (MD) - 1875
Carroll, Julian (KY) - 1975
Carroll, Robert P. (NY) - 1930
Carroll, William (TN) - 1821, 1823, 1825, 1829, 1831, 1833, 1835
Carruth, Walter L. (AR) - 1970
Carruthers, Garrey E. (NM) - 1986
Carson, Joseph K. Jr. (OR) - 1954
Carter, Jimmy (GA) - 1970
Carter, Jonathan K. (ME) - 1994
Carter, Yancy (GA) - 1908
Caruthers, Robert L. (TN) - 1863
Carvel, Elbert N. (DE) - 1948, 1952, 1960
Carville, Edward P. (NV) - 1938, 1942
Cary, Melbert B. (CT) - 1902
Case, Norman S. (RI) - 1928, 1930, 1932
Casey, Robert P. (PA) - 1986, 1990
Casey, Thomas B. (NV) - 1906
Cashin, John Logan (AL) - 1970
Castle, Michael N. (DE) - 1984, 1988
Castro, Raul H. (AZ) - 1970, 1974

Cate, Asa P. (NH) - 1858, 1859, 1860
Catlin, George S. (CT) - 1848
Catts, Sidney J. (FL) - 1916
Caulfield, Henry Stewart (MO) - 1928
Causey, Peter F. (DE) - 1846, 1850, 1854
Cayetano, Benjamin J. (HI) - 1994
Celebrezze, Anthony J. Jr. (OH) - 1990
Celeste, Richard F. (OH) - 1978, 1982, 1986
Center, John H. (VT) - 1900
Chace, Benjamin G. (RI) - 1873
Chace, James H. (RI) - 1889
Chafee, John H. (RI) - 1962, 1964, 1966, 1968
Chamberlain, Abiram (CT) - 1902
Chamberlain, Daniel H. (SC) - 1874, 1876
Chamberlain, Edwin M. (MA) - 1869, 1871
Chamberlain, George E. (OR) - 1902, 1906
Chamberlain, Henry (MI) - 1874
Chamberlain, Joshua L. (ME) - 1866, 1867, 1868, 1869
Chamberlain, Levi (NH) - 1849, 1850
Chamberlin, Robert (SD) - 1966, 1968
Chambers, Dr. Henry (AL) - 1821, 1823
Chambers, E. F. (MD) - 1864
Chambers, Ernest W. (NE) - 1974
Chambers, J. J. (TX) - 1851
Chambers, T. J. (TX) - 1853, 1861, 1863
Chambers, William (TX) - 1875
Chandler, Albert B. "Happy" (KY) - 1935, 1955
Chandler, Anson G. (ME) - 1852
Chandler, Zacharaiah (MI) - 1852
Chanler, Lewis Stuyvesant (NY) - 1908
Chapin, Josiah (RI) - 1851
Chapman, Horace L. (OH) - 1897
Chapman, Reuben (AL) - 1847
Chapn (CT) - 1854
Chase (WI) - 1849
Chase, Dudley (VT) - 1823
Chase, Ira J. (IN) - 1892
Chase, John C. (MA) - 1902, 1903
Chase, Ray P. (MN) - 1930
Chase, Salmon P. (OH) - 1855, 1857
Chavez, Fabian Jr. (NM) - 1968
Cheney, John M. (FL) - 1908
Cheney, Person C. (NH) - 1875, 1876
Cherry, Francis (AR) - 1952
Cherry, R. Gregg (NC) - 1944
Chiles, Lawton (FL) - 1990, 1994
Chittenden, Martin (VT) - 1811, 1812, 1813, 1814, 1815
Chittenden, Thomas (VT) - 1791, 1792, 1793, 1794, 1795, 1796
Christiancy, Isaac P. (MI) - 1852
Christianson, Theodore (MN) - 1924, 1926, 1928
Church, Daniel T. (RI) - 1897, 1898
Churchill, Thomas J. (AR) - 1880
Churchill, Winston (NH) - 1912
Chvala, Chuck (WI) - 1994
Cianci, Vincent A. (RI) - 1980
Claflin, William (MA) - 1868, 1869, 1870
Claiborne, W. C. C. (LA) - 1812
Clardy, W. A. (AL) - 1938
Clark (KY) - 1855
Clark (MD) - 1850
Clark (MO) - 1840
Clark, A. M. (WY) - 1934
Clark, Barzilla W. (ID) - 1936
Clark, Charles (MS) - 1863

Clark, Chase A. (ID) - 1940, 1942
Clark, D. M. (IA) - 1881
Clark, E. S. (AZ) - 1926
Clark, Ed (CA) - 1978
Clark, Edward (TX) - 1861
Clark, F. Davis (ME) - 1946
Clark, George (TX) - 1892
Clark, James (KY) - 1836
Clark, John (GA) - 1825
Clark, Jonas (VT) - 1849
Clark, Merritt (VT) - 1854, 1855
Clark, Myron H. (NY) - 1854
Clark, Nehemiah (DE) - 1836
Clark, William (MO) - 1820
Clarke, George W. (IA) - 1912, 1914
Clarke, J. P. (AR) - 1894
Clarke, John (DE) - 1816
Clauson, Clinton A. (ME) - 1958
Clay, Clement Comer (AL) - 1835
Clay, Green (KY) - 1808
Clayton (MS) - 1843
Clayton, Joshua (DE) - 1792
Cleaves, Henry B. (ME) - 1892, 1894
Clee, Lester H. (NJ) - 1937
Clement, Frank G. (TN) - 1952, 1954, 1962
Clement, Percival W. (VT) - 1902, 1906, 1918
Clements, Earle C. (KY) - 1947
Clements, William P. (TX) - 1978, 1980, 1986
Cleveland (CT) - 1886
Cleveland, A. C. (NV) - 1894, 1902
Cleveland, Chauncey F. (CT) - 1842, 1843, 1844
Cleveland, Grover (NY) - 1882
Clifford, John H. (MA) - 1852
Clifford, Tom (OH) - 1910
Clinch (GA) - 1847
Clinton, Bill (AR) - 1978, 1980, 1982, 1984, 1986, 1990
Clinton, De Witt (NY) - 1817, 1820, 1824, 1826
Clinton, George (NY) - 1789, 1792, 1801
Cloud, Roger (OH) - 1970
Clough, David M. (MN) - 1896
Clyde, George Dewey (UT) - 1956, 1960
Clymer, Hiester (PA) - 1866
Cobb, Howell (GA) - 1851
Cobb, Osro (AR) - 1936
Cobb, Rufus W. (AL) - 1878, 1880
Cobb, William T. (ME) - 1904, 1906
Coblentz, L. A. (ID) - 1912, 1914
Cobo, Albert E. (MI) - 1956
Coburn, Abner (ME) - 1862
Coburn, Berthold C. (VT) - 1946
Cochran, A. M. (TX) - 1886
Cochran, John P. (DE) - 1874
Cochran, Robert L. (NE) - 1934, 1936, 1938
Cochrane, John (WI) - 1886
Cooke, Edmund R. (VA) - 1893
Cocke, William (TN) - 1807, 1809
Coffin, Frank M. (ME) - 1960
Coffin, O. Vincent (CT) - 1894
Coghill, John B. "Jack" (AK) - 1994
Cogswell (NH) - 1886
Coke, Richard (TX) - 1873, 1875
Colby, Anthony (NH) - 1843, 1844, 1845, 1846, 1847
Colby, Everett (NJ) - 1913
Colcord, R. K. (NV) - 1890
Cole, A. L. (MA) - 1906
Cole, Charles H. (MA) - 1928
Cole, Charles S. (AR) - 1938
Coleman (WI) - 1920
Coleman, J. Marshall (VA) - 1981, 1989
Coleman, J. P. (MS) - 1955
Coler, Bird S. (NY) - 1902

Coles, Edward (IL) - 1822
Collier, Henry Watkins (AL) - 1849, 1851
Collins (WI) - 1849
Collins, James M. (CO) - 1920
Collins, John (DE) - 1820
Collins, John (IL) - 1904
Collins, Leroy (FL) - 1954, 1956
Collins, Martha Layne (KY) - 1983
Collins, P. V. (MN) - 1912
Collins, Susan M. (ME) - 1994
Collins, Timothy E. (MT) - 1892
Colquitt, Alfred Holt (GA) - 1876, 1880
Colquitt, Oscar B. (TX) - 1910, 1912
Colt, Samuel Pomeroy (RI) - 1903
Colton, Don B. (UT) - 1940
Combs, Bert T. (KY) - 1959
Comegys, Cornelius P. (DE) - 1836
Comer, B. B. (AL) - 1906
Comings, Herbert C. (VT) - 1926
Comstock, Charles C. (MI) - 1870
Comstock, William A. (MI) - 1926, 1928, 1930, 1932
Cone, Fred P. (FL) - 1936
Conley, William G. (WV) - 1928
Conlin, Roxanne (IA) - 1982
Connally, John B. (TX) - 1962, 1964, 1966
Conner, Martin S. (MS) - 1931
Conness, John (CA) - 1861
Connor, Selden E. (ME) - 1875, 1876, 1877, 1878
Conover, Simon B. (FL) - 1880
Conrad, Larry A. (IN) - 1976
Converse, Julius (VT) - 1872
Conway, Elias N. (AR) - 1852, 1856
Conway, James S. (AR) - 1836
Cony, Samuel (ME) - 1863, 1864, 1865
Cook, C. W. (KY) - 1879
Cook, Merrill (UT) - 1988, 1992
Cook, Rodney M. (GA) - 1978
Cooke, Lorrin A. (CT) - 1896
Coolidge, Arthur W. (MA) - 1950
Coolidge, Calvin (MA) - 1918, 1919
Coolidge, Carlos (VT) - 1848, 1849
Coon, Ken (AR) - 1974
Cooper, Job A. (CO) - 1888
Cooper, John R. (NE) - 1960
Cooper, Mark A. (GA) - 1843
Cooper, Myers Y. (OH) - 1926, 1928, 1930
Cooper, Prentice (TN) - 1938, 1940, 1942
Cooper, Robert A. (SC) - 1918, 1920
Cooper, William B. (DE) - 1840
Coopwood (MS) - 1845
Corbet, Leo (AZ) - 1980
Cornelius, T. R. (OR) - 1886
Cornell, Alonzo B. (NY) - 1879
Cornwell, John J. (WV) - 1904, 1916
Corwin, Thomas (OH) - 1840, 1842
Cosgrove, Samuel G. (WA) - 1908
Costigan, Edw. P. (CO) - 1912, 1914
Couch, Darius N. (MA) - 1865
Couchman, Peter (SD) - 1892
Coursey, Thomas B. (DE) - 1870
Courter, Jim (NJ) - 1989
Courtney, Thomas J. (IL) - 1944
Cowherd (MO) - 1908
Cowper, Steve J. (AK) - 1986
Cox, Channing H. (MA) - 1920, 1922
Cox, J. E. (NC) - 1908
Cox, Jack (TX) - 1962
Cox, Jacob D. (OH) - 1865
Cox, James M. (OH) - 1912, 1914, 1916, 1918
Cox, Thomas W. (FL) - 1912
Coxey, Jacob S. (OH) - 1895
Coy, John G. (CO) - 1890

Cozzens, William C. (RI) - 1863
Craddock, W. H. (KS) - 1902
Crafts, Samuel C. (VT) - 1828, 1829, 1830, 1832
Cragin, Charles R. (ME) - 1982
Craig, George N. (IN) - 1952
Craig, Locke (NC) - 1912
Craig, William H. (NH) - 1952
Crane, Elvin W. (NJ) - 1898
Crane, S. B. (IA) - 1895
Crane, Winthrop Murray (MA) - 1899, 1900, 1901
Crank, Marion (AR) - 1968
Crapo, Henry H. (MI) - 1864, 1866
Craswell, Ellen (WA) - 1996
Crawford, Coe I. (SD) - 1906
Crawford, George Walker (GA) - 1843, 1845
Crawford, Joel (GA) - 1829, 1833
Crawford, Samuel J. (KS) - 1864, 1866
Creager, R. B. (TX) - 1916
Creighton, Hobart (IN) - 1948
Crichton, Jack (TX) - 1964
Crill, Louis N. (SD) - 1904, 1922
Crittenden, John J. (KY) - 1848
Crittenden, Thomas Theodore (MO) - 1880
Croft, Chancy (AK) - 1978
Cronan (ND) - 1902
Crook, Abraham J. (ID) - 1892
Crosby, Robert B. (NE) - 1952
Crosby, William G. (ME) - 1850, 1852, 1853
Cross (WI) - 1857
Cross, Burton M. (ME) - 1952, 1954
Cross, Wilbur L. (CT) - 1930, 1932, 1934, 1936, 1938
Crossley, Randolph (HI) - 1966, 1974
Croswell, Charles M. (MI) - 1876, 1878
Crothers, Austin L. (MD) - 1907
Crounse, Lorenzo (NE) - 1892
Crowder, H. L. (TN) - 1966
Crowder, John S. (AL) - 1950
Crowe, G. B. (AL) - 1900
Crowley, Roger J. Jr. (NH) - 1970, 1972
Crowninshield, Benjamin W. (MA) - 1818, 1819
Croxton, J. H. (NE) - 1870
Cruce, Lee (OK) - 1910
Crumbie, J. T. (OK) - 1910
Crumpler, Shirley (NV) - 1974
Culberson, Charles A. (TX) - 1894, 1896
Culbertson, J. G. (TX) - 1920
Cullom, Shelby M. (IL) - 1876, 1880
Cummins, Albert B. (IA) - 1901, 1903, 1906
Cummins, Alva M. (MI) - 1922
Cunningham, C. E. (AR) - 1886
Cuomo, Mario M. (NY) - 1982, 1986, 1990, 1994
Curley, James M. (MA) - 1924, 1934, 1938
Currey, John (CA) - 1859
Currie, Ralph W. (TX) - 1950
Currier, Moody (NH) - 1884
Curry (DE) - 1882
Curry, Bill (CT) - 1994
Curtin, Andrew G. (PA) - 1860, 1863
Curtin, J. B. (CA) - 1914
Curtis, Kenneth M. (ME) - 1966, 1970
Curtis, Oakley C. (ME) - 1914, 1916
Cusey, James C. (KS) - 1874
Cushing, Caleb (MA) - 1847, 1848
Cutler, Charles R. (RI) - 1875
Cutler, John C. (UT) - 1904

D

Daddario, Emilio Q. (CT) - 1970
Daggett, David (CT) - 1825, 1826
Dahl, C. P. (ND) - 1960
Dahlman, James C. (NE) - 1910
Dahoney, E. L. (TX) - 1886
Dailey, Frank C. (IN) - 1928
Dale, Charles M. (NH) - 1944, 1946
Dale, David M. (KS) - 1904
Daley, John J. (VT) - 1968
Dalton, John (VA) - 1977
Dalton, John M. (MO) - 1960
Dalton, Ted (VA) - 1953, 1957
Daly, Lorraine (SD) - 1922
Dana, John W. (ME) - 1846, 1847, 1848, 1861
Daniel, John W. (VA) - 1881
Daniel, Mike (SC) - 1986
Daniel, Price (TX) - 1956, 1958, 1960
Darden, Colgate W. Jr. (VA) - 1941
Darnell, N. H. (TX) - 1847
Davenport, Charles N. (VT) - 1865, 1866
Davenport, Ira (NY) - 1885
Davey, Martin L. (OH) - 1928, 1934, 1936, 1940
Davidson, James O. (WI) - 1906, 1908
Davis, C. W. (ME) - 1904, 1906
Davis, Cushman K. (MN) - 1873
Davis, Daniel F. (ME) - 1879, 1880
Davis, David W. (ID) - 1916, 1918, 1920
Davis, Deane C. (VT) - 1968, 1970
Davis, E. J. (TX) - 1880
Davis, Edmund J. (TX) - 1869, 1873
Davis, Harry L. (OH) - 1920, 1924
Davis, Isaac (MA) - 1845, 1846, 1861
Davis, Jefferson (AR) - 1900, 1902, 1904
Davis, Jefferson (MS) - 1851
Davis, Jimmie H. (LA) - 1944, 1960
Davis, John E. (ND) - 1956, 1958
Davis, John (MA) - 1833, 1834, 1840, 1841, 1842
Davis, John W. (RI) - 1887, 1888, 1889, 1890, 1891
Davis, Jonathan M. (KS) - 1920, 1922, 1924, 1926
Davis, Nicholas (AL) - 1831, 1847
Davis, Reuben (MS) - 1863
Davis, Thomas E. (WV) - 1892
Davis, Westmoreland (VA) - 1917
Davis, William (AR) - 1916
Dawes, James W. (NE) - 1882, 1884
Dawson (LA) - 1834
Dawson, Charles I. (KY) - 1923
Dawson, Daniel Boone (WV) - 1940, 1944
Dawson, William C. (GA) - 1841
Dawson, William M. O. (WV) - 1904
Daxon, Tom (OK) - 1982
Dean, Gilbert B. (AL) - 1898
Dean, Howard (VT) - 1994, 1996
Dearborn, Henry (MA) - 1817
de Baca, Ezequiel C. (NM) - 1916
Debuys (LA) - 1846
Declouet (LA) - 1849
Defenbach (ID) - 1932
Delamater, George W. (PA) - 1890
Del Sesto, Christopher (RI) - 1956, 1958, 1960
Dempsey, John J. (NM) - 1942, 1944
Dempsey, John N. (CT) - 1962, 1966
Deneen, Charles S. (IL) - 1904, 1908, 1912
Denney, Edwin R. (KY) - 1955
Denney, William E. (DE) - 1920
Dennison, William Jr. (OH) - 1859
Dent, Louis (MS) - 1869
Depuy, Herbert C. (ND) - 1932

Depuy, William T. (ND) - 1944
Derbigny (LA) - 1855
Derbigny, Pierre (LA) - 1820, 1828
Dern, George H. (UT) - 1924, 1928
Derr, A. M. (ID) - 1958
Desha, Joseph (KY) - 1820, 1824
De Simone, Herbert F. (RI) - 1970, 1972
Destrehan, Jean Noel (LA) - 1820
Detweiler, W. H. (ID) - 1944
Deukmejian, George (CA) - 1982, 1986
Devens, Charles Jr. (MA) - 1862
Dever, Paul A. (MA) - 1940, 1948, 1950, 1952
Devereux, James Patrick (MD) - 1958
Dewey, Nelson (WI) - 1848, 1849
Dewey, Thomas E. (NY) - 1938, 1942, 1946, 1950
Dexter, Lemuel (MA) - 1814, 1815, 1816
Diamond, J. Jerome (VT) - 1980
Dickerson, D. S. (NV) - 1910
Dickie, Samuel (MI) - 1886
Dickinson, Luren D. (MI) - 1940
Dickson, David (MS) - 1823
Dickson, D. C. (TX) - 1855
Dietrich, Charles H. (NE) - 1900
Dill, Andrew H. (PA) - 1878
Dill, C. C. (WA) - 1940
Dill, William L. (NJ) - 1928, 1934
Dillingham, Paul (VT) - 1848, 1865, 1866
Dillingham, Paul Jr. (VT) - 1840, 1847
Dillingham, William P. (VT) - 1888
Dillman, Ray E. (UT) - 1936
Dillon, Richard C. (NM) - 1926, 1928, 1932
Dilworth, Richardson (PA) - 1950, 1962
Diman, Byron (RI) - 1846
Dimond, Francis M. (RI) - 1854
Dingley, Nelson Jr. (ME) - 1873, 1874
Dinsmoor, Samuel (NH) - 1823, 1831, 1832, 1833
Dinsmoor, Samuel Jr. (NH) - 1849, 1850, 1851
DiPrete, Edward D. (RI) - 1984, 1986, 1988, 1990
Dix, John A. (NY) - 1872, 1874, 1910
Dix, John (NY) - 1848
Dixon (NJ) - 1883
Dixon, Archibald (KY) - 1851
Dixon, Frank (AL) - 1938
Dixon, Joseph M. (MT) - 1920, 1924
Dixon, Sherwood (IL) - 1952
Dockery, Alexander Monroe (MO) - 1900
Dockery, Alfred (NC) - 1854, 1866
Dockery, Oliver H. (NC) - 1888
Docking, George (KS) - 1954, 1956, 1958, 1960
Docking, Robert (KS) - 1966, 1968, 1970, 1972
Docking, Tom (KS) - 1986
Dodge, A. C. (IA) - 1859
Dolloff, Maynard C. (ME) - 1962
Domenici, Pete V. (NM) - 1970
Donaghey, George W. (AR) - 1908, 1910
Donahey, Vic (OH) - 1920, 1922, 1924, 1926
Donaldson, J. Lyter (KY) - 1943
Donaugh, Carl C. (OR) - 1946
Donlan, Edward (MT) - 1908
Donnell, Forrest C. (MO) - 1940
Donnelly, Ignatius (MN) - 1892
Donnelly, Phil M. (MO) - 1944, 1952
Donovan, William J. (NY) - 1932

Doolittle, James R. (WI) - 1871
Doolittle, Joel (VT) - 1824, 1826, 1827, 1828, 1829
Doorley, Joseph A. Jr. (RI) - 1978
Dorn, W. J. Bryan (SC) - 1974
Dorsey, Hugh M. (GA) - 1916, 1918
Dougherty (GA) - 1835, 1839
Douglas, William L. (MA) - 1904
Dow, Robert C. (NM) - 1928
Dowd, Edward L. (MO) - 1972
Downey, J. G. (CA) - 1863
Doyle, S. J. (ND) - 1918
Drake, Francis M. (IA) - 1895
Draper, Eben S. (MA) - 1908, 1909, 1910
Drew, George F. (FL) - 1876
Drew, Thomas S. (AR) - 1844
Dreyfuss, Lee S. (WI) - 1978
Driscoll, Alfred E. (NJ) - 1946, 1949
Dryer, Edmund H. (AL) - 1934
Dubord, F. Harold (ME) - 1936
Dudley, Edward B. (NC) - 1836, 1838
Duff, James H. (PA) - 1946
Dukakis, Michael S. (MA) - 1974, 1982, 1986
Duke, David E. (LA) - 1991
Dummit, Eldon S. (KY) - 1947
Dumont, John (IN) - 1837
Dumont, Wayne Jr. (NJ) - 1965
Duncan, A. L. (LA) - 1820
Duncan, Joseph (IL) - 1834, 1842
Duncan, Lewis J. (MT) - 1912, 1916
Dunklin, Daniel (MO) - 1832
Dunlap, James (OH) - 1816, 1818
Dunlap, Robert P. (ME) - 1833, 1834, 1835, 1836
Dunn, Edward G. (IA) - 1912
Dunn, Robert C. (MN) - 1904
Dunn, Winfield (TN) - 1970, 1986
Dunne, Edward F. (IL) - 1912, 1916
Dunne, Joe E. (OR) - 1934
du Pont, Pierre S. "Pete" IV (DE) - 1976, 1980
Durand, Lorenzo T. (MI) - 1902
Durbin, Winfield T. (IN) - 1900, 1912
Durrette, Wyatt B. (VA) - 1985
Duryea, Perry B. (NY) - 1978
Dutton (CT) - 1853
Dutton, Henry (CT) - 1854, 1855
Dwinell, Lane (NH) - 1954, 1956
Dwyer, Thomas P. (MN) - 1916
Dyer (MO) - 1880
Dyer, Charles V. (IL) - 1848
Dyer, Elisha (RI) - 1857, 1858, 1897, 1898, 1899
Dyke, William D. (WI) - 1974

E

Eagle, James P. (AR) - 1888, 1890
Earl, Anthony S. (WI) - 1982, 1986
Earle, George H. (PA) - 1934
Earnest (AL) - 1853
Eastman (NH) - 1863
Easton, John (VT) - 1984
Eaton, A. E. (OR) - 1910
Eaton, Benjamin H. (CO) - 1884
Eaton, George E. (VT) - 1882
Eaton, Horace (VT) - 1846, 1847
Eberhart, Adolph O. (MN) - 1910, 1912
Ebright, Don H. (OH) - 1950
EchoHawk, Larry (ID) - 1994
Eckerd, Jack M. (FL) - 1978
Eden, John R. (IL) - 1868
Edgar, Jim (IL) - 1990, 1994
Edge, Walter E. (NJ) - 1916, 1943
Edgerly, M. V. B. (NH) - 1882
Edison, Charles (NJ) - 1940
Edmisten, Rufus (NC) - 1984

Edmondson, J. Howard (OK) - 1958
Edmunds, James M. (MI) - 1847
Edwards, Clark S. (ME) - 1886
Edwards, Cyrus (IL) - 1838
Edwards, Edward I. (NJ) - 1919
Edwards, Edwin W. (LA) - 1972, 1975, 1983, 1991
Edwards, Frank J. (MT) - 1912, 1916, 1924
Edwards, Henry W. (CT) - 1833, 1834, 1835, 1836, 1837
Edwards, James B. (SC) - 1974
Edwards, John Cummins (MO) - 1844
Edwards, John L. (VT) - 1867, 1868
Edwards, Ninian (IL) - 1826
Edwards, R. M. (TN) - 1878
Eels, Richard (IL) - 1846
Egan, William A. (AK) - 1958, 1962, 1966, 1970, 1974
Eggers, Paul (TX) - 1968, 1970
Eggleston, Beriah B. (MS) - 1868
Ehringhaus, J. C. B. (NC) - 1932
Eikenberry, Ken (WA) - 1992
Elder, P. P. (KS) - 1888
Elkin, Richard (ND) - 1976
Ellerbe, William H. (SC) - 1896, 1898
Ellington, Buford (TN) - 1958, 1966
Elliott, Howard (MO) - 1952
Ellis, John W. (NC) - 1858, 1860
Ellsworth, Oliver (CT) - 1796
Ellsworth, William W. (CT) - 1837, 1838, 1839, 1840, 1841, 1842
Elrod, Samuel H. (SD) - 1904
Ely, Joseph B. (MA) - 1930, 1932
Emberton, Tom (KY) - 1971
Emerson, Frank C. (WY) - 1926, 1930
Emerson, Lee E. (VT) - 1950, 1952
Emery, Lewis Jr. (PA) - 1906
Emmerson, Louis L. (IL) - 1928
Endicott, William C. (MA) - 1884
England, Paren (NE) - 1876
Engler, John (MI) - 1990, 1994
English, James E. (CT) - 1866, 1867, 1868, 1869, 1870, 1871, 1880
Epperson, B. H. (TX) - 1851
Erbe, Norman A. (IA) - 1960, 1962
Erickson, John E. (MT) - 1924, 1928, 1932
Erickson, Leif (MT) - 1944
Ertel, Allen E. (PA) - 1982
Ervin, Charles W. (NY) - 1918
Erwin, James S. (ME) - 1970, 1974
Erwin, S. B. (KY) - 1891
Estee, Morris M. (CA) - 1882, 1894
Etheridge, Emerson (TN) - 1867
Eustis, William (MA) - 1820, 1821, 1822, 1823, 1824
Eustis, William H. (MN) - 1898
Evans (TN) - 1906
Evans, Daniel J. (WA) - 1964, 1968, 1972
Evans, David H. (MN) - 1918
Evans, H. Clay (TN) - 1894
Evans, John Gary (SC) - 1894
Evans, John V. (ID) - 1978, 1982
Evans, L. D. (TX) - 1853
Evans, Walter (KY) - 1879
Everett, Edward (MA) - 1835, 1836, 1837, 1838, 1839
Everett, William (MA) - 1897
Evers, James Charles (MS) - 1971
Ewing, R. C. (MO) - 1856
Ewing, Thomas (OH) - 1879
Ewing, W. T. (AL) - 1888
Exon, J. James (NE) - 1970, 1974
Exum, Wyatt P. (NC) - 1892

F

Fairbanks, Erastus (VT) - 1852, 1853, 1860
Fairbanks, Horace (VT) - 1876
Fairchild, Lucius (WI) - 1865, 1867, 1869
Fairchild, Roger (ID) - 1990
Fairchild, Sherman D. (ID) - 1920
Fairfield, John (ME) - 1838, 1839, 1840, 1841, 1842
Fancher, F. B. (ND) - 1898
Fannin, Paul (AZ) - 1958, 1960, 1962
Farmer, Edward G. (MO) - 1960
Farnham, Roswell (VT) - 1880
Farnsworth, E. (MI) - 1839
Farrar, Frank L. (SD) - 1968, 1970
Farrar, Timothy (NH) - 1806
Farwell, Leonard J. (WI) - 1851
Fasi, Frank F. (HI) - 1982, 1994
Fassett, Jacob Sloat (NY) - 1891
Faubus, Orval E. (AR) - 1954, 1956, 1958, 1960, 1962, 1964
Feinstein, Dianne (CA) - 1990
Felch (MI) - 1856
Felch, Alpheus (MI) - 1845
Felker, Samuel D. (NH) - 1912
Fellows, Lynn (SD) - 1944
Fenner, Arthur (RI) - 1790, 1791, 1792, 1793, 1794, 1795, 1796, 1797, 1798, 1799, 1800, 1801, 1802, 1803, 1804, 1805
Fenner, James (RI) - 1807, 1808, 1809, 1810, 1811, 1812, 1824, 1825, 1826, 1827, 1828, 1829, 1830, 1831, 1832, 1843, 1844, 1845
Fenton, Reuben E. (NY) - 1864, 1886
Fenton, William H. (MI) - 1864
Ferency, Zolton A. (MI) - 1966
Ferguson (WI) - 1861
Ferguson, James E. (TX) - 1914, 1916
Ferguson, Jo O. (OK) - 1950
Ferguson, Miriam A. (TX) - 1924, 1932
Ferguson, Phil (OK) - 1958
Fernald, Bert M. (ME) - 1908, 1910
Ferris, Woodbridge N. (MI) - 1904, 1912, 1914, 1920
Ferry, Elisha P. (WA) - 1889
Ferry, William M. (UT) - 1904
Fessenden, Samuel (ME) - 1846, 1847, 1848
Fielder, James F. (NJ) - 1913
Fields, Cleo (LA) - 1995
Fields, John (OK) - 1914, 1922
Fields, William J. (KY) - 1923
Fife, Symington (AZ) - 1990
Fifer, Joseph W. (IL) - 1888, 1892
Fike, Ed (NV) - 1970
Files, A. W. (AR) - 1896
Files, J. R. (IA) - 1922
Fillmore, Millard (NY) - 1844
Finch, Cliff (MS) - 1975
Findlay, James (OH) - 1834
Findlay, William (PA) - 1817, 1820
Fine, John S. (PA) - 1950
Fink, Tom (AK) - 1982
Finkelnburg, Gustavus A. (MO) - 1876
Finney, Joan (KS) - 1990
Fish, Hamilton (NY) - 1848
Fishback, W. M. (AR) - 1892
Fisher, E. S. (MS) - 1865
Fisher, Jake (WV) - 1924
Fisher, John S. (PA) - 1926
Fisher, Spencer O. (MI) - 1894
Fisk (NJ) - 1886
Fitzgerald, David (CT) - 1922
Fitzgerald, Frank D. (MI) - 1934, 1936, 1938

Fitzgerald, Jerome D. (IA) - 1978
Fitzgerald, John F. (MA) - 1922
Fitzgerald, William (MI) - 1978
Fitzpatrick, Benjamin (AL) - 1841, 1843
Fizer, N. B. (AR) - 1890
Flaherty, David T. (NC) - 1976
Flaherty, Peter (PA) - 1978
Flanagan, Webster (TX) - 1890
Flandrau, Charles E. (MN) - 1867
Flegel, Austin F. (OR) - 1950
Fleming, A. Brooks (WV) - 1888
Fleming, Francis P. (FL) - 1888
Fletcher, Allen M. (VT) - 1912
Fletcher, Ryland (VT) - 1856, 1857
Fletcher, Thomas C. (MO) - 1864
Florio, James J. (NJ) - 1981, 1989, 1993
Flory (MO) - 1900
Flournoy (VA) - 1855, 1863
Flournoy, Houston I. (CA) - 1974
Flournoy, M. (KY) - 1836
Flower, Roswell P. (NY) - 1891
Floyd, Charles M. (NH) - 1906
Flynn, Olney R. (OK) - 1946
Flynn, William S. (RI) - 1922
Folger, Charles J. (NY) - 1882
Folk, Joseph Wingate (MO) - 1904
Folmar, Emory (AL) - 1982
Folsom, David S. (MT) - 1900
Folsom, James E. (AL) - 1946, 1954
Folsom, James E. Jr. (AL) - 1994
Fontaine, C. D. (MS) - 1855
Foot, Samuel A. (CT) - 1834, 1835
Foote, Henry S. (MS) - 1851
Foote, Ralph A. (VT) - 1964
Foraker, Joseph B. (OH) - 1883, 1885, 1887, 1889
Forbes, Malcolm S. (NJ) - 1957
Ford, Nicholas (MO) - 1884
Ford, Peter J. (DE) - 1900
Ford, Samuel C. (MT) - 1940, 1944, 1948
Ford, Seabury (OH) - 1848
Ford, Thomas (IL) - 1842
Ford, Wendell H. (KY) - 1971
Fordice, Kirk (MS) - 1991, 1995
Forgy, Larry E. (KY) - 1995
Forsyth, John (GA) - 1827
Fort, George F. (NJ) - 1850
Fort, John Franklin (NJ) - 1907
Fosheim, Oscar (SD) - 1938
Foss, Eugene N. (MA) - 1910, 1911, 1912
Foss, Joe (SD) - 1954, 1956
Foster (CT) - 1850, 1851
Foster (TN) - 1845
Foster, Charles (OH) - 1879, 1881
Foster, Henry D. (PA) - 1860
Foster, M. J. "Mike" (LA) - 1995
Foster, Murphy J. (LA) - 1892, 1896
Foster, Robert C. (TN) - 1815, 1817
Fowle, Daniel G. (NC) - 1888
Fowler (TN) - 1898
Fowler, Absalom (AR) - 1836
Francis, David Rowland (MO) - 1888
Francis, John Brown (R) - 1833, 1834, 1835, 1836, 1837, 1838
Frank, M. P. (ME) - 1896
Frankland, Herman C. (ME) - 1978
Frantz, Frank (OK) - 1907
Franzenburg, Paul (IA) - 1968, 1972
Fratt, Nicholas D. (WI) - 1881, 1884
Frazier, C. N. (TN) - 1942
Frazier, Clifford (NC) - 1932
Frazier, James B. (TN) - 1902, 1904
Frazier, Lynn J. (ND) - 1916, 1918, 1920, 1921
Fredericks, John D. (CA) - 1914
Freehafer, A. L. (ID) - 1924
Freeman (TN) - 1872

Freeman, Orville L. (MN) - 1952, 1954, 1956, 1958, 1960
Freeman, Woody (AR) - 1984
French (KY) - 1840
French, Augustus C. (IL) - 1846, 1848
French, N. B. (WV) - 1880
Frensdorf, Edward (MI) - 1924
Frink, J. M. (WA) - 1900
Frizzell, Kent (KS) - 1970
Frohmiller, Ana (AZ) - 1950
Frohnmayer, Dave (OR) - 1990
Frothingham, Louis A. (MA) - 1911
Fry, Edward J. (MI) - 1944
Fuhr, John D. (CO) - 1982
Fulks, Clay (AR) - 1918
Fuller, Alvan T. (MA) - 1924, 1926
Fuller, Levi K. (VT) - 1892
Fuller, Philo C. (MI) - 1841
Fulton, John A. (NV) - 1938
Fulton, Robert D. (IA) - 1970
Funk, Frank H. (IL) - 1912
Fuqua, Henry L. (LA) - 1924
Furches, David M. (NC) - 1892
Furcolo, Foster (MA) - 1956, 1958
Furnas, Robert W. (NE) - 1872
Furnish, W. J. (OR) - 1902
Futrell, Julius M. (AR) - 1932, 1934

G

Gable, Robert E. (KY) - 1975
Gage, Henry T. (CA) - 1898
Gage, Jack R. (WY) - 1962
Gainer, Joseph H. (RI) - 1926
Gaither (MD) - 1907
Gallagher, Thomas (MN) - 1938
Gallaway, Jim (NV) - 1990
Gallen, Hugh J. (NH) - 1978, 1980, 1982
Gallentine, P. W. (AZ) - 1911
Gallogly, Edward P. (RI) - 1964
Galloway, William (OR) - 1894
Galusha, Jonas (VT) - 1809, 1810, 1811, 1812, 1813, 1814, 1815, 1816, 1817, 1818, 1819
Garber, Silas (NE) - 1874, 1876
Garcelon, Alonzo (ME) - 1878, 1879
Garcia, Felix (NM) - 1918
Gardiner, William Tudor (ME) - 1928, 1930
Gardner, A. B. (VT) - 1872
Gardner, Augustus P. (MA) - 1913
Gardner, Booth (WA) - 1984
Gardner, Frederick Dozier (MO) - 1916
Gardner, H. P. (ME) - 1914
Gardner, Henry J. (MA) - 1854, 1855, 1856, 1857
Gardner, J. F. (NE) - 1874, 1876
Gardner, James C. (NC) - 1968
Gardner, Jim (NC) - 1992
Gardner, O. Max (NC) - 1928
Gardner, Obadiah (ME) - 1908
Garey (MD) - 1879
Garfield, James R. (OH) - 1914
Garford, Arthur L. (OH) - 1912
Garland, A. H. (AR) - 1874
Garland, R. K. (AR) - 1882
Garrahy, Joseph J. (RI) - 1976, 1978, 1980, 1982
Garrard, James (KY) - 1800
Gartrell (GA) - 1882
Garvey, Dan E. (AZ) - 1948
Garvin, Lucius F. C. (RI) - 1901, 1902, 1903, 1904, 1905
Gary, Raymond (OK) - 1954
Gaston, William (MA) - 1873, 1874, 1875, 1877
Gaston, William A. (MA) - 1902, 1903, 1926

Gates, Charles W. (VT) - 1914
Gates, Ralph F. (IN) - 1944
Gavin, Robert L. (NC) - 1960, 1964
Gay, George E. (FL) - 1920
Gayle, John (AL) - 1831, 1833
Gaylord, Winfield R. (WI) - 1906
Gear, John Henry (IA) - 1877, 1879
Geary, J. W . (CA) - 1849
Geary, John White (PA) - 1866, 1869
Geer, Theodore Thurston (OR) - 1898
Gegax, Henry F. (NV) - 1910
Gellatly, John A. (WA) - 1932
Gengras, E. Clayton (CT) - 1966
Gentry (TN) - 1855
Gentry, William (MO) - 1874
George, Hyland P. (DE) - 1948
Geringer, Jim (WY) - 1994
Gerry, Elbridge (MA) - 1800, 1801, 1802, 1803, 1810, 1811, 1812
Gibbons, Charles (MA) - 1958
Gibbons, Jim (NV) - 1994
Gibbs, Addison C. (OR) - 1862
Gibbs, Barnett (TX) - 1898
Gibbs, William C. (RI) - 1821, 1822, 1823
Gibson (AR) - 1844
Gibson, Ernest W. (VT) - 1946, 1948
Gidley, Townsend E. (MI) - 1851
Gilchrist, Albert W. (FL) - 1908
Gillaspie, George (IA) - 1869
Gillett, James N. (CA) - 1906
Gillette (CT) - 1853
Gillette, Lester S. (IA) - 1950
Gilligan, John J. (OH) - 1970, 1974
Gilman, John T. (NH) - 1793, 1794, 1795, 1796, 1797, 1798, 1799, 1800, 1801, 1802, 1803, 1804, 1805, 1806, 1808, 1812, 1813, 1814, 1815
Gilmer, George R. (GA) - 1829, 1831, 1837
Gilmer, John A. (NC) - 1856
Gilmore, James S. (VA) - 1997
Gilmore, Joseph A. (NH) - 1863, 1864
Glade, Earl J. (UT) - 1952
Glasscock, William E. (WV) - 1908
Glendening, Parris N. (MD) - 1994
Glenn, Hugh J. (CA) - 1879
Glenn, R. B. (NC) - 1904
Glick, George W. (KS) - 1868, 1882, 1884
Glynn, Martin H. (NY) - 1914
Goddard, Sam (AZ) - 1962, 1964, 1966, 1968
Goddard, Terry (AZ) - 1990
Godwin, Mills E. Jr. (VA) - 1965, 1973
Goebel, William (KY) - 1899
Goff, Nathan (WV) - 1876, 1888
Goggin (VA) - 1859
Goldberg, Arthur J. (NY) - 1970
Goldsborough (MD) - 1847
Goldsborough, Phillips Lee (MD) - 1911
Goldschmidt, Neil (OR) - 1986
Goldsmith, Stephen (IN) - 1996
Goodell, David H. (NH) - 1888
Goodenow, Daniel (ME) - 1831, 1832, 1833
Goodin, John R. (KS) - 1878
Gooding, Frank R. (ID) - 1904, 1906
Goodland, Walter S. (WI) - 1944, 1946
Goodnow, Windsor H. (NH) - 1922
Goodover, Pat M. (MT) - 1984
Goodrich, James P. (IN) - 1916
Goodwin (CT) - 1910
Goodwin, Frank A. (MA) - 1934
Goodwin, Ichabod (NH) - 1859, 1860
Goodwyn, Albert T. (AL) - 1896

Gordon (GA) - 1868
Gordon, George W. (MA) - 1856
Gordon, John B. (GA) - 1886, 1888
Gordy, William J. (DE) - 1980
Gore, Christopher (MA) - 1808, 1809, 1810, 1811
Gore, Howard M. (WV) - 1924
Gore, Louise (MD) - 1974
Gorman, Arthur Pue (MD) - 1911
Gossett, Charles C. (ID) - 1944
Goudy, Frank C. (CO) - 1900
Gould, Samuel W. (ME) - 1902
Gould, Vick (WA) - 1972
Grabiel, John W. (AR) - 1922, 1924
Gragson, Oran K. (NV) - 1962
Graham, Bob (FL) - 1978, 1982
Graham, Horace F. (VT) - 1916
Graham, William A. (NC) - 1844, 1846
Granai, Edwin C. (VT) - 1978
Granberry, Jim (TX) - 1974
Grandmaison, J. Joseph (NH) - 1990
Granger, Francis (NY) - 1830, 1832
Grant, Earle S. (ME) - 1950
Grant, James B. (CO) - 1882
Grantham, Everett (NM) - 1952
Grasso, Ella T. (CT) - 1974, 1978
Graves, Bibb (AL) - 1926, 1934
Graves, Bill (KS) - 1994
Graves, Richard Perrin (CA) - 1954
Gray, C. A. (TX) - 1906
Gray, Isaac P. (IN) - 1884
Gray, James (MN) - 1910
Grayson, Beverly R. (MS) - 1827
Grayson, William (MD) - 1838
Greaves, Charles D. (AR) - 1902
Green, Charles B. (MS) - 1821
Green, Dwight H. (IL) - 1940, 1944, 1948
Green, Fred W. (MI) - 1926, 1928
Green, J. A. (TX) - 1851
Green, Jesse (DE) - 1820
Green, John T. (SC) - 1874
Green, Robert S. (NJ) - 1886
Green, Theodore Francis (RI) - 1912, 1930, 1932, 1934
Green, Warren E. (SD) - 1930, 1932
Greene (CT) - 1875
Greene (WI) - 1934
Greene, George W. (RI) - 1899
Greene, William (RI) - 1802
Greenhalge, Frederic T. (MA) - 1893, 1894, 1895
Greenup, Christopher (KY) - 1800, 1804
Gregg, Andrew (PA) - 1823
Gregg, Hugh (NH) - 1952, 1966
Gregg, S. (AR) - 1886
Gregory, William (RI) - 1900, 1901
Grevemberg, F. C. (LA) - 1960
Griffen, Horace B. (AZ) - 1956
Griffin, S. Marvin (GA) - 1954
Griffith, Benjamin (CO) - 1922
Griffith, Leon (AR) - 1976
Griggs, John W. (NJ) - 1895
Grim, Webster (PA) - 1910
Grimball (MS) - 1837
Grimes, James W. (IA) - 1854
Grissom, Gilliam (NC) - 1936
Griswold, Dwight (NE) - 1932, 1934, 1936, 1940, 1942, 1944
Griswold, John A. (NY) - 1868
Griswold, Morley (NV) - 1934
Griswold, Roger (CT) - 1810, 1811, 1812
Groark, Eunice Strong (CT) - 1994
Groesbeck, Alexander J. (MI) - 1920, 1922, 1924
Groome, John C. (MD) - 1857
Gropper, John L. (VT) - 1996
Gross, Harold J. (RI) - 1922
Grout, Josiah (VT) - 1896

Grover, Hank C. (TX) - 1972
Grover, LaFayette F. (OR) - 1870, 1874
Grubb (NJ) - 1889
Gubbrud, Archie M. (SD) - 1960, 1962
Guild, Curtis Jr. (MA) - 1905, 1906, 1907
Gunby, E. R. (FL) - 1896
Gunderson, Carl (SD) - 1924, 1926
Gunderson, Carroll G. (NM) - 1944
Gunter, Julius C. (CO) - 1916
Gurham, George C. (CA) - 1867
Gurney, Chester (MI) - 1847
Guthrie, William A. (NC) - 1896
Guy, William L. (ND) - 1960, 1962, 1964, 1968

H

Hackel, Stella B. (VT) - 1976
Hackett, Luther F. (VT) - 1972
Hadley, Herbert Spencer (MO) - 1908
Haeder, Richard (SD) - 1946
Hafer, Barbara (PA) - 1990
Hagan, John N. (ND) - 1938
Hageman, Fred P. (IA) - 1930
Hagen, Oscar W. (ND) - 1942
Hager (KY) - 1907
Hagood, Johnson (SC) - 1880
Haight, H. H. (CA) - 1867, 1871
Haight, Raymond L. (CA) - 1934
Haigis, John W. (MA) - 1936
Haile, William (NH) - 1857, 1858
Haile, William H. (MA) - 1892
Haines, Daniel (NJ) - 1847
Haines, H. H. (TX) - 1926
Haines, John M. (ID) - 1912, 1914
Haines, William T. (ME) - 1912, 1914
Halcrow, Don (ND) - 1964
Haldiman, Joe C. (AZ) - 1952
Hale, Samuel W. (NH) - 1882
Hale, William (NH) - 1817, 1818, 1819
Hall, David (DE) - 1798, 1801
Hall, David (OK) - 1970
Hall, Fred (KS) - 1954
Hall, Hiland (VT) - 1858, 1859
Hall, John W. (DE) - 1878
Hall, Luther E. (LA) - 1912
Hall, W. Scott (ID) - 1926
Halsey (NJ) - 1874
Halsted, Charles L. (MN) - 1948
Halvorson, Halvor L. (ND) - 1924
Hamil, David A. (CO) - 1948
Hamilton, A. J. (TX) - 1869
Hamilton, Clark (ID) - 1954
Hamilton, John T. (IA) - 1914
Hamilton, W. S. (LA) - 1831
Hamilton, William T. (MD) - 1879
Hamlin, E. O. (MN) - 1861
Hamlin, Elijah L. (ME) - 1848, 1849
Hamlin, Hannibal (ME) - 1856
Hamman, william H. (TX) - 1878, 1880
Hammersley (WI) - 1930
Hammill, John (IA) - 1924, 1926, 1928
Hammond, Jay S. (AK) - 1974, 1978
Hammond, Winfield S. (MN) - 1914
Hampton, Wade (SC) - 1865, 1876, 1878
Hancock, John (MA) - 1788, 1789, 1790, 1791, 1792, 1793
Handley, Harold W. (IN) - 1956
Hanly, J. Frank (IN) - 1904
Hanna, Louis B. (ND) - 1912, 1914
Hanna, Richard H. (NM) - 1920
Hannay, R. E. (TX) - 1900
Hannett, Arthur T. (NM) - 1924, 1926

Hansen, Clifford P. (WY) - 1962
Hansen, Lewis G. (NJ) - 1946
Hanson, Stewart (UT) - 1992
Hardace, Sam (KS) - 1982
Hardee, Cary A. (FL) - 1920
Hardin (KY) - 1895
Hardin, Charles H. (MO) - 1874
Harding, Warren G. (OH) - 1910
Harding, William L. (IA) - 1916, 1918
Hardman, Lamartine Griffin (GA) - 1926, 1928
Hardwick, Thomas W. (GA) - 1920
Hardy, H. W. (NE) - 1886
Harlan, John M. (KY) - 1875
Harman, Rick (KS) - 1968
Harmon, Judson (OH) - 1908, 1910
Harper, John (KY) - 1987
Harriman (NH) - 1863
Harriman, Averell (NY) - 1954, 1958
Harriman, Walter (NH) - 1867, 1868
Harrington, Edward W. (NH) - 1864, 1865
Harrington, Emerson C. (MD) - 1915
Harris (CT) - 1874
Harris (MD) - 1875
Harris, Andrew L. (OH) - 1908
Harris, C. J. (NC) - 1904
Harris, C. O. (TX) - 1936
Harris, Edward (RI) - 1849, 1850
Harris, Elisha (RI) - 1847, 1848, 1852
Harris, Isham G. (TN) - 1857, 1859
Harris, Joe Frank (GA) - 1982, 1986
Harris, Nathaniel E. (GA) - 1914
Harris, Wiley (MS) - 1831
Harris, William A. (KS) - 1906
Harrison, Albertis S. Jr. (VA) - 1961
Harrison, Benjamin (IN) - 1876
Harrison, Carter H. (IL) - 1884
Harrison, Christopher (IN) - 1819
Harrison, Henry B. (CT) - 1884
Harrison, Hugh (MN) - 1888
Harrison, William H. (OH) - 1820
Harrison, Wm. B. (KY) - 1931
Hart, Louis F. (WA) - 1920
Hart, Ossian B. (FL) - 1872
Hart, William (CT) - 1804, 1805, 1806, 1807, 1808
Hartigan, Neil F. (IL) - 1990
Hartley, Roland H. (WA) - 1924, 1928, 1936
Hartness, James (VT) - 1920
Hartranft, John Frederick (PA) - 1872, 1875
Harvey, James M. (KS) - 1868, 1870
Harvey, Louis (WI) - 1861
Harvey, Matthew (NH) - 1830
Haskell, A. C. (SC) - 1890
Haskell, C. N. (OK) - 1907
Hastings, Daniel H. (PA) - 1894
Hatch, Francis W. (MA) - 1978
Hatfield, H. D. (WV) - 1912
Hatfield, Mark O. (OR) - 1958, 1962
Hathaway, Stanley K. (WY) - 1966, 1970
Hatton (TN) - 1857
Haucke, Frank (KS) - 1930
Haven (CT) - 1873
Hawkins, Alvin (TN) - 1880, 1882
Hawkins, Samuel W. (TN) - 1888
Hawley, James H. (ID) - 1910, 1912
Hawley, Joseph R. (CT) - 1866, 1867
Hay, John W. (WY) - 1922
Hay, M. E. (WA) - 1912
Hayden, Mike (KS) - 1986, 1990
Hayes, Kyle (NC) - 1956
Hayes, Robin (NC) - 1996
Hayes, Rutherford B. (OH) - 1867, 1869, 1875
Hays, George W. (AR) - 1913, 1914
Hayward, M. L. (NE) - 1898
Haywood (NJ) - 1853
Haywood, William D. (CO) - 1906

Hazard, Rowland (RI) - 1875
Hazelbaker, Frank A. (MT) - 1932, 1936
Hazelton, Harry (MT) - 1908
Hazlehurst, Isaac (PA) - 1857
Hazlett (NV) - 1874
Hazlett, Joseph (DE) - 1804, 1807, 1810, 1822
Hazzard, Daniel (DE) - 1823
Head, Douglas M. (MN) - 1970
Head, Natt (NH) - 1879
Headlee, Richard H. (MI) - 1982
Healey, Robert J. (RI) - 1994
Healy, Joseph (NH) - 1835
Heard, Dwight B. (AZ) - 1924
Heard, William Wright (LA) - 1900
Hearnes, Betty (MO) - 1988
Hearnes, Warren E. (MO) - 1964, 1968
Hearst, William R. (NY) - 1906
Heaton, Homer W. (VT) - 1869, 1870
Hebert, Paul O. (LA) - 1852
Hedges, Job E. (NY) - 1912
Hegge, M. F. (ND) - 1904
Heil, Julius P. (WI) - 1938, 1940, 1942
Heininger, Alfred H. (VT) - 1936
Heitfeld, Henry (ID) - 1904
Hellstrom, F. O. (ND) - 1912, 1914
Helm, John Larue (KY) - 1867
Helm, Joseph C. (CO) - 1892
Hemans, Lawton T. (MI) - 1908, 1910
Hemmings, Fred (HI) - 1990
Hemphill, John M. (PA) - 1930
Hempstead, Stephen (IA) - 1850
Henderson, Charles (LA) - 1914
Henderson, John B. (MO) - 1872
Hendon (AL) - 1872
Hendricks, Thomas Andrews (IN) - 1860, 1868, 1872
Hendricks, William (IN) - 1822
Hendrickson, Robert C. (NJ) - 1940
Henry (TN) - 1853
Henry, Dwight (TN) - 1990
Henry, Howard (ND) - 1948
Henry, Louis D. (NC) - 1842
Herbert, Thomas J. (OH) - 1946, 1948
Herreid, Charles N. (SD) - 1900, 1902
Herrick, D. Cady (NY) - 1904
Herrick, Myron T. (OH) - 1903, 1905
Herrick, Thomas F. (RI) - 1899
Herring, Clyde E. (IA) - 1954
Herring, Clyde L. (IA) - 1920, 1932, 1934
Herschler, Ed (WY) - 1974, 1978, 1982
Herseth, R. Lars (SD) - 1986
Herseth, Ralph (SD) - 1956, 1958, 1960, 1962
Hershey, Harry B. (IL) - 1940
Herter, Christian A. (MA) - 1952, 1954
Hess, Henry L. (OR) - 1938
Heyward, Duncan C. (SC) - 1902, 1904
Hichborn, N. G. (ME) - 1869
Hickel, Walter J. (AK) - 1966, 1978, 1990
Hickenlooper, Bourke B. (IA) - 1942
Hickey, J. J. (WY) - 1958
Hicks, L. C. (WA) - 1932
Hicks, Thomas Holliday (MD) - 1857
Hiester, Joseph (PA) - 1817, 1820
Higgins, Frank W. (NY) - 1904
Higgins, James H. (RI) - 1906, 1907
Higgins, John C. (DE) - 1896
High, Robert King (FL) - 1966
Hildreth, Horace A. (ME) - 1944, 1946, 1958
Hill (GA) - 1849, 1857

Hill (NH) - 1884
Hill, Ben F. (WA) - 1924
Hill, C. L. (NM) - 1922
Hill, David B. (NY) - 1885, 1888, 1894
Hill, Herbert W. (NH) - 1948
Hill, Ira A. (OK) - 1930
Hill, Isaac (NY) - 1836, 1837, 1838
Hill, John F. (ME) - 1900, 1902
Hill, John (TX) - 1978
Hillenbrand, John A. (IN) - 1980
Hills, Glenn R. (IN) - 1940
Hilton, Walter B. (WV) - 1912
Hinds, Thomas (MS) - 1819
Hines (GA) - 1902
Hines, J. K. (GA) - 1894
Hinkle, James F. (NM) - 1922
Hipple, John E. (SD) - 1926
Hisgen, Thomas L. (MA) - 1907
Hoadly, George (OH) - 1883, 1885
Hoan, Daniel W. (WI) - 1944, 1946
Hoard, William D. (WI) - 1888, 1890
Hobart, Harrison C. (WI) - 1859, 1865
Hobbs, Horace E. (RI) - 1966
Hobby, William P. (TX) - 1918
Hoch, Edward W. (KS) - 1904, 1906
Hocker, Lon (MO) - 1956
Hodge, Robert T. (WA) - 1912
Hodges, George H. (KS) - 1910, 1912, 1914
Hodges, Luther H. (NC) - 1956
Hodgson, L. C. (MN) - 1920
Hoegh, Leo A. (IA) - 1954, 1956
Hoey, Clyde R. (NC) - 1936
Hoff, Phillip H. (VT) - 1962, 1964, 1966
Hoffecker (DE) - 1886
Hoffecker, John H. (DE) - 1896
Hoffman, Harold G. (NJ) - 1934
Hoffman, John T. (NY) - 1866, 1868, 1870
Hogan (GA) - 1898
Hogan, Dan (AR) - 1910, 1914
Hogan, Mark (CO) - 1970
Hogan, Thomas S. (MT) - 1900
Hoge, J. Hampton (VA) - 1901
Hoge, S. Harris (VA) - 1925
Hogg, James S. (TX) - 1890, 1892
Hoit, Daniel (NH) - 1843, 1844
Hoke, Michael (NC) - 1844
Holbrook, Frederick (VT) - 1861, 1862
Holcomb, Marcus H. (CT) - 1914, 1916, 1918
Holcomb, Silas A. (NE) - 1894, 1896
Holden, William W. (NC) - 1864, 1865, 1868
Holland, Spessard L. (FL) - 1940
Holley, Alexander H. (CT) - 1857
Holley, Charles R. (FL) - 1964
Holliday, Frederick W. M. (VA) - 1877
Holliday, William H. (WY) - 1894
Hollings, Ernest F. (SC) - 1958
Hollis, Henry F. (NH) - 1902, 1904
Holloway (MI) - 1880
Holmes (ND) - 1898
Holmes, D. M. (ND) - 1926
Holmes, David (MS) - 1817, 1825
Holmes, Ezekiel (ME) - 1853
Holmes, Robert D. (OR) - 1956, 1958
Holmes, W. H. (TX) - 1928
Holshouser, James E. Jr. (NC) - 1972
Holt, Fred W. (OK) - 1914
Holt, Homer A. (WV) - 1936
Holt, John H. (WV) - 1900
Holt, Rush D. (WV) - 1952
Holton (MD) - 1883
Holton (WI) - 1853
Holton, Linwood (VA) - 1965, 1969
Hooker, John J. Jr. (TN) - 1970

Hooper, Ben W. (TN) - 1910, 1912, 1914
Hopkins, Arthur F. (AL) - 1839
Hopkins, Edward (FL) - 1860
Hopkins, G. C. (TX) - 1940
Hopkins, Larry J. (KY) - 1991
Hopkins, Raleigh (TN) - 1928
Hoppin, William W. (RI) - 1853, 1854, 1855, 1856
Horner, Henry (IL) - 1932, 1936
Horton, Henry H. (TN) - 1928, 1930
Hough, John S. (CO) - 1880
Housel, L. W. (IA) - 1928
Houston, George S. (AL) - 1874, 1876
Houston, James Ray (NV) - 1974
Houston, Sam (TX) - 1857, 1859
Houston, Samuel (TN) - 1827
Houx, Frank L. (WY) - 1918
Hovey, Alvin P. (IN) - 1888
Howard (MD) - 1861
Howard, Albert C. (RI) - 1876, 1880
Howard, Dean (VT) - 1992
Howard, Henry (RI) - 1873, 1874
Howard, Joseph (ME) - 1864, 1865
Howard, Tilghman, A. (IN) - 1840
Howe, Harland B. (VT) - 1912, 1914
Howe, Isaac (SD) - 1894
Howell, Henry (VA) - 1973, 1977
Howell, R. B. (NE) - 1914
Howes, W. W. (SD) - 1920
Howey (NJ) - 1886
Howey, W. J. (FL) - 1928, 1932
Hoyt, Daniel (NH) - 1842, 1845
Hoyt, Henry Martyn (PA) - 1878
Hubbard, Henry (NH) - 1842, 1843
Hubbard, John (ME) - 1849, 1850, 1852
Hubbard, Lucius F. (MN) - 1881, 1883
Hubbard, Richard D. (CT) - 1872, 1876, 1878
Hubbard, Samuel (MA) - 1826
Hubbert, Paul (AL) - 1990
Huber, Sherry E. (ME) - 1986
Hughes (CO) - 1876
Hughes, Charles E. (NY) - 1906, 1908
Hughes, Harold E. (IA) - 1962, 1964, 1966
Hughes, Harry (MD) - 1978, 1982
Hughes, James H. (DE) - 1916
Hughes, Richard J. (NJ) - 1961, 1965
Hughes, Robert W. (VA) - 1873
Hughes, Simon P. (AR) - 1884, 1886
Hultman, Evan (IA) - 1964
Humes, Albert H. (RI) - 1912
Humphrey, L. U. (KS) - 1888, 1890
Humphreys, Benjamin G. (MS) - 1865, 1868
Humphries (TN) - 1835
Hunn, John (DE) - 1900
Hunt, Frank W. (ID) - 1900, 1902
Hunt, George W. P. (AZ) - 1911, 1914, 1916, 1922, 1924, 1926, 1928, 1930
Hunt, Guy (AL) - 1978, 1986, 1990
Hunt, Guy (GA) - 1986
Hunt, James B. Jr. (NC) - 1976, 1980, 1992, 1996
Hunt, Lester C. (WY) - 1942, 1946
Hunt, Washington (NY) - 1850, 1852
Hunter (CT) - 1910
Huntington, Samuel (CT) - 1787, 1788, 1789, 1790, 1791, 1792, 1793, 1794, 1795
Huntington, Samuel (OH) - 1808
Hunton, Jonathan G. (ME) - 1829, 1830
Hurley, Charles F. (MA) - 1936

Hurley, Robert A. (CT) - 1940, 1942, 1944
Hurst, John E. (MD) - 1895
Hutchins, John C. (NH) - 1916
Hutchinson, Joseph (IA) - 1889
Hutchinson, Titus (VT) - 1841
Huxman, Walter A. (KS) - 1936, 1938
Hyde, Arthur Mastick (MO) - 1920
Hynson, George B. (DE) - 1912

I

Indrehus, Edward (MN) - 1922
Ingalls, David S. (OH) - 1932
Ingersoll, Charles R. (CT) - 1873, 1874, 1875
Ingersoll, E. P. (NE) - 1882
Ingersoll, Jonathan (CT) - 1796
Ingham (CT) - 1854, 1855, 1856, 1857
Inhofe, James M. (OK) - 1974
Ireland, John (TX) - 1882, 1884
Irick, John B. (NM) - 1982
Irish, John P. (IA) - 1877
Irwin, James (PA) - 1847
Irwin, William (CA) - 1875
Irwin, William W. (OH) - 1822
Isakson, Johnny (GA) - 1990
Iverson, Sherman A. (SD) - 1952
Ives, Irving M. (NY) - 1954
Ivinson, Edward (WY) - 1892

J

Jack, William (WY) - 1954
Jackson, Charles (RI) - 1845, 1846
Jackson, Claiborne Fox (MO) - 1860
Jackson, Ed (IN) - 1924
Jackson, Elihu E. (MD) - 1887
Jackson, Frank D. (IA) - 1893
Jackson, Frederick H. (RI) - 1907
Jackson, Hancock (MO) - 1860
Jackson, J. Henry (VT) - 1896
Jackson, J. Holmes (VT) - 1922
Jackson, Jacob B. (WV) - 1880
Jackson, Richard Jr. (RI) - 1806
Jackson, Samuel D. (IN) - 1944
Jacob, John J. (WV) - 1870, 1872
Jacobs (WI) - 1910
Jacobson, Jacob F. (MN) - 1908
Jacobson, Judy (MT) - 1996
Jacques, Alfred (MN) - 1926
James, Arthur H. (PA) - 1938
James, Forrest H. "Fob" Jr. (AL) - 1978, 1994
Jameson, C. D. (ME) - 1861, 1862
Jameson, Nathan C. (NH) - 1906
Janklow, William J. (SD) - 1978, 1982, 1994
Jarvis, Thomas J. (NC) - 1880
Jarvis, William C. (MA) - 1827
Jay, John (NY) - 1792, 1795, 1798
Jefferson (DE) - 1862
Jefferson, Warren (DE) - 1840
Jelks, William D. (AL) - 1902
Jenkins (GA) - 1853
Jenkins (WI) - 1879
Jenks, George A. (PA) - 1898
Jennings, Jonathan (IN) - 1816, 1819
Jennings, William S. (FL) - 1900
Jennison, Silas H. (VT) - 1836, 1837, 1838, 1839, 1840
Jensen, Leslie (SD) - 1936
Jepson, Melvin E. (NV) - 1946
Jerome, David H. (MI) - 1880, 1882
Jester, Beauford H. (TX) - 1946, 1948
Jewell, Marshall (CT) - 1868, 1869, 1870, 1871, 1872
Jewett, Hugh J. (OH) - 1861
Johnson (MD) - 1841

Johnson, Andrew (TN) - 1853, 1855
Johnson, C. A. (ND) - 1908, 1910
Johnson, C. W. (TX) - 1912
Johnson, Charles F. (ME) - 1892, 1894
Johnson, Edwin C. (CO) - 1932, 1934, 1954
Johnson, Edwin S. (SD) - 1912
Johnson, Gary E. (NM) - 1994
Johnson, George W. (AR) - 1958
Johnson, Henry (LA) - 1824, 1842
Johnson, Hershel Vespasian (GA) - 1853, 1855
Johnson, Hiram W. (CA) - 1910, 1914
Johnson, Isaac (LA) - 1846
Johnson, J. N. (CA) - 1855
Johnson, James (AR) - 1966
Johnson, John A. (MN) - 1904, 1906, 1908
Johnson, John W. (MN) - 1974
Johnson, Joseph (VA) - 1851
Johnson, Joseph B. (VT) - 1954, 1956
Johnson, Keen (KY) - 1939
Johnson, M. T. (TX) - 1851
Johnson, Magnus (MN) - 1922, 1926
Johnson, Ole S. (ND) - 1952
Johnson, Paul B. (MS) - 1939, 1963
Johnson, R. H. (AR) - 1860
Johnson, R. W. (MN) - 1881
Johnson, Thomas (TN) - 1815
Johnson, Tom L. (OH) - 1903
Johnson, Walter (KY) - 1949
Johnson, Walter W. (CO) - 1950
Johnston, Henry S. (OK) - 1926
Johnston, Joseph F. (AL) - 1896, 1898
Johnston, Olin D. (SC) - 1934, 1942
Johnston, William (OH) - 1850
Johnston, William F. (PA) - 1849, 1851
Johnston, William J. (NC) - 1862
Jones, Brereton C. (KY) - 1991
Jones, Buell F. (SD) - 1928
Jones, Charles Alvin (PA) - 1938
Jones, Daniel Webster (AR) - 1896, 1898
Jones, Dick (WY) - 1974
Jones, Frank (NY) - 1880
Jones, George W. (TX) - 1882, 1884
Jones, J. S. (NV) - 1894
Jones, James C. (TN) - 1841, 1843
Jones, Norman L. (IL) - 1924
Jones, R. T. (AZ) - 1938
Jones, Sam H. (LA) - 1940
Jones, Samuel M. (OH) - 1899
Jones, Thomas G. (AL) - 1890, 1892
Jones, William (RI) - 1811, 1812, 1813, 1814, 1815, 1816, 1817
Jordan, Chester B. (NH) - 1900
Jordan, Len B. (ID) - 1950
Jordan, Robert B. III (NC) - 1988
Joseph, J. M. (IA) - 1893
Judd, Gregg (NH) - 1988, 1990
Judge, Thomas L. (MT) - 1972, 1976, 1988
Jullien, Paul J. (ME) - 1944
Jump (DE) - 1874
Jungert, Philip W. (ID) - 1966
Junkins, Lowell L. (IA) - 1986

K

Kaldor, Lee (ND) - 1996
Kanouse, Theodore D. (WI) - 1881
Karel, John C. (WI) - 1912, 1914
Kariotis, George (MA) - 1986
Karpan, Kathy (WY) - 1994
Katterfeld, L. E. (WA) - 1916
Katzenbach (NJ) - 1907

Kay, Morris (KS) - 1972
Kean, John Jr. (NJ) - 1892
Kean, Thomas H. (NJ) - 1981, 1985
Kearby, Jerome C. (TX) - 1896
Keating, Frank (OK) - 1994
Keefe, F. Clyde (NH) - 1940, 1946
Keister, Stephen A. D. (WY) - 1906
Kelley, David (VT) - 1994
Kelley, Thomas F. (ID) - 1906
Kellogg, Daniel (VT) - 1843, 1844, 1845
Kellogg, William Pitt (LA) - 1872
Kelly, Harry F. (MI) - 1942, 1944, 1950
Kelly, James K. (OR) - 1866
Kelly, John (NY) - 1879
Kelly, Margaret (MO) - 1996
Kelly, Tom (AK) - 1978
Kelly, William (NY) - 1860
Kemper, James L. (VA) - 1873
Kendall, Nathan E. (IA) - 1920, 1922
Kendrick (CT) - 1852
Kendrick, John B. (WY) - 1914
Kennedy, John C. (IL) - 1912
Kennedy, Walter L. (VT) - 1974
Kennedy, William (MT) - 1892
Kennerly, T. E. (TX) - 1966
Kennon, Robert F. (LA) - 1952
Kent, Edward (ME) - 1836, 1837, 1838, 1839, 1840, 1841
Kent, Henry O. (NH) - 1894, 1896
Kent, Herman O. (WI) - 1926
Kent, William P. (VA) - 1909
Kern, John W. (IN) - 1900, 1904
Kernan, Francis (NY) - 1872
Kerner, Otto (IL) - 1960, 1964
Kerr, John (NC) - 1852
Kerr, Robert S. (OK) - 1942
Kerrey, Robert F. (NE) - 1982
Ketchum, Omar B. (KS) - 1934
Keyes, Henry (VT) - 1856, 1857, 1858
Keyes, Henry W. (NH) - 1916
Keyser, F. Ray Jr. (VT) - 1960, 1962
Kilbourne, James (OH) - 1901
Kilby, Thomas E. (AL) - 1918
Kilgo, J. W. (TN) - 1944
Kilpatrick, Thomas M. (IL) - 1846
Kimball, Charles Dean (RI) - 1902
Kimball, Charles P. (ME) - 1871, 1872
Kimball, E. E. (MO) - 1888
Kimball, Horace A. (RI) - 1880, 1881, 1882
Kimmerle, Charles H. (MI) - 1906
King (MS) - 1881
King, Angus (ME) - 1994
King, Austin A. (MO) - 1848
King, Bruce (NM) - 1970, 1978, 1990, 1994
King, Edward J. (MA) - 1978
King, John A. (NY) - 1856
King, John W. (NH) - 1962, 1964, 1966
King, Rufus (NY) - 1816
King, Sam (HI) - 1970
King, Samuel Ward (RI) - 1840, 1841, 1842
King, W. R. (OR) - 1898
King, Wayne D. (NH) - 1994
King, William (ME) - 1820, 1835
Kinkead, John H. (NV) - 1878
Kinkead, William B. (KY) - 1867
Kinney, Audrey L. (AR) - 1914
Kinney, J. C. (AZ) - 1932
Kinney, William (IL) - 1830, 1834
Kinnie, L. G. (IA) - 1881, 1883
Kinter (ND) - 1894
Kirby, Ephraim (CT) - 1802, 1803
Kirk, Claude R. Jr. (FL) - 1966, 1970
Kirker, Thomas (OH) - 1808

Kirkwood, Samuel Jordan (IA) - 1859, 1861, 1875
Kirman, Richard Sr. (NV) - 1934
Kitchin, W. W. (NC) - 1908
Kitzhaber, John (OR) - 1994
Kleihege, George W. (KS) - 1912
Kleindienst, Richard (AZ) - 1964
Knapp, J. C. (IA) - 1871
Kneip, Richard Francis (SD) - 1970, 1972, 1974
Knight, Goodwin J. (CA) - 1954
Knight, Jesse William (UT) - 1908
Knight, Nehemiah R. (RI) - 1816, 1817, 1818, 1819, 1820, 1834, 1835
Knott, J. Procter (KY) - 1883
Knott, W. V. (FL) - 1916
Knous, Robert L. (CO) - 1966
Knous, William Lee (CO) - 1946, 1948
Knowland, William F. (CA) - 1958
Knowles, Tony (AK) - 1990, 1994
Knowles, Warren P. (WI) - 1964, 1966, 1968
Knowlton, D. A. (IL) - 1852
Koener, Gust (IL) - 1872
Kohler, Terry J. (WI) - 1982
Kohler, Walter J. (WI) - 1928, 1932
Kohler, Walter J. Jr. (WI) - 1950, 1952, 1954
Kolb, R. F. (AL) - 1892, 1894
Koontz, Arthur B. (WV) - 1920
Kraschel, Nelson G. (IA) - 1936, 1938, 1942
Kreshtool, Jacob (DE) - 1988
Kuehn, Philip G. (WI) - 1960, 1962
Kulongoski, Ted (OR) - 1982
Kump, Herman G. (WV) - 1932
Kunin, Madeleine M. (VT) - 1982, 1984, 1986, 1988

L

Lachapelle, Eugene J. (RI) - 1950
Lacy, Arthur J. (MI) - 1934
Ladd, Herbert W. (RI) - 1889, 1890, 1891
La Follette, Bronson C. (WI) - 1968
La Follette, Philip F. (WI) - 1930, 1934, 1936, 1938
La Follette, Robert M. (WI) - 1900, 1902, 1904
Lafoon, Ruby (KY) - 1931
Lake, Everett J. (CT) - 1920
Lake, I. Beverly Jr. (NC) - 1980
Lambert, Louis (LA) - 1979
Lamm (MO) - 1916
Lamm, Richard D. (CO) - 1974, 1978, 1982
Lamontagne, Ovide M. (NH) - 1996
Landers, Franklin (IN) - 1880
Landon, Alfred M. (KS) - 1932, 1934
Landreth, S. Lloyd (VA) - 1945
Lane, Alvin H. (TX) - 1948
Lane, Franklin K. (CA) - 1902
Lane, George W. Jr. (ME) - 1942
Lane, Henry S. (IN) - 1860
Lane, William Preston Jr. (MD) - 1946, 1950
Laney, Ben (AR) - 1944, 1946
Langdon, John (NH) - 1788, 1793, 1802, 1803, 1804, 1805, 1806, 1807, 1808, 1809, 1810, 1811
Langdon, W. H. (CA) - 1906
Langer, Lydia (ND) - 1934
Langer, William (ND) - 1932, 1936
Langlie, Arthur B. (WA) - 1940, 1944, 1948, 1952
Lanhan, Samuel W. T. (TX) - 1902, 1904
Lansdon, W. C. (KS) - 1916, 1918

Larrabee, William (IA) - 1885, 1887
Larrazolo, Octaviano A. (NM) - 1918
Larrow, Robert W. (VT) - 1952
Larsen, Allan (ID) - 1978
Larsen, Richard (ND) - 1972
Larson, Morgan F. (NJ) - 1928
Lashkowitz, Herschel (ND) - 1960
Lasater, Ed C. (TX) - 1912
Latham, M. S. (CA) - 1859
Lathrop, Samuel (MA) - 1824, 1831, 1832
Lattimore, William (MS) - 1823
Lausche, Frank J. (OH) - 1944, 1946, 1948, 1950, 1952, 1954
Lausier, Louis B. (ME) - 1948
Lavington, Leon E. (CO) - 1946
Law, Richard (CT) - 1796, 1801
Lawler, Daniel W. (MN) - 1892
Lawrence, Amos A. (MA) - 1858, 1860
Lawrence, David L. (PA) - 1958
Lawrence, Isaac (RI) - 1878
Laxalt, Paul (NV) - 1966
Layton, L. (DE) - 1932
Lea (MS) - 1849
Lea, Preston (DE) - 1904
Leader, George M. (PA) - 1954
Leake, Walter (MS) - 1821, 1823
Leamy, James P. (VT) - 1932, 1934
Leavitt, Michael O. (UT) - 1992, 1996
Leche, Richard W. (LA) - 1936
Ledbetter, C. C. (AR) - 1934
Leddy, Bernard J. (VT) - 1958
Ledgerwood, Thomas D. II (OK) - 1990
Ledoux, Henri (NH) - 1932
Lee, Andrew E. (SD) - 1896, 1898, 1908
Lee, Fitzhugh (VA) - 1885
Lee, J. Bracken (UT) - 1944, 1948, 1952, 1956
Lee, Jerrie W. (AZ) - 1938, 1940, 1942, 1944
Lee, William E. (MN) - 1914
Leedy, John W. (KS) - 1896, 1898
Leffler, Shepherd (IA) - 1875
Lehman, Herbert H. (NY) - 1932, 1934, 1936, 1938
Lehrman, Lew (NY) - 1980
Lemke, William (ND) - 1922
Lemon, Robert S. (KS) - 1944
Leonard, A. H. (LA) - 1892
Leonard, Donald S. (MI) - 1954
Leonard, Elizabeth Ann (RI) - 1992
Leonard, L. (MO) - 1892
Leonard, Richard W. (NH) - 1974
Leopold, John (HI) - 1978
Leroy, David H. (ID) - 1986
Leslie, Harry G. (IN) - 1928
Leslie, Preston H. (KY) - 1871
Lester, J. T. (MS) - 1915
Letcher, John (VA) - 1859, 1861
Letcher, Robert P. (KY) - 1840
Lett, H. C. (NE) - 1872
Levander, Harold (MN) - 1966
Levin, Sander (MI) - 1970, 1974
Lewelling, L. D. (KS) - 1892, 1894
Lewis, Andrew L. "Drew" Jr. (PA) - 1974
Lewis, Austin (CA) - 1906
Lewis, David P. (AL) - 1872, 1874
Lewis, Dean J. (RI) - 1954
Lewis, James Hamilton (IL) - 1920
Lewis, James T. (WI) - 1863
Lewis, Joshua (LA) - 1816
Lewis, Lunsford L. (VA) - 1905
Lewis, Morgan (NY) - 1804, 1807
Lewis, Robert E. (MO) - 1896
Lewis, Samuel (OH) - 1851, 1853
Lewis, Tom J. (MN) - 1914
Lewis, Vivian M. (NJ) - 1910
Licht, Frank (RI) - 1968, 1970

Lien, Burre H. (SD) - 1900
Ligon, Thomas Watkins (MD) - 1853
Lilley, George L. (CT) - 1908
Lincoln, Enoch (ME) - 1826, 1827, 1828
Lincoln, Levi (MA) - 1825, 1826, 1827, 1828, 1829, 1830, 1831, 1832
Lincoln, Levi I (MA) - 1809
Lind, John (MN) - 1896, 1898, 1900
Lindley, John F. (SD) - 1964
Lindsay, Ben B. (CO) - 1906
Lindsay, H. B. (TN) - 1918
Lindsay, Robert B. (AL) - 1870
Lindsay, William (MT) - 1904
Link, Arthur A. (ND) - 1972, 1976, 1980
Linney, Frank A. (NC) - 1916
Lippitt, Charles Warren (RI) - 1895, 1896
Lippitt, Henry (RI) - 1875, 1876
List, Robert F. (NV) - 1978, 1982
Lister, Ernest (WA) - 1912, 1916
Little, Chauncey B. (KS) - 1928
Little, John S. (AR) - 1906
Littlefield, Alfred H. (RI) - 1880, 1881, 1882
Littlefield, George L. (RI) - 1895, 1896
Littlefield, Nathan W. (RI) - 1900
Littlejohn, Flavius (MI) - 1849
Littleton (TN) - 1904
Livesay, J. O. (AR) - 1930, 1932
Livingston, Robert R. (NY) - 1798
Lloyd, James (MA) - 1826
Lobeck, E. E. (MN) - 1912
Locke, Gary (WA) - 1996
Locke, Hugh A. (AL) - 1930
Lodge, John D. (CT) - 1950, 1954
Loftus, Thomas (WI) - 1990
Logan, Benjamin (KY) - 1800
Logan, William (KY) - 1820
London, Herbert I. (NY) - 1990
Long, Benjamin M. (AL) - 1890
Long, Earl K. (LA) - 1948, 1956
Long, Huey P. (LA) - 1928
Long, John D. (MA) - 1879, 1880, 1881
Long, Richard H. (MA) - 1918, 1919
Longino, Andrew H. (MS) - 1899
Longley, James B. (ME) - 1974
Longshore, William L. Jr. (AL) - 1958
Longstreth, Morris (PA) - 1848
Looker, Othniel (OH) - 1814
Loomis (CT) - 1861, 1862
Loomis, Orland S. (WI) - 1940, 1942
Lord, John F. (ND) - 1958
Lord, Samuel L. (ME) - 1898, 1900
Lord, William P. (OR) - 1894
Loucks, H. L. (SD) - 1890
Lounsbury, George E. (CT) - 1898
Lounsbury, Phineas C. (CT) - 1886
Love, John A. (CO) - 1962, 1966, 1970
Loveland, W. A. H. (CO) - 1878
Loveless, Herschel C. (IA) - 1952, 1956, 1958
Lovering, Henry B. (MA) - 1887
Low, Frederick F. (CA) - 1863
Lowden, Frank O. (IL) - 1916
Lowden, J. G. (TX) - 1904
Lowe, A. Lynn (AR) - 1978
Lowe, Enoch L. (MD) - 1850
Lowe, Ralph P. (IA) - 1857
Lowe, W. O. (TN) - 1946
Lowndes, Lloyd (MD) - 1895, 1899
Lowry, Mike (WA) - 1992
Lowry, Robert (MS) - 1881, 1885
Lubbock, Francis R. (TX) - 1861
Lucas, Robert (OH) - 1830, 1832, 1834
Lucas, William (MI) - 1986

Luce, Cyrus G. (MI) - 1886, 1888
Lucey, Patrick J. (WI) - 1966, 1970, 1974
Ludeman, Cal R. (MN) - 1986
Ludington, Harrison (WI) - 1875
Ludlow, George C. (NJ) - 1880
Lueck, Martin L. (WI) - 1924
Lueck, William L. (WI) - 1936
Lujan, Manuel (NM) - 1948
Luksik, Peg (PA) - 1994
Lumpkin, Wilson (GA) - 1831, 1833
Lundeen, Ernest (MN) - 1928
Lusk, T. E. (NM) - 1966
Lyman, Darius (OH) - 1832
Lynch, Andrew J. (DE) - 1920
Lynch, Charles (MS) - 1831, 1835
Lynch, Walter A. (NY) - 1950
Lyons, Charlton H. Sr. (LA) - 1964

M

Mabey, Charles R. (UT) - 1920, 1924
Mabry, Thomas J. (NM) - 1946, 1948
Mabus, Ray (MS) - 1987, 1991
MacCollum, Isaac J. (DE) - 1944
MacCorkle, William A. (WV) - 1892
MacFarlane, M. B. (FL) - 1900, 1904
Mackinnon, George (MN) - 1958
Macleod, Norman D. (RI) - 1944
Maddock, Thomas (AZ) - 1934
Maddock, Walter (ND) - 1928
Maddox, Lester (GA) - 1966
Madison, George (KY) - 1816
Magoffin, Beriah (KY) - 1859
Maguire, James G. (CA) - 1898
Mahone, William (VA) - 1889
Mahoney, George P. (MD) - 1966
Major, Elliott Woolfolk (MO) - 1912
Majors, T. J. (NE) - 1894
Makemson, W. K. (TX) - 1894
Maley, Anna A. (WA) - 1912
Mallberg, Leon (ND) - 1988
Mallory (WI) - 1877
Mandel, Marvin (MD) - 1970, 1974
Manly, Charles (NC) - 1848, 1850
Mann, Horace (MA) - 1852
Mann, William Hodges (VA) - 1909
Manning, Richard I. (SC) - 1914, 1916
Mansfield, Frederick W. (MA) - 1916, 1917
Marcy (NH) - 1876, 1877
Marcy, William L. (NY) - 1832, 1834, 1836, 1838
Marigny, Bernard (LA) - 1824, 1828
Markham, H. H. (CA) - 1890
Markle, Joseph (PA) - 1844
Marks, Albert S. (TN) - 1878
Marland, E. W. (OK) - 1934
Marland, William C. (WV) - 1952
Marmaduke, John Sappington (MO) - 1884
Marshall, Joseph G. (IN) - 1846
Marshall, Thomas R. (IN) - 1908
Marshall, William R. (MN) - 1865, 1867
Martin (NH) - 1918
Martin, Burleigh (ME) - 1932
Martin, Charles H. (OR) - 1934
Martin, Clarence D. (WA) - 1932, 1936
Martin, Ed C. (SD) - 1954
Martin, Edward (PA) - 1942
Martin, Fred C. (VT) - 1920, 1924, 1938
Martin, G. H. (ID) - 1912
Martin, J. (FL) - 1924
Martin, James (AL) - 1966
Martin, James G. (NC) - 1984, 1988
Martin, John (KS) - 1876, 1888
Martin, John A. (KS) - 1884, 1886

Martin, John W. (FL) - 1924
Martin, John W. (SD) - 1902
Martin, Joshua L. (AL) - 1845
Martin, Marion (TX) - 1888
Martin, Noah (NH) - 1852, 1853
Martin, Wheeler (RI) - 1824
Martineau, John E. (AR) - 1926
Martinez, Bob (FL) - 1986, 1990
Marty, John (MN) - 1994
Marvel, Joshua H. (DE) - 1894
Marvel, Josiah Jr. (DE) - 1940
Marvel, Richard D. (NE) - 1974
Mason, Charles (IA) - 1867
Mason, Jeremiah (NH) - 1817, 1818
Mason, Samuel R. (PA) - 1878
Mason, Stevens T. (MI) - 1835, 1837
Massie, Nathanael (OH) - 1807
Matheson, Scott M. (UT) - 1976, 1980
Mathews, Henry M. (WV) - 1876
Matson, Courtland C. (IN) - 1888
Matson, John A. (IN) - 1849
Matteson, Joel A. (IL) - 1852
Matthews, Claude (IN) - 1892
Mattocks, John (VT) - 1843
Maupin, Joseph H. (CO) - 1892
Maw, Herbert B. (UT) - 1940, 1944, 1948
Maxwell, Edwin (WV) - 1884
May (WI) - 1879
Maybank, Burnet R. (SC) - 1938
Maybury, William C. (MI) - 1900
Mayer, Edwin S. (TX) - 1958
Maynard, Horace (TN) - 1874
Mayo, William B. (VT) - 1916, 1918
Mazullo, Vincent (RI) - 1982
McAlister, Hill (TN) - 1932, 1934
McAllister (GA) - 1845
McArthur, D. H. (ND) - 1916
McArthur, Duncan (OH) - 1830
McBride, Henry (WA) - 1916
McCafferty, Matthew J. (MA) - 1884
McCall, John E. (TN) - 1900, 1932
McCall, R. K. (FL) - 1845
McCall, Samuel W. (MA) - 1914, 1915, 1916, 1917
McCall, Tom (OR) - 1966, 1970
McCarney, Robert P. (ND) - 1968
McCarter, J. W. (SD) - 1914
McCarty, Daniel T. (FL) - 1952
McCarty, Nicholas (IN) - 1852
McCary, Elvin (AL) - 1974
McCaull, Patrick H. (VA) - 1897
McClaughry, John (VT) - 1992
McClellan, George B. (NJ) - 1877
McClelland, Robert (MI) - 1851, 1852
McClung, James W. (AL) - 1841
McClure, P. F. (SD) - 1889
McClurg, Joseph W. (MO) - 1868, 1870
McColl, J. H. (NE) - 1896
McConaughy, James L. (CT) - 1946
McConnell, J. H. Tyler (DE) - 1956
McConnell, J. R. (CA) - 1861
McConnell, William J. (ID) - 1892, 1894
McCook, George W. (OH) - 1871
McCord, James N. (TN) - 1944, 1946, 1958
McCormack, Edward J. (MA) - 1966
McCormick, Vance C. (PA) - 1914
McCoy (WI) - 1920
McCrae, Duncan K. (NC) - 1858
McCray, Warren T. (IN) - 1920
McCreary, James B. (KY) - 1875, 1911
McCulloch, Carleton B. (IN) - 1920, 1924
McCullough, D. A. (SD) - 1930
McCullough, J. B. (NV) - 1898
McCullough, John G. (VT) - 1902

McCutchins, Luther (NH) - 1874
McDaniel, Henry D. (GA) - 1884
McDaniel, Larry (MO) - 1940
McDermott, James A. (WA) - 1980
McDonald, Charles James (GA) - 1839, 1841
McDonald (GA) - 1851
McDonald, Jesse F. (CO) - 1908
McDonald, Joseph E. (IN) - 1864
McDonald, W. C. (NM) - 1911
McDowell, J. L. (KS) - 1866
McEachern, Paul (NH) - 1986, 1988
McElroy, Hugh E. (ID) - 1914
McEnery, John (LA) - 1872
McEnery, Samuel D. (LA) - 1884, 1892
McEniry, Hugh (AL) - 1942
McFarland, Ernest W. (AZ) - 1954, 1956
McGettrick, Felix W. (VT) - 1902
McGill (NJ) - 1895
McGill, A. R. (MN) - 1886
McGonigle, Arthur I. (PA) - 1958
McGovern (WI) - 1940
McGovern, Francis E. (WI) - 1910, 1912
McGrath, J. Howard (RI) - 1940, 1942, 1944
McGrath, John (VT) - 1940
McGraw, John H. (WA) - 1892
McGreevey, James (NJ) - 1997
McGregor, T. H. (TX) - 1920
McIntire, Albert W. (CO) - 1894
McIntire, Bertrand G. (ME) - 1918, 1920
McIntyre, John J. (WY) - 1950
McKay, Douglas (OR) - 1948, 1950
McKean (NY) - 1878
McKean, Thomas (PA) - 1799, 1802, 1805
McKeever, Horace G. (OK) - 1918
McKeithen, John J. (LA) - 1964, 1968
McKeldin, Theodore R. (MD) - 1942, 1946, 1950, 1954
McKellips, Roger (SD) - 1978
McKelvie, Samuel R. (NE) - 1918, 1920
McKernan, John R. Jr. (ME) - 1986, 1990
McKinley, John C. (MO) - 1912
McKinley, William Jr. (OH) - 1891, 1893
McKinney, Luther F. (NH) - 1892
McKinney, Philip W. (VA) - 1889
McKnight, Thomas (IA) - 1846
McLane (SC) - 1882
McLane, John (NH) - 1904
McLane, Malcolm (NH) - 1972
McLane, Robert M. (MD) - 1883
McLaughlin, Robert H. (IL) - 1834
McLaurin, Anselm J. (MS) - 1895
McLean, Angus Wilton (NC) - 1924
McLean, Ernest L. (ME) - 1926
McLean, George P. (CT) - 1900
McLean, John R. (OH) - 1899
McLeod, Thomas G. (SC) - 1922, 1924
McLevy, Jasper (CT) - 1934, 1936, 1938, 1942
McManus, E. J. (IA) - 1960
McManus, James O. (RI) - 1942
McMaster, William H. (SD) - 1920, 1922
McMath, Sidney S. (AR) - 1948, 1950
McMillan, William (NV) - 1898
McMillin, Benton (TN) - 1898, 1900, 1912
McMinn, Joseph (TN) - 1815, 1817, 1819
McMinn, T. J. (TX) - 1900

McMullen, Adam (NE) - 1924, 1926
McMullen, Richard C. (DE) - 1936
McMurray, John (ID) - 1930
McNair, Alexander (MO) - 1820
McNair, Robert E. (SC) - 1966
McNeal, J. W. (OK) - 1910
McNeill, Robert H. (NC) - 1948
McNichols, Stephen L. R. (CO) - 1956, 1958, 1962
McNutt, Alexander G. (MS) - 1837, 1839
McNutt, Paul V. (IN) - 1932
McRae, Duncan K. (NC) - 1858
McRae, John J. (MS) - 1853, 1855
McRae, Thomas C. (AR) - 1920, 1922
McShane, J. A. (NE) - 1888
McSparran, John A. (PA) - 1922
McSweeney, John (OH) - 1942
McSweeney, Miles B. (SC) - 1900
McWane, Fred W. (VA) - 1933
McWherter, Ned R. (TN) - 1986, 1990
McWillie, William (MS) - 1857
Mead, Albert E. (WA) - 1904
Mead, Cowles (MS) - 1825
Mead, James M. (NY) - 1946
Mead, John A. (VT) - 1910
Mead, Mary (WY) - 1990
Meadows, Clarence W. (WV) - 1944
Meares, Iredell (NC) - 1912
Mecham, Evan (AZ) - 1978, 1986
Mechem, Edwin L. (NM) - 1950, 1952, 1956, 1958, 1960, 1962
Mechem, Merritt C. (NM) - 1920
Medill, William (OH) - 1853, 1855
Meech, Ezra (VT) - 1830, 1831, 1832, 1833
Meekins, I. M. (NC) - 1924
Meier, Julius L. (OR) - 1930
Meigs, Return J. Jr. (OH) - 1807, 1810, 1812
Meitzen, E. R. (TX) - 1914, 1916
Melich, Mitchell (UT) - 1964
Mellette, Arthur C. (SD) - 1889, 1890
Menario, John E. (ME) - 1986
Meredith, E. T. (IA) - 1916
Merriam, Frank F. (CA) - 1934, 1938
Merriam, William R. (MN) - 1888, 1890
Merrill, Samuel (IA) - 1867, 1869
Merrill, Steve (NH) - 1992, 1994
Merrimon, Augustus S. (NC) - 1872
Merritt, William H. (IA) - 1861
Merwin, S. E. (CT) - 1890, 1892
Meskill, Thomas J. (CT) - 1970
Messer, Asa (RI) - 1830
Metcalf (RI) - 1893
Metcalf, Ralph (NH) - 1855, 1856
Metcalfe (WI) - 1932
Metcalfe, Thomas (KY) - 1828
Metschan, Phil (OR) - 1930
Metzger, Frazer (VT) - 1912
Metzger, John W. (CO) - 1952
Meyer, William H. (CO) - 1886
Meyers, Harry H. (AR) - 1902, 1913
Meyner, Robert B. (NJ) - 1953, 1957, 1969
Mickelson, George S. (SD) - 1986, 1990
Mickelson, George T. (SD) - 1946, 1948
Mickey, John H. (NE) - 1902, 1904
Miera, Maurice (NM) - 1940
Mifflin, Thomas (PA) - 1790, 1793, 1796
Mikel, G. E. (AR) - 1912
Mildren, Jack (OK) - 1994
Miles, Frank (IA) - 1946
Miles, John E. (NM) - 1938, 1940, 1950
Miller, Alex R. (IA) - 1926

Miller, B. M. (AL) - 1930
Miller, Bob J. (NV) - 1990, 1994
Miller, Charles R. (DE) - 1912
Miller, J. B. (TX) - 1847
Miller, Jaffa (NM) - 1934, 1936
Miller, John (MO) - 1825, 1828
Miller, John (ND) - 1889
Miller, John F. (OR) - 1862
Miller, John H. (NV) - 1922
Miller, Keith H. (AK) - 1970
Miller, Leslie A. (WY) - 1930, 1932, 1934, 1938
Miller, Nathan L. (NY) - 1920, 1922
Miller, Stephen (MN) - 1863
Miller, Vern (KS) - 1974
Miller, Warner (NY) - 1888
Miller, William R. (AR) - 1876, 1878
Miller, Zell (GA) - 1990, 1994
Milliken, Carl E. (ME) - 1916, 1918
Milliken, William G. (MI) - 1970, 1974, 1978
Millner, Guy (GA) - 1994
Mills (TN) - 1894
Mills, John T. (TX) - 1849
Mills, Ogden L. (NY) - 1926
Mills, W. T. (AR) - 1946
Milton, John (FL) - 1860
Minor, William T. (CT) - 1855, 1856
Mitchell, Albert K. (NM) - 1938
Mitchell, D. P. (KS) - 1878
Mitchell, George (DE) - 1792
Mitchell, George J. (ME) - 1974
Mitchell, Henry L. (FL) - 1892
Mitchell, Hugh B. (WA) - 1952
Mitchell, James F. (NV) - 1906
Mitchell, James P. (NJ) - 1961
Mitchell, Nathanael (DE) - 1801, 1804
Mitchell, R. F. (IA) - 1944
Mitchell, Roy (AR) - 1956
Mitchell, Theo (SC) - 1990
Mobley, Al (OR) - 1990
Moehlenpah (WI) - 1918
Moeur, B. B. (AZ) - 1932, 1934
Moffett, Charles (TN) - 1966
Molleston, Henry (DE) - 1819
Mollohan, Robert H. (WV) - 1956
Moloney, Thomas W. (VT) - 1898
Molpus, Dick (MS) - 1995
Monaghan, Thomas M. (DE) - 1912
Mondragon, Roberto (NM) - 1994
Montague, A. J. (VA) - 1901
Montgomery, Samuel B. (WV) - 1920
Montgomery, Thomas (DE) - 1792
Moodie, Thomas H. (ND) - 1934
Moody, Dan (TX) - 1926, 1928
Moody, Zenas F. (OR) - 1882
Mooney, Thomas J. (MD) - 1986
Moonlight, Thomas (KS) - 1886
Moore, Andrew B. (AL) - 1857, 1859
Moore, Arch A. Jr. (WV) - 1968, 1972, 1980, 1984, 1988
Moore, Arthur Harry (NJ) - 1925, 1931, 1937
Moore, Charles C. (ID) - 1922, 1924
Moore, Dan K. (NC) - 1964
Moore, Gabriel (AL) - 1829
Moore, Harbin H. (IN) - 1828
Moore, James B. (IL) - 1822
Moore, John (MI) - 1868
Moore, Preston J. (OK) - 1966
Moore, Samuel B. (AL) - 1831
Moore, Thomas O. (LA) - 1859
Moran, Edward C. Jr. (ME) - 1928, 1930
Moran, J. Edward (VT) - 1950
Moran, John B. (MA) - 1906
Morehead, Charles S. (KY) - 1855
Morehead, John H. (NE) - 1912, 1914, 1920
Morehead, John M. (NC) - 1840, 1842

Morgan (CT) - 1898
Morgan (MS) - 1837
Morgan, David (MN) - 1912
Morgan, Edwin D. (NY) - 1858, 1860, 1876
Morgan, Ephraim F. (WV) - 1920
Morgan, George W. (OH) - 1865
Morgan, James (WI) - 1888
Morgan, W. A. (NV) - 1914
Morgan, W. S. (AR) - 1898
Morgan, W. Y. (KS) - 1922
Morgenthau, Robert M. (NY) - 1962
Morison, W. S. D. (IL) - 1848
Morley, Clarence J. (CO) - 1924
Morrill, Ansen P. (ME) - 1853, 1854, 1855
Morrill, David L. (NH) - 1824, 1825, 1826, 1827
Morrill, E. N. (KS) - 1894, 1896
Morrill, Lot M. (ME) - 1857, 1858, 1859
Morris, Buckner S. (IL) - 1856
Morris, Charles (CT) - 1924, 1926, 1928
Morris, George L. (NE) - 1956
Morris, Luzon B. (CT) - 1888, 1890, 1892
Morris, Nephi L. (UT) - 1912, 1916
Morrison, Bruce A. (CT) - 1990
Morrison, Cameron (NC) - 1920
Morrison, Frank B. (NE) - 1960, 1962, 1964
Morrison, John T. (ID) - 1902
Morrison, Robert (AZ) - 1958
Morrow, Edwin P. (KY) - 1915, 1919
Morrow, Jeremiah (OH) - 1820, 1822, 1824
Morrow, Thomas Z. (KY) - 1883
Morse, Allen B. (MI) - 1892
Morse, Freeman H. (ME) - 1845
Morse, Thomas J. (VT) - 1994
Morton, J. S. (NE) - 1866, 1882, 1884, 1892
Morton, Levi P. (NY) - 1894
Morton, Marcus (MA) - 1828, 1829, 1830, 1831, 1832, 1833, 1834, 1835, 1836, 1837, 1838, 1839, 1840, 1841, 1842, 1843
Morton, Oliver P. (IN) - 1856, 1864
Morton, Warren A. (WY) - 1982
Moseley, William D. (FL) - 1845
Moses, Franklin J. Jr. (SC) - 1872
Moses, John (ND) - 1936, 1938, 1940, 1942
Moses, Robert (NY) - 1934
Moss, A. B. (ID) - 1898
Motley, S. W. (ID) - 1910
Mount, James A. (IN) - 1896
Mouton, Alexander (LA) - 1842
Moyle, James H. (UT) - 1900, 1904
Muhlenberg, Frederick A. (PA) - 1793
Muhlenburgh, Henry (PA) - 1835
Muir (ND) - 1890
Mullen, W. E. (WY) - 1910
Mullikin, Addison E. (MD) - 1926
Muncy, T. J. (VA) - 1917
Munford (VA) - 1863
Muniz, Ramsey (TX) - 1972, 1974
Munroe Addison P. (RI) - 1916
Munson, Henry C. (ME) - 1877
Murphy, Ed (MN) - 1940
Murphy, Francis P. (NH) - 1936, 1938
Murphy, Frank (MI) - 1936, 1938
Murphy, Franklin (NJ) - 1901
Murphy, George W. (AR) - 1913
Murphy, Jack M. (ID) - 1974
Murphy, John (AL) - 1825, 1827
Murphy, John G. (RI) - 1946
Murphy, Robert F. (MA) - 1954
Murphy, Vincent J. (NJ) - 1943
Murrah, Pendleton (TX) - 1863
Murray, Johnston (OK) - 1950

Murray, William G. (IA) - 1958, 1966
Murray, William H. (OK) - 1930
Murtagh, J. C. (IA) - 1924
Muse (VA) - 1941
Muskie, Edmund S. (ME) - 1954, 1956
Musselman, Amos S. (MI) - 1912
Mutz, John M. (IN) - 1988
Myers, Harry H. (AR) - 1904

N

Nance, Albinus (NE) - 1878, 1880
Nash, George K. (OH) - 1899, 1901
Naudain, Arnold (DE) - 1832
Neal, John R. (TN) - 1950, 1954
Neal, Lawrence T. (OH) - 1893
Neal, William J. (NH) - 1942
Needham, Horatio (VT) - 1849
Neely, Harold E. (WV) - 1960
Neely, Matthew M. (WV) - 1940
Neff, Pat M. (TX) - 1920, 1922
Nelsen, Ancher (MN) - 1956
Nelson, A. T. (MO) - 1924
Nelson, Andrew (MN) - 1928
Nelson, Ben (NE) - 1990, 1994
Nelson, Gaylord A. (WI) - 1958, 1960
Nelson, Knute (MN) - 1892, 1894
Nelson, Martin A. (MN) - 1934, 1936
Nelson, Sheffield (AR) - 1990, 1994
Nestos, Ragnvald A. (ND) - 1921, 1922
Nelson (TN) - 1859
Netsch, Dawn Clark (IL) - 1994
Neville, Keith (NE) - 1916, 1918
Newell (NJ) - 1877
Newell, William A. (NJ) - 1856
Nice, Harry W. (MD) - 1919, 1934, 1938
Nicholls, Francis T. (LA) - 1876, 1888
Nichols, Alva W. (MI) - 1894
Nicks (AL) - 1853
Nicoll (CT) - 1841
Nigh, George (OK) - 1978, 1982
Niles (CT) - 1839, 1840, 1849
Niquette, Russell F. (VT) - 1960
Nixon, Richard M. (CA) - 1962
Noble, Noah (IN) - 1831, 1834
Noel, Edmond F. (MS) - 1907
Noel, Philip W. (RI) - 1972, 1974
Nolte, Eugene Jr. (TX) - 1946
Noone, Albert W. (NH) - 1914, 1930
Norbeck, Peter (SD) - 1916, 1918
Norcross (GA) - 1876
Norris, Edwin L. (MT) - 1908
North, J. E. (NE) - 1886
Northen, William J. (GA) - 1890, 1892
Norton, A. B. (TX) - 1878, 1884
Norton, J. N. (NE) - 1924
Nortoni, Albert D. (MO) - 1912
Norwood (GA) - 1880
Norwood, C. M. (AR) - 1888
Notte, John A. Jr. (RI) - 1960, 1962
Noyes, Edward F. (OH) - 1871, 1873
Nugent, James W. (RI) - 1892
Nugent, Thomas L. (TX) - 1892, 1894
Nunn, Louie B. (KY) - 1979
Nunn, Louis B. (KY) - 1963, 1967
Nutter, Donald G. (MT) - 1960

O

Oates, W. C. (AL) - 1894
O'Bannon, Frank L. (IN) - 1996
O'Brien, Leo Jr. (VT) - 1970
O'Callaghan, Mike (NV) - 1970, 1974
Ochiltree, W. B. (TX) - 1853
O'Connell, John J. (WA) - 1968
O'Conner, Frank (NY) - 1966

O'Connor, Herbert R. (MD) - 1938, 1942
O'Connor, J. F. T. (ND) - 1920
O'Connor, Michael J. (SD) - 1982
O'Daniel, W. Lee (TX) - 1938, 1940, 1956
Oddie, Tasker L. (NV) - 1910, 1914, 1918
Odell, Benjamin B. Jr. (NY) - 1900, 1902
O'Donnell, C. C. (CA) - 1886
O'Ferrall, Charles T. (VA) - 1893
Ogilvie, Richard B. (IL) - 1968, 1972
Oglesby, Richard J. (IL) - 1864, 1872, 1884
Olcott, Ben W. (OR) - 1922
Olden, Charles S. (NJ) - 1859
Olin, John M. (WI) - 1886
Oliver, James C. (ME) - 1952
Oliver, Samuel W. (AL) - 1837
Olsen, Arnold H. (MT) - 1956
Olsen, George W. (NE) - 1944
Olson, Allen I. (ND) - 1980, 1984
Olson, Culbert L. (CA) - 1938, 1942
Olson, Floyd B. (MN) - 1924, 1930, 1932, 1934
Olson, Jack B. (WI) - 1970
Olson, John E. (SD) - 1974
O'Malley, Malcolm A. (MT) - 1904
Oman, J. R. (WA) - 1924
O'Neal, Edward A. (AL) - 1882, 1884
O'Neal, Emmet L. (AL) - 1910
O'Neal, W. (FL) - 1924
O'Neal, William R. (FL) - 1912
O'Neill, C. William (OH) - 1956, 1958
O'Neill, William A. (CT) - 1982, 1986
Orear, E. C. (KY) - 1911
Orman, James B. (CO) - 1900
Ormsbee, Ebenezer J. (VT) - 1886
O'Rourke, Andrew P. (NY) - 1986
Orr, James L. (SC) - 1865
Orr, Kay A. (NE) - 1986, 1990
Orr, Robert D. (IN) - 1980, 1984
Orr, Sample (MO) - 1860
Osborn, Chase S. (MI) - 1910, 1914
Osborn, Sidney P. (AZ) - 1940, 1942, 1944, 1946
Osborn, Thomas A. (KS) - 1872, 1874
Osborne, John E. (WY) - 1892, 1904
Osgood, William N. (MA) - 1908
Ostlund, John C. (WY) - 1978
Otero, Manuel B. (NM) - 1924
Otis, George L. (MN) - 1869
Otis, Harrison G. (MA) - 1823
Otjen, William J. (OK) - 1942
Ottinger, Albert (NY) - 1928
Overall, John W. (TN) - 1916
Overby (GA) - 1855
Overmyer, David (KS) - 1894
Owen, Sidney M. (MN) - 1890, 1894
Owens, Wayne (UT) - 1984
Owsley, William (KY) - 1844

P

Packard, Stephen B. (LA) - 1876
Packer, Asa (PA) - 1869
Packer, William F. (PA) - 1857
Padelford, Seth (RI) - 1860, 1869, 1870, 1871, 1872
Page, Carroll S. (VT) - 1890
Page, John (NH) - 1839, 1840, 1841
Page, John B. (VT) - 1867, 1868
Paine, Charles (VT) - 1835, 1841, 1842
Paine, Henry W. (MA) - 1863, 1864
Paine, Robert Treat (MA) - 1899, 1900
Pajcic, Steve (FL) - 1986
Palfrey, John G. (MA) - 1851

Palmer, Henry L. (WI) - 1863
Palmer, Joel (OR) - 1870
Palmer, John M. (IL) - 1868, 1888
Palmer, Linwood E. (ME) - 1978
Palmer, William A. (VT) - 1830, 1831, 1832, 1833, 1834, 1835
Pardee, George C. (CA) - 1902
Park, Guy Brasfield (MO) - 1932
Parker, Amasa J. (NY) - 1856, 1858
Parker, Crawford F. (IN) - 1960
Parker, Joel (NJ) - 1862, 1871
Parker, John J. (NC) - 1920
Parker, John M. (LA) - 1916, 1920
Parkhurst, Frederick H. (ME) - 1920
Parks (AR) - 1880
Parks, C. C. (CO) - 1912
Parks, Gorham (ME) - 1837
Parnell, Harvey J. (AR) - 1928, 1930
Parriott, James D. (CO) - 1932
Parris, Albion K. (ME) - 1821, 1822, 1823, 1824, 1825, 1854
Parsons, Enoch (AL) - 1835
Parsons, Enoch (TN) - 1819
Partridge, Azariah S. (MI) - 1890
Pascal, Robert A. (MD) - 1982
Pastore, John O. (RI) - 1946, 1948
Pataki, George E. (NY) - 1994
Pattangall, William R. (ME) - 1922, 1924
Patten, George F. (ME) - 1856
Pattengill, Henry R. (MI) - 1914
Patterson, I. L. (OR) - 1926
Patterson, Jack A. (ND) - 1940
Patterson, John (AL) - 1958
Patterson, Malcolm R. (TN) - 1906, 1908
Patterson, Paul (OR) - 1954
Patterson, T. M. (CO) - 1888, 1914
Patteson, Okey L. (WV) - 1948
Pattison, John (WA) - 1908
Pattison, John M. (OH) - 1905
Pattison, Robert E. (PA) - 1882, 1890, 1902
Patton, Frank C. (NC) - 1944
Patton, Paul E. (KY) - 1995
Patton, Robert Miller (AL) - 1865
Patton, W. S. (MS) - 1865
Patty, Hubert D. (TN) - 1962
Paulen, Ben S. (KS) - 1924, 1926
Paulus, Norma (OR) - 1986
Payne, Frederick G. (ME) - 1948, 1950
Payne, H. B. (OH) - 1857
Paynter, Rowland G. (DE) - 1908
Paynter, Samuel (DE) - 1823
Peabody, Endicott (MA) - 1962
Peabody, James H. (CO) - 1902, 1904
Peabody, Oliver (NH) - 1798
Peabody, Thomas H. (RI) - 1887, 1896, 1897
Pearson, H. Clyde (VA) - 1961
Pearson, Linley E. (IN) - 1992
Pease, Elisha M. (TX) - 1853, 1855, 1865, 1866
Peasley, B. J. (TX) - 1944
Peay, Austin (TN) - 1922, 1924, 1926
Peck (GA) - 1892
Peck, Asahel (VT) - 1874
Peck, George W. (WI) - 1890, 1892, 1894, 1904
Peck, Lucius B. (VT) - 1850
Peck, T. F. (TN) - 1924
Peckham, G. E. (NV) - 1894
Peckham, William (RI) - 1837
Peery, George C. (VA) - 1933
Peery, Harman W. (UT) - 1936
Pendleton, George H. (OH) - 1869
Pennewill, Caleb S. (DE) - 1904
Pennewill, Simeon S. (DE) - 1908
Pennoyer, Sylvester (OR) - 1886, 1890

Pennypacker, Samuel W. (PA) - 1902
Percy, Charles H. (IL) - 1964
Perham, Sidney (ME) - 1870, 1871, 1872
Perkins, George C. (CA) - 1879
Perkins, Jared (NH) - 1854
Perpich, Rudy (MN) - 1978, 1982, 1986, 1990
Perry, Charles B. (WI) - 1926
Perry, Edward A. (FL) - 1884
Perry, Madison S. (FL) - 1856
Pershing, Cyrus L. (PA) - 1875
Persons, Gordon (AL) - 1950
Peters, John S. (CT) - 1831, 1832, 1833
Petersen, George C. (FL) - 1960
Petersen, Hjalmar (MN) - 1940, 1942
Peterson, Harry H. (MN) - 1950
Peterson, Russell W. (DE) - 1968, 1972
Peterson, Val (NE) - 1946, 1948, 1950
Peterson, Walter (NH) - 1968, 1970
Pettigrew, A. J. (FL) - 1908
Pettus, John J. (MS) - 1859, 1861
Pharr, Henry N. (LA) - 1908
Pharr, John N. (LA) - 1896
Phelps, Edward J. (VT) - 1880
Phelps, John S. (MO) - 1868, 1876
Phelps, T. G. (CA) - 1875
Philip, John W. (TX) - 1914
Philipp, Emanuel L. (WI) - 1914, 1916, 1918
Phillip, Stephen L. (MA) - 1848
Phillips, John C. (AZ) - 1928, 1930
Phillips, Joseph B. (IL) - 1822
Phillips, Kirk G. (SD) - 1898
Phillips, Leon C. (OK) - 1938
Phillips, Rubel L. (MS) - 1963, 1967
Phillips, Stephen C. (MA) - 1849, 1850
Phillips, T. J. (IA) - 1901
Phillips, Wendell (MA) - 1870
Pickens (AL) - 1880
Pickens, Israel (AL) - 1821, 1823
Pickering, John (NH) - 1789, 1790
Pierce, Benjamin (NH) - 1826, 1827, 1828, 1829
Pierce, Lymon (RI) - 1866, 1867, 1868, 1869, 1870, 1874
Pierce, Nathan (OR) - 1894
Pierce, Walter M. (OR) - 1918, 1922, 1926
Pike, James (NH) - 1871
Pilcher, Zind (MI) - 1843
Pillsbury, Albert (ME) - 1853
Pillsbury, Eben F. (ME) - 1866, 1867, 1868
Pillsbury, John (NH) - 1962, 1964
Pillsbury, John S. (MN) - 1875, 1877, 1879
Pinchot, Gifford (PA) - 1922, 1930
Pine, William B. (OK) - 1934
Pingree, Hazen S. (MI) - 1896, 1898
Pingree, Samuel E. (VT) - 1884
Pitkin, Frederick W. (CO) - 1878, 1880
Pitkin, Timothy (CT) - 1824, 1825
Pitman, Robert C. (MA) - 1877
Pittman, Vail (NV) - 1946, 1950, 1954
Plaisted, Frederick W. (ME) - 1910, 1912
Plaisted, Harris M. (ME) - 1880, 1882
Platt, Jonas (NY) - 1810
Pleasant, Ruffin G. (LA) - 1916
Plumer, William (NH) - 1812, 1813, 1814, 1815, 1816, 1817, 1818
Poindexter, George (MS) - 1819
Polk, James K. (TN) - 1839, 1841, 1843
Polk, Trusten (MO) - 1856
Pollard, John Garland (VA) - 1929

Pollard, Park H. (VT) - 1930, 1942
Pollock, James (PA) - 1854
Pond, E. B. (CA) - 1890
Ponder, James (DE) - 1870
Pool, John (NC) - 1860
Pope (FL) - 1884
Pope, Lewis S. (TN) - 1932, 1934
Pope, Sampson (SC) - 1894, 1896
Porter, Albert Gallatin (IN) - 1880
Porter, Claude R. (IA) - 1906, 1910, 1918
Porter, David R. (PA) - 1838, 1841
Porter, Eli H. (VT) - 1904
Porter, James D. Jr. (TN) - 1874, 1876
Porter, T. R. (NE) - 1868
Porter, W. D. (SC) - 1868
Porter, Wilber E. (NY) - 1896
Posey, Thomas (IN) - 1816
Pothier, Aram J. (RI) - 1908, 1909, 1910, 1911, 1912, 1924, 1926
Potter, Americus V. (RI) - 1855, 1856, 1857
Potter, Elisha R. (RI) - 1818, 1858, 1859
Potter, Frederick E. (NH) - 1900
Potts (NJ) - 1880
Powell, D. Frank (WI) - 1894
Powell, Lazarus W. (KY) - 1848, 1851
Powell, Ray B. (NM) - 1986
Powell, Thomas E. (OH) - 1887
Powell, Wesley (NH) - 1958, 1960
Power, Thomas C. (MT) - 1889
Powers, J. H. (NE) - 1890
Powers, James J. (NH) - 1944
Powers, Llewellyn (ME) - 1896, 1898
Poynter, William A. (NE) - 1898, 1900
Pratt (CT) - 1858, 1859
Pratt, Thomas G. (MD) - 1844
Prescott, Benjamin F. (NH) - 1877, 1878
Pressman, Hyman A. (MD) - 1966
Preston, David (MI) - 1884
Preus, Jacob A. O. (MN) - 1920, 1922
Prewitt, R. K. (MS) - 1899
Price, Bill (OK) - 1990
Price, James H. (VA) - 1937
Price, Rodman M. (NJ) - 1853
Price, Sterling (MO) - 1852
Price, Thomas L. (MO) - 1864
Prieur (LA) - 1838
Prince, Frederick O. (MA) - 1885
Pritchard, George M. (NC) - 1948
Pritt, Charlotte Jean (WV) - 1992, 1996
Proctor, Fletcher D. (VT) - 1906
Proctor, Mortimer R. (VT) - 1944
Proctor, Redfield (VT) - 1878, 1922
Prouty, George H. (VT) - 1908
Proxmire, William (WI) - 1952, 1954, 1956
Pryor, David (AR) - 1974, 1976
Putnam, A. L. (SD) - 1924
Putnam, Roger L. (MA) - 1942
Putnam, William L. (ME) - 1888
Pyle, Howard (AZ) - 1950, 1952, 1954

Q

Quick, Williamk F. (WI) - 1924
Quie, Albert H. (MN) - 1978
Quillen, William T. (DE) - 1984
Quimby, Smith (RI) - 1895
Quinby, Henry B. (NH) - 1908
Quincy, Josiah (MA) - 1901
Quinn, Patrick H. (RI) - 1914
Quinn, Robert E. (RI) - 1936, 1938

Quinn, William F. (HI) - 1959, 1962
Quitman, John A. (MS) - 1849

R

Racicot, Marc (MT) - 1992, 1996
Raecke, Walter R. (NE) - 1950, 1952
Ralston, Samuel M. (IN) - 1912
Ramirez, Jack (MT) - 1980
Rampton, Calvin L. (UT) - 1964, 1968, 1972
Ramsdell, George A. (NH) - 1896
Ramsey, Alexander (MN) - 1857, 1859, 1861
Randall, Alexander W. (WI) - 1857, 1859
Randall, Charles H. (NE) - 1922
Randall, David (LA) - 1831
Randolph, Richard L. (AK) - 1982
Randolph, Theodore F. (NJ) - 1868
Rankin, Wellington D. (MT) - 1928
Ranney, Rufus P. (OH) - 1859
Ransom, Epaphroditus (MI) - 1847
Ratner, Payne (KS) - 1938, 1940
Ray, Dixy Lee (WA) - 1976
Ray, James Brown (IN) - 1825, 1828
Ray, Robert D. (IA) - 1968, 1970, 1972, 1974, 1978
Read, James G. (IN) - 1831, 1834
Reading, P. B. (CA) - 1851
Reagan, Ronald (CA) - 1966, 1970
Reams, Frazier Jr. (OH) - 1966
Rector, Henry M. (AR) - 1860
Redfield, Timothy P. (VT) - 1851, 1863, 1864
Redman, Fulton J. (ME) - 1940
Redman, John B. (ME) - 1884
Reed, Clyde M. (KS) - 1928, 1958
Reed, Harrison (FL) - 1868
Reed, Isaac (ME) - 1854, 1855
Reed, Jack (MS) - 1987
Reed, John H. (ME) - 1960, 1962, 1966
Regan, John E. (MN) - 1932, 1934
Reid (TN) - 1884
Reid, David S. (NC) - 1848, 1850, 1852
Reid, James P. (RI) - 1898, 1900
Remmel, H. L. (AR) - 1894, 1896, 1900
Remmel, Pratt C. (AR) - 1954
Renne, Roland (MT) - 1964
Rennebohm, Oscar (WI) - 1948
Reynolds, John (IL) - 1830
Reynolds, John W. (WI) - 1962, 1964
Reynolds, Robert J. (DE) - 1890
Reynolds, Stephen N. (IN) - 1912
Reynolds, Thomas (MO) - 1840
Rhodes, James A. (OH) - 1954, 1962, 1966, 1974, 1978, 1986
Ribicoff, Abraham A. (CT) - 1954, 1958
Rice, Alexander H. (MA) - 1875, 1876, 1877
Rice, Edmund (MN) - 1879
Rice, H. M. (MN) - 1865
Rice, John S. (PA) - 1946
Rich, John T. (MI) - 1892, 1894
Richards, Ann W. (TX) - 1990, 1994
Richards, C. L. (NV) - 1930
Richards, DeForest (WY) - 1898, 1902
Richards, John G. (SC) - 1926
Richards, L. D. (NE) - 1890
Richards, R. O. (SD) - 1914, 1924
Richards, W. S. (OR) - 1910
Richards, William A. (WY) - 1894
Richardson (DE) - 1890
Richardson, Friend William (CA) - 1922

Richardson, John P. (SC) - 1886, 1888
Richardson, Noble A. (CA) - 1914
Richardson, R. B. (ND) - 1896
Richardson, William A. (IL) - 1856
Rickards, John E. (MT) - 1892
Ricketts, Willis (AR) - 1962
Riddle, James (DE) - 1813, 1866
Ridge, Tom J. (PA) - 1994
Ridgely, Hilliard S. (WY) - 1914
Riley, Richard (SC) - 1978, 1982
Rinehart (SD) - 1916
Rinfret, Pierre A. (NY) - 1990
Ringdal, Peter M. (MN) - 1912
Ringsrud, A. O. (SD) - 1896
Ristine, Richard O. (IN) - 1964
Ritchie, Albert C. (MD) - 1919, 1923, 1926, 1930, 1934
Ritchie, William (NE) - 1954
Ritner, Joseph (PA) - 1829, 1832, 1835, 1838
Rivers, Eurith D. (GA) - 1936, 1938
Rizley, Ross (OK) - 1938
Roach, William (ND) - 1899, 1890
Roane, Archibald (TN) - 1801, 1803, 1805
Roane, John S. (AR) - 1849
Robb, Charles S. (VA) - 1981
Robbie, Joe (SD) - 1950
Roberts, Albert H. (TN) - 1918, 1920
Roberts, Barbara (OR) - 1990
Roberts, Charles W. (ME) - 1870, 1875
Roberts, Dennis J. (RI) - 1950, 1952, 1954, 1956, 1958
Roberts, Henry (CT) - 1904
Roberts, Hiram R. (NH) - 1875
Roberts, John (VT) - 1850
Roberts, Oran M. (TX) - 1878, 1880
Robertson, A. Heaton (CT) - 1904, 1908
Robertson, J. B. A. (OK) - 1918
Robertson, Thomas B. (LA) - 1820
Robie, Frederick (ME) - 1882, 1884
Robins, Charles A. (ID) - 1946
Robinson (CT) - 1876
Robinson (WV) - 1916
Robinson, C. R. (AL) - 1966
Robinson, Charles (KS) - 1882, 1890
Robinson, Charles D. (WI) - 1869
Robinson, Edward (ME) - 1842, 1843, 1844
Robinson, George D. (MA) - 1883, 1884, 1885
Robinson, James C. (IL) - 1864
Robinson, Joe T. (AR) - 1912
Robinson, John S. (VT) - 1851, 1852, 1853
Robinson, Jonathan (VT) - 1804, 1805
Robinson, Lucius (NY) - 1876, 1879
Robinson, Moses (VT) - 1798
Robinson, Robert P. (DE) - 1924
Robsion, John M. (KY) - 1959
Rochester, William B. (NY) - 1826
Rock, Robert L. (IN) - 1968
Rockefeller, John D. "Jay" IV (WV) - 1972, 1976, 1980
Rockefeller, Nelson A. (NY) - 1958, 1962, 1966, 1970
Rockefeller, Winthrop (AR) - 1964, 1966, 1968, 1970
Rockwell, Julius (MA) - 1855
Rockwell, Robert F. (CO) - 1930
Rodney, Daniel (DE) - 1810, 1813
Rogers (MS) - 1853
Rogers, E. E. (CT) - 1930
Rogers, John R. (WA) - 1896, 1900
Rogers, Joseph O. Jr. (SC) - 1966
Roland, Andrew I. (AR) - 1910, 1912
Rollins, Frank W. (NH) - 1898
Rollins, J. S. (MO) - 1857

Rollins, James S. (MO) - 1848
Rollins, John W. (DE) - 1960
Rolph, James Jr. (CA) - 1930
Rolvaag, Karl F. (MN) - 1962, 1966
Roman, Andre B. (LA) - 1831, 1838
Rome, Lewis B. (CT) - 1982
Romer, Roy (CO) - 1986, 1990, 1994
Romney, George (MI) - 1962, 1964, 1966
Romney, L. C. (UT) - 1956
Romney, Vernon B. (UT) - 1976
Rooney, Charles (KS) - 1952
Rooney, John J. (WY) - 1970
Roos, Lawrence K. (MO) - 1968
Roosevelt, Franklin D. (NY) - 1928, 1930
Roosevelt, Franklin Jr. (NY) - 1966
Roosevelt, James (CA) - 1950
Roosevelt, Mark (MA) - 1994
Roosevelt, Theodore (NY) - 1898
Roosevelt, Theodore Jr. (NY) - 1924
Rose, David S. (WI) - 1902
Rose, Robert E. (NV) - 1978
Rosellini, Albert D. (WA) - 1956, 1960, 1964, 1972
Rosing, Leonard A. (MN) - 1902
Ross, C. Ben (ID) - 1928, 1930, 1932, 1934, 1938
Ross, Edmund G. (KS) - 1880
Ross, F. Clair (PA) - 1942
Ross, James (PA) - 1799, 1802, 1808
Ross, Lawrence S. (TX) - 1886, 1888
Ross, Nellie T. (WY) - 1924, 1926
Ross, Wiliam H. (DE) - 1850
Ross, William B. (WY) - 1922
Rothman, Kenneth J. (MO) - 1984
Routt, John L. (CO) - 1876, 1890
Rowland, John G. (CT) - 1990, 1994
Royall, J. Powell (VA) - 1937
Royce, Stephen (VT) - 1854, 1855
Ruerat, Albert P. (RI) - 1948
Runk (NJ) - 1850
Runnels, Hardin R. (TX) - 1857, 1859
Runnels, Hiram G. (MS) - 1831, 1833, 1835
Runvon (NJ) - 1865
Runyon (NJ) - 1922
Rusk, Jeremiah M. (WI) - 1881, 1884, 1886
Russell, Charles H. (NV) - 1950, 1954, 1958
Russell, Daniel L. (NC) - 1896
Russell, Donald (SC) - 1962
Russell, George (WI) - 1898
Russell, John E. (MA) - 1893, 1894
Russell, Lee M. (MS) - 1919
Russell, Richard B. (GA) - 1930
Russell, William (KY) - 1824
Russell, William E. (MA) - 1888, 1889, 1890, 1891, 1892
Ruthenberg, C. E. (OH) - 1912
Ryan, Charles F. (VT) - 1948
Rye, Tom C. (TN) - 1914, 1916
Rzewnicki, Janet C. (DE) - 1996

S

Sackett, Adnah (RI) - 1848, 1849
Sadler, Reinhold (NV) - 1898
Saffels, Dale E. (KS) - 1962
Safford, Edward L. (NM) - 1946
Saiki, Patricia F. (HI) - 1994
Salmon, Thomas P. (VT) - 1972, 1974
Saltonstall, Leverett (MA) - 1938, 1940, 1942
Samford, William F. (AL) - 1859
Samford, William J. (AL) - 1900
Sampson, Flem D. (KY) - 1927
Samuels, Ben M. (IA) - 1857

Samuels, H. F. (ID) - 1918, 1922, 1924
Samuelson, Bob L. (SD) - 1990
Samuelson, Don (ID) - 1966, 1970
Sanders, Bernard J. (VT) - 1976, 1986
Sanders, Carl E. (GA) - 1962
Sanders, Jared Y. (LA) - 1908
Sandman, Charles W. (NJ) - 1973
Sanford, Terry (NC) - 1960
SanSouci, Emery J. (RI) - 1920
Sarasin, Ronald A. (CT) - 1978
Sargent (CT) - 1896
Sargent, Eaton D. (NH) - 1926, 1928
Sargent, Francis W. (MA) - 1970, 1974
Sarles, Elmore Y. (ND) - 1904, 1906
Sauerbrey, Ellen R. (MD) - 1994
Saulsbury, Gove (DE) - 1866
Saunders, George E. (CO) - 1940
Saunders, Phil (SD) - 1958
Saunders, Romulus M. (NC) - 1840
Sawyer, Charles (OH) - 1938
Sawyer, Charles H. (NH) - 1886
Sawyer, Grant (NV) - 1958, 1962, 1966
Sawyer, Hiram Wilson (WI) - 1898
Sawyer, Thomas E. (NH) - 1851, 1852
Saxe, John G. (VT) - 1859, 1860
Sayers, Joseph D. (TX) - 1898, 1900
Scales, Alfred M. (NC) - 1884
Schaben, James F. (IA) - 1974
Schaefer, William D. (MD) - 1986, 1990
Schafer, Edward T. (ND) - 1992, 1996
Schley, William (GA) - 1835, 1837
Schmedeman, Albert G. (WI) - 1928, 1932, 1934
Schmidt, Henry R. (CA) - 1946
Schmitz (WI) - 1910
Schnader, William A. (PA) - 1934
Schoeppel, Andrew F. (KS) - 1942, 1944
Schreiber, Martin G. (WI) - 1978
Schricker, Henry F. (IN) - 1940, 1948
Schulz, Bill (AZ) - 1986
Schulze, John Andrew (PA) - 1823
Schwinden, Ted (MT) - 1980, 1984
Scofield, Edward (WI) - 1896, 1898
Scott, Abram M. (MS) - 1831, 1833
Scott, Charles (KY) - 1808
Scott, Gary B. (DE) - 1992
Scott, George W. (FL) - 1868
Scott, Robert K. (SC) - 1868, 1870
Scott, Robert W. (NC) - 1968
Scott, Thomas (OH) - 1812
Scott, Tom (CT) - 1994
Scott, W. Kerr (NC) - 1948
Scranton, William W. (PA) - 1962, 1986
Scrugham, James G. (NV) - 1922, 1926
Scruple, Eugene (WA) - 1889
Seabury, Samuel (NY) - 1916
Sears, John W. (MA) - 1982
Seaton, Fred A. (NE) - 1962
Seawell, H. F. (NC) - 1928
Seawell, H. F. Jr. (NC) - 1952
Seay, Thomas (AL) - 1886, 1888
See, Clyde M. Jr. (WV) - 1984
Seegmiller, William W. (UT) - 1932
Segar, Thomas W. (RI) - 1879, 1884
Seidel (WI) - 1918
Seligman, Arthur (NM) - 1930, 1932
Senter, De Witt Clinton (TN) - 1869
Settle, Thomas (NC) - 1876, 1912
Sevier, John (TN) - 1796, 1797, 1799, 1803, 1805, 1807
Sewall, Samuel E. (MA) - 1842, 1843, 1844, 1845, 1846, 1847

Sewall, Sumner (ME) - 1940, 1942
Seward, William H. (NY) - 1834, 1838, 1840
Seymour (CT) - 1860
Seymour, Horatio (NY) - 1850, 1852, 1854, 1862, 1864
Seymour, Horatio (VT) - 1834
Seymour, James M. (NJ) - 1901
Seymour, Origen S. (CT) - 1864, 1865
Seymour, Thomas H. (CT) - 1849, 1850, 1851, 1852, 1853, 1863
Shafer, George F. (ND) - 1928, 1930
Shafer, Raymond P. (PA) - 1966
Shafroth, John F. (CO) - 1908, 1910
Shafter, Oscar L. (VT) - 1848
Shafter, William R. (VT) - 1844, 1845
Shaheen, Jeanne (NH) - 1996
Shallenberger, Ashton C. (NE) - 1906, 1908
Shannon, James C. (CT) - 1948
Shannon, Wilson (OH) - 1838, 1840, 1842
Shapiro, Peter (NJ) - 1985
Shapiro, Samuel H. (IL) - 1968
Shapp, Milton (PA) - 1966, 1970, 1974
Sharp, Isaac (KS) - 1870
Sharp, Summers H. (WV) - 1936
Sharpe, Merrell Q. (SD) - 1942, 1944
Shattuck, D. O. (MS) - 1841
Shaw, Henry (MA) - 1845
Shaw, John (NH) - 1954, 1956
Shaw, Leslie M. (IA) - 1897, 1899
Shaw, Theodore M. (ID) - 1904
Shaw, Warren W. (KS) - 1956
Sheafe, James (NH) - 1816, 1817
Sheffield, Bill (AK) - 1982
Sheffield, J. L. (AL) - 1882
Shelby, Isaac (KY) - 1812
Sheldon, Charles H. (SD) - 1892, 1894
Sheldon, George L. (NE) - 1906, 1908
Shelton, A. C. (AL) - 1970
Shepard, James B. (NC) - 1846
Shepard, William S. (MD) - 1990
Shepley, Ethan A. H. (MO) - 1964
Sherman, Buren R. (IA) - 1881, 1883
Sherwood, W. S. (CA) - 1849
Shields, James (AL) - 1851
Shields, John B. (AL) - 1914
Shipman, V. J. (FL) - 1888
Shipstead, Henrik (MN) - 1920
Shively, Benjamin F. (IN) - 1896
Shivers, Allan (TX) - 1950, 1952, 1954
Sholtz, David (FL) - 1932
Short, Isaac Dolphus (DE) - 1936
Shorter, John Gill (AL) - 1861, 1863
Shortridge (AL) - 1855
Shortridge, Eli C. D. (ND) - 1892
Shotts, Ron (OK) - 1978
Shoup, G. L. (ID) - 1890
Shoup, Oliver H. (CO) - 1918, 1920, 1926
Shulze, John Andrew (PA) - 1826
Shunk, Francis R. (PA) - 1844, 1847
Shurtleff, Harry C. (VT) - 1928
Shurtleff, Stephen C. (VT) - 1886, 1888
Sibley, Henry H. (MN) - 1857
Sigler, Kim (MI) - 1946, 1948
Silber, John (MA) - 1990
Siler, Eugene (KY) - 1951
Silverthorn, Willis C. (WI) - 1896
Silzer, George S. (NJ) - 1922
Simms, John F. Jr. (NM) - 1954, 1956
Simms, Mit (AZ) - 1920
Simpson, John N. (TX) - 1908

Simpson, Milward L. (WY) - 1954, 1958
Simpson, Pete (WY) - 1986
Sinclair, John G. (NH) - 1866, 1867, 1868
Sinclair, Upton (CA) - 1934
Singel, Mark S. (PA) - 1994
Singerly, William M. (PA) - 1894
Sinner, George (ND) - 1984, 1988
Sisson, Charles P. (RI) - 1936
Skeen, Joseph R. (NM) - 1974, 1978
Skinner, Richard (VT) - 1820, 1821, 1822
Slack, W. D. (AR) - 1882
Slade, George H. (RI) - 1885, 1886
Slade, James M. (VT) - 1855
Slade, William (VT) - 1844, 1845
Slaton, John M. (GA) - 1912
Slattery, Jim (KS) - 1994
Slaughter, Gabriel (KY) - 1812
Slayton, John W. (PA) - 1910
Sleeper, Albert E. (MI) - 1916, 1918
Sligh, Charles R. (MI) - 1896
Slocum, Ziba O. (RI) - 1885
Sloo, Thomas Jr. (IL) - 1826
Small, Frank Jr. (MD) - 1962
Small, Len (IL) - 1920, 1924, 1932
Smalley, B. B. (VT) - 1892
Smalley, B. H. (VT) - 1861, 1862
Smart, E. K. (ME) - 1860
Smilie, Nathan (VT) - 1839, 1841, 1842
Smith (AL) - 1918
Smith (AR) - 1852
Smith (CT) - 1912
Smith (ME) - 1829
Smith (MI) - 1878
Smith (OR) - 1882
Smith, Abram W. (KS) - 1892
Smith, Alfred E. (NY) - 1918, 1920, 1922, 1924, 1926
Smith, Benjamin H. (WV) - 1866
Smith, C. J. (OR) - 1914
Smith, Charles M. (VT) - 1934
Smith, Denny (OR) - 1994
Smith, Ed (MT) - 1972
Smith, Edward (OH) - 1850
Smith, Edward C. (VT) - 1898
Smith, Elmo (OR) - 1956
Smith, Forrest (MO) - 1948
Smith, Franklin (ME) - 1869
Smith, George W. (VT) - 1894
Smith, Henry (RI) - 1806
Smith, Hoke (GA) - 1906, 1910
Smith, Hulett (WV) - 1964
Smith, Israel (VT) - 1800, 1802, 1806, 1807, 1808
Smith, James Milton (GA) - 1872
Smith, James Y. (RI) - 1861, 1863, 1864, 1865
Smith, Jeremiah (NH) - 1809, 1810, 1811, 1824
Smith, John (VT) - 1846
Smith, John A. W. (AL) - 1902
Smith, John B. (NH) - 1892
Smith, John C. (CT) - 1813, 1814, 1815, 1816, 1817
Smith, John Gregory (VT) - 1863, 1864
Smith, John Walter (MD) - 1899
Smith, Joseph L. (ME) - 1878, 1879
Smith, Manassah H. (ME) - 1857, 1858, 1859
Smith, Nathan (CT) - 1825
Smith, Nels H. (WY) - 1938, 1942
Smith, Peter (VT) - 1986
Smith, Preston (TX) - 1968, 1970
Smith, Robert B. (MT) - 1896
Smith, Samuel E. (ME) - 1830, 1831, 1832, 1833
Smith, Vernon K. (ID) - 1962
Smith, W. J. (OR) - 1914

Smith, William (VA) - 1863
Smith, William E. (WI) - 1877, 1879
Smith, William Hugh (AL) - 1868, 1870
Smith, William R. (AL) - 1865
Smylie, Robert E. (ID) - 1954, 1958, 1962
Smyth, Frederick (NH) - 1865, 1866
Snell, Earl (OR) - 1942, 1946
Snelling, Richard A. (VT) - 1966, 1976, 1978, 1980, 1982, 1990
Snively, Henry J. (WA) - 1892
Snow, Wilbert (CT) - 1946
Snyder, Simon (PA) - 1805, 1808, 1811, 1814
Solomon, Anthony J. (RI) - 1984
Sorensen, Philip C. (NE) - 1966
Sorlie, Arthur G. (ND) - 1924, 1926
Sorrell, Frank (NE) - 1946, 1948, 1956
Southwick, Solomon (NY) - 1828
Spaeth, Nicholas (ND) - 1992
Spaight, Richard D. (NC) - 1836
Spalding, Asa (CT) - 1809, 1810
Spanos, Harry V. (NH) - 1976
Sparks, Chauncey (AL) - 1942
Sparks, John (NV) - 1902, 1906
Sparks, Reuben K. (OK) - 1954
Spaulding, Huntley N. (NH) - 1926
Spaulding, Rolland H. (NH) - 1914
Speck, Jefferson W. (AR) - 1950, 1952
Spellacy, Thomas (CT) - 1918
Spellman, John D. (WA) - 1976, 1980, 1984
Spence, Gene (NE) - 1994
Spirou, Chris (NH) - 1984
Spooner, John C. (WI) - 1892
Sprague, Amasa (RI) - 1886
Sprague, Charles A. (OR) - 1938
Sprague, Peleg (ME) - 1834
Sprague, William (RI) - 1832, 1838, 1839, 1860, 1861, 1862, 1883
Springer, Raymond S. (IN) - 1932, 1936
Sproul, William C. (PA) - 1918
Sprouse, James M. (WV) - 1968
Spry, William (UT) - 1908, 1912
St. Clair, Arthur (PA) - 1790
St. John, John P. (KS) - 1878, 1880, 1882
Staebler, Neil (MI) - 1964
Stafford (LA) - 1864
Stafford, Robert T. (VT) - 1958
Stallard, H. H. (OR) - 1926
Stanchfield, John B. (NY) - 1900
Standrod, D. W. (ID) - 1900
Stanford, Leland (CA) - 1859, 1861
Stanford, R. C. (AZ) - 1936
Stanley, Augustus Owsley (KY) - 1915
Stanley, Thomas B. (VA) - 1953
Stanley, W. E. (KS) - 1898, 1900
Stanly, Edw. (CA) - 1857
Stapp, Milton (IN) - 1831
Stark (NH) - 1861, 1862
Stark, Lloyd Crow (MO) - 1936
Stassen, Harold E. (MN) - 1938, 1940, 1942
Stearns, Marcellus L. (FL) - 1876
Stearns, Onslow (NH) - 1869, 1870
Steele, John A. (AL) - 1900
Steele, John H. (NH) - 1844, 1845
Steele, John L. (MD) - 1838
Steele, Robert H. (CT) - 1974
Steere, Thomas (RI) - 1871
Steger, Frank L. (ID) - 1934, 1936
Stephen, John B. (CO) - 1910
Stephens, Alexander H. (GA) - 1882

Stephens, Lawrence Vest (MO) - 1896
Stephens, Stan (MT) - 1988
Stephens, William D. (CA) - 1918
Stepovich, Mike (AK) - 1962
Sterling, Ross (TX) - 1930
Steunenberg, Frank (ID) - 1896, 1898
Stevens, Enos (NH) - 1840, 1841, 1842
Stevens, John L. (IA) - 1912
Stevenson, Adlai E. (IL) - 1908
Stevenson, Adlai E. II (IL) - 1948
Stevenson, Adlai E. III (IL) - 1982, 1986
Stevenson, C. C. (NV) - 1886
Stevenson, Coke R. (TX) - 1942, 1944
Stevenson, Edward A. (ID) - 1894
Stevenson, John A. (LA) - 1884
Stevenson, John W. (KY) - 1868
Stevenson, William E. (WV) - 1868, 1870
Steward, Lewis (IL) - 1876
Stewart (DE) - 1878
Stewart, James Garfield (OH) - 1944
Stewart, John (PA) - 1882
Stewart, John W. (VT) - 1870
Stewart, R. M. (MO) - 1857
Stewart, Samuel V. (MT) - 1912, 1916
Stickney, William W. (VT) - 1900
Stimson, E. C. (CO) - 1902
Stimson, Henry L. (NY) - 1910
Stockley, Charles C. (DE) - 1882
Stockslager, Charles O. (ID) - 1906
Stockton, Alvin (NM) - 1954
Stockton, Thomas (DE) - 1844
Stokes, Edward C. (NJ) - 1904, 1913
Stokes, William B. (TN) - 1869
Stone, Charles F. (NH) - 1898
Stone, John M. (MS) - 1877, 1889
Stone, William A. (PA) - 1898
Stone, William Joel (MO) - 1892
Stone, William M. (IA) - 1863, 1865
Stoneman, George (CA) - 1882
Storrs, Zalmon (CT) - 1831, 1833, 1834
Story, William J. Jr. (VA) - 1965
Stout (MI) - 1862
Stransky, John A. (SD) - 1906
Stratton, Asa E. (AL) - 1906
Stratton, Charles C. (NJ) - 1844
Stratton, William G. (IL) - 1952, 1956, 1960
Straub, Robert W. (OR) - 1966, 1970, 1974, 1978
Straus, Oscar S. (NY) - 1912
Straw, Ezekiel A. (NH) - 1872, 1873
Street, James A. (UT) - 1908
Street, O. D. (AL) - 1922
Strickland, Ted (CO) - 1978, 1986
Strike, Nicholas L. (UT) - 1972
Stringer, Lawrence B. (IL) - 1904
Strong, Caleb (MA) - 1800, 1801, 1802, 1803, 1804, 1805, 1806, 1807, 1812, 1813, 1814, 1815
Strong, Samuel (VT) - 1816
Strother, Enoch (NV) - 1882
Strutz, Alvin C. (ND) - 1944
Stuart (MI) - 1858
Stuart, Edwin S. (PA) - 1906
Stuart, Henry C. (VA) - 1913
Stubbs, Daniel P. (IA) - 1877
Stubbs, W. R. (KS) - 1908, 1910
Studley (CT) - 1912
Stuenenberg, Frank (ID) - 1898
Stump, H. C. (AR) - 1940, 1944
Sturgiss, George C. (WV) - 1880
Sturgulewski, Arliss (AK) - 1986, 1990
Suit, Hal (GA) - 1970

Sullivan (WI) - 1942
Sullivan, E. J. (WY) - 1924
Sullivan, Edward M. (RI) - 1920
Sullivan, J. B. (IA) - 1903
Sullivan, James (MA) - 1797, 1798, 1804, 1805, 1806, 1807, 1808
Sullivan, John (NH) - 1788, 1789
Sullivan, John D. (MN) - 1942
Sullivan, John L. (NH) - 1934, 1938
Sullivan, Michael J. (WY) - 1986, 1990
Sullivan, P. C. (WA) - 1896
Sulzer, William (NY) - 1912, 1914
Summers (VA) - 1851
Sumner, Increase (MA) - 1796, 1797, 1798, 1799
Sundlun, Bruce (RI) - 1986, 1988, 1990, 1992
Sundquist, Don (TN) - 1994
Sununu, John H. (NH) - 1982, 1984, 1986
Suthon, H. S. (LA) - 1912
Sutter, J. A. (CA) - 1849
Sutton, Abraham L. (NE) - 1916
Swainson, John B. (MI) - 1960, 1962
Swallow, Silas C. (PA) - 1898
Swan, Harry S. (FL) - 1952
Swann, Thomas (MD) - 1864
Swanson, Claude A. (VA) - 1905
Sweet, Edwin F. (MI) - 1916
Sweet, W. D. (ND) - 1912
Sweet, William E. (CO) - 1922, 1924
Sweetser, Theodore H. (MA) - 1866
Swift, John F. (CA) - 1886
Swisher, Perry (ID) - 1966
Switzer, Carroll O. (IA) - 1948
Swope, King (KY) - 1935, 1939
Symington, Fife (AZ) - 1994

T

Taft, Charles P. (OH) - 1952
Taft, James L. (RI) - 1976
Taft, Royal C. (RI) - 1888
Talbot, George F. (ME) - 1849, 1850
Talbot, John C. (ME) - 1876
Talbot, Thomas (MA) - 1874, 1878
Talbot, W. E. (TX) - 1930
Taliaferro, James G. (LA) - 1868
Tallmadge, John J. (WI) - 1867
Tallman, A. V. (NV) - 1942
Talmadge, Eugene (GA) - 1932, 1934, 1940, 1946
Talmadge, Herman E. (GA) - 1948, 1950
Tannehill, R. H. (LA) - 1892
Tanner, John R. (IL) - 1896
Tappan, Benjamin (OH) - 1826
Tawes, J. Millard (MD) - 1958, 1962
Taylor, Alfred A. (TN) - 1886, 1920, 1922
Taylor, J. Alfred (WV) - 1928
Taylor, Maris (SD) - 1890
Taylor, Robert L. (TN) - 1886, 1888, 1896, 1910
Taylor, T. N. (UT) - 1920
Taylor, William R. (WI) - 1873, 1875
Taylor, William S. (KY) - 1899
Teasdale, Joseph P. (MO) - 1976, 1980
Templeton, Charles A. (CT) - 1922
Tener, John K. (PA) - 1910
Terral, T. J. (AR) - 1924
Terrell, J. O. (TX) - 1910
Terrell, Joseph M. (GA) - 1902, 1904
Terry, Charles L. Jr. (DE) - 1964, 1968
Terry, Mary Sue (VA) - 1993
Terry, Nathaniel (AL) - 1845
Thach, P. H. (TN) - 1936
Thacher, Solon O. (KS) - 1864

Tharp, William (DE) - 1844, 1846
Thayer, Charles (CT) - 1906
Thayer, John M. (NE) - 1886, 1888
Thayer, William Wallace (OR) - 1878
Theodore, Nick A. (SC) - 1994
Thomas (TN) - 1876
Thomas, Charles S. (CO) - 1898
Thomas, Francis (MD) - 1841
Thomas, George M. (KY) - 1871
Thomas, Jerry (FL) - 1974
Thomas, Philemon (LA) - 1828
Thomas, Philip Francis (MD) - 1847
Thompson (NJ) - 1844
Thompson, Carl D. (WI) - 1912
Thompson, Carl W. (WI) - 1948, 1950
Thompson, Carmi A. (OH) - 1922
Thompson, Carveth (SD) - 1972
Thompson, Charles P. (MA) - 1880, 1881
Thompson, D. P. (OR) - 1890
Thompson, Floyd E. (IL) - 1928
Thompson, Hugh S. (SC) - 1882, 1884
Thompson, Jacob (MS) - 1861
Thompson, James L. (IA) - 1850
Thompson, James R. (IL) - 1978, 1982, 1986
Thompson, Joseph O. (AL) - 1910
Thompson, Murray E. (MO) - 1948
Thompson, Ronnie (GA) - 1974
Thompson, Smith (NY) - 1828
Thompson, Tommy G. (WI) - 1986, 1990, 1994
Thompson, W. R. (WV) - 1912
Thompson, William H. (NE) - 1902
Thompson, William P. (ME) - 1890
Thomson, Meldrim Jr. (NH) - 1970, 1972, 1974, 1976, 1978, 1980
Thomson, Vernon W. (WI) - 1956, 1958
Thone, Charles (NE) - 1978, 1980
Thornburgh, Dick (PA) - 1978, 1982
Thornton, Dan (CO) - 1950, 1952
Thornton, Robert Y. (OR) - 1962
Throckmorton, J. W. (TX) - 1865, 1866
Throop, Enos T. (NY) - 1830
Thurman, A. G. (OH) - 1867
Thurmond, J. Strom (SC) - 1946
Thye, Edward J. (MN) - 1944
Tichenor, Isaac (VT) - 1793, 1794, 1795, 1797, 1798, 1799, 1800, 1801, 1802, 1803, 1804, 1805, 1806, 1807, 1808, 1809, 1810, 1817
Tidball, Lewis C. (WY) - 1894
Tiemann, Norbert T. (NE) - 1966, 1970
Tierney, James (ME) - 1986
Tiffin, Edward (OH) - 1803, 1805
Tilden, Samuel J. (NY) - 1874
Tilghman, William (PA) - 1811
Tillman, Benjamin Ryan (SC) - 1890, 1892
Tillman, G. N. (TN) - 1896, 1908
Tilton, Charles E. (NH) - 1920
Timmerman, George Bell Jr. (SC) - 1954
Tingier, Lyman (CT) - 1914
Tingley, Clyde (NM) - 1934, 1936
Tipton, T. W. (NE) - 1880
Titcomb, Joseph (ME) - 1873, 1874
Tobey, Charles W. (NH) - 1928
Tobin, Maurice J. (MA) - 1944, 1946
Tod, David (OH) - 1844, 1846, 1861
Todd (MO) - 1825
Todd, Levi G. (NE) - 1878
Todd, Thomas (KY) - 1800
Tolman, J. C. (OR) - 1874
Tolton, John F. (UT) - 1912
Tome, Jacob (MD) - 1871

Tomkins, Daniel (NY) - 1807, 1810, 1813, 1816, 1820
Tomlinson, Gideon (CT) - 1827, 1828, 1829, 1830, 1836
Tomlinson, Reuben (SC) - 1872
Tompkins, Christopher (KY) - 1824
Tondre, Joseph F. (NM) - 1942
Toole, Joseph K. (MT) - 1889, 1900, 1904
Toucey, Isaac (CT) - 1845, 1846
Toupin, Felix L. (RI) - 1924
Towns, George Washington (GA) - 1847, 1849
Townsend, John G. Jr. (DE) - 1916
Townsend, Maurice Clifford (IN) - 1936
Townsend, T. C. (WV) - 1932
Townsend, W. Wayne (IN) - 1984
Townsend, Wallace (AR) - 1916, 1920
Tracy, Andrew (VT) - 1861
Trafton, W. A. Jr. (ME) - 1956
Trammell, Park (FL) - 1912
Trayler, George W. (GA) - 1900
Treadwell, John (CT) - 1810, 1811
Treen, David C. (LA) - 1972, 1979, 1983
Tribbitt, Sherman W. (DE) - 1972, 1976
Trimble, Allen (OH) - 1822, 1824, 1826, 1828, 1855
Trimble, Henry H. (IA) - 1879
Trinkle, Elbert Lee (VA) - 1921
Triplow, Annie E. (ID) - 1916
Tritte, F. A. (NV) - 1870
Troast, Paul L. (NJ) - 1953
Troup, George M. (GA) - 1825
Trousdale, William (TN) - 1849, 1851
Trowbridge, Charles C. (MI) - 1837
Truitt, George (DE) - 1807
Trumbull, John H. (CT) - 1926, 1928, 1932
Trumbull, Jonathan II (CT) - 1796, 1798, 1799, 1800, 1801, 1802, 1803, 1804, 1805, 1806, 1807, 1808, 1809
Trumbull, Joseph (CT) - 1849
Trumbull, Lyman (IL) - 1880
Tuck, William M. (VA) - 1945
Tucker, Jim Guy (AR) - 1994
Tucker, Merle H. (NM) - 1964
Tucker, Ralph (IN) - 1956
Tucker, Tilghman M. (MS) - 1841
Tunnell, Ebe W. (DE) - 1894, 1896
Turner, Dan W. (IA) - 1930, 1932, 1934
Turner, Edward (MS) - 1839
Turner, George (WA) - 1904
Turner, James M. (MI) - 1890
Turner, Roy J. (OK) - 1946
Turner, Thomas G. (RI) - 1859
Turney, Peter (TN) - 1892, 1894
Tuttle, Charles H. (NY) - 1930
Tuttle, Hiram A. (NH) - 1890
Tuttle, James M. (IA) - 1863
Tuxbury, Albert (NE) - 1874
Tweedy (WI) - 1848
Tyler, James Hoge (VA) - 1897
Tyler, Rollin U. (CT) - 1920
Tynan (CO) - 1918
Tyree, Randy (TN) - 1982

U

Ullman, Daniel (NY) - 1854
Umstead, William B. (NC) - 1952
Underwood, Cecil H. (WV) - 1956, 1964, 1976, 1996
Unruh, Jess (CA) - 1970
Untermann, Ernest (ID) - 1908

Upham (NH) - 1830
Upham (WI) - 1851
Upham, William H. (WI) - 1894
Utter, George H. (RI) - 1904, 1905, 1906

V

Vahey, James H. (MA) - 1908, 1909
Vail, Henry W. (VT) - 1952
Vale, J. G. (IA) - 1873
Valentine, John (IA) - 1940
Vallandigham, C. L. (OH) - 1863
Van Buren, Martin (NY) - 1828
Vance, Joseph (OH) - 1836, 1838
Vance, Zebulon B. (NC) - 1862, 1864, 1876
Vanderbilt, William H. (RI) - 1938, 1940
Vanderhoof, John D. (CO) - 1974
Vandiver, S. Ernest (GA) - 1958
Van Ness, Cornelius P. (VT) - 1823, 1824, 1825
Van Nort (MD) - 1891
Vanosdel, A. L. (SD) - 1892
Van Renssalaer, Stephen (NY) - 1801, 1813
Van Sant, Samuel R. (MN) - 1900, 1902
Van Wagoner, Murray D. (MI) - 1940, 1942, 1946
Van Wyck, Augustus (NY) - 1898
Van Wyck, Charles Henry (NE) - 1892
Van Zandt, Charles C. (RI) - 1877, 1878, 1879
Vardaman, James K. (MS) - 1903
Varnum, Joseph B. (MA) - 1813
Vessey, Robert S. (SD) - 1908, 1910
Vickery, Stephen (MI) - 1845
Villere, Jacques (LA) - 1812, 1816, 1824
Vinton, Samuel F. (OH) - 1851
Vivian, John C. (CO) - 1942, 1944
Vogler, Joseph E. (AK) - 1974, 1986
Voinovich, George V. (OH) - 1990, 1994
Volpe, John A. (MA) - 1960, 1962, 1964, 1966
Volz, Harold J. (SD) - 1948
Voorhees, Foster M. (NJ) - 1898
Vrooman, H. P. (KS) - 1880

W

Wadsworth, James S. (NY) - 1862
Wagstaff, W. R. (KS) - 1862
Waihee, John (HI) - 1986, 1990
Waite, Davis H. (CO) - 1892, 1894
Walbridge, Cyrus P. (MO) - 1904
Walde, William (CA) - 1853
Walker (GA) - 1872
Walker, Clifford M. (GA) - 1922, 1924
Walker, Daniel (IL) - 1972
Walker, David S. (FL) - 1856, 1865
Walker, Gilbert C. (VA) - 1869
Walker, Joseph (LA) - 1849
Walker, Joseph (MA) - 1912, 1914
Walker, Samuel (FL) - 1868
Walker, Thaddeus H. (KS) - 1872
Walker, Timothy (NH) - 1798, 1800, 1801
Wall, Thomas P. (TN) - 1958
Wallace (ND) - 1894
Wallace, David (IN) - 1837
Wallace, George C. (AL) - 1962, 1970, 1974, 1982
Wallace, Lew (OR) - 1942, 1948
Wallace, Lurleen B. (AL) - 1966
Waller, Thomas M. (CT) - 1882, 1884
Waller, William L. (MS) - 1971

Walley, Samuel H. (MA) - 1855
Wallgren, Monrad C. (WA) - 1944, 1948
Walsh, Cornelius (NJ) - 1871
Walsh, David I. (MA) - 1913, 1914, 1915
Walsh, John J. (MA) - 1920
Walter, H. W. (MS) - 1859
Walters, David (OK) - 1986, 1990
Walters, Ted A. (ID) - 1920
Walton, John C. (OK) - 1922
Walworth, Reuben (NY) - 1848
Ward, Edward (TN) - 1821
Ward, George T. (FL) - 1852
Ward, Henry (KY) - 1967
Ward, James A. (SD) - 1894
Ward, Joseph D. (MA) - 1960
Ward, Lyman (AL) - 1946
Ward, Marcus L. (NJ) - 1862, 1865
Wardell, Justus S. (CA) - 1926
Wardwell, William T. C. (RI) - 1892
Warfield, Edwin (MD) - 1903
Warmoth, Henry C. (LA) - 1868, 1888
Warner, Carolyn (AZ) - 1986
Warner, Charles J. (NE) - 1938
Warner, Fred M. (MI) - 1904, 1906, 1908
Warner, Wallace E. (ND) - 1956
Warner, William (MO) - 1892
Warren, Earl (CA) - 1942, 1946, 1950
Warren, Francis E. (WY) - 1890
Warren, Fuller (FL) - 1948
Warren, Nate C. (CO) - 1934
Washburn, Cadwallader C. (WI) - 1871, 1873
Washburn, Emory (MA) - 1853, 1854
Washburn, Israel Jr. (ME) - 1860, 1861
Washburn, Peter T. (VT) - 1869
Washburn, William A. Jr. (FL) - 1956
Washburn, William B. (MA) - 1871, 1872, 1873
Waterman, Lewis A. (RI) - 1910, 1911
Watkins, John A. (IN) - 1952
Watkins, Lucius Whitney (MI) - 1912
Watkins, Wes (OK) - 1994
Watson, Albert (SC) - 1970
Watson, Charles D. (VT) - 1910
Watson, Cyrus B. (NC) - 1896
Watson, J. Tom (FL) - 1954
Watson, James E. (IN) - 1908
Wattis, William H. (UT) - 1928
Watts, Cornelius C. (WV) - 1896
Watts, Thomas Hill (AL) - 1861, 1863
Wayne, Isaac, (PA) - 1814
Weakley, Robert (TN) - 1815
Weaver, Arthur J. (NE) - 1928, 1930
Weaver, James B. (IA) - 1883
Weaver, Rae (WI) - 1916
Webb, E. B. (IL) - 1852
Webber (MI) - 1876
Webber, J. Emil (AR) - 1913
Webster, J. V. (CA) - 1894
Webster, W. H. (NE) - 1878
Webster, William L. (MO) - 1992
Weeks, John E. (VT) - 1926, 1928
Weicker, Lowell P. Jr. (CT) - 1990
Welch, Peter (VT) - 1990
Weld, William F. (MA) - 1990, 1994
Welford, Walter (ND) - 1936
Weller, J. B. (CA) - 1857
Weller, John B. (OH) - 1848
Weller, Ovington E. (MD) - 1915
Wells (CT) - 1856
Wells (LA) - 1859
Wells, Edward W. (AZ) - 1911
Wells, H. H. (VA) - 1869
Wells, Heber M. (UT) - 1896, 1900
Wells, Henry T. (MN) - 1863
Wells, James Madison (LA) - 1865

Wells, John S. (NY) - 1856, 1857
Wells, Samuel (ME) - 1855, 1856
Welsh, Matthew E. (IN) - 1960, 1972
Wene, Elmer H. (NJ) - 1949
Wentworth, Joshua (NH) - 1790
Werts, George T. (NJ) - 1892
West, A. M. (MS) - 1863
West, John C. (SC) - 1970
West, Oswald (OR) - 1910
West, Will G. (KS) - 1936
West, William H. (OH) - 1877
Weston, Harry R. (WY) - 1932
Weston, James A. (NH) - 1871, 1872, 1873, 1874
Wetherby, Lawrence W. (KY) - 1951
Wetmore, George Peabody (RI) - 1885, 1886, 1887
Wharton, Charles M. (DE) - 1928
Wharton, Jesse (TN) - 1815
Wheaton, Fred E. (MN) - 1918
Wheaton, Seth (RI) - 1807
Wheeler, Burton K. (MT) - 1920
Wheeler, Herman C. (IA) - 1891
Whelan, Gerald T. (NE) - 1978
Whipple, W. G. (AR) - 1892
Whitcomb, Edgar D. (IN) - 1968
Whitcomb, James (IN) - 1843, 1846
White, A. B. (WV) - 1900
White, Edward D. (LA) - 1834
White, Frank (AR) - 1986
White, Frank (ND) - 1900, 1902
White, Frank D. (AR) - 1980, 1982
White, Fred E. (IA) - 1897, 1899, 1908
White, George (OH) - 1930, 1932
White, Hugh L. (MS) - 1935, 1951
White, John H. (NH) - 1842, 1843, 1853
White, Kevin H. (MA) - 1970
White, Mark (TX) - 1982, 1986
White, Walter (TN) - 1926
White, William Allen (KS) - 1924
White, William F. (CA) - 1879
Whiteaker, John (OR) - 1858
Whitfield, Henry L. (MS) - 1923
Whiting, Charles (IA) - 1885
Whiting, Justin R. (MI) - 1898
Whitman, Charles S. (NY) - 1914, 1916, 1918
Whitman, Christine Todd (NJ) - 1993, 1997
Whitman, Ezekiel (ME) - 1821, 1822
Whitney, Arthur (NJ) - 1925
Whitney, Henry M. (MA) - 1907
Whitney, Wheelock (MN) - 1982
Whittier, Sumner G. (MA) - 1956
Whittlesey (CT) - 1847
Whyte, William P. (MD) - 1871

Wickliffe, Charles A. (KY) - 1863
Wickliffe, Robert C. (LA) - 1855
Wicks, W. A. (FL) - 1896
Wight, E. M. (TN) - 1878
Wilder, L. Douglas (VA) - 1989
Wiles, Harry G. (KS) - 1964
Wiley, Alexander (WI) - 1936
Wiley, Calvin (CT) - 1832
Wilkerson, Ernest (WY) - 1966
Wilkinson, Wallace G. (KY) - 1987
Willard, Ashbel P. (IN) - 1856
Williams (MI) - 1866
Williams, Arnold (ID) - 1946
Williams, Bob (WA) - 1988
Williams, Burt (WI) - 1916
Williams, Charles K. (VT) - 1843, 1850, 1851
Williams, Clayton (TX) - 1990
Williams, Daniel (MS) - 1827
Williams, G. Mennen (MI) - 1948, 1950, 1952, 1954, 1956, 1958
Williams, George Fred (MA) - 1895, 1896, 1897
Williams, J. A. (ND) - 1914
Williams, Jack (AZ) - 1966, 1968, 1970
Williams, James Douglas (IN) - 1876
Williams, Jared W. (NH) - 1846, 1847, 1848
Williams, John Bell (MS) - 1967
Williams, Joseph H. (ME) - 1877
Williams, M. D. (AL) - 1819
Williams, Robert L. (OK) - 1914
Williams, Russell (AZ) - 1974
Williams, S. A. (MD) - 1903
Willis, Frank B. (OH) - 1914, 1916, 1918
Willis, Simeon S. (KY) - 1943
Willits, J. F. (KS) - 1890
Wills, William H. (VT) - 1940, 1942
Willson, August E. (KY) - 1907
Wilmot, David (PA) - 1857
Wilson (AR) - 1849
Wilson (ID) - 1890
Wilson (TN) - 1880
Wilson, Asher B. (ID) - 1926
Wilson, E. Willis (WV) - 1884
Wilson, Eugene M. (MN) - 1888
Wilson, Francis M. (MO) - 1928
Wilson, George (IA) - 1936, 1938, 1940
Wilson, Harry L. (MT) - 1912
Wilson, Henry (MA) - 1853
Wilson, J. (NH) - 1838, 1839
Wilson, J. Stitt (CA) - 1910
Wilson, Malcolm (NY) - 1974
Wilson, Pete (CA) - 1990, 1994

Wilson, Stanley C. (VT) - 1930, 1932
Wilson, Ted (UT) - 1988
Wilson, Thomas (MN) - 1890
Wilson, Woodrow (NJ) - 1910
Wiltz, Louis A. (LA) - 1879
Winans, Edward B. (MI) - 1890
Winant, John G. (NH) - 1924, 1930, 1932
Winchester, George W. (MS) - 1829
Wingate, Joshua Jr. (ME) - 1821
Winsted, George W. (TN) - 1892
Winston, James (MO) - 1852
Winston, John A. (AL) - 1853, 1855
Winter, Edward H. (MO) - 1932
Winter, William (MS) - 1979
Winters, John D. (NV) - 1866
Winters, Theodore (NV) - 1894
Winters, Thomas (NV) - 1890
Winthrop, Robert C. (MA) - 1851
Wipperman, M. A. (ND) - 1900
Wise, Henry A. (VA) - 1855
Wise, John S. (VA) - 1885
Wisener, W. H. (TN) - 1870
Wisner, Moses (MI) - 1858
Withycombe, James (OR) - 1906, 1914, 1918
Witt, R. Beecher (TN) - 1952
Wittpenn (NJ) - 1916
Wolcott, Henry R. (CO) - 1898
Wolcott, Oliver Jr. (CT) - 1816, 1817, 1818, 1819, 1820, 1821, 1822, 1823, 1824, 1825, 1826, 1827
Wolcott, Oliver Sr. (CT) - 1796, 1797
Wolcott, Roger (MA) - 1896, 1897, 1898
Wolf, George (PA) - 1829, 1832, 1835
Wolpe, Howard (MI) - 1994
Wood, Andrew T. (KY) - 1891
Wood, Chauncey L. (SD) - 1910
Wood, G. T. (TX) - 1853
Wood, George T. (TX) - 1847, 1849
Wood, Lloyd H. (PA) - 1954
Wood, Reuben (OH) - 1850, 1851
Woodahl, Robert (MT) - 1976
Woodbridge, William (MI) - 1839
Woodbury, Levi (NH) - 1823, 1824
Woodbury, Urban A. (VT) - 1894
Woodford, Stewart L. (NY) - 1870
Woodman (MI) - 1880
Woodring, Harry H. (KS) - 1930, 1932, 1946
Woodruff (AL) - 1876
Woodruff, Rollin S. (CT) - 1906

Woods, George L. (OR) - 1866
Woodson, Silas (MO) - 1872
Woodward, George W. (PA) - 1863
Woodward, Gilbert M. (WI) - 1886
Woolwine, Thomas Lee (CA) - 1922
Worcester, Franklin (NY) - 1912
Workman, W. D. (SC) - 1982
Worth, Jonathan (NC) - 1865, 1866
Worthington, John I. (AR) - 1906, 1908
Worthington, Thomas (OH) - 1808, 1810, 1814, 1816
Wray, Arthur G. (NE) - 1920
Wright (TN) - 1880
Wright, Bob (UT) - 1980
Wright, Calvin E. (ID) - 1950
Wright, Earl (WY) - 1946
Wright, Fielding L. (MS) - 1947
Wright, Joseph A. (IN) - 1849, 1852
Wright, Seaborn (GA) - 1896
Wright, Silas (NY) - 1844, 1846
Wright, William (NJ) - 1847, 1859

Y

Yaple, George L. (MI) - 1886
Yates, Joseph C. (NY) - 1822
Yates, Richard (IL) - 1860, 1900
Yates, Robert (NY) - 1789, 1795
Yeaman, Caldwell (CO) - 1890
Yell (AR) - 1856
Yell, Archibald (AR) - 1840
Yerger, William (MS) - 1857
Yerkes, John W. (KY) - 1900
York, Myrth (RI) - 1994
York, Tyre (NC) - 1884
Young, C. C. (CA) - 1926
Young, C. W. (WA) - 1892
Young, Edward L. (SC) - 1978
Young, George U. (AZ) - 1914
Young, John (NY) - 1846
Young, Milton K. (CA) - 1930
Young, Samuel (NY) - 1824
Young, Winthrop (MN) - 1871
Youngdahl, Luther W. (MN) - 1946, 1948, 1950
Younger, Evelle J. (CA) - 1978
Youngman, William Sterling (MA) - 1932

Z

Zeller, Fred R. (CT) - 1958
Zimmerman, Fred R. (WI) - 1926
Zimmerman, Peter (OR) - 1934

Primary Candidates Index

The Primary Candidates Index includes all candidates appearing in Gubernatorial Primary Election Returns, 1919-1997. The index includes candidates' names followed by state abbreviations and the years of candidacy. To locate a candidate's returns, turn to pages 95 to 154 where the returns are arranged alphabetically by state (*State Abbreviations below*) and in chronological order of election for each state.

A

Abel, Hazel (NE) - 1960
Abernathy, Lee Roy (GA) - 1958
Acker, Bert L. (FL) - 1944, 1948, 1952
Ackerman, Lee (AZ) - 1960
Ackermann, Barbara (MA) - 1978
Acuff, Roy (TN) - 1948
Adams (SC) - 1938
Adams, Alto (FL) - 1952
Adams, Mary (ME) - 1994
Adams, Paul L. (NY) - 1970
Adams, Roy C. (MS) - 1971
Adams, Tom (FL) - 1974
Addington, William H. (KS) - 1960
Adkins, Homer M. (AR) - 1940, 1942
Agnew, Spiro T. (MD) - 1966
Albertazzie, Ralph D. (WV) - 1976
Albright, R. Mayne (NC) - 1948
Alexander, J. F. (NC) - 1976
Alexander, Lamar (TN) - 1974, 1978, 1982
Alford, Dale (AR) - 1962, 1966
Alioto, Joseph L. (CA) - 1974
Allain, William A. (MS) - 1983
Allen, Carrol V. "Red" (SD) - 1994
Allen, Clifford R. (TN) - 1950, 1952, 1958
Allen, Jim (AL) - 1954
Allen, Oscar K. (LA) - 1932
Allen, Thomas H. (ME) - 1994
Allen, William C. (NV) - 1978
Allensworth, Don (MD) - 1994
Allred, James V. (TX) - 1934, 1936
Almond, J. Lindsay Jr. (VA) - 1957
Almond, Lincoln C. (RI) - 1978, 1994
Altofer, John H. (IL) - 1968

Altvater, George (OR) - 1962
Amaimo, Morgan L. (MD) - 1958
Anaya, Toney (NM) - 1982
Andersen, Elmer L. (MN) - 1960, 1962
Anderson, A. C. (MS) - 1927
Anderson, Bob (IA) - 1986
Anderson, Bruce (NH) - 1986
Anderson, D. G. (HI) - 1982, 1986
Anderson, Emmett T. (WA) - 1956
Anderson, Forrest H. (MT) - 1968
Anderson, John (KS) - 1960, 1962, 1972
Anderson, LeRoy (MT) - 1968
Anderson, Sigurd (SD) - 1964
Anderson, Victor E. (NE) - 1956, 1958
Anderson, Wendell R. (MN) - 1970, 1974
Andrews, John (CO) - 1990
Andrews, Lloyd J. (WA) - 1960
Andrews, Mark (ND) - 1962
Andrews, Robert E. (NJ) - 1997
Andrus, Cecil D. (ID) - 1966, 1970, 1974, 1986, 1990
Annable, Robert W. (OH) - 1970
Apodaca, Jerry (NM) - 1974
Ariyoshi, George R. (HI) - 1974, 1978, 1982
Armstrong, Bob (TX) - 1982
Arnall, Ellis (GA) - 1942, 1966
Arnesen, Deborah A. (NH) - 1992
Arnold, Remmie L. (VA) - 1949
Aronson, J. Hugo (MT) - 1956
Ashcroft, John (MO) - 1984, 1988
Ashworth, Emily (OR) - 1978
Askew, Reubin (FL) - 1970, 1974

Atiyeh, Victor G. (OR) - 1974, 1978, 1982
Atkinson, David (VT) - 1990
Atkinson, W. P. (OK) - 1958
Austin, Gene (NV) - 1962
Avenson, Donald D. (IA) - 1990
Avery, William H. (KS) - 1964, 1966
Aycock, A. A. (LA) - 1971

B

Babbage, Bob (KY) - 1995
Babbitt, Bruce (AZ) - 1978, 1982
Babcock, Robert S. (VT) - 1960, 1964
Babcock, Tim M. (MT) - 1964, 1968
Baca, Jim (NM) - 1994
Bachrach, George A. (MA) - 1994
Badgett, Joseph M. (MO) - 1964
Baer, Steven (IL) - 1990
Baesler, Scott (KY) - 1991
Bafalis, L. A. "Skip" (FL) - 1970, 1982
Baggett, Bryce (OK) - 1970
Bagley, Hugh G. (CA) - 1986
Bagwell, Paul D. (MI) - 1958, 1960
Bailey, Carl E. (AR) - 1936, 1938, 1940
Bailey, Joseph W. (TX) - 1920
Bailey, Josiah W. (NC) - 1924
Bailey, Thomas L. (MS) - 1939, 1943
Bailey, Wendell (MO) - 1992
Bakalis, Michael (IL) - 1978
Baker, J. Edwin (FL) - 1944
Balentine, Karla (MD) - 1962
Bangerter, Norman H. (UT) - 1984
Barbee, James (FL) - 1940
Bardacke, Paul (NM) - 1990

Barlocker, W. A. (UT) - 1960
Barnes, Ben (TX) - 1972
Barnes, Clarence E. (OK) - 1958
Barnes, Roy E. (GA) - 1990
Barnes, Wallace (CT) - 1970
Barnes, Wilson K. (MD) - 1974
Barnett, Ross R. (MS) - 1951, 1955, 1959, 1967
Barr, Burton S. (AZ) - 1986
Barrett, Barbara (AZ) - 1994
Barrett, Michael J. (MA) - 1994
Barringer, Richard E. (ME) - 1994
Barron, W. W. (WV) - 1960
Barry, James J. (NH) - 1966
Barry, Jonathan B. (WI) - 1986
Bartlett, Dewey F. (OK) - 1966, 1970
Basha, Eddie (AZ) - 1994
Batchelder, Clifton B. (NE) - 1970
Bateman, Raymond H. (NJ) - 1977
Bates (SC) - 1950, 1954
Bates, Charles A. (NE) - 1960, 1964
Batt, Phillip (ID) - 1982, 1994
Battle, John S. (VA) - 1949
Battle, Laurie C. (AL) - 1958
Battle, William C. (VA) - 1969
Baum, Ted (NE) - 1956
Baxley, Bill (AL) - 1978, 1986
Bayh, Evan (IN) - 1988, 1992
Beall, Carlton (MD) - 1978
Beall, J. Glenn Jr. (MD) - 1978
Beasely, Jere (AL) - 1978
Beasley, David (SC) - 1994
Beasley, Leonard W. (KY) - 1987
Becht, Paul F. (NM) - 1986
Beck, Robert K. (IA) - 1966, 1968
Beddow, Jim (SD) - 1994
Bedsole, Ann (AL) - 1994
Begley, Elmer (KY) - 1975

State Abbreviations

Alabama	.AL	Illinois	.IL	Montana	.MT	Rhode Island	.RI
Alaska	.AK	Indiana	.IN	Nebraska	.NE	South Carolina	.SC
Arizona	.AZ	Iowa	.IA	Nevada	.NV	South Dakota	.SD
Arkansas	.AR	Kansas	.KS	New Hampshire	.NH	Tennessee	.TN
California	.CA	Kentucky	.KY	New Jersey	.NJ	Texas	.TX
Colorado	.CO	Louisiana	.LA	New Mexico	.NM	Utah	.UT
Connecticut	.CT	Maine	.ME	New York	.NY	Vermont	.VT
Delaware	.DE	Maryland	.MD	North Carolina	.NC	Virginia	.VA
Florida	.FL	Massachusetts	.MA	North Dakota	.ND	Washington	.WA
Georgia	.GA	Michigan	.MI	Ohio	.OH	West Virginia	.WV
Hawaii	.HI	Minnesota	.MN	Oklahoma	.OK	Wisconsin	.WI
Idaho	.ID	Mississippi	.MS	Oregon	.OR	Wyoming	.WY
		Missouri	.MO	Pennsylvania	.PA		

Beitelspacher, Ron (ID) - 1994
Belaga, Julie D. (CT) - 1986
Beliveau, Severin M. (ME) - 1986
Bell, Bob (GA) - 1982
Bell, Howard L. (OK) - 1982
Bell, Percey (MS) - 1923
Bell, Robert K. "Buster" (AL) - 1950
Bell, Samuel (LA) - 1971
Bellmon, Henry L. (OK) - 1962, 1986
Bellotti, Francis X. (MA) - 1964, 1970, 1990
Benedict, Cleveland K. (WV) - 1992
Bennett (SC) - 1938
Bennett, Andrea (MT) - 1992
Bennett, Bruce (AR) - 1960, 1968
Bennett, Robert F. (KS) - 1974, 1978
Benson, Bruce (CO) - 1994
Bentley, Helen D. (MD) - 1994
Bentley, James L. (GA) - 1970
Berentson, Duane (WA) - 1980
Berg, Philip J. (PA) - 1990
Berkman, Craig (OR) - 1994
Bernhardt, Michael (VT) - 1900
Beshear, Steven L. (KY) - 1987
Bethea, A. W. (SC) - 1962
Beutler, Chris (NE) - 1986
Bickerstaff, William (NV) - 1974
Bicknell, Gene (KS) - 1986, 1994
Bilbo, Theodore G. (MS) - 1923, 1927
Bird, Michael C. (CO) - 1994
Bishop, Al (MT) - 1980
Blackburn, Ben (GA) - 1982
Blacketor, Paul (NH) - 1990
Blackwell, Earl (MO) - 1972
Blackwood, D. H. (AR) - 1932
Blackwood, Ibra C. (SC) - 1926, 1930
Blair, C. Stanley (MD) - 1970
Blair, George (MS) - 1991
Blair, James T. (MO) - 1956
Blanchard, James J. (MI) - 1982, 1986, 1990
Blanton, Ray (TN) - 1974
Blaylock, Chet (MT) - 1996
Blaylock, Len E. (AK) - 1972
Blease, Coleman L. (SC) - 1922, 1934, 1938
Blenski, Roman R. (WI) - 1970
Blevens, Clarence G. (NH) - 1996
Bloom, Jeremiah B. (NY) - 1978
Blount, Winton (AL) - 1994
Blunt, Roy D. (MO) - 1992
Bodenhamer, William T. (GA) - 1958
Boe, Nils A. (SD) - 1964, 1966
Boggs, Hale (LA) - 1952
Bohner, Robert J. (NY) - 1982
Bond, Christopher S. "Kit" (MO) - 1972, 1976, 1980
Bond, Frank M. (NM) - 1986, 1990
Bonner, John W. (MT) - 1956
Bonser, Robert A. (NH) - 1990
Boosalis, Helen (NE) - 1986
Boozer, Elbert (AL) - 1946, 1950
Boren, David L. (OK) - 1974
Boswell, Ted (AR) - 1968
Bouanchaud, Hewitt (LA) - 1924
Boucher, H. A. (AK) - 1982
Bourgois, Anna Belle (ND) - 1984
Boutin, Bernard L. (NH) - 1958, 1960
Bouza, Tony (MN) - 1994
Bowen, Otis R. (IN) - 1976
Bowen, Peter (IL) - 1986
Bowles, Hargrove Jr. "Skipper" (NC) - 1972
Boyce, Sam (AR) - 1966
Boyd, Jim (GA) - 1994
Boyd, McDill (KS) - 1960, 1964
Boyden, John S. (UT) - 1956
Boyle, Mike (NE) - 1990
Bozzuto, Richard C. (CT) - 1986

Bradley, Dorothy (MT) - 1992
Bradley, Tom (CA) - 1982, 1986
Bramante, Fred (NH) - 1994
Bramlett, Leon (MS) - 1979, 1983
Brandon, William W. (AL) - 1922
Branon, E. Frank (VT) - 1956
Branstad, Terry E. (IA) - 1982, 1986, 1990, 1994
Brashear, Kermit (NE) - 1986
Breathitt, Edward T. (KY) - 1963
Bredesen, Phil (TN) - 1994
Brennan, Joseph E. (ME) - 1974, 1978, 1982, 1990, 1994
Brett, George J. (PA) - 1966
Brewer, Albert (AL) - 1970, 1978
Brickley, James H. (MI) - 1982
Brier, Jack H. (KS) - 1986
Brimmer, Clarence (WY) - 1974
Briscoe, Andrew C. (TX) - 1986
Briscoe, Dolph (TX) - 1968, 1972, 1974, 1978
Britt, Henry M. (AR) - 1960
Britt, Maurice (AR) - 1986
Brock, Art (AZ) - 1964
Broderick, Raymond (PA) - 1970
Brooks, Mrs. Ralph G. (NE) - 1962
Brooks, Ralph G. (NE) - 1958
Brotzman, Donald G. (CO) - 1956
Broughton, J. Melville (NC) - 1940
Broughton, J. Melville Jr. (NC) - 1968
Brown, Bonn (NV) - 1964
Brown, Charlie (NV) - 1990
Brown, Clarence Jr. (OH) - 1982
Brown, David Andrew (MO) - 1996
Brown, Edmund G. (CA) - 1958, 1962, 1966
Brown, Edmund G. Jr. (CA) - 1974, 1978
Brown, Glenn B. (MN) - 1958
Brown, James H. (LA) - 1987
Brown, Jerry (OK) - 1990
Brown, John W. (OH) - 1956
Brown, John Y. Jr. (KY) - 1979, 1987
Brown, Kathleen (CA) - 1994
Brown, Paul W. (OH) - 1970
Brown, William J. (OH) - 1982
Browning, Chauncey H. (WV) - 1984
Browning, Gordon (TN) - 1936, 1938, 1946, 1948, 1950, 1952, 1954
Bruce, Walter E. (NM) - 1974
Bryan, Richard (NV) - 1982
Bryant, Farris (FL) - 1956, 1960
Buck, Gilbert (NV) - 1974
Buckley, Thomas H. (MA) - 1956
Buckson, David P. (DE) - 1972
Budd, Bill (WY) - 1986
Buehner, Carl W. (UT) - 1968
Bumpers, Dale (AR) - 1970, 1972
Bunning, Jim (KY) - 1983
Burbach, J. W. (NE) - 1966, 1970
Burch, Palmer L. (CO) - 1958
Burch, Robert L. (OH) - 1994
Burdett, Joe F. (WV) - 1956
Burg, Jim (SD) - 1994
Burgess, Larry (IL) - 1986
Burke, Howard L. (WY) - 1966
Burke, Joe (WY) - 1966
Burney, Dwight W. (NE) - 1964
Burns, Brian D. (VT) - 1976
Burns, Edward P. (ND) - 1972
Burns, Haydon (FL) - 1960, 1964, 1966
Burns, John A. (HI) - 1959, 1962, 1966, 1970
Burns, Lester (KY) - 1983
Burris, Roland W. (IL) - 1994
Burroughs, John (NM) - 1958, 1960, 1966
Burrows, George (NE) - 1982
Bursey, Joseph A. (NM) - 1958, 1960
Burton, Grady (FL) - 1936

Burton, Marvin L. (AZ) - 1958
Busbee, George D. (GA) - 1974, 1978
Bush, George W. (TX) - 1994
Bush, Hilary A. (MO) - 1964
Bush, Jeb (FL) - 1994
Bussey, Elmer E. (NH) - 1962
Bussiere, Emile R. (NH) - 1968
Butcher, Jake (TN) - 1974, 1978
Butera, Bob (PA) - 1978
Butrovich, John (AK) - 1958
Butte, George C. (TX) - 1930
Buttrick, John (AZ) - 1994
Byer, George H. (AK) - 1962
Byrd, Garland T. (GA) - 1966
Byrd, Harry F. (VA) - 1925
Byrd, Jesse M. (MS) - 1947, 1951
Byrne, Brendan T. (NJ) - 1973, 1977
Byrnes, James F. (SC) - 1950

C

Cafferata, Patty (NV) - 1986
Cahill, Pamela A. (ME) - 1994
Cahill, William T. (NJ) - 1969, 1973
Cain, Mary D. (MS) - 1951, 1955
Caldwell, Millard F. (FL) - 1944
Caldwell, Sam S. (LA) - 1944
Caldwell, Stafford (FL) - 1932, 1936
Camp, John N. H. (OK) - 1966
Campbell, Bonnie D. (IA) - 1994
Campbell, Bruce S. (MD) - 1958
Campbell, Carroll (SC) - 1986, 1990
Campbell, Edward L. (IA) - 1982
Campbell, Jack M. (NM) - 1962, 1964
Campbell, James O. "Jim" (AK) - 1990, 1994
Cannon, D. James (UT) - 1964
Cannon, Joe (OK) - 1970
Cannon, Paul (MT) - 1960
Caperton, Gaston (WV) - 1988, 1992
Card, Andrew (MA) - 1982
Cardinale, Gerald (NJ) - 1989
Carey, Hugh L. (NY) - 1974, 1978
Carey, Richard J. (ME) - 1978
Cargo, David F. (NM) - 1966, 1968, 1994
Carley, David (WI) - 1966, 1978
Carlin, John (KS) - 1978, 1982, 1990
Carlson, Arne (MN) - 1990, 1994
Carlton, Doyle E. (FL) - 1928
Carmichael (AL) - 1926
Carmichael, Gil (MS) - 1979
Carmichael, J. V. (GA) - 1946
Carnahan, Mel (MO) - 1984, 1992, 1996
Carnley, J. A. (AL) - 1930
Carpenter, Terry (NE) - 1960
Carper, Thomas R. (DE) - 1992, 1996
Carr, Larry (AK) - 1970
Carr, Waggoner (TX) - 1968
Carroll, Julian (KY) - 1975, 1987
Carruthers, Garrey E. (NM) - 1986
Carstens, C. J. (NC) - 1980
Carswell, George H. (GA) - 1926, 1930
Carter, Doug (AL) - 1986
Carter, Jerry W. (FL) - 1936
Carter, Jimmy (GA) - 1966, 1970
Cartwright, Wilburn (OK) - 1970
Carwile, Howard H. (VA) - 1957
Cary, Hudson (VA) - 1941
Casey, Robert P. (PA) - 1966, 1970, 1978, 1986, 1990
Cason, William (MO) - 1976
Castle, Michael N. (DE) - 1984, 1988
Castro, Raul H. (AZ) - 1970, 1974
Catts, Sidney J. (FL) - 1924, 1928
Caudell, James A. (NM) - 1990
Cavanagh, Jerome P. (MI) - 1974
Cayetano, Benjamin J. (HI) - 1994

Cazort, Lee (AR) - 1924
Cecil, J. N. R. (KY) - 1963
Celebrezze, Anthony J. (OH) - 1958, 1990
Celeste, Richard F. (OH) - 1978, 1982, 1986
Chafee, John H. (RI) - 1962, 1964, 1966, 1968
Chamberlin, Robert (SD) - 1966, 1968
Champagne, Alfred J. (NH) - 1958
Chance, Simon W. (SD) - 1972
Chandler, Albert B. (KY) - 1963, 1967
Chandler, Barton E. (NE) - 1982
Chaney, Bert (KS) - 1978
Chapman, Bruce (WA) - 1980
Chapman, Philip F. (ME) - 1956, 1958
Chappell, Dan (FL) - 1936
Chavez, Fabian (NM) - 1968, 1982
Chavez, Tibo J. (NM) - 1974
Cheever, R. E. (NV) - 1962
Cheney, Dick (NM) - 1994
Cherry, Francis (AR) - 1952, 1954
Cherry, R. Gregg (NC) - 1944
Childs, Dana W. (ME) - 1966
Chiles, Lawton (FL) - 1990, 1994
Chrisman, Marshall (AR) - 1980, 1982
Christensen, Kathryn A. (WI) - 1986
Christensen, Richard G. (WA) - 1964
Christopher, George (CA) - 1966
Chrysler, Dick (MI) - 1986
Chrystal, John (IA) - 1990
Chvala, Chuck (WI) - 1994
Cibes, William J. (CT) - 1990
Clack, Robert W. (KS) - 1974
Clanton, Bobby (MS) - 1991
Clark, Don (OR) - 1982
Clark, Newman (WA) - 1960
Clark, William H. R. (CA) - 1986
Clark, William J. (NJ) - 1965
Clarke, George A. (NE) - 1962
Clauson, Clinton A. (ME) - 1958
Clear, Tom (NM) - 1970
Clem, Chester (FL) - 1986
Clement, Bob (TN) - 1978
Clement, Frank G. (TN) - 1952, 1954, 1962
Clements, William P. (TX) - 1978, 1982, 1986
Clingman, Ron (WY) - 1990
Clinton, Bill (AR) - 1978, 1980, 1982, 1984, 1986, 1990
Cloud, Drew (NM) - 1974
Cloud, Roger (OH) - 1970
Clyde, George D. (UT) - 1956, 1960
Cobo, Albert E. (MI) - 1956
Cochran, Frank (TN) - 1994
Coe, Earl S. (WA) - 1956
Coe, William O. (OK) - 1958
Coffin, Frank M. (ME) - 1960
Coffin, J. Donald (KS) - 1964
Cogdill, John L. (FL) - 1948
Coghill, John B. "Jack" (AK) - 1994
Coghill, John B. (AK) - 1990
Coleman, J. Marshall (VA) - 1989
Coleman, James P. (MS) - 1955, 1963
Coleman, Kevin (RI) - 1962
Collins, Hal H. (TX) - 1942
Collins, Leroy (FL) - 1954, 1956
Collins, Martha Layne (KY) - 1983
Collins, Ross A. (MS) - 1919
Collins, Susan M. (ME) - 1994
Colton, Stan (NV) - 1982
Combs, Bert T. (KY) - 1959, 1971
Compton, Charles E. (LA) - 1954
Concannon, Donald O. (KS) - 1974
Cone, Fred P. (FL) - 1936
Cone, J. Carrol (AR) - 1928

Conlin, Roxanne (IA) - 1982
Connally, John B. (TX) - 1962, 1964, 1966
Conner, Martin S. (MS) - 1923, 1927, 1931, 1939, 1943
Connor, Edward (MI) - 1960
Connor, Eugene "Bull" (AL) - 1950
Connor, James A. (NH) - 1976
Connor, Kenneth L. (FL) - 1994
Conrad, Larry A. (IN) - 1976
Conrad, Robert (NE) - 1960
Cook, Marlow W. (KY) - 1967
Cook, R. A. (AR) - 1936, 1938
Cook, Rodney M. (GA) - 1978
Coolidge, W. M. "Bill" (GA) - 1974
Coon, Ken (AR) - 1974
Cooper, John R. (NE) - 1960
Cooper, Prentice (TN) - 1938, 1940, 1942
Cooper, Richard H. (IL) - 1976
Cooper, Robert A. (SC) - 1920
Cooper, Thomas E. (NC) - 1940
Cope, Norah M. (PA) - 1974
Copeland, David Y. (TN) - 1994
Copenhaver, John T. (WV) - 1956
Corbet, Leo (AZ) - 1982
Coté, Armand (RI) - 1958, 1960
Cotten, Sam (AK) - 1994
Courter, James A. (NJ) - 1989
Cowper, Steve (AK) - 1982, 1986
Cox, Jack (TX) - 1960, 1962
Crabtree, W. R. (TN) - 1920
Cragin, Charles L. (ME) - 1978, 1982
Craig, William G. (VT) - 1976
Crank, Marion (AR) - 1968
Craswell, Ellen (WA) - 1996
Creer, John P. (UT) - 1976
Crenshaw, Ander (FL) - 1994
Crichton, Jack (TX) - 1964
Crispe, A. Luke (VT) - 1960
Criss, Vernon (WV) - 1992
Crockett, Hudley (TN) - 1974
Croft, Chancy (AK) - 1978
Crookham, George L. (ID) - 1962
Crossley, Randolph (HI) - 1966, 1974
Crouch, Harvey F. (KS) - 1962
Crowder, A. Don (TX) - 1986
Crowell, Charles M. (WY) - 1962
Crowley, Roger J. (NH) - 1970, 1972
Crozier, Dell (KS) - 1966
Crumpler, Shirley (NV) - 1974
Crutcher, John (KS) - 1968
Cunningham, Minnie F. (TX) - 1944
Cuomo, Mario M. (NY) - 1982, 1986, 1990, 1994
Cupp, Harry (WV) - 1964
Curb, Mike (CA) - 1982
Curran, Paul J. (NY) - 1982
Curry, Bill (CT) - 1994
Curtis, Kenneth M. (ME) - 1966, 1970
Curtis, Robert B. (MO) - 1968
Cutright, Harold G. (WV) - 1964

D

Dahl, C. P. (ND) - 1960
Daily, Stephen J. (IN) - 1988
Daley, John J. (VT), 1968, 1970
D'Allesandro, Louis C. (NH) - 1980, 1982
Dalton, John M. (MO) - 1960
D'Amours, Norman E. (NH) - 1992
Daniel, Mike (SC) - 1986
Daniel, Price (TX) - 1956, 1958, 1960, 1962
Daniels, Jack (NM) - 1970
Daniels, Robert W. (CO) - 1974
Dantin, Maurice (MS) - 1975, 1987
Darden, Colgate W. Jr. (VA) - 1941
David, Thomas E. (FL) - 1960

Davids, Vernon (FL) - 1982
Davidson, Lynch (TX) - 1924, 1926
Davidson, T. W. (TX) - 1924
Davis, Deane C. (VT) - 1968, 1970
Davis, Ed (CA) - 1978
Davis, Erwin (AR) - 1984
Davis, Guy (GA) - 1986
Davis, Jimmie H. (LA) - 1944, 1959, 1960, 1971
Davis, John (FL) - 1990
Davis, John E. (ND) - 1956, 1958
Davis, W. C. (AL) - 1930
Dawson, Bert (OH) - 1974
Daxon, Tom (OK) - 1982
Deal, J. T. (VA) - 1933
Dean, Ernest Howard (UT) - 1964
Dean, Howard B. (VT) - 1992, 1994, 1996
Dean, Roscoe Emory (GA) - 1978
Dear, Cleveland (LA) - 1936
DeBoer, Stan (NE) - 1982
DeCamp, John (NE) - 1994
Dee, William J. (ID) - 1966
Degnan, John J. (NJ) - 1981
deGraffenried, Ryan (AL) - 1962
Del Sesto, Christopher (RI) - 1956, 1958, 1960
Del Tufo, Robert J. (NJ) - 1985
Demarest, Eugene E. (NJ) - 1961
Dempster (TN) - 1940
Dendahl, John (NM) - 1994
Depue, Stephen (PA) - 1974
DeRose, Ralph C. (NJ) - 1973, 1977
Derr, A. M. (ID) - 1958
Derryberry, Larry (OK) - 1978
DeRushe, William (AK) - 1990
DeSimone, Herbert F. (RI) - 1970, 1972
Deukmejian, George (CA) - 1982, 1986
DeVault, Jack (AZ) - 1968
Devereux, James (MD) - 1958
D'Ewart, Wesley A. (MT) - 1960
Diamond, G. William (ME) - 1986
Diamond, M. Jerome (VT) - 1980
Dickerson, Harvey (NV) - 1958
Dickinson, Fred (FL) - 1960, 1964
Dickson, Earl L. (OR) - 1956
Dietrich, Theresa F. (CA) - 1978
Dilley, Robert D. (IA) - 1972
Dillon, Denis E. (NY) - 1986
Dilworth, Richardson (PA) - 1962
DiPrete, Edward D. (RI) - 1984, 1986, 1988, 1990
DiSalle, Michael V. (OH) - 1956, 1958, 1962
Dixon, Frank M. (AL) - 1934, 1938
Dixon, Jeanne (WA) - 1988
Docking, George (KS) - 1956, 1958, 1960
Docking, Robert (KS) - 1966, 1968, 1970, 1972
Docking, Thomas R. (KS) - 1986
Dodd, William J. (LA) - 1952, 1959
Doenges, Bill (OK) - 1958
Doherty, Edward W. (ND) - 1968
Dolloff, Maynard C. (ME) - 1958, 1962
Domenici, Peter V. (NM) - 1970
Domina, David A. (NE) - 1986
Donahue, Maurice A. (MA) - 1970
Donley, Russ (WY) - 1986
Dorn, Doug (CA) - 1994
Dorn, William Jennings Bryan (SC) - 1974, 1978
Dorsey, Ervin Odell (AR) - 1964
Dosek, Edward A. (NE) - 1958
Dossett, Burgin E. (TN) - 1936
Doty, Jules V. (KS) - 1964
Dougerty, Bill (SD) - 1974
Dougherty, Dan P. (CA) - 1982
Douglas, Steve (PA) - 1982

Douglass, Gus R. (WV) - 1988
Dow, Robert C. (NM) - 1958
Dowd, Edward L. (MO) - 1972
Dowdy, Wayne (MS) - 1991
Downing, Delbert F. (NH) - 1978
Dreyfus, Lee Sherman (WI) - 1978
Driggs, John R. (AZ) - 1974
Dubord, Richard J. (ME) - 1962
Dudley, Michael Kioni (HI) - 1994
Duggan, Lester W. "Les" Jr. (MO) - 1996
Dukakis, Michael S. (MA) - 1974, 1978, 1982, 1986
Duke, David E. (LA) - 1991
Dumont, Wayne (NJ) - 1957, 1961, 1965
Duncan, J. T. (SC) - 1924
Dunkle, Frank (MT) - 1972
Dunn, Aubrey L. (NM) - 1982
Dunn, Gary M. (NC) - 1992
Dunn, Vincent P. (NH) - 1968
Dunn, Winfield (TN) - 1970, 1986
Dupay, Robert L. (NH) - 1984
du Pont, Edward C. (NH) - 1992
du Pont, Pierre S. "Pete" IV (DE) - 1980
Durfee, Louise (RI) - 1994
Durkan, Martin J. (WA) - 1968, 1972
Durning, Marvin (WA) - 1976
Durrance, Charles M. (FL) - 1932
Duryea, Perry B. (NY) - 1978
Dwinell, Lane (NH) - 1956
Dye, Harold (GA) - 1974
Dyer, Margie (NV) - 1970
Dyke, William D. (WI) - 1974
Dzivi, Dick (MT) - 1972

E

Earl, Anthony S. (WI) - 1982, 1986
Early, Rex (IN) - 1996
Easley, Mack (NM) - 1968
Eastham, John P. (NM) - 1974
Eastland, Larry (ID) - 1994
Easton, John J. (VT) - 1984
Easton, Roger L. (NH) - 1986
Eastvold, Don (WA) - 1956
Eaves, John Arthur (MS) - 1975, 1979, 1987
Echols, Odis (NM) - 1974
Eckerd, Jack M. (FL) - 1970, 1978
Edgar, Jim (IL) - 1990, 1994
Edmisten, Rufus (NC) - 1984
Edmondson, J. Howard (OK) - 1958
Edwards, Cary (NJ) - 1989, 1993
Edwards, Edwin W. (LA) - 1971, 1975, 1987, 1991
Edwards, Horace H. (VA) - 1949
Edwards, James B. (SC) - 1974
Edwards, Stanley (WY) - 1958
Egan, William A. (AK) - 1958, 1962, 1966, 1970, 1974
Eggers, Paul W. (TX) - 1968, 1970
Ehringhaus, J. C. B. (NC) - 1932
Eikenberry, Ken (WA) - 1992
Elgin, Julian (AL) - 1978
Elkin, Richard (ND) - 1976
Ellington, Buford (TN) - 1958, 1966
Elliott, Carl (AL) - 1966
Ellis, Greeley (GA) - 1990
Ellis, Handy (AL) - 1946
Emberton, Thomas (KY) - 1971
Embs, Lowell D. (TX) - 1982
Engler, Colleen (MI) - 1986
Engler, John (MI) - 1990, 1994
English, Colin (FL) - 1948
Eppes, Frank (SC) - 1986
Erbe, Norman A. (IA) - 1960, 1962
Erhart, Milton E. (ID) - 1990
Ertel, Allen E. (PA) - 1982

Erwin, James S. (ME) - 1966, 1970, 1974
Eskind, Jane (TN) - 1986
Espinosa, Gary (TX) - 1994
Euge, Harvey F. (MO) - 1968, 1976
Evans, Daniel J. (WA) - 1964, 1968, 1972
Evans, Dwight (PA) - 1994
Evans, H. Dean (IN) - 1992
Evans, John V. (ID) - 1978, 1982
Evans, Roger Q. (TX) - 1948
Everett, Clif (OR) - 1982
Ewald, William B. (MO) - 1960, 1964
Exon, J. James (NE) - 1970, 1974
Exum, H. E. (TX) - 1930
Eyre, Richard M. (UT) - 1992

F

Fadeley, Edward N. (OR) - 1986
Fair, Mike (OK) - 1986
Fair, Robert J. (IN) - 1976
Fairchild, Roger (ID) - 1990
Faircloth, D. M. (NC) - 1984
Faircloth, Earl (FL) - 1970
Fallon, James F. (NH) - 1984
Fannin, Paul (AZ) - 1958, 1960, 1962
Farenthold, Frances (TX) - 1972, 1974
Farley, Thomas (CO) - 1974
Farmer, Edward G. (MO) - 1960
Farrar, Frank (SD) - 1968, 1970
Farris, William W. (TN) - 1962
Faryniasz, Kirk E. (VT) - 1980
Fasi, Frank F. (HI) - 1974, 1978, 1982, 1994
Faubus, Orval E. (AR) - 1954, 1956, 1958, 1960, 1962, 1964, 1970, 1974, 1986
Faulkner, Jimmy (AL) - 1954, 1958
Fay, Albert B. (TX) - 1972
Feder, Jack (OR) - 1994
Feinstein, Dianne (CA) - 1990
Fenwick, Charles R. (VA) - 1953
Ferency, Zoltan A. (MI) - 1966, 1970, 1978, 1982
Ferguson, Jim G. (AR) - 1924
Ferguson, Milton J. (WV) - 1956
Ferguson, Miriam A. (TX) - 1924, 1926, 1930, 1932, 1940
Ferguson, Philip (OK) - 1958
Ferguson, Robert E. (NM) - 1978
Ferguson, William M. (KS) - 1964
Fields, Cleo (LA) - 1995
Fike, Ed (NV) - 1970
Finan, Thomas B. (MD) - 1966
Finch, Cliff (MS) - 1975
Finch, Raymond (SC) - 1978
Fingold, George (MA) - 1958
Fink, Tom (AK) - 1978, 1982, 1994
Finkbeiner, Chris (AR) - 1958
Finnell, W. (AL) - 1930
Finney, Joan (KS) - 1990
Fischer, F. W. (TX) - 1936
Fisher, Leslie (OK) - 1986
Fisher, Mike (PA) - 1994
Fitzgerald, Jerome D. (IA) - 1978, 1982
Fitzgerald, William (MI) - 1978, 1982
Fitzmorris, James E. (LA) - 1979
Flaherty, David T. (NC) - 1976
Flaherty, Francis X. (RI) - 1990, 1992
Flaherty, Peter (PA) - 1978
Fleischli, Gus (WY) - 1978
Flippo, Ronnie G. (AL) - 1990
Florio, James J. (NJ) - 1977, 1981, 1989, 1993
Flournoy, Houston I. (CA) - 1974
Flowers, Richmond M. (AL) - 1966
Floyd, J. C. (AR) - 1920
Folcarelli, Giovani (RI) - 1976

Foley, John (NV) - 1978
Folks, Ken (FL) - 1964
Folmar, Emory (AL) - 1982
Folsom, James E. (AL) - 1942, 1946, 1954, 1962
Folsom, James E. Jr. (AL) - 1994
Fontes, G. J. (HI) - 1966
Foote, Ralph A. (VT) - 1964
Forbes, Malcolm S. (NJ) - 1957
Ford, Art (ND) - 1958
Ford, Wendell H. (KY) - 1971
Fordice, Kirk (MS) - 1991, 1995
Foreman, Dale (WA) - 1996
Forgy, Larry E. (KY) - 1991, 1995
Formby, Marshall (TX) - 1962
Fortson, Blanton (GA) - 1936
Foss, Joe J. (SD) - 1956
Foss, Judith C. (ME) - 1994
Foster, H. B. (FL) - 1964
Foster, M. J. "Mike" (LA) - 1995
Fountain, R. T. (NC) - 1932
Frami, Edward J. (WI) - 1994
Francisco, James L. (KS) - 1994
Franklin (MS) - 1935, 1939, 1943
Franklin, George E. (NV) - 1958
Franklin, L. C. (MS) - 1923
Franzenburg, Paul (IA) - 1968, 1972
Fraser, W. B. (FL) - 1940
Fraser, Willard E. (MT) - 1960, 1968
Freauf, Betty (OR) - 1986
Freeman, Orville L. (MN) - 1956, 1958, 1960
Freeman, Woody (AR) - 1984
Frey, Louis (FL) - 1978, 1986
Frinzi, Dominic H. (WI) - 1964, 1966
Frisbie, Ray E. (KS) - 1972
Fritz, Milo H. (AK) - 1962
Frizzell, Kent (KS) - 1970
Frohnmayer, Dave (OR) - 1990
Fry, Charles E. (OH) - 1970
Fuhr, John D. (CO) - 1982
Fuhrig, Joseph (CA) - 1986
Fulani, Lenora B. (NY) - 1994
Fulton, Richard (TN) - 1978, 1986
Fulton, Robert (IA) - 1970
Funston, Bob (OK) - 1978
Fuqua, Henry L. (LA) - 1924
Furcolo, Foster (MA) - 1956, 1958
Furman, Roy E. (PA) - 1958
Futrell, J. Marion (AR) - 1932, 1934

G

Gable, Robert E. (KY) - 1975, 1995
Gage, Jack R. (WY) - 1962, 1966
Gagnon, Paul M. (NH) - 1986
Galbraith, Gatewood (KY) - 1991, 1995
Gallagher, Tom (FL) - 1986, 1994
Gallaway, Jim (NV) - 1990
Gallen, Hugh (NH) - 1974, 1976, 1978, 1980, 1982
Gallion, MacDonald (AL) - 1962
Gallogly, Edward P. (RI) - 1964
Gambrell, David H. (GA) - 1966
Gandy, Evelyn (MS) - 1979, 1983
Gannon, William (IA) - 1970, 1974
Garamendi, John (CA) - 1982, 1994
Gardner, Booth (WA) - 1984, 1988
Gardner, Earl S. (VT) - 1978
Gardner, James C. (NC) - 1968, 1972, 1992
Gardner, Kem C. (UT) - 1984
Gardner, O. Max (NC) - 1920, 1928
Gargan, Jack (FL) - 1994
Garrahy, J. Joseph (RI) - 1976, 1978, 1982
Garrison, Denzil D. (OK) - 1974
Gartin, Carroll (MS) - 1959
Gary, Raymond (OK) - 1962, 1966
Gavin, Robert L. (NC) - 1960, 1964

Geisinger, Harry (GA) - 1974
Geringer, Jim (WY) - 1994
Geving, Herb (ND) - 1976
Gibbons, Charles (MA) - 1958
Gibbons, Jim (NV) - 1994
Gibson, Kenneth A. (NJ) - 1981, 1985
Gigler, Andrew R. (OR) - 1970
Gilbert, Andrew J. (AZ) - 1966
Gilbert, Rachel S. (ID) - 1990
Gilchrist, Bob (AL) - 1966
Gill, Thomas P. (HI) - 1970, 1974
Gill, Warren (OR) - 1958
Gilligan, John J. (OH) - 1970, 1974
Gillmor, Paul E. (OH) - 1986
Gilmore, Thomas O. (NC) - 1984
Ginn, Bo (GA) - 1982
Glasby, John (ID) - 1958
Glendening, Parris N. (MD) - 1994
Goddard, Sam (AZ) - 1962, 1964, 1966, 1968
Goddard, Terry (AZ) - 1990, 1994
Goetz, Phyllis (OH) - 1982
Goldberg, Arthur J. (NY) - 1970
Goldsby, Dean (AR) - 1986
Goldschmidt, Neil (OR) - 1986
Goldsmith, Stephen (IN) - 1996
Goldstein, Mark K. (FL) - 1986
Gonzalez, Henry B. (TX) - 1958
Goode, R. J. (AL) - 1938
Goodenough, Keith B. (WY) - 1986
Goodover, Pat M. (MT) - 1984
Goodwin, Gregory (HI) - 1994
Gordy, William J. (DE) - 1980
Gore, Louise (MD) - 1974, 1978
Gorman, Robert N. (OH) - 1958
Gormley, Bill (NJ) - 1989
Gottlieb, Richard F. (VT) - 1982, 1984, 1986, 1988, 1990, 1992, 1994
Gowen, Charlie (GA) - 1954
Graddick, Charles (AL) - 1986
Gragson, Oran K. (NV) - 1962
Graham, A. H. (NC) - 1936
Graham, Bob (FL) - 1978
Graham, E. F. (ND) - 1944
Graham, Milton H. (AZ) - 1974
Granai, Edwin C. (VT) - 1978
Granberry, Jim (TX) - 1974
Grandmaison, J. Joseph (NH) - 1990
Grandy, Fred (IA) - 1994
Grant, John F. (TX) - 1930
Grant, Philip R. (NM) - 1978
Grass, Calvin F. (ME) - 1970
Grasso, Ella T. (CT) - 1978
Gravely, Lee (NC) - 1940
Graves, Bibb (AL) - 1922, 1926, 1934
Graves, Bill (KS) - 1994
Gray, James H. (GA) - 1966
Greely, Mike (MT) - 1988
Green, James C. (NC) - 1984
Green, Norman (AZ) - 1966
Green, Robert A. "Lex" (FL) - 1944
Greene, Keith H. (CA) - 1970
Greenspan, Elliot (NJ) - 1984
Greenspun, H. M. (NV) - 1962
Greenstein, Hyman (HI) - 1962
Gregg, Hugh (NH) - 1958, 1960, 1966
Gregg, Judd (NH) - 1988, 1990
Grevemberg, Francis C. (LA) - 1956, 1959
Griffen, Horace B. (AZ) - 1956
Griffin, Ben Hill (FL) - 1974
Griffin, James C. (CA) - 1982
Griffin, S. Marvin (GA) - 1954, 1962
Griffith, Leon (AR) - 1976
Griisser, Frederick M. (MD) - 1990
Gropper, John L. (VT) - 1994, 1996
Groszer, Andrew J. (MD) - 1966
Grover, Henry C. (TX) - 1972

Grunseth, Jon (MN) - 1990
Gubbrud, Archie M. (SD) - 1960, 1962
Guion, George Seth (LA) - 1932
Gundersen, Lamont B. (UT) - 1960
Guy, William L. (ND) - 1960, 1962, 1964, 1968
Gwin, William (VT) - 1990
Gwinn, L. E. (TN) - 1922, 1930

H

Hackel, Stella B. (VT) - 1976
Hackett, Luther F. (VT) - 1972
Haegen, Florence (MT) - 1980
Hafer, Barbara (PA) - 1990
Hagemeister, Bruce (NE) - 1966
Hagen, Orville W. (ND) - 1980
Hagen, Oscar W. (SD) - 1974
Hager, Elizabeth (NH) - 1992
Hager, Henry (PA) - 1978
Haines, H. H. (TX) - 1926
Halcrow, Donald M. (ND) - 1964
Haldiman, Joe (AZ) - 1962
Hale, Virginia (OK) - 1994
Haley, J. Evetts (TX) - 1956
Halford, Rick (AK) - 1990
Hall, Chuck (FL) - 1970
Hall, David (OK) - 1966, 1970, 1974
Hall, Fred (KS) - 1956, 1958
Hall, John (TX) - 1972
Hamburg, Al (WY) - 1986
Hamil, David A. (CO) - 1962
Hamlin, Thurman J. (KY) - 1959, 1971, 1987
Hamm, Philip J. (AL) - 1950
Hammond, Jay S. (AK) - 1974, 1978
Hance, Kent (TX) - 1986, 1990
Hand, Fred (GA) - 1954
Haney, Franklin (TN) - 1974
Hannah, Harvey (TN) - 1922
Hansen, Clifford P. (WY) - 1962
Hansen, Gracie (OR) - 1970
Hansen, Lowell (SD) - 1986
Hansen, Robert V. (NE) - 1978
Hanson, H. Max (ID) - 1958
Hanson, Stewart (UT) - 1992
Hao, Joseph K. (HI) - 1974
Harbour, Mack (AR) - 1972
Hardage, Sam (KS) - 1982
Hardee, Cary A. (FL) - 1920, 1932
Hardin, Joe C. (AR) - 1960
Hardman, Lamartine G. (GA) - 1926, 1928
Hardwick, Chuck (NJ) - 1989
Hardwick, Thomas W. (GA) - 1920, 1922, 1932
Hardy, Paul (LA) - 1979
Hare, James M. (MI) - 1960
Hargis, Burns (OK) - 1990
Harman, Rick (KS) - 1968, 1970
Harmon, David S. (WI) - 1994
Harper, John (KY) - 1987
Harris, Bill (NE) - 1990
Harris, Carmon C. (OK) - 1958
Harris, Fred R. (OK) - 1962
Harris, Joe Frank (GA) - 1982, 1986
Harrison, Albertis S. Jr. (VA) - 1961
Hart, Edwin L. (NE) - 1956
Hart, George (KS) - 1962, 1964, 1966
Hartigan, Neil F. (IL) - 1990
Hartman, Edward M. (NM) - 1970
Hartnett, Thomas F. (SC) - 1994
Harvey, W. Brantley (SC) - 1978
Hatch, Francis W. (MA) - 1978
Hatch, Mike (MN) - 1990, 1994
Hatfield, Mark O. (OR) - 1958, 1962
Hathaway, Fons A. (FL) - 1928
Hathaway, Stan (WY) - 1966, 1970
Haugh, John (AZ) - 1966

Hawkins, Reginald A. (NC) - 1968, 1972
Hawley, Clifford J. (NM) - 1966, 1968
Hayden, Mike (KS) - 1986, 1990
Hayden, Tom (CA) - 1994
Hayes, Bert (AL) - 1978
Hayes, Joe L. (AK) - 1986
Hayes, Kyle (NC) - 1956
Hayes, Robin (NC) - 1996
Hayes, Thomas L. (VT) - 1966, 1970
Haynie, G. R. (AR) - 1920
Hays, Brooks (AR) - 1928, 1930, 1966
Head, Douglas M. (MN) - 1970
Head, Jim (OK) - 1978
Headlee, Richard H. (MI) - 1982
Heard, Paul (GA) - 1994
Hearnes, Betty C. (MO) - 1988
Hearnes, Warren E. (MO) - 1964, 1968
Hechler, Ken (WV) - 1976
Hechtner, Howard D. (ID) - 1962
Hector, Louis H. (NE) - 1958
Heftel, Cecil (HI) - 1986
Heigaard, Bill (ND) - 1992
Helbing, Stephen C. (NM) - 1970
Hellstoski, Henry (NJ) - 1969
Helms, Ned (NH) - 1992
Hemmings, Fred (HI) - 1990
Henderson, Frank E. (SD) - 1970
Henderson, J. Bruce (AL) - 1950, 1954
Henkle, Joseph W. (KS) - 1964
Henry, Dwight (TN) - 1990
Henry, E. L. (LA) - 1979
Henzler, Jude (AK) - 1994
Herbert (SC) - 1930
Herbert, Mary Alice (VT) - 1996
Herndon, Charles (ID) - 1962, 1966
Herrin, Bud (GA) - 1978
Herring, Jim (MS) - 1979
Herschler, Ed (WY) - 1974, 1978, 1982
Herseth, R. Lars (SD) - 1986
Herseth, Ralph (SD) - 1956, 1958, 1960, 1962
Hewlett, Steve (TN) - 1994
Hickel, Walter J. (AK) - 1966, 1974, 1978, 1986
Hickey, J. J. (WY) - 1958
Higby, Lester H. (CA) - 1974
Higgins, George N. (MI) - 1964
High, Robert King (FL) - 1964, 1966
Hildreth, Horace (ME) - 1958
Hill, John (TX) - 1968, 1978
Hillenbrand, John A. (IN) - 1980
Hines, Harry (TX) - 1940
Hitchcock, E. D. (HI) - 1959
Hobbs, Horace, E. (RI) - 1966
Hobby, Wilbur (NC) - 1972
Hoch, Ed (AK) - 1986
Hoch, Nancy (NE) - 1986
Hocker, Lon (MO) - 1956
Hodges, Luther H. (NC) - 1956
Hodges, William C. (FL) - 1936
Hoegh, Leo A. (IA) - 1956
Hoey, Clyde R. (NC) - 1936
Hoff, Philip H. (VT) - 1962, 1964, 1966
Hoffman (NC) - 1940
Hoffman, Joseph A. (NJ) - 1977
Hoffman, LeRoy G. (SD) - 1978
Hogan, Lawrence J. (MD) - 1974
Hogan, Mark (CA) - 1970
Hogan, Mike (CO) - 1970
Holder, John N. (GA) - 1920, 1926, 1930, 1932
Holdiman, Al (OR) - 1970
Holland, Spessard L. (FL) - 1940
Holland, Thomas E. (NM) - 1960
Hollenbach, Todd (KY) - 1975
Holley, Charles R. (FL) - 1964

Hollings, Ernest F. (SC) - 1958
Hollingsworth, Marvin J. (OR) - 1978
Hollis, Ray (TX) - 1994
Holloway, Clyde C. (LA) - 1991
Holmes, Robert D. (OR) - 1956, 1958
Holshouser, James E. (NC) - 1972
Holt, Frank (AR) - 1966
Holt, Jack (AR) - 1948, 1952
Hooker, John J. (TN) - 1966, 1970
Hooper, Ruby T. (NC) - 1984, 1992
Hopkins, Larry J. (KY) - 1991
Hoppe, Harley (WA) - 1976
Hoppner, Bill (NE) - 1990
Horn, Calvin (NM) - 1968
Horton, Henry H. (TN) - 1928, 1930
Horton, W. P. (NC) - 1940
Houck, L. R. (SD) - 1958
Hou-Seye, Edmond E. (WI) - 1974, 1986
Houston, Les (NM) - 1990
Howald, Edwin W. (MO) - 1996
Howard, Marlene (FL) - 1990
Howell, Henry (VA) - 1969, 1977
Howell, Hugh (GA) - 1938
Howlett, Michael J. (IL) - 1976
Hubbard, Carroll (KY) - 1979
Hubbard, Joe (AR) - 1964
Hubbert, Paul R. (AL) - 1990, 1994
Huber, Sherry F. (ME) - 1982
Huggins, Ira A. (UT) - 1960
Hughes, Harold E. (IA) - 1960, 1962, 1964, 1966
Hughes, Harry R. (MD) - 1978, 1982
Hughes, James L. (NM) - 1974
Hughes, Maury (TX) - 1934
Hughes, Richard J. (NJ) - 1961, 1965
Hulley, Lincoln (FL) - 1920
Hultman, Evan (IA) - 1964
Hume, David (MD) - 1962
Hunt, Guy (AL) - 1978, 1986, 1990
Hunt, James B. "Jim" Jr. (NC) - 1976, 1980, 1992, 1996
Hunter, Tom F. (TX) - 1932, 1934, 1936, 1938
Hurst, Q. Byrum (AR) - 1972
Huss, Walter (OR) - 1982
Hutchinson, John G. (WV) - 1976
Hutchison, Ray (TX) - 1982
Hyatt, Gregory S. (MA) - 1986

I

Ingram, John (NC) - 1984
Inhofe, James M. (OK) - 1974
Inslee, Jay (WA) - 1996
Irick, John B. (NM) - 1982
Isakson, Johnny (GA) - 1990

J

Jaccaci, August (VT) - 1994
Jack, William (WY) - 1962
Jackson, Clingan (OH) - 1958
Jackson, Edmund B. (SC) - 1926
Jackson, Larry (ID) - 1978
Jackson, Lowell B. (WI) - 1982
Jackson, Shelby M. (LA) - 1963
Jackvony, Louis (RI) - 1962
Jacobsen, Alan (NE) - 1994
Jacobson, Alvin J. (PA) - 1974
Jacquin, William C. (AZ) - 1974
James, Forrest H. "Fob" Jr. (AL) - 1978, 1986, 1990, 1994
James, Peter (MD) - 1970
James, Ted (MT) - 1968
Jancek, Steve (AZ) - 1982
Janklow, William J. (SD) - 1978, 1982, 1994
Jarman, Maxey (TN) - 1970
Jeffords, James M. (VT) - 1972

Jenkins, William (TN) - 1970
Jennings, Frank E. (FL) - 1924
Jester, Beauford H. (TX) - 1946, 1948
Johns, Charley E. (FL) - 1954
Johnson, Carl A. (WY) - 1982
Johnson, Charles M. (NC) - 1948
Johnson, Donald E. (IA) - 1968
Johnson, Gary E. (NM) - 1994
Johnson, George W. (AR) - 1958
Johnson, James D. (AR) - 1956, 1966
Johnson, John A. (IN) - 1992
Johnson, John W. (MN) - 1974
Johnson, Joseph B. (VT) - 1956
Johnson, Joseph E. (KY) - 1987
Johnson, Paul (AZ) - 1994
Johnson, Paul B. Jr. (MS) - 1947, 1951, 1955, 1963
Johnson, Pete (MS) - 1991
Johnson, Robert W. (MN) - 1978
Johnson, Virginia (AR) - 1968
Johnson, W. L. (MI) - 1958
Johnston, Harry (FL) - 1986
Johnston, Harvey F. (PA) - 1962, 1974
Johnston, J. Bennett (LA) - 1971
Johnston, Olin D. (SC) - 1930, 1934, 1942
Johnston, Oscar (MS) - 1919
Johnston, William C. (SC) - 1958
Jondahl, Lynn (MI) - 1994
Jones, Brereton C. (KY) - 1991
Jones, Dick (WY) - 1974
Jones, Guy (AR) - 1954
Jones, Jan L. (NV) - 1994
Jones, Larry (KS) - 1986
Jones, Robert R. (LA) - 1975
Jones, Sam H. (LA) - 1940, 1948
Jones, Walter H. (NJ) - 1961
Jones, William L. (AR) - 1994
Jordan, Robert B. (NC) - 1988
Judge, Thomas L. (MT) - 1972, 1976, 1980, 1988
Juelfs, Stanley R. (NE) - 1978
Junkins, Lowell L. (IA) - 1986

K

Kaiser, Edmon V. (CA) - 1974
Kaldor, Lee (ND) - 1996
Karcher, Alan J. (NJ) - 1989
Kariotis, George (MA) - 1986
Karl, Frederick B. (FL) - 1964
Karpan, Kathy (WY) - 1994
Kasten, Bob (WI) - 1978
Katz, Sam (PA) - 1994
Kaufman, Paul J. (WV) - 1968
Kay, Morris (KS) - 1972
Kay, Wendell P. (AK) - 1966
Kealoha, James K. (HI) - 1962
Kean, Thomas H. (NJ) - 1977, 1981, 1985
Keathley, Elizabeth (CA) - 1974
Keating, Frank (OK) - 1994
Kecskemethy, Laszlo (CA) - 1978
Keenan, Edward T. (FL) - 1944
Keith (SC) - 1930
Keith, A. M. (MN) - 1966
Kelleher, Robert "Bob" Carlson (MT) - 1984, 1996
Keller, Fred (AR) - 1942
Kelley, David F. (VT) - 1994
Kelley, Doug (MN) - 1990
Kelley, Harry W. (MD) - 1982
Kelley, Peter S. (ME) - 1974
Kelley, V. A. (IL) - 1982
Kelly, Francis E. (MA) - 1960
Kelly, Margaret (MO) - 1996
Kelly, Scott (FL) - 1964, 1966
Kelly, William F. (NJ) - 1969

Kendall, Bruce (AK) - 1966
Kenna, Lee M. (WV) - 1972
Kennedy, John F. (MA) - 1960
Kennedy, Walter L. (VT) - 1974
Kennerly, T. E. (TX) - 1966
Kennon, Robert F. (LA) - 1948, 1952, 1963
Kerner, Otto (IL) - 1960, 1964
Kerr, Fred (KS) - 1994
Kerrey, Bob (NE) - 1982
Kerttula, Jalmar M. (AK) - 1978
Keyser, F. Ray (VT) - 1960, 1962
Kezer, Pauline R. (CT) - 1994
Kihei, David (HI) - 1959
Kilgo, John W. (TN) - 1944
Killian, Robert K. (CT) - 1978
King, Bruce (NM) - 1968, 1970, 1978, 1990, 1994
King, C. B. (GA) - 1970
King, Edward F. (MA) - 1978
King, Edward J. (MA) - 1978, 1982
King, Jean (HI) - 1982
King, Joe (WA) - 1992
King, John W. (NH) - 1962, 1964, 1966
King, R. J. (MO) - 1972
King, Samuel P. (HI) - 1970
King, Wayne D. (NH) - 1994
Kingsbury, Robert (NH) - 1996
Kinley, George R. (IA) - 1986
Kinney, Harry F. (NM) - 1990
Kirk, Claude R. Jr. (FL) - 1966, 1970, 1978
Kirkland, Mickey (AL) - 1994
Kirscht, Bob (CO) - 1986
Kitchenmaster, Leslie (KS) - 1994
Kitzhaber, John (OR) - 1994
Kitzmiller, Elmore F. (FL) - 1952
Klein, Ann (NJ) - 1973
Klein, T. William (KY) - 1975
Kleindienst, Richard (AZ) - 1964
Kline, Ernest P. (PA) - 1978
Kneip, Richard F. (SD) - 1970, 1972, 1974, 1986
Knight, Harold (KS) - 1978
Knobel, Ralph (NE) - 1994
Knoll, Catherine B. (PA) - 1994
Knous, Robert L. (CO) - 1966
Knowland, William F. (CA) - 1958
Knowles, Tony (AK) - 1990, 1994
Knowles, Warren P. (WI) - 1964, 1966, 1968
Knox, Eugene (PA) - 1982
Knox, H. Edward (NC) - 1984
Knox, John (GA) - 1994
Knutson, Milo G. (WI) - 1964
Koch, Edward I. (NY) - 1982
Kohler, Terry J. (WI) - 1982
Koory, Fred (AZ) - 1990
Kramer, Lawrence F. (NJ) - 1981
Kreshtool, Jacob (DE) - 1988
Krupsak, Mary Anne (NY) - 1978
Kryzan, Frank X. (OH) - 1956
Kuchera, Mike (MT) - 1960, 1964
Kuehn, Philip G. (WI) - 1960, 1962
Kuhlmann, Henry E. (NE) - 1966
Kuhn, Fred (FL) - 1982
Kulongowski, Ted (OR) - 1982
Kundert, Alice (SD) - 1986
Kunin, Madeleine M. (VT) - 1982, 1984, 1986, 1988
Kunst, Robert P. (FL) - 1982
Kurfess, Charles F. (OH) - 1978

L

Labriola, Gerald (CT) - 1986
Lacey, Charles (SD) - 1958
Lader, Phil (SC) - 1986
Lady, Frank (AR) - 1976, 1978
Lady, Wendell (KS) - 1982

LaFleur, Alexander A. (KY) - 1956
La Follette, Bronson C. (WI) - 1968
LaFountain, Lloyd P. (ME) - 1974
Lake, I. Beverly (NC) - 1960, 1964
Lake, I. Beverly Jr. (NC) - 1980
Lakian, John R. (MA) - 1982
Lambert, Louis (LA) - 1979
Lamm, Richard D. (CO) - 1974, 1978, 1982
Lamontagne, Ovide M. (NH) - 1996
Lance, Bert (GA) - 1974
Landrieu, Mary L. (LA) - 1995
Laney, Ben T. (AR) - 1944, 1946, 1950
Laney, George K. (SC) - 1922, 1926
Lanier, Wayne (AR) - 1986
Lankford, George (GA) - 1974
Lannon, T. James (VT) - 1974
La Riva, Gloria Estela (CA) - 1994
Larkins, John D. (NC) - 1960
Larry, Jackson (ID) - 1978
Larsen, Allan (ID) - 1978
Larsen, Richard (ND) - 1972
Larsen, Richard R. (NE) - 1970
Larson, John B. (CT) - 1994
Latimer, George (MN) - 1986
Lau, Cheryl A. (NV) - 1994
Lauve, John (MI) - 1990
Lavelle, Edward P. (PA) - 1958
Lawrence, David (PA) - 1958
Lawton, Edwin G. (OH) - 1970
Laxalt, Paul (NV) - 1966
Layne, Donald D. (AR) - 1958
Leatherman, Hugh (SC) - 1986
Leavitt, Dixie L. (UT) - 1976
Leavitt, Mike (UT) - 1992
Leavitt, Myron E. (NV) - 1982
LeBlanc, Dudley J. (LA) - 1932, 1944, 1952
Leche, Richard W. (LA) - 1936
Leddy, Bernard J. (VT) - 1958
Lee, Blair (MD) - 1978
Lee, Charles A. (MO) - 1956
Lee, J. Bracken (UT) - 1956
Lees, Jim (WV) - 1996
Lehrman, Lew (NY) - 1982
Leighton, Porter D. (ME) - 1986
Leimback, Harry E. (WY) - 1974
Leinemann, Del (NE) - 1960
Lemon, Doug (MS) - 1987
Leonard, Donald S. (MI) - 1956
Leonard, Elizabeth Ann (RI) - 1992
Leonard, Paul J. (MO) - 1972
Leonard, Richard W. (NH) - 1974
Leopold, John (HI) - 1978
Leota, Alema (HI) - 1978
Leroy, David H. (ID) - 1986
LeVander, Harold (MN) - 1966
Lever (SC) - 1930
Levesque, J. Michael (RI) - 1992
Levin, Sander (MI) - 1970, 1974
Lewallen, John (CA) - 1994
Lewin, John (HI) - 1994
Lewis, Andrew L. (PA) - 1974
Lewis, Steve (OK) - 1990
Lewter, V. Gene (AZ) - 1978
Ley, Henry E. (NE) - 1966
Licht, Frank (RI) - 1968, 1970
Lim, John K. (OR) - 1990
Lindau, James H. (MN) - 1986
Lindauer, John (AK) - 1990
Linder, Tom (GA) - 1954
Lindley, John F. (SD) - 1964
Lindquist, Elvin A. (ID) - 1962
Lindsay, Roderick (WA) - 1956
Lindsey, Jim (AR) - 1976
Lindstedt, Martin (MO) - 1996
Link, Arthur A. (ND) - 1972, 1976, 1980
Lint, Lewis E. (IA) - 1962
Lipman, Sumner H. (ME) - 1994
List, Robert F. (NV) - 1978, 1982

Livengood, William S. (PA) - 1958
Livingston, Bob (LA) - 1987
Locke, Bobby (TX) - 1986
Locke, Eugene (TX) - 1968
Locke, Gary (WA) - 1996
Loeffler, Tom (TX) - 1986
Loeta, Alema (HI) - 1978
Loftus, Thomas (WI) - 1990
Lohman, Joseph D. (IL) - 1960
Londen, Jack (AZ) - 1978
London, Herbert I. (NY) - 1990
Long (SC) - 1946
Long, Earl K. (LA) - 1940, 1948,
   1956
Long, Gillis W. (LA) - 1963, 1971
Long, Huey P. (LA) - 1924, 1928
Long, Speedy O. (LA) - 1971
Longino, A. H. (MS) - 1919
Looney, Ben F. (TX) - 1920
Lopez, Junio (NM) - 1970
Lord, John F. (ND) - 1958
Lord, Michael H. (OH) - 1990
Love, John A. (CO) - 1962, 1966,
   1970
Love, T. B. (TX) - 1930
Loveless, Herschel C. (IA) - 1956,
   1958
Loveless, Wayne L. (ID) - 1978
Lovett, Billy (GA) - 1982
Lovett, Sid (NH) - 1996
Lowe, A. Lynn (AR) - 1978
Lowe, W. O. (TN) - 1944, 1946
Lowery, H. C. (TN) - 1944
Lowery, Sumter L. (FL) - 1956
Lowry, Mike (WA) - 1992
Lucas, William (MI) - 1986
Luce, Tom (TX) - 1990
Lucey, Patrick J. (WI) - 1966, 1970,
   1974
Ludeman, Cal R. (MN) - 1986
Luelf, Steve (AR) - 1994
Lukens, Donald E. (OH) - 1970
Luksik, Marguerite A. (PA) - 1990
Lumpkin, Sam (MS) - 1951
Luna, Casey E. (NM) - 1994
Lusk, Thomas E. (NM) - 1966
Lyons, Charlton H. Sr. (LA) - 1963

M

Mabus, Ray (MS) - 1987, 1991
MacBride, Roger (VT) - 1964
Machtley, Ronald K. (RI) - 1994
MacKinnon, George (MN) - 1958
Maddox, Lester (GA) - 1966, 1974
Maddy, Ken (CA) - 1978
Mahoney, Eugene H. (MT) - 1968
Mahoney, George P. (MD) - 1962,
   1966
Maleng, Norm (WA) - 1988
Maleng, Norm (WA) - 1996
Mallberg, Leon L. (ND) - 1988
Malone, J. M. (AR) - 1946
Manchin, Joe III (WV) - 1996
Mandel, Marvin (MD) - 1970
Mangan, Michael J. (WI) - 1994
Mangham, J. J. (GA) - 1938
Mangiamelli, Tony (NE) - 1962
Manning, Wyndham (SC) - 1934,
   1938, 1942
Mantooth, Donald W. (IN) - 1984
Mapp, G. Walter (VA) - 1925, 1929
March, Caso (TX) - 1948, 1950
Marriott, Dan (UT) - 1984
Marshall, Edward G. (NV) - 1966
Marston, David W. (PA) - 1978
Martin, Billy (NC) - 1988
Martin, James G. (NC) - 1984, 1988
Martin, John W. (FL) - 1924, 1932
Martin, Paul (TX) - 1970
Martin, Ried (KY) - 1971

Martin, Roddy T. (SC) - 1982
Martin, Roger (OR) - 1978
Martin, Verne O. (AK) - 1962
Martin, Wade O. (LA) - 1975
Martineau, John E. (AR) - 1924,
   1926
Martinez, Bob (FL) - 1986, 1990
Martinez, Elizabeth (CA) - 1982
Marty, John (MN) - 1994
Marvel, Richard D. (NE) - 1974
Marzullo, Vincent (RI) - 1982
Masel, Bennett A. (WI) - 1990
Mash, Jerry L. (OK) - 1978
Mason, Tony (AZ) - 1986
Matheson, Scott M. (UT) - 1976
Mathews, John E. (FL) - 1964, 1970
Mathis, John (IL) - 1972
Mattox, Jim (TX) - 1990
Maxwell, A. J. (NC) - 1940
Maxwell, Allen J. (NC) - 1932
Maybank, Burnet R. (SC) - 1938,
   1962
Mayer, Edwin S. (TX) - 1958
Mayfield, Bobby M. (NM) - 1968,
   1974
Mayfield, E. B. (TX) - 1930
McAlister, Hill (TN) - 1926, 1928,
   1932, 1934
McAlpine, Stephen (AK) - 1990,
   1994
McBrayer, Odell (TX) - 1974
McBrayer, Terry (KY) - 1979
McBride, Jon (WV) - 1996
McCaleb, Neal A. (OK) - 1982
McCall, Charles C. (AL) - 1930
McCall, Tom (OR) - 1966, 1970,
   1978
McCarney, Robert P. (ND) - 1964,
   1968, 1972
McCarty, Daniel T. (FL) - 1948, 1952
McCarty, John M. (FL) - 1960
McCarty, Virginia Dill (IN) - 1984
McCary, Elvin (AL) - 1974
McClaughry, John (VT) - 1992
McClerkin, Hayes C. (AR) - 1970
McCord, James N. (TN) - 1944,
   1946, 1948
McCord, Leon (AL) - 1934
McCormack, Edward J. (MA) - 1966
McCormick, James L. (MI) - 1970
McCorquodale, Joe C. (AL) - 1982
McCraw, William (TX) - 1938
McCready, Jerome (CA) - 1990,
   1994
McCullough, Patrick (MI) - 1978
McDermott, Francis X. (NJ) - 1969
McDermott, James A. (WA) - 1972,
   1980, 1984
McDonald, C. C. (TX) - 1934
McDonald, Dan (WA) - 1992
McDonald, Ed F. (AR) - 1936
McDonald, John K. (MT) - 1976
McDonald, Lauren (GA) - 1990
McDonald, Leo J. (WI) - 1970
McDonald, Ralph (NC) - 1936, 1944
McDonald, Sid (AL) - 1978
McDonald, Thomas E. (MN) - 1974
McDonnell, Jessop (WA) - 1964
McDowell (AL) - 1926
McDowell, Earl S. (PA) - 1982
McEachern, Paul (NH) - 1984, 1986,
   1988
McElroy, Mark (OH) - 1962, 1970
McElroy, Tom (TX) - 1972
McFarland, Ernest W. (AZ) - 1956
McGeever, Francis T. (PA) - 1970
McGonigle, A. T. (PA) - 1958
McGrath, Mike (MT) - 1992
McGraw, Warren R. (WV) - 1984
McGreevey, James (NJ) - 1997
McGuire, Pat (WY) - 1982, 1986
McGuirk, Harry J. (MD) - 1982

McIlwain, Harry H. (OH) - 1966
McKeithen, John J. (LA) - 1963,
   1964, 1967
McKellips, Roger (SD) - 1978
McKernan, John R. (ME) - 1986,
   1990
McKinley, David (WV) - 1996
McKinstry, Margaret (WY) - 1978
McKrell, James (AR) - 1948
McLain, Gene (AL) - 1974
McLean, Angus Wilton (NC) - 1924
McLemore, James M. (LA) - 1952,
   1956
McLeod, James C. (SC) - 1946
McLeod, Thomas G. (SC) - 1922,
   1924
McManus, E. J. (IA) - 1960
McMath, Sidney S. (AR) - 1948,
   1950, 1952, 1962
McMillan (AR) - 1954
McMillan, Benton (TN) - 1922
McMillan, Colin R. (NM) - 1986
McMillan, George (AL) - 1982, 1986
McMurry, Robert M. (TN) - 1948
McNair, Nimrod (GA) - 1994
McNair, Robert E. (SC) - 1966
McNary, Gene (MO) - 1972, 1984
McNeill, Robert H. (NC) - 1940
McNichols, Stephen (CO) - 1956,
   1958, 1962
McQuown, Sally (WA) - 1992
McRae, Thomas C. (AR) - 1920,
   1922
McRae, Tom (AR) - 1990
McSpadden, Clem R. (OK) - 1974
McSparren, J. Collins (PA) - 1962
McWherter, Ned (TN) - 1986, 1990
Mead, Ed V. (NM) - 1962
Mead, Mary (WY) - 1990
Mecham, Evan (AZ) - 1964, 1974,
   1978, 1982, 1986, 1990
Mechem, Edwin L. (NM) - 1956,
   1958, 1960, 1962
Medlock, T. Travis (SC) - 1994
Melich, Mitchell (UT) - 1964
Mercer, Joseph H. (NM) - 1986
Merdes, Edward A. (AK) - 1978
Merlino, Joseph P. (NJ) - 1981
Merrell, Norman L. (MO) - 1984
Merrill, Philip L. (ME) - 1984
Merrill, Steve (NH) - 1992, 1994
Meskill, Thomas J. (CT) - 1970
Meyner, Robert B. (NJ) - 1957, 1969
Mickelson, George S. (SD) - 1986,
   1990
Miedusiewski, American Joe (MD) -
   1994
Mildren, Jack (OK) - 1994
Miles, Clarence W. (MD) - 1966
Miller, Andrew P. (VA) - 1977
Miller, B. M. (AL) - 1930
Miller, Barry (TX) - 1930
Miller, Charles S. (MO) - 1972
Miller, Francis P. (VA) - 1949
Miller, Gary V. (CA) - 1986
Miller, Keith (AK) - 1970, 1974
Miller, O. D. (AZ) - 1956
Miller, Robert J. (NV) - 1990, 1994
Miller, Terry (AK) - 1982
Miller, Tom (IA) - 1990
Miller, Vern (KS) - 1974
Miller, Walter D. (SD) - 1994
Miller, Zell (GA) - 1990, 1994
Milliken, William G. (MI) - 1970,
   1974, 1978
Millner, Guy W. (GA) - 1994
Mink, Patsy T. (HI) - 1986
Miskovsky, George (OK) - 1958
Mitchell (MS) - 1931
Mitchell, George J. (ME) - 1974
Mitchell, J. Ridley (TN) - 1942
Mitchell, James P. (NJ) - 1961

Mitchell, Stephen A. (IL) - 1960
Mitchell, Theo (SC) - 1990
Moffett, Charles R. (TN) - 1990
Mollohan, Robert H. (WV) - 1956
Molpus, Dick (MS) - 1995
Mongan, John C. (NH) - 1964
Monier, Robert B. (NH) - 1982
Montague, Harry R. (VT) - 1974
Montgomery, George F. (MI) - 1970
Montgomery, Jimmy D. (KS) - 1982
Moody, Dan (TX) - 1926, 1928
Moody, Mike (NV) - 1982
Mooney, Thomas J. (MD) - 1986
Moore, Arch A. Jr. (WV) - 1968,
   1972, 1980, 1984, 1988
Moore, Dan K. (NC) - 1964
Moore, John (HI) - 1978
Moore, Preston (OK) - 1962, 1966
Moretti, Robert (CA) - 1974
Morgan, Lewis L. (LA) - 1944
Morris, Bill (TN) - 1994
Morris, Earle E. Jr. (SC) - 1974
Morris, J. M. (AZ) - 1962, 1964
Morris, Milton (MO) - 1968
Morris, William S. (MO) - 1972
Morrison, Bruce A. (CT) - 1990
Morrison, Cameron (NC) - 1920
Morrison, deLesseps S. (LA) - 1956,
   1959, 1960, 1963, 1964
Morrison, Edward (NY) - 1974
Morrison, Frank (MT) - 1988, 1992
Morrison, Frank B. (NE) - 1960,
   1962, 1964
Morrison, James H. (LA) - 1940,
   1944, 1948
Morrison, Robert (AZ) - 1958
Morrison, Sid (WA) - 1992
Morsa, Chuck (CA) - 1990
Morse, Thomas J. (VT) - 1994, 1996
Morton, Warren A. (WY) - 1982
Moss, David R. (AZ) - 1974, 1978,
   1986, 1990
Moss, Kermit (AR) - 1984
Mouton, Edgar G. (LA) - 1979
Muldrew, Richard B. (FL) - 1966
Mullen, Martin P. (PA) - 1974
Munoz, Maria E. (CA) - 1986, 1990
Murphree, Dennis (MS) - 1927, 1935,
   1943
Murphy, Dan (MI) - 1986
Murphy, Jack M. (ID) - 1974
Murphy, Leo T. (NM) - 1962
Murphy, Michael (NJ) - 1997
Murphy, Nyla (WY) - 1990
Murphy, Robert F. (MA) - 1960
Murray, Erwin L. (PA) - 1966
Murray, Roger (TN) - 1978
Murray, William G. (IA) - 1958, 1966
Murry (AR) - 1952
Musa, Ben (OR) - 1966
Muskie, Edmund S. (ME) - 1956
Mutz, John M. (IN) - 1988
Myers, Clay (OR) - 1974
Myers, J. Howard (WV) - 1956
Myers, Robert (WV) - 1972

N

Nader, George (AZ) - 1970
Nance, Carroll D. (SC) - 1926
Natelson, Rob (MT) - 1996
Nation, Bill (WY) - 1966
Neal, John R. (TN) - 1924, 1944
Neely, Harold E. (WV) - 1960
Neff, Pat M. (TX) - 1920, 1922
Nelsen, Ancher (MN) - 1956
Nelson, Ben (NE) - 1990, 1994
Nelson, Bill (FL) - 1990
Nelson, Donovan D. (IA) - 1978
Nelson, Gaylord (WI) - 1958, 1960
Nelson, Sheffield (AR) - 1990, 1994

Nereim, Robert L. (IA) - 1970
Nesbitt, Charles (OK) - 1966
Netsch, Dawn C. (IL) - 1994
Neuman, Ted (MT) - 1988
New, Jack L. (IN) - 1976
Nicholas, David R. (WY) - 1986
Nicholas, W. H. (IA) - 1956, 1960, 1962
Nielsen, Warren A. (CA) - 1970
Nigh, George (OK) - 1962, 1978, 1982
Nimic, Robb (NE) - 1994
Niquette, Russell F. (VT) - 1960
Nix, Abit (GA) - 1932, 1940
Nixon, David L. (NH) - 1974
Nixon, Richard M. (CA) - 1962
Noe, J. A. (LA) - 1940
Noe, James A. (LA) - 1959
Noel, Philip W. (RI) - 1972, 1974
Nolan, James D. (OH) - 1974
Nordhougen, Orris G. (ND) - 1960
Notte, John A. (RI) - 1960, 1962
Nugent, James W. (RI) - 1974
Nunn, Louie B. (KY) - 1963, 1967, 1979
Nutter, Donald G. (MT) - 1960

O

Oakes, James L. (VT) - 1968
O'Bannon, Frank L. (IN) - 1988, 1996
O'Brannon, Mary (AK) - 1986
O'Brien, Anna Belle Clement (TN) - 1982
O'Brien, Leo (VT) - 1970
O'Brien, Robert (VT) - 1976
O'Callaghan, Mike (NV) - 1970, 1974
O'Connell, John J. (WA) - 1968
O'Connor, Michael J. (SD) - 1982
O'Connor, Timothy J. (VT) - 1980
O'Daniel, W. Lee (TX) - 1938, 1940, 1956, 1958
Odham, Brailey (FL) - 1952, 1954
O'Donnell, Kenneth P. (MA) - 1966, 1970
Ogelsby, J Mark (MO) - 1996
Ogilvie, Richard B. (IL) - 1968, 1972
Ogle, James (CA) - 1994
O'Hara, Shawn (MS) - 1995
O'Herron, Edward M. (NC) - 1976
Oldham, Dortch (TN) - 1974
Olgiati, P. R. (TN) - 1962
Olive, Hubert E. (NC) - 1952
Olmstead, Ralph (ID) - 1982
Olsen, Arnold H. (MT) - 1956
Olson, Allen I. (ND) - 1980, 1984
Olson, Jack B. (WI) - 1970
Olson, John E. (SD) - 1974
O'Neal (SC) - 1946
O'Neill, C. William (OH) - 1956, 1958
O'Neill, Danny (MT) - 1956
Orgill, Edmund (TN) - 1958
O'Rouke, Andrew P. (NY) - 1986
Orr, Kay (NE) - 1986, 1990
Orr, Robert D. (IN) - 1980, 1984
Orza, Vince (OK) - 1990
O'Shea, Bernard G. (VT) - 1978
Ostlund, John C. (WY) - 1978
Otter, C. L. (ID) - 1978
Ouzts, D. A. G. (SC) - 1926
Owen, Dave (KS) - 1982
Owen, Larry (MI) - 1994
Owens, Wayne (UT) - 1984

P

Page, R. N. (NC) - 1920
Page, Vivian L. (VA) - 1937, 1941
Pajcvie, Steve (FL) - 1986
Palmer, Linwood E. (ME) - 1978
Palumbo, Mario J. (WV) - 1988, 1992

Paolino, Joseph R. (RI) - 1990
Parker, Barry T. (NJ) - 1981
Parker, John M. (LA) - 1920
Parnell, Harvey J. (AR) - 1928, 1930
Parris, George N. (MI) - 1970
Parris, Stanford E. (VA) - 1989
Parsekian, Ned J. (NJ) - 1969
Pascal, Robert A. (MD) - 1982
Paschen, Herbert C. (IL) - 1956
Passailaigue, Ernie (SC) - 1990
Pataki, George E. (NY) - 1994
Patric, John (WA) - 1960
Patterson (AL) - 1926
Patterson, John (AL) - 1958
Patterson, L. Brooks (MI) - 1982
Patterson, M. R. (TN) - 1932
Patton, Paul E. (KY) - 1995
Patty, Hubert D. (TN) - 1962, 1990
Paty, B. F. (FL) - 1936, 1940
Paulus, Norma (OR) - 1986
Pavlock, Joseph L. (MD) - 1962
Peabody, Endicott (MA) - 1960, 1962, 964
Peabody, George (HI) - 1994
Pearce (SC) - 1934
Pearl, Art (OR) - 1970
Pearson, Linley E. (IN) - 1992
Pearson, Walter J. (OR) - 1962
Peay, Austin (TN) - 1922, 1924, 1926
Peck, Roy (WY) - 1974
Peckham, Richard J. (KS) - 1986, 1990
Pedersen, Richard (MN) - 1978
Peeples, Thomas H. (SC) - 1926
Percy, Charles H. (IL) - 1964
Perpich, Rudy (MN) - 1978, 1982, 1986, 1990
Perry, George C. (VA) - 1933
Perry, John (WY) - 1994
Perry, John F. (PA) - 1994
Persons, Gordon (AL) - 1946, 1950
Peters, Robert L. (TN) - 1958
Peterson, Donald O. (WI) - 1970
Peterson, George C. (FL) - 1960
Peterson, John C. (MN) - 1960
Peterson, Russell W. (DE) - 1972
Peterson, Val (NE) - 1966
Peterson, Walter R. (NH) - 1968, 1970, 1972
Pettaway, Raleigh (FL) - 1936
Pfeifer, Paul E. (OH) - 1986
Phares, Robert A. (NE) - 1978
Phelan, Richard (IL) - 1994
Phelps, Fred (KS) - 1990
Phelps, William (MO) - 1980
Phillips, Joseph A. (MD) - 1958
Phillips, Rubel L. (MS) - 1963, 1967
Pickett, Ingram B. (NM) - 1956, 1958
Pickrell, Robert W. (AZ) - 1966
Pierce, Edward C. (MI) - 1982
Pierce, Jerry (OK) - 1994
Pierce, Richard H. (ME) - 1982
Pierce, Steven D. (MA) - 1990
Pierpont, Ross Z. (MD) - 1982, 1990
Pillsbury, John (NH) - 1962, 1964
Pineda, Charles (CA) - 1986
Pittman, Claude (GA) - 1934
Pittman, Ed (MS) - 1971, 1987
Plawecki, David A. (MI) - 1982
Plock, Richard (CO) - 1978
Plomis, Wilfred (DE) - 1992
Plummer, Lawrence E. (IA) - 1956
Plunkett, Moss A. (VA) - 1945
Poag, Charles (GA) - 1994
Pohwell, Ray B. (NM) - 1986
Pollard, Fred G. (VA) - 1969
Pollard, John Garland (VA) - 1929
Pollock, Howard W. (AK) - 1962, 1970

Poole, Joe N. (AL) - 1946
Poore, Floyd G. (KY) - 1991
Pope (SC) - 1950
Pope, Lewis S. (TN) - 1928, 1932, 1934
Pore, Frank (HI) - 1978
Porter, Albert S. (OH) - 1958
Porteus, Hebden (HI) - 1970
Powell, Smead (AR) - 1920
Powell, Wesley (NH) - 1956, 1958, 1960, 1962, 1964, 1968, 1978
Preate, Ernie (PA) - 1994
Preaus, Frederick T. (LA) - 1956
Preis, Phil (LA) - 1995
Preston, Robert F. (NH) - 1990
Preyer, Richardson (NC) - 1964
Price, Bill (OK) - 1990
Price, BraDa Ji (HI) - 1982
Price, James H. (VA) - 1937
Priddy, A. B. (AR) - 1932
Pritchard (NC) - 1940
Pritt, Charlotte (WV) - 1992, 1996
Privette, Coy C. (NC) - 1976
Proffitt, Hansell (TN) - 1958
Proxmire, William (WI) - 1956
Pryor, David (AR) - 1974, 1976
Purcell, Joe (AR) - 1970, 1982

Q

Quarterman, Kenneth B. (GA) - 1986
Quie, Albert H. (MN) - 1978
Quillen, William T. (DE) - 1984
Quinn, Robert (MA) - 1974
Quinn, William F. (HI) - 1959, 1962
Quist, Allen (MN) - 1994

R

Racicot, Marc (MT) - 1992, 1996
Raese, John R. (WV) - 1988
Raiche, Robert E. (NH) - 1972
Rainach, William M. (LA) - 1959
Rainey, Homer P. (TX) - 1946
Rains, Jack (TX) - 1990
Ralls, William (MI) - 1978
Ramirez, Jack (MT) - 1980
Rampton, Calvin L. (UT) - 1964, 1968, 1972
Randolph, Richard (AK) - 1986
Rappa, Daniel D. (DE) - 1992
Rarick, John R. (LA) - 1967
Rasmussen, Clark (IA) - 1974
Ravenel, Arthur (SC) - 1994
Ravenel, Charles D. (SC) - 1974
Ravenscroft, Vernon (ID) - 1970, 1978
Rawlings, Lamar A. (UT) - 1968
Ray, Dixy Lee (WA) - 1976, 1980
Ray, Robert (IA) - 1968, 1970, 1972, 1974, 1978
Reagan, David (TX) - 1972
Reagan, Ronald (CA) - 1966, 1970
Reams, Frazier Jr. (OH) - 1966
Rebsamen, Raymond (AR) - 1966
Redden, Jim (OR) - 1974
Redel, Ruth (MO) - 1996
Redmond, David E. (ME) - 1986
Redwine, Charles D. (GA) - 1936
Reed, Carlton D. (ME) - 1966
Reed, Clyde M. (KS) - 1958
Reed, Howard (AR) - 1934
Reed, Jack (MS) - 1987
Reed, John H. (ME) - 1960, 1962, 1966
Reed, Lavoy (MO) - 1988
Reeser, Gregory (HI) - 1978
Rego, John L. (RI) - 1964
Reichardt, William J. (IA) - 1994
Reider, Robert W. (OH) - 1956
Reilly, John F. (VT) - 1974

Reinecke, Ed (CA) - 1974
Relph, Robert G. (NY) - 1994
Rendell, Edward G. (PA) - 1986
Renk, Wilbur N. (WI) - 1962
Renne, Roland (MT) - 1964
Reusch, Dale (OH) - 1978
Revercomb, Chapman (WV) - 1960
Reynolds, John L. (OR) - 1966
Reynolds, John W. (WI) - 1962, 1964
Rhodes, James A. (OH) - 1962, 1966, 1974, 1978, 1986
Rice, Norman (WA) - 1996
Richards, Ann (TX) - 1990, 1994
Richards, Bob (AK) - 1986
Richards, John G. (SC) - 1926
Richardson, Harrison L. (ME) - 1974
Riche, John E. (IL) - 1982
Ricketts, Willis (AR) - 1962
Rider, Richard (CA) - 1994
Ridge, Tom J. (PA) - 1994
Riley, Bob (AR) - 1974
Riley, Clement A. (MA) - 1962
Riley, Joe (SC) - 1994
Riley, Richard (SC) - 1978, 1982
Rinehart, Jim A. (OK) - 1958
Rinfret, Pierre A. (NY) - 1990
Rivers, Eurith D. (GA) - 1928, 1930, 1936, 1938, 1946
Rivers, Victor (AK) - 1958
Roach, Pam (WA) - 1996
Roberts, Albert H. (TN) - 1920
Roberts, Barbara (OR) - 1990
Roberts, Betty (OR) - 1974
Roberts, Clint (SD) - 1978, 1986
Roberts, Columbus (GA) - 1940
Roberts, Dennis J. (RI) - 1956, 1958
Robertson, C. Donald (WV) - 1968
Robertson, Claude (TN) - 1970
Robertson, F. D. (TX) - 1924
Robertson, Hayes (IL) - 1960
Robinson, Forrest J. (KS) - 1974
Robinson, Paul W. (NM) - 1960
Robinson, Tommy F. (AR) - 1990
Robsion, John M. (KY) - 1959
Roche, John E. (IL) - 1982
Rockefeller, John D. "Jay" IV (WV) - 1972, 1976, 1978
Rockefeller, Nelson A. (NY) - 1970
Rockefeller, Winthrop (AR) - 1964, 1966, 1968, 1970
Roe, Robert A. (NJ) - 1977, 1981
Roemer, Charles "Buddy" (LA) - 1987, 1991, 1995
Roeser, Jack (IL) - 1994
Rogers, Cleeta J. (OK) - 1966
Rogers, Emmet T. (OR) - 1966
Rogers, Fred S. (TX) - 1922
Rogers, H. John (WV) - 1980
Rogers, Sharon (MO) - 1992
Rogers, Vance D. (NE) - 1978
Rolvaag, Karl F. (MN) - 1962, 1966
Romans, Jack (NE) - 1964
Romer, Roy (CO) - 1986, 1990, 1994
Romney, George W. (MI) - 1962, 1964, 1966
Romney, L. C. (UT) - 1956
Romney, Vernon B. (UT) - 1976
Romo, Ricardo (CA) - 1970
Rooney, John J. (WY) - 1970, 1974
Roos, Lawrence K. (MO) - 1968
Roosevelt, Mark (MA) - 1994
Rose, John "Eck" (KY) - 1995
Rose, Robert E. (NV) - 1978
Rosellini, Albert D. (WA) - 1956, 1960, 1964, 1972
Rosenbaum, Richard M. (NY) - 1994
Ross, Albert (LA) - 1971
Ross, Jack (AZ) - 1970, 1974
Roth, William M. (CA) - 1974
Rothman, Kenneth J. (MO) - 1984
Rotthaus, Finlay (NH) - 1996
Rowe, Al (AK) - 1994

Rowland, John G. (CT) - 1994
Rubega, Al (NH) - 1996
Rupert, Emerson H. (FL) - 1960
Russell, Charles H. (NV) - 1958
Russell, Donald S. (SC) - 1958, 1962
Russell, Lee M. (MS) - 1919
Russell, Richard B. (GA) - 1930
Russo, John F. (NJ) - 1985
Rust, Jerry (OR) - 1982
Rzewnicki, Janet C. (DE) - 1996

S

Sachs, Morris B. (IL) - 1956
Sachs, Stephen H. (MD) - 1986
Sadler, Jerry (TX) - 1940, 1946
Saffels, Dale E. (KS) - 1962
Saiki, Patricia F. (HI) - 1994
Salmon, Thomas P. (VT) - 1972, 1974
Sampson, Jessica (AZ) - 1978
Samuels, Howard J. (NY) - 1970, 1974
Samuelson, Bob L. (SD) - 1990
Samuelson, Don (ID) - 1966, 1970
Sanderford, Roy (TX) - 1936
Sanders, Bernard (VT) - 1976
Sanders, Carl E. (GA) - 1962, 1970
Sanders, Robert R. (KS) - 1978
Sandman, Charles W. (NJ) - 1965, 1969, 1973
Sanford, Terry (NC) - 1960
Saposhnek, Trudy (CA) - 1974
Sarcone, C. Robert (NJ) - 1977
Sargent, Dick (CO) - 1994
Sargent, Francis W. (MA) - 1970, 1974
Sauerbrey, Ellen R. (MD) - 1994
Saunders, Phil (SD) - 1958
Sawyer, Grant (NV) - 1958, 1962, 1966
Sawyer, Tom (NC) - 1956
Sceresse, Alexander F. (NM) - 1970
Schaben, James F. (IA) - 1974
Schaefer, William D. (MD) - 1986, 1990
Schafer, Edward T. (ND) - 1992, 1996
Schmitt, Charles J. (PA) - 1962
Schmitz, Richard D. (NE) - 1974
Schnell, Ray (ND) - 1956
Schoemehl, Vince (MO) - 1992
Schofield, Jack (NV) - 1978
Schreiber, Martin J. (WI) - 1978, 1982
Schroeder, Fred (WY) - 1986
Schroeder, Jack (IA) - 1960
Schuck, Steve (CO) - 1986
Schuller, Peter M. (OH) - 1994
Schwartzlose, Monroe A. (AR) - 1980
Schwegmann, John G. (LA) - 1971
Schwinden, Ted (MT) - 1980, 1984
Scott, B. Gary (DE) - 1992
Scott, Charles K. (WY) - 1994
Scott, E. P. (TX) - 1926
Scott, Robert W. (NC) - 1968, 1980
Scott, W. Kerr (NC) - 1948
Scott, William J. (IL) - 1964
Scranton, William W. (PA) - 1962
Scranton, William W. (PA) - 1986
Screen, John P. (NV) - 1966
Seals, Marilyn (CA) - 1978
Searles, Dick (AZ) - 1958
Sears, Harry L. (NJ) - 1969
Sears, John W. (MA) - 1982
Seaton, Fred A. (NE) - 1962
Seawell, Malcolm B. (NC) - 1960
See, Clyde M. (WV) - 1984, 1988
Sego, William A. (NM) - 1982
Seidman, Peter (WI) - 1982
Selawsky, John T. (CA) - 1994

Sellers, Grover (TX) - 1946
Selstad, Tom A. (MT) - 1972
Sensenbrenner, M. E. (OH) - 1958
Shafer, Raymond P. (PA) - 1966
Shaheen, Jeanne (NH) - 1996
Shands, W. A. (FL) - 1948
Shapiro, Peter (NJ) - 1985
Shapiro, Samuel H. (IL) - 1968
Shapp, Milton (PA) - 1966, 1970, 1974
Shaw, John (NH) - 1956, 1958, 1960
Shaw, Robert F. (NH) - 1988
Shaw, Warren W. (KS) - 1956
Shea, Patrick (UT) - 1992
Shearer, William K. (CA) - 1970
Shedrick, Bernice (OK) - 1994
Sheehan, Carroll P. (MA) - 1974
Sheets, Weldon R. (NJ) - 1961
Sheffield, Bill (AK) - 1982, 1986
Sheffield, J. C. (AR) - 1930
Sheldon, Raymond (FL) - 1944
Shell, Joseph C. (CA) - 1962
Shepard, William S. (MD) - 1990, 1994
Shepley, Ethan (MO) - 1964
Sherlock, Chris J. (AL) - 1942
Shevin, Robert L. (FL) - 1978, 1982
Shields, Currin V. (AZ) - 1968
Shivers, Allan (TX) - 1950, 1952, 1954
Sholtz, David (FL) - 1932
Shotts, Ron (OK) - 1978
Shultz, Reynolds (KS) - 1972
Sickles, Carlton R. (MD) - 1966
Sidebotham, Winford (MO) - 1956
Siegelman, Don (AL) - 1990
Sigman, Bruce M. (WA) - 1960
Sigmund, Barbara Boggs (NJ) - 1989
Silber, John (MA) - 1990
Simms, John F. (NM) - 1956
Simon, Paul (IL) - 1972
Simpson, Milward L. (WY) - 1958
Simpson, O. H. (LA) - 1928
Simpson, Peter (WY) - 1986
Simpson, W. A. (VT) - 1960
Sims, J. Bryan (AR) - 1944
Singel, Mark S. (PA) - 1994
Singleton, Julius V. (WV) - 1964
Sinner, George A. (ND) - 1984, 1988
Sisk, Wallace (TX) - 1968
Skeen, Joe (NM) - 1974, 1978
Skeen, Orel (WV) - 1960
Skoien, Leslie C. (OK) - 1962
Slattery, Jim (KS) - 1994
Sloane, Harvey (KY) - 1979, 1983
Small, Clint C. (TX) - 1930, 1934
Small, Frank (MD) - 1962
Smathers, Bruce (FL) - 1978
Smiley, Larry (WI) - 1982
Smith, Denny (OR) - 1994
Smith, Dick (ID) - 1970
Smith, Ed (MT) - 1972
Smith, Elmo E. (OR) - 1956
Smith, George T. (GA) - 1974
Smith, Hulett C. (WV) - 1960, 1964
Smith, Jim (FL) - 1986, 1994
Smith, John Lee (TX) - 1946
Smith, Peter (VT) - 1986
Smith, Preston (TX) - 1968, 1970, 1972, 1978
Smith, Thomas F. X. (NJ) - 1981
Smith, Triaka-Don (HI) - 1990
Smith, Vernon K. (ID) - 1962
Smith, W. Worth (VA) - 1933
Smith, Wiley W. (OR) - 1958
Smylie, Robert E. (ID) - 1958, 1962, 1966
Snelling, Richard A. (VT) - 1966, 1976, 1978, 1980, 1982, 1990
Snider (MS) - 1939
Snoddy, Jim (AR) - 1956

Snodgrass, Stanley (TN) - 1970, 1974
Snyder, John (IN) - 1984
Solomon, Anthony J. (RI) - 1984
Sorenson, Philip C. (NE) - 1966
Sorrell, Frank (NE) - 1956
Spaeth, Nicholas (ND) - 1992
Spaht, Carlos G. (LA) - 1952
Spainhower, James I. (MO) - 1980
Spannaus, Warren (MN) - 1982
Spanos, Harry V. (NH) - 1974, 1976
Sparks, Chauncey (AL) - 1938, 1942, 1950
Specter, Arlen (PA) - 1978
Speers, Jerrold B. (ME) - 1978
Spellman, John (WA) - 1976, 1980, 1984
Spence, Gene (NE) - 1994
Spirou, Chris (NH) - 1984
Springer, Charles E. (NV) - 1966
Springer, Jerry (OH) - 1982
Sprouse, James M. (WV) - 1968, 1976
Stabenow, Debbie (MI) - 1994
Staebler, Neil (MI) - 1964
Stafford, Robert T. (VT) - 1958
Stanley, Thomas B. (VA) - 1953
Stassen, Harold E. (MN) - 1982
Stassen, Harold E. (PA) - 1958, 1966
Steinberg, Melvin A. (MD) - 1994
Stelger, Sam (AZ) - 1982, 1990
Stephens, A. E. S. (VA) - 1961
Stephens, Robert F. (NM) - 1956
Stephens, Stan (MT) - 1988
Stepovich, Mike (AK) - 1962, 1966
Sterling, Harold (TN) - 1978
Sterling, Ross S. (TX) - 1930, 1932
Stevenson, Adlai E. III (IL) - 1982, 1986
Stevenson, Coke R. (TX) - 1942, 1944
Stikley, John L. (NC) - 1968
Stofferahn, Kenneth D. (SD) - 1986
Stokely, Harry P. (NC) - 1956
Stone, Jim (NV) - 1986
Stoner, J. B. (GA) - 1978
Stovall, Thelma (KY) - 1979
Strait, Warren D. (IA) - 1978
Stratton, William G. (IL) - 1956, 1960, 1968
Straub, Robert W. (OR) - 1966, 1970, 1974, 1978
Strickland, Ted (CO) - 1978, 1986
Strike, Nicholas L. (UT) - 1972
Strom, Harold (MN) - 1958
Strong, Charles W. (NC) - 1964
Strumbo, Grady (KY) - 1983
Strunk, Leonard M. (PA) - 1974
Stubbs, Frank P. (LA) - 1920
Stumbo, Grady (KY) - 1987
Sturdivant, Mike P. (MS) - 1983, 1987
Sturgulewski, Arliss (AK) - 1986, 1990
Suit, Hal (GA) - 1970
Sullivan, Charles L. (MS) - 1959, 1963, 1971
Sullivan, Dennis J. (NH) - 1970
Sullivan, Henry P. (NH) - 1968
Sullivan, Joseph (NJ) - 1981
Sullivan, Mike (WY) - 1986, 1990
Sullivan, Mort (NE) - 1990
Sundlun, Bruce G. (RI) - 1986, 1988, 1990, 1992, 1994
Sunquist, Don (TN) - 1994
Sununu, John H. (NH) - 1982, 1984, 1986
Swainson, John B. (MI) - 1960, 1962
Swan, Harry S. (FL) - 1952
Swan, James E. "Jimmy" (MS) - 1967, 1971
Swearingen, V. C. (FL) - 1920

Swed, Abe L. (WI) - 1966
Sweeney, John E. (OH) - 1956
Sweeney, Robert E. (OH) - 1970
Swenson, John M. (MO) - 1996
Switzler, Royall H. (MA) - 1986
Sykes, Jim (AK) - 1994
Symington, Fife (AZ) - 1990, 1994

T

Tackett (AR) - 1952
Taft, Alexander M. (NH) - 1966
Taft, Charles P. (OH) - 1958
Taft, James L. (RI) - 1976
Taft, Seth (OH) - 1982
Talmadge, Eugene (GA) - 1932, 1934, 1940, 1942, 1946
Talmadge, Herman E. (GA) - 1948
Tanous, Wakine G. (ME) - 1974
Tanzler, Hans (FL) - 1978
Taok, Epifanio (HI) - 1959
Tapscott, John (IA) - 1972
Tate, Mark (GA) - 1994
Tauzin, W. J. (LA) - 1987
Tawes, J. Millard (MD) - 1958, 1962
Taylor (SC) - 1946
Taylor, Andrew T. (TN) - 1958
Taylor, H. P. "Pat" 1972
Taylor, John S. (FL) - 1928
Taylor, Robert L. (TN) - 1970
Taylor, Warren A. (AK) - 1962
Teasdale, Joseph P. (MO) - 1972, 1976, 1980
Teater, Robert W. (OH) - 1982
Temple, Buddy (TX) - 1982
Terral, Thomas J. (AR) - 1920, 1924, 1926, 1928, 1932, 1936
Terry, David L. (AR) - 1944
Theodore, Nick A. (SC) - 1994
Thomas, Granville (KY) - 1959, 1975
Thomas, Jerry (FL) - 1974
Thomasello, Peter Jr. (FL) - 1936
Thomason, Robert E. (TX) - 1920
Thompson, Carveth (SD) - 1972
Thompson, Clifford (VT) - 1980, 1982
Thompson, Dennis (CA) - 1990
Thompson, Ernest O. (TX) - 1938, 1940
Thompson, Horace (AR) - 1948
Thompson, James R. (IL) - 1976, 1978, 1982, 1986
Thompson, M. E. (GA) - 1948, 1950, 1954
Thompson, Ronnie (GA) - 1974
Thompson, Tommy G. (WI) - 1986, 1990, 1994
Thomson, Meldrim Jr. (NH) - 1968, 1970, 1972, 1974, 1976, 1978, 1980
Thomson, Vernon W. (WI) - 1956, 1958
Thone, Charles (NE) - 1978, 1982
Thornburg, Lacy H. (NC) - 1992
Thornburgh, Richard L. (PA) - 1978, 1982
Thornley, Hank (NV) - 1970
Thornton, Robert Y. (OR) - 1962
Thurmond, J. Strom (SC) - 1946
Tice, Merton B. (SD) - 1964
Tiemann, Norbert T. (NE) - 1966, 1970
Tierney, James (ME) - 1986
Timmerman, George Bell Jr. (SC) - 1954
Timmerman, Harry C. (MO) - 1960, 1964, 1968
Tobman, Herb (NV) - 1986
Todd, A. W. (AL) - 1958
Toney, E. P. (AR) - 1922

Tonti, D. Louis (NJ) - 1969
Toole, Jack (MT) - 1960
Townsend, W. Wayne (IN) - 1980, 1984
Trafton, Willis A. (ME) - 1956
Trammell, Worth W. (FL) - 1924
Treen, David C. (LA) - 1971, 1979
Tribbitt, Sherman W. (DE) - 1984
Trible, Paul S. (VA) - 1989
Trice, John R. (TX) - 1968
Trinkle, Elbert Lee (VA) - 1921
Tripp, Alice (MN) - 1978
Truman, Plato (ME) - 1970
Trump, Fred (AZ) - 1956
Tuck, William M. (VA) - 1945
Tucker, Harry St. George (VA) - 1921
Tucker, Jan B. (CA) - 1982
Tucker, Jim Guy (AR) - 1982
Tucker, Merle H. (NM) - 1964
Tudisco, Belmont (MN) - 1960, 1962
Turner, Carroll (TN) - 1990
Turner, James C. (MI) - 1970
Turner, Lonnie (AR) - 1984
Turpen, Mike (OK) - 1986
Tyree, Randy (TN) - 1982

U

Uhlman, Wes (WA) - 1976
Umstead, William B. (NC) - 1952
Unander, Sig (OR) - 1958
Underwood, Cecil H. (WV) - 1956, 1964, 1968, 1976, 1996
Underwood, Norman (GA) - 1982
Unruh, Jess (CA) - 1970
Unz, Ron K. (CA) - 1994
Upchurch, F. D. (FL) - 1944
Upham, William H. (WI) - 1974

V

Vaaler, Martin (ND) - 1976
Van Daam, Peter (RI) - 1988
Van de Kamp, John (CA) - 1990
Vanderhoof, John D. (CO) - 1974
Vandiver, S. Ernest (GA) - 1958
Van Meter, Thomas A. (OH) - 1982
Varilek, Elvern R. (SD) - 1982
Venetoulis, Theodore G. (MD) - 1978
Vinroot, Richard (NC) - 1996
Vogler, Joe (AK) - 1986
Voinovich, George (OH) - 1990, 1994
Voll, Connie (AR) - 1982
Volpe, John A. (MA) - 1960, 1962, 1964, 1966
Vope, Charles (PA) - 1994

W

Waggoner, D. E. (TX) - 1934
Wagnon, Joan (KS) - 1994
Waihee, John (HI) - 1986, 1990
Waldie, Jerome R. (CA) - 1974
Waldo, Jim (WA) - 1996
Walker, Clifford M. (GA) - 1920, 1922, 1924
Walker, Daniel (IL) - 1972, 1976
Walker, Edwin A. (TX) - 1962
Walker, Lloyd (ID) - 1970
Wallace, George C. (AL) - 1958, 1962, 1970, 1974, 1982
Wallace, Lew (OR) - 1956, 1958
Wallace, Lurleen B. (AL) - 1966
Waller, William L. (MS) - 1967, 1971, 1987
Wallop, Malcolm (WY) - 1974
Wallwork, Bill (NJ) - 1993
Wallwork, Jim (NJ) - 1981
Walsh, Alexander R. (RI) - 1964
Walsh, Joseph W. (RI) - 1984
Waltermire, Jim (MT) - 1988
Walters, David (OK) - 1986, 1990
Walters, John G. (ID) - 1962
Wampler, Robert H. (OR) - 1970
Wangberg, Lou (MN) - 1982
Warburton, Calvin (NH) - 1994
Ward, Conley (ID) - 1962
Ward, Henry (KY) - 1967
Ward, Joseph D. (MA) - 1960
Ward, Lee (AR) - 1958
Wardlaw, Louis J. (TX) - 1928
Warner, Carolyn (AZ) - 1986
Warner, Harry T. (TX) - 1922
Warner, Wallace E. (ND) - 1956
Warren, Fuller (FL) - 1940, 1948, 1956
Washburne, W. A. Jr. (FL) - 1956
Waterfield, Harry Lee (KY) - 1959, 1967
Watkins, Wes (OK) - 1990
Watson, Andrew J. (PA) - 1970
Watson, J. Tom (FL) - 1948, 1954
Watson, Jack (GA) - 1982
Watson, Robert O. (TN) - 1990
Watts, George (WI) - 1986
Watumull, David (HI) - 1970
Webb, John C. (MD) - 1970
Weber, C. T. (CA) - 1974
Webster, Charles M. (ME) - 1994
Webster, William L. (MO) - 1992
Weigand, Nestor (KS) - 1990
Wein, Louis P. (NY) - 1990
Welborn, Jack (MI) - 1982
Welch, Peter (VT) - 1990
Weld, William F. (MA) - 1990, 1994
Wells, Bill (AR) - 1970
Wells, James E. (MI) - 1974
Wells, Paul D. (OR) - 1994
Welty, Rex G. (WY) - 1982

West, John C. (SC) - 1970
Westmoreland, William (SC) - 1974
Weston, Joseph H. (AR) - 1974, 1976
Whealen, Joseph M. (MO) - 1956
Whelan, Gerald T. (NE) - 1978
Whitaker, Raymond B. (WY) - 1966
Whitbeck, Frank (AR) - 1968
White, Frank D. (AR) - 1980, 1982, 1986
White, Hugh L. (MS) - 1931, 1935, 1951
White, Kevin H. (MA) - 1970
White, Mark (TX) - 1982, 1986, 1990
White, Ray B. (KY) - 1979
White, Steve (RI) - 1986, 1990
White, William L. (OH) - 1962, 1966
Whitehair, Francis P. (FL) - 1940
Whitfield, Henry L. (MS) - 1923
Whitman, Christine Todd (NJ) - 1993, 1997
Whitney, Tom (IA) - 1978
Whitney, Wheelock (MN) - 1982
Whittemore, Charles F. (NH) - 1970
Whitten, Vernon H. (AR) - 1962
Whittenburg, Roy (TX) - 1962
Whittier, Sumner G. (MA) - 1956
Wick, Hilton (VT) - 1984
Wickham, Elizabeth (KY) - 1983
Wickstrom, James P. (WI) - 1982
Wiggins, Donald (KY) - 1983
Wiles, Harry G. (KS) - 1964, 1978
Wiley, Albert L. (WI) - 1986
Wiley, Stephen B. (NJ) - 1985
Wilkerson, Ernest (WY) - 1966
Wilkinson, Wallace G. (KY) - 1987
Wille, Floyd L. (WI) - 1968
Williams (SC) - 1930, 1946
Williams, Bob (WA) - 1988
Williams, Clayton (TX) - 1990
Williams, Danny (OK) - 1994
Williams, David M. (CA) - 1990
Williams, Dwain (NE) - 1960
Williams, G. Mennen (MI) - 1956, 1958
Williams, H. E. (AR) - 1960
Williams, Hamp (AR) - 1924
Williams, J. G. (AK) - 1958
Williams, Jim (FL) - 1978
Williams, John Bell (MS) - 1967
Williams, John R. (AZ) - 1966, 1968, 1970
Williams, Russell (AZ) - 1974
Williams, Terry A. (TN) - 1990
Williams, W. Dakin (IL) - 1978
Williamson, Ronald F. (SD) - 1974
Willson, Jacob R. (AR) - 1924
Wilson, Henry (MI) - 1986
Wilson, Malcolm (NY) - 1974

Wilson, Pete (CA) - 1978, 1990, 1994
Wilson, Riley J. (LA) - 1928
Wilson, Will (TX) - 1962
Winder, Charles L. (ID) - 1994
Wines, Marcia J. (NV) - 1986
Wingate, Thomas B. (NH) - 1980
Winingar, Robert F. (NE) - 1994
Winslow, Cal (MT) - 1988
Winston, Nat (TN) - 1974
Winter, Steve (NH) - 1994
Winter, William (MS) - 1967, 1975, 1979
Wiseman, Tom (TN) - 1974
Witt, Edgar E. (TX) - 1934
Witwer, George (IN) - 1996
Wollman, Harvey (SD) - 1978
Wolpe, Howard (MI) - 1994
Wong, Edwina A. (HI) - 1994
Woo, Merle (CA) - 1990
Wood, Bob (GA) - 1990
Wood, George (NC) - 1976
Wood, J. O. (GA) - 1926
Wood, James B. (WI) - 1982
Woodahl, Robert (MT) - 1976
Woodall, Perry B. (WA) - 1972
Woodbury, Robert L. (ME) - 1994
Woodring, Harry H. (KS) - 1956
Woods, Charles (AL) - 1970
Woods, Stanley C. (TX) - 1966
Woodward, Joe D. (AR) - 1978
Workman, W. D. (SC) - 1982
Wright, Fielding L. (MS) - 1947, 1955
Wright, Warren E. (IL) - 1956
Wunsch, Paul R. (KS) - 1964
Wyckoff, Robert L. (CA) - 1962
Wyman, Jasper S. (ME) - 1994

Y

Yarborough, Don (TX) - 1962, 1964, 1968
Yarborough, Ralph W. (TX) - 1952, 1954, 1956
Yeakel, Lynn (PA) - 1994
York, Myrth (RI) - 1994
Yorty, Samuel W. (CA) - 1966, 1970
Young, Andrew (GA) - 1990
Young, Edward L. (SC) - 1978
Young, James (TX) - 1930
Young, Paul R. (ME) - 1994
Younger, Evelle J. (CA) - 1978

Z

Zeiller, Gerald J. (NH) - 1976
Zeliff, Bill (NH) - 1996
Zimmerman, Eugene R. (WI) - 1978
Zuur, Cheryl (CA) - 1986